SHIFTING PARADIGMS IN INTERNATIONAL INVESTMENT LAW

Shifting Paradigms in International Investment Law

More Balanced, Less Isolated, Increasingly Diversified

Edited by
STEFFEN HINDELANG
and
MARKUS KRAJEWSKI

OXFORD
UNIVERSITY PRESS

Great Clarendon Street, Oxford, OX2 6DP,
United Kingdom

Oxford University Press is a department of the University of Oxford.
It furthers the University's objective of excellence in research, scholarship,
and education by publishing worldwide. Oxford is a registered trade mark of
Oxford University Press in the UK and in certain other countries

© The several contributors 2016

The moral rights of the authors have been asserted

First Edition published in 2016

Impression: 1

All rights reserved. No part of this publication may be reproduced, stored in
a retrieval system, or transmitted, in any form or by any means, without the
prior permission in writing of Oxford University Press, or as expressly permitted
by law, by licence or under terms agreed with the appropriate reprographics
rights organization. Enquiries concerning reproduction outside the scope of the
above should be sent to the Rights Department, Oxford University Press, at the
address above

You must not circulate this work in any other form
and you must impose this same condition on any acquirer

Crown copyright material is reproduced under Class Licence
Number C01P0000148 with the permission of OPSI
and the Queen's Printer for Scotland

Published in the United States of America by Oxford University Press
198 Madison Avenue, New York, NY 10016, United States of America

British Library Cataloguing in Publication Data

Data available

Library of Congress Control Number: 2015951219

ISBN 978–0–19–873842–8

Printed and bound by
CPI Group (UK) Ltd, Croydon, CR0 4YY

Links to third party websites are provided by Oxford in good faith and
for information only. Oxford disclaims any responsibility for the materials
contained in any third party website referenced in this work.

Preface

Twenty years ago, international investment law was a field for a few specialist lawyers and government officials. Ten years ago, academic interest in investment law began to rise; in particular with ever faster growing numbers of investment disputes and newly signed investment agreements. Five years ago, voices critical of the investment regime became more vocal and States began to reform their model investment agreements. The debate that emerged concerned the impact of investment law on sustainable development and regulatory autonomy. Today, people march in the streets against 'private investment courts' and sign online petitions against trade agreements with investment protection chapters. The defenders of the status quo first ignored the protest, then belittled it, and now claim that the protesters are missing the point. At the heights of a heated public debate about the future of international investment law, academia should provide room for an honest, constructive, but also fact-based reflection and exchange of ideas.

Based on this philosophy, the editors of this volume—which might be placed in different 'camps' of the debate about the future of investment law—decided to organize an international conference in Berlin in October 2013 entitled 'International Investment Agreements: Balancing Sustainable Development and Investment Protection'. We thought that the Investment Policy Framework for Sustainable Development published by the United Nations Conference on Trade and Development (UNCTAD) in 2012 provided a good basis for academic reflection of the investment regime and also linked academic analysis with political reforms. The conference attracted a large audience ranging from international scholars to government officials and civil society representatives. The presentations sketched the entire spectrum of the debate and allowed for controversial, but fruitful discussions.

When pondering possible ways of how to best present the innovative and thought-provoking ideas evolving from the conference in an edited volume which ideally would not just reflect but meaningfully continue these debates and fit into a larger one on the future of international investment law, we knew from the outset that some aspects would not be possible to cover at the conference, others were too narrowly treated.

When approaching additional authors to fill the gaps we acted in the same spirit of looking for a wide spectrum of views. However, the present volume is not a collection of everything. Instead, all authors embarked on the quest for the future of investment law. Some would call only for minor reforms but would nevertheless concede that these reforms might be necessary to save the system as a whole. Others would opt for fundamentally new approaches. Yet others are of the opinion that pushing the 'reset'-button is not required if significant reforms are undertaken.

On this basis, this volume's value could be seen in identifying, analysing, and evaluating current lines of developments that suggest yet another fundamental change of the predominant paradigms in international investment law. Framed in the style of a working hypothesis, international investment law appears to face attempts of a more fundamental, long-term recalibration towards a more balanced, less isolated, and in terms of regulatory approaches increasingly diversified regime.

While one can agree or disagree with the UNCTAD Policy Framework's stocktaking and respective policy recommendations advanced or omitted therein, due to its relative comprehensiveness also for this volume it provides a valuable crystallization point and catalyst for a broader discussion aiming at the question of whether we will witness a more fundamental shift in the dominant mindset in international investment law. Hence, when the individual authors of this volume analyse and evaluate efforts undertaken to recalibrate the weight attributed to private property interests compared to other interests such as environmental, cultural, and social interests they will do so against the background of the UNCTAD Policy Framework. Their contributions are grouped into three distinct, but inter-linked strands of thought which concern: (1) efforts to change treaty language with a view to addressing concerns related to the impact of existing international investment agreements and related dispute settlement on policies directed at other interests, such as those of an environmental, cultural, and social nature; (2) the more vigorously emphasized importance of general public international law for refocusing international investment law; and (3) an amplified reliance on alternative or hybrid methods for investment protection through national law, regional arrangements, or a mix of national and international instruments, again with the view to achieving what these States perceive as a more harmonious coordination of interests at stake in case of foreign investment.

As with any project of this magnitude, the editors relied on substantial help from others. First and foremost, we need to thank the individual contributors to this volume—those who had to put up with us since the autumn of 2013 and those who joined the project later. We are especially grateful to those who accepted last minute invitations to contribute to our common effort. The 2013 Berlin conference was made possible through financial support of the *German Research Foundation (DFG), Center for International Cooperation* of the *Freie Universität Berlin*, the *Ernst-Reuter-Gesellschaft der Freunde, Förderer und Ehemaligen der Freien Universität Berlin*, and the *Universität Erlangen-Nürnberg* for which we are grateful. *Pauline Brosch, Ciaran Cross, Tanja Herklotz, Rita Nunes, Franziska Oehm,* and *Sebastian Schreiber* contributed to the organization of the conference in numerous ways and many extra hours. *Daniel-Thabani Ncube* worked tirelessly to prepare the manuscript, check the language of the contributions, and to make sure the citation guidelines were followed. We are grateful to OUP, in particular, *Emma Endean, Rosie Chambers, Jenifer Payne, Cheryl Prophett, Nicole Leyland,* and *Rajeswari Siva,* for accepting our proposal and guiding us through the production steps as painlessly as possible. We also owe thanks to the anonymous book proposal reviewers providing us with valuable feedback.

Finally, now that our work appears to have come to a close for a moment, we very much hope that the volume with its diverse, but in total balanced contributions adds in many meaningful ways to the current debate on the future of the investment law regime. For what we can only wish for is moving a bit closer to achieving a more informed public discourse and better policymaking in the years to come.

SH and MK

Berlin and Erlangen
May 2015

Summary Contents

Contents	xi
Table of Cases	xix
Table of Legislation	xxix
List of Abbreviations	xxxix
List of Contributors	xli

Towards a More Comprehensive Approach
in International Investment Law   1
Steffen Hindelang and Markus Krajewski

PART I

I. Investment Protection and Sustainable Development: Key Issues   19
   Giorgio Sacerdoti

II. Negotiating New Generation International Investment Agreements:
    New Sustainable Development Oriented Initiatives   41
    Peter Muchlinski

PART II

Section 1

III. Revising Treatment Standards—Fair and Equitable Treatment
     in Light of Sustainable Development   65
     Roland Kläger

IV. Expropriation in the Light of the UNCTAD Investment
    Policy Framework for Sustainable Development   81
    Lukas Stifter and August Reinisch

Section 2

V. Investment Arbitration: Learning from Experience   97
   Jonathan Ketcheson

VI. The European Commission and UNCTAD Reform Agendas:
    Do They Ensure Independence, Openness, and Fairness
    in Investor–State Arbitration?   128
    Gus Van Harten

Section 3

VII. Sustainable Development Provisions in International Trade Treaties: What Lessons for International Investment Agreements?   142
J Anthony VanDuzer

PART III

VIII. Reconciling Investment Protection and Sustainable Development: A Plea for an Interpretative U-Turn   177
Katharina Berner

IX. Investment Protection and Sustainable Development: What Role for the Law of State Responsibility?   204
Helmut Philipp Aust

X. Termination and Renegotiation of International Investment Agreements   227
Karsten Nowrot

PART IV

XI. The Emergence of a New Approach to Investment Protection in South Africa   266
Sean Woolfrey

XII. Reliance on Alternative Methods for Investment Protection through National Laws, Investment Contracts, and Regional Institutions in Latin America   291
María José Luque Macías

XIII. Jumping Back and Forth between Domestic Courts and ISDS: Mixed Signals from the Asia-Pacific Region   316
Leon E. Trakman and Kunal Sharma

XIV. The 'Generalization' of International Investment Law in Constitutional Perspective   339
Peter-Tobias Stoll and Till Patrik Holterhus

XV. The Contribution of EU Trade Agreements to the Development of International Investment Law   357
Frank Hoffmeister

Conclusion and Outlook: Whither International Investment Law?   377
Steffen Hindelang and Markus Krajewski

Bibliography   393
Index   435

Contents

Table of Cases	xix
Table of Legislation	xxix
List of Abbreviations	xxxix
List of Contributors	xli

Towards a More Comprehensive Approach
in International Investment Law   1
Steffen Hindelang and Markus Krajewski

PART I

**I. Investment Protection and Sustainable Development:
Key Issues**   19
Giorgio Sacerdoti

    I. Introduction: The Role of Foreign Direct Investment
in Promoting Development   19
    II. The Concept of 'Sustainable Development':
Economic Background   23
    III. Content and Legal Definitions of 'Sustainable Development'   25
    IV. Foreign Investment: International Protection and Regulation   28
    V. The Evolution of BITs: From Just Protecting Investors
to Safeguarding also the Rights of Host States to pursue
their General Interest   32
    VI. The International Protection of Foreign Investment
and Sustainable Development: Interference
and Support   37

**II. Negotiating New Generation International Investment Agreements:
New Sustainable Development Oriented Initiatives**   41
Peter Muchlinski

    I. Introduction   41
    II. Sustainable Development and IIA Reform   43
    III. Treaty Design and Sustainable Development   46
        a) Preamble   46
        b) Pre-establishment rights   47
    IV. Resolving Controversial Interpretations of Existing Provisions   48
        a) Fair and equitable treatment (FET)   48
        b) Regulatory takings   50

	c) Most-favoured-nation (MFN) treatment	53
	d) National treatment	54
	e) Scope and definition	54
V.	The Inclusion of New Sustainable Development Oriented Provisions	56
	a) General exceptions	56
	b) Investor responsibilities	57
	c) State obligations and institutional structures	59
	d) Special and differential treatment provisions	60
	e) Sustainability assessment	60
VI.	Reform of Investor-State Dispute Settlement	61
VII.	Concluding Remarks	63

PART II

Section 1

III. Revising Treatment Standards—Fair and Equitable Treatment in Light of Sustainable Development   65
Roland Kläger

I.	Introduction	65
II.	What is Fair and Equitable Treatment and What are the Problems?	65
III.	Policy Options in the IPFSD	68
	a) Unqualified commitment of fair and equitable treatment	68
	b) Reference to international law/minimum standard	70
	c) Exhaustive list of fair and equitable treatment obligations	74
	d) Interpretative guidance to arbitral tribunals	75
	e) Omit fair and equitable treatment clause	77
IV.	Conclusion	79

IV. Expropriation in the Light of the UNCTAD Investment Policy Framework for Sustainable Development   81
Lukas Stifter and August Reinisch

I.	Introduction	81
II.	The Role of Sustainable Development in the Context of Expropriation	84
	a) Pre-modern (indirect) expropriation clauses	85
	aa) The sole effects doctrine	86
	bb) The police powers doctrine	88
	b) Modern expropriation clauses	90
III.	Conclusion	96

Section 2

V. Investment Arbitration: Learning from Experience   97
Jonathan Ketcheson

I.	Introduction	97

	II.	ISDS and Sustainable Development	98
	III.	Should there be Adjudication of Investment Disputes?	101
	IV.	Is Arbitration Ill Suited for Investment Disputes?	104
	V.	The Need for Transparency and Public Participation	110
	VI.	The Need for an Appellate Body?	115
	VII.	A Reintroduction of the Local Remedies Rule?	121
	VIII.	Conclusion	126

VI. **The European Commission and UNCTAD Reform Agendas: Do They Ensure Independence, Openness, and Fairness in Investor–State Arbitration?**   128
Gus Van Harten

I.	Introduction	128
II.	The Approaches to Reform	130
III.	Independence and Impartiality	131
IV.	Openness	136
V.	Procedural Fairness	139
VI.	Conclusion	140

Section 3

VII. **Sustainable Development Provisions in International Trade Treaties: What Lessons for International Investment Agreements?**   142
J Anthony VanDuzer

I.	Introduction	142
II.	Sustainable Development	144
III.	Survey of Sustainable Development Provisions in International Trade and Investment Treaties Related to Labour Standards and the Environment	145
	a) A taxonomy of sustainable development provisions—focusing on environmental protection and labour rights	145
	b) Environmental and labour rights protection provisions in PTIAs and BITs	147
IV.	Summary of Survey of Labour Rights and Environmental Protection Provisions in PTIAs and BITs	171
V.	Factors Affecting the Likelihood that PTIA Provisions Regarding Labour Rights and Environmental Protection will be Adopted in BITs	172
	a) Introduction	172
	b) Factors encouraging the adoption of labour rights and environmental protection provisions in BITs	172
	c) Factors discouraging the adoption of labour rights and environmental protection provisions in BITs	175
VI.	Conclusion	175

PART III

VIII. Reconciling Investment Protection and Sustainable Development: A Plea for an Interpretative U-Turn — 177
Katharina Berner

    I. Introduction — 177
    II. The Vienna Rules as a Gateway for Sustainable Development — 178
        a) Applicability of the Vienna rules — 179
        b) Meaning and legal status of sustainable development — 181
        c) The Vienna rules' potential to reconcile investment protection and sustainable development concerns — 183
            aa) Interpretation and conflicts of norms — 183
            bb) The Vienna rules and international investment agreements — 185
    III. Putting Theory into Practice: A Critical Review of Arbitral Jurisprudence — 188
        a) No single combined operation for sustainable development — 189
        b) Inadequate consideration of contextual arguments — 195
        c) The prominent role of de facto precedents — 200
    IV. Conclusion — 202

IX. Investment Protection and Sustainable Development: What Role for the Law of State Responsibility? — 204
Helmut Philipp Aust

    I. Remedies and Regulatory Space: The UNCTAD Suggestions for Sustainable Development — 204
    II. Legal Consequences in General International Law — 207
    III. Legal Consequences of Treaty Breaches in International Investment Law — 210
        a) Applicability of the ASR remedies — 210
        b) The choice between restitution and compensation in the practice of investment arbitration — 213
        c) Analysis — 216
    IV. Rethinking the Role of State Responsibility in the Context of Investment Protection and Sustainable Development — 220
        a) Restitution—an undue infringement of State sovereignty? — 220
        b) State responsibility as a set of secondary rules — 222
        c) State sovereignty and the development of international law — 224
    V. Conclusion — 225

X. Termination and Renegotiation of International Investment Agreements — 227
Karsten Nowrot

    I. Introduction — 227
    II. Reasons for the Current Importance of Termination and Renegotiation of Investment Agreements — 229
        a) Current shift from 'second generation' to 'third generation' investment agreements — 230

		b) The rise of regionalism in international investment treaty-making	235
	III.	'Termination without Renegotiation': Legal Issues Arising from the Denunciation of Investment Agreements	238
		a) Investment treaty provisions stipulating requirements of a lawful termination	239
		b) 'Survival clauses': treaty provisions addressing the consequences arising from denunciations	241
	IV.	'Termination as a Result of Renegotiation': Normative Implications of Investment Treaty Termination by Mutual Consent	245
		a) Mutually agreed terminations in accordance with the relevant treaty provisions	245
		b) Terminations by mutual consent in disregard of applicable treaty provisions	247
		aa) Doctrinal and practical relevance	247
		bb) A closer look at Article 54 (b) VCLT and its normative limitations	249
		cc) 'Starting all over again': on the past and present scope of application of termination clauses	254
	V.	'Renegotiation without (simultaneous) Termination': Treaty Amendments and Suspensions in Light of Termination Clauses	260
		a) 'Ordinary' treaty amendments and authoritative interpretations	260
		b) Treaty practice aimed at 'circumventing' termination clauses	263
	VI.	Conclusion	264

PART IV

XI.	The Emergence of a New Approach to Investment Protection in South Africa	266
Sean Woolfrey		
I.	Introduction	266
II.	South Africa and BITs	267
III.	South Africa Faces International Investment Arbitration under its BITs	270
IV.	South Africa Reviews its BIT Policy Framework	272
	a) The main findings of the Review	272
	b) The 2010 Cabinet Decision	276
V.	The Emergence of a New Approach to Investment Protection in South Africa	276
VI.	The Draft Promotion and Protection of Investment Bill	278
	a) Interpretation	278
	b) Security of investment	279
	c) Expropriation	280
	d) Dispute settlement	282
	e) Sovereign right to regulate in the public interest	282

	VII.	A South African Model BIT	283
	VIII.	A Dual Investment Protection Regime?	285
	IX.	Conclusion	286
		a) Balancing investment protection and sustainable development in South Africa	287
		b) What does replacing BITs with the PPI Bill mean?	287
		c) A dual approach to investment protection	289
		d) South Africa and the shifting paradigm in international investment law	289

XII. Reliance on Alternative Methods for Investment Protection through National Laws, Investment Contracts, and Regional Institutions in Latin America   291
María José Luque Macías

- I. Introduction   291
- II. Recent Developments in Investment Treaty and Contractual Practice in Latin America   292
- III. Investment Contracts and National Laws as Legal Means for the Protection and Regulation of Foreign Investment in Latin America   295
  - a) Investment laws and dispute settlement through arbitration   295
  - b) Stabilization clauses   298
  - c) Addressing non-economic concerns   300
  - d) The future of IIAs   302
- IV. Regional Initiatives in Latin America for Challenging the Status Quo of ISDS   303
  - a) The UNASUR Centre for the Settlement of Investment Disputes   304
    - aa) Background   304
    - bb) Structure and basic principles   306
    - cc) Potential scope of jurisdiction   308
    - dd) Relationship between inter-State and investor–state disputes   310
    - ee) Outlook   312
  - b) Observatory on Transnational Corporations   313
- V. Conclusion   314

XIII. Jumping Back and Forth between Domestic Courts and ISDS: Mixed Signals from the Asia-Pacific Region   316
Leon E. Trakman and Kunal Sharma

- I. Introduction   316
- II. The Practical Value of ISDS   318
- III. Domestic Policies—Australia and the Asia Pacific   320
  - a) Australian Labor Party's 2011 trade policy   320
  - b) The Coalition Government's current policy   322
  - c) Australia's regional investment interests   323
  - d) Australia not alone—Indonesia's apparent aversion to ISDS   327
  - e) Regional concerns—the Trans-Pacific Partnership Agreement   328
- IV. ISDS or Domestic Courts   330

V.	The Future of ISDS for Australia	334
VI.	Conclusion	336

XIV. The 'Generalization' of International Investment Law in Constitutional Perspective — 339
Peter-Tobias Stoll and Till Patrik Holterhus

I.	Introduction	339
II.	From Splendid Isolation to Centre Stage	340
	a) Splendid isolation and reform	340
	b) Interlinkages to other areas of international economic law and general international law	340
	c) Recent experiences of the application of international investment law	341
	d) Generalization: CETA, TTIP, and others	342
III.	A 'Constitutional' View	343
IV.	Aspects of Sovereignty, Democracy, and Legitimation	345
V.	Review of the Exercise of Public Authority— by an Arbitral Body?	346
	a) The Autonomy of the EU Legal Order	346
	b) The Arbitration Procedure	347
VI.	A Fast Track to Compensation?	349
VII.	'Reverse discrimination' as an Aspect of Non-discrimination	351
VIII.	International Constitutional Dimensions	353
	a) Investors' rights as a substitute for a human right to property—or the other way round?	353
	b) A proper role for the individual in an international economic law for the global marketplace	355
IX.	Outlook	356

XV. The Contribution of EU Trade Agreements to the Development of International Investment Law — 357
Frank Hoffmeister

I.	Introduction	357
II.	The Concept of Sustainable Development in EU Agreements	
	a) Definition of sustainable development	359
	aa) UNCTAD Report 2012	359
	bb) The Brussels Consensus	360
	b) The EU sustainable development chapter	361
	aa) Free Trade Agreements (FTAs)	361
	bb) Investment Protection Agreements	363
	c) Further EU reforms	365
	aa) Fair and equitable treatment	366
	bb) Expropriation	367
III.	Importance of International Law	369

IV.	Enforcement	371
	a) Mediation	372
	b) Domestic Remedies	373
	c) Improved Enforcement Mechanism	375
V.	Conclusion	375

Conclusion and Outlook:
Whither International Investment Law? 377
Steffen Hindelang and Markus Krajewski

I.	Where Do We Stand?	377
	a) More balanced	379
	b) More diversified	382
	c) Less isolated?	384
II.	Where Do We Go from Here?	386
	a) The protection of the State's ability to regulate	386
	b) Reform of the dispute settlement system	387
	c) Relationship between investment protection and domestic legal remedies	389

Bibliography 393
Index 435

Table of Cases

INTERNATIONAL ARBITRATIONS

Abaclat and Others v Argentine Republic, ICSID Case No ARB/07/5, Decision on
  Jurisdiction and Admissibility (4 August 2011) 54
AbitibiBowater Inc v Government of Canada, Claimant submission (23 April 2009)..........139
ADC Affiliate Limited and ADC & ADMC Management Limited v Republic of
  Hungary, ICSID Case No ARB/03/16, Award (2 October 2006)..............76, 210, 215
ADF Group Inc v United States of America, ICSID Case No ARB (AF)/00/1, Award
  (9 January 2003) 261, 311
ADF Group Inc v United States of America, ICSID Case No ARB (AF)/00/1, Decision
  on Respondent´s Proposal to Disqualify Arbitrator (19 January 2001)................293
Aguas del Tunari SA v Bolivia, ICSID Case No ARB/02/3, Decision on Respondent's
  Objections to Jurisdiction (21 October 2005) 258
Alex Genin, Eastern Credit Limited, Inc and AS Baltoil v Republic of Estonia, ICSID
  Case No ARB/99/2, Award (25 June 2001) 76
Ambiente Ufficio SPA and Others v Argentine Republic, ICSID Case No ARB/08/9,
  Decision on Jurisdiction and Admissibility (8 February)...........................122
Amco Asia Corporation and Others v Republic of Indonesia, ICSID Case No ARB/81/1,
  Award (20 November 1984)..122
Amco v Republic of Indonesia (Resubmitted Case) Award (5 June 1990)
  1 ICSID Rep 569..297
Archer Daniels Midland Company and Tate & Lyle Ingredients Americas, Inc v
  United Mexican States, ICSID Case No ARB(AF)/04/05, Award
  (21 November 2007) 212, 214–15
Asian Agricultural Products Ltd (AAPL) v Republic of Sri Lanka, ICSID Case No ARB/
  87/3, Award (27 June 1990)..181, 188, 367
Azurix Corp v Argentina, ICSID Case No ARB/01/12, Award (14 July 2006)........72, 252, 293

Bayindir Insaat Turizim Ticaret ve Sanayi AS v Islamic Republic of Pakistan, ICSID
  Case No ARB/03/29, Award (24 August 2009) 74, 78
Bernhard von Pezold and Others v Republic of Zimbabwe, ICSID Case No ARB/10/15,
  Procedural decision (26 June 2012) 139
BG Group Plc v Argentina, UNCITRAL, Award (24 December 2007) 214, 245
Biloune and Marine Drive Complex Ltd v Ghana Investments Centre and the
  Government of Ghana, UNCITRAL, Award on Jurisdiction and Liability
  (27 October 1989)..200
Biwater Gauff (Tanzania) Ltd v United Republic of Tanzania, ICSID Case No ARB/05/22,
  Procedural Order No 5 (2 February 2007)...45
Biwater Gauff (Tanzania) Ltd v United Republic of Tanzania, ICSID Case No ARB/05/22,
  Award (24 July 2008)..45, 72, 74, 189
BP Exploration Company (Libya) Ltd v Government of the Libyan Arab Republic,
  Award (1 August 1974) (1979)..297
Burlington Resources Inc v Republic of Ecuador, ICSID Case No ARB/08/5
  (formerly Burlington Resources Oriente Limited v Ecuador and Empresa Estatal
  Petroleos del Ecuador), Procedural Order No 1 (29 June 2009) 215
Burlington Resources Inc v Republic of Ecuador, ICSID Case No ARB/08/5 (formerly
  Burlington Resources Oriente Limited v Ecuador and Empresa Estatal Petroleos del
  Ecuador), Decision on Liability (14 December 2012) 116

Table of Cases

Cargill, Incorporated v United Mexican States, ICSID Case No ARB (AF)/05/2, Award
(18 September 2009) 73
CC/Devas (Mauritius) Ltd, Devas Employees Mauritius Private Limited and Telecom
Devas Mauritius Limited v India, UNCITRAL, Decision on the Respondent's
Challenge to the Hon. Marc Lalonde and Prof. Francisco Orrego Vicuña
(30 September 2013) 106
Chemtura Corporation v Government of Canada, UNCITRAL, Award
(2 August 2010)..190–93, 200
Chevron Corporation (USA) and Texaco Petroleum Company (USA) v Republic of
Ecuador, PCA Case No 34877, Interim Award (1 December 2008)..................370
Chevron Corporation (USA) and Texaco Petroleum Company (USA) v Republic of
Ecuador, PCA Case No 34877, Partial Award on Merits (30 March 2010)..............308
Churchill Mining PLC and Planet Mining Pty Ltd v Republic of Indonesia, ICSID
Case Nos ARB/12/14 and 12/40 327
Clayton v Canada, PCA Case No 2009-04, Award on Jurisdiction and Liability
(17 March 2015) 180
CME Czech Republic BV v Czech Republic, UNCITRAL, Partial Award
(13 September 2001) 214
CME Czech Republic BV v Czech Republic, UNCITRAL, Final Award
(14 March 2003) 215, 221
CMS Gas Transmission Company v Argentine Republic, ICSID Case No ARB/01/8,
Decision of the Tribunal on Objections to Jurisdiction (17 July 2003) 292
CMS Gas Transmission Company v Argentine Republic, ICSID Case No
ARB/01/8, Award (12 May 2005) 33, 113, 215
Compana de Aguas del Aconquija & Vivendi Universal v The Argentine
Republic, ICSID Case No ARB/97/3, Decision on the Challenge to the President
of the Committee (3 October 2001) 293
Compañía del Desarrollo de Santa Elena SA v Republic of Costa Rica, ICSID
Case No ARB/96/1, Award (17 February 2000)............................51, 193, 198
Corn Products International Inc v Mexico, ICSID Case No ARB(AF)/04/01,
Decision on Responsibility (15 January 2008) 245

Daimler Financial Services AG v Argentine Republic, ICSID Case No ARB/05/1,
Award (22 August 2012) 257–58
Daimler Financial Services AG v Argentine Republic, ICSID Case No ARB/05/1,
Decision for Annulment (7 January 2015) 181

Eastern Sugar BV v Czech Republic, UNCITRAL, SCC No 088/2004, Partial Award
(27 March 2007) 236, 241, 244, 248, 253–54, 257
EDF (Services) Limited v Romania, ICSID Case No ARB/05/13, Award
(2 October 2009)..80
EDF (Services) Limited v Romania, ICSID Case No ARB/05/13, Award and
Dissenting Opinion (8 October 2009) 96
El Paso Energy International Company v Argentine Republic, ICSID Case No ARB/03/15,
Decision on Jurisdiction (27 April 2006) 116, 292
El Paso Energy International Company v Argentine Republic, ICSID Case No ARB/03/15,
Award (27 October 2011) 89, 95
Electrabel SA v Republic of Hungary, ICSID Case No ARB/07/19, Decision on
Jurisdiction, Applicable Law and Liability (30 November 2012) 87, 114
Eli Lilly and Company v Government of Canada, UNCITRAL, ICSID Case No UNCT/14/2....... 2
Eli Lilly and Company v Government of Canada, UNCITRAL, ICSID
Case No UNCT/14/2, Canada's Statement of Defence (30 June 2014) 346
Emilio Agustín Maffezini v The Kingdom of Spain, ICSID Case No ARB/97/7,
Decision on Objections to Jurisdiction (25 January 2000) 53

Table of Cases   xxi

Emilio Agustín Maffezini v The Kingdom of Spain, ICSID
    Case No ARB/97/7, Award (13 November 2000)..................................76
Enron Corporation and Ponderosa Assets, LP v Argentine Republic, ICSID
    Case No ARB/01/03, Award (22 May 2007) 215
Eureko BV v Republic of Poland, Rajski separate opinion (19 August 2005) 139
Eureko BV v Slovak Republic, PCA Case No 2008-13, Award on Jurisdiction,
    Arbitrability and Suspension (26 October 2010) 236, 241

Franck Charles Arif v Republic of Moldova, ICSID Case No ARB/11/23, Award
    (8 April 2013) 110, 215–16, 222
FTR Holdings SA (Switzerland) v Oriental Republic of Uruguay, ICSID
    Case No ARB/10/7, Request for Arbitration (19 February 2010).....................321

Generation Ukraine, Inc v Ukraine ICSID Case No ARB/00/9, Award
    (16 September 2003) 280
Glamis Gold, Ltd v United States of America, UNCITRAL..............................73
Glamis Gold, Ltd v United States of America, UNCITRAL, Award (14 May 2009) 72, 200
Government of the Province of East Kalimantan v PT Kaltim Prima Coal et al,
    ICSID Case No ARB/07/3, Award (28 December 2009) 253
Grand River Enterprises Six Nations Ltd v United States of America, ICSID
    Case No ARB/10/5, Award (12 January 2011)................................196–97

ICS Inspection and Control Services Limited v United Kingdom, PCA Case No 2010-9
    (UNCITRAL Rules), Award on Jurisdiction (10 February 2012).....................258
Industria Nacional de Alimentos SA and Indalsa Perú SA (formerly Empresas
    Lucchetti SA and Lucchetti Peru SA) v The Republic of Peru, ICSID
    Case No ARB/03/4, Award (7 February 2005)............................308, 312
International Thunderbird Gaming Corporation v United Mexican States,
    UNCITRAL, Award (26 January 2006)..76
Iran-US Claims Tribunal, Shahin Shaine Ebrahimi v Government of the Islamic
    Republic of Iran, Award (12 October 1994) Award No 569-44/46/47-3 221

Jan de Nul NV/Dredging International NV v Egypt, ICSID Case No ARB/04/13,
    Decision on Jurisdiction (16 June 2006) 248
Jan de Nul NV/Dredging International NV v Egypt, ICSID Case No ARB/04/13,
    Award (6 November 2008)..248
Joseph Charles Lemire v Ukraine, ICSID Case No ARB/06/18, Decision on
    Jurisdiction and Liability (14 January 2010)................................186, 194

Kiobel v Royal Dutch Petroleum decision of 17 April 2013, 133 SCt 1659 (2013) 22
Kuwait v American Independent Oil Company (Aminoil), Award (24 March 1982) 221

LG&E Energy Corp, LG&E Capital Corp, and LG&E International Inc v Argentine
    Republic, ICSID Case No ARB/02/1, Decision on Liability (26 September 2006) 46
LG&E Energy Corp, LG&E Capital Corp, and LG&E International Inc v Argentine
    Republic, ICSID Case No ARB/02/1, Decision on Liability (3 October 2006) 90
LG&E Energy Corp, LG&E Capital Corp, and LG&E International Inc v Argentine
    Republic, ICSID Case No ARB/02/1, Award on Damages (25 July 2007)...........215–18
LG&E Energy Corp, LG&E Capital Corp, and LG&E International Inc v Argentine
    Republic, ICSID Case No ARB/02/1, Award (8 July 2008).......................103
Libyan American Oil Company (LIAMCO) v Government of the Libyan Arab Republic,
    Award (12 April 1977) (1981) 297
Lone Pine Resources Inc v The Government of Canada, UNCITRAL, Notice of
    Arbitration (6 September 2013) 341

Malaysian Historical Salvors Sdn Bhd v Government of Malaysia, ICSID
   Case No ARB/05/10 181
Malaysian Historical Salvors Sdn Bhd v Government of Malaysia, ICSID
   Case No ARB/05/10, Decision on the Application for Annulment (16 April 2009).......181
Mamidoil Jetoil Greek Petroleum Products Society SA v Republic of Albania, ICSID
   Case No ARB/11/24, Award (30 March 2015)...................................201
Marion Unglaube and Reinhard Unglaube v Republic of Costa Rica, ICSID
   Case Nos ARB/08/1 and ARB/09/20, Award (16 May 2012).......................193
Marvin Feldmann v Mexico, ICSID Case No ARB(AF)/99/1, Award
   (16 December 2002) 88
Merrill & Ring Forestry LP v Government of Canada, UNCITRAL, Award
   (31 March 2010) 261
Merrill & Ring Forestry LP v Government of Canada, UNCITRAL, Award
   (31 July 2010) 73
Metalclad Corporation v The United Mexican States, ICSID Case No ARB(AF)/97/1.........200
Metalclad Corporation v The United Mexican States, ICSID Case No ARB(AF)/97/1,
   Award (30 August 2000) 51, 84, 86, 195–96, 200, 369
Methanex Corp v United States of America, UNCITRAL......................88, 89, 192–93
Methanex Corp v United States of America, UNCITRAL, Decision of the Tribunal on
   Petitions from Third Persons to intervene as 'amici curiae' (15 January 2001)............113
Methanex Corp v United States of America, UNCITRAL, Partial Award
   (7 August 2002)..191
Methanex Corp v United States of America, UNCITRAL, Final Award of the
   Tribunal on Jurisdiction and Merits (3 August 2005)................88–89, 191, 200, 311
Mondev International Ltd v USA, ICSID Case No ARB(AF)/99/2, Award
   (11 October 2002)..224, 252, 258
MTD Equity Sdn Bhd and MTD Chile SA v Republic of Chile, ICSID
   Case No ARB/01/7, Award (25 May 2004) 77, 301
MTD Equity Sdn Bhd and MTD Chile SA v Republic of Chile, ICSID Case
   No ARB/01/7, Decision on Annulment (21 March 2007)..........................213

National Grid Plc v The Argentine Republic, UNCITRAL, Decision on Jurisdiction
   (20 June 2006)..292
Nycomb Synergetics Technology Holding AB v The Republic of Latvia, SCC, Award
   (16 December 2003) 214–15

Occidental Exploration and Production Company v Republic of Ecuador, London Court
   of International Arbitration Case No UN 3467, Final Award (1 July 2004)...............72
Occidental Petroleum Corporation and Occidental Petroleum and Exploration
   Company v Republic of Ecuador, ICSID Case No ARB/06/11, Decision on
   Provisional Measures (17 August 2007) 215
Oostergetel and Laurentius v Slovak Republic, UNCITRAL, Decision on Jurisdiction
   (30 April 2010) 241

Pantechniki SA Contractors and Engineers (Greece) v Republic of Albania, ICSID
   Case No ARB/07/21, Award (28 July 2009).....................................77
Parkerings-Compagniet AS v Republic of Lithuania, ICSID Case No ARB/05/8,
   Award (11 September 2007)..76, 96
Perenco Ecuador Limited v Republic of Ecuador and Empresa Estatal Petróleos del
   Ecuador, ICSID Case No ARB/08/6, Decision on the Remaining Issues of
   Jurisdiction and on Liability (12 September 2014).............................115–16
Petrobart Limited v Kyrgyz Republic, SCC Case No 126/2003, Award
   (29 March 2005) 120, 214, 253
Philip Morris Asia Limited v The Commonwealth of Australia, UNCITRAL,
   PCA Case No 2012-12...97, 110, 321

Table of Cases   xxiii

Piero Foresti, Laura de Carli & Others v The Republic of South Africa, ICSID
  Case No ARB (AF)/07/1, Award (4 August 2010) 54, 270–72
Ping An Life Insurance Company of China, Limited and Ping An Insurance
  (Group) Company of China, Limited v Kingdom of Belgium, ICSID
  Case No ARB/12/29 ....2, 174, 357
Plama Consortium Limited v Republic of Bulgaria, ICSID Case No
  ARB/03/24, Decision on Jurisdiction (8 February 2005) 122, 231, 257
Plama Consortium Limited v Republic of Bulgaria, ICSID Case No ARB/03/24,
  Award (27 August 2008) 370
Pope & Talbot Inc v The Government of Canada, UNCITRAL, Final Merits Award
  (10 April 2001) 80
Pope & Talbot Inc v The Government of Canada, UNCITRAL, Merits, Phase 2
  (10 April 2001) 138
Pope & Talbot Inc v The Government of Canada, UNCITRAL, Award in
  Respect of Damages (31 May 2002)..................................120, 261, 311
Poštová banka, a.s. and Istrokapital SE v Hellenic Republic, ICSID
  Case No ARB/13/8 174

Rachel S Grynberg et al v Grenada, Award (10 December 2010) 253
Railroad Development Corporation v Republic of Guatemala, ICSID
  Case No ARB/07/23, Award (29 June 2012) 93
Renta 4 SVSA et al v Russia, Arbitration Institute of the Stockholm Chamber
  of Commerce, Award on Preliminary Objections to Jurisdiction (20 March 2009)........258
Repsol SA and Repsol Butano SA v Argentine Republic, ICSID
  Case No ARB/12/38, Decision on the Proposal for the Disqualification
  of Francisco Orrego Vicuña and Claus von Wobeser (13 December 2013)..............106
Republic of Ecuador v United States of America, PCA Case No 2012-5...................119
Republic of Ecuador v United States of America, PCA Case No 2012-5, Expert
  Opinion with Respect to Jurisdiction, Prof. W. Michael Reisman (24 April 2012) 315
Republic of Italy v Republic of Cuba, Ad Hoc Arbitration, Dissenting Opinion
  of Attila Tanzi, Sentence préliminaire [Interim Award] (15 March 2005) 309, 311
Republic of Italy v Republic of Cuba, Ad Hoc Arbitration, Sentence finale
  [Final Award] (1 January 2008) 309
Revere Copper & Brass, Inc v Overseas Private Investment Corporation, Award
  (24 August 1978)...200
Robert Azinian and others v United Mexican States, ICSID Case No ARB(AF)/97/2,
  Award (1 November 1999)...301
RosInvestCo UK Ltd v The Russian Federation, SCC Case no V079/2005, Award on
  Jurisdiction (1 October 2007) 122
Rumeli Telekom AS and Telsim Mobil Telekomikasyon Hizmetleri AS v Kazakhstan,
  ICSID Case No ARB/05/16, Award (29 July 2008).........................72, 74, 254

Saint Marys VCNA v Government of Canada, Claimant submission (13 May 2011)..........139
Saipem SpA v Bangladesh, ICSID Case No ARB/05/07, Decision on Jurisdiction
  and Recommendation on Provisional Measures (21 March 2007) 252
Salini Costruttori SpA and Italstrade SpA v Kingdom of Morocco, ICSID
  Case No ARB/00/4, Decision of Jurisdiction (23 July 2001) 340
Saluka Investments BV v The Czech Republic, UNCITRAL, Partial Award
  (17 March 2006) 46, 69, 76, 80, 88–89, 102, 224, 239, 363
SD Myers v Government of Canada, UNCITRAL, Procedural Orders No 3 and 11
  (10 June 1999 and 11 November 1999)...138
SD Myers v Government of Canada, UNCITRAL, First Partial Award
  (13 November 2000) 76, 80, 194
Sempra Energy International v Argentine Republic, ICSID Case No ARB/02/16,
  Award (28 September 2007)..95, 215

SGS Société Générale de Surveillance SA v Islamic Republic of Pakistan, ICSID
    Case No ARB/01/13, Decision of the Tribunal on Objections to
    Jurisdiction (6 August 2003) 115
SGS Société Générale de Surveillance SA v Republic of the Philippines, ICSID Case No
    ARB/02/6, Decision of the Tribunal on Objections to Jurisdiction
    (29 January 2004) 115
Siemens AG v The Argentine Republic, ICSID Case No ARB/02/8 293
Siemens AG v The Argentine Republic, ICSID Case No ARB/02/8, Award
    (6 February 2007) 214, 369
Suez, Sociedad General de Aguas de Barcelona SA and Vivendi Universal SA v Argentine
    Republic, ICSID Case No ARB/03/19, Order in response to a Petition for
    Participation as Amicus Curiae (19 May 2005) 110, 112

Tecnicas Medioambientales Tecmed SA v Mexico, ICSID Case No ARB(AF)/00/2,
    Award (29 May 2003) 67, 94, 252, 369
Telenor Mobile Communications AS v Hungary, ICSID Case No ARB/04/15,
    Award (13 September 2006)..89, 258, 369
Texaco Overseas Petroleum Company and California Asiatic Oil Company v
    Government of the Libyan Arab Republic, Award (19 January 1977) (1978)............297
The Loewen Group et al v USA, ICSID Case No ARB(AF)/98/3, Decision on Hearing
    of Respondent's Objection to Competence and Jurisdiction (5 January 2001) 258

Urbaser SA and Consorcio de Aguas Bilbao Bizkaia, Bilbao Biskaia Ur Partzuergoa v The
    Argentine Republic, ICSID Case No ARB/07/26................................122
Urbaser SA and Consorcio de Aguas Bilbao Bizkaia, Bilbao Biskaia Ur Partzuergoa v The
    Argentine Republic, ICSID Case No ARB/07/26, Decision on Jurisdiction
    (19 December 2012) 123

Vattenfall AB and others v Federal Republic of Germany, ICSID
    Case No ARB/12/12 ....2, 97, 174, 266, 390
Vattenfall AB and others v Federal Republic of Germany, ICSID
    Case No ARB/12/12, Notice of Arbitration (31 May 2012).......................341

Walter Bau AG (In Liquidation) v Kingdom of Thailand, UNCITRAL, Award
    (1 July 2009) 254
Waste Management, Inc v United Mexican States, ICSID Case No ARB (AF)/00/3,
    Award (30 April 2004)...200, 261
Wintershall Aktiengesellschaft v Argentine Republic, ICSID Case No ARB/04/14,
    Award (8 November 2008)..214

Yukos Universal Limited (Isle of Man) v The Russian Federation, UNCITRAL,
    PCA Case No AA 227, Interim Award on Jurisdiction and Admissibility
    (30 November 2009) 243
Yukos Universal Limited (Isle of Man) v The Russian Federation, UNCITRAL, PCA
    Case No AA 227, Award (18 July 2014).................................173, 243

INTERNATIONAL COURTS AND TRIBUNALS

PCIJ and ICJ
Application of the Convention on the Prevention and Punishment of the Crime of Genocide
    (Bosnia and Herzegovina v Serbia and Montenegro) (Merits) (2007) ICJ Rep 43...........209
Application of the Convention on the Prevention and Punishment of the Crime of
    Genocide (Bosnia and Herzegovina v Yugoslavia (Serbia and Montenegro) (1993)
    ICJ Rep 325 (Separate opinion of Judge ad hoc Lauterpacht).......................106

Barcelona Traction, Light and Power Company, Limited (Belgium v Spain) (Judgment)
  (1970) ICJ Rep 3 .... 102, 309
Case Concerning Avena and other Mexican Nationals (Mexico v United States of
  America) (2004) ICJ Rep 12 218
Case Concerning Kasikili/Sedudu Island (Botswana v Namibia) (1999) ICJ Rep 1045 261
Case concerning Right of Passage over Indian Territory (Portugal v India) (Merits) (1960)
  ICJ Rep 6.. 198
Case Concerning the Arrest Warrant of 11 April 2000 (Democratic Republic of the
  Congo v Belgium) (2002) ICJ Rep 3 218
Case Concerning the Factory at Chorzów (Germany v Poland) (Jurisdiction) PCIJ
  Rep Series A No 9 208
Case Concerning the Factory at Chorzów (Germany v Poland) (Merits) PCIJ
  Rep Series A No 17 208
Case Concerning the Factory at Chorzów (Germany v Poland) (Judgment) PCIJ
  Rep Series A No 17 85
Case Concerning the Gabčíkovo-Nagymaros Project (Hungary v Slovakia)
  (1997) ICJ Rep 7 .... 7, 98, 183, 241, 244, 380
Case Concerning the Land and Maritime Boundary between Cameroon and Nigeria
  (Cameroon v Nigeria) (1998) ICJ Rep 275 253
Case Concerning the Payment of Various Serbian Loans Issued in France/Case
  Concerning the Payment in Gold of the Brazilian Federal Loans Issued in France
  (Judgment No 14) PCIJ Rep Series A No 20 297
Case Concerning the Temple of Preah Vihear (Cambodia v Thailand) (1962) ICJ Rep 5 218
Case Concerning the Temple of Preah Vihear (Cambodia v Thailand) (1962) ICJ Rep 6 253
Case Concerning United States Diplomatic and Consular Staff in Tehran (United States
  of America v Iran) (1980) ICJ Rep 1 218
Dispute regarding Navigational and Related Rights (Costa Rica v Nicaragua) (Judgment)
  (2009) ICJ Rep 213.. 39
Interhandel (Switzerland v United States of America) (1959) ICJ Rep 6.................. 122
Interpretation of Peace Treaties with Bulgaria, Hungary, and Romania (Advisory
  Opinion) (1950) ICJ Rep 65 308
LaGrand Case (Germany v United States of America) [2001] ICJ Rep 466 108
Legal Consequences of the Construction of a Wall in the Occupied Palestinian Territory
  (Advisory Opinion) (2004) ICJ Rep 38 180
Mavrommatis Palestine Concessions (Greece v Great Britain) (1924) PCIJ Series A No 2 308
Prince von Pless Administration (Germany v Poland) (Preliminary Objection) (1933)
  PCJI Rep Series A/B no 54.. 123
Pulp Mills on the River Uruguay (Argentina v Uruguay) (2010) ICJ Rep 14 100
S.S. 'Wimbledon' Case (1923) PCIJ Rep A No 1... 103
Sovereignty over Pulau Litigan and Pulau Sipadan (Indonesia/Malaysia) (2002) ICJ Rep 625 ... 180
Territorial Dispute (Libyan Arab Jamahiriya v Chad) (1994) ICJ Rep 6................... 120

European Court of Human Rights
Agoudimos and Cefallonian Sky Shipping Co v Greece App no 38703/97 (ECtHR,
  28 June 2001) 120
Akdivar v Turkey App no 21893/93 (ECtHR, 16 September 1996)................... 123, 125
Burden v The United Kingdom App no 13378/05 (ECtHR, 29 April 2008) 124
Golder v UK App no 4451/70 (ECtHR, 27 September 1973)............................ 180
Iovchev v Bulgaria App no 41211/98 (ECtHR, 2 February 2006) 124
Ireland v The United Kingdom App No 5310/71 (ECtHR, 18 January 1978) Separate
  Opinion of Judge Fitzmaurice 109
Kemmache v France (No 3) App no 17621/91 (ECtHR 24 November 1994) 123
Roche v The United Kingdom App no 32555/96 (ECtHR, 19 October 2005) 124
Stran Greek Refineries and Stratis Andreadis v Greece App no 13427/87 (ECtHR,
  9 December 1994).. 120

Table of Cases

European Court of Justice

Case 104/81, Hauptzollamt Mainz v Kupferberg, ECR 1982 3641 374
Case C-149/96, Portugal v Council, ECR [1999] I-8395..............................374
Case C-162/96 Racke, ECJ Reports [1998] I-3688 370
Case C-366/10, ATAA, ECJ Reports [2011] I-13755................................370
Opinion 1/09, ECR 2009 I-1137...347, 371
Opinion 1/91, ECR 1991 I-6079..371

WTO Dispute Settlement Body

Appellate Body, EC and certain Member States, Measures affecting trade in certain
　large civil aircraft, WT/DS316/AB/R..370
Certain Measures Concerning Trademarks and Other Plain Packaging Requirements
　Applicable to Tobacco Products and Packaging (9 May 2014) WT/DS434 321
China—Measures Affecting Trading Rights and Distribution Services for Certain
　Publications and Audiovisual Entertainment Products, WT/DS363/AB/R..............258
China—Measures Related to the Exportation of Rare Earths, Tungsten and Molybdenum
　(26 March 2014) WT/DS431/R; WT/DS432/R; WT/DS433/R....................38
China—Measures Related to the Exportation of Various Raw Materials (30 January
　2012), WT/DS394/AB/R; WT/DS395/AB/R; WT/DS398/AB/R 38
EC—Measures Concerning Meat and Meat Products (Hormones), Report of the
　Appellate Body (16 January 1998) WT/DS26 and DS48/AB/R...................258–59
Japan—Alcoholic Beverages II, Report of the Appellate Body, 4 October 1996,
　WT/DS8/AB/R, WT/DS10/AB/R, WT/DS11/AB/R 180
United States—Import Prohibition of Certain Shrimp and Shrimp Products
　(12 October 1998) WT/DS 58/AB/R 39
United States—Sunset Reviews of Anti-Dumping Measures on Oil Country Tubular
　Goods from Argentina: Report of the Appellate Body (29 November 2004)
　WT/DS268/AB/R [173] 114
WTO Appellate Body, 'Working Procedures for Appellate Review', WT/AB/WP/6...........118

International Tribunal for the Law of the Sea

Camouco (Panama v France) (ITLOS, 7 February 2000) Dissenting Opinion
　of Judge Anderson 123
Responsibilities and Obligations of States Sponsoring Persons and Entities with Respect
　to Activities in the Area (Request for Advisory Opinion submitted to the Seabed
　Disputes Chamber) ITLOS Case No 16 (1 February 2011)........................180

NATIONAL COURTS AND TRIBUNALS

Australia

Philip Morris Limited and Prime Minister [2011] AATA 556 321

Brazil

Resp. No 612.439 (Special Appeal), 2d Chamber of the Superior Court of Justice,
　reporting Justice João Otávio de Noronha, Decision of October 25, 2005,
　11 Revista de Arbitragem e Mediação 176 (2007) 296

Colombia

Demanda de Inconstitucionalidad contra los artículos 1, 2, 3, 4 y 6 (parciales) de la
　Ley 963 de 2005 por la cual se instaura una ley de estabilidad jurídica para los
　inversionistas en Colombia, Corte Constitucional, Sentencia C-320 de 2006
　(Gaceta de la Corte Constitucional, 24 de abril de 2006)..........................295

South Africa

Agri South Africa v Minister for Minerals and Energy (CCT 51/12) [2013]
 ZACC 9 .... 275, 279, 281

United Kingdom

R v Inland Revenue Commissioners, ex parte National Federation of Self-employed
 and Small Businesses Ltd [1982] AC 617 114

United States

Penn Central Transportation Co v New York City, 438 US 104 (1978) 88

Table of Legislation

BITS AND FTAS

Albania–Croatia FTA
  Art 23 156
Albania–United States BIT 82
Albania–Croatia BIT 78
Algeria–Indonesia BIT
  Art XIII(1) 240
Argentina–South Africa BIT 268
Argentina–United States BIT 31, 83, 115
Armenia–Canada BIT
  Art XVII 155
Armenia–United States BIT 82
ASEAN–Australia–New Zealand
  FTA 328
  Annex on Expropriation and
    Compensation 151
Australia–Chile FTA 235
  Annex 10-B 151
  Annex 10-E 235, 263
Australia–China FTA 317, 325–26
  Ch 9 317
Australia–Hong Kong BIT 266, 321
Australia–Japan EPA 317, 324–25, 329, 337
Australia–Korea FTA 317, 325
  Art 18.1(1) 153
  Ch 11 317
Australia–Singapore FTA 78
Australia–Hong Kong BIT 266, 321
  Art 14 255
  Art 14(3) 255
  Art 14(4) 255
Australia–United States FTA 101, 103, 162, 331
  Art 11.11 .... 151, 152
  Art 18.1 166
  Art 18.5 169
  Art 18.7 .... 160, 166
  Art 19.1 168
  Art 19.2 163
  Art 19.4 168
  Art 19.6 169
  Art 21.11(1) 161
  Art 21.11(2) 161
  Ch 21 161

Austria–Bosnia and Herzegovina BIT 148
Austria–South Africa BIT 268
Austria–Tajikistan BIT
  Art 5 162
Austrian Model BIT 163
  Art 5 162
Azerbaijan–United States BIT 82
Bangladesh–Turkey BIT 235
  Art 13(1) 259
  Art 13(2) 248
  Art 13(5) 259
Belgian–Luxembourg–Economic
  Union–Ethiopia BIT
  Art 1 164
  Art 1(6) 166
  Art 5(3) 157, 169
  Art. 6 .... 163, 166
Belgian–Luxembourg–Economic
  Union–Mauritius BIT
  Art 6(4) 163, 167
  Art 12 163
  Art 13 163
Belgian–Luxembourg–Economic
  Union–South Africa
  BIT 234, 268, 271, 277
Belgium–Luxembourg Model BIT
  Art 5(3) 169
Belgian Model BIT
  Art 5.2 162
Belgium–Indonesia BIT
  Art 13 243
Benin–Canada BIT
  Art 52(3) 261
Bolivia–United States BIT 82, 234
Brazil–Moçambique BIT 16
Canada–Chile FTA
  Art A-04 157
  Art G-14.1 151
Canada–China BIT 173, 336
  Art 28(1) 137
  Art 33.2 153
Canada–Colombia FTA
  Preamble 149
  Art 816 168
  Art 1601 162
  Art 1602 162

Art 1603 162
Art 1604 162
Canada–EFTA FTA
  Art 22 152
Canada–Honduras FTA 161
  Art 16 165
  Art 17 166
  Art 19.4 166
  Annex II 166
Canada–Korea FTA 155, 164
  Art 17.1 161
  Art 17.2 167–68
  Art 17.5(2) 162
  Art 17.10 .... 166, 170
  Art 17.11 170
  Art 17.17 164
  Art 18.2 .... 164, 167–68
  Art 18.11 169
  Art 18.24 .... 160, 165
  Ch 17 159
  Ch 18 159
  Annex 8-B 92
  Annex 18-A 169
Canada–Kuwait BIT
  Art 32(1) 261
Canada–Nigeria BIT
  Art 42 261
Canada–Panama FTA 152, 154
  Art 9.38 264
  Art 23. 2(3) 153
Canada–Peru BIT
  Art 16(4) 310
  Art 810 168
  Art 845 264
Canada–Tanzania BIT
  Art 10(5) 92
  Art 40(2) 243
Canadian Model BIT (2004) 56, 91–92,
                        94–95, 150, 154, 266
  Preamble 148
  Art 5 .... 70, 198
  Art 10 .... 4, 56, 152–54
  Art 11 163
  Art 13 91
  Annex B.13(1) 91, 150, 192
CARICOM–Cuba BIT 66
CARIFORUM–EC EPA 148, 162,
                         165, 167, 361
  Art 3(1) 361
  Art 72 361
  Art 72(b) 165
  Art 72(c) 165
  Art 73 .... 162–63, 361
  Art 115 170
  Art 116 170
  Art 184.1 168
  Art 188.1(a) 163
  Art 188.1(b) 163
  Art 191 361
  Art 192 361
  Art 193 .... 162, 361
  Art 194 361
  Art 195 361
  Art 196 .... 170, 361
  Art 230 170
Central America–Dominican
    Republic–United States
    FTA 93–94, 160
  Art 10.7(1) 93
  Art 16.1 166
  Art 16.2 162
  Art 16.5 169
  Art 16.8 166
  Annex 10 150–51
  Annex 10-C para 4(b) 92–93
  Annex 10-F 119
  Annex 16.5 169
Central American States–EFTA FTA
  Art 5.6 293
Chad–Italy BIT 256
Chile–Denmark BIT
  Art 16(1) 255
  Art 16(2) 255
Chile–EC FTA
  Art 91 152
Chile–EFTA FTA 156
Chile–Korea FTA 235
  Art 21.4 248
Chile–Mexico FTA
  Art 1.6 157
Chile–United States FTA
  Art 1 170
  Art 2 170
  Art 18.1 166
  Art 18.2 162
  Art 18.5 169
  Art 18.8 166
  Art 19.1 168
  Art 19.2 163
  Art 19.5 .... 160, 170
  Art 19.10 168–69
  Art 22.13 161
  Art 22.14 161
  Art 22.15(1) 161
  Art 22.15(2) 161
  Ch 22 161
  Annex 18.5 169
  Annex 19.3 170

China–Cuba BIT
  Art 9(4) 108
China–New Zealand FTA
  Annex 13 150–51
China–Norway BIT
  Art 9(2) 239
China–Panama FTA
  Art 1.03 157
China–Peru FTA
  Annex 9 150
China–South Africa BIT 268
Colombia–EU–Peru TA
  Art 268 361
  Art 277 361
  Art 281 361
  Art 282 361
Colombia–India BIT
  Art VI.2(c) 150
  Art 8(H) 150
Colombia–Panama BIT
  Art 14.5 293
Colombia–Peru FTA 361
Colombia–Singapore BIT
  Art 4 293
Colombia–United States TPA
  Preamble 149
Colombian Model BIT
  Art VI.2 150
Costa Rica–Germany BIT 193
Croatia–Ukraine BIT................. 78
Cuba–South Africa BIT 268
Czech Republic–South Africa BIT 268
Denmark–India BIT
  Art 18(1) 255
  Art 18(2) 255
Denmark–South Africa BIT........... 268
Ecuador–United States BIT 82, 119
  Art 7 para 1 306
EFTA–Jordan FTA
  Art 10 155
EFTA–Montenegro FTA
  Art 34(1) 158
EFTA–Tunisia FTA
  Art 21 155
Egypt–Germany BIT
  Art 11(4) 230
Egypt–Latvia BIT................... 242
Egypt–Japan BIT 78
El Salvador–United States BIT 82
Estonia–United States BIT.............. 82
Ethiopia–Germany BIT
  Art 12(3) 255
Ethiopia–South Africa BIT............ 274
EU–Korea FTA 149, 155, 361

Art 13.1 149
Art 13.3 168
Art 13.4 .... 162, 166–67
Art 13.6 149
Art 13.7 .... 161–63, 361
Art 13.11 .... 165, 170
Art 13.12 .... 165, 170
Art 13.13 .... 165, 170, 361
Art 13.13 .... 165, 170
Annex 13 .... 165, 170
EU-Singapore FTA............ 28, 36, 237,
                                342, 358
Finland–Kuwait BIT
  Art 15(1) 240
Finland–Nicaragua BIT 148
Finland–South Africa BIT 268
France–Korea BIT
  Art 9(4) 243
France–South Africa BIT............ 268
France-Mexico BIT 66
Gabon–Turkey BIT
  Art 14 (3)....................... 261
German Model BIT (2008)
  Art 2(2) 66
  Art 10(1) 79
Germany–Pakistan BIT 3, 31
  Art 9(2) 306
  Art 9(3) 306
  Art 14(2) 256
  Art 14(3) 256
Germany–South Africa BIT....... 268, 277
Greece–South Africa BIT............ 268
Guatemala–Trinidad and Tobago BIT
  Preamble 293
  Art 16 293
  Art 17 293
Hong Kong–Korea BIT
  Art 14(2) 255
Hong Kong–New Zealand BIT
  Art 13 255
Hong Kong–Thailand BIT
  Art 12(2) 255
  Art 12(3) 255
India–Japan EPA
  Art 96 324
India–Sri Lanka FTA
  Art IV 154
Indonesia–Japan EPA
  Art 69 324
Indonesia–Netherlands BIT 234, 317,
                                327, 337
Italy–South Africa BIT........... 268, 271
Italy–Korea BIT
  Art 14(2) 243

Italy–Malaysia BIT
  Art 15(2) 243
Japan–Malaysia EPA
  Art 85 324
Japan–Peru BIT
  Art 26 164
  Art 29(3) 242
Jordan–Korea BIT
  Art 12(3) 243
Jordan–United States BIT
  Art XVI(2) 240
Jordan–United States FTA 157
  Art 5.2 167
  Art 6 .... 162, 166
  Art 6.1 166
Kazakhstan–United States BIT 82
Korea–Peru FTA
  Art 9.17 .... 235, 248
  Art 18.2(1) 158
  Art 18.2(2) 162
  Art 18.7 165
Korea–South Africa BIT 268
Korea–United States FTA
  Art 11.10 152
  Art 19.2 168
  Art 19.2(1) 164
  Art 19.2(2) 163
  Art 19.7(5) 161, 165
  Art 20.1 167
  Art 20.2 168
  Art 20.3 161
  Art 20.3(1)(b) 162
  Art 20.3(2) 163
  Art 20.9(5) 161, 165
  Art 20.10 157
  Art 22.4 .... 161, 163, 165
  Ch 19 159
  Annex 19-A 166
  Annex 20.2 167
Kuwait–South Africa BIT 286
Malaysia–New Zealand FTA 151
Malaysia–United Arab Emirates BIT
  Art 15(1) 240
Mauritius–South Africa BIT 268, 286
Morocco–United States FTA
  Preamble 148
  Art 16.1 166
  Art 16.2 162
  Art 16.5 169
  Art 16.7 166
  Annex 16-A 169
Netherlands–South Africa
  BIT 234, 268, 273, 277

New Zealand–Singapore FTA 78
Nigeria–South Africa BIT 268, 274, 286
Norwegian Model BIT (2007) 4
OECD Model BIT 268
Panama–Peru BIT
  Art 12.10 293
  Annex 12.10 293
Panama–Taiwan FTA
Panama–United States TPA
  Art 16.2 168
  Art 16.2(2) 163, 168
  Art 16.6 169
  Art 17.2 168
  Art 17.3(2) 163
  Annex 16.6 169
Peru–Singapore FTA
  Art 10.19 259
  Art 10.20 .... 235, 248
Peru–United States TPA
  Art 16.2(2) 163
  Art 17.2(2) 163
  Art 17.3(1)(b) 162
  Art 17.7(7) 161
  Art 18.3 161
  Art 18.4 159
  Art 18.5 159
  Art 18.8 159
  Art 18.9 159
  Art 18.12(7) 161
  Art 21.2 .... 161, 163
  Annex 18.3.4 165
Protocol amending the Panama–United
  States BIT 260
Rwanda–United States BIT 82
  Art 12 163
  Art 13 163
  Art 30(3) 261
  Annex B 92
SADC Model BIT 283–84, 289
Singapore–United States FTA
  Art 15.10 151
  Art 15.21(2) 261
  Art 17.2(1)(b) 161
  Art 17.5 169
  Art 18.1 168
  Art 18.2 163
  Art 18.6 169
  Art 18.7 160
  Art 18.9 169
  Art 20.6(1) 161
  Art 20.6(2) 161
  Ch 20 161
  Annex 17A 169

Singapore–Taipei FTA
  Art 22.1(1)...................... 153
South Africa–Spain BIT........... 234, 268, 274, 277
South Africa–Sweden BIT 268
South Africa–Switzerland
  BIT 234, 268, 270, 277, 279
South Africa–Tanzania BIT 269, 274
South Africa–United Kingdom BIT 268
South Africa–Zimbabwe BIT ... 268, 274, 286
Spain–United States BIT
  Art IV(1) 90
Tanzania–United Kingdom BIT..... 189, 190
Trans-Pacific Strategic EPA
  Art 20 para 6 302
United States–Ukraine BIT 194
United States–Uruguay BIT
  Art 12 163
  Art 12(2) 151
  Art 13 163
  Art 13(1) 162
  Art 13(3) 151
  Art 14 156
  Art 24 .... 163, 165
  Art 24(1) 162
  Art 37(5) 162
  Art 37 163
  Annex B........................ 92
United States Model BIT (2004) 92
  Art 12 4
  Art 13 4
  Art 14 4
United States Model BIT (2012)
  Preamble 148
  Art 1 55
  Art 5(2) 198
  Art 6 92
  Art 12 .... 157, 163, 341
  Art 13 .... 157, 163, 166
  Annex B............... 92–93, 115, 120, 150, 192
  Annex B 3 85

INTERNATIONAL AND REGIONAL CONVENTIONS, TREATIES, AGREEMENTS AND OTHER INSTRUMENTS

African Charter on the Rights and
  Welfare of the Child............. 190
American Convention on Human
  Rights (1969)
  Art 25 123

ASEAN Comprehensive Investment
  Agreement 34, 173, 328
  Art 9 156
  Art 17 152–53
  Art 27 306
  Art 34(3) 312
  Art 40(3) 261
  Annex 2 151
ASEAN Protocol on Enhanced Dispute
  Settlement Mechanism
  Art 1 para 1 306
  Art 2 306
  Appendix I para 31............... 306
Canada–Chile Agreement on
  Environmental Cooperation
  Art 14 159
  Art 15 159
Canada–Chile Agreement on Labour
  Cooperation
  Art 3 160
Canada–Colombia Agreement on
  Labour Cooperation............. 162
  Art 1 168
  Art 3 160
Canada–Costa Rica Agreement on
  Labour Cooperation
  Art 4 160
Canada–Honduras Agreement on
  Environmental Cooperation........ 159
  Art 3 168
  Art 4 161
  Art 7 170
  Art 10 169
  Art 13 170
  Art 17 170
Canada–Honduras Agreement on
  Labour Cooperation............. 169
  Art 1 168
  Art 3 161
  Art 9 .... 166, 170
  Annex 1 170
Canada–Panama Agreement on the Environment
  Art 16 166
  Annex II....................... 166
Canada–Peru Agreement on Labour
  Cooperation................... 159
  Art 2 162
  Art 9 169
  Annex 1 169
Central American Regional Convention
  for the Management and
  Conservation of the Natural Forest
  Ecosystems and the Development
  of Forest Plantations............. 199

Charter of Economic Rights and
   Duties of States
   Art 2(2)(c) 51
Charter of the United Nations 201
COMESA Investment
   Agreement 57, 154, 162, 173, 306
   Art 5 163
   Art 20.6 150
   Art 22.1 154
Comprehensive Economic and Trade
   Agreement (CETA) 2, 13,
      17–18, 36, 62, 66, 94, 98, 114,
      118–21, 127–31, 135, 138–40, 149,
      162, 176, 207, 237, 248, 339, 342, 344,
      351, 355–56, 359, 362, 371, 376, 380,
      383, 385, 387–89
   Preamble 7, 98, 362
   Art X.07 .... 237, 248
   Art X.08 98
   Art X.2 152–53
   Art X.02.2(b) 153
   Art X.7.4 121
   Art X.9 .... 35, 40, 66, 83, 120
   Art X.11 .... 88, 94–95, 367, 368
   Art X.19 372
   Art X.21 .... 351, 373
   Art X.25 .... 108, 133, 134, 135
   Art X.27 120
   Art X.27(1) 385
   Art X.33 .... 114, 138
   Art X.42 .... 119, 126
   Ch IX 342
   Ch XX 7
Constitutive Treaty of the Union
   of South American Nations
   Preamble para 6 304–5
   Preamble para 7 304
   Art 2 304
   Art 3 lit.(a) 305
   Art 4 304
   Art 5 304
   Art 8 304
   Art 9 304
   Art 10 304
   Art 12 para 1 304
   Art 12 para 2 304
   Art 12 para 6 304
   Art 13 para 2 305
   Art 14 para 2 305
   Art 21 305
Convention concerning the Protection
   of the World Cultural and
   Natural Heritage 188, 199

Convention for the Protection of
   Human Rights and Fundamental
   Freedoms 123, 347
Convention for the Safeguarding of
   Intangible Cultural Heritage 188
Convention on Access to Information,
   Public Participation in Decision-
   Making and Access to Justice in
   Environmental Matters
   Preamble 100
Convention on Biological Diversity 187, 199
Convention on Long-range
   Transboundary Air Pollution 187
Convention on Nature Protection
   and Wildlife Preservation in the
   Western Hemisphere 198
Convention on the Elimination of All
   Forms of Discrimination against
   Women 190
Convention on the Protection of the
   Underwater Cultural Heritage 188
Convention on the Rights
   of the Child 190
Convention on the Settlement of
   Investment Disputes between
   States and Nationals of other States
   (ICSID Convention) 32, 98,
      107, 109, 112, 118, 217, 233,
      241, 291, 340, 349, 371
   Travaux préparatoires 181
   Preamble 102
   Art 11 306
   Art 14 105
   Art 14 para 1 307
   Art 26 350
   Art 27 312
   Art 27 para 1 310
   Art 37(2)(b) 107
   Art 38 107
   Art 40 105
   Art 42(1) 181, 214
   Art 48(5) 112
   Art 52 118
   Art 53(1) 117, 332
   Art 54(1) 216
   Art 57 105
   Art 75 332
Convention on Wetlands of
   International Importance, especially
   as Waterfowl Habitat 199
EC-South Africa Agreement on Trade,
   Development and Cooperation
   Art 27 155

Table of Legislation

Energy Charter Treaty 66, 87, 187, 342, 371
   Art 13(1) 86
   Art 47(1) 239–40
   Art 47(3) 243
Energy Charter Protocol on
   Energy Efficiency and Related
   Environmental Aspects
   Preamble 149
General Agreement on Tariffs and
   Trade (GATT 1947)
   Art XX 143
   Art XX(e) 154
General Agreement on Tariffs and
   Trade (GATT 1994)
   Art XX 34, 56–57,
           146, 151–55, 171, 176, 285
   Art XX(b) 152
   Art XX(g) 38, 152
   Art XXI 31
Hague Convention for the Pacific
   Settlement of International
   Disputes (1899)
   Art 22 306
   Art 28 306
Hague Convention for the Pacific
   Settlement of International Disputes (1907)
   Art 43 306
   Art 49 306
Hong Kong–EFTA Agreement on Labour
   Art 2 162
   Art 6(2) 165
ICSID Additional Facility Rules 332
   Art 53 para 3 307
ICSID Arbitration Rules (2006) 112, 269
   Rule 6 307
   Rule 37 112
   Rule 48 para 4 .... 112, 307
ILC Draft Articles on Diplomatic Protection
   Art 1 309
   Art 9 309
   Art 11 309
ILC Draft Articles on the Responsibility
   of International Organizations 370
ILC Draft Articles on the Responsibility
   of States for Internationally
   Wrongful Acts 370
ILO Freedom of Association and
   Protection of the Right to Organise
   Convention 370
India-Singapore Comprehensive
   Economic Cooperation Agreement ... 149
   Art 6.11 152–53
   Art 6.16 156

Inter-American Convention for the
   Protection and Conservation
   of Sea Turtles 199
International Covenant on Civil
   and Political Rights
   Art 2(3) 123
International Covenant on Economic,
   Social and Cultural Rights 354
Marrakesh Agreement Establishing the
   World Trade Organization 31,
                    143, 217, 285
North American Agreement
   on Environmental Cooperation
   (NAAEC) 158–60, 167, 196
   Art 2 167
   Art 14 159
   Art 15 159
   Art 22 160
   Art 23 160
   Art 24 161
   Art 25 161
   Art 26 161
   Art 27 161
   Art 28 161
   Art 29 161
   Art 30 161
   Art 31 161
   Art 32 161
   Art 33 161
   Art 34 161
   Art 34(4)(b) 161
   Art 35 161
   Art 36 161
North American Agreement on Labour
   Cooperation (NAALC) 158–60, 166
   Art 2 .... 158, 166
   Art 3 158
   Art 8 169
   Art 9 169
   Art 10 169
   Art 11 169
   Art 12 169
   Art 13 169
   Art 14 169
   Art 15 169
   Art 16 169
   Art 17 169
   Art 18 169
   Art 19 169
   Annex 1 166
North American Free Trade Agreement
   (NAFTA) 28, 66, 149, 187, 293
   Art 104 157

Art 1105 . . . . 72, 195–97
Art 1105(1) 72–73, 70, 77,
          191, 197
Art 1108 156
Art 1110 . . . . 86, 190–92, 195, 200
Art 1110(1) 86, 191, 192
Art 1114 151
Art 1114(1) 196
Art 1114(2) 163
Art 1131(1) 181
Art 1131(2) 180, 261
Art 1206 156
Ch XI 245–46
Art 2001(2)(c) 261
Art 2101 . . . . 152, 153
Annex 1120.1(a) 124
Pacific Alliance Cali Declaration
 Art 10.6 293
 Art 10.30 293
 Art 10.31 293
Pacific Alliance Framework Agreement
 Art 1 293
 Art 3 para 1 lit a 293
 Art 3 para lit b 293
Pacific Alliance Framework Agreement,
 Additional Protocol
 Art 1.1 293
 Art 1.4 293
Statute of the International Court of Justice
 Art 31 105
 Art 38(1)(d) 70
Transatlantic Trade and Investment
 Partnership (TTIP) 2, 17,
    27–28, 34, 38, 66, 130, 132, 135,
    224, 237, 339, 342–44, 355–56,
    365, 368, 372, 376, 383, 389
Treaty on European Union (TEU) 347
 Art 21 . . . . 7, 33, 360
 Art 21(2)(b) 363
 Art 21(2)(d) 360
 Art 21(2)(f) 360
Treaty on the Functioning of the
 European Union (TFEU) 390
 Art 206 353
 Art 207(1) 33, 236, 350,
         353, 358, 360
 Art 205 33
Universal Declaration of Human Rights
 Art 17 354
UNCITRAL Arbitration Rules
 (2010) 112, 306
 Art 6 107
 Art 9 . . . . 107, 307
 Art 11 307

UNCITRAL Rules on Transparency
 in Treaty-based Investor-State
 Arbitration (2014) 12, 62,
   112–14, 126, 128, 137, 307, 387–88
 Art 1(2) 112
 Art 1(4) 114
 Art 4 113
 Art 4(3) 113
 Art 6 113
 Art 7 113
Vienna Convention for the Protection
 of the Ozone Layer 187
Vienna Convention on the Law of
 Treaties (VCLT) 239, 362, 385
 Art 1 180
 Art 2(1)(a) 180, 184
 Art 2(1)(g) 187
 Art 4 180
 Art 26 . . . . 184, 241
 Art 31 . . . . 148, 179–80,
        185, 189, 201–2,
        219, 239, 369
 Art 31(1) 78, 147, 183, 194, 362
 Art 31(2) 186
 Art 31(3)(a) 180, 261
 Art 31(3)(b) 259, 261
 Art 31(3)(c) 39, 69 70,
     75, 77, 186, 190, 196–97,
     199, 220, 369, 370
 Art 31(4) 183
 Art 32 . . . . 179–81, 189, 201–2,
          219, 239
 Art 33 . . . . 179–80, 202, 219, 239
 Art 36 250
 Art 37 . . . . 184, 250
 Art 37(2) 244, 249–50, 252
 Art 42(2) 239–40
 Art 54(a) 239, 245
 Art 54(b) 249–50, 252–53
 Art 59 . . . . 241, 244
 Art 60 241
 Art 60(5) 241, 365
 Art 62 . . . . 240–41, 244, 249, 252
 Art 70(1)(b) 251–52
 Art 72 260
WTO Dispute Settlement
 Understanding
 Art 6 307
 Art 8 307
 Art 11 307
 Art 22.1 31
WTO Dispute Settlement
 Understanding Rules of Conduct
 Provision IV 307

NATIONAL LEGISLATION

Antigua and Barbuda
The Investment Authority Act, 2006
(Antigua and Barbuda)
    Sch 4 300

Bolivia
Ley de Inversiones (Bolivia) No 1182
    (17 September 1990) 295
    Art 13 300

Brazil
Brazilian Arbitration Act, Law No
9.307/Lei de Arbitragem—Lei
9307 (1996)
    Art 2 297
    Art 5 297
Brazilian Clean Companies Act, Lei No
L12846 (2013). 300
Constituição da República Federativa
do Brasil de 1988
    Art 5 296
    Art 4 subpara XXIV 296
Decreto No 55.762
    Art 2 296
Lei do Capital Estrangeiro No 4.131
    Art 2 296

Chile
Estatuto de la Inversion Extranjera
(Chile) Decreto Ley N 600
    Art 7 298
    Art 11 298

Colombia
Ley 1607 'Por la cual se expiden normas
en materia tribuaria y se dictan otras
disposiciones', Diario Oficial No
48.655 (26 de diciembre de 2012) 295

Ecuador
Código Orgánico de la Producción,
Comercio e Inversiones (2010)
    (Ecuador)...................... 296
    Art 17 para 1 296
    Art 17 para 3 296
    Art 18 296
    Art 21 300
    Art 25 para 1 297
    Art 25 para 2 296
    Art 26 para 1 296
    Art 27 296
    Art 27 para 1 297
    Art 27 para 2 297
    Art 27 para 3 297
Constitución de la República del Ecuador
    Art 422 296
Contrato de Inversión de Sectores
Productivos (extranjera) 296
    Cl 20, subpara 20.1 lit. (e) 301
    Cl 20, subpara 20.1 lit. (f) 300
    Cl 21 301
    Cl 28 para 1 296–97
    Cl 28 para 2 296–97
    Cl 28 subpara 28.3. .... 296, 297
Executive Decree No 1506 of
21 May 2013 (Ecuador)
    Art 2 302

El Salvador
Ley de Inversiones Decreto
Legislativo 732 (El Salvador)
    Art 14 300

Germany
Basic Law for the Federal Republic
of Germany (1949)
    Art 20 para 3 344
    Art 20 para 1 344
    Art 19 para 4 344
    Art 92 344
    Art 101 para 1 344

Panama
Estabilidad jurídica de las inversiones
(Panama) Ley No 54
    Art 10 para 2 298
    Art 10 para 3 298
    Art 10 para 5 298

Paraguay
Ley de Inversiones (Paraguay)
Ley No 117/91
(6 December 1991) 295
    Art 11 300

Peru
Constitución Política del Perú
    Art 38 para 2 298
Ley Marco para el Crecimiento
de la Inversion Privada Decreto
Legislativo (Peru) No 757.......... 295
    Art 51 300
    Art 52 300
    Art 53 300
    Art 39 298

Ley de Promoción de las Inversiones
 Extranjeras (Peru) Decreto
 Legislativo No 662
 (29 August 1991)................ 295
 Art 10 lit.(a)...................... 298
 Art 12 lit.(a)...................... 298
 Art 15 298

South Africa
Broad-Based Black Economic
 Empowerment Act 53 of 2003...... 269
Constitution of the Republic of South
 Africa, 1996................. 268, 274
 s 25 274
 s 25(1)........................ 275
 s 25(3)........................ 275
Draft 'Promotion and Protection of
 Investment Bill, 2013' (PPI Bill) 16,
          267, 277–83, 285, 287–89
 s 8(2) 281
 s 8(3) 281
Minerals and Petroleum Resources
 Development Act 28 of 2002
 (MPRDA) 54, 271–72

United Kingdom
UK Senior Courts Act 1981
 s 319(2) 114

United States
Foreign Relations Law of the
 United States 88

Ukraine
2006 Ukrainian Law on Television and
 Broadcasting (LRT) 194

OTHER

United Nations
UN Doc A/Res/S-19/2 (19 September
 1997) adopting the Programme
 for the Further Implementation of
 Agenda 21 99
United Nations General Assembly Res
 56/83 (12 December 2001) U.N.
 Doc.A/RES/56/83, 'Responsibility
 of States for Internationally
 Wrongful Acts'................... 349
United Nations General Assembly
 Resolution 68/109 307

United Nations General Assembly, 'Rio
 Declaration on Environment and
 Development' UNGA/CONF.151/
 26 Vol I (12 August 1992) 23, 100
United Nations General Assembly,
 'World Commission on
 Environment and Development'
 UNGA Res 42/87
 (11 December 1987) 23

European Union
Council Opinion (ECAA) 1/00 [2002]
 OJ I-3493 346
Council Opinion (EEC) 1/91 opinion
 pursuant to Art 228 of the EEC
 treaty [1991] OJ I-6099.......... 346
Council Opinion (EEC) 1/92 opinion
 of the court [1992] OJ I-2838 346
Council Opinion (European and
 Community Patents Court) 1/09
 [2011] OJ I-1137................ 346
Council Opinion 1/00, EU:C:2002:231....347
Council Opinion 1/09,
 EU:C:2011:123 347
Council Opinion 2/13 (ECtHR) [2014]
 ECLI:EU:C:2014:2454 347
European Parliament resolution 'On
 the Future European International
 Investment Policy', 2010/2203
 (INI) of 6 April 2011.............. 33
European Parliament Resolution P7_
 TA(2010)0434 of 25 November
 2010......................... 364
European Parliament Resolution P7_
 TA(2011)0257 of 8 June 2011........ 2
European Parliament Resolution P7_
 TA(2011)0141 of 6 April 2011 360
European Parliament Resolution P7_
 TA(2012)0249 of 13 June 2012..... 364
European Parliament Resolution
 P7_TA-PROV(2013)0411
 of 9 October 2013 .... 364, 372
Regulation (EU) No 1219/2012
 Establishing Transitional
 Arrangements for Bilateral
 Investment Agreements between
 Member States and Third
 Countries, OJ L 351/40 of 20
 December 2012 236
Regulation No 912/2014 of the
 European Parliament and of the
 Council of 23 July 2014........... 372

List of Abbreviations

BITs	bilateral investment treaties
CETA	EU–Canada Comprehensive Economic and Trade Agreement
CJEU	Court of Justice of the European Union
EC	European Commission
ECHR	European Convention for the Protection of Human Rights and Fundamental Freedoms
ECtHR	European Court of Human Rights
EU	European Union
FDI	foreign direct investment
FET	fair and equitable treatment
FTA	free trade agreements
HDI	Human Development Index
ICSID	International Centre for Settlement of Investment Disputes
IIA	International Investment Agreements
IISD	International Institute for Sustainable Development
IPFSD	Investment Policy Framework for Sustainable Development
ISDS	investor–State dispute settlement
SD	sustainable development
TEU	Treaty on the European Union
TFEU	Treaty on the Functioning of the European Union
TTIP	Transatlantic Trade and Investment Partnership
UNCITRAL	United Nations Commission on International Trade Law
UNCTAD	United Nations Conference on Trade and Development
UNGA	United Nations General Assembly
VCLT	Vienna Convention on the Law of Treaties
WGI	Worldwide Governance Indicators

List of Contributors

Helmut Philipp Aust is a senior research fellow at Humboldt University Berlin, Faculty of Law.

Katharina Berner is a legal trainee at the Kammergericht (Higher Regional Court Berlin). As a research fellow at Humboldt-University Berlin, she contributed to a project of the United Nations' International Law Commission on 'Treaties over Time'.

J Anthony VanDuzer is a professor at the Common Law Section of the Faculty of Law, University of Ottawa.

Gus Van Harten is an associate professor at Osgoode Hall Law School, York University.

Steffen Hindelang is associate professor of law at the Department of Law of Free University Berlin.

Frank Hoffmeister head of unit of Trade Defence Investigations II—Anti-circumvention at the European Commission and a part-time Professor of Law at the Free University of Brussels.

Till Patrik Holterhus is a senior research fellow at the Department of International Economic Law and Environmental Law in the Institute of Public International Law and European Law at the Georg-August-University in Göttingen.

Jonathan Ketcheson is currently a senior associate in Hogan Lovells' international arbitration group in London.

Roland Kläger is a lawyer specializing in international arbitration and litigation.

Markus Krajewski is a professor of German Public Law and Public International Law at the Friedrich-Alexander University Erlangen-Nürnberg.

María José Luque Macías is a PhD student in Public International Law at the Faculty of Law of the Friedrich-Alexander University Erlangen-Nürnberg.

Peter Muchlinski is a professor of International Commercial Law at the School of Law, SOAS, University of London.

Karsten Nowrot is a professor of Public Law, European Law and International Economic Law as well as Head of the Department of Law at the School of Socio-Economics of the Faculty of Business, Economics and Social Sciences at Hamburg University, Germany.

August Reinisch is a professor of International and European Law at the University of Vienna as well as an arbitrator and expert adviser in Austrian and foreign court litigation.

Giorgio Sacerdoti is currently a senior professor of International Law at Bocconi University in Milan and a senior arbitrator (ICSID).

Kunal Sharma is a graduate student and Rhodes Scholar at the University of Oxford. He has previously lectured in Private Law at the University of New South Wales and practised at the law firm Herbert Smith Freehills.

Lukas Stifter is a researcher and lecturer for Public International Law at the University of Vienna.

Peter-Tobias Stoll is a professor of International Economic Law and Environmental Law and the director of the Department of International Economic Law and Environmental Law in the Institute of Public International Law and European Law at the Georg-August-University in Göttingen.

Leon E Trakman is a professor of Law and Past Dean, Faculty of Law, University of New South Wales, Sydney, Australia.

Sean Woolfrey is a policy officer in the Food Security and Economic Transformation and Trade Programmes at the European Centre for Development Policy Management in Maastricht.

Towards a More Comprehensive Approach in International Investment Law

Steffen Hindelang and Markus Krajewski

If we want things to stay as they are, things will have to change.[1]

The Italian novelist *Giuseppe Tomasi di Lampedusa* had his character *Tancredi Falconeri* use this phrase in his novel '*Il gattopardo*' in order to describe a dramatic turn of two epochs and the futile quest for perpetuity. While not quite so dramatic, but arguably no less of a struggle for change, at present the international investment law regime has abandoned relative stability. Running into rougher seas, it sees further consolidation and proliferation, but also mounting contestation or even outright rejection.

Rising numbers of investor–State-disputes and newly signed investment agreements suggest the continuous importance, attractiveness, and further growth of this field of law. In 2012 and 2013 record numbers of new investor–State claims were filed—fifty-four and fifty-nine cases respectively, the latter number being the highest number of disputes ever registered in one year—confirming foreign investors' steadily increasing reliance on this system of property protection abroad.[2] Ever since, the number of newly registered claims has remained high.[3] Equally, the number of bilateral investment treaties (BITs) and so-called comprehensive free trade agreements (FTAs), which include chapters on investment, is also still on the rise.[4] Recent events, such as the accession of Canada to the Convention on the Settlement of Investment Disputes between States and Nationals of Other

---

[1] '*Se vogliamo che tutto rimanga com'è bisogna che tutto cambi.*' G Di Lampedusa, *The Leopard* (Pantheon 1991) 40.
[2] UNCTAD, *World Investment Report 2015, Reforming International Investment Governance* (United Nations 2015) 112.
[3] After the record fifty-nine new claims of 2013, claims went back slightly in 2014, with a total of forty-two known initiated claims, see UNCTAD, 'Recent Trends in IIAs and ISDS' (2015) 1 IIA Issues Note 1 <http://unctad.org/en/PublicationsLibrary/webdiaepcb2015d1_en.pdf> accessed 23 April 2015.
[4] Currently 3,281 such agreements in total, UNCTAD *Investment Policy Hub, International Investment Agreements* <http://investmentpolicyhub.unctad.org/IIA> accessed 21 August 2015.

States (ICSID),[5] the inclusion of an investment protection chapter in the negotiation agendas of both the European Union (EU) and the United States of America (USA) on the Transatlantic Trade and Investment Partnership (TTIP)[6] as well as the opening of negotiations between the EU and China on an investment agreement highlight this trend.[7]

At the same time, the current regime of international investment law is increasingly contested: On one end of the spectrum, some countries chose to maintain the status quo or embark on minor reforms. On the other end countries such as South Africa[8] or Indonesia[9] did not renew or even terminated existing BITs while others, for instance Ecuador, have withdrawn from ICSID.[10] In addition, high-profile cases against industrialized countries such as *Vattenfall v Germany*,[11] *Ping An v Kingdom of Belgium*,[12] or *Eli Lilly and Company v The Government of Canada*[13] have led to some noticeable public opposition to investor–State dispute settlement (ISDS).[14] Moreover, treaty negotiations such as those of the EU with Canada and the US on investment chapters in comprehensive trade agreements have attracted far more public attention and steered more controversial debate than any other investment agreement in recent years.[15] Over the last years, the

---

[5] Foreign Affairs, Trade and Development Canada Press Release, 'Canada Ratifies Important International Treaty on Investment Disputes' (1 November 2013) <www.international.gc.ca/media/comm/news-communiques/2013/11/01a.aspx?lang=eng> accessed 23 April 2015.

[6] The EU Negotiation Mandate ('Directives for the negotiation on the Transatlantic Trade and Investment Partnership between the European Union and the United States of America', ST 11103/13 RESTREINT UE/EU RESTRICTED) can be viewed at <http://data.consilium.europa.eu/doc/document/ST-11103-2013-DCL-1/en/pdf> accessed 23 April 2015.

[7] European Commission Memo, 'EU Investment Negotiations with China and ASEAN' (18 October 2013) <http://europa.eu/rapid/press-release_MEMO-13-913_en.htm> accessed 23 April 2015. See also the text of the Comprehensive Economic and Trade Agreement (CETA) on which negotiations were concluded in late 2014, <http://trade.ec.europa.eu/doclib/docs/2014/september/tradoc_152806.pdf> accessed 23 April 2015.

[8] See S Woolfrey's chapter in this volume.

[9] See LE Trakman and K Sharma's chapter in this volume.

[10] On the situation in Latin America see MJ Luque Macías' chapter in this volume. See also S Clarkson and S Hindelang, 'How Parallel Lines Intersect: Investor-State Dispute Settlement and Regional Social Policy' in AC Bianculli and A Ribeiro Hoffmann (eds), *Regional Organizations and Social Policy in Europe and Latin America: A Space for Social Citizenship?* (Palgrave 2015) 25–45.

[11] *Vattenfall AB and others v Federal Republic of Germany*, ICSID Case No ARB/12/12.

[12] *Ping An Life Insurance Company of China, Limited and Ping An Insurance (Group) Company of China, Limited v Kingdom of Belgium*, ICSID Case No ARB/12/29.

[13] *Eli Lilly and Company v The Government of Canada*, UNCITRAL, ICSID Case No UNCT/14/2.

[14] C Olivet and P Eberhardt, *Profiting from Injustice: How Law Firms, Arbitrators and Financiers are Fuelling an Investment Arbitration Boom* (Transnational Institute 2012) <www.tni.org/briefing/profiting-injustice> accessed 1 September 2014; T McDonagh, *Unfair, Unsustainable and Under the Radar—How Corporations use Global Investment Rules to Undermine a Sustainable Future* (The Democracy Center 2013) <http://democracyctr.org/wp/wp-content/uploads/2013/05/Under_The_Radar_English_Final.pdf> accessed 23 April 2015.

[15] See, for example, the European Parliament resolution of 8 June 2011 on EU–Canada trade relations (P7_TA(2011)0257); Bundesverband der Deutschen Industrie e.V., *Positionspapier: Schutz europäischer Investitionen im Ausland: Anforderungen an Investitionsabkommen der EU* (BDI 2014) <www.bdi.eu/download_content/GlobalisierungMaerkteUndHandel/Schutz_europaeischer_Investitionen_im_Ausland.pdf> accessed 23 April 2014; European Trade Union Confederation Press Release, 'European Trade Union Calls for a Fundamental Rethink of Canadian and US Trade

body of legal literature on international investment law has expanded tremendously both in terms of quantity as well as scrutiny. In scholarly writing, calls for reform with a view to preserving (more) policy-space or for rebalancing private and public interests[16] crescendo and are yet another indication that the perception of international investment law might undergo a profound change. Latest signs of this trend are policy proposals by inter-governmental organizations such as the United Nations Conference on Trade and Development (UNCTAD)[17] or the Commonwealth Secretariat[18] advocating for 'systemic reform'—to use UNCTAD-language[19]—of the investment law regime with a stronger focus on sustainable development.[20]

In the light of these developments one may say with some confidence that the international investment law regime is currently in a 'state of transition'. Even more, the developments sketched above appear not only to suggest the emergence of a more complex, heterogeneous, or ambiguous international investment law regime but they may herald long-term shifting paradigms.

While the principles and basic functions of international investment law can be traced to the 'classic' international law of aliens,[21] a first major evolutionary step towards the paradigm of international investment law substantially challenged today can be envisaged in the emergence of BITs in the late 1950s.[22] However, it was not until the 1970s, when investor–State dispute settlement clauses were frequently included in BITs[23] and, subsequent to the fall of the Iron Curtain, that

---

Deals' (17 November 2014) <www.etuc.org/press/european-trade-union-calls-fundamental-rethink-canadian-and-us-trade-deals#.VTjoyfAgcg8> accessed 23 April 2015; see for the national debate in Germany also S Hindelang, *Stellungnahme, Öffentliche Anhörung des Ausschusses für Wirtschaft und Energie des Deutschen Bundestages zum Comprehensive Economic and Trade Agreement ('CETA') zwischen der EU und Kanada* <https://www.bundestag.de/blob/345496/2f9d17704429c70693d11e18755bbc3b/steffen-hindelang-fu-berlin-data.pdf> accessed 23 April 2015.

[16] Such long-standing critics as Muthucumaraswamy Sornarajah or, more moderate, Peter Muchlinski (also a contributor to this volume) have been joined by Gus van Harten, cf his chapter in this volume, or the contributions of Luke Peterson and William Burke-White to M Waibel, A Kaushal, K Chung, and C Balchin (eds), *The Backlash against Investment Arbitration* (Kluwer 2010).

[17] UNCTAD, *Investment Policy Framework for Sustainable Development* (United Nations 2012 (IPFSD)) <http://unctad.org/en/PublicationsLibrary/diaepcb2012d5_en.pdf>, accessed 23 April 2015; UNCTAD, 'Reform of Investor-State Dispute Settlement: In Search of a Roadmap' (2013) 2 IIA Issues Note <http://unctad.org/en/PublicationsLibrary/webdiaepcb2013d4_en.pdf> accessed 23 April 2015; UNCTAD, 'Reform of the IIA Regime: Four Paths of Action and a Way Forward' (2014) 3 IIA Issues Note <http://unctad.org/en/PublicationsLibrary/webdiaepcb2014d6_en.pdf> accessed 23 April 2015.

[18] JA VanDuzer, P Simons, and G Mayeda (eds), *Integrating Sustainable Development into International Investment Agreements: A Commonwealth Guide for Developing Country Negotiators* (Commonwealth Secretariat 2013).

[19] UNCTAD, 'Reform of the IIA Regime' (n 17) 1.

[20] See on this P Muchlinski's chapter in this volume.

[21] R Dolzer, *Eigentum, Enteignung und Entschädigung im geltenden Völkerrecht/Property, Expropriation and Compensation in Current International Law* (Springer 1985).

[22] Treaty between the Federal Republic of Germany and Pakistan for the Promotion and Protection of Investments (signed 25 November 1959, entered into force 28 April 1962) ('Germany–Pakistan BIT').

[23] J Pohl, K Mashigo, and A Nohen, 'Dispute Settlement Provisions in International Investment Agreements: A Large Sample Survey' 2012/2 OECD Working Papers on International Investment 11.

those treaties gained real practical significance. The geographical scope of the regime was even further amplified when countries both in the Global North and Global South—aided by international organizations such as UNCTAD[24]—embarked on another round of proliferating investment protection agreements during the 1990s, bringing their total numbers from 385 at the end of 1989 to 3,268 in 2014.[25]

The key to understanding and possibly also the foundation of the regime's success in terms of practical significance has been its dispute settlement mechanism; still exceptional in public international law. It allows individuals—that is, investors—to challenge State measures which had adverse effects on their investment in international fora. At the same time, this unique feature of the regime is probably also the most significant reason for public controversy.[26]

Since more significant changes to treaty language pointing more clearly to public interest considerations can only be witnessed since the mid-2000s,[27] the vast majority of investment agreements in force, by their text and nature, have basically been concerned with protecting economic interests of an investor vis-à-vis a host State. This predetermination is also reflected—arguably even reinforced[28] by a small set of adjudicators exercising a dominant position in coining the regime's orientation[29]—in investor–State arbitration. Consequently, the current international investment law regime may be broadly described as being preoccupied with the protection of private property against political risk; the latter often understood in a very broad sense.[30] At the same time, it should not be forgotten that placing a State measure interfering with private property interests under 'suspicion', that is, obliging a State to justify such interference

---

[24] Z Elkins, AT Guzman, and BA Simmons, 'Competing for Capital: The Diffusion of Bilateral Investment Treaties 1960–2000' (2006) 60 Intl Org 818–19.

[25] UNCTAD, Bilateral Investment Treaties 1959–1999 (United Nations 2000) 1 <http://unctad.org/en/Docs/poiteiiad2.en.pdf> accessed 23 April 2015; UNCTAD, 'Recent Trends in IIAs and ISDS' (n 3) 1.

[26] See n 14.

[27] cf, for example, Art 12 on environment, Art 13 on labour rights, and Art 14 on opt-out clause for non-conforming measures, all of the US American Model BIT 2004, Art 10 providing for a GATT Art XX-style general exception clause in the Canadian Model BIT 2004. Note also the 2007 Norwegian Model BIT, which places an even stronger emphasis on public interests. See also UNCTAD (n 2) 102–103; UNCTAD, *World Investment Report 2014, Investing in the SDGs: An Action Plan* (United Nations 2014) 116 which notices that most if not all investment agreements signed in 2012 und 2013 exhibit some features devoted to aspects of sustainable development; UNCTAD (n 2) 112 confirms these findings for IIAs concluded in 2014 in stating that 'most of the treaties include provisions safeguarding the right to regulate for sustainable development objectives'.

[28] See K Berner's chapter in this volume; she argues that the existing potential inherent in general public international law to balance property protection and competing interests has not sufficiently been leveraged.

[29] S Puig, 'Social Capital in the Arbitration Market' (2014) 25 EJIL 387–424.

[30] See for the challenges arbitral tribunals faced when distinguishing and delineating protection against regulatory risk from the ordinary commercial risk of an adjustment of the regulatory environment in the host State, the latter to be borne by the investor, for example, JE Viñuales, 'The Environmental Regulation of Foreign Investment Schemes under International Law' in P-M Dupuy and JE Viñuales (eds), *Harnessing Foreign Investment to Promote Environmental Protection: Incentives and Safeguards* (CUP 2013) 273–320.

by demonstrating that it pursues other (competing) legitimate public interests in an appropriate manner, may rightly be seen as an instrument to control the exercise of sovereign powers not to excessively curtail individual freedom. Such approach, however, also indicates that freedom can be meaningfully coordinated and balanced in order not to cause harm to other interests, private and public alike.[31] This balancing process—or some may say the insufficiency or even lack thereof—is at the heart of much critique on the current investment law regime's basic orientation.

If the focus on the protection of the economic interests of individual investors is understood as the underlying paradigm of the international investment law regime up until recently, new developments and changing perceptions can be framed as deviations from this paradigm. On this basis, this volume identifies, analyses, and evaluates lines of developments that suggest yet another fundamental change of the predominant paradigm in international investment law. In a nutshell, international investment law appears to face attempts of a more fundamental, long-term recalibration towards a more balanced, less isolated, and in terms of regulatory approaches increasingly diversified regime.

The balance of the international investment law regime may shift away from a strong emphasis on interests of private property protection towards a more comprehensive approach. The latter may lead to property protection 're-joining'—some others may say though property protection is relegated to—the ranks of the band of interests to be balanced when regulating in the general public interest.

This recalibration may be described as an attempt to more firmly securing a State's right to regulate in the public interest. Others have chosen to coin this recalibration attempt as a shift towards 'sustainable development', most prominently UNCTAD.[32] UNCTAD set out its core concept in the 'Investment Policy Framework for Sustainable Development' ('UNCTAD Policy Framework or IPFSD') of 2012 in which it puts forward its views on perceived or real imperfections in the current system of international investment law. It also proposes potential remedies in the areas of national policy agenda-setting and international treaty-making.[33] While one can agree or disagree with the UNCTAD Policy Framework's stocktaking and respective policy recommendations advanced or omitted therein, due to its relative comprehensiveness it provides a valuable point of departure, crystallization point, and catalyst for a broader discussion aiming at the question of whether we will witness a more fundamental shift in

---

[31] J Zhan, 'Investment Policies for Sustainable Development: Addressing Policy Challenges in a New Investment Landscape' in R Echandi and P Sauvé (eds), *Prospects in International Investment Law and Policy* (CUP 2013) 13, 22–24.
[32] See n 17.
[33] In the meanwhile, UNCTAD has continued its effort and put forward more detailed analysis and policy recommendations on dispute settlement in investor–State conflicts, see UNCTAD, 'Reform of Investor–State Dispute Settlement' (n 17).

the predominant paradigm in international investment law towards a more balanced, less isolated, and in terms of regulatory approaches increasingly diversified regime.

Hence, when the individual contributions to this volume analyse and evaluate efforts undertaken to re-calibrate the weight attributed to private property interests compared to other interests such as environmental, cultural, and social interests they will do so against the background of the UNCTAD Policy Framework, utilizing the Framework in various ways, from starting point up to object of scrutiny. Their contributions are grouped into three distinct, but interlinked strands of thought which concern

- efforts to change treaty language with a view to addressing concerns related to the impact of existing international investment agreements and related dispute settlement on policies directed at other interests, such as those of an environmental, cultural, and social nature;
- the more vigorously emphasized importance of general public international law for refocusing international investment law; and
- an amplified reliance on alternative or hybrid methods for investment protection through national law, regional arrangements, or a mix of national and international instruments, again with the view to achieving what these States perceive as a more harmonious coordination of interests at stake in case of foreign investment.

Obviously, these three lines of development do not cover exhaustively all recent changes and challenges aimed at fostering a shift in the fundamental paradigm underlying the current international investment law regime, but they appear to capture and group the most relevant legal occurrences in this regard.

Inevitably, when relying on and operating with the concept of sustainable development we face the concept's inherent weaknesses. While, arguably, one can in few words explain what international investment law is about and what its main features are, the task of definition becomes immediately more difficult when turning to sustainable development.

One might justifiably form the impression that the international policy circus cannot do without it anymore: the term is echoed, for example, in Agenda 21 from the United Nations Conference on Environment and Development,[34] and in the Johannesburg Plan of Implementation adopted by the 2002 World Summit on Sustainable Development.[35] We also find it in the G8 2009 declaration on Responsible

---

[34] United Nations Conference on Environment and Development, *Agenda 21: Programme of Action for Sustainable Development* (United Nations 1992) <https://sustainabledevelopment.un.org/content/documents/Agenda21.pdf> accessed 8 May 2015 para 2.23.

[35] United Nations World Summit for Sustainable Development, *Plan of Implementation of the World Summit for Sustainable Development* (United Nations 2002) <www.un.org/esa/sustdev/documents/WSSD_POI_PD/English/WSSD_PlanImpl.pdf> accessed 8 May 2015 para 4.

Leadership for a Sustainable Future[36] and in the G20 Core Values for Sustainable Economic Activity.[37]

Sustainable development is identified as an explicit objective in dozens of international treaties; most notably in Article 21 Treaty on European Union and in the preamble of the 1995 WTO Agreement, as well as in numerous soft-law instruments.[38] And, it would appear that the number of references to sustainable development is set to increase even further, as the concept is now spreading into the realm of international investment law.[39]

Despite the concept's obvious popularity, its content and meaning is uncertain and heavily disputed. The 1987 Brundtland-Report defined sustainable development as 'development that meets the needs of the present without compromising the ability of future generations to meet their own needs'. A more detailed understanding of the concept alludes to three pillars—(1) economic development, (2) social well-being and social development, and (3) environmental protection. While certain smaller elements or fragments of the concept might indeed form customary international law,[40] one can however surely doubt that there is any general all-embracing customary international law principle of sustainable development.[41] Hence, when talking about sustainable development *at large* we must be aware that we are operating also with a political and not just a legal concept. Hence, when claiming that international investment law, as it stands today, does not conform to and must be brought in line with the concept of sustainable development *at large*, then this is first and foremost not a formal conflict of legal norms. Rather, it is a claim that the law *should* be formulated or interpreted in a certain way.

When relating sustainable development *at large* to foreign investment, there seems to be a widespread political consensus that foreign investment is one of the key elements in furthering the development of States, their economies and societies.[42] However, controversy has long existed around the question of precisely which qualities an investment should exhibit in order to fulfil its function without compromising competing public interests.

---

[36] Group of Eight, 'Responsible Leadership for A Sustainable Future' <www.g8italia2009.it/static/G8_Allegato/G8_Declaration_08_07_09_final,0.pdf> accessed 27 April 2015, paras 49–53.

[37] Group of Twenty, 'G20 Leaders Statement: The Pittsburgh Summit, September 24–25, 2009, Pittsburgh, Annex: Core Values for Sustainable Economic Activity' <www.g20.utoronto.ca/2009/2009communique0925.html#annex> accessed 27 April 2015, paras 3, 5.

[38] M-C Cordonier Segger and A Khalfan, *Sustainable Development Law: Principles, Practices & Prospects* (OUP 2004) 32–36.

[39] For example, in the Preamble and Ch XX of CETA ('Trade and Sustainable Development').

[40] U Beyerlin, 'Sustainable Development' in Rüdiger Wolfrum (ed), *The Max Planck Encyclopedia of Public International Law* (2nd edn, OUP 2013) paras 6, 18, 19, 20.

[41] B Braune, *Rechtsfragen der nachhaltigen Entwicklung im Völkerrecht* (Peter Lang 2005) 70f; *Case Concerning the Gabčíkovo-Nagymaros Project (Hungary v Slovakia)* (1997) ICJ Rep 7 para 140.

[42] A Newcombe, 'Sustainable Development and Investment Treaty Law' (2008) 8 J World Inv & Tr 357; United Nations, *Monterrey Consensus of the International Conference on Financing for Development, Report of the International Conference on Financing for Development, Monterrey, Mexico, 18-22 March 2002 (UN Doc. A/CONF.198/11, chapter 1, resolution 1, annex)* (United Nations 2003) <www.un.org/esa/ffd/monterrey/MonterreyConsensus.pdf> accessed 27 April 2015 para 1.

Foreign investment is essentially about the acquisition of a cross-border claim to income in the hope of getting a return in the future. And, in very simple terms, an investment will be made where it generates the highest returns.[43] However, economic rationales do not always go easily hand in hand with the objectives pursued by the host State. Taxes generated by foreign investments are certainly highly appreciated, as are any transfers of technology or of knowledge. But foreign investment may be accompanied by environmental pollution, or poor labour and health standards. Regulatory measures taken in the interests of preserving the environment, of safeguarding labour standards, or for other non-investment concerns—no matter how necessary or indispensable these may be—also have the capacity to negatively impact on investment returns. It is the host State's right to reach an appropriate balance of the diverse interests at play for the benefit of its people. This is to be achieved, among others, by means of establishing a regulatory framework which maximizes positive and minimizes negative impacts from foreign investment. Such regulatory framework does not only comprise national measures but also includes international treaties.

It is hardly possible to overestimate the value of international investment treaties with regard to certain aspects: on the micro-level, they provide investors with a tool to manage and mitigate political risk and host States believe they offer an advantage when competing with one another to attract investments.[44] On the macro-level, many would argue that these treaties promote the rule of law and good governance standards; they make public international law even more meaningful for the individual, beyond the narrow elite of States and international organizations, and beyond the fragmentary protection of human rights.[45]

However, the question arises whether these benefits might ultimately come at too high a price. Some claim that the current body of international investment law, in particular its application in the context of investor–State dispute settlement, curtails or even frustrates the sustainable development of host States. At the extreme, international investment agreements are depicted as hegemonic instruments, straitjackets preventing host States from taking much-needed measures to secure the well-being of their populations.[46]

Yet others would maintain that while foreign investors are certainly not motivated by altruism, they can nevertheless contribute to the economic and social development of their chosen host State in many different and meaningful ways.

---

[43] Debate on whether host States benefit from inward FDI, cf B Jin, F Garcia, and R Salomon, 'Do Host Countries Really Benefit from Inward Foreign Direct Investment?' (2013) 98 Columbia FDI Perspectives; S Pathak, A Laplume, and E Xavier-Oliviera, 'Inward Foreign Direct Investment: Does it Enable or Constrain Domestic Technology Entrepreneurship?' (2012) 84 Columbia FDI Perspectives.

[44] UNCTAD, *World Investment Report 2003, FDI Policies for Development: National and International Perspectives* (United Nations 2003) 171.

[45] See for a call to intensify the protection of property by means of human rights the contribution of P-T Stoll and TP Holterhus to this volume.

[46] AT Guzman, 'Why LDCs Sign Treaties that Hurt them: Explaining the Popularity of BITs' (1998) 38 Va JIL 639; E Benvinisti and GW Downs, 'The Empire's New Clothes: Political Economy and the Fragmentation of International Law' (2007) 60 Stan L Rev 595, 611 et seq, 616 et seq; the IPFSD also uses the term 'straightjacket', cf UNCTAD *IPFSD* (n 17) 37.

If, however, the host State would suddenly adopt protectionist or discriminatory measures to the detriment of the foreign investor, international investment agreements could deter the host State from this type of conduct or would at least lead to come kind of compensation.[47] From this perspective, the demand to 'balance' investor protection and sustainable development might be characterized as an ill-camouflaged attempt to get rid of the bonds of the international rule of law and accountability by maximizing regulatory arbitrariness.

However, as is often the case, the 'truth' might be found somewhere in between these extremes, warranting a more balanced approach. In this light, the present volume wants to trace, chart, and evaluate recalibration attempts in international investment law to bring about a shift in its fundamental paradigm away from a pre-occupation with the protection of private property interests towards 'sustainable development'. The latter is understood broadly in the sense of a harmonious pursuit of a diverse set of economic, environmental, cultural, and social interests without attributing a priori more weight to one or the other. In doing so, we also aim at bringing closer together two debates which have been dealt with as separate issues for far too long. Over the past decades, sustainable development and the protection of foreign investment have been addressed in parallel discourses. Only gradually have these two policy strands, each with its own perspectives and distinct socialization processes, started to take notice of each other. With the set of contributions in this volume, diverse in their political orientation in the debate, in their authors' professional background, and not least in their geographical provenience, we hope to contribute to a more balanced, fact-oriented, and less ideology-driven appreciation of the question of whether we might see a shift in international investment law's fundamental paradigm.

Part I of the volume provides for the foundations, background, and framework for the discussion in subsequent Parts that are devoted to specific issues. In the opening chapter *Georgio Sacerdoti* critically assesses the development and interrelation of the two key concepts of this volume, that is, the current status of the investment protection regime and the principle of sustainable development. In a tour d'horizon, the chapter sketches not only the historic background of these concepts and highlights their potentials for cross-fertilization, but also addresses shortcomings and ambiguities. It argues that the legal value of the concept of sustainable development is often unclear. Yet, sustainable development remains an important normative principle which can serve as a tool to adjust imbalances within the current system preoccupied with investment protection. And, indeed, adjustments increasingly materialize which might be capable of shifting the current balance between investment protection and sustainable development in the long-run.

---

[47] S Hindelang, 'Study on Investor-State Dispute Settlement ('ISDS') and Alternatives of Dispute Resolution in International Investment Law' in EU Directorate-General for External Policies, *Investor-State Dispute Settlement (ISDS) Provisions in the EU's International Investment Agreements* (European Parliament 2014) <http://ssrn.com/abstract=2525063> accessed 24 April 2013.

Peter Muchlinski introduces us to the UNCTAD's Investment Policy Framework for Sustainable Development, which will be summarized, contextualized, and critically assessed. By way of comparison, *Muchlinski* also explores a further important international initiative aimed at recalibrating the current regime commissioned by Commonwealth Secretariat, that is, the study entitled 'Integrating Sustainable Development into International Investment Agreements: A Guide for Developing Countries'.[48] Overall, he remains an optimistic sceptic that both initiatives will have a significant impact on what he describes as a 'rather unedifying reality of a world apparently incapable of leaving behind the nostrums of neoliberalism'.

Part II addresses changes, implemented or suggested, to the treaty language which has predominantly been used in investment protection agreements over the last fifty years. This approach also lies at the heart of UNCTAD's Investment Policy Framework for Sustainable Development of 2012. The common denominator of this and other reform proposals in that direction is that the preoccupation of international investment agreements, in terms of their text and application, with individual investors' economic interests may challenge or impede policies directed at environmental protection, poverty reduction, equality and justice, health and social policy, or the protection of cultural heritage. What has been perceived as particularly problematic is the open and vague language of many terms in investment agreements, a lack of coordination with other fields of law concerned with the accommodation of interests other than those of the investor, as well as a certain tendency towards judicial activism in investor–State dispute settlement. The individual contributions in this part—split in three Sections dealing with substantive, procedural, and contextual issues—will critically assess reform proposals in light of both the question of whether they would achieve their aims pursued, that is, balancing investment protection and policies directed at other interests and, furthermore, of whether a stronger emphasis on the concept of sustainable development could serve as the basis of a new paradigm in international investment law.

Section 1 of Part II addresses the impact of substantive provisions in international investment agreements on sustainable development, their shortcomings, and possible remedies. In this regard, important questions such as whether the protection of legitimate expectations of an investor is truly at odds with sustainable development or rather whether such safeguard is a basic element of the rule of law and, hence, an indispensable part of any investment agreement, need to be addressed. Out of several policy options on how to design and structure substantive provisions in a fashion more friendly to sustainable development, this volume places an emphasis on two of them: Among the different treaty standards in international investment agreements, the fair and equitable treatment (FET) standard is the most important one. Yet, its language in treaties is often very vague and open for a variety of interpretations; at times to the detriment of State regulatory

---

[48] JA VanDuzer, P Simons, and G Mayeda, *Integrating Sustainable Development into International Investment Agreements: A Guide for Developing Countries, Prepared for the Commonwealth Secretariat* (August 2012) <www.iisd.org/pdf/2012/6th_annual_forum_commonwealth_guide.pdf>.

autonomy, some may argue. Clarifying and lending contours to the FET standard as well as increasing the threshold of liability has therefore moved to the centre of the reform debate. Using UNCTAD's range of policy proposal as a starting point, *Roland Kläger* analyses and assesses the different options, sketches their theoretical basis, and discusses their implications, and practical value for recalibrating the current investment law regime. *Kläger* argues that the proposals of the UNCTAD Policy Framework are only of limited value to the aims to be achieved. Instead, he calls for a vigorous implementation of the concept of proportionality in investment treaties and arbitration.

Despite the growth in importance of FET in investment treaty arbitration, direct and indirect expropriation remain the historic root and backbone of the investment protection system. Similar to FET, indirect expropriation has increasingly been viewed by critics as a tool to reduce State discretion and regulatory autonomy. It is therefore not surprising that reform proposals have also focused on expropriation clauses. In particular, while the UNCTAD Policy Framework does not suggest an omission of such a clause in an investment agreement, it centres on the difficult delineation of a State measure qualifying as compensable indirect expropriation and such measures to be borne by the investor as an ordinary risk of doing business in the host State. *Lukas Stifter* and *August Reinisch* analyse and assess the reform proposals and their implications and practicality against the background of arbitral awards and in the light of a growing trend towards a stronger emphasis on non-economic interest in international investment law.

Section 2 of Part II focuses on procedural issues. More specifically, it elaborates on the current practice of dispute resolution and its implications and perceived or real shortcomings in light of the promotion of sustainable development. Investor–State dispute settlement provisions are at the heart of international investment law and, at the same time, they are perhaps the main focal point of criticism.

International investment law is one of the very few areas of public international law endowed with a rather effective enforcement mechanism. If there were no such mechanism, or if IIAs were to provide only for State-to-State dispute settlement, the field would probably lose much of its controversy, and also its appeal to businesses, legal practitioners, and to academia.

Investor–State dispute settlement practice is criticized in many aspects: for a lack of coherence and consistency, for a lack of transparency, for a lack of respect towards democratically elected governments implementing policies in the public interest,[49] and, last but not least, for having created an oligopolistic dispute resolution industry.[50] At least part of this criticism is shared by UNCTAD's Investment Policy Framework.[51] Indeed, many reform proposals place investor–State dispute settlement at their core. However, the debate on appropriate changes in the

---

[49] See for a comprehensive discussion and possible remedies Hindelang, 'Study on Investor-State Dispute Settlement' (n 48).
[50] Puig (n 30).
[51] UNCTAD *IPFSD* (n 18) 8, 38, 40, 56 et seq; without, though, providing much evidence for the critique.

investor–State dispute settlement system has not always been highly factual, but appears rather heated in practice and literature alike. Considering the importance and controversy of this issue this volume contains two chapters on investor–State dispute settlement with, while not directly opposing, certainly not mutually affirming views on the need for reform.

Wanting to preserve the basic structure of dispute settlement in investment law, *Jonathan Ketcheson* draws some lessons from the concept of sustainable development for investor–State dispute settlement from past experience. The most important lesson to be learnt from taking the concept of sustainable development into account more seriously is that investment agreements should not be biased in favour of the protection of foreign investment; sustainable development requires that a balance be struck between economic considerations and environmental, social, and other concerns. To this end, he suggests that participants in the system, including States, investors, counsel, and arbitrators have engaged with public criticisms to improve the system. He identifies a number of areas where his main proposition would have to be spelled out in more detail. For example, sustainable development would suggest that the public should have access to information about arbitrations, and there should be mechanisms for their participation. Furthermore, *Ketcheson* argues that until a well-designed investment court becomes a realistic possibility, attention should be focused on a number of areas, including ensuring that the ethical rules for arbitrator conduct are appropriately designed to cater for the unique features of the investment treaty system. He also calls for an appellate body and for the incorporation of the UNCITRAL Rules on Transparency into the existing investment agreements. However, he also cautions: investment treaties need to provide an effective means for investors to enforce their rights. This will inevitably constrain State actions, he claims, but need not undermine sustainable development.

In contrast, *Gus van Harten* suggests that the current model of dispute resolution by ad hoc arbitration cannot be reformed but must be replaced by a permanent court model firmly based on institutional safeguards securing independence and impartiality well known to developed domestic systems. Consequently, *van Harten* concludes that current reform agendas—referring to UNCTAD's Policy Framework und the consultation on the Transatlantic Trade and Investment Partnership of the European Commission[52] as cases in point—'would not make investment treaty arbitration independent and fair'. He, however, acknowledges that the implementation of both reform proposals would improve the openness or transparency of investor–State arbitration.

Section 3 of Part II addresses contextual issues of treaty language. In the area of trade law the concept of sustainable development has been receiving attention for a considerable period of time. Certain elements thereof have even been part of

---

[52] European Commission, 'Report on the Online Public Consultation on Investment Protection and Investor-State Dispute Settlement in the Transatlantic Trade and Investment Partnership (TTIP)' (July 2014) <http://trade.ec.europa.eu/doclib/docs/2014/july/tradoc_152693.pdf> accessed 28 October 2014. But note the recent EC draft text on an investment chapter for TTIP which includes some type of a permanent mechanism: European Commission, 'Commission draft text TTIP-investment' (September 2015) <http://trade.ec.europa.eu/doclib/docs/2015/september/tradoc_153807.pdf> accessed 1 October 2015.

treaty language since early days of the international trade regime. More recently, bilateral or regional free trade arrangements pay more substantial regard to aspects of sustainable development. *Anthony Van Duzer* broadens the horizon beyond the realm of investment agreements and puts up the question of whether something can be learned from developments in the area of trade by providing a survey of recent bilateral and regional treaty making practice in respect of provisions specifically addressing aspects of sustainable development, such as labour standards or the environment. This is especially relevant as such trade agreements increasingly include investment protection chapters as, for example, seen in the text of the EU–Canada Comprehensive Economic and Trade Agreement (CETA). The numbers of provisions explicitly addressing aspects of sustainable development will increase in line with the further proliferation of comprehensive bilateral or regional trade agreements. Some of these provisions—less frequent though—will also migrate to stand-alone investment protection agreements.

Part III of the volume is devoted to the wider corpus of public international law. The relevance of general public international law for refocusing international investment law has only recently been more broadly recognized. While in academia it was hardly disputed that investment agreements would be agreements governed by public international law, investor–State tribunals did not take this understanding sufficiently into account when deciding individual cases. In fact, the private commercial law provenience of investor–State arbitration seems to have contributed to what some may describe as a 'clinical isolation' of international investment law. Hence, the potential present in general public international law to reassess and refocus international investment law and provide for linkages to other bodies of international law, such as environmental law, human rights or trade law has so far been neglected. This also holds largely true for UNCTAD's Policy Framework.

Several policy proposals are found in UNCTAD's Policy Framework on how to make the texts of international investment agreements more friendly to sustainable development. This is to be achieved, for example, by balancing State commitments with investor obligations, promoting responsible investment, or explicitly preserving more regulatory space for development. Such textual re-design would supposedly be called for, because the current investment agreement regime has produced 'unexpected' interpretations of provisions or has allowed for 'unwanted' challenges to national measures in pursuit of a public purpose. However, is this perceived 'unfairness' really due to the text and wording of international investment agreements? Or is it due to the interpretation and, ultimately, due to those people who interpret them? UNCTAD is rather brief in its Policy Framework on the realities of dispute settlement; referring by and large to 'ambiguities' in these processes.

Katharina Berner fills this gap by critically examining the current system of dispute settlement and laying bare its weaknesses and shortcomings in respect of treaty interpretation. In contrast to UNCTAD, she comes to the conclusion that what UNCTAD is calling for—that is, sustainable development-friendly substantive standards in international investment agreements—might also be achieved without tinkering with the design of the substantive standards encompassed in the current regime. She suggests that the Vienna rules on the interpretation of treaties constitute a workable gateway for integrating sustainable development into international investment agreements; if applied correctly instead of just paying lip-service to them. Hence, the real problems of the current system are not necessarily the indeterminacy of substantive standards, but methodological weaknesses in their interpretation. What seems to be particularly problematic is the backward looking, path-dependent, quasi-precedence system and the refusal of some arbitrators to pronounce on points of law—perhaps because they might fear that this would negatively impact on their future nominations.

Moreover, UNCTAD's Policy Framework is rather silent on the question of the potential role of the law of State responsibility in accommodating sustainable development concerns. It includes, though, some policy recommendations on remedies, which appear to favour compensation over restitution.[53] Indeed, the choice of a certain type of remedy might not only have an impact on a State's policy space, but also significantly influence the legitimacy of the investment protection regime. There is perhaps nothing more devastating for this legitimacy than excessive damages awards. *Helmut Aust* takes a fresh look at the issue of choice of remedies in international investment law. While the rules provided under general public international law contain a variety of possible remedies, in investment arbitration mainly compensation is granted. He argues that

> it is not convincing... that compensation would generally be more conductive for sustainable development than reparation. Rather, the general rules of State responsibility do not stand in the way of the accommodation of sustainable development concerns which have been translated into primary rules of international investment law.

Bringing change to the current regime of over 3,000 international investment agreements with a view to recalibrating it inevitably requires their termination and/or renegotiation. Until recently, these two subjects had not attracted much public attention, despite the fact that international investment agreements were frequently updated, replaced, or even terminated over the last decades. One possible explanation might be that the power distribution or political convictions of State parties were structured in such ways that the conclusion of ever-stronger investment protection agreements was hardly resisted, or even explicitly welcomed. Today, approaches to adapting and reforming the current investment law regime not only display a greater diversity,[54] but also occur in the context of strong trends towards regionalization, and towards more comprehensive treaty regimes covering also trade, services, intellectual property, and other economic relations. Hardly surprising then, termination and

---

[53] UNCTAD *IPFSD* (n 18) 57.

[54] Not just that certain countries such as Bolivia, Ecuador, and Venezuela completely withdraw from the current regulatory regime on foreign investment, we also see an overall decline of concise wordings and abstract language in favour of more elaborated provisions on fair and equitable treatment and indirect expropriation. At the heart of these 'chatty' provisions is a desire to regain policy space, to accommodate commercial and non-commercial regulatory concerns in an even broader fashion. This trend has been triggered by increased security concerns, a changing perception of strategic industries, state measures in cases of economic crisis, and an increasing trend that former capital exporting countries turn increasingly also into host States for capital from developing countries and emerging market economies, see UNCTAD IPFSD (n 18).

renegotiation of treaties generates more debate than in the past. Not just the international investment agreements themselves frequently inhibit rules on termination and the consequences flowing therefrom, but public international law offers a rich body of rules and principles also relevant to the issue. *Karsten Nowrot* explores the chances and challenges of an attempt to escape the relative isolation of the current investment law regime and to open it up more broadly to non-commercial concerns by means of the rules in public international law on termination and renegotiation of treaties. Overcoming the weight of history and the force of inertia might, however, take some doing. It would hardly be surprising if we can soon witness the emergence of an intensified debate, including also some shrilly contributions, in particular in and among investor–State arbitral tribunals, whether and to which degree States are—under public international law—still the masters of the treaties in a sense that they can *freely* restrict or even end with *immediate* effect protections previously afforded to investors in international investment agreements.

In Part IV the contributions are devoted to current trends in investor protection in selected regions of the world. To begin with, what we are witness to is a trend towards regionalization of international investment law with the negotiation of major preferential trade and investment treaties already under way—to name a few, the proposed Trans-Pacific Partnership Agreement,[55] the Regional Comprehensive Economic Partnership,[56] as well as the Transatlantic Trade and Investment Partnership.[57] Moreover, trade and investment policy is integrating; for better or worse. Notions such as special and differential treatment will gain importance. Chapters on sustainable development will more often be included in treaties with references to internationally agreed principles and rules, particularly in the area of labour and the environment.[58] The European Union, as a new major player in this field, decided to embark on both a modest reform of the current international regime itself by suggesting new treaty language[59] and, otherwise, it has allowed for no less than a little revolution: international investment agreements shall not anymore predominantly be concluded between developed and less developed countries but basically among all States, irrespective of their level of development, also in terms of the domestic rule of law.[60]

---

[55] As of writing, TPP officials had last met for a meeting in Hawaii from 9–15 March 2015 'to advance remaining technical issues', Foreign Affairs, Trade and Development Canada, 'Trans-Pacific Partnership (TPP) Free Trade Negotiations' <http://www.international.gc.ca/trade-agreements-accords-commerciaux/agr-acc/tpp-ptp/rounds-series.aspx?lang=eng> accessed 24 April 2015.
[56] The sixth round of negotiations took place from 1–5 December 2014 in India, Department of Foreign Affairs and Trade Australia, 'Regional Comprehensive Economic Partnership' <http://dfat.gov.au/trade/agreements/rcep/Pages/regional-comprehensive-economic-partnership.aspx#news> accessed 24 April 2015.
[57] The ninth round of negotiations came to a close on 24 April 2015, European Commission Memo, '9th Round Transatlantic Trade and Investment Partnership Negotiations' (7 April 2015) <http://trade.ec.europa.eu/doclib/events/index.cfm?id=1287> accessed 24 April 2015.
[58] cf this volume's chapters by G VanDuzer and F Hoffmeister.
[59] cf F Hoffmeister in this volume; see also Hindelang, 'Study on Investor-State Dispute Settlement' (n 47).
[60] cf P-T Stoll and TP Holterhus in this volume, see also Hindelang, 'Study on Investor-State Dispute Settlement' (n 47).

States in other regions of the world have chosen to go down a different road: In practice, most States consider some form of protection of foreign investors and investment to be desirable. Yet, some governments are beginning to ask whether the current system, relying predominantly on public international law instruments, can be complemented with or even replaced by systems which would allow for another balance to be struck between legitimate private property interests and important public concerns. While some States withdraw from the international system and rely on domestic legal protections only, others experiment with new forms of investment protection through regional arrangements. Again others jump back and forth between international and domestic instruments. In such diversified environment, it should be promising to analyse how these new systems differ from the existing model both substantially and procedurally. In doing so, the contributions in this Part, again, analyse whether a proliferation of alternative models of investment protection may be taken as a herald of a paradigmatic shift in international investment law.

Sean Woolfrey addresses South Africa's new approach to investment protection that relies on investment-specific domestic legislation and a new model BIT to be developed soon. South Africa signed a number of investment agreements in the immediate post-Apartheid era to re-establish its international credibility. Currently the country—after a comprehensive review process—is terminating or not renewing these BITs. As an alternative means, the country is implementing domestic law—that is, the Promotion and Protection of Investment Bill—that the South African Government believes strikes a better balance between investment protection standards and the Government's capacity to regulate in the public interest. As a rule, protection standards would be enforceable through domestic court proceedings. At the same time the Government is developing a new model BIT relying on a template devised by the Southern African Development Community. *Woolfrey* explains that this model BIT will probably provide considerably more regulatory leeway than previous South African BITs. Strikingly, while the EU—together with countries such as Canada and the USA—aim at establishing investment protection through means of public international law as a standard feature irrespective of the level of development of a specific country, South Africa proceeds quite selectively by promoting investment protection by domestic law as the default rule.

Latin American countries have always displayed a wide ideational variety of approaches to foreign investment. This can be illustrated, on the one hand, by the *Calvo*-doctrine aiming at limiting the protection of foreign investors to national treatment, the unique role of Brazil as an eminent emerging market economy not having ratified any BIT as of yet,[61] or the more recent withdrawals from ICSID by

---

[61] The Brazilian position seems to be shifting, however, as it signed two investment protection agreements with Mozambique and Angola early 2015. ISDS mechanisms commonly found in BITs and FTAs seem not to be part of these agreements. As of writing, both agreements await ratification by Brazilian Congress. Acordo Brasil-Moçambique de Cooperação e Facilitação de Investimentos (ACFI) <www.itamaraty.gov.br/index.php?option=com_content&view=article&id=8511&catid=42&Itemid=280&lang=pt-BR> accessed 24 April 2015; Portal Brasil, 'Brasil e Angola assinam acordo bilateral'

Bolivia, Ecuador, or Venezuela. On the other hand, there are those countries coming together in the Pacific Alliance—Chile, Peru, Colombia, and Mexico—which support investor protection through international treaties.[62] Against the background of these diverse developments *Maria José Luque Macias* introduces and assesses recent regional approaches in Latin America relying on national laws and investment contracts and regional institutions to create alternative regimes for investor protection which would deviate from the current dominant system of investment arbitration through international treaties.

Leon E Trakman and *Kunal Sharma* address the recent developments in the Pacific Rim area in the light of the overall theme of the volume. In particular, they critically discuss the policy changes of the Australian Government, having jumped back and forth between domestic courts and investor–State dispute settlement in international investment treaties in recent years. Instead of considering including investor–State dispute settlement provisions in BITs and FTAs on a case-by-case basis, as Australia's current investment doctrine suggests, they would prefer to include such dispute settlement mechanisms in all agreements and rather work on improving it.[63] Moreover, *Trakman* and *Sharma* refer to the developments in Indonesia, which has shown a stronger resistance against the present investment law regime lately. Nevertheless, according to them, it appears unlikely that Indonesia will follow the path of some South American countries in abandoning investment protection by means of public international law. Rather, Indonesia will seek more favourable deals in upcoming international investment agreement negotiation rounds. In bringing their chapter to a close, *Trakman* and *Sharma* embed these two strands of development in a greater context, that is, the ongoing negotiations on the Trans-Pacific Partnership Agreement.

It took some years following the signing of the Lisbon Treaty in 2007 before the European Commission could finally include investment protection in its international negotiating agenda. CETA, TTIP, and other comprehensive free trade agreements, if and once entered into force, will—from a European perspective—break new ground by including full-fledged investment protection chapters. Furthermore, the EU began negotiating the first European stand-alone BIT with China in 2013. In defining its policy priorities the EU Commission's Directorate General for Trade has to align different visions on investment protection found in the European institutions,[64] among the Member State governments,

---

(2 April 2015) <www.brasil.gov.br/governo/2015/04/brasil-e-angola-assinam-acordo-bilateral> accessed 24 April 2015. See also Brasil, Ministério do Desenvolvimento, Indústria e Comércio Exterior, Cooperation and Facilitation Investment Agreement (CFIA), Presentation at the UNCTAD World Investment Forum 2015, <http://unctad-worldinvestmentforum.org/wp-content/uploads/2015/03/Brazil_side-event-Wednesday_model-agreements.pdf> accessed 24 April 2015.

[62] cf Clarkson and Hindelang (n 10).

[63] See on a similar approach suggested in respect of Europe, while attributing a stronger role to *functioning* domestic courts Hindelang, 'Study on Investor-State Dispute Settlement' (n 47).

[64] See, for example, the studies produced on behalf of the European Parliament PJ Kuijper, 'Part I: Study on Investment Protection Agreements as Instruments of International Economic Law', in European Parliament, Directorate General for External Policies of the Union, *Study Investor-State Dispute Settlement (ISDS) Provisions in the EU's International Investment Agreements* (European

in corporate lobby organizations, and civil society. In doing so the European Union has, among others, to address an increasingly critical reflection of the impact of international investment agreements and related dispute settlement on policies directed at sustainable development. Embedding investment protection into comprehensive economic agreements, containing lengthy texts on the environment or labour standards, puts sustainable development, according to *Frank Hoffmeister*, 'on par with an investment protection chapter'. At the same time, by embarking on a reform of current investment treaty language employed in respect of substantive as well as procedural rules, the European Union emphasizes the continuing importance of public international law for refocusing international investment law; other methods for investment protection fade somewhat in the background.

Peter-Tobias Stoll and *Till Holterhus* invite us to take a 'constitutional view' on international investment law and its recalibration attempts. Such approach is warranted as the EU and other major players are turning international investment law from a 'special regime' predominantly aimed at countries with a weak domestic rule of law into a general system of controlling and reviewing the exercise of governmental powers, irrespective of the level of development of the domestic rule of law. Such development renders questions relating to concepts such as sovereignty, democracy, legitimacy, due process, and the rule of law, all developed in the context of constitutional law and thought, even more pressing. As *Stoll* and *Holterhus* have difficulties finding adequate answers addressing the aforementioned concerns in the purported texts on the Comprehensive Economic and Trade Agreement between the EU and Canada, and similar undertakings, they suggest an alternative avenue. Instead of turning international investment law into a global standard—without considering the level of development in terms of the domestic rule of law—they advocate for intensifying efforts in further developing the human rights approach to property protection.

Bringing the volume to a close, in the last chapter, by tying together the individual contributions to this book, it is for the editors to revisit the initial working hypothesis. We are certainly not giving away any secrets when we say here that the question of whether we do indeed see shifting paradigms, towards a more balanced, less isolated and increasingly diversified investment law regime warrants a nuanced answer. As always with ongoing processes, their assessment is inevitably provisional. Necessarily speculative are the remarks on possible lines of future development of and in the field of international investment law. Caveat lector.

Commission 2014) <www.jura.fu-berlin.de/fachbereich/einrichtungen/oeffentliches-recht/lehrende/hindelangs/Studie-fuer-Europaeisches-Parlament/Volume-2-Studies.pdf> accessed 24 April 2015; I Pernice, 'Part III: Study on International Investment Protection Agreements and EU Law', in European Parliament, Directorate General for External Policies of the Union, *Study Investor-State Dispute Settlement (ISDS) Provisions in the EU's International Investment Agreements* (European Commission 2014) <www.jura.fu-berlin.de/fachbereich/einrichtungen/oeffentliches-recht/lehrende/hindelangs/Studie-fuer-Europaeisches-Parlament/Volume-2-Studies.pdf> accessed 24 April 2015; Hindelang, 'Study on Investor-State Dispute Settlement' (n 47).

I

Investment Protection and Sustainable Development

Key Issues

Giorgio Sacerdoti

I. Introduction: The Role of Foreign Direct Investment in Promoting Development

This introductory chapter aims at assessing critically in perspective and in their mutual relations two key concepts within the subject matter of this volume, that is, the current status of the investment protection regime and the principle of sustainable development (SD). This chapter sketches the historical background of these principles and highlights their potentials, but addresses also shortcomings and ambiguities in their interrelation. The legal value of the concept of SD is often unclear. Yet, SD represents an important normative principle, which can serve as a tool to adjust imbalances within the current investment protection system. The chapter will also consider the notion of State regulatory autonomy, which is an important tool to ensure a host State's capacity to adapt its policies to the changing needs of SD while there is concern that international commitments to foreign investors may unduly limit this flexibility.[1]

A central issue of growing concern in the area of legal regulation of international investments is, indeed, how to ensure that also through treaty making and treaty application the promotion and protection of foreign direct investment (FDI) is beneficial for the recipient host countries, especially developing countries.

Seen from the point of view of those in charge of promoting the development of host countries, the issue is how to ensure that those treaties effectively promote

---

[1] See generally MC Cordonnier Segger, MW Gehring, and A Newcombe (eds), *Sustainable Development in World Investment Law* (Wolters Kluwer 2011); for an exercise in policy guidance see Commonwealth Secretariat, *Integrating Sustainable Development into International Investment Agreements: A Guide for Developing Countries* (2012) <www.iisd.org/pdf/2012/6th_annual_forum_commonwealth_guide.pdf> accessed 25 August 2015.

the contribution of foreign investment to the development goals of the recipient countries and do not represent a hurdle for their efforts in that direction.

Generally speaking, the positive role of FDI for development appears at present to be taken for granted. The emphasis is rather, on one hand, on the responsibility of enterprises engaged in direct foreign investment to pursue responsible policies irrespective of the applicable legal framework in the host country and, on the other hand, on instruments and rules that would encourage SD.

As an example of the first proposition, the importance of foreign investment for development has been stressed recently by none other than UN Secretary-General Ban Ki-moon in his preface to the United Nations Conference on Trade and Development (UNCTAD) 2014 World Investment Report. After noting that 'after a decline in 2012 global foreign direct investment flows rose by 9% in 2013, with growth expected to continue in the years to come', the Secretary-General goes on to conclude as follows:

> This demonstrates the great potential of international investment, along with other financial resources, to help reach the goals of a post-2015 agenda for sustainable development. Transnational corporations can support this effort by creating decent jobs, generating exports, promoting rights, respecting the environment, encouraging local content, paying fair taxes and transferring capital, technology and business contacts to spur development.[2]

As to the role of rules and institutions one can quote an eloquent statement that appears as the 'key message' on the website of the International Institute for Sustainable Development (IISD), an NGO active in the field, based in Canada:[3]

> Without investment, sustainable development is impossible. Well planned, high quality foreign investment in developed and developing countries can help make current economic practices more sustainable. Inappropriate investment, however, can undermine communities and the environment, as well as domestic development strategies. IISD examines how the rules and institutions that govern international investment flows can be improved so as to help developing countries, in particular attract the sort of investment that promotes sustainable development.

This ambitious statement reflects a policy approach to the issue that calls for the structuring of domestic policies as well as instruments of economic cooperation that will maximize the contribution of foreign investment to the needs of developing countries. According to the parameters of 'sustainable development' this goes beyond just promoting economic growth.

Before going further into the subject matter a few basic points should be made. My exposé and analysis is a *legal* one: it is beyond my scope to address the economic policy issues underpinning the choice that a given country sets for itself, as well as the domestic instruments put in place to attain a country's development objectives and the role given therein to foreign investment. In respect of

---

[2] UNCTAD, *World Investment Report 2014. Investing in the SDGs* [Sustainable Development Goals]: *An Action Plan* (United Nations 2014) iii.

[3] See <www.iisd.org/investment> accessed 5 October 2014.

encouraging and selecting FDI, this includes not only international instruments but foremost also domestic measures. Among these are financial or tax incentives in order to stimulate the flow of FDI in general, or to promote it in certain sectors (such as mining or manufacturing), in certain parts of the territory of that country, or in certain forms (such as joint-ventures). Institutions such as UNCTAD, as evidenced by its annual World Investment Report, and the World Bank have done great work in this area but studying the implications of such policies would go beyond the scope of the present contribution by a lawyer.[4]

Generally speaking, everybody, and not just lawyers, should be aware of the limits that legal instruments and legal analysis inherently have when addressing policy issues and evaluating the contribution of legal instruments to complex economic goals, whose content is debated among economist and policy makers, such as 'sustainable development'. While the first term of my theme 'investment protection' is essentially legal, the second term 'sustainable development' is essentially economic or policy-based, although consistent efforts have been devoted to elaborate on its legal implications. A caveat is, thus, appropriate as to 'balancing' such diverse, somehow heterogeneous concepts: at first sight, the title seems to imply a link, be it correlation or causation, possibly even an inverted one: an equation where the greater the protection of foreign investments, the lesser will or might be their contribution to development, and vice versa. However, there is no support generally for this approach in policy documents by international organizations focusing on development, as the above quotations from authoritative statements show. Such an approach would leave out, moreover, an important term, that is the correlation between protection, be it under international instruments or domestic law (including the looser, comprehensive, and currently popular concept of 'good governance')[5] and investment flows in a host country.

Traditionally, bilateral investment treaties (BITs) and other International Investment Agreements (IIAs), including investment chapters of more comprehensive regional agreements, have been mute as their relationship with SD. Moreover, liberalization of FDI has not been a prerequisite, nor an outright goal of these agreements, notwithstanding the statements found usually

---

[4] See UNCTAD, *The Role of IIAs in Attracting FDI to Developing Countries* (2009).
[5] See the World Bank, *Governance Indicators* <http://info.worldbank.org/governance/wgi/index.aspx#home> accessed 25 August 2015. The website gives the following definition:

> Governance consists of the traditions and institutions by which authority in a country is exercised. This includes the process by which governments are selected, monitored and replaced; the capacity of the government to effectively formulate and implement sound policies; and the respect of citizens and the state for the institutions that govern economic and social interactions among them.

The Worldwide Governance Indicators (WGI) project reports are described as follows: They
> aggregate and individual governance indicators for 215 economies over the period 1996–2013, for six dimensions of governance: Voice and Accountability; Political Stability and Absence of Violence; Government Effectiveness; Regulatory Quality; Rule of Law: Control of Corruption. These aggregate indicators combine the views of a large number of enterprise, citizen and expert survey respondents in industrial and developing countries.

in their preambles in favour of the reciprocal promotion of foreign investment among the parties. They have not been conceived as policy instruments but rather as a framework of minimum standards expressing in general terms a pro-investment protective approach.

Any evaluation of the impact of *international* legal instruments focused on the protection of FDI and on the promotion of SD in a host country should consider moreover that such instruments, because of how they have been traditionally drafted, though potentially significant, tend to play a more limited role than focused domestic instruments and policies, such as specific incentives and the quality of the legal and institutional environment in terms of good governance.

Recent agreements tend to be more detailed and tend to take into account the specific needs, economic structure, and policy goals of the signatories, as will be highlighted and discussed later, also in respect of the development implications of this change of approach. This makes the issue set forth in the above quotation from the website of the IISD more pressing, since more detailed investment agreements call for a more careful 'custom-made' approach to their drafting so as to reflect better any development policy and needs of the parties and their right to modify such policies in the future. On the other hand, the ability of policy makers to structure the normative framework for foreign investment so as to ensure the contribution of actual investments to the attainment of defined economic and social development objectives is a challenge that cannot be met just by a more accurate drafting of legal instruments. Economic and financial incentives may be called for, as well as rules of conduct for multinational enterprises by home countries.[6] Finally a 'favourable investment climate' in the host country as may result from

---

[6] Thus, as to the role and responsibility of home countries, the Columbia Center on Sustainable Investment (CCSI) in presenting the Ninth Annual Columbia International Investment Conference, entitled 'Raising the Bar: Home Country Efforts to Regulate Foreign Investment for Sustainable Development' at Columbia University, 12–13 November 2014, has described its aims as follows:

> In recent years there has been growing dialogue over whether, in addition to supporting their firms in making foreign direct investments, home countries should also monitor or regulate the activities of companies operating abroad, for example, with regards to the disclosure of tax payments, or impacts on human rights, the environment, or development. Legal experts have argued that home countries have extraterritorial obligations under international law, including with respect to regulating the activities of both publicly controlled as well as private companies. The increasing pressure on home countries to monitor or regulate the overseas activities of multinational companies also results from a sense of moral duty, the desire for greater coherency of governmental policies and actions, and perceptions of potential political or economic self-interest. Yet, while home countries have influence over outward investors, are willing to exercise extraterritorial power in certain contexts, and are often committed to sustainable development, their policies and actions are not always coherent.

See CCSI, Annual Report 2014–2015, 24, <http://ccsi.columbia.edu/files/2013/10/CCSI-Annual-Report-2014-2015-FINAL.compressed.pdf> accessed 9 October 2015. The limits of extraterritorial legislation of home countries in protecting human rights affected by the conduct of multinational companies abroad has been made evident by the restrictive interpretation of the Alien Tort Statute by the US Supreme Court in the well-known *Kiobel v Royal Dutch Petroleum* decision of 17 April 2013, 133 SCt 1659 (2013).

domestic instruments and good governance policies (such as reducing the level of corruption) is also required.[7]

This leads us to defining the terms of the relationship: 'sustainable development' on the one hand and 'investment agreements' and the protection they afford to foreign investors on the other.

II. The Concept of 'Sustainable Development': Economic Background

As is well known, the concept of 'sustainable development' stems from the Bruntland Commission Report 'Our Common Heritage' of 1987, where it was defined as 'development that meets the needs of the present without compromising the ability of future generations to meet their own needs'.[8] The Rio Declaration on Environment and Development of 1992 and the Agenda 21 stemming therefrom heavily endorsed and elaborated the concept as a road map for a global development strategy.[9] Principle 4 of the Rio Declaration clarifies that the concept aims at incorporating environmental concerns and protection into purely economic development strategies. Today

SD is broadly understood as a concept that is characterized by (1) the close linkage between policy goals of economic and social development and environmental protection; (2) the qualification of environmental protection as an integral part of any developmental measure, and vice-versa; and (3) the long-term perspective of both political goals, that is the State's inter-generational responsibility.[10]

The subsequent elaboration of the concept of SD in operative terms by international organizations focusing on developmental policies should also be considered. Other concepts have been added to for measuring economic development in addition to the rate of GDP growth and other purely economic quantitative indicators. Besides environmental protection there is also the concept of social development with all its multi-faceted aspects. Broader 'welfare' indicators are now considered, as reflected in the Human Development Index (HDI), a composite statistic of life expectancy, education, and income indices developed by the UNDP since the 1990s, to which in 2010 inequality measurement has been added (including gender inequality). Growth in extractive industries and manufacturing, and building of large infrastructures, which used to be synonymous of development, where often foreign technological

---

[7] See Transparency International, *Corruption Perception Index*, annually, <www.transparency.org/cpi2013> accessed 4 November 2014, showing least developed countries in the bottom part of the listing.
[8] United Nations General Assembly (UNGA), 'World Commission on Environment and Development' UNGA Res 42/87 (11 December 1987).
[9] UNGA, 'Rio Declaration on Environment and Development' UNGA/CONF.151/26 Vol I (12 August 1992).
[10] See U Beyerlin, 'Sustainable Development', *Max Planck Encyclopedia of Public International Law* (OUP 2009) para 9.

and capital contribution is crucial, have given way to other priorities and agendas. Thus, the rate of poverty reduction has become the focus of the UN Global Compact, following the Millennium Summit (2000), and of the policies of the World Bank and other development agencies, not to speak of criteria which are difficult to measure in quantitative terms, such as good governance and the rule of law. From respect and promotion of core labour standards to empowerment of women and indigenous populations, the list of what is included here is quite substantial. Democratic representative government and respect for fundamental human rights and liberties should also be high on this list but it must be noted with regret that this is not often the case. Finally, the concept of financial stability has recently become a predominant concern, an element that had been totally neglected until then.

The more ambitious the objectives and multi-faceted the policies meant to attain them, the more difficult it is to pinpoint a univocal meaning for SD. On the one hand, centralized industrial policies have been abandoned, as well as those based on import substitution,[11] in view of their poor results and the social cost often associated with them. On the other hand, liberal market-based policies of the type advocated in the 1990s by the 'Washington Consensus'[12] have also often failed. It is clear that countries pursue their development strategies in different ways, as to institutional set-up, priorities, and strategies or mix of policies. While the progress of individual countries towards certain quantitative objectives can be measured, the debate goes on as to the policies that for a given country would stimulate SD. A good example is the divide between countries in relation to the Kyoto Protocol to the protection of the environment and the lack of consensus on the causes, responsibilities, and policies to fight global warming. A recent debate between Nobel Prize winners for economy as to the biggest problems facing the global economy of the future do not pay any specific attention to SD, but rather focus directly on some of its objectives such as coping with global warming (George A Akerlof), promoting inclusiveness (Michael Spencer), and reducing inequality (Joseph E Stiglitz).[13] The focus of another Nobel Prize winner, Amartya Sen, on (self) empowerment of the poor and on recognition of individual and collective rights as keys to overcoming underdevelopment and extreme poverty should not be overlooked.

---

[11] Import substitution industrialization is a trade and economic policy that advocates replacing foreign imports with domestic production, also by raising tariffs and other barriers against imports, see N Brian (ed), *A Comprehensive Dictionary of Economics* (Abhishek Publications 2009) 88. This policy is based on the premise that a country should attempt to reduce its foreign dependency through the local production of industrialized products to foster economic independence and endogenous development.

[12] This is the set of ten policies that the US Government, the International Monetary Fund (IMF), and the World Bank especially considered were necessary elements of 'first stage policy reform' that all countries should adopt to increase economic growth. At its heart is an emphasis on the importance of macroeconomic stability, fiscal discipline, and integration into the international economy—in other words a neo-liberal view of globalization, <www.who.int/trade/glossary/story094/en/> accessed 24 October 2014.

[13] See IMF, 'Looming Ahead. Five Nobel Prize winners discuss what they each see as the biggest problem facing the global economy of the future' (September 2014) 51 Finance & Development (IMF) 14.

It is not surprising that the impact of FDI on economic growth is debated among qualified economists, although the importance of FDI as an important source of capital, managerial and technological know-how, and employment is acknowledged, as well as its positive impact on the improvement of the competitive environment in closed local markets.[14]

The adoption of liberal market-based economic models and the opening of markets worldwide have rendered out of fashion centralized industrial policies such as the import substitution approach. As a result, in the context of globalization, the instruments available to most countries to promote independently a definite model of (sustainable) development are limited and of dubious effectiveness. Direct investment spreads throughout the world propelled by market opportunities, cost efficiency (such as outsourcing due to high labour costs in industrialized countries), different levels of productivity and of rates of return, which individual host countries can hardly influence. Uncoordinated, unilateral regulatory efforts may be inefficient to govern and select the flows of inward FDI; on the contrary, such policies may fuel undesired regulatory arbitrage by multinational companies. These enterprises are able to shift the location of their investments in response to the diversity of incentives and the inherent advantages of different markets, thus favouring some countries at the expense of others.

One should also consider that globalization has not only encouraged FDI as a means of internationalizing production: the development of industrial capabilities also in least developed countries has allowed the establishment of transnational supply chains of production (value chains) based on long-term contractual arrangements rather than direct investment controlled by the masterminds of such schemes. There are multinational companies based in advanced economies which own the brands under which these products are sold worldwide.[15]

III. Content and Legal Definitions of 'Sustainable Development'

There are conflicting views among legal authors as to the normative content of SD and its binding scope, although one can agree that, in general terms, SD has

---

[14] See E Borensztein, J De Gregorio, and J Lee, 'How does Foreign Direct Investment Affect Economic Growth?' (1998) 45 J Int Econ 115–35; TH Moran, EM Graham, and M Blomstrom (eds), *Does Foreign Direct Investment Promote Development?* (IIE 2005); L Resmini, 'Il ruolo degli investimenti esteri' in G Venturini (ed), *Le nuove forme di sostegno allo sviluppo nella prospettiva del diritto internazionale* (Giappichelli 2009) 67–80.

[15] The effect of this change can be seen when recollecting the disastrous collapse in Bangladesh on 13 May 2013 of a building hosting textile factories, the deadliest garment-factory accident in history, with a toll of more than 1,000 clothing workers, mostly women, due to poor labour conditions and inexistent health, building, and environmental controls, in patent breach of any sustainable development policy. No foreign investor was directly and legally implicated although most of those factories worked under exclusive contracts for international brands. The reaction was a voluntary but binding 'Accord on Factories and Buildings Safety in Bangladesh', signed by a number of foreign buyers (but refused by Walmart), in order to ensure standards which local authorities do not care about enforcing; see <www.bangladeshaccord.org> accessed 4 November 2014.

won international recognition as a broad legal principle, beyond being a policy principle.[16] But what about its specific content and effects on the interpretation and application of norms and obligations? The International Court of Justice (ICJ) has been cautious in the *Gabcicovo-Nagymaros* decision as to the consequences that can be derived from the 'concept of sustainable development', when recognizing it as a basis for the 'need to reconcile economic development with protection of the environment'. The Court just concluded that 'the parties should look afresh at the effects on the environment of the operation of the Gabcicovo plant'.[17]

One of the most elaborate legal reflections is found in the ILA New Delhi Declaration of 2002 on 'Principles of International Law Relating to Sustainable Development', which lists seven principles, each articulated in more detailed sub-principles:

1. The duty of States to ensure sustainable use of natural resources;
2. The principle of equity and eradication of poverty;
3. The principle of common but differentiated responsibilities;
4. The principle of the precautionary approach to human health, natural resources, and ecosystems;
5. The principle of public participation and access to information and justice;
6. The principle of good governance; and
7. The principle of integration and interrelationship, in particular in relation to human rights and social, economic, and environmental objectives.

This definition is not exhaustive. The absence of any specific principle on the right to regulate foreign investment and the responsibility of investors is striking.[18] The latter concern has been somehow covered by putting the responsibility to protect, respect, and enhance human rights directly on multinational enterprises by the UN 'Guiding Principles on Business and Human Rights' of 2011.[19]

This broad approach to the coverage, implication, and methods to promote SD underlines the responsibility of host States in respect of foreign investment. It is understandable that concern has been voiced as to the possible interference of legal commitments stemming out of IIAs, especially directly in favour of foreign

---

[16] See P Sands, *Principles of International Environmental Law* (2nd edn, CUP 2003) 254.
[17] *Gabcicovo-Nagymaros Project (Hungary v Slovakia)* (Judgment) [1997] ICJ Rep 7 at para 140.
[18] See the text at <www.ila-hq.org/en/committees/index.cfm/cid/25> accessed 4 November 2014; also as an Appendix to the volume discussing the issue in N Schrijver and F Weiss (eds), *International Law and Sustainable Development, Principles and Practice* (Martinus Nijhoff 2004). The focus on sustainable development as a set of principles seems to indicate a change of perspective in respect of the approach to the 'right to development' as an individual 'inalienable' human right, expressed in the UNGA Resolution A/RES/41/128 of 4 December 1986. See recently C Tietje, 'The Right to Development within the International Legal Order' in M Cremona and others (eds), *Reflections on the Constitutionalisation of International Economic Law: Liber Amicorum, EU Petersmann* (Brill 2014) 381.
[19] HR/PUB/11/04, implementing the UN 'Protect, Respect and Remedy Framework', annexed to the Special Representative of the Secretary-General's 'Final Report on the issue of human rights and transnational corporations and other business enterprises' (UNHCR A/HRC/17/31), endorsed by the Council in its resolution 17/4 of 16 June 2011.

investors, with the right and ability of host States to pursue policies aimed at promoting or safeguarding SD. This right and ability is often understood in the broadest sense, protecting the use of a State 'policy space' for an almost indefinite range of reasons and ends.[20] However, if governments consider that it is in the interest of their economy to give assurances, backed by international law, of 'reasonable' treatment to investors from abroad, they have to take into account this hurdle when adopting new policies that may infringe existing rights, as well as deterring new investments.

Finally, is SD a concept essentially applicable only to 'developing countries', assuming that this category still reflects reality and is of conceptual usefulness? In this respect, one must note from the heart of the European Union that there are doubts whether there is a single concept of SD applicable throughout countries with diverse levels of development. In Europe we rarely hear about this concept in the political and economic debate. Sustainability is rather declined with debt or pensions and linked to growth, stability, and unemployment.

In EU countries it is taken for granted that any (economic) development—and hence public and private decision making—must respect other priorities and values, including the respect of fundamental individual rights, both civil and social. Our complex political democratic systems, the elaborate formation of our administrative decisions, the multiple rights of recourse granted to those potentially affected to national and European courts for redress are meant to ensure this balance. On the other hand, the European Union subscribes to the concept of SD in its international relations, including in 'North–North' contexts. Thus, the EU Council mandate to the Commission for the negotiations of the Transatlantic Trade and Investment Partnership (TTIP)[21] with the USA states as Objective no. 8 that:

This Agreement should recognize that sustainable development is an overarching objective of the Parties and that they will aim at ensuring and facilitating respect of international environmental and labour agreements and standards while promoting high levels of protection for the environment, labour and consumers, consistent with the EU acquis and Member States' legislation. The Agreement should recognize that the Parties will not encourage trade or foreign direct investment by lowering domestic environmental, labour or occupational health and safety legislation and standards, or by relaxing core labour standards or policies and legislation aimed at protecting and promoting cultural diversity.

Reverting to the global level, a recent elaboration by UNCTAD of the 'Sustainable Development Goals' states that these goals are

meant to galvanize action by government, the private sector, international organizations, non-governmental organizations (NGOs) and other stakeholders worldwide by providing direction and setting concrete targets in areas ranging from poverty reduction to food

---

[20] See A Newcombe, 'The Boundaries of Regulatory Expropriation in International Investment Law' (2005) 20 ICSID Rev 1.
[21] The mandate of 17 June 2013 has been declassified in October 2014, see <http://data.consilium.europa.eu/doc/document/ST-11103-2013-DCL-1/en/pdf> of 8 October 2014, accessed 4 November 2014.

security, health, education, employment, equality, climate change, ecosystems and biodiversity, among others.²²

These goals, adopted at the 2015 Summit in furtherance of the Millennium Development Goals agreed in 2000 at the UN Millennium Summit, point to objectives which are key for developing economies. They have, clearly, a different focus than those listed by the EU as objectives in the negotiations of the TTIP under the same heading of sustainable development.

IV. Foreign Investment: International Protection and Regulation

Let us turn now to the second term, namely 'investment protection', focusing on the scope and limits of 'international legal protection', thus under international instruments.

Two categories of instruments have to be considered here: (a) self-standing treaties, essentially BITs, and, especially more recently, (b) regional investment treaties and investment chapters of treaties covering also trade. The latter may be bilateral (such as the Free Trade Agreements (FTAs) which the EU has been negotiating with Canada and Singapore and the Transatlantic Trade and Investment Partnership or TTIP with the USA), or among several parties (such as the North American Free Trade Agreement (NAFTA)), some being currently concluded in South-East Asia, especially the Transpacific Partnership (TPP).

Starting with BITs, let's consider first their typical format—initiated by Germany at the end of the 1950s, as they have been traditionally framed and still mostly are. The texts of these treaties are rather short and contain mostly general provisions which provide for their coverage (definitions), the substantive rights granted directly to the investors and the remedies made available to them. The terms used must be interpreted in the light of relevant international customary concepts when no specific definitions under the treaty, or as guidance to arbitral tribunals, are included in the text.²³ I would point out to the following features as being relevant for the present analysis:

1. The stated *purpose* of these BITs is to promote and protect foreign (direct) investments. However, their content, the object of their provisions, that is the legal obligation they create, is aimed at providing for general and specific levels/standards/duties of *protection* for the investors, who are nationals of

---

²² UNCTAD (n 2) 136. The Sustainable Development Summit held within the UN General Assembly on 25–27 September 2015 adopted seventeen global goals 'to end poverty, protect the planet and ensure prosperity for all', as elaborated in the preparatory document and draft A/69/L.85 of 12 August 2015. No mention was made of the role of foreign investment.

²³ This is notably the case of the more articulated and considerably longer text of the current 2012 US Model of BIT (going back to the previous one of 2004) <www.state.gov/documents/organization/188371.pdf> accessed 24 October 2014. The arbitral case law is also relevant to interpret standard terms such as 'fair and equitable treatment', although arbitral case law does not have a precedential value *stricto sensu*; see G Sacerdoti, 'Precedent in the Settlement of International Economic

either party and their investments in the other party. Promotional provisions, such as incentives by the signatories, are extraneous to the structure of such BITs. One could define them as 'static' instruments; they are not dynamic policy instruments meant to promote economic cooperation between the parties.[24]

2. As to *definitions*, investments are broadly defined, usually including existing investments, through a non-exclusive list of any kind of assets that may qualify as an investment of an investor of one party in the territory of the other party.

3. *Nationality* of the protected investors is also broadly defined: natural and legal persons, private and public entities (to which State-Owned Enterprises (SOEs), and Sovereign Wealth Funds (SWFs), mostly from developing nations are an important recent addition) are included, based usually on formal links, such as place of incorporation, making the nationality of shareholders and the origin of the capital invested immaterial. This allows recourse to 'treaty shopping' by investors especially in cases of disputes: investors from one country can establish holding companies in a third country as a conduit for their investments in the host country when the country of the holding company has a BIT with the host country, while their home country has none or it contains less favourable terms.

4. The treaties are all *reciprocal* so that investments by investors of both parties are covered and subject to the same standards, irrespective of the prevailing direction of investment flows. This aspect had not been considered by industrialized countries when they had initially promoted these instruments since their concern was to protect their outward private direct investments in developing countries. Those countries have realized only recently that countries labelled traditionally as 'developing economies' have also become the origin of FDI, including by SOEs and SWFs. As a consequence they had to cease viewing themselves exclusively as home countries.

5. BITs contain *only obligations on the States which are parties* thereto, essentially the host country, not on investors. The only obligation on investors, which is rather a condition for their protection, is that an investment be made in conformity with the domestic law of the host country. This reflects the fact that foreign investments are generally subject in their daily operations to the law of the host State, as the law of the place of establishment. Host countries are thus able to enforce any general or specific requirement and obligations laid down by them upon foreign investors through domestic judicial, administrative, and any other enforcement means, without the need to initiate arbitration against a foreign investor under the BIT. The treaty

---

Disputes: the WTO and the Investment Arbitration Models' in A Rovine (ed), *Contemporary Issues in International Arbitration and Mediation: The Fordham Papers 2010* (Martinus Nijhoff 2011) 225.

[24] This is usually true also for the home country. However, separate domestic investment support facilities (such as foreign investment public insurance in Germany) may be subject to the condition that a BIT exists with the host country of the investment concerned.

provisions are in substance relevant only as a guarantee for the investors, when those internal provisions and requirements fall below what the treaty requires, the latter operates thus as a kind of 'safety net'.[25]

6. BITs do not usually include among the obligations listed the right of an investor from the other signatory to make an investment, that is they do not grant 'market access' (in trade law terminology) or 'pre-establishment' rights (in investment law terminology). Those BITs that do include this right (the US approach) contain detailed 'negative' lists, specific to each signatory, setting forth the sectors excluded. The right of a host country to restrict access by foreign investors in specific sectors of its economy and thus to reserve certain activities to nationals is thereby safeguarded.

7. Substantive rights granted by BITs to foreign investors may be distinguished according to the following criteria:

   (a) *Contingent standards*, that is rights whose content depends on how the host State treats other similarly situated investors. Basically, these are the Most-Favoured Nation (MFN) and the National Treatment (NT) standards.

   (b) *Absolute standards*, such as 'fair and equitable treatment' (sometimes limited or specified with reference to 'conformity with international law' or to 'the minimum standard provided by international law') and 'full protection and security'. Since the contingent and absolute 'standards' listed are rather undetermined as to their content in the abstract, the import of the obligations to be respected by the host State in a given situation requires an analysis of what is generally practised and is considered lawful or due under different yardsticks (customary international law, practice based on a comparative law evaluation, general principles of law, the treatment made to similarly situated other investors).

   (c) *Absolute general rights:* first of all the right to compensation (full, effective) for direct expropriation (transfer of property to public entities for public purposes), as well as for indirect takings/acts equivalent to expropriation.

   (d) *Absolute specific rights*, which focus on the specific needs for the carrying out of foreign investments, such as the right to repatriate dividends, profits, royalties, fees and the proceeds of divesting; the right to obtain necessary permits and visa for key foreign personnel.

8. As to procedural rights (settlement of disputes), the key, innovative feature of the BITs has been the availability of direct arbitration (Investor-State Dispute Settlement (ISDS) mechanism) by any aggrieved foreign investor covered by the treaty against the host State for breach of the investor's rights stemming

---

[25] See G Sacerdoti, 'Bilateral Treaties and Multilateral Instruments on Investment Protection' (1997) 269 Recueil des Cours de l'Académie de Droit International 255, 368 ff.

from the BIT. A notable feature in this respect is that the institutional setting of the arbitration provided (such as International Centre for Settlement of Investment Disputes (ICSID) or international commercial arbitration models) is such as to allow (international) proceedings to take place and a binding decision to be issued, unimpeded by any obstruction of the host State, without usually any need to exhaust previously its domestic remedies.

This basic model, simple and 'light', has been the blueprint for the conclusion of thousands of such BITs in the last decades. They have been concluded by most countries of the world irrespective of the actual or potential flow of investments between the signatories, their level of development, complementary of their economies, geographical proximity, and political relations. From being an instrument to support the flow of investments from one of the signatories to the other, within a policy of promotion of such investment—as was probably the intent of Germany and Pakistan when they entered into the first of such treaties in 1959—they have become an almost normal feature of the existing level playing field applicable to international investments in the global economy worldwide.

This success cannot be understood without considering two key factors, which after so many years are often forgotten: first, that BITs are traditionally 'static' and 'light'. For a long time host countries had not anticipated that the obligations they were subscribing to could really tie their hands in legitimate law making, granting rather to foreign investors special remedies in case of breaches.[26] An additional element supporting the view that BITs were not considered unduly restraining the regulatory powers of the signatories is that in case of breach the host State is liable to pay monetary compensation to the investor affected in accordance with the principles of State responsibility as determined in direct arbitration but not to restitution or reestablishment of the *status quo ante*. By contrast, breach of WTO obligations in the area of trade entails no compensation for past wrongful damages but the more constraining obligation to withdraw (with no retroactive effects however) the objectionable measure or to modify any domestic regulation found to be in breach of WTO provisions, so as to make it compliant.[27]

Well-run States (which comprise those with the highest level of governance and respect for property rights) recognize in theory and practice in their domestic system the rights listed in the BITs, to both domestic and foreign investors irrespective of their nationality and origin. The small number of disputes over several decades, the very few disputes brought against industrialized market

---

[26] This can explain the lack of safeguard/exception clauses in BITs such as could be patterned after Art XX GATT. The US model clause safeguarding 'essential security interest' reflects rather the military concerns of a world power (cf Art XXI GATT), although it could and has been invoked in case of economic emergency by host States, notably by Argentina under the BIT with the US.

[27] See Understanding on Rules and Procedures Governing the Settlement of Disputes, Marrakesh Agreement Establishing the World Trade Organization, Annex 2, 1869 UNTS 401, 33 ILM 1226 (1994) (Dispute Settlement Understanding, DSU) Art 22.1. Another fundamental difference is that the WTO dispute settlement system is only intergovernmental.

economies (which are also those where the rule of law and non-discrimination is or should be best observed), is evidence thereof. As to developing countries with weak public institutions, adopting internationally recognized best practices may improve and lock-in connected improvements in governance for the benefit also of their domestic enterprises.[28]

Moreover, for countries interested in promoting FDI to developing countries, BITs were meant to supplement customary principles as to the protection of economic rights of foreigners that communist regimes' nationalizations and the promotion of the New International Economic Order by decolonized developing countries had badly shaken in the 1950s to 1960s. In addition, direct arbitration, to be conducted in a neutral framework by aggrieved foreign investors, to present an important political benefit. It was meant to avoid the pitfalls of diplomatic protection, the politicization of investment disputes, the risk of resort to political pressure, and even subversion by powerful nations against small countries for economic reasons that had exacerbated North-South post-decolonization relations.

This is evidenced by the fact that it was the foremost development financial organization, namely the World Bank, which took the initiative to launch the ICSID Convention in 1965[29] as a specific instrument for settling investment disputes, as stated in its preamble and clarified by the accompanying explicatory report of the Bank's Executive Directors. ICSID was proposed to interested Members of the organization as an optional procedural framework based on their free choice, expressed in contracts or in domestic investment statutes. The development of BITs, laying down substantive standards of protection and opening arbitration to any present and future protected investor against the signatories based just on the treaty clauses, was only starting at that time.[30]

V. The Evolution of BITs:
From Just Protecting Investors to Safeguarding also the Rights of Host States to pursue their General Interest

Things have changed in part because of several reasons. First, industrialized countries, starting with the US and Canada, have realized, after the introduction of direct investment arbitration under the NAFTA, that they had to view themselves as host countries also. They have accordingly amended their model BITs restricting

---

[28] See Americans for Tax Reform Foundation, *International Property Rights Index* <http://internationalpropertyrightsindex.org> accessed 24 November 2014; see also AT Guzman, 'Why LDCs Sign Treaties That Hurt Them: Explaining the Popularity of BITs' (1998) 38 Va JIL 639–88. Tellingly no developing country is listed in the first twenty positions of the Index.

[29] Convention on the Settlement of Investment Disputes between States and Nationals of Other States (opened for signature 18 March 1965, entered into force 14 October 1966) ('ICSID Convention').

[30] For a historical perspective see Sacerdoti (n 25).

the scope of the most flexible standards (fair and equitable treatment and compensation for indirect expropriation) in order to prevent extensive interpretation of the terms by arbitral tribunals. The aim was to align them to the level of protection granted generally under their domestic law, safeguarding their ability to regulate without discrimination in the general interest.[31]

In many other countries which had concluded BITs in order to protect their investors abroad, critical positions have emerged in non-business circles (civil society, NGOs, trade unions) as to the purpose of BITs in general. The awareness has spread that the protection that BITs grant may interfere with the pursuit of non-economic values (such as the protection of the environment and health).[32] This criticism has been fuelled by some awards where tribunals have found, under the traditional BITs, that by introducing more restrictive domestic regulation in order to pursue legitimate purposes signatories were subject to the obligation to pay compensation to affected foreign investors even in the absence of discrimination, expropriation, or arbitrary conduct.[33]

As to legislators, these concerns have been forcefully expressed in the European Parliament,[34] when discussing the future investment treaty policy of the EU, after the granting by the Lisbon Treaty of competence to the EU in the field of the regulation of FDIs within the Common Commercial Policy.[35] Since this new competence is moreover part of the broader 'External Action of the Union' it must be carried out according to the principles and objectives laid down in that respect by the Treaty on the European Union (TEU) as amended in Lisbon.[36] The EU investment policy must therefore respect and pursue the predominantly ultimate non-economic dimension of the same.[37]

This approach hints at more complex, lengthy but also balanced BITs to be concluded by the EU, replacing BITs of individual Member States in force with third countries. The same applies to investment chapters in FTAs (Economic Partnership Agreements). The impact of envisaged obligations has to be accurately evaluated

---

[31] See the well-known clause in the US 2004 and 2012 Model BIT stating that 'except in rare circumstances' non-discriminatory regulatory action to protect legitimate public welfare objectives (health, safety, and environment) does not constitute indirect expropriation.

[32] For a discussion of these issues see the various contributions published in G Sacerdoti and others (eds), *General Interests of Host States in International Investment Law* (CUP 2014).

[33] Or at least this has been the interpretation of these decisions. See *CMS Gas Transmission Company v The Republic of Argentina*, ICSID Case No ARB/01/8, Award (12 May 2005), criticized but not annulled by the Ad Hoc Annulment Committee of 25 September 2007. See generally R Pavoni, 'Environment Rights, Sustainable Development and Investor-State Case Law: A Critical Appraisal' in PM Dupuy, EU Petersmann, and F Francioni (eds), *Human Rights in International Investment Law and Arbitration* (OUP 2009) 525.

[34] See European Parliament resolution 'On the Future European International Investment Policy', 2010/2203 (INI) of 6 April 2011.

[35] Art 207.1 of the Treaty on the Functioning of the European Union (TFEU).

[36] See Art 205 TFEU, in conjunction with Art 21 TEU.

[37] See A De Luca, 'Integrating non-trade objectives in the oncoming EU Investment Policy: what policy options for the EU?' (2013/14) CLEER Working Papers (Asser Institute); A Perfetti, 'Ensuring the consistency of the EU Investment Policy within the EU External Action: The Relevance of Non-Trade Values' in Sacerdoti and others (n 32) 308–23.

beforehand as to their effects on non-economic values, leading to more carefully drafted and detailed provisions. Issues emerge concerning the mutual interaction of the various clauses, their effect on the regulatory powers of the parties, to be balanced with their effectiveness in protecting national investors abroad.[38]

Especially in the context of investment chapters of bilateral or regional treaties establishing free trade areas or economic partnerships, investment provisions are meant to go beyond minimal, static protection. They are meant to stimulate mutual investment flows, just as is the case for trade and other forms of economic cooperation under the other chapters.[39]

The transformation of traditional 'protection treaties' into a different species is, however, not easy, as negotiations currently under way show. This implies, first of all, granting the right of making investment, just as market access is provided to products and services, possibly in the form of progressive liberalization.

Protective clauses (safeguards, exceptions) which are rarely found in traditional BITs become appropriate, such as Article XX GATT-type clauses included in recent agreements in South-East Asia,[40] to parallel similar clauses concerning trade.[41] Under these provisions the host State may exclude from coverage measures taken for certain public purposes or in certain sectors or circumstances. A caveat here is that these clauses have not been tested yet in respect of investments: if not well calibrated, they might deprive investors from protection even in the face of discriminatory measures.

Within FTAs further instruments are available to make the investment provisions more responsive to the specific development and other needs of the signatories. This is the case of the institutional setting normally provided therein to monitor the application of the agreement, such as joint commissions. They may be empowered to address and resolve issues at an early stage and control (or even 'rectify') the interpretation given to any provision by arbitral tribunals.[42]

Finally, direct arbitration has become an issue in view of the increasing number of cases brought by investors under BITs. Host States, especially developing countries, are faced with real challenges from an evolution they had not anticipated.

---

[38] The negotiating mandate for the EU–USA TTIP in respect of the investment chapter (n 21) provides that the provisions of the investment chapters should be 'without prejudice to the right of the EU and the Member States to adopt and enforce…measures necessary to pursue legitimate public policy objectives such as social, environmental, security, stability of the financial system, public health and safety in a non-discriminatory manner'.

[39] See the text of the negotiating mandate of 17 June 2013 by the EU Council to the Commission for the TTIP with the USA (n 21). For the proposals of the EU Commission of September 2015 replacing ISDS with a permanent tribunal (with appeal) following the EP recommendations see <http://trade.ec.europa.eu/doclib/docs/2015/september/tradoc_153807.pdf> accessed 9 October 2015.

[40] See the ASEAN Comprehensive Investment Agreement 2012 (ACIA) <www.asean.org/news/asean-secretariat-news/item/asean-comprehensive-investment-agreement> accessed 4 November 2014.

[41] See B Legum and I Petculescu, 'GATT Art. XX and International Investment Law' in A de Mestral and C Levesque (eds), *Improving International Investment Agreements* (Routledge 2013) 340–62.

[42] The well-known initiatives of the NAFTA Tripartite Commission in respect of the interpretation of the NAFTA by arbitral tribunals (as to the 'minimum' standard of international law, transparency and against the carrying over of principles found in other chapters to the investment chapter) show a clear pro-host State approach/bias shared by the three countries, reducing the scope of their obligations towards ISDS to investors to the detriment of the latter's protection.

This relates to the number of disputes to be handled, costs, financial implications in case of loss, political reactions against what is perceived outside the business community as a preferential treatment for foreign investors, who can opt out of domestic jurisdiction. The number of decisions rendered brings to the forefront the inconsistency of interpretation of similar provisions by different tribunals, which adds an element of unpredictability for legislators and business. In the current setting this is inevitable, in view of the (intentional) vagueness of many key terms (which may be moreover defined differently in different treaties) and the entrusting the resolution of individual disputes to ad hoc tribunals. Being composed of a variety of arbitrators chosen mostly by the parties themselves, not subject to an obligation to follow previous decisions, nor controlled by some appeals mechanism capable of developing consistent case law, the outcome is inevitably somehow unpredictable and inconsistent.[43]

On the other hand the availability of effective adjudication in the hands of investors is a key feature of BITs for their effective protection. Reverting to diplomatic protection or resorting to State-to-State arbitration or to a system of panels such as in the WTO, would subject to political interference and pressures the effectivity of mechanisms meant to impartially adjudicate claims of breaches of substantive standards of protection of BITs.

No prompt and generally accepted solution is currently on the table to address the perceived shortcoming of the current system in view of the conflicting interests present among actors (investors, home, and host countries) and the different objective of different groups of States. Opting-out of BITs is a radical choice that is not appealing to most countries. Elimination of direct investors-State disputes settlement would undermine substantially investors' protection and entangle again signatories in investment disputes. Replacing or amending existing BITs should be the preferred avenue for States which consider their existing treaties inappropriate but still would like to retain the BIT approach. This is or would be, however, a slow and cumbersome process in view of the massive number of existing BITs and the diversity of views on the advisable changes.[44] Such changes involve revising both the substantive obligations of host States towards investors as well as the dispute settlement mechanism.[45]

---

[43] See G Sacerdoti and M Recanati, 'From Annulment to Appeal in Investor-State Arbitration: Is the WTO Appeal Mechanism a Model?' in JA Huerta-Goldman, A Romanetti, and F Stirnimann (eds), *WTO Litigation, Investment and Commercial Arbitration* (Kluwer 2013) 327–56.

[44] For practical proposals and for a full review of solutions to improve the 'development-friendliness' of the BIT system see the Report by KP Sauvant and F Ortino, *Improving the International Investment Law and Policy Regime: Options for the Future* (Formin 2013), sponsored by the Ministry of Foreign Affairs of Finland.

[45] Thus Art X.9 of the Canada-EU Comprehensive Economic and Trade Agreement (CETA), as negotiated and released on 26 September 2014 (<http://trade.ec.europa.eu/doclib/docs/2014/september/tradoc_152806.pdf> accessed 4 November 2014) provides that

> A Party breaches the obligation of fair and equitable treatment referenced in paragraph 1 where a measure or series of measures constitutes: Denial of justice in criminal, civil or administrative proceedings; Fundamental breach of due process, including a fundamental breach of transparency, in judicial and administrative proceedings; Manifest arbitrariness;

In respect of the latter, minds and interests are especially divided. The current debate within the EU as to ISDS is telling of the new awareness that BITs and direct dispute settlement mechanisms should be responsive to broader concerns, shared societal values and should not become an instrument to grant privileges to foreign investors. The text which has emerged from the negotiations between the EU Commission and Canada, as concluded in September 2014, retains direct arbitration. At the same time the need and appropriateness of ISDS in North–North relations, between countries whose courts are generally impartial towards foreigners in their dealings with local public authorities, is being questioned.

The text includes in any case many innovative features which should be considered also in North-South relations. Foremost among them are more detailed procedural rules in order to increase the transparency of proceedings (such as the right of affected non-disputing parties to have a role as *amici curiae*) and to ensure the independence of arbitrators and the absence of conflicts of interests. Carve-outs of specific matters and measures from ISDS (such as prudential measures to ensure the stability of the financial system) also go in the direction of granting more flexibility to host States in regulating key aspects of their economic system in the interest of the society at large. It is notable that the new format has been agreed in the North–North context, where the need of ISDS is questioned in view of the satisfactory operation of justice also in respect of foreigners challenging local authorities' acts, rather than the North-South or South-South context, where SD is a more pressing issue. The result of this engagement of the EU may well result in an EU de facto model which may set the standard beyond the direct reach of the EU.[46]

Proposals have also been made to transform radically the format of BITs, such as introducing obligations on investors or subjecting the exercise of their treaty rights to an assessment of their contribution to development, although these suggestions have failed until now to be effectively considered in treaty drafting.[47] In our view, the case for using BITs to impose obligations on investors and transforming them into instruments for the selective promotion of investment flows which are coherent with the economic policy of the recipient economy, has not yet been made persuasively. Other mechanisms, domestic incentives, international economic cooperation schemes (such as direct financial contribution to technical assistance by international organizations, NGOs, foreign developmental agencies) remain

---

Targeted discrimination on manifestly wrongful grounds, such as gender, race or religious belief; Abusive treatment of investors, such as coercion, duress and harassment; or A breach of any further elements of the fair and equitable treatment obligation adopted by the Parties in accordance with paragraph 3 of this Article.

No such specifications are found in traditional BITs of EU Member States. The Investment Chapter of CETA is made of forty-three mostly long articles plus various annexes, compared to the maximum fifteen articles of traditional BITs of European countries.

[46] See M Bungenberg and A Reinisch, 'Special Issue: The Anatomy of the (Invisible) EU Model BIT' (2014) 15 J World Inv & Trade. The draft text of the EU–Singapore FTA released in October 2014 follows the approach of the EU-Canada FTA in matters of investment and ISDS, rendering the procedural requirements even stricter, see <http://trade.ec.europa.eu/doclib/press/index.cfm?id=961> accessed 17 October 2014.

[47] See the review of proposals in Sauvant and Ortino (n 44).

paramount and are more coherent with these objectives. This notwithstanding, changes in substantive standards and the regulation of procedural mechanisms, such as those promoted by the EU, are a relevant turnaround to update the BIT scheme to current needs and concerns of host countries, especially in the developing world. They will thereby contribute to making BITs more 'development-friendly'.

VI. The International Protection of Foreign Investment and Sustainable Development: Interference and Support

Some final reflections

The purpose of an opening contribution is not to draw conclusions but rather to present the issues and to point to a road map.[48] Before doing so a general remark is appropriate at this stage.

The primary responsibility for the SD of a country rests on its political institutions, more specifically on its government. It is for it to set priorities, standards, conditions for economic activity by locals and foreigners alike, while it is the duty of foreign investors to respect those parameters. In this regard it must be recalled that one of the main problems hindering development in many parts of the world is that governments are often not accountable to their citizens; respect for democratic principles and fundamental human rights is far from being universal; corruption in ruling elites is widespread; fighting poverty is often just a slogan.[49]

It is also for the government to set a framework and incentives that may be conducive to the entry and the positive contribution of foreign investment to development, not just in economic terms. Investors from abroad usually bring in more advanced technology and management methods. They should be expected to bring in also the higher standards of their country of origin as to environment, labour and industrial relations, health, security, as well as to comply with tax obligations, respect human rights, and social standards.[50]

This is the approach pursued under the UN agenda following the Millennium Summit. It is advocated by the 2011 *Guiding principles on business and human rights*, which promote the direct engagement of enterprises in this direction, as mentioned above.[51] On the other hand, the laying of specific requirements by the host States only upon foreign

---

[48] For further reflection see A Van Aaken and TA Lehmann, 'Sustainable Development and International Investment Law: A Harmonious View from Economists' in R Echandi and P Sauvé (eds), *Prospects in International Investment Law and Policy* (CUP 2013) 317–39; MW Gehring and A Kent, 'Sustainable Development and IIAs: From Objective to Practice' in de Mestral and Levesque (n 41) 284–302.

[49] See the World Bank Governance Indicators (n 5) and the Transparency Corruption Perception Index (n 7).

[50] See generally Dupuy, Petersmann, and Francioni (n 33). However, substantial FDI into developing countries currently originates from emerging economies (such as the BRICs countries) whose corporate investors' accountability to these criteria cannot be taken for granted.

[51] See (n 18).

investors, especially if they upset the competitive balance with local entrepreneurs, may deter investment from abroad. It is in any case accepted that host countries should not lower their standards and in any case cannot derogate from internationally recognized ones (such as the ILO core labour standards), in order to attract investment from abroad. BITs may be the appropriate instruments to obtain the cooperation of home countries in this respect and statements to this effect have found their way into BITs and investment chapters of trade agreements.[52]

Another limit of bilateral instruments, including BITs, is that by definition they have no effect beyond the bilateral context and their application is delimited by the territory of the host country. Sustainable development involves, however, addressing the protection of global commons (public goods), first of all the environment and climate change issues, that involve broader geographical dimensions where multilateral cooperation and taking into account the interest of neighbouring countries is paramount.[53] Irrespective of assistance provided by international organizations (intergovernmental or NGOs) or other countries, SD cannot be pursued in isolation from, or disregarding, international obligations binding upon a host State, including those concerning investments, international economic cooperation, and trade relations, by beggar-thy-neighbour policies or otherwise.[54]

A catalogue or milestones of a road map to improve the pro-development features of international investment law instruments could look as follows:

1. The balancing of investment protection and sustainable development does not imply the existence of a conflict in principle. There is rather a need to reconcile possible areas of interference or friction in order to make the contribution of foreign investment supportive of the efforts of host developing countries to pursue sustainable development policies.[55]

---

[52] See above the quote from objective of the EU mandate for the TTIP (n 21), See also P Acconci, 'The "Unexpected" Development-Friendly Definition of Investment in the 2013 Resolution of the Institut de droit international' (2014) 23 Italian Ybk Int L 69ff.

[53] See F Francioni, 'Foreign Investments, Sovereignty and the Public Good' (2014) 23 Italian Ybk Int L 3ff; I Dubava, 'The Future of International Investment Protection Law: The Promotion of Sustainable (Economic) Development as a Public Good' in Cremona and others (n 18) 381.

[54] A recent example might be the disputes brought by various WTO members against China challenging the latter's restrictions to the export of certain raw materials and rare earths, which China justified as necessary to protect its permanent right to natural resources, originally developed by the developing countries at the UN in the 1960s and 1970s as an integral part of the New International Economic Order strategy. The panel and the Appellate Body denied to China, however, the right to justify its measures under Art XX-g GATT, finding that the restrictions (export bans, quotas, and duties) were not 'made effective in conjunction with restrictions on domestic production or consumption'. See WTO, *China—Measures Related to the Exportation of Various Raw Materials* (30 January 2012), WT/DS394/AB/R; WT/DS395/AB/R; WT/DS398/AB/R and WTO, *China—Measures Related to the Exportation of Rare Earths, Tungsten and Molybdenum* (26 March 2014) WT/DS431/R; WT/DS432/R; WT/DS433/R. The Chinese restrictions appear not to be dictated by conservationist policies of those resources, which are in short supply worldwide and in high demand for advanced technological use, but rather part of an industrial policy aimed at developing China's domestic transformation industry to the detriment of those of the importing countries.

[55] See International Chamber of Commerce, *ICC Guidelines for International Investment* (2012) ch I.

2. International cooperation, multilateral, regional and bilateral instruments—such as investment chapters within FTAs—are key in order to promote investments which conform to these objectives, something that traditional BITs are not meant to, nor capable of ensuring.

3. Changes in BIT format and innovative drafting of investment chapters, most recently by the EU, point to the possibility of making BITs more respectful of the policy space of host States in the pursuit of legitimate general interest, balancing these values while maintaining the essential protection from arbitrary, discriminatory conduct and outright expropriation without compensation of foreign investors by host countries.

4. These changes, however, cannot transform BITs into development cooperation instruments, since their structure, object, and purpose are geared to investment protection through the laying down of general obligations on the host country and access to effective remedies for the investors. BITs are not the appropriate instruments to stimulate and regulate specific investments, a task which pertains to the host country, possibly with the cooperation of the home country.

5. Irrespective of texts' changes, protection provisions in existing BITs can and should be interpreted in the light of sustainable development objectives shared by the signatories. They should not be viewed and interpreted in isolation but rather in context, in the light of other instruments (notably treaties on human rights, environment, health, labour standards) binding upon the signatories or to which they have broadly subscribed (including non-binding acts). International rules on interpretation of treaties require to take into account 'any relevant rules of international law applicable in the relations between the parties' (Article 31(3)(c) of the Vienna Convention on the Law of Treaties[56]) which include those instruments. An evolutionary interpretation of old treaties in the light of the current context is an accepted approach to treaty interpretation, followed both by the ICJ and the WTO Appellate Body.[57]

6. When it comes to reconciling the right of host States to regulate the economy in the pursuit of general interests with the right of foreign investors to protection under an applicable BIT, principles found in the sources mentioned above can be an appropriate yardstick, considering the object and purpose of the various instruments in a broad perspective, including resorting to an evolutionary interpretation.

7. While 'legitimate expectations' of foreign investors cannot constrain the competence and duty of States to resort 'reasonably' to their regulatory

---

[56] Vienna Convention on the Law of Treaties (adopted 23 May 1969, entered into force 27 January 1980) 1155 UNTS 331.
[57] See *Dispute regarding Navigational and Related Rights (Costa Rica v Nicaragua)* (Judgment) [2009] ICJ Rep 213; WTO, *United States—Import Prohibition of Certain Shrimp and Shrimp Products* (12 October 1998) WT/DS 58/AB/R.

powers if these investors are not beneficiaries of specific commitments,[58] indemnification of losses suffered by foreign investors when substantially affected in their operations or specifically singled out must be anticipated by host States when planning substantial changes of policies. This does not stem just from the duty of States to observe their obligations under BITs but is, most of the time, also in conformity with a good governance approach to the carrying out of their activities in the furtherance of the general interest.

---

[58] See Art X.9.4 CETA (n 45) on fair and equitable treatment:
> When applying the above fair and equitable treatment obligation, a tribunal may take into account whether a Party made a specific representation to an investor to induce a covered investment, that created a legitimate expectation, and upon which the investor relied in deciding to make or maintain the covered investment, but that the Party subsequently frustrated.

II
Negotiating New Generation International Investment Agreements
New Sustainable Development Oriented Initiatives

Peter Muchlinski

I. Introduction

It is now commonplace to suggest that International Investment Agreements (IIAs) are in need of substantial reconsideration. First generation agreements, with their emphasis on investor rights and host State obligations, are said to be past their best and should give way to new agreements that seek to balance investor rights and duties, preserve the State's right to regulate in the public interest and to acknowledge the importance of not only economic but also social and environmental goals in their design. This position was once the preserve of critical scholars and non-governmental organizations.[1] Now, it appears to have gone mainstream with bodies such as the United Nations Conference on Trade and Development (UNCTAD) and the Commonwealth Secretariat offering detailed models for the recalibration of IIAs.[2]

---

[1] See further, for example, M Sornarajah, *The International Law on Foreign Investment* (3rd edn, CUP 2010); SP Subedi, *International Investment Law: Reconciling Policy and Principle* (2nd edn, Hart Publishing 2012); Osgoode Hall Law School, 'Public Statement on the International Investment Regime' (31 August 2010) available at: <www.transnational-dispute-management.com/article.asp?key=1657>; see the International Institute for Sustainable Development (IISD), *Model International Agreement on Investment for Sustainable Development. Negotiators Handbook* (2nd edn, IISD 2005, revised 2006), available at: <www.iisd.org/pdf/2005/investment_model_int_agreement.pdf> accessed 12 November 2014. The Model Agreement is reproduced in 20 ICSID Rev-FILJ 91 (2005); see also H Mann, 'Introductory Note', ibid 84. For a detailed analysis of the IISD Model Agreement see further PT Muchlinski, 'Holistic Approaches to Development and International Investment Law: the Role of International Investment Agreements' in J Faundez and C Tan (eds), *International Economic Law, Globalization and Developing Countries* (Edward Elgar 2010) 180, M Malik, 'IISD Model International Agreement on Investment for Sustainable Development' in MC Cordonier Segger, M Gehring, and A Newcombe (eds), *Sustainable Development in World Investment Law* (Kluwer Law International 2011) 561.

[2] See UNCTAD *Investment Policy Framework for Sustainable Development* (United Nations 2012) UN Pub. UNCTAD/DIAE/PCB/2012/5 available at: <http://unctad.org/en/PublicationsLibrary/diaepcb2012d5_en.pdf> accessed 12 November 2014 (cited as IPFSD 2012); UNCTAD *Investment Policy Framework for Sustainable Development* UN Pub. UNCTAD/WEB/DIAE/PCB/2015/3

At the core of this development lies the fear that an unaccountable, privatized, system of Investor-State Dispute Settlement (ISDS), rooted in IIAs and tasked with resolving disputes involving possibly far-reaching public policy implications, is acquiring a role in international life that surpasses anything that a system of administration of justice would be permitted to do without close oversight based on open, public, and fully accountable procedures and judicial personnel. Indeed, some have advocated an international investment court as an alternative to investment arbitration.[3]

Against this background UNCTAD has produced its comprehensive *Investment Policy Framework for Sustainable Development* (IPFSD).[4] It too expresses concern over investor-state arbitration, saying that ISDS can create unjustified liabilities and high procedural costs. Together, these put a significant economic and procedural burden on respondent host countries and exacerbate concerns over the balance between investor protection and the preservation of national policy space for development, especially in the case of less developed host countries.[5] In addition, UNCTAD asserts that ISDS claims have been used by investor claimants in hitherto unanticipated ways to challenge measures adopted in the public interest (such as measures to promote social equity, foster environmental protection, or protect public health) showing that, 'the borderline between protection from political risk and undue interference with legitimate domestic policies is becoming increasingly blurred'.[6] Accordingly, UNCTAD asserts that this problem needs a solution involving treaty design that looks at options both in ISDS provisions and in the scope and application of substantive clauses.[7]

In a similar vein, the Commonwealth Secretariat, as part of its programme of trade assistance to less-developed member countries, has published an extensive study

---

available at <http://investmentpolicyhub.unctad.org/Upload/Documents/INVESTMENT%20POLICY%20FRAMEWORK%202015%20WEB_VERSION.pdf> accessed 13 August 2015 (cited as IPFSD 2015); see too UNCTAD *World Investment Report 2015, Reforming Inernational Investment Governance* (United Nations 2015) Ch.IV 'Reforming the International Investment Regime: An Action Menu'; JA VanDuzer, P Simons, and G Mayeda, *Integrating Sustainable Development into International Investment Agreements: A Guide for Developing Countries* (Commonwealth Secretariat 2012) (cited as VanDuzer and others) available at: <http://www.iisd.org/pdf/2012/6th_annual_forum_commonwealth_guide.pdf> accessed 12 November 2014. Also published as a Commonwealth Secretariat book *Integrating Sustainable Development into International Investment Agreements: A Guide for Developing Country Negotiators* (Commonwealth Secretariat 2013). See too OECD Informal Ministerial Meeting on Responsible Business Conduct, 'Investment treaty law, sustainable development and responsible business conduct: A fact finding survey' (26 June 2014) available at: <www.oecd.org/investment/2014RBCMinisterial-TreatyRBC.pdf> accessed 12 November 2014; European Commission Concept Paper 'Investment in TTIP and beyond—the path for reform' (May 2015) available at <http://trade.ec.europa.eu/doclib/docs/2015/may/tradoc_153408.PDF> accessed 24 August 2015.

[3] The *locus classicus* of this position is G Van Harten, *Investment Treaty Arbitration and Public Law* (OUP 2007). See too the German Federal Ministry for Economic Affairs and Energy Memorandum (Gutachten) on a Model BIT (cited in UNCTAD World Investment Report 2015 (n 2) at 109) which discusses a possible bilateral tribunal or court composed of independently appointed judges as an alternative to ISDS.

[4] UNCTAD 2012 (n 2); UNCTAD 2015 (n 2).   [5] UNCTAD 2012 (n 2) 39–40.
[6] UNCTAD 2012 (n 2) 40.   [7] UNCTAD 2012 (n 2) 40.

authored by three leading Canadian legal scholars entitled *Integrating Sustainable Development into International Investment Agreements: A Guide for Developing Countries* ('the Guide').[8] As with the UNCTAD IPFSD, the Guide lays the problem with current IIAs at the feet of the outcomes of ISDS claims.[9] The proposed solution is again to rebalance new IIAs taking into account such concerns, though with some more prescriptive, and potentially more radical, new provisions than the UNCTAD model, as will be seen below.[10]

Both organizations seek to place sustainable development at the heart of the IIA reform project. They do not reject ISDS outright. Rather ISDS is seen to have a role but one that needs to address the shortcomings identified above so that it fits in with the wider sustainable development agenda.[11] Equally, substantive provisions may need reformulation so as better to meet the goals of sustainable development.

This chapter explores the scope and core content of the UNCTAD and Commonwealth Secretariat initiatives. It begins by looking at the changing investment environment and why this may require a recalibration of IIAs to be more sensitive to sustainable development. It will then consider the implications of these changing circumstances on the design and content of new IIAs and on resolving controversial interpretations of existing provisions, as well as on the introduction of new provisions that may be required to further sustainable development goals. Finally, proposed reforms of ISDS procedures will be briefly reviewed.

II. Sustainable Development and IIA Reform

Both the UNCTAD and Commonwealth Secretariat frameworks assert two core justifications for IIA reform: first that there exists a changing international investment environment[12] which requires the proposed rethink and, second, that the principle of sustainable development is becoming the overriding goal of new policy initiatives, a goal conspicuously absent from first generation IIAs with their emphasis on investor rights only and economic development as the sole policy justification.[13]

---

[8] VanDuzer and others (n 2). See too Commonwealth Secretariat Press Release, 'Commonwealth investment guide launched at trade workshop in Vanuatu' (7 February 2013) at: <http://thecommonwealth.org/media/news/commonwealth-investment-guide-launched-trade-workshop-vanuatu#sthash.zGBw9CG9.dpuf> accessed 12 November 2014.
[9] ibid 7.   [10] ibid.
[11] UNCTAD 2012 (n 2) 43; VanDuzer and others (n 2) Section 4.5 'Dispute Settlement'.
[12] According to UNCTAD this is characterized by changes in the destination of foreign investment with many developing countries now receiving the bulk of FDI, new types of investors including State-owned enterprises from emerging and transitional economies, greater government involvement in regulating and steering the economy, a greater need for global coordination of investment policy, and emerging 'new generation' investment policies that place inclusive growth and sustainable development at their heart as well as investor responsibilities: UNCTAD 2012 (n 2) 3–6.
[13] On which see further Muchlinski in Faundez and Tan (n 1) and ibid 'Towards a Coherent International Investment System: Key Issues in the Reform of International Investment Law' in R Echandi and P Suave (eds), *Prospects in International Investment Law and Policy: World Trade Forum* (CUP 2013) 411.

To date, few IIAs expressly mention sustainable development, or, indeed, development as such, while some investment arbitration awards have mentioned a significant contribution to the host State's development as a factor in defining an 'investment' that merits protection under an IIA, though this has not been uniformly followed or accepted.[14] Thus, the elucidation of what 'development' and 'sustainable development' should mean in the context of IIAs is a new area. Both UNCTAD and the Commonwealth Secretariat seek to fill this gap, albeit in distinctive ways.

The Commonwealth Secretariat Guide offers a working definition of sustainable development adapted for use in relation to IIAs.[15] Instead of focusing purely on economic growth or environmental sustainability, the Guide

> employs a holistic and comprehensive notion of development that encompasses a broad range of considerations, such as environmental protection, human health and welfare, human rights and the rights of indigenous peoples.[16]

This does not, however, entail abandoning a commitment to increasing inward investment flows to developing countries, and accepts that IIA investor protection provisions play a role in encouraging and promoting economic growth. On the other hand, the potential negative effects of increased foreign investment, and the need to mitigate them, are also accepted. According to the Guide, this approach is consistent with the international obligations that most countries have accepted by ratifying major international treaties in the area of human rights, labour rights, environmental sustainability and the rights of indigenous peoples. In taking on these obligations, 'these countries accept part of the responsibility for regulating the negative effects of foreign investment'.[17]

In sum, the Guide offers a functional definition that requires a balancing between the positive and negative impacts of foreign investment on sustainable development and the need to protect the regulatory discretion of States to achieve the social and environmental goals of such development through their policies.

By contrast, the UNCTAD IPFSD does not elaborate in much detail on the definition of sustainable development. Rather, UNCTAD relies on the wider UN initiative of Sustainable Development Goals (SDGs), to be adopted in 2015, to orient the policy focus of its IIA reform programme.[18] These are outlined in Chapter IV of the UNCTAD *World Investment Report 2014*.[19] The SDGs are seen as the next step from the Millennium Development Goals offering a concerted effort to shift the global economy, both developed and developing, onto a more sustainable trajectory of long-term growth and development.[20] The main focus

---

[14] See Muchlinski in Echandi and Sauve (eds) (n 13) 415–17; OECD (n 2).
[15] See VanDuzer and others (n 2) 24–30 on which this account draws.   [16] ibid 30.
[17] ibid.
[18] See UNCTAD, *IIA Issues Note No.3* (June 2014) 7 available at <http://unctad.org/en/PublicationsLibrary/webdiaepcb2014d6_en.pdf> accessed 12 November 2014.
[19] UNCTAD, *World Investment Report 2014*, ch IV, 'Investing in SDGs: An Action Plan for Promoting Private Sector Contributions' (United Nations 2014).
[20] ibid 136.

areas are the economic infrastructure for power, transport, telecoms, water and sanitation in developing countries, food security, the social infrastructure of health and education, environmental sustainability involving climate change adaptation and mitigation, the conservation and safeguarding of ecosystems, and sustainable agriculture.[21] In addition, investment to assist marginalized groups, such as isolated communities or the excluded poor, and gender and equality issues are considered.[22]

The role of the private sector is seen as key to investment in these areas, given the significance of such investment in global capital flows, and its ability to reduce pressure on public funding.[23] On the other hand the essential role of the public sector is stressed. This appears in two key ways. First, the use of Public Private Partnerships (PPPs) may need to be widened, but with caution over the well-known financial risks run by the public partner which need to be adequately addressed in the applicable contractual arrangements.[24] Second, effective regulation will be required to avoid negative private sector impacts. This is particularly relevant in relation to maintenance of standards and capabilities, effective competition, and consumer protection, including affordability to the poorest, especially in basic needs sectors such as water and sanitation.[25] This requires guiding principles for investment in SDGs to offer clear direction and to ensure that the needs of all stakeholders are met.[26]

Here the IPFSD provides a set of principles specifically focused on designing sound SDG-friendly investment policies. This requires coordination between national and international investment policies and commitments in IIAs. In particular, such treaties must not unduly undermine the regulatory space required for sustainable development policies.[27] Indeed, they must be designed to be proactive in mobilizing and channelling investment into projects furthering SDGs.[28]

Against this background both the UNCTAD and Commonwealth Secretariat initiatives concentrate mainly on detailed technical analysis of substantive clauses and dispute settlement procedures that may be adapted to serve the overarching goal of sustainable development. The result, as will be seen below, is a rather complex set of alternative formulations that also include retaining the status quo found

---

[21] ibid 140–43.   [22] ibid 144–45.   [23] ibid 146.   [24] ibid 167–68.
[25] ibid 150. These sectors have attracted attention over the relationship between investor rights and responsibilities and the right to regulate in investment awards. Notably in *Biwater Gauff (Tanzania) Ltd v United Republic of Tanzania*, ICSID Case No ARB/05/22, Procedural Order No 5 (2 February 2007) para 52, the Tribunal accepted, at the procedural stage, that human rights considerations might be raised by the dispute, in that it concerned the operation of a privatized water company and that this involved significant public interests in relation to the right to water and to health. At the award stage, in *Biwater Gauff (Tanzania) Ltd v United Republic of Tanzania*, ICSID Case No ARB/05/22, Award (24 July 2008) para 358, the Tribunal noted that the public interest issues surrounding the right to water in this case were admissible though the Tribunal did not explore the United Republic of Tanzania's human rights law obligations in further detail holding, rather, that the claimants had not made out their case on the facts.
[26] UNCTAD, *World Investment Report 2014* (n 19) 151–52.   [27] ibid 152.
[28] ibid 181.

in first generation treaty provisions. Thus, the degree to which these initiatives really do represent a radical rethink of IIA contents remains open to discussion. That said some interesting new options are there. To these we now turn.[29]

III. Treaty Design and Sustainable Development

In this section the main questions that arise are how to formulate the preamble of the treaty and whether or not the treaty should extend to pre-establishment rights.

a) Preamble

The preamble is a key element in the interpretation of a treaty as it sets out its key goals, making the preamble a significant factor in the way that governments and tribunals will read its provisions. To date the preambles of first generation IIAs have tended to be short with emphasis on the primary goal of investment stability or favourable conditions for investment and cooperation rather than wider sustainable development goals. Thus IIAs say little about development save for generally accepting that a quantitative increase in foreign investment equates with development.[30]

The UNCTAD model offers a choice of approaches from retaining the standard first generation formulation to a new formulation that stresses the complementary goals of investment promotion and protection and sustainable development or the Contracting Parties right to regulate. The aim is to create conditions favourable to a more balanced approach to interpretation that allows for the consideration of this wider policy context.[31]

The Commonwealth Secretariat Guide also stresses the need for reformed preambles, though it offers a more detailed model than UNCTAD.[32] Like the UNCTAD model, this sees no contradiction between increased foreign investment and sustainable development so long as this is read in the light of other sustainability goals. Two

---

[29] It would be impossible, in the space available, to discuss all aspects of the proposed UNCTAD and the Commonwealth Secretariat models. Thus, the less prominent issues of transparency, performance requirements, full protection and security, funds transfer, and foreign personnel and staff are omitted.

[30] Muchlinski in Echandi and Sauve (n 13) 416. Tribunals have had relatively little to say about the preamble as a source of interpretation see: JW Salacuse, *The Law of Investment Treaties* (OUP 2nd ed 2015) at 163 noting the different conclusions arrived at by the tribunals in *LG&E Energy Corp, LG&E Capital Corp, and LG&E International, Inc v Argentine Republic*, ICSID Case No ARB/02/1, Decision on Liability (26 September 2006) para 124 and *Saluka Investments BV v The Czech Republic*, UNCITRAL, Partial Award (17 March 2008) para 298 as to the object and purpose of investment agreements with the former demanding that a stable investment environment is essential in the light of the preamble, while the latter stressed the need for a balanced interpretation of the treaty to avoid excessive investor protection such as might hamper the extension of the parties mutual economic relations as stated in the preamble.

[31] UNCTAD 2012 (n 2) 48; UNCTAD 2015 (n 2) 89.

[32] VanDuzer and others above (n 2) 49.

elements are central to this objective: cooperation among the host State, the home State and investors, and the existence of favourable conditions for investment.[33] In addition, the Guide model lists other values inherent in a commitment to sustainable development and which are to inform interpretation of the treaty. These are: the protection of health, safety, and the environment; the promotion and protection of internationally and domestically recognized human rights; labour rights; the rights of indigenous peoples; the commitment of the parties to democracy; the rule of law; and the parties' determination to prevent and combat corruption and to promote corporate social responsibility. The sample preamble also specifically refers to the right of party States to regulate to achieve their development objectives.[34]

b) Pre-establishment rights

Here a significant policy difference arises between the UNCTAD and Commonwealth Secretariat. The former accepts that treaty negotiators can extend the scope of the treaty to the pre-establishment stage and offers concrete proposals for this option if taken. By contrast the Commonwealth Secretariat does not include any sample provision on this issue in its Guide on the grounds that, 'only a few developed countries seek a right of establishment, and even for those that do, the right is always a qualified one'.[35] Also, the Guide sees the challenge of drafting adequate reservations (a negative list approach) or listing commitments (a positive list approach) to provide sufficient policy flexibility regarding the host State's right to refuse entry of foreign investors as significant and one that will be hard for many host States to meet.[36]

This difference may be attributed to the distinctive aims of the Commonwealth Secretariat Guide as a means, 'to assist developing countries to negotiate IIAs that do a better job of promoting their sustainable development'.[37] This results in a more prescriptive approach which has some significant and rather radical results, as will be seen further below. On the other hand UNCTAD self-limits as regards prescription and prefers an 'a la carte' approach, offering a range of choices to negotiators without specifically expressed preferences. This difference may also be attributed to the distinctive processes by which the UNCTAD and Commonwealth Secretariat models have been developed, with the former arising out of the intergovernmental and multi-stakeholder consultation and research process usual to UNCTAD activity in this field, as opposed to the use, by the Commonwealth Secretariat, of a detailed and authoritative academic study by a group of selected Commonwealth-based academic experts, as its policy guidance.

As a result, the UNCTAD model concentrates not on whether there should, or should not, be a pre-establishment clause in the treaty, but on the modalities of creating a sustainable development-friendly one, should negotiators decide to extend their IIA to pre-establishment matters.[38] This is stressed by the inclusion

---

[33] ibid.   [34] ibid.   [35] ibid 111.   [36] ibid.   [37] ibid 7.
[38] UNCTAD 2012 (n 2) 61; UNCTAD 2015 (n 2) 76, 77, 112–13.

of these options in a separate section, Part B, in its Policy Options Framework appended to the IPFSD.

Here the main issue is whether a negative or positive list approach should be taken to the question of sectoral inclusion or exclusion from pre-establishment rights.[39] UNCTAD expresses no particular preference highlighting only that a negative list approach is, 'more demanding in terms of resources' and requires a 'sophisticated domestic regulatory regime and sufficient institutional capacity for properly designing and negotiating the scheduling of liberalization commitments'.[40]

IV. Resolving Controversial Interpretations of Existing Provisions

Given the constraints of space, only the most significant recent controversies of interpretation will be covered in detail. These are: the wide interpretation of the Fair and Equitable Treatment (FET) standard, creating the potential for far-reaching review of State administrative action that may be incompatible with the State's right to regulate for development; the protection of investors against regulatory takings undertaken for legitimate policy reasons under the taking of property clause; the use of the Most-Favoured-Nation (MFN) clause to allow for the importation of wider protection standards from third party IIAs into the IIA applicable to the dispute before the tribunal; the possible application of the national treatment standard to prevent legitimate development policies that favour indigenous undertakings; and the extension of the concept of 'investment' to cover cases involving mainly contractual claims and multiple claims by corporate groups. Both the UNCTAD and Commonwealth Secretariat models offer options for redrafting of existing provisions to tackle any interpretations that may not be consistent with the goal of sustainable development.

a) Fair and Equitable Treatment (FET)

A common criticism is that tribunals have gone too far in a creative interpretation of FET provisions that is not warranted by the usually general wording of such clauses or by the negotiating intention behind them.[41] The result has been the development of a generalized standard of administrative review that goes beyond the traditional international minimum standard of treatment for aliens, based, usually, on a gross denial of justice. It has been argued that this general standard is becoming the overarching standard of protection enjoyed by investors and that

---

[39] On the issue of negative and positive lists in pre-establishment clauses see further P Muchlinski, *Multinational Enterprises and the Law* (2nd edn, OUP 2007) 254.
[40] UNCTAD 2012 (n 2) 61; UNCTAD 2015 (n 2) 113.
[41] See further for examples Subedi (n 1) 168–71; UNCTAD, *Fair and Equitable Treatment: A Sequel* (United Nations 2012).

it supplants claims made under other provisions.[42] In particular the concept of investor's legitimate expectations has been developed by some tribunals to encompass a general expectation of a good investment environment rather than a more specific standard based on actual representations made to investors.[43] Given that other tribunals have applied this more restrictive approach, while still others have applied the international minimum standard of treatment, the result is considerable confusion and uncertainty as to the precise scope of this standard.[44] In order to resolve such uncertainties, both the UNCTAD and Commonwealth Secretariat proposals seek to reform FET clauses to leave less discretion for a creative extension of the standard that might, in practice, lead to legitimate administrative action being treated as a treaty violation where it impedes on the interests of investors.

Thus UNCTAD offers three options depending on the degree of discretion that negotiators wish to leave to tribunals.[45] The first is to include an express reference to the international minimum standard with its high liability threshold of egregious misconduct as defined by international jurisprudence. This approach is also included in the Commonwealth Secretariat Guide model.[46] However, using the international minimum standard is open to the criticism that it fails to meet modern issues of good governance and is also a source of uncertainty.[47]

Perhaps that is why investment tribunals have felt it right to evolve the FET standard along the lines of contemporary judicial review, based on modern notions of good governance, rather than limit themselves to the condemnation of the worst kinds of maladministration and denial of justice. In practice what may be needed is a set of administrative law-based standards so that the legitimate claims of investors can be balanced against those of the State to regulate.[48] This informs the second UNCTAD option, which is to offer FET with an exhaustive list of State obligations under FET. These include an obligation: not to deny justice in judicial or administrative proceedings, treat investors in an arbitrary manner, flagrantly violate due process, engage in manifestly abusive treatment involving continuous, unjustified coercion or harassment and infringing investors legitimate expectations based on investment-inducing representations or measures.[49]

In addition the clause could contain clarifications that FET does not preclude legitimate, good faith regulatory action, that investors' conduct may be relevant in determining whether the FET standard is breached, that the host country's level of

---

[42] See TJ Greierson-Weiler and IA Laird, 'Standards of Treatment' in P Muchlinski, F Ortino, and C Schreuer (eds), *The Oxford Handbook of International Investment Law* (OUP 2008) 259.
[43] UNCTAD (n 41) 64–67.
[44] ibid 67–78 and on the international minimum standard at 44–58; VanDuzer and others (n 2) 140 and 149.
[45] See UNCTAD 2012 (n 2) 51; UNCTAD 2015 (n 2) 80, 94–95.
[46] See VanDuzer and others (n 2) 152.
[47] See UNCTAD, *Fair and Equitable Treatment* (n 41) 105, VanDuzer and others (n 2) 150.
[48] On which see further SW Schill, *The Multilateralization of International Investment Law* (CUP 2009) 372–78; B Kingsbury and SW Schill, 'Investor–State Arbitration as Governance: Fair and Equitable Treatment, Proportionality and the Emerging Global Administrative Law' (2009) New York University School of Law Institute for International Law and Justice, Working Paper 2009/6.
[49] UNCTAD 2012 (n 2) 51; UNCTAD 2015 (n 2) 94.

development is to be taken into account and that breach of another provision or IIA is not proof of breach of the standard.[50] Seeing this approach, one is left feeling that the new provision would be equally challenging to interpret. For example what level of development would qualify as a reason for relaxing the highest standards of good governance? What type of investor conduct would negate a breach of FET?[51] And what is legitimate regulatory action? These remain fact-based and highly subjective assessments for a tribunal to make.

The approach taken by the Commonwealth Secretariat Guide defines fair and equitable treatment as meaning, 'treatment that is not manifestly arbitrary, unreasonable or discriminatory or a gross denial of justice or due process'.[52] It then lists explicit limitations on FET that create a high threshold for breach including the host country's level of development and the right to regulate. Unlike the UNCTAD model the Commonwealth Secretariat model does not include any reference to legitimate expectations, even though the accompanying discussion accepts that the concept has a role in the interpretation of the standard.[53] In addition it offers a novel provision requiring the tribunal to set compensation for breach on an equitable basis taking account of all relevant circumstances. These would include the investor's behaviour, such as whether it had been duly diligent in informing itself regarding the risks associated with the investment.[54]

The exhaustive list of State obligations formulation, followed both by UNCTAD and the Commonwealth Secretariat models, has the advantage of demanding a more focused factual enquiry but continues the disadvantage of the first generation provision by leaving major questions of factual judgement to the tribunal. Thus the final UNCTAD option is to omit the FET clause altogether. This would undoubtedly reduce the exposure of host countries from investor claims but would also send out a negative message as regards the country's investment climate and would not absolve that country from observing the customary international law minimum standard of treatment.[55]

b) Regulatory takings

A major historical motivation for the development of IIAs has been the risk of expropriation of foreign owned assets by the host State.[56] The development of the international law relating to the taking of property by the major capital-exporting States was the initial response, but was also the source of major disagreements about the extent of State obligations to foreign investors during the mid-twentieth

---

[50] ibid.
[51] On which see PT Muchlinski, '"Caveat Investor"? The Relevance of the Conduct of the Investor under the Fair and Equitable Treatment Standard' (2006) 55 ICLQ 527.
[52] VanDuzer and others (n 2) 151.   [53] ibid 145–47.   [54] ibid 152 and 151.
[55] UNCTAD 2012 (n 2) 51; UNCTAD 2015 (n 2) 95 and UNCTAD, *Fair and Equitable Treatment* (n 41) 104.
[56] See further C Lipson, *Standing Guard: Protecting Foreign Capital in the Nineteenth and Twentieth Centuries* (University of California Press 1985).

century. This culminated in the call for a New International Economic Order in the early 1970s, which challenged, among other matters, the idea that expropriation of foreign-owned assets should be for a public purpose carried out in accordance with the applicable law, be non-discriminatory and give rise to a right of full, adequate and effective compensation, the essential elements of the customary international law norm regulating this practice.[57] In response IIAs sought to bind host States to the international norm by treaty.

In relation to IIA claims, the main issue of contention has centred on takings short of outright nationalization or expropriation, so-called indirect or regulatory takings/expropriations.[58] This has led to wide interpretations by tribunals as to what constitutes a regulatory taking. According to UNCTAD, on the basis of State practice, doctrine, and arbitral awards, an indirect expropriation contains the following elements:

(a) an act attributable to the State;
(b) interference with property rights or other protected legal interests;
(c) of such degree that the relevant rights or interests lose all or most of their value or the owner is deprived of control over the investment;
(d) even though the owner retains the legal title or remains in physical possession.[59]

In principle, protection against such a taking is unobjectionable. However, in arbitral practice, some tribunals have given a broad meaning to expropriation with the effect of restricting the ability of States to regulate in the public interest. For example, in *Compania del Desarrollo de Santa Elena SA* v *Costa Rica* the tribunal held that the fact that the property was taken for environmental reasons did not affect, 'either the nature or the measure of compensation to be paid for the taking'.[60] This could lead to the effective negation of regulatory action by reason of the risk of liability on the part of the State to the investor for taking legitimate action to further environmental goals. In order to guard against the possible striking down of a legitimate regulatory measure both the UNCTAD and Commonwealth Secretariat models propose formulations that restrict tribunal discretion in making such a finding.[61]

---

[57] See Muchlinski (n 39) 597 and Art 2(2)(c) of the Charter of Economic Rights and Duties of States, UNGA Res 3281 (XXIX) 12 December 1974 14 ILM 251 (1975) which speaks of 'appropriate compensation'.

[58] For the purposes of this paper the phrase indirect/regulatory taking/expropriation will be used interchangeably. On issues of terminology see further UNCTAD, *Expropriation: A Sequel* (United Nations 2012) 5–6.

[59] ibid at 12.

[60] *Compania del Desarrollo de Santa Elena SA v The Republic of Costa Rica*, ICSID Case No ARB/96/1, Award (17 February 2000), available at: <www.worldbank.org/icsid/cases/santaelena_award.pdf> accessed 12 November 2014 or 15 ICSID Rev-FILJ 169 (2000), paras 71–72. See also *Metalclad Corporation v The United Mexican States*, ICSID Case No ARB (AF)/97/1(NAFTA), Award (30 August 200) para 111 40 ILM 36 (2001): 'The Tribunal need not decide or consider the motivation or intent of the adoption of the Ecological Decree.'

[61] UNCTAD 2012 (n 2) 52; UNCTAD 2015 (n 2) 80, 96; VanDuzer and others (n 2) 173.

The main method used by both models is to clarify the elements of a legitimate regulatory taking in the expropriation provision or in an interpretative provision, as has been the case in some existing model agreements.[62] This follows broadly the criteria listed above. In addition lists of exceptions may be added to clarify the types of regulatory actions that would not normally be considered as compensable takings.

The Commonwealth Secretariat Guide offers a more detailed approach than the UNCTAD version, which is surprisingly short. The Commonwealth Secretariat provision states that the expropriation provision does not apply to, 'the issuance of compulsory licences granted in relation to intellectual property rights, or to the revocation, limitation, or creation of intellectual property rights' provided these are consistent with international agreements on intellectual property rights agreed to by both parties to the IIA. In addition:

Non-discriminatory measures by a party that are designed and applied to achieve legitimate public objectives, such as the economic security of residents, public health, safety, the protection or promotion of internationally and domestically recognised human rights, labour rights, the rights of indigenous peoples, social justice and the protection of the environment, do not constitute indirect expropriations.[63]

This constitutes a wide list of measures. It offers a response to the kind of reasoning exemplified by the tribunal in the *Santa Elena Case* by making the objective of the measure a relevant consideration.

Exempting such measures altogether from the operation of the expropriation clause may be a cause for concern among investors. The existence of an indirect expropriation is said to be a case-by-case question in the Commonwealth Secretariat model and it makes clear that the international law standard still applies.[64] Thus if the public purpose measure fails to observe the requirements of non-discrimination or is not in fact taken for a public purpose, despite being such a measure on its face, it will constitute an unlawful expropriation. Equally a right of compensation should arise where the regulatory action adversely affects the tangible or intangible property rights of the investor and that action does not fall within the international law notion of the 'police power' of the State, which allows for such an interference without compensation, as in the case of a punitive confiscation of assets under lawful criminal sanctions or a compulsory licence of intellectual property rights consistent with WTO rules. Thus the exclusion of the above types of public policy measures from the indirect expropriation concept may not offer the clarity that this appears to give at first sight. Claimants may well still question whether the economic loss they suffer at the hands of, for example, an environmental measure is just the outcome of legitimate regulation or is in fact expropriatory in nature.

---

[62] See, for example, the US Model Bilateral Investment Treaty 2012 Annex B para 4 available at: <www.ustr.gov/sites/default/files/BIT%20text%20for%20ACIEP%20Meeting.pdf> accessed 12 November 2014.
[63] VanDuzer and others (n 2) 177.   [64] ibid.

c) Most-favoured-nation (MFN) treatment

The MFN treatment standard aims to ensure equality of competitive conditions between investors of differing nationalities. It offers the investor a means by which to challenge material measures taken by the host country that favour specific foreign investors on the grounds of their nationality.[65] However, investment tribunals have interpreted the standard as allowing investors to invoke more investor-friendly provisions from treaties between the host country and a third country, sidelining the 'base' treaty between the investor's home and host country.[66] Most controversially this was extended to the invocation of more favourable procedural provisions from a third party treaty into the ISDS clause of the base treaty in *Maffezini v Spain*.[67]

Such a development has been seen as evidence of the mulitlateralization of investor protection standards through IIAs.[68] It has also been criticized as undermining individually negotiated treaties by adding higher protection standards from third treaties contrary to the intentions of the parties to the base treaty.[69] Moreover, the approach in *Maffezini* has not been uniformly followed in subsequent arbitral decisions.[70]

In response, some more recent treaties have restricted the operation of the MFN clause to exclude procedural matters.[71] This option is offered in the UNCTAD and Commonwealth Secretariat model clauses.[72] In addition, other exclusions can be included to heighten the development friendliness of the MFN clause by way of carve-outs for selected policies and measures, such as subsidies, specific sectors or industries and issues of a social character such as minorities, rural populations, and marginalized or indigenous peoples.[73] Also more favourable treatment offered in agreements concluded prior to and/or after the conclusion of the base agreement can be specifically excluded.[74] Finally both models stress that only more favourable treatment accorded to investors/investments that are comparable or 'in like circumstances' should be covered so as to avoid widening the application of the standard to cases that lack true comparability.[75]

---

[65] UNCTAD, *Most-Favoured-Nation Treatment: A Sequel* (United Nations 2010) 18.
[66] UNCTAD 2012 (n 2) 42; UNCTAD 2015 (n 2) 79–80, 93–94 and see *World Investment Report 2015* (n 2) 136–37.
[67] ICSID Case No ARB/97/7, Decision on Objections to Jurisdiction (25 January 2000): 16 ICSID Rev-FILJ 212 (2001).
[68] See Schill above (n 48) 173–96.
[69] UNCTAD 2012 (n 2) 42; UNCTAD 2015 (n 2) 80.
[70] UNCTAD, *Most-Favoured-Nation Treatment* (n 65) 73–84; VanDuzer and others (n 2) 127.
[71] UNCTAD, *Most-Favoured-Nation Treatment* (n 65) 84–87.
[72] UNCTAD 2012 (n 2) 51; UNCTAD 2015 (n 2) 93–94; VanDuzer and others (n 2) 136 and 138.
[73] UNCTAD 2012 (n 2); UNCTAD 2015 (n 2) 51.
[74] ibid. See too VanDuzer and others (n 2) 139.
[75] UNCTAD 2012 (n 2); UNCTAD 2015 (n 2) and VanDuzer and others (n 2) 136. The Commonwealth Secretariat model offers a detailed provision on relevant factors in determining 'like circumstances': ibid 138.

d) National treatment

National treatment shares the same goal as MFN, in promoting an equal competitive environment in the host country, by preventing differential treatment between domestic and foreign investors who are in like circumstances.[76] However, an unqualified national treatment clause has the potential to be applied in a way that undermines legitimate development oriented policy goals that offer preferential treatment to domestic, as opposed to foreign, investors.

This risk was well illustrated in *Foresti and others v the Republic of South Africa*.[77] The claimants, Italian mining investors, who had invested after the fall of apartheid, argued that their investment had been indirectly expropriated as a result of South Africa's post-apartheid equal opportunities and land rights policy. Under the Minerals and Petroleum Resources Development Act (MPRDA) existing mining rights were converted into 'new order' mining rights and required 26 per cent of mining assets to be transferred to black owners over the next decade. The Italian claimants argued that their rights in a number of quarries could be expropriated and also that, as foreign investors, they were being subjected to more onerous requirements than domestic firms in breach of the fair and equitable and national treatment principles. The claimants informed the ICSID of their wish to discontinue proceedings in 2009. South Africa objected to the claimants' request for discontinuance and filed an application for a default award. The tribunal awarded the default, ordering a partial recovery of fees and costs by South Africa from the claimants.[78]

Future claims of this kind can be avoided by the use of qualified national treatment clauses. Both the UNCTAD and Commonwealth Secretariat models propose qualified provisions that allow for derogations by way of reservations for specific sectors or specific measures from national treatment.[79] As with MFN, the Commonwealth Secretariat model also contains a detailed provision on relevant factors in determining 'like circumstances'.

e) Scope and definition

In this area arbitral awards have accepted transactions such as government debt securities as covered 'investments', which some treaties have included, but others have expressly excluded, from the definition of 'investment' and which, according to UNCTAD, were generally not envisaged to benefit from IIA protection.[80]

---

[76] UNCTAD 2012 (n 2) 41–42; UNCTAD 2015 (n 2) 79, 92–93.
[77] *Piero Foresti, Laura de Carli & Others v The Republic of South Africa*, ICSID Case No ARB (AF)/07/1, Award (4 August 2010).
[78] On this case and South Africa's reaction see the contribution by Woolfrey in this book.
[79] UNCTAD 2012 and UNCTAD 2015 (n 76); VanDuzer and others (n 2) 125.
[80] See *Abaclat and Others v Argentine Republic*, ICSID Case No ARB/07/5, Decision on Jurisdiction and Admissibility (4 August 2011); UNCTAD 2012 (n 2) 41; UNCTAD, 'Sovereign debt restructuring and international investment agreements' (2011) IIA Issues Note No 2 July 2011 at <http://

In addition the term has been used to allow for multiple claims from corporate groups based on the same actions of the host country, arising out of the interlocking share structures of companies in such groups.[81] Such structures can also be used to allow for 'treaty-shopping' where an affiliate in a third country, that has an investment agreement with the host country, can be used as a vehicle for a claim arising out of losses to another affiliate in the group, that has the nationality of a country which does not have an investment agreement with the host, on the grounds that the claimant affiliate is an 'investor' in the host country by reason of the group structure of the enterprise.[82] Some arbitral tribunals have accepted this development on the basis of a strict application of the principles of incorporation and by a refusal to lift the corporate veil between affiliates, while others have done so.[83]

To avoid such complications the UNCTAD and Commonwealth Secretariat models offer a series of qualifications to the scope and definition clause. Thus, in relation to investments, a list of excluded types of investments can be added which ensure that purely contractual claims and other controversial types of claims (for example claims based on portfolio investments, sovereign debt instruments or intellectual property rights not covered by domestic laws) are excluded.[84] In addition, following the practice of certain tribunals and more recent model BITs, a set of characteristics may be listed that identify an investment that should be protected. This includes a reference to a commitment of capital, expectation of profit and assumption of risk (following the 2012 US Model BIT[85]) and, possibly, a reference to its development contribution.[86] In relation to corporate investors, both models propose the exclusion of legal persons that do not have their legal seat or any real economic activity in the home country and the inclusion of a denial-of-benefits clause which denies treaty protection, inter alia, to legal entities that are owned or controlled by third country nationals or host country nationals and that do not have any real economic activity in the home country.[87]

---

unctad.org/en/Docs/webdiaepcb2011d3_en.pdf> accessed 12 November 2014 which suggests that a claim based on a sovereign debt instrument cannot be ruled out from a broad asset based definition of 'investment' even if it does not expressly refer to government debt. See too D Strik, 'Investment Protection of Sovereign Debt and its Implications on the Future of Investment Law in the EU' (2012) 29 (2) J Intl Arb 183.

[81] See further UNCTAD, *Scope and Definition: A Sequel* (United Nations 2011) 66–72.
[82] ibid 86–92.   [83] ibid and cases there cited.
[84] UNCTAD 2012 (n 2) 49; UNCTAD 2015 (n 2) 79, 90; VanDuzer and others (n 2) 91. As a separate issue, the umbrella clause may also need to be modified, or omitted, so as to exclude contractual claims arising out of the investment contract from being turned into treaty violations subject to ISDS: see UNCTAD 2012 (n 2) 54; UNCTAD 2015 (n 2) 99.
[85] See (n 62) article 1.
[86] UNCTAD 2012 (n 2) 49; UNCTAD 2015 (n 2) 90; VanDuzer and others (n 2) 76.
[87] UNCTAD 2012 (n 2); UNCTAD 2015 (n 2) 90–91; VanDuzer and others (n 2) 88–89 and 92–93.

V. The Inclusion of New Sustainable Development Oriented Provisions

In order to evolve beyond the limitations of first generation IIAs as instruments for sustainable development, the reform of existing provisions is not enough. New provisions that seek to further such goals are also needed. In this regard both the UNCTAD and the Commonwealth Secretariat models propose the inclusion of general exceptions clauses to supplement the abovementioned exceptions in investor protection clauses, the addition of investor responsibilities either as voluntary or mandatory standards and the inclusion of State obligations and institutional structures. In addition, the UNCTAD model offers provisions on special and differential treatment of less developed country parties to IIAs, while the Commonwealth Secretariat model introduces the completely new concept of sustainable development assessments.

a) General exceptions

At present only a few, more recent, IIAs contain exceptions clauses. For example, the Canadian model agreement of 2004 has a clause based on Article XX GATT.[88] According to UNCTAD, provisions that protect the host country's right to regulate in the public interest are more conducive to the achievement of sustainable development goals and protect against claims where the host country's legitimate exercise of regulatory powers may interfere with the interests of the investor.[89] In addition such clauses may safeguard certain sovereign actions that would otherwise be prohibited by the agreement but which may be necessary to protect vital national security interests or the furtherance of State's obligations under the UN Charter.[90]

A major difficulty in the use of a provision modelled on Article XX GATT is that it retains a significant degree of discretion for the adjudicator in determining whether a public policy measure is consistent with the exception. For example, Article 10 of the Canadian model investment agreement requires that all measures coming within the excepted categories of public policy, 'are not applied in a manner that would constitute arbitrary or unjustifiable discrimination between investments or between investors, or a disguised restriction on international trade or investment'. This requires a tribunal to determine whether a particular measure is arbitrary or discriminatory, proportionate to the aim involved, and does not unduly interfere with investment protection.

---

[88] VanDuzer and others (n 2) 225.
[89] UNCTAD 2012 (n 2) 55; UNCTAD 2015 (n 2) 74–75, 78, 100–02.
[90] UNCTAD 2012 (n 2) 55, UNCTAD 2015 (n 2) 74–75, 78, 100–02.

Indeed, a public policy exception clause, modelled on Article XX GATT, creates a perception that regulatory action which restricts investor rights is prima facie inconsistent with these rights unless the respondent State can discharge the burden of proving that its measures come within the exception. So as to avoid such complexities the UNCTAD model suggests that the IIA could require that the measure in question is 'related' to the policy objective. However, the model also notes that, 'in order to prevent abuse of exceptions, it is useful to clarify that "exceptional" measures must be applied in a non-arbitrary manner and not as disguised investment protectionism'.[91] This appears to restate the problem with GATT exceptions rather than avoiding it.

However, negotiators could make the exceptions self-judging, so that the necessity or appropriateness of the measure is judged only by the respondent State itself.[92] In the alternative, as suggested by the Commonwealth Secretariat model, the requirement that the measures be 'necessary' to achieve the listed objectives can be replaced with a requirement that they be 'designed and applied' to achieve the indicated objectives, following the COMESA Investment Agreement.[93]

This alternative formulation applies to measures to protect human, animal, or plant life or health, internationally and domestically recognized human rights, labour rights, or the rights of indigenous peoples, to ensure compliance with laws and regulations that are not inconsistent with the provisions of the IIA in question and to protect the environment, including but not limited to the conservation of living or non-living exhaustible natural resources.[94] Other exceptions include prudential financial measures, public finance safeguards, cultural industries, essential security, and taxation.[95]

b) Investor responsibilities

Section 7 of the UNCTAD model provides a clause on investor obligations and responsibilities.[96] This can include a general obligation to obey host State laws with a concomitant denial of rights under the treaty if an investment is made in violation of host country law.[97] In addition, following the adoption by the UN Human Rights Council of Guiding Principles for Business and Human Rights, a provision could be included encouraging (or, in the alternative, requiring) an investor to follow the corporate human rights due diligence process contained in the Guiding Principles relating to economic development social and environmental

---

[91] UNCTAD 2012 ibid; UNCTAD 2015 ibid 101.
[92] UNCTAD 2012 ibid, UNCTAD 2015 ibid.
[93] VanDuzer and others (n 2) 249–50. [94] ibid.
[95] ibid. UNCTAD mentions, in addition, public morals, linguistic/cultural diversity, ensuring provision of essential social services, broader developmental safeguards, and cultural heritage: UNCTAD 2012 (n 2) 55; UNCTAD 2015 (n 2) 100.
[96] UNCTAD 2012 ibid 58; UNCTAD 2015 ibid 74–75, 106–08.
[97] UNCTAD 2012 ibid; UNCTAD 2015 ibid. See too VanDuzer and others (n 2) 287–90.

risks.[98] Furthermore, investors may be encouraged (or required) to observe applicable corporate social responsibility standards.[99]

The Commonwealth Secretariat model follows a similar path emphasizing the impact of the UN Guiding Principles on investor responsibilities under future IIAs.[100] However, unlike the UNCTAD model, it adds a further provision outlining the investor obligation to refrain from complicity in grave human rights violations.[101] This draws upon the *UN Norms on the Responsibilities of Transnational Corporations and Other Business Enterprises* of 2003,[102] which is somewhat surprising, given that this instrument never had any recognized normative status and has been superseded by the UN Guiding Principles. The main justification for this additional provision is to avoid local enforcement difficulties, especially in weak governance zones, and to target specific conduct requiring criminal sanctions thus differing from the general provision on human rights responsibilities.[103] However, it may be considered unnecessary. The corporate responsibility to carry out human rights due diligence under the general human rights provision would cover grave human rights violations in any case.

A further, apparently unnecessary, provision in the Commonwealth Secretariat model covers the civil liability of investors. This is designed to ensure that multinational corporate groups cannot escape liability for breaches of their obligations and responsibilities under the investment agreement by requiring them to purchase liability insurance on behalf of their local subsidiary and to post a bond in favour of the host State in situations where the sustainability assessment (see below) reveals that, 'potential adverse impacts on human rights, labour rights, indigenous

---

[98] See UN Human Rights Council Seventeenth Session 21 March 2011: *Guiding Principles on Business and Human Rights Implementing the United Nations 'Protect, Respect and Remedy' Framework* available at: <www.ohchr.org/documents/issues/business/A.HRC.17.31.pdf> accessed 12 November 2014; Guiding Principle 17, adopted by Resolution 17/4 of the Human Rights Council 16 June 2011 UN Doc A/HRC/RES/17/4 6 July 2011 available at: <www.business-humanrights.org/media/documents/un-human-rights-council-resolution-re-human-rights-transnational-corps-eng-6-jul-2011.pdf> accessed 12 November 2014. See further P Muchlinski, 'Implementing the New UN Corporate Human Rights Framework: Implications for Corporate Law, Governance and Regulation' (2012) 22(1) Bus Ethics Q 145; Business and Human Rights Initiative, *How to Do Business with Respect for Human Rights* (Global Compact Network Netherlands 2010); International Finance Corporation, *Guide to Human Rights Impact Assessment and Management (HRIAM)* available at: <www.ifc.org/wps/wcm/connect/8ecd35004c0cb230884bc9ec6f601fe4/hriam-guide-092011.pdf?MOD=AJPERES> accessed 12 November 2014. See too OECD Guidelines for Multinational Enterprises (2011 revision) Ch VI 'Human Rights' available at: <www.oecd.org/daf/inv/mne/48004323.pdf> accessed 12 November 2014.

[99] UNCTAD 2012 (n 2) 58; UNCTAD 2015 (n 2) 107.

[100] VanDuzer and others (n 2) 290–311.

[101] ibid 315. The Commonwealth Secretariat model also includes a separate provision on observance of fundamental labour rights (ibid 318–29) while the UNCTAD model incorporates reference to core labour standards in its general investor obligations and responsibilities provision.

[102] Norms on the Responsibilities of Transnational Corporations and Other Business Enterprises with Regard to Human Rights, ECOSOC, UN Doc E/CN.4/Sub.2/2003/12/Rev.2 (2003); Commentary on the Norms on the Responsibilities of Transnational Corporations and Other Business Enterprises with Regard to Human Rights, UN Doc E/CN.4/Sub.2/2003/38/Rev.2, (2003).

[103] VanDuzer and others (n 2) 312–16.

peoples' rights or the environment are sufficiently serious to require extra available funds to satisfy any judgment against the investor for breach of the investor's obligations under the treaty'.[104]

While securing the liability of investors through litigation at the domestic level is difficult,[105] it has to be asked whether an IIA is the right place for the development of a new field of transnational liability law. Domestic legal liability, despite the difficulties involved, is already available and leads to more immediate results in terms of the settlement of claims. The attempt to develop a new field of liability at the international level would, surely, need a separate treaty expressing a clear international consensus to create transnational corporate liability law that operates above domestic law. However, there is nothing to stop States from enacting this provision in their agreements, though it would be surprising to see such a provision in place.

c) State obligations and institutional structures

Three types of provisions fall under this heading: no lowering of standards clauses, specialized home State obligations, and the establishment of institutional structures for cooperation between the State Contracting Parties to the IIA. No lowering of standards clauses have been used in some IIAs so as to prevent competition over inward investment through a lowering of regulatory standards in relation to labour and environment in particular. The UNCTAD model offers a wider range of issues by including health and human rights.[106] The Commonwealth Secretariat does not offer a sample provision in its Guide, because of political sensitivity, but accepts that States may wish to include a no lowering of standards clause, or to commit to raising domestic law standards where these fall below international norms.[107] As regards home State obligations the UNCTAD model includes a provision for technical assistance to be given by a more developed Contracting Party to a less developed Contracting Party to implement IIA obligations and facilitate investment flows.[108] Finally, UNCTAD also proposes a cooperative institutional structure under which the parties can discuss the interpretation of the IIA, so as to facilitate consistency in awards, and to provide a forum for cooperation in the furtherance of the sustainable development goals of the agreement.[109]

---

[104] ibid 390.
[105] On which see further P Muchlinski and V Rouas, 'Foreign Direct-Liability Litigation Toward the Transnationalisation of Corporate Legal Responsibility' in L Blecher, NK Stafford, and GC Bellamy (eds), *Corporate Responsibility for Human Rights Impacts: New Expectations and Paradigms* (ABA Chicago 2014) 357–91.
[106] UNCTAD 2012 (n 2) 59; UNCTAD 2015 (n 2) 109.
[107] VanDuzer and others (n 2) 363.
[108] UNCTAD 2012 (n 2) 63; UNCTAD 2015 (n 2) 109.
[109] UNCTAD 2012 ibid 60; UNCTAD 2015 ibid 110. Such institutional arrangements as also proposed in Brazil's continuing review of investment agreements and in the new Norwegian draft BIT of May 2015: *World Investment Report 2015* (n 2) 108 and 110.

d) Special and differential treatment provisions

This element is unique to the UNCTAD model.[110] It is designed to give expression to the concerns of least developed countries. It transports ideas already found in the WTO agreements, and other areas of international law, to IIAs. It has four elements: the delayed implementation of certain obligations, such as pre-establishment obligations, national treatment, transfer of funds, performance requirements, transparency or ISDS which represent a significant application of scarce governmental resources; replacing binding obligations in these areas with best endeavour clauses; carve-outs for these obligations; and the development friendly interpretation of protection standards taking into account the States' level of development. Again there is nothing in principle to rule out such provisions and they have the merit of growing out of existing precedents in other international economic agreements. However, it would not remove judgments over what a development friendly interpretation of the agreement would mean for a tribunal unless the question were removed from the tribunal by full carve-outs from protection provisions, or the use of best endeavour clauses, thus reducing the investor friendliness of the agreement. The balance to be struck here is not easy to define.

e) Sustainability assessment

This provision is unique to the Commonwealth Secretariat model. It is accepted that such a provision is novel and untested, creating an additional burden on investors and host countries alike, and so may not be readily accepted by countries negotiating IIAs.[111] Nonetheless, the benefits of requiring a sustainability assessment are seen as outweighing these concerns in that this will help to realize the policy goals of the IIA in this area.[112]

The sustainability assessment develops the approach of environmental and human rights impact assessments, requiring the investor to determine the impact of their investment on sustainable development goals. The State Contracting Parties should pass legislation regulating the use of such assessments. The assessment would have to be made before the investment is established. It is to take into account the following criteria:

(i) the promotion of sustainable development;
(ii) the need to respect national and international human rights, labour rights, the rights of indigenous peoples and environmental standards consistent with a Party's international obligations under treaty and customary international law;
(iii) the precautionary principle;
(iv) the principle that the polluter should bear the costs of pollution;

---

[110] UNCTAD 2012 (n 2) 63; UNCTAD 2015 (n 2) 117–18.
[111] VanDuzer and others (n 2) 262.   [112] ibid 262–63.

(v) the requirement that affected communities fully participate in decisions regarding aspects of the investment that could potentially affect them;

(vi) the requirement that indigenous peoples give their free, prior, and informed consent to the investment on issues that could potentially affect them;

(vi) the promotion of effective environmental, social, and human rights performance of investors through the effective integration of risk prevention and mitigation strategies in the investor's management systems; and

(vii) respect for and promotion of the dignity, human rights, cultures, and livelihoods of indigenous peoples as recognized in the national law of the host State and international law, and other international instruments including but not limited to the UN Declaration on the Rights of Indigenous Peoples and ILO Convention (No 169) concerning Indigenous and Tribal Peoples in Independent Countries, 1989.[113]

The assessment must involve public consultation and will result in a management plan that is subject to a grievance procedure.[114]

This proposal is indeed far beyond what an IIA might be reasonably expected to cover. It is, in effect, mandating a screening law to be adopted by the host country that examines investment proposals based on the listed criteria. Given that the 'promotion of sustainable development' inevitably involves an examination of the economic impact of the proposed investment, and given that social and environmental criteria do play a role in existing screening laws,[115] the list covers most issues that such laws cover. Far from making IIAs more development-friendly and reducing the risk of investment disputes, this provision makes for new potential trouble. No IIA has ever mandated a particular system of economic regulation for foreign investors. Even pre-establishment obligations do not prevent screening laws from being adopted, as long as they are not used as vehicles for discrimination against foreign investors. This proposal, on the other hand, requires States to adopt a comprehensive screening law, as a matter of international obligation. It may be said with some confidence that this provision will indeed not be used, as predicted by the Guide itself.

VI. Reform of Investor-State Dispute Settlement

The reform of ISDS is potentially very wide-ranging. The Commonwealth Secretariat Guide devotes eighty-seven pages to this topic.[116] More succinctly, the UNCTAD proposal focuses on three key issues: conditions of access to investment arbitration, ISDS institutions and procedures, and remedies and compensation.[117]

---

[113] ibid 284–85.   [114] ibid 285 and 378–79.
[115] On which see Muchlinski (n 39) 201–13.
[116] VanDuzer and others (n 2) 398–485.
[117] UNCTAD 2012 (n 2) 56–57; UNCTAD 2015 (n 2) 76, 103–105.

As to conditions of access, these can be restricted so as to avoid the costs of investor-State arbitration to the host country, mentioned in the introduction. In some cases this may lead to the exclusion of ISDS altogether, or to its availability only for a limited list of claims, and/or the exclusion of certain types of claims, such as those arising out of measures to protect health or human rights, which are key to sustainable development.

In addition, the availability of ISDS could be conditional on the prior exhaustion of domestic remedies in the host country,[118] and/or be made subject to a 'fork-in-the-road' provision by which the investor agrees not to bring, or a 'no U-turn' provision, by which the investor undertakes to discontinue, proceedings in the same case before another forum. In addition strict limitation periods could be added to prevent 'old' cases from being brought. UNCTAD is keen to stress that the use of alternative dispute resolution mechanisms should be encouraged, especially as resort to investor-State arbitration often results in the breakdown of the relationship between the investor and the host country.[119]

Both the UNCTAD and Commonwealth Secretariat models suggest the availability of counterclaims arising out of investors' non-compliance with domestic laws or a breach of investors' obligations under the treaty.[120]

On the issue of institutions and procedures the Commonwealth Secretariat model offers sample provisions of a highly detailed kind covering all major aspects of investor-State arbitration.[121] Space prevents a detailed exposition of these questions.[122] Of the many reforms proposed to make ISDS more legitimate and consistent the most important are: the adoption of an appellate mechanism; accessibility to proceedings, including public documentation and hearings and *amicus curiae* participation; a means of disposing of frivolous claims, consolidation of multiple claims arising from the same facts, and a joint interpretation mechanism for the Contracting Parties to control tribunal interpretations of IIA clauses.

Finally, as regards remedies and compensation, at present most IIAs do not specify any rules on this issue. This may allow a tribunal to require, for example, the

---

[118] See too VanDuzer and others (n 2) 413.
[119] UNCTAD 2012 (n 2) 43 and 56; UNCTAD 2015 (n 2) 105.
[120] UNCTAD 2012 ibid 57; UNCTAD 2015 ibid 103 and VanDuzer and others (n 2) 468–69.
[121] Van Duzer and others (n 116).
[122] See further A Joubin-Bret and JE Kalicki, 'Introduction TDM Special issue on "Reform of Investor-State Dispute Settlement: In Search of a Roadmap"' (January 2014) 11(1) Transnatl Disp Mgmt available at: <www.transnational-dispute-management.com> accessed 12 November 2014. For an advanced model of reformed ISDS provisions see the draft Canada–EU Comprehensive Economic and Trade Agreement: European Commission, 'Investment Provisions in the EU-Canada Free Trade Agreement' (3 December 2013) available at: <http://trade.ec.europa.eu/doclib/docs/2013/november/tradoc_151918.pdf> accessed 12 November 2014 and see too the EU consultation document over the Transatlantic Trade and Investment Partnership (TTIP) at <http://trade.ec.europa.eu/doclib/docs/2014/march/tradoc_152280.pdf> accessed 12 November 2014 especially the Annex containing draft CETA. See too the UNCITRAL Rules on Transparency in Treaty-based Investor-State Arbitration available at: <www.uncitral.org/pdf/english/texts/arbitration/rules-on-transparency/Rules-on-Transparency-E.pdf> accessed 12 November 2014. Note too the German proposal (n 3) which also advocates an exhaustion of local remedies requirement. In addition, India suggests this requirement in its continuing BIT review: *World Investment Report 2015* (n 2) 109.

modification or annulment of laws or regulations thus unduly intruding into host country sovereignty.[123] To avoid such consequences the dispute settlement clause can limit available remedies to monetary compensation and restitution of property, or compensation only. Guidance as to the measure of compensation may also be provided, as it already is for expropriation. Thus the clause could specify that compensation will be equitable and take into account all relevant circumstances, including the host country's level of development, and exclude certain types of damages by agreement of the parties such as moral damages and lost profits past a certain date.[124]

VII. Concluding Remarks

It is hard to question that the world has changed since the first Bilateral Investment Treaties were pioneered in the early 1960s, nor that the universe of IIAs has evolved in ways that its founders may not have foreseen and which may, in fact, be the result of historical accident.[125] However, as the interpretation of these changing circumstances unfolds in the new model provisions discussed above, one is left wondering whether these initiatives simply sidestep the hard and rather unedifying reality of a world apparently incapable of leaving behind the nostrums of neoliberalism, and offers, instead, a romantic vision of what could be, but which will not be, as neither organization is willing to assert that the vision put forward is anything other than a policy option for negotiators to follow. There is no real guidance as to how and why negotiators should choose a particular approach over another, though, to be fair, the Commonwealth Secretariat Guide tends towards a degree of prescription and the UNCTAD IFPSD is supplemented by a web-based Handbook for IIA Negotiators that contains all the concrete formulations needed to implement all of the policy options.[126]

Of course, as organizations composed of, and accountable to, the member States, nothing can be imposed. What these initiatives represent is an attempt to stretch the envelope of what may be possible in a policy environment dominated by neoliberal values to mitigate, to some degree, their perceived negative impacts. Thus both initiatives have an air of aspiration about them and of an attempt to accommodate some broadly social values in a predominantly market-based system that is still focused on the facilitation of business freedom and private enterprise without much concern for externalities, and into which first generation IIAs,

---

[123] UNCTAD 2012 (n 2) 57; UNCTAD 2015 (n 2) 106.
[124] UNCTAD 2012 ibid; UNCTAD 2015 ibid; VanDuzer and others (n 2) 467–68.
[125] On which see further P Muchlinski, 'The Role of Preferential Trade and Investment Agreements in International Investment Law: From Unforeseen Historical Developments to Uncertain Future' in R Hofman, SW Schill, and CJ Tams (eds), *Preferential Trade and Investment Agreements: From Recalibration to Reintegration* (Nomos 2013) 211.
[126] *International Investment Agreements Negotiators Handbook* (APEC Project CTI 15/2010T APEC/UNCTAD, 2013) (IIA Handbook) at http://investmentpolicyhub.unctad.org/Upload/Documents/UNCTAD_APEC%20Handbook.pdf accessed 12 November 2014.

accidentally, fit very well as devices for the protection of corporate freedom and the restriction of national policy space and regulatory discretion.[127]

That said, there is no necessary contradiction between goals of economic growth, investment protection, and the furtherance of sustainable development values. Indeed, the investment-sustainable development 'trade-off' may be an inaccurate and exaggerated contestation. Rather, the balance between the two needs to be further clarified.[128] In this regard the two models of new generation investment agreements discussed in this chapter do offer at least the first comprehensive guides to what could be done. The time is ripe for becoming more concrete on how new generations of IIAs should like and both UNCTAD and the Commonwealth Secretariat have a key role in this debate. To that extent these organizations have earned, and will continue to earn, their keep.

---

[127] On which see further VanDuzer and others (n 2) 25–26.
[128] See further J Bonnitcha, *Substantive Protection under Investment Treaties: A Legal and Economic Analysis* (CUP 2014).

III

Revising Treatment Standards— Fair and Equitable Treatment in Light of Sustainable Development

Roland Kläger

I. Introduction

Investment treaty makers face the challenge of shaping international investment agreements (IIAs) under a two-fold objective. On the one hand, the conclusion of an IIA is intended to display a State's commitment to the creation and preservation of a good investment climate. On the other hand, a State may wish to retain a certain flexibility to adopt measures it deems appropriate in light of the public interest. In between these two poles, the United Nations Conference on Trade and Development (UNCTAD) Investment Policy Framework on Sustainable Development[1] (IPFSD) provides and discusses a number of policy options available to treaty makers in order to achieve the conclusion of IIAs which are tailored to their needs and which are capable of ensuring sustainable development.

This article critically reviews the different policy options presented in the IPFSD with a focus on the provision granting fair and equitable treatment to foreign investors and investments. In particular, the article seeks to test the IPFSD's assumption that some policy options are less conducive to sustainable development than others. To do so, the article will describe, in an introductory part, the relationship between fair and equitable treatment and sustainable development and will then take a closer look at the sustainable development dimension of each of the IPFSD's policy options.

II. What is Fair and Equitable Treatment and What are the Problems?

Fair and equitable treatment is a core standard in IIAs protecting foreign investors and investments. It is a standard which regularly appears in the vast majority

---

[1] UNCTAD, *International Policy Framework for Sustainable Development* (2012) available at: <http://unctad.org/en/Pages/DIAE/International%20Investment%20Agreements%20%28IIA%29/IIA-IPFSD.aspx> accessed on 7 October 2015.

of bilateral investment agreements (BITs) as well as in multilateral investment agreements such as the North American Free Trade Agreement (NAFTA) and the Energy Charter Treaty. In empirical exercises, a considerable number of BITs have been reviewed and it was determined that only a negligible amount of treaties does not incorporate a fair and equitable treatment clause. In one study, it has been identified that nineteen out of 365 BITs[2] do not refer to fair and equitable treatment; an earlier study came to a similar conclusion.[3] Therefore, at this superficial level, great consensus seems to exist that fair and equitable treatment is an important element of international investment law.

Much more diversity exists when taking a closer look at the way in which IIAs refer to fair and equitable treatment. There are a number of different formulations of fair and equitable treatment clauses which may be found in IIAs, insofar as there are unqualified provisions of fair and equitable treatment in which this standard is free-standing or juxtaposed to other standards like full protection and security.[4] Another frequent type of fair and equitable treatment clause combines this standard with a reference to general international law[5] or to the minimum standard of customary international law.[6] Only a few treaties make fair and equitable treatment contingent on domestic law.[7]

This shows that the landscape of fair and equitable treatment provisions is diverse and one of increasing variety.[8] There are clauses consisting of only a few words and clauses which fill a couple of pages. Especially in Northern and Latin America, a strong tendency exists towards more complex fair and equitable treatment clauses often referring to the international minimum standard. This is certainly a reaction to investor–State claims brought against a number of States. More recently, the European Union strongly favours complex fair and equitable treatment clauses, which are used for instance as a basis for the negotiation of the EU–Canada Comprehensive Economic Trade Agreement (CETA) and the EU–USA Transatlantic Trade and Investment Partnership (TTIP).[9] However, this is not a uniform trend, as China especially seems to have abandoned reservations against unqualified fair and equitable treatment provisions.

---

[2] I Tudor, *The Fair and Equitable Treatment Standard in the International Law of Foreign Investment* (OUP 2008) 23.
[3] MI Khalil, 'Treatment of Foreign Investment in Bilateral Investment Treaties' (1992) 8 ICSID Rev 351ff, finding that twenty-eight out of 335 BITs omit fair and equitable treatment.
[4] See, for example, Treaty between the Federal Republic of Germany and—concerning the Encouragement and Reciprocal Protection of Investments (2008) ('2008 Germany Model BIT') Art 2(2).
[5] See, for example, Agreement between the Government of the Republic of France and the Government of the United Mexican States on the Reciprocal Promotion and Protection of Investments (signed 12 November 1998, entered into force 12 October 2000) ('1998 France–Mexico BIT') Art 4(1).
[6] See, for example, Treaty between the Government of the United States of America and—concerning the Encouragement and Reciprocal Protection of Investment (2012) ('2012 US Model BIT').
[7] See, for example, Agreement on Reciprocal Promotion and Protection between the Caribbean Community (CARICOM) and the Republic of Cuba (1997) ('CARICOM–Cuba BIT') Art IV.
[8] See also UNCTAD, 'International Investment Rule-Making' UNCTAD/ITE/IIT2007/3 (2008) 28ff.
[9] See the draft fair and equitable treatment provisions in Art X.9 of the Consolidated CETA Text as published on 26 September 2014 (available at: <http://ec.europa.eu/trade/policy/in-focus/ceta/>

The driver of these developments in treaty making is the dynamic evolution of arbitral jurisprudence on fair and equitable treatment. Within the last decade, different sub-elements of fair and equitable treatment or patterns of argumentation in case law have emerged which provide certain contours to the scope and content of this provision. Despite remaining uncertainty as to the details and labelling of each of the sub-elements, there is considerable agreement within arbitral jurisprudence that fair and equitable treatment entails these or similar principles. Considering furthermore the relatively short period of time from the first arbitral awards at the end of the 1990s until now, remarkable progress has been made in clarifying the meaning of fair and equitable treatment.

Nevertheless, the dynamic development of international investment has also caused problems and concerns as the case law, especially on fair and equitable treatment but also on other investment protection standards, is often perceived as being too far-reaching and inconsistent.[10] Fair and equitable treatment is by its nature a general clause and, therefore, inherently vague. This poses problems on how to apply such a vague clause for which, in the beginning, no case law existed. Boosted by some demanding interpretations by early arbitral tribunals of what fair and equitable treatment may possibly entail,[11] this provision quickly became a prominent cause of action for investor–State claims.

On account of such demanding interpretations and due to the fact that developed States were also held liable for breaching fair and equitable treatment, concerns rose that this provision may constrict a State's sovereignty considerably and that this threatens sustainable development.[12] Such concerns are not entirely unfounded as it has soon become clear that, under fair and equitable treatment, arbitral tribunals may potentially scrutinize all sorts of State action irrespective of whether it pertains to the administrative, legislative, or judicative branch and irrespective of the policy area concerned.[13] Fair and equitable treatment is therefore sometimes considered as a 'black box' which is full of surprises. However, one should also not forget the ideological divide which existed on the international level with regard to foreign investments. General clauses like fair and equitable treatment are a tool to bridge this divide and to create flexibility with regard to the manifold problems foreign investors may encounter within a host State.

---

accessed 7 October 2015), and in Art 3 of the EU Commission's TTIP draft as released on 16 September 2015 (available at: <http://trade.ec.europa.eu/doclib/docs/2015/september/tradoc_153807.pdf>); see also European Commission, 'Investment Protection and Investor-to-State Dispute Settlement in EU Agreements—Fact Sheet' (November 2013) 8 available at: <http://trade.ec.europa.eu/doclib/cfm/doclib_results.cfm?docid=151916> accessed 7 October 2015.

[10] See, for example, S Franck, 'The Legitimacy Crisis in Investment Treaty Arbitration: Privatizing Public International Law Through Inconsistent Decisions' (2005) 73 Fordham L Rev 1521.

[11] See, for example, *Técnicas Medioambientales TECMED SA v The United Mexican States*, ICSID Case No ARB(AF)/00/2, Award (29 May 2003), para 154.

[12] The notion of sustainable development is not defined in the IPFSD but understood in this chapter as referring to the environmental, economic, and social development implications of foreign investment; thereon see UN, 'Johannesburg Declaration on Sustainable Development' (2002) UN Doc A/CONF.199/20 (2002) para 5.

[13] See also R Dolzer, 'The Impact of International Investment Treaties on Domestic Administrative Law' (2005) 37 NYU J Intl L & Pol 954.

The IPFSD also emphasizes the problems arising out of the vagueness of fair and equitable treatment.[14] Accordingly, the IPFSD complains that there is a great deal of legal uncertainty concerning the precise meaning of fair and equitable treatment. This is said to be because notions of 'fairness' and 'equity' would allow for a significant degree of subjective judgement.[15] Such discretion would have induced arbitral tribunals to read a taxing list of disciplines into the provision of fair and equitable treatment creating further ambiguity regarding the appropriate threshold of liability. Particular concern is expressed in relation to the sub-element of protecting an investor's legitimate expectations as this could threaten a host State's liability to change and introduce investment-related policies for the public good.

III. Policy Options in the IPFSD

To accommodate these concerns and in order to enhance sustainable development, the IPFSD lists and recommends certain policy options for fair and equitable treatment clauses in IIAs: (a) unqualified commitment of fair and equitable treatment, (b) reference to the minimum standard or international law, (c) exhaustive list of fair and equitable treatment obligations, (d) interpretative guidance to arbitral tribunals, and (e) omit fair and equitable treatment. These options are reviewed in the following.

a) Unqualified commitment of fair and equitable treatment

The IPFSD takes a critical view on unqualified fair and equitable treatment clauses. The concern is that such a clause would entail a low level of liability to provide maximum protection and that it would therefore unduly limit the policy space of host States:

> Through an unqualified promise to treat investors 'fairly and equitably', a country provides maximum protection for investors but also risks posing limits on its policy space, raising its exposure to foreign investors' claims and resulting financial liabilities. Some of these implications stem from the fact that there is a great deal of uncertainty concerning the precise meaning of the concept, because the notions of 'fairness' and 'equity' do not connote a clear set of legal prescriptions and are open to subjective interpretations. A particularly problematic issue concerns the use of the FET standard to protect investors' 'legitimate expectations', which may restrict the ability of countries to change policies or to introduce new policies that—while pursuing SD objectives—may have a negative impact on foreign investors.[16]

In this quote, the IPFSD draws a scenario in which a host State is liable for introducing new policies pursuing sustainable development objectives which negatively affect an investor's expectation that the legal environment of its investment remains unchanged. Liability of a host State under such a scenario is generally possible as the law at the time of the investment represents the basis of an investor's

---

[14] UNCTAD (n 1) 43.
[15] See also Katharina Berner, 'Treaty Interpretation', in Ch 8 of this book.
[16] UNCTAD (n 1) 51.

expectations and as these expectations may also extend to the overall legal framework of the host State.[17]

However, a realistic assessment of the sustainable development implications of unqualified fair and equitable treatment provisions needs to be aware of the fact that such provisions are status quo in many IIAs. Considering the huge number of BITs already concluded and the long period for which such treaties usually remain in force, it is likely that unqualified provisions remain an important reference point in the future. This appears true in particular for BITs of European States such as Germany, which traditionally incorporated unqualified clauses.[18] Moreover, as long as a State has concluded at least one IIA including an unqualified fair and equitable treatment provision, this may be incorporated as the relevant standard also into other IIAs via a most-favoured-nation clause.

Against this background, the question arises whether unqualified fair and equitable treatment clauses mean that there is a threat to sustainable development or a low level of liability as the quote from the IPFSD might imply. Of course, this is not necessarily the case.[19] As indicated in the preamble of investment agreements, fair and equitable treatment or other substantive provisions of investment agreements aim at the promotion and protection of foreign investment but certainly not at 'maximum protection'. Moreover, the notions of 'fairness' and 'equity' clearly indicate the need for a comprehensive balancing of interests which makes the level of protection dependent on the weight of the particular interests at stake.

This is recognized by the prevailing trend in arbitral jurisprudence and, accordingly, arbitral tribunals increasingly find that principles like sovereignty and sustainable development influence the application of fair and equitable treatment clauses. An important example of this approach is presented by the *Saluka* case in which the Arbitral Tribunal emphasized in relation to an unqualified fair and equitable treatment clause:

The protection of foreign investment is not the sole aim of the treaty, but rather a necessary element alongside the overall aim of encouraging foreign investment and intensifying the parties' economic relations. That in turn calls for a balanced approach to the interpretation of the treaty's substantive provisions for the protection of investments, since an interpretation which exaggerates the protection to be accorded to foreign investments may serve to dissuade host States from admitting foreign investments and so undermine the overall aim of extending and intensifying the parties' mutual economic relations.[20]

The interpretative toolbox to accommodate the need for balancing is provided by Article 31(3)(c) of the Vienna Convention on the Law of Treaties (VCLT),[21] which

---

[17] For a review of case law, see R Kläger, *'Fair and Equitable Treatment' in International Investment Law* (CUP 2011) 169ff.

[18] On the traditional structure of German BITs, see M Füracker, 'Relevance and Structure of Bilateral Investment Treaties—The German Approach' (2006) SchiedsVZ 236, 240ff.

[19] See R Kläger, '"Fair and Equitable Treatment" and Sustainable Development', in MC Cordonier Segger, M Gehring, and A Newcombe (eds), *Sustainable Development in World Investment Law* (Kluwer 2011) 241.

[20] *Saluka Investments BV v Czech Republic*, UNCITRAL, Partial Award (17 March 2006), para 300.

[21] Vienna Convention on the Law of Treaties (adopted 23 May 1969, entered into force 27 January 1980) (VCLT) 1155 UNTS 331.

stipulates that any relevant rules of international law applicable in the relations between the parties shall be taken into account in the interpretation of a treaty provision. Article 31(3)(c) VCLT allows for the systemic integration of sustainable development law, human rights, or other principles into the concept of fair and equitable treatment.[22] This means that even under an unqualified fair and equitable treatment provision a broad range of principles may be invoked as a defence by host States to influence the threshold of liability to be applied in a particular case.[23]

In conclusion, the IPFSD is certainly right in observing that the notions of 'fairness' and 'equity' are open to subjective interpretation and that they do not connote a clear set of legal prescriptions. On the one hand, this creates a certain degree of uncertainty, but only to the extent that the interpretation and application of fair and equitable treatment is not clarified already by the rapidly increasing body of arbitral case law.[24] On the other hand, the notions of 'fairness' and 'equity' are the windows that arbitrators may use in order to apply arguments in favour of sovereignty, sustainable development, human rights, or other principles, even if such principles are not mentioned in the particular investment agreement relevant for the case to be decided.[25]

b) Reference to international law/minimum standard

As a first alternative policy option to enhance the sustainable development dimension of an investment agreement, the IPFSD recommends to qualify a fair and equitable treatment provision by reference to (principles of) international law or to the minimum standard of treatment of aliens under customary international law. The IPFSD emphasizes:

> The reference to customary international law may raise the threshold of State liability and help to preserve States' ability to adapt public policies in light of changing objectives (except when these measures constitute manifestly arbitrary conduct that amounts to egregious mistreatment of foreign investors), but the exact contours of MST/CIL remain elusive.[26]

This policy option resembles the wording that is used, for instance, in Article 1105(1) NAFTA and the drafting approaches of a number of more recent Model BITs of the US, Canada, and other countries. Such provisions regularly provide that host States shall accord foreign investors or investments treatment in accordance with (customary) international law, including fair and equitable treatment, whereby (customary) international law is equated with the customary international law minimum standard of treatment of aliens.[27]

---

[22] See C McLachlan, L Shore, and M Weininger, *International Investment Arbitration* (OUP 2007) 67, 222–23.

[23] See, for example, A Diehl, *The Core Standard of International Investment Protection* (Kluwer 2012) 511ff; S Karamanian, 'The Place of Human Rights in Investor-State Arbitration' (2013) 17 Lewis & Clark L Rev 423.

[24] International decisions are relevant as a subsidiary means of interpretation according to Art 38(1)(d) ICJ Statute.

[25] See Kläger (n 17) 110 ff.   [26] UNCTAD (n 1) 51.

[27] See Art 5 of the Agreement between Canada and—for the Promotion and Protection of Investments (2004) ('2004 Canada Model BIT'), which provides one of the more concise drafting examples of that type:

By suggesting the inclusion of language referring to customary international law, the IPFSD tries to tackle two main problems of the fair and equitable treatment concept: first, the vagueness and, second, the presumably low liability threshold. However, it is highly uncertain and controversial whether such clauses are able to achieve the envisaged result.

First, in relation to the vagueness problem, the minimum standard requires further explanation and concretization itself. In this context, arbitral tribunals traditionally invoked the definition of the customary international law minimum standard in the 1926 *Neer* case:

> The treatment of an alien, in order to constitute an international delinquency should amount to an outrage, to bad faith, to wilful neglect of duty, or to an insufficiency of governmental action so far short of international standards that every reasonable and impartial man would readily recognize its insufficiency.[28]

In the contemporary context of foreign investment, arbitral tribunals have however regularly held that physical violence, bad faith or wilful intent is (conducive but) not required to establish a breach of fair and equitable treatment.[29] If these elements are therefore taken out from the *Neer* definition, the standard of a reasonable and impartial man remains. While reasonableness and impartiality certainly have a role to play in the application of fair and equitable treatment, the *Neer* definition is nevertheless insufficient to help to concretize the meaning of fair and equitable treatment. The replacement of notions of 'fairness' and 'equity' by notions of 'reasonableness' and 'impartiality' rather appears as an attempt to define fair and equitable treatment by reference to another black box of which the content is unknown or at least opaque. The cases on State responsibility from the 1920s or 1930s, of which the *Neer* case is the most prominent one, may be of limited relevance for the areas of compensation for expropriation, violent interference with the investment by non-State actors, or denial of justice. However, beyond that, the minimum standard and the pertinent case law seem to be of little use to guide arbitrators in complex modern investor–State arbitrations on foreign investment possibly involving a very broad range of matters.[30]

Second, the IPFSD considers the references to international law or the minimum standard as a tool to raise the liability threshold.[31] Many commentators and host States trying to limit the scope of fair and equitable treatment to the status

1. Each Party shall accord to covered investments treatment in accordance with the customary international law minimum standard of treatment of aliens, including fair and equitable treatment and full protection and security.
2. The concepts of 'fair and equitable treatment' and 'full protection and security' in paragraph 1 do not require treatment in addition to or beyond that which is required by the customary international law minimum standard of treatment of aliens.
3. [...].

[28] *LFH Neer and Pauline Neer* (*USA v United Mexican States*) (1926) IV RIAA 60, 61f.
[29] See K Vandevelde, 'A Unified Theory of Fair and Equitable Treatment' (2010) 42 Intl L & Pol 43, 55.
[30] See also M Sornarajah, *The International Law on Foreign Investment* (3rd edn, CUP 2010) 346.
[31] See also UNCTAD, Fair and Equitable Treatment, *UNCTAD Series on Issues in International Investment Agreements II* (2012) 13.

of customary international law share this view.³² This was also the declared aim of the NAFTA Free Trade Commission Note of Interpretation on Article 1105(1) NAFTA of 31 July 2001, which was a direct reaction to some early far-reaching arbitral awards in which, for the first time, developed States were held liable for breaches of fair and equitable treatment.³³ Interestingly, this development turned the initial impetus of the minimum standard upside down which, in the times of the *Neer* case, was employed as a tool to establish and not to prevent liability of host States for their acts against foreign nationals. As such, the minimum standard was heavily contested by developing countries.

When considering the arbitral case law discussing the threshold issue, the actual effect of such clauses referring to the minimum standard remains controversial and uncertain. In this context, a number of fundamental questions arises that complicate the application of this treaty provision in an individual case: What is the status of customary international law? To what extent (if at all) did customary international law evolve since the *Neer* case? Does fair and equitable treatment (or parts of it) form part of customary international law? Arguably, fair and equitable treatment was initially established as a conventional norm exactly to avoid the difficulties surrounding the minimum standard.³⁴ The drafting approach connecting fair and equitable treatment to the minimum standard necessarily reintroduces such questions into the application of this provision. Moreover, this drafting approach may also have the effect of stimulating the evolution of customary international law. Consequently, many arbitral tribunals have held that the customary international law minimum standard has evolved in the past and that, therefore, a real difference between the treaty provision of fair and equitable treatment and the minimum standard cannot be identified.³⁵ All this has led to considerable uncertainty as to the threshold arbitral tribunals should apply.

An extreme example advocating a high liability threshold is presented by the reasoning in the *Glamis Gold* case.³⁶ In this decision, the Arbitral Tribunal emphasized that the threshold of liability is still the same as in the *Neer* case:

It therefore appears that, although situations may be more varied and complicated today than in the 1920s, the level of scrutiny is the same. The fundamentals of the Neer standard thus still apply today: to violate the customary international law minimum standard of treatment codified in Article 1105 of the NAFTA, an act must be sufficiently egregious and

---

[32] See, for example, with further references H Haeri, 'A Tale of Two Standards: "Fair and Equitable Treatment" and the Minimum Standard in International Law' (2011) 27 Arb Int 27.

[33] On the development of the case law on Art 1105(1) NAFTA, see comprehensively P Dumberry, *The Fair and Equitable Treatment Standard: A Guide to NAFTA Case Law on Article 1105* (Kluwer 2013).

[34] See G Sacerdoti, 'Bilateral Treaties and Multilateral Instruments on Investment Protection' (1997) 269 RdC 251, 341.

[35] See, for example, *Occidental Exploration and Production Co v The Republic of Ecuador*, London Court of International Arbitration Case No UN 3467, Final Award (1 July 2004) para 187; *Azurix Corp and other v Argentine Republic*, ICSID Case No ARB/01/12, Award (14 July 2006) paras 364ff; *Rumeli Telekom SA and others v Republic of Kazakhstan*, ICSID Case No ARB/05/16, Award (29 July 2008) para 611; *Biwater Gauff Ltd v United Republic of Tanzania*, ICSID Case No ARB/05/22, Award (24 July 2008) para 592.

[36] *Glamis Gold Ltd v United States of America*, UNCITRAL, Award (14 May 2009).

shocking—a gross denial of justice, manifest arbitrariness, blatant unfairness, a complete lack of due process, evident discrimination, or a manifest lack of reasons—so as to fall below accepted international standards and constitute a breach of Article 1105 (1). The Tribunal notes that one aspect of evolution from Neer that is generally agreed upon is that bad faith is not required to find a violation of the fair and equitable treatment standard, but its presence is conclusive evidence of such.[37]

To establish this high hurdle, the tribunal in the *Glamis Gold* case first placed the burden of proof for the issue of whether the minimum standard had evolved or not on the investor.[38] At the same time, the Tribunal left a back door open by asserting that 'it is entirely possible, however that, as an international community, we may be shocked by State actions now that did not offend us previously'.[39]

At the other extreme, the *Merrill & Ring* case stands out as one in which the Tribunal emphasized the evolutionary nature of customary law.[40] The Tribunal found that, except for cases of safety and due process, today's minimum standard is broader than the above definition in the *Neer* case.[41] In particular, the minimum standard was said to comprise fair and equitable treatment, which itself had become part of customary law and which required a reasonable justification for a State measure:

A requirement that aliens be treated fairly and equitably in relation to business, trade and investment is the outcome of this changing reality and as such it has become sufficiently part of widespread and consistent practice so as to demonstrate that it is reflected today in customary international law as opinio juris. In the end, the name assigned to the standard does not really matter. What matters is that the standard protects against all such acts or behavior that might infringe a sense of fairness, equity and reasonableness. Of course, the concepts of fairness, equitableness and reasonableness cannot be defined precisely: they require to be applied to the facts of each case.[42]

In conclusion, this means for treaty makers that there is no certainty as to whether a reference to the international minimum standard ultimately leads to a higher liability threshold. An UNCTAD study suggests that within NAFTA (and therefore under a provision with reference to the minimum standard) a breach of fair and equitable treatment is determined less often than outside.[43] The reasons for this finding are, however, unknown and may be diverse. Moreover, it is also questionable whether the aim of this policy option to achieve a high but, at the same time, inflexible threshold for liability is conducive to sustainable development across the board. It seems that the discussion on the important question, in which areas judicial self-restraint is appropriate and in which it is not, is just starting and that it has not received sufficient attention so far.

---

[37] ibid para 616.   [38] ibid para 601.
[39] ibid para 616; see similar *Cargill Inc v United Mexican States*, ICSID Case No ARB(AF)/05/2, Award (18 September 2009) para 282.
[40] *Merrill & Ring Forestry LP v The Government of Canada*, UNCITRAL, Award (31 July 2010).
[41] ibid para 213.   [42] ibid para 210.
[43] UNCTAD, 'Fair and Equitable Treatment' *UNCTAD Series on Issues in International Investment Agreements II* (2012) 61.

c) Exhaustive list of fair and equitable treatment obligations

The IPFSD also provides for an option to incorporate an exhaustive list of State obligations under fair and equitable treatment. This option focuses more strongly on the content of fair and equitable treatment rather than on the level of scrutiny, and may be applied in addition, or as an alternative to the reference to (customary) international law. Possible examples for the list of State obligations are commitments not to:

- deny justice in judicial or administrative proceedings;
- treat investors in a manifestly arbitrary manner;
- flagrantly violate due process;
- engage in manifestly abusive treatment involving continuous, unjustified coercion or harassment;
- infringe investors' legitimate expectations based on investment-including representations or measures.[44]

This list reflects the more recent developments in arbitral jurisprudence and the continuous emergence of certain sub-elements of fair and equitable treatment. In fact, it seems to be widely acknowledged in scholarly literature and case law that fair and equitable treatment comprises these or similar principles.[45] For example, the Tribunal in the *Rumeli Telekom* case affirmed:

> The parties rightly agree that the fair and equitable treatment standard encompasses inter alia the following concrete principles: the State must act in a transparent manner; the State is obliged to act in good faith; the State's conduct cannot be arbitrary, grossly unfair, unjust, idiosyncratic, discriminatory, or lacking in due process; the State must respect procedural propriety and due process. The case law also confirms that to comply with the standard, the State must respect the investor's reasonable and legitimate expectations."[46]

Of course, it is debatable whether fair and equitable treatment should comprise each and every one of these principles and to what extent protection should be granted thereunder. Treaty makers may wish to influence this debate by stipulating an exhaustive list and possibly by omitting certain more controversial sub-elements from the list (such as transparency or the protection of legitimate expectations). However, striking out established sub-elements from an exhaustive fair and equitable treatment clause will arguably constitute a difficult task in treaty negotiations and will depend on the negotiation power of the States involved.

The added value of a list of sub-elements in a fair and equitable treatment clause depends on a number of factors. For instance, if none of the established principles

---

[44] UNCTAD (n 1) 51.
[45] See, for example, UNCTAD, 'Fair and Equitable Treatment' *UNCTAD Series on Issues in International Investment Agreements II* (2012) 62; SW Schill, 'Fair and Equitable Treatment, The Rule of Law and Comparative Public Law', in SW Schill (ed), *International Investment Law and Comparative Public Law* (OUP 2010) 151; K Vandevelde, 'A Unified Theory of Fair and Equitable Treatment' (2010) 43 Intl L & Pol 43.
[46] *Rumeli* (n 35) para 609; similar *Biwater Gauff Ltd v Tanzania*, ICSID Case No ARB/05/22 (Award of 18 July 2008) para 60; *Bayindir Insaat Turizim Ticaret ve Sanayi AS v Islamic Republic of Pakistan*, ICSID Case No ARB/03/29; Award (24 August 2009) para 178.

are omitted, the question arises whether there is a difference to an unqualified fair and equitable treatment provision. Even though a strict rule of *stare decisis* does not apply in international investment arbitration, there is a high probability that arbitral tribunals rely on the established principles of fair and equitable treatment and pertinent case law when deciding an investment dispute.[47] Further, if certain principles are left out from an exhaustive list, the question is whether arbitral tribunals are still able to draw from such elements. This may be possible because the principle is rooted in customary law or another source of international law, which an arbitral tribunal considers to be relevant for the decision of the case and which, thus, may influence the interpretation of fair and equitable treatment. Taking into account other sources of international law when interpreting fair and equitable treatment is feasible pursuant to Article 31(3)(c) VCLT. It may also be possible that certain factors are sometimes treated as a proper sub-element of fair and equitable treatment but, if this is excluded, the factor is still relevant under another element of the list.

This shows that the drafting of a particular list of sub-elements of fair and equitable treatment does not yet predict the outcome of future arbitrations under this cause of action. Moreover, further room for interpretation exists with regard to the meaning of the individual terms included in the list, such as 'due process', 'denial of justice', 'harassment', or 'manifest arbitrary treatment'. These are all very general terms which are subject to the same interpretational problems like fair and equitable treatment itself. This notwithstanding, the consistent use of lists of fair and equitable treatment principles will certainly concretize the application of this norm over time, and will help to consolidate the already existing trend in arbitral jurisprudence on the emerging principles of fair and equitable treatment.

Another question is whether the additional use of adjectives like 'manifest', 'evident', or 'flagrant' implies that arbitral tribunals should apply a rather high standard of review.[48] Serious doubts exist whether such an approach will prove to be successful, or whether it adds anything to general interpretative guidelines like in dubio mitius. Moreover, an arbitral tribunal will not find a breach of an investment treaty provision lightly, but only if the claiming party has proven and if the tribunal is sufficiently convinced that there are good reasons for establishing liability. Under these circumstances, the added value of a label like 'manifest' is questionable if it is not further specified in the treaty what exactly counts as manifest.

d) Interpretative guidance to arbitral tribunals

The IPFSD highlights another policy option and suggests amending fair and equitable treatment clauses by interpretative guidelines for arbitrators. To this end, it is proposed to clarify in the text of the respective provision that

- the fair and equitable treatment clause does not preclude States from adopting good faith regulatory or other measures that pursue legitimate policy objectives;

---

[47] On the de facto rule of precedent, see, for example, A Newcombe and L Paradell, *Law and Practice of Investment Treaties—Standards of Treatment* (Kluwer 2009) 59, at § 1.46.

[48] See UNCTAD, 'Fair and Equitable Treatment' *UNCTAD Series on Issues in International Investment Agreements II* (2012) 110.

- the investor's conduct including the observance of universally recognized standards[49] is relevant in determining whether the fair and equitable treatment clause has been breached;
- a breach of another provision of the international investment agreement or of another international agreement cannot establish a claim for breach of the clause.[50]

This option is inspired by the legal reasoning in arbitral practice. By stipulating interpretative guidelines in the text of the treaty, the option attempts to make such considerations mandatory for arbitral tribunals and to achieve greater legal certainty in this regard. While this is certainly an innovative drafting approach, the benefit of such guidelines depends on the question as to whether they differ from the current state of arbitral practice.

In this context, the first guideline appears to be firmly established in arbitral jurisprudence. Tribunals are already enquiring whether there is a legitimate objective for a State measure and frequently recognize that host States have a wide regulatory space.[51] Tribunals have held that State measures impairing the business of a foreign investor were justified, for instance, because the measures pursued the objective to tackle the problems of economic and political transition in a country's banking sector;[52] because they were carried out to ensure the observance of legal requirements to protect the environment;[53] or because the measures aimed at preserving a country's cultural heritage.[54] However, it is equally clear from arbitral practice that the right to regulate or the pursuance of legitimate objectives may not be abused by host States to justify all means in achieving such ends.[55] It is a basic principle of concluding international investment agreements that this implies certain boundaries to a host State's regulatory freedom. Accordingly, as the interpretative guideline is formulated in a broad way, it will remain debatable under such a fair and equitable treatment clause what, in the end, constitutes a legitimate objective and what means are justified to pursue this objective.

With regard to the second guideline, the matters appear to be more diverse. As the application of fair and equitable treatment requires a comprehensive balancing process and as this provision is rooted in the ideas of fairness and equity, the conduct of the investor may be a relevant element to be considered by an arbitral tribunal. At least, this is increasingly emphasized in scholarly literature.[56] However, there are only few arbitral decisions in which this issue is explicitly discussed in the legal reasoning

---

[49] The IPFSD points to the following examples: the ILO Tripartite Declaration of Principles concerning Multinational Enterprises and Social Policy, the UN Guiding Principles on Business and Human Rights, and corporate social responsibility standards; see UNCTAD (n 1) 58.

[50] ibid 51.

[51] See, for example, *SD Myers Inc v Government of Canada*, UNCITRAL, First Partial Award (13 November 2000) para 255; *International Thunderbird Gaming Corp v The United Mexican States*, UNCITRAL, Award (26 January 2006) para 127; *Saluka* (n 20) paras 298, 305.

[52] See *Alex Genin and others v The Republic of Estonia*, ICSID Case No ARB/99/2, Award (25 June 2001) para 370.

[53] See *Emilio Augustín Maffezini v The Kingdom of Spain*, ICSID Case No ARB/97/7, Award (13 November 2000) paras 67, 71.

[54] See *Parkerings-Compagniet AS v Republic of Lithuania*, ICSID Case No ARB/05/8, Award (11 September 2007) para 392.

[55] See *ADC Affiliate Ltd. and others v The Republic of Hungary*, ICSID Case No ARB/03/16, Award (2 October 2006) para 423.

[56] See, for example, P Muchlinski, 'Caveat Investor? The Relevance of the Conduct of the Investor under the Fair and Equitable Treatment Standard' (2006) 55 ICLQ 527; Sornarajah (n 30) 466ff.

relating to fair and equitable treatment.[57] This is even more so in relation to the question of whether the host State's level of development should be taken into account.[58] As, therefore, considerable uncertainty remains, it is, on the one hand, certainly helpful for arbitrators to receive guidance from the treaty makers on these questions. On the other hand, the suggested interpretative guideline does not provide any particulars as to the concrete criteria how and under what circumstances the matters should be taken into account by arbitral tribunals. These criteria will evolve over time through the continuous development of case law.

The third guideline addresses the difficult question of the interrelationship of different investment protection standards. Thereby, it is clear that, for instance, expropriation, national treatment, or full protection and security clauses cannot be considered in clinical isolation from fair and equitable treatment. Many arguments relevant for the determination of a breach of these other clauses are also related to the concept of fair and equitable treatment and vice versa. Therefore, this guideline may be of more importance in the context of free trade agreements or of other international agreements exceeding the scope of the arbitration clause in the investment chapter or agreement. Then, however, the question is no longer one of how to interpret fair and equitable treatment but one of the scope of jurisdiction of the arbitral tribunal. With regard to the interpretation of fair and equitable treatment, a paramount interpretative guideline concerning the taking into account of other international agreements is already provided by Article 31(3)(c) VCLT. It is not to be assumed that the above interpretative guideline for fair and equitable treatment is intended to deviate from the universally accepted principles of the VCLT.

In conclusion, the guidelines appear as innovative and soft tools to influence the balancing of interests by arbitral tribunals. However, as the guidelines are quite broad and open to interpretation themselves, they cannot avoid a certain level of legal uncertainty or subjective judgement by arbitrators. Ultimately, it is also unclear what the legal consequences are if a tribunal openly refuses to comply with the interpretative guidelines. A more invasive tool for State parties to guide or to react to the interpretation of arbitral tribunals would be foreseeing a mechanism in the investment agreement to issue binding notes of interpretations. However, such notes of interpretation are to be used very cautiously, as they may threaten the consistency of case law or provoke interpretations bypassing the note.[59]

e) Omit fair and equitable treatment clause

The IPFSD's most radical policy option is to omit completely any reference to fair and equitable treatment in the text of an international investment agreement. The IPFSD proposes 'an omission of the FET clause would reduce States' exposure to investor claims, but foreign investors may perceive the country as not offering

---

[57] See, however, *MTD Equity Sdn Bhd and others v Republic of Chile*, ICSID Case No ARB/01/7, Award (25 May 2004) para 178.
[58] See with respect to full protection and security *Pantechniki SA Contractors and Engineers v The Republic of Albania*, ICSID Case No ARB/07/21, Award (28 July 2009) paras 76–77.
[59] For a complete review of the discussion following the FTC note of interpretation on Art 1105(a) NAFTA, see P Dumberry, *The Fair and Equitable Treatment Standard: A Guide to NAFTA Case Law on Article 1105* (Kluwer 2013).

a sound and reliable investment climate'.[60] Fair and equitable treatment clauses have a long tradition as one of the most frequently used provisions in international investment agreements.[61] Accordingly, there are only few exceptional cases in the current landscape of international investment agreements which do not include a fair and equitable treatment clause in the treaty text or, at least, a reference to it in the preamble. Examples are provided by BITs concluded by Germany in the 1960s, the 1977 Japan–Egypt BIT,[62] the 1993 Croatia–Albania BIT,[63] or the 1997 Croatia–Ukraine BIT.[64] More recently, a few free trade agreements entered into by Singapore omit fair and equitable treatment provisions, namely the 2001 Singapore–New Zealand FTA[65] or the 2003 Singapore-Australia FTA.[66]

As the IPFSD indicates, the policy implications of omitting fair and equitable treatment as a core element of international investment agreements are uncertain and difficult to assess. At the same time, the reduction of a host State's exposure to investor claims again depends heavily on the scope and interpretation of other investment protection provisions in the respective international investment agreement.

In particular, most-favoured-nation clauses enable arbitral tribunals to apply fair and equitable treatment of investment agreements concluded by the host State with other States, even if the investment agreement in relation to which the dispute arose does not grant fair and equitable treatment. This has happened with regard to Turkish BITs, which refer to fair and equitable treatment only in their preamble.[67] In this context, the Tribunal in the *Bayindir* case noted:

It is true that the reference to FET in the preamble together with the absence of a FET clause in the Treaty might suggest that Turkey and Pakistan intended not to include an FET obligation in the Treaty. The Tribunal is, however, not persuaded that this suggestion rules out the possibility of importing an FET obligation through the MFN clause expressly included in the Treaty. The fact that the States parties to the Treaty clearly contemplated the importance of the FET rather suggests the contrary. Indeed, even though it does not establish an operative obligation, the preamble is relevant for the interpretation of the MFN clause in its context and in the light of the Treaty's object and purpose pursuant to Article 31(1) of the VCLT.[68]

Even if fair and equitable treatment is not applied in toto through a most-favoured-nation clause, the sub-elements or principles behind this standard are usually similarly

---

[60] UNCTAD (n 1) 51.
[61] See R Dolzer and M Stevens, *Bilateral Investment Treaties* (Nijhoff 1995) 58.
[62] Agreement between Japan and the Arab Republic of Egypt concerning the Encouragement and Reciprocal Protection of Investment (signed 28 January 1977, entered into force 14 January 1978) ('1977 Japan–Egypt BIT').
[63] Agreement between the Government of the Republic of Albania and the Government of the Republic of Croatia for the Encouragement and Reciprocal Protection of Investments (signed 10 May 1993, entered into force 16 April 1994) ('1993 Croatia–Albania BIT').
[64] Agreement between the Government of the Republic of Croatia and the Government of Ukraine for the Promotion and Reciprocal Protection of Investments (signed 15 December 1997, entered into force 5 June 2001) ('1997 Croatia–Ukraine BIT').
[65] Agreement between New Zealand and Singapore on a Closer Economic Partnership (signed 14 November 2000, entered into force 1 January 2001) ('2001 Singapore–New Zealand FTA').
[66] Singapore–Australia Free Trade Agreement (SAFTA) (signed 17 February 2003, entered into force 28 July 2003) ('2003 Singapore–Australia FTA').
[67] See *Rumeli* (n 35) para 575.
[68] *Bayindir* (n 46) para 155.

relevant under other provisions. For instance, the often discussed element of protecting an investor's legitimate expectations may equally be considered by an arbitral tribunal when examining a violation of an expropriation clause.[69] Consequently, an omission of fair and equitable treatment may have the consequence that many of the issues embraced by this provision will be discussed under the heading of another cause of action. Many principles of fair and equitable treatment (or indeed fair and equitable treatment itself) are also deemed part of customary international law. Whether or not customary law itself forms a suitable cause of action for investors depends on the scope of the applicable arbitration clause, as such clauses are not always limited to breaches of the investment agreement.[70]

This shows that the individual principles of fair and equitable treatment are indeed fundamental to the entire system of international investment law, and that they cannot be eliminated simply by omitting the words 'fair and equitable treatment' from a treaty text. Accordingly, if a host State chooses to participate in this system, it also makes sense to commit to the fundamental principle of treating foreign investors fairly and equitably.

IV. Conclusion

The policy options provided and explained in the IPFSD offer a good overview of the different possibilities to formulate a fair and equitable treatment clause. This is to be welcomed as a valuable step to raise the awareness of the implications of certain approaches to the drafting of international investment agreements. Thereby, the IPFSD focuses on how to make a 'good' investment agreement that contributes to (or at least not interferes with) the general objective of sustainable development. However, the above analysis has also shown that the complex problems in applying fair and equitable treatment largely defy a simple solution.

The policy options mainly aim at reducing legal uncertainty by concretizing the general clause of fair and equitable treatment and, at the same time, limiting the discretion of arbitration. Another aim is to ensure the policy space of host States and to raise the liability threshold for the finding of a breach of fair and equitable treatment. However, the options mentioned in the IPFSD are able to achieve these goals only to a limited extent. This is because the amendment or change of treaty language usually leads to the replacement or overlaying of fair and equitable treatment with other general terms that are equally open to interpretation and subjective judgement. The vagueness of treaty language is a problem that affects all policy options in a similar way.

The same is true with regard to the threshold of liability. It has been demonstrated above that the use of certain policy options is not necessarily connected with a high or a low level of scrutiny by arbitral tribunals.[71] Accordingly, even under clauses referring to the customary international law minimum standard

---

[69] See, for example, *Azurix* (n 35) paras 316 and 372.
[70] See, for example, Art 10(1) 2008 Germany Model BIT (n 4).
[71] On the different approaches to the standard of review, see also C Henckels, 'Balancing Investment Protection and the Public Interest: The Role of the Standard of Review and the Importance of Deference in Investor-State Arbitration' (2013) 4 JIDS 197.

arbitral tribunals may apply a demanding test to scrutinize individual State measures. On the other side, it is perfectly possible to balance principles of sustainable development and sovereignty against principles of investment protections under an unqualified fair and equitable treatment clause without unduly limiting policy space. As the facts underlying investment disputes may relate to all kinds of different sectors or State measures, the question arises whether it is at all possible or reasonable to try to define the applicable threshold beforehand for all future disputes under a particular investment agreement, or whether the threshold is rather to be determined by considering the individual facts of the case at hand.

A proportionality test appears as an important tool to address exactly these issues on the threshold of liability in an individual case and to structure the balancing process of arbitral tribunals. The traditional three steps of a proportionality test ((1) suitability of a State measure to pursue a legitimate goal; (2) necessity; and (3) proportionality stricto sensu) are only partly reflected in the suggested interpretative guidelines for arbitral tribunals. However, proportionality is increasingly a topic and explicitly or implicitly addressed in many arbitral decisions[72] and academic publications.[73] Despite the considerable deficiencies in the application of the concept of proportionality by arbitral tribunals, it is submitted that this concept provides impulses to strengthen the legitimacy of arbitral decisions and their definition of the standard of review. The concept of proportionality, therefore, reveals a considerable potential to foster the sustainable development dimension of fair and equitable treatment.

Generally, the discussion of the IPFSD's policy options has shown that the drafting of investment protection clauses is only one element affecting the relationship between international investment agreements and sustainable development. Therefore, the different approaches to the drafting of international investment agreements are arguably also influenced by different perceptions of common and civil lawyers on whether treaty clauses should be rather specific or general. The task to strengthen the sustainable development dimension of foreign investments is, however, not only a task of treaty makers, as their influence is mainly limited to the text of international investment agreements, which are necessarily only a broad legal framework for foreign investment. It is rather a joint task of States, investors, and arbitrators to ensure that international investment law avoids blind spots that could impair the economic, social, or environmental sustainable development of all parties involved.

---

[72] See, for example, *SD Myers* (n 51) para 255; *Pope & Talbot Inc v The Government of Canada*, UNCITRAL, Final Merits Award (10 April 2001) paras 123, 125, 128, 155; *TECMED* (n 11), paras 122ff; *Saluka* (n 21) paras 304–07; *EDF (Services) Ltd v Romania*, ICSID Case No ARB/05/13, Award (2 October 2009) para 293.

[73] See comprehensively G Bücheler, *Proportionality in Investor-State Arbitration* (OUP 2015); see also AS Sweet, 'Investor-State Arbitration: Proportionality's New Frontier' (2010) 4 L & Ethics Hum Rts 47; B Kingsbury and SW Schill, 'Public Law Concepts to Balance Investors' Rights with State Regulatory Actions in the Public Interest—The Concept of Proportionality', in SW Schill (ed), *International Investment Law and Comparative Public Law* (OUP 2010) 75; Kläger (n 17) 236ff; for criticism on this approach, see M Sornarajah, 'Mutations of Neo-Liberalism in International Investment Law' (2011) 3 Trade L & Dev 203.

IV

Expropriation in the Light of the UNCTAD Investment Policy Framework for Sustainable Development

*Lukas Stifter and August Reinisch**

I. Introduction

For several years, there has been a discussion on sustainable development in investment law which can be understood as reflecting a broader debate on sustainable development in general.[1]

This debate is not new, but has gained renewed attention through the negotiation of the post-Millennium Development Goals agenda, which shall achieve sustainable development.[2] Even though the precise content of the concept established by the World Commission on Environment and Development in the 1980s[3] is disputed, one can still find a consensus on its core meaning. Development will be deemed sustainable if it can harmonize economic, environmental, and social concerns.[4]

In this vein the attention has shifted from mostly publicly pursued development aid, in the form of development cooperation, mainly through the OECD, to the

---

* The authors wish to thank Andrea Bockley for valuable input.

[1] Generally on sustainable development in investment law see UNCTAD, *Foreign Direct Investment and Development*, UNCTAD/ITE/IIT/10 (vol I, 1999); S Puvimanasinghe, *Foreign Investment, Human Rights and the Environment: A Perspective from South Asia on the Role of Public International Law for Development* (Martinus Nijhoff Publishers 2007); MC Segger, M Gehring, and A Newcombe (eds), *Sustainable Development in World Investment Law* (Wolters Kluwer 2011); L Cotula and K Tienhaara, 'Reconfiguring Investment Contracts to Promote Sustainable Development' in K Sauvant (ed), *Yearbook on International Investment Law and Policy 2011–2012* (2013); Special Issue: Towards Better BITs?—Making International Investment Law Responsive to Sustainable Development Objectives (2014) J World Inv & Tr; SW Schill, 'International Investment Law and International Development Law' in A Bjorklund (ed), *Yearbook on International Investment Law and Policy 2012-2013 (5–6)* (2014).

[2] UNGA Res 66/288 (27 July 2012) UN Doc A/RES/66/288.

[3] World Commission on Environment and Development, *Report of the World Commission on Environment and Development: Our Common Future* (1987).

[4] D Clifton, 'Representing a Sustainable World—A Typology Approach' (2010) 3 J Sustainable Dev 40, 46.

private sector.[5] It has been recognized that foreign direct investment (FDI) by far outnumbers the official development assistance (ODA) and is therefore crucial to achieving sustainable development.[6]

In reaction to these considerations the United Nations Conference on Trade and Development (UNCTAD) has adopted an investment policy framework for sustainable development in 2012 which proposes to create a new generation of investment treaties taking into account sustainable development concerns.[7]

Due to the double function of international investment law which aims, first and foremost, at the protection of investments on the one hand and at the promotion of economic growth on the other, there is an inherent tension between a State's regulatory interests in general and, arguably, with regard to sustainable development in particular, and the investors' interest in a relatively unchanged and thus predictable legal framework. Under the standards set by international investment agreements (IIAs), these conflicting interests are sometimes difficult to reconcile.

While most IIAs make references to the economic development of the host State, only few refer to social and environmental development.[8] In this regard,

---

[5] UN Human Rights Council 'Report of the Special Representative of the Secretary-General on the issue of human rights and transnational corporations and other business enterprises, John Ruggie' (21 March 2011) UN Doc A/HRC/17/31.

[6] The worldwide FDI inflow 2013 amounted to US$1.45 trillion, see UNCTAD 'World Investment Report 2014. Investing in the SDGs: An Action Plan' (2014), 2. In comparison, the Official Development Assistance ODA in the same year only reached US$138.4 billion, see: OECD 'Official Development Assistance 2013' available at: <www.oecd.org/statistics/datalab/oda2012.htm> accessed 5 November 2014.

[7] UNCTAD 'World Investment Policy Framework for Sustainable Development' (2012).

[8] See, for example, Treaty between the Government of the United States of America and the Government of the Republic of Albania concerning the Encouragement and Reciprocal Protection of Investment (signed 11 January 1995, entered into force 4 January 1998) ('USA–Albania BIT'), Treaty between the United States of America and the Argentine Republic concerning the Reciprocal Encouragement and Protection of Investment (signed 14 November 1991, entered into force 20 October 1994) ('USA–Argentina BIT'), Treaty between the United States of America and the Republic of Armenia concerning the Encouragement and Reciprocal Protection of Investment (signed 23 September 1992, entered into force 29 March 1996) ('USA–Armenia BIT'), Treaty between the Government of the United States of America and the Government of the Republic of Azerbaijan concerning the Encouragement and Reciprocal Protection of Investment (signed 1 August 1997, entered into force 2 August 2001) ('USA–Azerbaijan BIT'), Treaty between the Government of the United States of America and the Government of the Republic of Bolivia concerning the Encouragement and Reciprocal Protection of Investment (signed 17 April 1998, entered into force 6 June 2001) ('USA–Bolivia BIT'), Treaty between the United States of America and the Republic of Ecuador concerning the Encouragement and Reciprocal Protection of Investment (signed 27 August 1993, entered into force 11 May 1997) ('USA–Ecuador BIT'), Treaty between the Government of the United States of America and the Government of the Republic of El Salvador concerning the Encouragement and Reciprocal Protection of Investment (signed 10 March 1999) ('USA–El Salvador BIT'), Treaty between the Government of the United States of America and the Government of the Republic of Estonia concerning the Encouragement and Reciprocal Protection of Investment (signed 19 April 1994, entered into force 16 February 1997) ('USA–Estonia BIT'), Treaty between the United States of America and the Republic of Kazakhstan concerning the Encouragement and Reciprocal Protection of Investment (signed 19 May 1992, entered into force 12 January 1994) ('USA–Kazakhstan BIT'), Treaty between the Government of the United States of America and the Government of the Republic of Rwanda concerning the Encouragement and Reciprocal Protection of Investment (signed 19 February 2008, entered into force 1 January 2012) ('USA–Rwanda BIT').

Introduction

it is important to note that these references are usually made in the preamble of the respective BITs. Hence, they do not directly impose legal obligations but may potentially assist in interpreting the treaty.

Furthermore, even if IIAs imposed legally binding obligations promoting sustainable development upon investors, substantial enforcement issues would remain. Investor–State Dispute Settlement (ISDS) arguably constitutes an immediate procedural obstacle to the enforcement of such obligations. In the light of the arbitration pedigree of ISDS, the consent of the investor would (independently from the host State's consent to arbitrate a certain dispute most commonly expressed in the IIAs) be required for the initiation of any arbitral proceeding.[9]

Based on these findings, the core question with regard to sustainable development is whether existing substantive commitments undertaken by States within IIAs, that is, provisions on expropriation for the purpose of the present article, restrain their regulatory power.

According to the UNCTAD study, regulation is not only 'a State right, but also a necessity'[10] since '[w]ithout an adequate regulatory framework, a country will not be attractive for foreign investors, because such investors seek clarity, stability and predictability of investment conditions in the host country'.[11]

With regard to the core protection standards usually contained in investment agreements, the proposed UNCTAD framework emphasizes balanced rights and obligations of States and investors in the interest of development for all. Equally, particular emphasis is laid on the right to regulate understood as the sovereign right of each country to establish both entry conditions as well as operational conditions for foreign investments in the interest of the public good and to minimize potential negative effects.

In the analytical part of the UNCTAD Framework concerning policy options for IIAs, it is interesting to note that UNCTAD does not consider omitting an expropriation clause to be an available option.[12] Whether this will shift the attention of investment tribunals to indirect expropriation claims will depend upon the degree to which the currently most often invoked standard of fair and equitable treatment will be curtailed or even omitted in future investment agreements.[13]

---

[9] See, for example, M Toral and T Schultz, 'The State, a Perpetual Respondent in Investment Arbitration? Some Unorthodox Considerations' in M Waibel, A Kaushal, KH Chung, and C Balchin (eds), *The Backlash against Investment Arbitration: Perceptions and Reality* (Kluwer 2010), 577–602 at 579.
[10] UNCTAD (n 7) 13.   [11] ibid.
[12] UNCTAD (n 7) 52. By contrast, such omission is specifically mentioned as an option with regard to national treatment, fair and equitable treatment, for protection and security, as well as clauses concerning transparency protection from strife and others, see UNCTAD (n 7) 50–51.
[13] Omitting a fair and equitable treatment clause entirely or limiting its scope are mentioned as specific policy options in UNCTAD (n 7) 52. The alternative to severely limit its scope has been recently adopted in the negotiations between the EU and Canada. See Art X.9 Consolidated CETA Text, published on 26 September 2014, available at <http://trade.ec.europa.eu/doclib/docs/2014/september/tradoc_152806.pdf> accessed 5 November 2014.

II. The Role of Sustainable Development in the Context of Expropriation

The law on the protection of aliens (foreigners) and their property has arguably been a main pillar of both customary international law and treaty law governing the law of foreign investments in the past.[14] It has been generally accepted within both sources of international law that expropriations are lawful if they are carried out for a public purpose, in a non-discriminatory manner, in accordance with due process, and accompanied by the payment of compensation.[15]

In this context, two forms of expropriation can be distinguished: (i) direct expropriation which involves a formal seizure of the foreign investor's rights and a transfer of those rights to the State or a State-mandated third party[16] and (ii) indirect expropriation which commonly does not entail the formal seizure of the investor's rights but concerns State measures that interfere with the usage of investor rights 'with the effect of depriving the owner, in whole or in significant part, of the use or reasonably-to-be-expected economic benefit of property even if not necessarily to the obvious benefit of the host State'.[17]

As a starting point for the following analysis, it is, first of all, important to note that virtually all IIAs cover both forms of expropriation.[18] Arguably, since both forms of expropriation trigger an obligation to compensate, usually the full value of the investment taken, States may refrain from implementing new regulation where such regulation may amount to indirect expropriation. In this regard one also speaks of regulatory chill.[19]

---

[14] See, for example, A Lowenfeld, *International Economic Law* (2nd edn, OUP 2008) 559; R Dolzer and C Schreuer, *Principles of International Investment Law* (2nd edn, OUP 2012) 1ff.

[15] See UNCTAD, *Taking of Property* (2000) 12 ('In customary international law, there is authority for a number of limitations or conditions that relate to: the requirement of a public purpose for the taking; the requirement that there should be no discrimination; the requirement that the taking should be accompanied by payment of compensation; and, the requirement of due process'); UNCTAD, *International Investment Agreements: Key Issues* (2004) 235 ('Under customary international law and typical international investment agreements, three principal requirements need to be satisfied before a taking can be considered to be lawful: it should be for a public purpose; it should not be discriminatory; and compensation should be paid').

[16] See, for example, A Newcombe, 'The Boundaries of Regulatory Expropriation in International Law' (2005) 20 ICSID Rev 1, 7.

[17] *Metalclad Corporation v The United Mexican States*, ICSID Case No ARB(AF)/97/1, Award (30 August 2000) para 103.

[18] See Newcombe (n 16) 16; A Reinisch, 'Expropriation' in P Muchlinski, F Ortino, and C Schreuer (eds), *The Oxford Handbook of International Investment Law* (OUP 2008) 407; LY Fortier and SL Drymer, 'Indirect Expropriation in the Law of International Investment: I Know it When I See it, or Caveat Investor' (2004) 19 ICSID Rev—FILJ 293; U Kriebaum, 'Regulatory Takings: Balancing the Interests of the Investor and the State' (2007) 8 J World Inv and Tr 717; K Yannaca-Small, 'Indirect Expropriation and the Right to Regulate: How to Draw the Line?' in K Yannaca-Small (ed), *Arbitration under International Investment Agreements: A Guide to Key Issues* (OUP 2010) 445.

[19] See M Paparinskis, 'Regulatory Expropriation and Sustainable Development' in Segger and others (n 1) 295; L Dhooge, 'Foreign Investors versus Environmentalists: Whose Green Counts in the North American Free Trade Agreement?' (2001) 10 Minn J Global Trade 209; BW Jenkins 'The Next

While sustainable development is usually not expressly covered by IIAs,[20] public interest does play a crucial role in the context of expropriation. Since the former may arguably fall under the ambit of the latter the considerations with regard to public interest can apply to the question if and to what extent sustainable development should be a decisive factor in determining whether an expropriation had occurred.

The following analysis elaborates on the role of public interest and, therefore, the notion of sustainable development within the two distinct forms of expropriation. However, the focus will be on indirect expropriation.

Direct expropriations are rarely encountered in recent practice, notably because they clearly trigger a compensation obligation and, if done without compensation, will negatively impact the investment climate of a State due to its publicity.[21] As mentioned above, the fact that an expropriatory measure serves public interest, for example sustainable development, merely constitutes one of four legality requirements.[22] Thus, the possible role of sustainable development considerations in the context of direct expropriations is fairly unambiguous and limited: it does not relieve a State from its obligation to compensate as this constitutes a precondition for the legality of the measure in questions in its own right. However, the fact that the measure at stake contributes to sustainable development may influence the amount of compensation due to be paid.[23]

a) Pre-modern (indirect) expropriation clauses

While it is clearly recognized that most IIAs regularly treat direct (or formal) expropriation in the same way as indirect expropriation,[24] most contemporary investment treaties do not provide guidance for the determination of the latter. Such expropriation clauses are referred to as 'pre-modern' for the purpose of this contribution.

Direct expropriation can be easily identified by the requirement of the actual transfer of title of a property.[25] The situation with regard to indirect expropriation is more complex.

Generation of Chilling Uncertainty: Indirect Expropriation Under CAFTA and its Potential Impact on Environmental Protection' (2007) 12 (2) Ocean and Coastal LJ 269.

[20] See n 8.   [21] See Reinisch, 'Expropriation' (n 18) 407ff.
[22] See also A Reinisch, 'Legality of Expropriations' in A Reinisch (ed), *Standards of Investment Protection* (OUP 2008) 171–204.
[23] An unlawful expropriation not serving public interests triggers the duty to pay damages. Thus, the *Chorzów*-principle would apply: an expropriating but non-compensating State would have to eliminate all the consequences of the illegal act and re-establish the situation which would have existed if that act had not been committed. See *Case Concerning the Factory at Chorzów (Germany v Poland)* (Judgment) PCIJ Rep Series A No 17. See also Kriebaum (n 18) 721.
[24] U Kriebaum, 'Expropriation' in M Bungenberg, J Gabriel, S Hobe, and A Reinisch (eds), *International Investment Law* (Nomos 2015) 959–1027.
[25] See also Annex B 3. US Model BIT 2012 ('...direct expropriation, where an investment is nationalized or otherwise directly expropriated through formal transfer of title or outright seizure').

Indirect expropriations can occur in various forms and treaties often refer to it as 'measures tantamount or equivalent to expropriation'.[26] In the light of sustainable development, the most important forms are regulatory takings. These may qualify as indirect expropriations when a State implements a regulation leading to a (quasi-total) deprivation of property.

Against this background, the practical application of expropriation clauses has caused controversy because a broad reading of indirect expropriation can arguably be used 'to challenge general regulation with an alleged negative effect on the value of an investment. This raises the question of the proper borderline between expropriation and legitimate public policy making (for example, environmental, social or health regulations)'.[27]

aa) The sole effects doctrine

The sole effects doctrine is based on the assumption that there is no difference between the adverse effects on an investment caused by general regulation or by (formal) State conduct directed at the investment.[28] The only decisive factor is the degree of interference of the State measure with the investor's rights. Regardless of the contemplated purpose, there will be an indirect expropriation if a certain threshold is met by the measure in question and the investor will be eligible for full compensation or for damages if the expropriation is unlawful.

This view seems to have been confirmed by the NAFTA Chapter 11 Tribunal in *Metalclad v Mexico* which decided not to consider the State's intent behind a decree declaring the land where the investor held a hazardous landfill facility a conservation area for the sake of protecting rare plants:

> The Tribunal need not decide or consider the motivation or intent of the adoption of the Ecological Decree. Indeed, a finding of expropriation on the basis of the Ecological Decree is not essential to the Tribunal's finding of a violation of NAFTA Article 1110. However, the Tribunal considers that the implementation of the Ecological Decree would, in and of itself, constitute an act tantamount to expropriation.[29]

It is important to note that this finding does not concern the basic requirements for the lawfulness of the expropriation in question which do take into account the intention of a State measure *via* the notion of public interest. The question at stake

---

[26] See, for example, Art 1110(1) North American Free Trade Agreement between the USA, Canada, and Mexico (adopted 17 December 1992, entered into force 1 January 1993) 32 ILM 289 (NAFTA) ('No Party may directly or indirectly nationalize or expropriate an investment of an investor…') or Art 13(1) of the Energy Charter Treaty (signed 17 December 1994, entered into force 16 April 1998) 2080 UNTS 100 ('Investments of Investors of a Contracting Party in the Area of any other Contracting Party shall not be nationalized, expropriated or subjected to a measure or measures having effect equivalent to nationalization or expropriation (hereinafter referred to as "Expropriation") except where such Expropriation is: (a) for a purpose which is in the public interest; (b) not discriminatory; (c) carried out under due process of law; and (d) accompanied by the payment of prompt, adequate and effective compensation').

[27] UNCTAD (n 7) 52.   [28] See Paparinskis (n 19) 305.

[29] *Metalclad Corporation v The United Mexican States* (n 17) para 111.

was whether the existence of a public interest limits the ambit of the underlying treaty provision in a way that regulatory measures serving public interest would be excluded from treaty protection and thus would not trigger the duty to pay compensation. As it was demonstrated, the Tribunal solely focused on the effects, the severity of the interference with the investor's rights.[30]

In this regard, investment Tribunals, even when applying 'pre-modern' expropriation clauses, often set a very high threshold in order to find that State measures amount to expropriation. Most important in this context, it appears that investment tribunals continue to apply a very strict effects doctrine requiring that host State measures must amount to a total or quasi-total deprivation of the economic benefits of an investment in order to constitute indirect expropriation. What is required has traditionally been labelled to be a 'substantial loss of control or value'[31] or a 'severe economic impact'.[32] In more recent case law this seems to have become a more demanding test for claimants.

For instance, in 2012, the tribunal in *Electrabel v Hungary*,[33] applying the Energy Charter Treaty (ECT),[34] stressed that an indirect expropriation can only be contemplated if the investor was substantially deprived of its investment. Relying on previous investment cases as well as scholarly writings, the Tribunal was of the opinion

...that the accumulated mass of international legal materials, comprising both arbitral decisions and doctrinal writings, describe for both direct and indirect expropriation, consistently albeit in different terms, the requirement under international law for the investor to establish the substantial, radical, severe, devastating or fundamental deprivation of its rights or the virtual annihilation, effective neutralisation or factual destruction of its investment, its value or enjoyment.[35]

In the specific case, the Tribunal found that the termination of specific long-term power purchase agreements by Hungary did not constitute such a radical deprivation of the investor's rights. In fact, the *Electrabel* Tribunal does not only speak of 'substantial loss' or 'severe impact'; rather, it speaks of 'substantial, radical, severe, devastating or fundamental deprivation' and 'virtual annihilation, effective

---

[30] For more details on the 'sole effects doctrine' see Kriebaum (n 18) 725–26; Paparinskis (n 19) 305ff; R Dolzer, 'Indirect Expropriations: New Developments?' (2003) 11 NYU Env LJ, 79–80.
[31] UNCTAD (n 15) 41.
[32] C Yannaca-Small, '"Indirect Expropriation" and the "Right to Regulate" in International Investment Law' in OECD (ed), *International Investment Law. A Changing Landscape* (OECD Paris 2005) 43, 55.
[33] *Electrabel SA v Republic of Hungary*, ICSID Case No ARB/07/19, Decision on Jurisdiction, Applicable Law and Liability (30 November 2012).
[34] Article 13(1) ECT ('Investments of Investors of a Contracting Party in the Area of any other Contracting Party shall not be nationalized, expropriated or subjected to a measure or measures having effect equivalent to nationalization or expropriation (hereinafter referred to as "Expropriation") except where such Expropriation is: (a) for a purpose which is in the public interest; (b) not discriminatory; (c) carried out under due process of law; and (d) accompanied by the payment of prompt, adequate and effective compensation').
[35] *Electrabel* (n 33) para 6.62.

neutralisation or factual destruction' of an investment. These demands make successful invocations of an indirect expropriation already very unlikely.

bb) The police powers doctrine

Under the police powers doctrine the existence of an underlying public interest excludes a regulatory measure from constituting an indirect expropriation.[36]

Following this assumption, investment tribunals have also accepted that certain non-discriminatory 'measures of a Party that are designed and applied to protect legitimate public welfare objectives, such as health, safety and the environment, do not constitute indirect expropriations'.[37] For instance, the NAFTA Tribunal in *Feldman v Mexico*[38] stated that

> ...governments must be free to act in the broader public interest through protection of the environment, new or modified tax regimes, the granting or withdrawal of government subsidies, reductions or increases in tariff levels, imposition of zoning restrictions and the like. Reasonable governmental regulation of this type cannot be achieved if any business that is adversely affected may seek compensation, and it is safe to say that customary international law recognizes this.[39]

It is particularly relevant that the *Feldman* Tribunal came to this conclusion in a situation where the applicable treaty, NAFTA Chapter 11, did not contain express language carving out regulatory measures from the reach of indirect expropriation.

In a similar vein, *Methanex*[40] and *Saluka*[41] can also be viewed as a transposition of the so-called police powers doctrine of the US Supreme Court[42] to international investment law, aiming at specifying what constitutes an expropriation and what does not.[43]

According to the *Methanex* Tribunal,

> ...as a matter of general international law, a non-discriminatory regulation for a public purpose, which is enacted in accordance with due process and, which affects, inter alios, a foreign investor or investment is not deemed expropriatory and compensable unless specific commitments had been given by the regulating government to the then putative

---

[36] See Restatement (Third) of the Foreign Relations Law of the United States, § 712 Comment g, at 201 ('A state is not responsible for loss of property or for other economic disadvantage resulting from bona fide general taxation, regulation, forfeiture for crime, or other action of the kind that is commonly accepted as within the police power of states...'). See also Kriebaum (n 18); Newcombe (n 16) 18ff.
[37] Annex X.11.3 CETA.
[38] *Marvin Feldmann v Mexico*, ICSID Case No ARB(AF)/99/1, Award (16 December 2002).
[39] ibid para 103.
[40] *Methanex Corporation v United States of America*, NAFTA Arbitral Tribunal, Final Award on Jurisdiction and Merits (3 August 2005).
[41] *Saluka Investments BV v The Czech Republic*, UNCITRAL, Partial Award (17 March 2006).
[42] See *Penn Central Transportation Co v New York City*, 438 US 104 (1978).
[43] See C Lévesque and A Newcombe, 'Canada' in C Brown (ed), *Commentaries on Selected Model Investment Treaties* (2013) 53, 95.

foreign investor contemplating investment that the government would refrain from such regulation.[44]

Similarly, the *Saluka* tribunal reasoned that as a matter of international law

States are not liable to pay compensation to a foreign investor when, in the normal exercise of their regulatory powers, they adopt in a non-discriminatory manner *bona fide* regulations that are aimed at the general welfare.[45]

At the time these cases were decided they caused some irritation because they seemed to incorporate the traditional legality requirements as a test to assess whether an expropriation had taken place at all.[46] In fact, some tribunals continued to stress the traditional 'intensity of interference' test.[47]

This *Methanex/Saluka* approach clearly contrasts with the sole effect doctrine espoused by many other tribunals which would only look at the intensity of the interference in order to ascertain whether an indirect expropriation has taken place.[48] Obviously, the effect of such an approach is likely to be considerably narrowing the scope of indirect expropriation and thus investment protection against expropriation.

The *Methanex/Saluka* doctrine has been refined by some tribunals. In *El Paso v Argentina*[49] an ICSID Tribunal suggested the following:

1. Some general regulations can amount to indirect expropriation
   a. As a matter of principle, general regulations do not amount to indirect expropriation.
   b. By exception, unreasonable general regulations can amount to indirect expropriation.
2. A necessary condition for expropriation is the neutralisation of the use of the investment
   a. This means that at least one of the essential components of the property rights must have disappeared.
   b. This means also, *a contrario*, that a mere loss in value of the investment, even an important one, is not an indirect expropriation.[50]

---

[44] *Methanex* (n 40) IV D para 7. [45] *Saluka Investments* (n 41) para 255.
[46] See, for example, Kriebaum (n 18), 726.
[47] See *Azurix v Argentine Republic*, ICSID Case No ARB/01/12, Award (14 July 2006); *Telenor Mobile Communications AS v Republic of Hungary*, ICSID Case No ARB/04/15, Award (13 September 2006) paras 64–65. See also A Reinisch, 'Back to Basics: From the Notion of "Investment" to the Purpose of Annulment—ICSID Arbitration in 2007' (2008) 8 The Global Community. Yearbook of International Law & Jurisprudence 1591, 1599.
[48] cf R Dolzer (n 30) 64ff; Y Fortier and St Drymer (n 18) 293; C Yannaca-Small (n 32).
[49] *El Paso Energy International Company v Argentine Republic*, ICSID Case No ARB/03/15, Award (27 October 2011).
[50] *El Paso* (n 49) para 233.

Again, it is important to take into consideration that this interpretation was given on the basis of the Spain–Argentina BIT[51] which only contained a 'pre-modern' expropriation clause without an elaborate understanding on indirect expropriation.

The core task for treaty makers as well as treaty enforcers is a balancing exercise to determine the delimitation of lawful and non-compensable regulation and indirect regulatory expropriation which triggers a duty to compensate. Such a balancing test was already alluded to by the ICSID Tribunal in *LG&E v Argentina*[52] which held that

[i]n order to establish whether State measures constitute expropriation…, the Tribunal must balance two competing interests: the degree of the measure's interference with the right of ownership and the power of the State to adopt its policies.[53]

More specifically it added:

With respect to the power of the State to adopt its policies, it can generally be said that the State has the right to adopt measures having a social or general welfare purpose. In such a case, the measure must be accepted without any imposition of liability, except in cases where the State's action is obviously disproportionate to the need being addressed. The proportionality to be used when making use of this right was recognized in *Tecmed*, which observed that 'whether such actions or measures are proportional to the public interest presumably protected thereby and the protection legally granted to investments, taking into account that the significance of such impact, has a key role upon deciding the proportionality'.[54]

b) Modern expropriation clauses

It is obvious that any reduction in the number of instances that may be qualified as indirect expropriation will give a broader scope to host States to adopt regulations promoting public policy goals, including sustainable development, at the same time such a broadening of the regulatory scope may deprive investors of effective protection against interference with their investments.

Hence, the main issue is to what extent expropriation clauses may require recalibrating in order to ensure that they are not interpreted in a fashion possibly qualifying general regulatory measures in the public interest as compensable indirect expropriations.

As a result of such considerations, the UNCTAD Framework proposes under 'policy options for international investment agreements' to limit investment

---

[51] See Art IV(1) of the USA–Spain BIT ('1. Investments shall not be expropriated or nationalized either directly or indirectly through measures tantamount to expropriation or nationalization ('expropriation') except for a public purpose; in a non-discriminatory manner; upon payment of prompt, adequate and effective compensation; and in accordance with due process of law and the general principles of treatment provided for in Article II').
[52] *LG&E Energy Corp, LG&E Capital Corp, LG&E International Inc v The Argentine Republic*, ICSID Case No ARB/02/1, Decision on Liability (3 October 2006).
[53] ibid para 189.   [54] ibid para 195.

Role of Sustainable Development in the Context of Expropriation   91

protection in case of indirect expropriation (regulatory taking) by various techniques. It specifically suggests the following:

- establishing criteria that need to be met for indirect expropriation to be found
- defining in general terms what measures do not constitute indirect expropriation (non-discriminatory good faith regulations relating to public health and safety, protection of the environment, etc.)
- clarifying that certain specific measures do not constitute an indirect expropriation (for example, compulsory licensing in compliance with WTO rules).[55]

It is such considerations that have already been taken into account in the past by the Model BITs adopted by Canada and the US in 2004 in particular via the technique of including in the annexes to their substantive investment protection chapters so-called understandings in which the parties have confirmed their understanding of what amounts to an indirect expropriation.

The Canada Model FIPA 2004[56] contains a classic expropriation clause treating both direct and indirect expropriation in the same way:

1. Neither Party shall nationalize or expropriate a covered investment either directly, or indirectly through measures having an effect equivalent to nationalization or expropriation (hereinafter referred to as 'expropriation'), except...[57]

Its Annex B.13(1) formulates the 'shared understanding' of the parties as follows:

a) Indirect expropriation results from a measure or series of measures of a Party that have an effect equivalent to direct expropriation without formal transfer of title or outright seizure;
b) The determination of whether a measure or series of measures of a Party constitute an indirect expropriation requires a case-by-case, fact-based inquiry that considers, among other factors:
   i) the economic impact of the measure or series of measures, although the sole fact that a measure or series of measures of a Party has an adverse effect on the economic value of an investment does not establish that an indirect expropriation has occurred;
   ii) the extent to which the measure or series of measures interfere with distinct, reasonable investment-backed expectations; and
   iii) the character of the measure or series of measures;
c) Except in rare circumstances, such as when a measure or series of measures are so severe in the light of their purpose that they cannot be reasonably viewed as having been adopted and applied in good faith, non-discriminatory measures of a Party that are designed and applied to protect legitimate public welfare objectives, such as health, safety and the environment, do not constitute indirect expropriation.[58]

---

[55] UNCTAD (n 7) 52.
[56] Agreement between Canada and... for the Promotion and Protection of Investments—Foreign Investment and Protection Agreements (FIPA), available at: <http://investmentpolicyhub.unctad.org/Download/TreatyFile/2820> accessed 5 November 2014.
[57] Article 13 Model FIPA 2004, ibid.   [58] Annex B 13(1) Model FIPA 2004, ibid.

The 2004 US Model BIT contains, also in its most recent 2012 version,[59] an expropriation clause that equally assimilates the legal consequences of direct and indirect expropriation:

1. Neither Party may expropriate or nationalize a covered investment either directly or indirectly through measures equivalent to expropriation or nationalization ('expropriation'), except:...[60]

Similar to the Canadian Model FIPA, the US Model BIT also contains an annex specifying the meaning of indirect expropriation. It provides:

4. The second situation addressed by Article 6 [Expropriation and Compensation] (1) is indirect expropriation, where an action or series of actions by a Party has an effect equivalent to direct expropriation without formal transfer of title or outright seizure.
   (a) The determination of whether an action or series of actions by a Party, in a specific fact situation, constitutes an indirect expropriation, requires a case-by case, fact-based inquiry that considers, among other factors:
      (i) the economic impact of the government action, although the fact that an action or series of actions by a Party has an adverse effect on the economic value of an investment, standing alone, does not establish that an indirect expropriation has occurred;
      (ii) the extent to which the government action interferes with distinct, reasonable investment-backed expectations; and
      (iii) the character of the government action.
   (b) Except in rare circumstances, non-discriminatory regulatory actions by a Party that are designed and applied to protect legitimate public welfare objectives, such as public health, safety, and the environment, do not constitute indirect expropriations.[61]

Both the Canadian as well as the US negotiation templates have been included in several recent IIAs.[62] Neither the US nor the Canadian models strictly follow the sole effects doctrine or the police powers doctrine. The factors to be used under such clauses combine elements stemming from both approaches.

---

[59] 2012, Treaty between the Government of the United States of America and the Government of (Country) Concerning the Encouragement and Reciprocal Protection of Investment, available at: <http://investmentpolicyhub.unctad.org/Download/TreatyFile/2870> accessed 5 November 2014. The US has released a new Model BIT in 2012, the provision on expropriation and the respective text in the Annex however remain identical.

[60] Article 6 US Model BIT 2012.   [61] Annex B US Model BIT 2012.

[62] See, for example, para 4(b) of Annex 10-C of the US–Dominican Republic-Central America Free Trade Agreement (signed 5 August 2004, entered into force 1 March 2007) (CAFTA); Annex 8-B of the July 2014 Final Text of the Canada–Korea Free Trade Agreement (signed 11 March 2014, entered into force 1 January 2015); Art 10(5) of the Agreement between the Government of Canada and the Government of the United Republic of Tanzania for the Promotion and Reciprocal Protection of Investments (signed 17 May 2013, entered into force 9 December 2013) ('Canada–Tanzania BIT'); Annex B of the USA–Rwanda BIT and Annex B of the Treaty between the United States of America and the Oriental Republic of Uruguay concerning the Encouragement and Reciprocal Protection of Investment (signed 4 November 2005, entered into force 1 November 2006) ('USA–Uruguay BIT').

In the form as they appear in the last sentence of the common understanding in the US and Canada model treaties, however, it is made clear that this refers to an extreme situation and that the effects or impact test remains valued as a general consideration with regard to the determination of indirect expropriation. It just clarifies that bona fide or good faith measures adopted in a non-discriminatory fashion in order to protect legitimate public welfare objectives are generally considered to be non-expropriatory and thus non-compensable.

In arbitral practice, awards based on the application of 'modern expropriation clauses' are just beginning to be delivered. One example can be found in *Railroad Development Corporation (RDC) v Republic of Guatemala*[63] based on the US–Dominican Republic–Central America Free Trade Agreement (CAFTA). The case concerned a concession agreement including a contract for the use of the infrastructure and other rail assets to provide railway services in Guatemala. The government of Guatemala issued a presidential decree which declared the contract to be against the State's interests. Based on this decree, the contract was revoked by the Attorney General. The investor claimed that this measure constituted an indirect expropriation pursuant to Article 10.7 CAFTA.[64]

In its analysis the Tribunal did not conclusively answer the question whether the measure at stake served public interest, mainly based on the ambiguity of the facts put forth by the disputing party.[65] It thus put the emphasis on the investor's investment backed expectations[66] and the decree's economic impact on the investment. It concluded that the threshold for an indirect expropriation was not met. Based on the assertion that some contracts related to the investment were still in effect and that the claimant still possessed railway equipment and received rents based on real-estate rights, the Tribunal stated that the claimant had not been 'deprived substantially of the use and benefits of the investment'.[67] Hence, there was no indirect expropriation.

Thus, it is hard to say whether the inclusion of a 'modern expropriation clause' actually provides for additional regulatory flexibility. In fact, the *RDC v Guatemala* Tribunal did not use other factors for the determination of an indirect expropriation different from those deployed by other tribunals.[68]

---

[63] *Railroad Development Corporation v Republic of Guatemala*, ICSID Case No ARB/07/23, Award (29 June 2012).

[64] Article 10.7 (1) of CAFTA ('No Party may expropriate or nationalize a covered investment either directly or indirectly through measures equivalent to expropriation or nationalization ("expropriation"), except:

(a) for a public purpose; (b) in a non-discriminatory manner; (c) on payment of prompt, adequate, and effective compensation in accordance with paragraphs 2 through 4; and (d) in accordance with due process of law and Article 10.5.').

Corresponding with the content of Annex B of the US Model BIT, Annex 10-C of CAFTA provides for a number of factors to be taken into account for the determination of an indirect expropriation.

[65] See *Railroad Development Corporation* (n 63) paras 93ff.
[66] See *Railroad Development Corporation* (n 63) paras 112ff.
[67] See *Railroad Development Corporation* (n 63) paras 151–52.
[68] See *Railroad Development Corporation* (n 63) para 81 ('[The tribunal will] analyze the nature of the Lesivo Declaration, its public purpose, whether the Government interfered with reasonable investment backed expectations and their economic impact on Claimant's investment...').

For instance, already the Tribunal in *Tecmed SA v Mexico* established that the economic effect of a measure is not the only factor to be taken into account.[69] Referring to the case law of the European Court of Human Rights, the Tribunal considered whether the measure in question is 'proportional to the public interest presumably protected thereby and to the protection legally granted to investments, taking into account that the significance of such impact has a key role upon deciding the proportionality'.[70] Furthermore, the investor's legitimate expectations were taken into account.[71]

However, it is important to note that the Tribunal in *RDC v Guatemala* considered these factors pursuant to the underlying expropriation clause of CAFTA and not as a matter of discretion.[72]

Consequently, expropriation clauses containing a defined scope of the notion of indirect expropriation scale down the arbitrators' discretion with regard to the method for identifying the existence of an indirect expropriation. This is an important feature. The application of either the sole effects doctrine or the police powers doctrine in their extreme forms may lead to unwelcome results for the investor or for the State. Thus, the more balanced approach enshrined in the shared understandings on the concept of indirect expropriation contained in some IIA annexes arguably prepares the ground for more legal certainty and predictability and for more balanced awards.

More recently, in the first investment agreement negotiated by the European Union so far, the Comprehensive Economic and Trade Agreement with Canada (CETA),[73] the EU and Canada have agreed on a similar provision with regard to the concept of expropriation in order to protect the regulatory freedom of host countries. They have included a normal expropriation clause which is similar to the ones Member States have included in their BITs in the past.

Article X.11 on Expropriation provides:

1. Neither Party may nationalize or expropriate a covered investment either directly, or indirectly through measures having an effect equivalent to nationalization or expropriation (hereinafter referred to as 'expropriation'), except: ...[74]

In addition, the CETA includes an apparent novelty for European States, that is, an annex on expropriation in which the parties confirm their shared understanding which reflects the earlier Canadian Model FIPA language.

Annex X.11: 'Expropriation' of the CETA provides:

2. The determination of whether a measure or series of measures of a Party, in a specific fact situation, constitutes an indirect expropriation requires a case-by-case, fact-based inquiry that considers, among other factors:

---

[69] See *Tecnicas Medioambientales Tecmed SA v The United Mexican States*, ICSID Case No ARB (AF)/00/2, Award (29 May 2003), para 118.
[70] ibid para 122. [71] ibid para 149. [72] See n 64.
[73] Consolidated CETA Text, published on 26 September 2014, available at: <http://trade.ec.europa.eu/doclib/docs/2014/september/tradoc_152806.pdf> accessed on 5 November 2014.
[74] Article X.11 Consolidated CETA Text, ibid.

the economic impact of the measure or series of measures, although the sole fact that a measure or series of measures of a Party has an adverse effect on the economic value of an investment does not establish that an indirect expropriation has occurred;
the duration of the measure or series of measures by a Party;
the extent to which the measure or series of measures interferes with distinct, reasonable investment-backed expectations; and
the character of the measure or series of measures, notably their object, context and intent.

3. For greater certainty, except in the rare circumstance where the impact of the measure or series of measures is so severe in light of its purpose that it appears manifestly excessive, nondiscriminatory measures of a Party that are designed and applied to protect legitimate public welfare objectives, such as health, safety and the environment, do not constitute indirect expropriations.[75]

This language clearly intends to ensure regulatory freedom by limiting the scope of what may be considered to constitute indirect expropriation; in particular it contains a rule of thumb which corresponds to the earlier ones found in the Canada and US Model BITs, according to which good faith regulation designed to protect legitimate public welfare objectives normally does not constitute indirect expropriation. The merely illustrative mentioning of 'health, safety, and the environment' indicates that other public welfare objectives such as sustainable development would also be covered. It thus appears that modern expropriation clauses are unlikely to pose a major obstacle to host States adopting measures aimed at sustainable development.

Also the fact that 'distinct, reasonable investment-backed expectations' of investors are specifically mentioned as one of the considerations to be taken into account by investment tribunals when assessing whether a host State's measures amount to indirect expropriation does not seem to unduly put them into a straitjacket of investor expectations. The careful wording clearly refers to 'distinct, reasonable' expectations only and arbitral jurisprudence on the related concept of 'legitimate expectations' has been explicit that

... legitimate expectations cannot be solely the subjective expectations of the investor, but have to correspond to the objective expectations than can be deduced from the circumstances and with due regard to the rights of the State. In other words, a balance should be established between the legitimate expectation of the foreign investor to make a fair return on its investment and the right of the host State to regulate its economy in the public interest.[76]

This approach developed in the context of fair and equitable treatment has stressed that only reasonable expectations grounded on host State assurances may reduce the latter's regulatory freedom and that normally investors cannot rely on the expectation that a host State's regulatory framework will not change.[77] In a similar

---

[75] Annex X.11 Consolidated CETA Text, ibid.   [76] *El Paso* (n 49) para 358.
[77] See, for example, *Sempra Energy International v The Argentine Republic*, ICSID Case No ARB/02/16, Award (28 September 2007) para 298 ('... the foreign investment must be treated in a manner such that it "will not affect the basic expectations that were taken into account by foreign

way, investor expectations in the context of expropriation will only be reasonable if specifically induced by a host State.

III. Conclusion

Expropriation is clearly a side-show in the broader quest for sustainable development. But because expropriation is so deeply entrenched in IIAs as one of the core standards of investment protection, it may have received disproportionate attention.

It is obvious that the fine-tuning of IIA provisions on expropriation, in particular, their delimitation of what may constitute indirect expropriation has the potential to enlarge the policy space of host States, by clarifying that ordinary regulatory measures in the public interest should not be considered as expropriatory measures.

This is certainly a core task that can be fulfilled by IIA language. As acknowledged by UNCTAD, it is, however, questionable whether such 'defensive' drafting will actually contribute to sustainable development. Obviously, it will increase regulatory space, but such greater freedom of a host State can be used in different forms and there is no guarantee that general regulatory measures will have a positive impact on (sustainable) development. It will remain the regulatory task falling to the host State to ensure that its measures will serve the goal of sustainable development.

---

investor to make the investment." This requirement becomes particularly meaningful when the investment has been attracted and induced by means of assurances and representations, as has been established in the jurisprudence that the Claimant has invoked'); *Parkerings-Compagniet AS v Republic of Lithuania*, ICSID Case No ARB/05/8, Award (11 September 2007) para 331 ('...expectation is legitimate if the investor received an explicit promise or guaranty from the host-State, or if implicitly, the host-State made assurances or representation that the investor took into account in making the investment. Finally, in the situation where the host-State made no assurance or representation, the circumstances surrounding the conclusion of the agreement are decisive to determine if the expectation of the investor was legitimate'); *EDF (Services) Limited v Romania*, ICSID Case No ARB/05/13, Award and Dissenting Opinion (8 October 2009) para 217 ('The idea that legitimate expectations, and therefore FET, imply the stability of the legal and business framework, may not be correct if stated in an overly-broad and unqualified formulation. The FET might then mean the virtual freezing of the legal regulation of economic activities, in contrast with the State's normal regulatory power and the evolutionary character of economic life. Except where specific promises or representations are made by the State to the investor, the latter may not rely on a bilateral investment treaty as a kind of insurance policy against the risk of any changes in the host State's legal and economic framework. Such expectation would be neither legitimate nor reasonable').

V

Investment Arbitration: Learning from Experience

Jonathan Ketcheson

I. Introduction

Investor–State dispute settlement (ISDS) provisions in investment treaties provide a mechanism for investors to commence arbitration against a host State without any need for further consent on the part of the host State. Since the early 1990s there has been rapid growth in the use of ISDS to resolve disputes between investors and States.[1] Accompanying this increased use of ISDS has been a growing awareness of the potentially significant implications of investment treaties for States. In particular, a number of high profile cases[2] have drawn attention to the investment treaty regime and contributed to what might be described as a 'backlash' against investment treaties.

Concerns have arisen that investment treaties negatively impact on sustainable development because such treaties constrain a State's ability to adopt measures in the public interest. An investor can challenge measures, including those adopted in the public interest, before an investment treaty tribunal.[3] Furthermore, even the threat of such a claim may dissuade a State from adopting a measure in the public interest. More specific criticisms have been directed at ISDS in particular (as opposed to substantive investment protection standards).[4] Many of the criticisms

---

[1] The United Nations Conference on Trade and Development (UNCTAD) regularly publishes information on the number of known ISDS cases. See, for example, UNCTAD, 'Recent Developments in Investor-State Dispute Settlement' (2014) 1 IIA Issues Note available at: <http://unctad.org/en/PublicationsLibrary/webdiaepcb2014d3_en.pdf> accessed 24 April 2015.

[2] High-profile cases include a challenge by a tobacco company to the introduction of plain packaging laws by Australia (*Philip Morris Asia Limited v The Commonwealth of Australia*, UNCITRAL, PCA Case no 2012-12) and a claim brought by a Swedish company against Germany following a decision to phase out nuclear power generation (*Vattenfall AB and others v Federal Republic of Germany*, ICSID Case No ARB/12/12).

[3] It should not be assumed that all measures engage the public interest to the same degree. Indeed, a State measure might have been adopted by governmental officials for private reasons. Nevertheless, there remains a minimum degree of public interest in all investor–State disputes to the extent that the State, and therefore taxpayers, may be held liable and required to pay compensation to an investor.

[4] See, for example, G Van Harten, *Investment Treaty Arbitration and Public Law* (OUP 2007); P Eberhardt and C Olivet, 'Profiting from Injustice' (2012) available at: <http://corporateeurope.

directed at ISDS are not unique to the investment treaty regime; they might be levelled at commercial litigation, commercial arbitration, and public international law adjudication.[5] However, given the nature of adjudication under investment treaty arbitration, and the public interest which is engaged in many cases, arguably these concerns are more acute.

It is important that participants in the system, including States, investors, counsel and arbitrators engage with these criticisms. The drafters of the Convention on the Settlement of Investment Disputes between States and Nationals of other States ('ICSID Convention') and (older) investment treaties did not envisage how the system would be operate. States—in light of their experiences in ISDS—have begun to negotiate treaties which are more balanced and which address many of the criticisms that have been levelled at the investment treaty system. An example of such a treaty is the Comprehensive Economic and Trade Agreement (CETA) which has been negotiated between Canada and the European Union.[6] CETA includes recognition (at least in the preamble) of the importance of sustainable development.[7]

II. ISDS and Sustainable Development

Sustainable development[8] as a concept reflects the need to find a balance between economic development and the protection of the environment.[9] The most commonly cited definition of sustainable development is provided by the Brundtland Report: 'development that meets the needs of the present without compromising the ability of future generations to meet their needs'.[10] More recent definitions of sustainable development have extended the concept beyond reconciling development

---

org/sites/default/files/publications/profiting-from-injustice.pdf> accessed 8 March 2015; R French, 'Investor-State Dispute Settlement—A Cut Above the Courts?' (Supreme and Federal Court Judges' Conference, Darwin 2014) available at <www.hcourt.gov.au/assets/publications/speeches/current-justices/frenchcj/frenchcj09jul14.pdf> accessed 8 March 2015.

[5] See, for example, E Posner and M de Figueiredo, 'Is the International Court of Justice Biased?' (2005) 34 Journal of Legal Studies 599 (considering whether or not there is evidence of bias on the part of judges of the International Court of Justice).

[6] In this chapter reference will be made to the Consolidated CETA text which was published by the European Commission on 26 September 2014 available at: <http://trade.ec.europa.eu/doclib/docs/2014/september/tradoc_152806.pdf> accessed 8 March 2015.

[7] CETA also contains a general carve out with respect to water on the basis that it is 'not a good or product' and with the exception of one chapter, water is not subject to the terms of CETA. See CETA (Initial Provisions and General Definitions) Art X.08.

[8] On the concept of sustainability and its relation to international investment law see also the chapter by Sacerdoti in this volume.

[9] See *Case Concerning the Gabčíkovo-Nagymaros Project (Hungary v Slovakia)* (1997) ICJ Rep 7, 78, 140: 'This need to reconcile economic development with protection of the environment is aptly expressed in the concept of sustainable development.'

[10] World Commission on Environment and Development, *Our Common Future* (1987).

and environmental concerns, to a more integrated concept of social development incorporating human rights, public participation, and good governance.[11]

There remains a significant degree of controversy as to the normative status of sustainable development in international law.[12] For example, Sands has considered that '[t]here can be little doubt that the concept of "sustainable development" has entered the corpus of international customary law'.[13] By contrast Lowe points to the difficulty in couching sustainable development in normative terms and suggests that it instead operates as an interstitial norm that helps to resolve overlaps or conflicts between primary norms.[14] Leaving the debate as to its normative status aside, the concept of sustainable development can be used to both critique the design of the present system of ISDS and to inform policy choices as to the future design of the system.[15]

Admittedly, the concept of sustainable development provides only limited guidance for the design of ISDS.[16] Private investment has been recognized as a key component of the development strategy of developing countries.[17] Sustainable development suggests the need for a balance between the rights of investors and the protection of the environment (and other interests). It does not however indicate how such a balance is to be struck. This indicates that ISDS should not be 'biased' in favour of private investment (including foreign investment), as this may undermine the balance which needs to be struck between competing interests.

Sustainable development may also provide a broad indication of the standard of review that should be applied by investment tribunals. Prominent commentators have observed that 'one of the main attractions of sustainable development as a concept is that both sides in any legal argument will be able to rely on it'.[18] The absence of justiciable standards for review as to what is and is not sustainable

---

[11] See International Law Association, Declaration of Principles of International Law Relating to Sustainable Development, 2 April 2002 ('ILA Delhi Declaration on Sustainable Development').

[12] P Birnie, A Boyle, and C Redgwell, *International Law and the Environment* (3rd edn, OUP 2009) 125: 'No easy answer can be given to the question whether international law now requires that all development should be sustainable, or if so, what that would mean in specific terms.'

[13] P Sands, *Principles of International Environmental Law* (2nd edn, CUP 2003) 256.

[14] V Lowe, 'Sustainable Development and Unsustainable Arguments' in A Boyle and D Freestone (eds), *International Law and Sustainable Development: Past Achievements and Future Challenges* (OUP 1999) 31.

[15] J Crawford, *Brownlie's Principles of Public International Law* (8th edn, OUP 2012) 358 (sustainable development is best understood as a collection, or collocation, of different legal categories, and as a 'general guideline').

[16] A Ziegler, 'Better BITS?—Making International Investment Law Responsive to Sustainable Development Objectives' (2014) 15 JWIT 803, 808: 'the notion of sustainable development itself sometimes lacks precision that might be useful to get proper guidance on how to reform existing BITs and negotiate better BITs in the future'.

[17] UN Doc A/Res/S-19/2 (19 September 1997) adopting the Programme for the Further Implementation of Agenda 21 [81]: 'Private capital is a major tool for achieving economic growth in a growing number of developing countries. Higher levels of foreign...To ensure that such investments are supportive of sustainable development objectives, it is essential that the national Governments of both investor and recipient countries provide appropriate regulatory frameworks and incentives for private investment.'

[18] Birnie, Boyle, and Redgwell (n 12) 116.

suggests that such decisions should reside with a host State.[19] This position is further reinforced by the principle of subsidiarity:[20] the balancing of social, economic, and environmental impacts is best undertaken by those who are most closely affected by a decision.[21] Both of these concepts suggest that investment treaty tribunals should afford a 'margin of appreciation' to the decisions of States seeking to reconcile social, environmental, and economic interest.[22]

More concrete procedural and substantive elements of sustainable development have been identified in international instruments, such as the Rio Declaration on Environment and Development. These 'elements', such as the principles of sustainable use, the principle of intergenerational equity, and the principle of equitable use, do not directly engage the design of ISDS, and are more germane to developing primary rules of investment law. However, one important aspect of sustainable development that does inform ISDS is the principle of public participation and access to information.[23] The Aarhus Convention recognizes that improved access to information and public participation in decision making is likely to improve the quality of decision making.[24] This appears to be fundamental to ensure that decisions support sustainable development. Aside from improving legitimacy, decision-makers cannot reconcile competing interests without being informed about those interests.

In July 2012 UNCTAD published an Investment Policy Framework for Sustainable Development (IPFSD), which identifies a number of core principles for investment policymaking for sustainable development. The IPFSD identifies various problems, and sets out policy options open to States to address these

---

[19] ibid 126.
[20] While the principle of subsidiarity is a highly developed legal concept in the field of European law, arguably it reflects the residual freedom which States retain in areas not regulated by general international law. See Y Shany, 'Towards a General Margin of Appreciation Doctrine in International Law' (2006) 16 EJIL 907, 921. In any event, the principles is useful for informing policy when States design international institutions.
[21] A Newcombe, 'An Integrated Agenda for Sustainable Development in International Law' in M-C Cordonier Segger, M Gehrig, and A Newcombe (eds), *Sustainable Development in World Investment Law* (Kluwer 2011) 115.
[22] By contrast, procedural rules in the area of environmental law are more concretized, which suggests that an international tribunal can more closely scrutinize whether a State has adopted an adequate procedure, and afforded due process. This emphasis on ensuring compliance with procedure echoes the approach adopted by the International Court of Justice in the *Pulp Mills* case. The International Court of Justice found that Uruguay had breached various procedural obligations. However, although Uruguay was required to undertake an environmental impact assessment, the Court recognized that it was for each State to determine the content of the environmental impact assessment. See *Pulp Mills on the River Uruguay (Argentina v Uruguay)* (2010) ICJ Rep 14, 83, 205.
[23] See ILA Delhi Declaration on Sustainable Development, Principle 5.1: 'Public participation is essential to sustainable development and good governance in that it is a condition for responsive, transparent and accountable governments as well a condition for the active engagement of equally responsive, transparent and accountable civil society organizations, including industrial concerns and trade unions. The vital role of women in sustainable development should be recognized.'
[24] See the preamble to the Convention on Access to Information, Public Participation in Decision-Making and Access to Justice in Environmental Matter (adopted 25 June 1998, entered into force 30 October 2001) 2161 UNTS 447.

problems. Many of the problems identified in the IPFSD focus on substantive standards of protection. In addition, a number of concerns specific to ISDS are also identified including inconsistent and unintended interpretations of treaty provisions and limited or no transparency in ISDS.[25] However, the IPFSD fails to address one of the most significant criticisms made against ISDS, namely that an arbitral model is fundamentally ill-suited for the adjudication of investment disputes.[26]

This chapter seeks to address the most significant criticisms levelled at ISDS which potentially impact on sustainable development:[27]

a. there is a lack of independence on the part of arbitrators—arbitrators have a financial stake in the system as they are dependent on repeat appointments, therefore they may interpret their jurisdiction broadly to ensure future appointments;

b. the lack of transparency in proceedings—arbitrations typically occur behind closed doors and awards are confidential, which is inappropriate for proceedings which engage the public interest, as this undermines public participation; and

c. inconsistent decisions—arbitral tribunals are constituted for each dispute and different tribunals have reached different conclusions as to the meaning of terms contained in investment treaties.

In addition, this chapter also considers whether a requirement to exhaust local remedies, prior to commencing arbitration, could have benefits for sustainable development.

III. Should there be Adjudication of Investment Disputes?

A threshold issue is whether investment treaties should include ISDS at all. The IPFSD suggests that one option open to States is to consider 'in light of the quality of the host country's administrative and judicial system, the option of "no ISDS"'.[28] This was the solution adopted in the US–Australia Free Trade Agreement, the investment chapter of which omitted an ISDS provision. According to the Australian Government, ISDS was omitted on the basis that 'both countries have robust, developed legal systems for resolving disputes between foreign investors'.[29]

---

[25] See IPFSD 43.   [26] See Van Harten (n 4) ch 7.
[27] For a discussion of these criticisms see also the chapter by Van Harten in this volume.
[28] IPFSD 44.
[29] Australian Department of Foreign Affairs and Trade, 'AUSFTA fact sheets: investment' (31 December 2012) available at: <www.dfat.gov.au/fta/ausfta/outcomes/09_investment.html> accessed 20 December 2014; see on the current situation in Australia (and the Pacific rim region) also the chapter by Trakman and Sharma in this volume.

In the absence of an investment treaty containing ISDS an investor would typically be left with two options. First, an investor could seek relief before the domestic courts of the host State (or perhaps before a contractually agreed forum such as an arbitral tribunal established pursuant to an investment contract). Second, an investor could request its State of nationality to exercise diplomatic protection. The limitations of diplomatic protection are well known. Under international law, a State has no obligation to either pursue diplomatic protection or pay any damages that it recovers to an injured investor.[30] Furthermore, there may be no standing tribunal which would have jurisdiction over a diplomatic protection claim. Any settlement may be 'wrapped up' into other political issues. Therefore, neither of these two options may present an appealing remedy for a foreign investor.

The protection of foreign investment should not be conceived as an end in itself.[31] Investment treaties protect foreign investment in order to encourage foreign investment.[32] This is reflected in the preamble to the ICSID Convention which recognizes the role of private investment in economic development.[33] However, in the absence of investor–State dispute resolution, an investment treaty is unlikely to fulfil this purpose of encouraging foreign investment.[34] The existence of an investment treaty with ISDS will not be the sole factor for an investor in deciding whether or not to invest in a particular State. Instead, it is likely to be one of a number of factors which an investor might take into account.[35] Although there is disagreement as to whether investment treaties do in fact encourage foreign investment, some studies have concluded that an investment treaty can influence a company's decision whether to invest.[36] From the perspective of an investor, the key benefits of investment treaties are that they provide standards of protection that are independent of domestic law, and a system of adjudication which is independent of domestic courts. However, in the absence of independent adjudication, the existence of an investment treaty is unlikely to provide an incentive to

---

[30] On the shortcomings of diplomatic protection, see *Barcelona Traction, Light and Power Company Limited (Belgium v Spain)* (1970) ICJ Rep 3, 44.

[31] More generally on the justifications for investment treaties see J Bonnitcha, *Substantive Protection under Investment Treaties—A Legal and Economic Analysis* (CUP 2014) 39ff.

[32] *Saluka Investments BV v The Czech Republic*, UNCITRAL, Partial Award (17 March 2006) para 300: 'The protection of foreign investments is not the sole aim of the Treaty, but rather a necessary element alongside the overall aim of encouraging foreign investment and extending and intensifying the parties' economic relations.'

[33] Preamble to the Convention on the Settlement of Investment Disputes between States and Nationals of Other States (adopted 18 March 1965, entered into force 14 October 1966) 575 UNTS 159 ('ICSID Convention'): 'Considering the need for international cooperation for economic development, and the role of private international investment therein.'

[34] An investor might discover long after a dispute has arisen that it has the ability to bring a claim under an investment treaty. In such a situation it cannot be said that the existence of an investment treaty encouraged the foreign investor to make the investment, or reduced the risk of that investment (potentially leading to a better deal for the host State).

[35] See UNCTAD, *The Role of Investment Agreements in Attracting Foreign Direct Investment* (United Nations 2009) 110.

[36] ibid.

an investor to make an investment in a host State.[37] Indeed, the absence of ISDS in the investment chapter of the US–Australia Free Trade Agreement has led one commentator to describe the chapter as a 'ghost'.[38]

Investment treaties do constrain State conduct; the ability of States to enter into agreements which constrain future activity is an essential attribute of State sovereignty.[39] Although it is doubtful that an investment treaty tribunal has the power to 'annul' a domestic regulatory act,[40] the threat of a significant damages award against a State may achieve much the same result. In the absence of some type of enforcement mechanism, investment treaties would be unlikely to impose a significant constraint on State activity. The extent to which substantive investment protection standards constrain States measures in pursuit of sustainable development is more fully explored in other chapters in this volume.[41] However, investment protection standards afford significant latitude to States to adopt measures in pursuit of the public interest, unless the measures place a disproportionate burden on foreign investors, are discriminatory or unreasonably change a State's regulatory framework.[42]

It is a non-legal question as to whether it is in the best interests of a State to enter into an investment treaty that provides for ISDS.[43] States need to weigh the potential benefits of entering into investment treaties (for example, encouragement of inbound investment; protection of their investors abroad) against the potential costs (for example, potential claims against it; constraints on its regulatory autonomy). However, if a State decides that it is in its interest to enter into an investment treaty containing ISDS, then the question shifts to different questions such as the form that this adjudication should take. This chapter proceeds on the assumption that there should be adjudication of investment disputes, and focuses on the question of how investment disputes should be adjudicated consistently with the concept of sustainable development.

---

[37] C Brower and S Schill, 'Is Arbitration a Threat or a Boon to the Legitimacy of International Investment Law?' (2009) 9 Chicago Journal of International Law 471, 477: 'without the investor having the option of recourse to arbitration, investment treaties would be mere political declarations (albeit with some implications on the diplomatic level) instead of a set of rules enforceable against states'.

[38] W Dodge, 'Investor-State Dispute Settlement between Developed Countries: Reflections on the Australia-United States Free Trade Agreement' (2006) 39 Vanderbilt Journal of Transnational Law 1, 26.

[39] *SS 'Wimbledon'* (1923) PCIJ Rep A No 1 16, 25.

[40] See *LG&E Energy Corp, LG&E Capital Corp, and LG&E International Inc.v Argentine Republic*, ICSID Case No ARB/02/1, Award (8 July 2008) para 87. See on the available remedies under the law of state responsibility the chapter by Aust in this volume.

[41] See chapters by Kläger and Stifter and Reinisch in this volume.

[42] See S Schill, 'Do Investment Treaties Chill Unilateral State Regulation to Mitigate Climate Change?' (2007) 24 Journal of International arbitration 469, 477.

[43] Another option for States may be to exclude certain classes of disputes from the scope of the offer to arbitrate. See UNCTAD, *Investor-State Dispute Settlement* (United Nations 2014) 174 and n 6. However, it may be difficult to classify a dispute in order to identify whether it falls within or outside the excluded class of disputes.

IV. Is Arbitration Ill Suited for Investment Disputes?

It has been argued that the asymmetric nature of investment treaty arbitration—only investors can commence arbitration—leads to unacceptable bias.[44] It is not just investor-appointed arbitrators who are compromised, the asymmetric structure compromises all of the tribunal members; decisions favourable to investors will lead to more claims and increase the opportunities open to all arbitrators.[45] While it may not be possible to establish actual bias, critics of the system point to these structural features as creating an unacceptable appearance of bias. If the system of investor–State arbitration did institutionalize such bias then the system would undermine sustainable development, as it would favour one group of interests (for example, foreign investors) over others.

Independence and impartiality are related concepts. Independence is an instrument to achieving the goal of impartiality,[46] which relates to the 'the absence of favour, bias or prejudice in the consideration of cases'.[47] While it is accepted that international tribunals should be both independent and impartial, these concepts do not necessarily operate in the same way that they operate in a domestic system.[48] For example, domestic judges—absent guarantees of independence—would be subject to the influence of the legislative and executive without adequate safeguards. By contrast, members of international tribunals are subject to different threats to their independence and impartiality. Arbitration, when compared to other types of dispute resolution, has both its advantages and disadvantages. It is a system of dispute resolution that rests on the consent of the parties. However, notwithstanding the parties' ability to control (to a degree) the process, as will be explained, arbitration possesses sufficient mechanisms to ensure that disputes are adjudicated independently and impartially, and that the parties should have sufficient confidence in the outcome of the arbitration process.

It is difficult to establish that there is actual bias in favour of investors (or States) generally in investment treaty arbitration. One can point to awards that might be conceived as pro-State or pro-investor. It might be expected that the high costs of

---

[44] G Van Harten, 'Arbitrator Behaviour in Asymmetrical Adjudication: An Empirical Study of Investment Treaty Arbitration' (2012) Osgoode Hall Law Journal 211, 219.
[45] Van Harten (n 4) 172.
[46] See P Pasquino, 'Prolegomena to a Theory of Judicial Power' (2003) 2 The Law and Practice of International Courts and Tribunals 11, 25: 'independence of the judicial power has always to be understood as an instrument to achieve the goal of impartiality; and that independence has to be conceived of as neutrality, and absence of the subordination of the judge a) from the parties to the conflict, b) from any other power interested in a given resolution of the conflict, and as far as possible c) from the bias of passions and partiality of the judge himself or herself'.
[47] P Mahoney, 'The International Judiciary: Independence and Accountability' (2008) 7 The Law and Practice of International Courts and Tribunals 303, 305.
[48] J Crawford and J McIntyre, 'The Independence and Impartiality of the International Judiciary' in S Shetreet and C Forsyth (eds), *The Culture of Judicial Independence: Conceptual Foundations and Practical Challenges* (Nijhoff 2011) 189, 191: 'the critical issue is not whether the principles of judicial independence and impartiality apply to the international judiciary, but rather what those principles demand'.

investment treaty arbitration would act as a disincentive for unmeritorious claims, and therefore investors would only proceed with claims that are likely to succeed. A recent study found that before 2001, investors prevailed in about 63 per cent of cases, whereas since this time respondents have prevailed in 59 per cent of cases.[49] There is burgeoning literature on the subject of arbitrator independence, including in the field of investment treaty arbitration. Empirical studies have been done to try and identify whether there is evidence of bias.[50] However, such studies are subject to significant limitations,[51] and it would seem impossible to find conclusive proof of bias from such studies.[52]

One particular source of controversy is the ability of parties to appoint arbitrators. This is of course a right that applies to both an investor and the respondent State. Subject to the applicable rules relating to the qualification and disqualification of arbitrators,[53] the parties have complete freedom to decide who they wish to appoint as an arbitrator. A party can therefore appoint an arbitrator that they consider has the appropriate expertise to adjudicate on a particular dispute.[54] In addition, party input might be expected to increase the confidence of that party in the decision making of the tribunal.[55] For example, the International Court of Justice allowed the use of chambers in order to make this a more attractive forum for States at a time when the court was under-utilized.[56] The use of such chambers allowed States to influence both the size and composition of chambers.[57]

There are misconceptions about the role of party-appointed arbitrators. A party having the power to appoint a member of a tribunal may, at first sight, ring alarm bells for observers more familiar with domestic litigation. In domestic litigation against a State, it will often be the State (directly or indirectly) who has appointed all of the members of the court. In contentious proceedings before the International Court of Justice a State has the right to appoint an ad hoc judge if there is no judge of that State's nationality on the court.[58] However, given the size of the court, the influence of an ad hoc judge is typically more limited than as is the case with

---

[49] M Hodgson, 'Counting the costs of investment treaty arbitration' (2014) 9(2) Global Arbitration Review.
[50] See, for example, Van Harten (n 44) 211; S Franck, 'Development and Outcomes of Investment Treaty Arbitration' (2009) 50 HILJ 435.
[51] C Rogers, 'The Politics of International Investment Arbitrators' (2014) 12 Santa Clara Journal of International Law 223, 234: '[Empirical research] cannot, however, isolate what legal outcome would otherwise have resulted in the absence of any hypothesized influences.'
[52] Van Harten (n 44) 215.
[53] See ICSID Convention Arts 14, 40, and 57. Under the ICSID Convention, the burden for obtaining the disqualification of an arbitrator is high, as it must be demonstrated that they 'manifestly' lack the necessary qualities, including independent judgement.
[54] See E Lauterpacht, *Aspects of the Administration of International Justice* (CUP 1991) 78.
[55] W Park, 'Arbitrator Integrity' in M Waibel, A Kaushal, K Chung, and C Balchin (eds), *The Backlash against Investment Arbitration* (Kluwer 2010) 213; J Paulsson, 'Moral Hazard in International Dispute Resolution' (2010) 25 ICSID Review 339, 350 (unilateral appointments may increase the likelihood of acceptance but is unnecessary as a marketing strategy for mature institutions).
[56] E Valencia-Ospina, 'The Use of Chambers of the International Court of Justice' in V Lowe and M Fitzmaurice (eds), *Fifty years of the International Court of Justice* (CUP 1996) 506–07.
[57] See S Schwebel, 'Ad Hoc Chambers of the International Court of Justice' (1987) 81 AJIL 831.
[58] Statute of the International Court of Justice Art 31.

a party appointed arbitrator sitting on a three person tribunal. Like an ad hoc judge, party-appointed arbitrators can play a role in ensuring that the arguments of the party which appointed them have been fully understood and considered by the tribunal.[59] However, party appointed members of a tribunal have the same obligations of independence and impartiality as the president of a tribunal.[60]

A study by one prominent arbitrator has pointed to the fact that nearly all dissents are written in favour of the party which appointed that arbitrator.[61] This is not altogether unexpected. Legal counsel for parties will typically spend a significant amount of time researching arbitrators, and appoint an arbitrator who has views which might be considered favourable to the party appointing them. Unlike with commercial arbitration, investment treaty awards are not only often public but similar issues arise in different investment treaty cases. This might therefore facilitate appointing an arbitrator who is favourably disposed to a party's position on a point of law.[62] However, it is often not possible to distil an arbitrator's precise views given that it is typically the case that three members of the tribunal subscribe to a single decision or award which may in some respects represent a compromise position. If an arbitrator has clearly expressed their views on a particular subject then they might be disqualified on the basis that they had prejudged that question.[63]

Is it a problem that parties can seek to appoint an arbitrator which might have expressed favourable views on questions of law? This is of course a right which applies to both parties to a proceeding. However, saying that both parties have the power to appoint a 'pro-investor' or 'pro-State' arbitrator, as the case may be, does not solve the problem. In this respect, the role of a third presiding arbitrator is critical to ensuring the integrity of the arbitral process. It provides an incentive

---

[59] *Application of the Convention on the Prevention and Punishment of the Crime of Genocide (Bosnia and Herzegovina) v Yugoslavia (Serbia and Montenegro)* (1993) ICJ Rep 325, 409 (Separate opinion of Judge *ad hoc* Lauterpacht): 'consistently with the duty of impartiality by which the ad hoc judge is bound, there is still something specific that distinguishes his role. He has, I believe, the special obligation to endeavour to ensure that, so far as is reasonable, every relevant argument in favour of the party that has appointed him has been fully appreciated in the course of collegial consideration and, ultimately, is reflected—though not necessarily accepted—in any separate or dissenting opinion that he may write.'

[60] Park (n 55) 202.

[61] See A van den Berg, 'Dissenting Opinions by Party-Appointed Arbitrators in Investment Arbitration' in M Arsanjani, J Katz Cogan, R Sloane, and S Wiessner (eds), *Looking to the Future: Essays in Honour of W. Michael Reisman* (Brill 2010) 824.

[62] Arguably an arbitrator should not be disqualified if they have expressed a view on abstract legal questions, but only if they have prejudged a particular factual scenario. See the approach taken in *Repsol SA and Repsol Butano SA v Argentine Republic*, ICSID Case No ARB/12/38 Decision on the Proposal for the Disqualification of Francisco Orrego Vicuña and Claus von Wobeser (13 December 2013) para 79.

[63] *CC/Devas (Mauritius) Ltd, Devas Employees Mauritius Private Limited and Telecom Devas Mauritius Limited v India*, UNCITRAL Case, Decision on the Respondent's Challenge to the Hon Marc Lalonde and Prof Francisco Orrego Vicuña, (30 September 2013) para 64 (finding that Professor Orrego Vicuña's consistent position on the meaning of an 'essential security interests' clause, affirmed in an academic article, raised doubts as to whether he could approach the issue with an open mind and justified his disqualification).

for both parties to appoint an arbitrator who is perceived to be sufficiently independent and impartial. An investor who needs to rely on a most favoured nation (MFN) clause to establish the jurisdiction of a tribunal will not appoint an arbitrator who has expressly rejected the view that an MFN clause can apply to dispute settlement. However, if an investor appoints an arbitrator who is seen as too pro-claimant then they are unlikely to be an influential member of a tribunal.[64] Neither an investor-appointed arbitrator nor a State-appointed arbitrator can decide the case on their own. If a State—which presumably is capable of representing the public interest—has agreed to the selection of a majority of the members of a tribunal, any concern of bias in favour of investors is likely to be lessened.

A system in which the chairperson of a tribunal is appointed with the agreement of both parties is likely to inspire greater confidence. The appointment of the chairperson or presiding arbitrator occurs in different ways under different rules. For example, under the ICSID Convention, the president of the tribunal is to be appointed by the agreement of the parties.[65] However, in the absence of agreement ICSID will appoint the president.[66] Under the 2010 UNCITRAL Arbitration Rules, the presiding arbitrator is appointed by the two party-appointed arbitrators.[67] However, some type of deadlock breaking mechanism is required in the event that neither party agrees. Under the ICSID Convention, the president will be appointed by the Chairman of the Administrative Council, on the recommendation of the Secretary-General of ICSID.[68] Under the 2010 UNCITRAL Arbitration Rules, the Secretary-General of the Permanent Court of Arbitration may be called upon to designate an appointing authority.[69]

It is suggested that not only do arbitrators need to appeal to investors to ensure the growth of the system, and future appointments, but they also have an interest in safeguarding their reputation with appointing authorities.[70] Concerns have been expressed about the (perceived) lack of independence of the appointing authority.[71] The ICSID Secretary-General is appointed by the World Bank, an organization in which the voting structure favours certain capital exporting States. Certainly a handful of Latin American States have alleged that ICSID is biased, and withdrawn from the ICSID Convention.[72] If the problem is the appointing authority, then this would not seem to necessitate scrapping arbitration as a mechanism for ISDS. Instead, it suggests conferring functions on an institution which has wide acceptance amongst not only capital exporting States but also capital importing States. For example, a number of

---

[64] Brower and Schill (n 37) 493. [65] ICSID Convention Art 37(2)(b).
[66] ICSID Convention Art 38. [67] UNCITRAL Arbitration Rules 2010 Art 9.
[68] ICSID Convention Art 38. See C Schreuer, L Malintoppi, A Reinisch, and A Sinclair, *The ICSID Convention: A Commentary* (2nd edn, CUP 2009) 494.
[69] UNCITRAL Arbitration Rules 2010 Art 6. [70] Van Harten (n 4) 169.
[71] Van Harten (n 4) 170–71.
[72] On the reasons for the denunciation of the ICSID Convention see R Polanco Lazo, 'Is There a Life for Latin American Countries After Denouncing the ICSID Convention?' (2014) 11(1) Transnational Dispute Management.

investment treaties designate the President of the International Court of Justice as the designating authority.[73]

Aside from the function played by the presiding member of the tribunal, an arbitrator's reputation is an important mechanism for ensuring independence and impartiality.[74] The importance of arbitrators' reputations should not be underestimated. In a sense arbitration is a meritocracy. If arbitrators issue poor or biased decisions, they are unlikely to be reappointed. Furthermore, if they are not perceived to be independent, an arbitrator is unlikely to be an influential member of a tribunal; their views are more likely to be ignored by the other arbitrators. The retort is that investors and appointing institutions (which are biased in favour of investors) have the greatest influence over the appointment of arbitrators, and therefore arbitrators will seek to enhance their reputation with these parties, presumably at the expense of States.[75] However, this would seem to ignore the important role that States play in the appointment of arbitrators and tribunal presidents. Arbitrators need to be seen to be independent, otherwise a State will not consent to their appointment as president of a tribunal (assuming that it's the parties that appoint the president). One mechanism which is becoming increasingly common is for the State parties to designate arbitrators to a 'pre-approved' list, from which appointments might be made.[76] States may remove arbitrators from designated lists from which arbitrators might be appointed.

A proposed alternative to the current system of party-appointed arbitration is the creation of a permanent investment court.[77] If properly designed, this proposal has merit.[78] However, lessons from general public international law suggest that creating an investment court should not be seen as a panacea. Arguably all adjudicators have a proclivity to expand their jurisdiction.[79] For example, faced with jurisdictional competition from other tribunals that had the power to order binding provisional measures, the International Court of Justice found that its power to 'indicate' provisional measures was in fact binding.[80] The WTO Appellate Body and the Court of Justice of the European Union have been criticized for judicial

---

[73] See, for example, agreement between the People's Republic of China and the Republic of Cuba concerning the encouragement and reciprocal protection of investments (adopted 25 April 1995, entered into force 1 August 1996) Art 9(4).

[74] Park (n 55) 212–13: 'Reputations tarnished by deviation form duty do not bring reappointment, at least when both host states and investor have a role in the process.... if arbitrator incentives operate at all in large international cases, they work to promote accuracy and honesty.' Brower and Schill (n 37) 491.

[75] Van Harten (n 4) 169.

[76] The CETA text provides for a list of potential arbitrators from which the president might be appointed (if the parties cannot agree). CETA Investment Chapter Art X.25.

[77] Paulsson has proposed the abandonment of party-appointed arbitrators generally in arbitration. This ultimately transfers significant power to the appointing authority. Paulsson (n 55) 339.

[78] There are various important questions such as who will appoint the judges, and who will decide on the configuration of individuals chambers. The process for the appointment of judges to international tribunals is often highly politicized. See, for example, R McKenzie, K Malleson, P Martin, and P Sands, *Selecting International Judges: Principles, Process, and Politics* (OUP 2010) 173.

[79] See Rogers (n 51) 250.

[80] *LaGrand (Germany v United States of America)* (2001) ICJ Rep 466, 506 para 109.

policymaking.⁸¹ The European Court of Human Rights, which provides individuals with standing and is therefore one of the most comparable regimes to the investment treaty regime, has been criticized for the expansive interpretations of the European Convention on Human Rights.⁸² Indeed, one potential reason why States may prefer an arbitral model of dispute resolution over a permanent investment court is because this limits the power of tribunals. A permanent investment court may exceed its mandate, and States may lack sufficient control to address this.⁸³ In a decentralized system, such as the present ISDS system, the role of arbitral tribunals is weaker than that of a permanent court. States may have difficulty controlling arbitral tribunals and their use of de facto precedent, however they would have a more difficult time controlling a permanent investment court.

The mechanisms that arbitration has to ensure impartiality and independence are different to those in domestic legal systems. They are also admittedly less concrete than measures adopted in many legal systems, such as providing for tenure of appointment. However, this is not to say that arbitration is ill-suited as a mechanism for dispute settlement in investment disputes. Ultimately those best situated to determine whether an arbitral model is biased are the parties to the dispute. They have the fullest knowledge of the facts and arguments. The best evidence that arbitration is not a fundamentally ill-suited mechanism in investment disputes is that States which have been respondents in investment treaty proceedings continue to be prepared to enter into investment treaties that provide for investor–State arbitration. For example, the United States and Canada are amongst the most frequent respondents in investment treaty cases, yet they continue to negotiate investment treaties providing for investor–State arbitration. While their investors abroad might desire 'strong' investment protection, such States might also be subject to significant liabilities. They therefore have an interest in entering into investment treaties which strike an appropriate 'balance'.

Some of the strongest critics of the current system are Latin American countries, including Bolivia, Ecuador, and Venezuela.⁸⁴ These countries have withdrawn from the ICSID Convention and sought to terminate a number of investment treaties.⁸⁵ However, rather than withdrawing from a system of international investment protection altogether, a new model has been proposed. In particular, Ecuador has led efforts within the Union of South American Nations (UNASUR) to create a

---

⁸¹ See E Voeten, 'The Politics of International Judicial Appointments' (2007) 61 International Organisation 669, 670 (noting that the assumptions that judges share an interest in expanding the reach of their court and that governments seek to prevent such occurrences have remained unchallenged).

⁸² See, for example, Sir Gerald Fitzmaurice describing the European Court of Human Rights as engaging in a 'quasi-legislative operation exceeding the normal judicial function' (*Ireland v The United Kingdom* App No 5310/71 (ECHR, 18 January 1978) Separate Opinion of Judge Fitzmaurice para 6).

⁸³ See J Katz Cogan, 'Competition and Control in International Adjudication' (2009) 48 Virginia Journal of International Law 411, 419: '[control mechanisms] provide States with the comfort they seek... that an international court will not venture beyond its assigned mandate'.

⁸⁴ See for a more detailed discussion of the situation in Latin America the chapter by Luque Macías in this volume.

⁸⁵ See UNCTAD, 'Denunciation of the ICSID Convention and BITs' (2010) 2 IIA Issues Note.

regional arbitration centre, as an alternative to ICSID.[86] The retention of arbitration suggests that in the eyes of these States—which have been amongst the most vocal critics of the present regime—an arbitral model is suited to the resolution of investment disputes. Admittedly, consent should not be seen as obviating the need for an appropriate system of impartiality and independence.[87] However, it would seem difficult to believe that States with experience in the system would propose the continuation of a system that they knew was biased against them. This suggests that, at least in the eyes of the users of the system, arbitration is not a fundamentally flawed model. Until a well-designed international investment court becomes a realistic prospect, reform efforts should be directed in a number of areas to improve the arbitral process and address concerns, such as:

a. addressing arbitrator ethics to deal with problems specific to ISDS, such as the 'double hat' problem created by lawyers acting as both arbitrators and counsel and 'issue conflict';
b. removing the power of co-arbitrators to decide on challenges to an arbitrator;
c. increasing transparency to reduce any disparity in information when it comes to the appointment of arbitrators; if both parties are informed and adequately represented, this will reduce the possibility that one party may obtain an advantage through the appointment process.

V. The Need for Transparency and Public Participation

The ILA Delhi Declaration on Sustainable Development recognizes the principle of public participation and access to information as instrumental in pursuing sustainable development.[88] Investment treaty disputes often raise issues of general public importance, such as protection of the environment and public health.[89] Not all cases engage the public interest to the same extent; the public interest in plain packaging of tobacco[90] is clearly greater than that for the operation of duty free stores.[91] However, at a minimum, public taxpayers will usually have an interest in the outcome of a dispute, as they will bear the burden of paying an adverse award against a State. Increased transparency and public participation is one solution to address the perception that investment treaty arbitration suffers from a

---

[86] See S Fiezzoni, 'UNASUR Arbitration Centre: The Present Situation and the Principal Characteristics of Ecuador's Proposal' (*International Institute for Sustainable Development*, 12 January 2012) available at <www.iisd.org/itn/2012/01/12/unasur/> accessed 8 March 2015.
[87] cf Park (n 55) 196 (observing that a lack of independence may be waived, up to a point).
[88] ILA Delhi Declaration on Sustainable Development, Principle 5.
[89] See *Suez, Sociedad General de Aguas de Barcelona SA and Vivendi Universal SA v Argentine Republic*, ICSID Case No ARB/03/19, Order in response to a Petition for Participation as Amicus Curiae (19 May 2005) para 19.
[90] *Philip Morris Asia Limited v The Commonwealth of Australia*, UNCITRAL, PCA Case no 2012-12.
[91] *Mr Franck Charles Arif v Republic of Moldova*, ICSID Case No ARB/11/23.

democratic deficit: private arbitrators, who are not accountable to a domestic polity, can review the decisions of that polity, without allowing for those affected by a decision to participate.[92]

Transparency and participation might be considered separately but they go hand in hand.[93] Any effective public participation in ISDS requires access to information (although there can be a significant degree of transparency without participation).[94] If a person does not know of the existence of an arbitration, let alone the issues at stake, they cannot effectively participate in that arbitration. Transparency is also important for a number of other reasons, including improving the perceived legitimacy of decision making,[95] and ensuring accountability of arbitrators. While the publication of awards is not uniform, arbitrators know that there is a significant likelihood that their awards and decisions may be made public and subject to scrutiny by academics and others. This encourages arbitrators to issue well-reasoned decisions. An arbitrator will consider the implications of what they do for their own reputation and the reputation of the system.[96] As discussed above, this is an important mechanism for ensuring the independent and impartiality of arbitrators.

One perceived advantage of arbitration is confidentiality. Investors may prefer that their disputes be kept private so as to protect confidential information and their reputation. However, this does not appear to be an overwhelming consideration when it comes to a choice of forum. Businesses often agree to adjudicate disputes before the English courts, where the existence of proceedings will be known and the public may have access to a number of court documents as well as the hearing.[97] States may also oppose increased transparency for a number of reasons.[98] States wishing to present themselves as a friendly environment for investment do not wish potential investors to know about claims against them by other foreign investors.

Representing and accommodating the public interest in a system of dispute resolution originally aimed at confidentially resolving a dispute between two private parties presents difficulties. Initially improvements occurred on an ad hoc basis with various investment treaty tribunals allowing the admission of amicus

---

[92] N Blackaby and C Richard, 'Amicus Curiae: A Panacea for Legitimacy in Investment Arbitration?' in M Waibel, A Kaushal, K Chung, and C Balchin (eds), *The Backlash against Investment Arbitration* (Kluwer 2010) 268.

[93] Transparency and public participation is relevant not only for ISDS but also for the negotiation of investment agreements.

[94] ILA Delhi Declaration on Sustainable Development, Principle 5.2.

[95] C Rogers, 'Transparency in International Commercial Arbitration' (2005–06) 54 University of Kansas L Rev 1301, 1308.

[96] Van Harten (n 4) 161.

[97] See M Kantor, 'The Transparency Agenda for UNCITRAL Investment Arbitrations Looking in all the Wrong Places' (2011) available at: <www.iilj.org/research/documents/IF2010-11.Kantor.pdf> accessed 8 March 2015.

[98] State practice varies as to the transparency of domestic judicial proceedings, and some States may place more weight on the procedural autonomy of parties as a guiding principle.

briefs based on broad procedural powers conferred on those tribunals.[99] In addition to tribunals interpreting their powers broadly to allow the receipt of amicus briefs, certain States have published pleadings and information about cases,[100] and opened hearings to the public.[101] ICSID has made a number of improvements to its Arbitration Rules to allow the publication of basic information about a dispute and to set out the circumstances in which a submission from a non-disputing party will be received.[102] However, attempts to reform the ICSID Arbitration Rules are constrained by the terms of the ICSID Convention. For example, the ICSID Convention prevents ICSID from publishing an award without the consent of the parties.[103]

The most significant recent initiative has been adoption of the Rules on Transparency in Treaty-based Investor–State Arbitration ('UNCITRAL Transparency Rules') by UNCITRAL in July 2013. The UNCITRAL Transparency Rules provide rules for access to information about investor–State arbitrations, as well as setting out rules for participation by third persons. However, the UNCITRAL Transparency Rules only apply automatically to arbitrations initiated under the UNCITRAL Arbitration Rules pursuant to investment treaties concluded on or after 1 April 2014. States and investors can agree to the application of the UNCITRAL Transparency Rules to treaties concluded prior to 1 April 2014.[104] This therefore limits the operation of the Rules, as the parties to a dispute or State parties to an investment treaty would need to agree to the application of the Rules with respect to investment treaties concluded prior to 1 April 2014, or to arbitrations operating under rules other than the UNCITRAL Rules. On 10 December 2014 the General Assembly adopted the United Nations Convention on Transparency in Treaty-based Investor-State Arbitration (the 'Mauritius Convention') which provides a mechanism for States to apply the UNCITRAL Transparency Rules to arbitrations under investment treaties entered into prior to 1 April 2014, as well as non-UNCITRAL arbitrations. The Mauritius Convention therefore facilitates States opting into the regime of transparency and participation created by the UNCITRAL Transparency Rules.

The UNCITRAL Transparency Rules (where applicable) will ensure that a significant amount of information is available to the dispute. This will ensure that awards can be scrutinized, and that third parties can participate more effectively in arbitrations. The UNCITRAL Transparency Rules provide for the publication

---

[99] See *Suez, Sociedad General de Aguas* de Barcelona *SA and Vivendi Universal SA v Argentine Republic*, ICSID Case No ARB/03/19, Order in response to a Petition for Participation as Amicus Curiae (19 May 2005) paras 11, 15f.

[100] NAFTA Free Trade Commission, 'Notes of Interpretation of Certain Chapter 11 Provisions', 31 July 2001.

[101] See NAFTA Free Trade Commission, 'Joint Statement on the Decade of Achievement', 16 July 2004.

[102] ICSID Arbitration Rules Rule 37.

[103] ICSID Convention Art 48(5). However, ICSID has amended its Arbitration Rules to require the publication of 'excerpts of legal reasoning'. See ICSID Arbitration Rules Rule 48(4).

[104] UNCITRAL Transparency Rules Art 1(2).

of certain basic information about a case once a notice of arbitration has been submitted, as well as the publication of certain key documents (notice of arbitration, pleadings etc). Hearings are 'public'.[105] There are however exceptions to this transparency to protect confidential information, as well as certain other categories of information.[106] Investors (and States) might complain about the increased costs associated with redacting documents, and non-parties might raise concerns about the potential for the parties to the dispute to abuse these exceptions to withhold information from the public. Ultimately, it will be for arbitrators to find an appropriate balance between these competing interests.

As well as ensuring that information about a dispute is publicly available, the UNCITRAL Transparency Rules provide a procedure for third persons to file submissions.[107] The Rules do not provide for an automatic entitlement to file such a submission. Furthermore, third parties do not have the right to participate in public hearings, by, for example, making oral submissions or presenting evidence. Arguably, the UNCITRAL Transparency Rules could have gone further and made it clear that a tribunal has discretion to allow a third person to participate more fully in proceedings.

In *Methanex v USA* a NAFTA tribunal observed that:

There is...a broader argument, as suggested by the Respondent and Canada: the Chapter 11 arbitral process could benefit from being perceived as more open or transparent or conversely be harmed if seen as unduly secretive. In this regard, the Tribunal's willingness to receive amicus submissions might support the process in general and this arbitration in particular; whereas a blanket refusal could do positive harm.[108]

However, contrary to what was suggested by the *Methanex* tribunal, it is doubtful whether the admission of amicus briefs improves transparency per se. The primary role of participation by third persons in arbitral proceedings should be to improve arbitral decision making. It could do this in a number of ways. The UNCITRAL Transparency Rules provide that in determining whether or not to allow a submission by a third person a tribunal is to take into account the extent to which that person has a significant interest in the proceedings, and whether the submission would assist the tribunal by bringing a perspective, particular knowledge or insight that is different from that of the disputing parties.[109] However, the Respondent State in any arbitration is capable of representing the public interest. States have called on a variety of different organizations to provide evidence in support of their case.[110]

---

[105] UNCITRAL Transparency Rules Art 6.   [106] UNCITRAL Transparency Rules Art 7.
[107] UNCITRAL Transparency Rules Art 4.
[108] *Methanex Corporation v United States of America*, UNCITRAL, Decision of the Tribunal on Petitions from Third Persons to intervene as 'amici curiae' (15 January 2001) para 49.
[109] UNCITRAL Transparency Rules Art 4(3).
[110] See, for example, *CMS Gas Transmission Company v The Republic of Argentina*, ICSID Case No ARB/01/8, Award (12 May 2005) para 211. Presenting such views as evidence may be preferable as it allows those views to be tested through cross-examination. See Blackaby and Richard (n 92) 269.

The UNCITRAL Transparency Rules could have gone further and granted 'full standing' to third persons to participate in an arbitration as if they were a party. Admittedly, there may be situations in which States might not adequately represent the interest of minorities. However, if a third person's (or group's) rights or interests are directly affected by a decision then that third person is likely to have a 'significant interest'.[111] If a State does not represent the interest of such a person or group, then that person or group is likely to be able to assist the tribunal by bringing a perspective, knowledge or insight different from the disputing parties.[112] In most cases the filing of a written submission is likely to be adequate to ensure that that parties interests are taken into account, particularly if that party has access to the submission of the parties to the arbitration. Therefore, the circumstances in which such participation might be justified are likely to be quite limited.

The UNCITRAL Transparency Rules represent an accommodation between competing concerns: the public interest in transparency and the disputing parties' interest in a fair and efficient resolution of their dispute.[113] As the product of negotiations between States (with input from NGOs) they also represent a compromise position.[114] However, States can opt for a higher level of transparency as they have done under CETA. For example, the CETA text designates additional documents to be made available to the public, and allows documents to be published at an earlier stage of the proceedings.[115] Assuming they are adopted, the UNCITRAL Transparency Rules represent a relatively robust baseline for ensuring transparency and public participation. The Transparency Rules ultimately confer significant discretion on tribunals, and will rely on tribunals for their effective operation.

However, debate about transparency and participation in ISDS should not obscure the importance of transparency and participation at a domestic level. ISDS cannot offer a substitute for this. Investment treaty tribunals might be called upon to consider measures which have been adopted through transparent processes and with public participation. The European Court of Human Rights has been prepared to afford a greater 'margin of appreciation' to legislative acts which constitute a deliberative choice by a democratic government.[116] Investment treaty tribunals should afford similar deference.

---

[111] In many domestic legal systems parties do not have an entitlement to appear. Under English law an applicant can only has standing to apply for judicial review if they can demonstrate 'sufficient interest' (Senior Courts Act 1981, s 319(2)). Admittedly, this is interpreted liberally. See *R v Inland Revenue Commissioners, ex parte National Federation of Self-employed and Small Businesses Ltd* [1982] AC 617.

[112] In recent times, the European Commission has taken a more active role in presenting views on European Union law which might not coincide with those of the State parties to the relevant treaty. See, for example, *Electrabel SA v Republic of Hungary*, ICSID Case No ARB/07/19, Decision on Jurisdiction, Applicable Law and Liability (30 November 2012) paras 5.26–5.30.

[113] UNCITRAL Transparency Rules Art 1(4).

[114] See J Salasky and C Montineri, 'UN Commission on International Trade Law and Multilateral Rule-making' (2014) 11(1) Transnational Dispute Management.

[115] CETA Art X.33.

[116] See A Legg, *The Margin of Appreciation in International Human Rights Law* (OUP 2012) 75. See similarly WTO, *United States—Sunset Reviews of Anti-Dumping Measures on Oil Country Tubular Goods from Argentina: Report of the Appellate Body* (29 November 2004) WT/DS268/AB/R [173].

VI. The Need for an Appellate Body?

The IPFSD identifies inconsistent and unintended interpretations of investment treaty provisions as one of the shortcomings of the present system.[117] Investment treaty tribunals have interpreted similar or identical provisions of investment treaties in divergent ways.[118] For example, in *SGS v Pakistan* an ICSID tribunal interpreted an umbrella clause narrowly, finding that the relevant umbrella clause did not allow the claimant to bring a claim with respect to breaches of State contracts.[119] The narrow interpretation of this clause was not shared by at least one of the parties to the relevant investment treaty.[120] By contrast, in the subsequent decision of *SGS v Philippines* an ICSID tribunal found that a differently worded umbrella clause made it 'a breach of the BIT for the host State to fail to observe binding commitments, including contractual commitments, which it has assumed with regard to specific investments'.[121] It however found the case to be inadmissible due to the existence of a dispute resolution clause in the relevant contract, and stayed the proceedings.[122] Although the outcome of these two cases was substantially the same, the differences between the interpretations cannot be explained by differences in the wording of the relevant clauses.

The problem of inconsistent decisions should not be overestimated. On many issues the decisions of investment treaty tribunals are relatively consistent.[123] Different interpretations may be attributable to differences in treaty wording and differences in the jurisdictional mandate of tribunals. Furthermore, the application of broad and vaguely worded investment protection standards is often a fact-specific exercise.[124] Even when applying the same standard, different tribunals may have a different appreciation of the underlying factual scenario.[125]

---

[117] IPFSD 45.

[118] For example, investment treaty tribunals have adopted very different interpretations as to the meaning of the emergency clause in the US–Argentina BIT. See, for example, J Alvarez and T Brink, 'Revisiting the Necessity Defense' (2010–2011) Yearbook on International Law and Investment Policy 315.

[119] *SGS Société Générale de Surveillance SA v Islamic Republic of Pakistan*, ICSID Case No ARB/01/13, Decision of the Tribunal on Objections to Jurisdiction (6 August 2003) para 173.

[120] Switzerland sent a letter to ICSID objecting to the narrow interpretation given by the tribunal. See Letter for the Swiss Secretariat for Economic Affairs to the ICSID Deputy Secretary-General of 1 October 2003, Mealey's International Arbitration Reports (February 2003).

[121] *SGS Société Générale de Surveillance SA v Republic of the Philippines*, ICSID Case No ARB/02/6, Decision of the Tribunal on Objections to Jurisdiction (29 January 2004) para 128.

[122] ibid paras 169, 175.

[123] C Schreuer and M Weiniger, 'A Doctrine of Precedent?' in P Muchnlinksi, F Ortino, and C Schreuer (eds), *The Oxford Handbook of International Investment Law* (OUP 2008) 1198: 'Fortunately, the problem of inconsistency is not pervasive.' See ICSID Secretariat, 'Possible Improvements of the Framework for ICSID Arbitration' (22 October 2004) [21]: 'Significant inconsistencies have not to date been a general feature of the jurisprudence of ICSID.'

[124] See 2012 United States Model Bilateral Investment Treaty annex B: 'The determination of whether an action or series of actions by a Party, in a specific fact situation, constitutes an indirect expropriation, requires a case-by case, fact-based inquiry…'

[125] For example in *Perenco v Ecuador* and *Burlington v Ecuador* both tribunals considered the same underling factual scenario. In *Burlington v Ecuador* the tribunal found that the occupation of the oil

Nevertheless inconsistent decisions, and decisions which do not accord with the intentions of the parties to a treaty, have the potential to negatively impact on sustainable development. UNCTAD has identified policy coherence as one of the core principles for investment policymaking: 'All policies that may impact on investment should be coherent and synergetic at both the national and international level.'[126] Uncertainty as to the scope or content of investment treaty obligations may undermine the ability of States to exercise their regulatory autonomy in pursuit of sustainable development (that is, so-called 'regulatory chill').[127] For example, in light of uncertainty as to its international obligations, a State may be dissuaded from adopting a particular measure in order to avoid possible claims.[128]

Two features of investment treaty arbitration may explain a significant degree of the inconsistency: the ad hoc constitution of arbitral tribunals and the vague, open textured provisions contained in many investment treaties.[129] Investment treaty tribunals are constituted ad hoc for each dispute. There is no hierarchy between different investment treaty tribunals, or system of binding precedent. Notwithstanding statements by tribunals to the effect that that they will 'take into account' earlier decisions,[130] there is an inherent risk of inconsistent decisions.[131] This institutional feature of investment treaty arbitration is compounded by the

---

blocks by Ecuador amounted to an expropriation. (*Burlington Resources Inc v Republic of Ecuador*, ICSID Case No ARB/08/5, Decision on Liability (14 December 2012) para 537.) Whereas in *Perenco v Ecuador* the tribunal considered that this did not amount to an expropriation, and an expropriation occurred only with the subsequent declaration of *caducidad*. (*Perenco Ecuador Limited v Republic of Ecuador and Empresa Estatal Petróleos del Ecuador*, ICSID Case No ARB/08/6, Decision on the Remaining Issues of Jurisdiction and on Liability (12 September 2014) para 710).

[126] IPFSD 11.
[127] A distinction could be drawn between the chilling of measures which would give rise to liability and the chilling of measures which might give rise to liability. See J Bonnitcha, 'Outline of normative framework for evaluating interpretations of investment treaty protections' in C Brown and K Miles (eds), *Evolution in Investment Treaty Law and Arbitration* (CUP 2011) 135.
[128] Chilling effects are difficult to identify because they require evidence as to what would have happened in the absence of the so-called chilling. Ibid, 134. It is also difficult to identify whether the threat of investment treaty arbitration led to regulatory chill, as other factors may explain the decision not to pursue a measure. See K Tienhaara, 'Regulatory Chill and the Threat of Arbitration: A View from Political Science' in C Brown and K Miles (eds), *Evolution in Investment Treaty Law and Arbitration* (CUP 2011) 609.
[129] This would suggest that measures to ameliorate inconsistencies might be directed at either of these two features of the system.
[130] See *El Paso Energy International Company v The Argentine Republic*, ICSID Case No ARB/03/15, Decision on Jurisdiction (27 April 2006) para 39: 'ICSID arbitral tribunals are established ad hoc, from case to case, in the framework of the Washington Convention, and the present Tribunal knows of no provision, either in that Convention or in the BIT, establishing an obligation of *stare decisis*. It is, nonetheless, a reasonable assumption that international arbitral tribunals, notably those established within the ICSID system, will generally take account of the precedents established by other arbitration organs.' See M Paparinskis, *The International Minimum Standard* (OUP 2013) 120ff (explaining why recourse to case law in investment arbitration is difficult to accommodate within the rules of treaty interpretation).
[131] C Tams, 'An Appealing Option? A debate about an ICSID Appellate System' (2006) Essays in Transnational Economic Law No 57, 19 available at: <http://papers.ssrn.com/sol3/papers.cfm?abstract_id=1413694>: 'The risk of inconsistent decisions therefore is inherent in the system, it is part and parcel of a process of decentralized, non-hierarchical dispute resolution, such as that of investment arbitration.'

nature of the rules which tribunals are called on to apply. Investment treaty tribunals are called on to determine the meaning of open textured rules.[132] At least with substantive standards of protection this may be an inevitable feature given the diverse forms of State conduct which investment treaties are intended to regulate. A notable feature of many investment treaties, particularly older treaties, is that they contain broadly worded provisions that contain little interpretative guidance. Recourse to tools of treaty interpretation does not lead to a particular uncontroverted meaning being ascribed to such treaty provisions. Such judging inevitably involves an element of choice.[133]

There are a variety of mechanisms that might be adopted to address the problem of inconsistency.[134] Many of the solutions that have been proposed are institutional. For example, the creation of an investment appellate body has been suggested as a means to ensure greater consistency.[135] Another suggested solution is some type of preliminary ruling procedure based on the model provided by European Union law;[136] this would circumvent possible problems arising from Article 53 of the ICSID Convention, which excludes any form of appeal against an award.[137]

The WTO Appellate Body offers a possible model for an investment appellate mechanism.[138] However, there are important differences between the WTO system and the investment treaty regime. First, individuals or corporations cannot bring a claim before a WTO panel—the system is State-centric. This impacts on who should appoint members of an investment treaty appellate body. Second, the WTO Appellate Body adjudicates over a coherent set of rules.[139] Similarly worded treaty provisions may need to be interpreted in different ways because of

---

[132] On open textured rules see H Hart, *The Concept of Law* (2nd edn, OUP 1994) 136: 'In every legal system a large and important field is left open for the exercise of discretion by courts and officials in rendering initially vague standards determinate....'

[133] In the context of applying open textured rules and resolving conflicts between competing principles, the concept of sustainable development may have a role to play as an interstitial norm. See V Lowe, 'Sustainable Development and Unsustainable Arguments' in A Boyle and D Freestone (eds), *International Law and Sustainable Development: Past Achievements and Future Challenges* (OUP 1999) 31.

[134] An appellate mechanism might also improve decision making by correcting errors (for example, an incorrect interpretation of domestic law). This is not a function which could be performed by a preliminary ruling procedure.

[135] See ICSID Secretariat, 'Possible Improvements of the Framework for ICSID Arbitration' (22 October 2004) [21].

[136] See, for example, Schreuer and Weiniger (n 123) 1203–05.

[137] It is argued that the parties to an IIA could amend this rule inter se, as to do so would not undermine the object and purpose of the ICSID Convention. ICSID Secretariat, 'Possible Improvements of the Framework for ICSID Arbitration' (22 October 2004) annex [2].

[138] See references to the WTO system in the ICSID Secretariat, 'Possible Improvements of the Framework for ICSID Arbitration' (22 October 2004) annex.

[139] Legum argues that standing international tribunals have typically been created in the context of a single multilateral instrument with a single set of provisions to be consistently applied, and that in the absence of such an environment the idea of an appellate mechanism will have little traction. (B Legum, 'Options to Establish an Appellate Mechanism for Investment Disputes' in K Sauvant (ed), *Appeals Mechanism in International Investment Disputes* (OUP 2008) 236).

the context and structure of investment treaties. Third, there are fewer WTO cases compared to investment cases.[140] This means that a smaller group of judges can deal with appellate work in the WTO. The larger workload in investment treaty cases is likely to require a large investment appellate body, which in itself creates problems for consistency. What if one panel of appellate body members disagrees with an earlier panel of appellate body members?[141] There are a number of difficult questions associated with the design of such a system, such as the grounds of appeal[142] and the appointment of members to an investment appellate body. Nevertheless an appropriately designed appellate body could reduce inconsistency in decision making. It may also serve other beneficial functions such as improving the legitimacy of the investment treaty system.[143]

Any legal system needs to balance the competing desire for finality with the quest for accuracy and consistency. A key advantage of the ICSID system (at least in the eyes of an investor) is the finality of investment treaty awards.[144] Awards can only be annulled on narrow grounds, which focus on the procedural propriety of the arbitral proceedings.[145] Investment treaty proceedings are typically lengthy. Adding an appeal phase will lengthen the time between initiation of proceedings and an investor having a final enforceable decision.[146] Ideally, any appellate mechanism would replace the present annulment system under the ICSID Convention.[147] A potentially problematic situation would arise where an appellate mechanism is not adopted universally—which seems likely. Investors might then be incentivized to treaty shop.[148] If, for example, the decisions of an appellate body were not favourable to an investor, the investor might to submit its claim under a treaty which is not subject to such a mechanism.

When the proposal for an appellate mechanism was first floated by ICSID, States showed little interest in this reform.[149] However, a number of investment treaties, including CETA, refer to the possibility of the State parties adopting some type

---

[140] The WTO publishes information on the number of Panel Reports appealed. See <www.wto.org/english/tratop_e/dispu_e/stats_e.htm>.

[141] To an extent this problem is mitigated in the context of the WTO body by the system of exchange of views. See WTO Appellate Body, 'Working Procedures for Appellate Review', WT/AB/WP/6, Rule 4.

[142] For example, if appeal is only available in relation to a 'manifest error of law', rather than any error of law, then this might undermine the role of such a mechanism in increasing consistency. Consideration also needs to be given to the extent to which an appellate body might have a corrective function in relation to errors of fact.

[143] See G Bottini, 'Reform of the investor-State arbitration regime: the appeal proposal in Reform of Investor-State Dispute Settlement: In Search of A Roadmap' (2014) 11(1) Transnational Dispute Management.

[144] L Reed, J Paulsson, and N Blackaby, *Guide to ICSID Arbitration* (Kluwer 2010) 15.

[145] ICSID Convention Art 52.

[146] See ICSID Secretariat, 'Possible Improvements of the Framework for ICSID Arbitration', (22 October 2004) [21].

[147] Non-ICSID awards would still be subject to annulment proceedings at the seat of arbitration.

[148] See I Ten Cate, 'International Arbitration and the Ends of Appellate Review' (2012) 44 International Law and Politics 1109, 1196–98.

[149] See ICSID Secretariat, 'Suggested Changes to the ICSID Rules and Regulations' 12 May 2005 [4].

of appellate mechanism.[150] One possible reason why States may wish to maintain the status quo relates to their interest in not ceding too much power to permanent institutions. In the context of the WTO Trachtman has explained that less specific standards are consistent with a transfer of power to a dispute resolution body while more specific standards are more consistent with the reservation of continuing power by member States.[151] Similarly, Alvarez has described the phenomenon of treaty makers using dispute settlers to 'complete' their treaty contracts.[152] Do States want to leave it to an appellate body to decide 'definitively' on the extent to which the fair and equitable treatment standard protects legitimate expectations?

An appellate body may arrive at an unintended interpretation of an investment treaty but being permanent it is far harder to correct such a decision. For example, even if it were possible to correct the decision with a bilateral 'amendment' of the relevant investment treaty at issue, one State may be happy with the decision, or at least not agree with the alternative interpretation offered by the other State party to the treaty.[153] The one-off nature of adjudication limits the interpretative power of investment tribunals.[154] States may therefore prefer a limited amount of inconsistency to unintended and consistent interpretations of investment treaties. Therefore, States as repeat players in the investment system may have an interest in a fragmented system of adjudication.

A different but perhaps less effective solution to the problem of inconsistency is for States to use their powers as (international) law makers. In other words, a solution can be sought at the normative rather than an institutional level. Rather than leaving it to investment treaty tribunals or some type of appellate body to determine the meaning of vague provisions and resolve inconsistencies, States can clarify the rules contained in investment treaties.[155] In this way, States retain greater power rather than ceding this power to a permanent appellate body.

States can be seen utilizing their law making powers in two ways.

a. entering into investment treaties which contain more detailed provisions; and/or

b. providing a mechanism for the treaty parties to issue a binding interpretation of the investment treaty.[156]

We can see both of these mechanisms being utilized in the CETA text. For example, CETA provides illustrative examples of conduct that will breach the fair

---

[150] See CETA Investment Chapter Art X.42; The Dominican Republic-Central America—United states Free Trade Agreement (adopted 5 August 2004, entered into force 1 March 2006) annex 10-F.
[151] J Trachtman, 'The Domain of WTO Dispute Resolution' (1999) 40 HILJ 333, 335.
[152] J Alvarez, *International Organizations as Law-Makers* (OUP 2006) 532.
[153] cf Ecuador's failed attempt to obtain an interpretation of the US–Ecuador BIT. *Republic of Ecuador v United States of America*, PCA Case no 2012-5.
[154] S Schill, 'The Virtues of Investor-State Arbitration' (*EJIL: Talk!*, 19 November 2013) available at: <www.ejiltalk.org/the-virtues-of-investor-state-arbitration/> accessed 8 March 2015.
[155] These solutions are not of course mutually exclusive and could be combined.
[156] An alternative is for States to issue non-binding interpretations that tribunals are required to 'take into account'.

and equitable treatment standard.[157] Similarly, Annex B to the US Model BIT, which has proved influential, gives guidance as to the circumstances in which a State measure will amount to an indirect expropriation.[158] In addition, the CETA text provides for the Trade Committee to adopt an 'interpretation' which will be binding on a Tribunal from a specified date.[159]

Negotiating investment treaties with more detailed rules is likely to provide greater consistency. However, there is always the risk that by using more concrete rules that such rules will be either under-inclusive or over-inclusive (that is, exclude or include situations which the treaty negotiators might not have foreseen).[160] However, the adoption of 'interpretation' may raise various due process and rule of law concerns.[161] The distinction between an interpretation and an amendment is often elusive.[162] A retroactive amendment to a treaty, particularly for the purpose of gaining an advantage in a pending dispute is problematic. States have in diverse circumstances passed retroactive legislation for the purpose of obtaining an advantage in pending litigation.[163] For example, in a domestic context, this has taken the form of legislation purporting to decisively interpret the parties' rights and obligations under domestic law. The European Court of Human Rights stated that 'the principle of the rule of law and the notion of fair trial enshrined in aticle 6 preclude any interference by the legislature—other than on compelling grounds of the general interest—with the administration of justice designed to influence the judicial determination of a dispute'[164] Ideally any interpretations would be prospective to minimize due process and rule of law concerns.[165]

Many investment treaties were drafted and entered into at a time when there had been no investment treaty cases, or very few such cases. There is now a considerable body of arbitral practice. While there may be disagreement on a number of issues, there is at least greater clarity as to where this disagreement lies.[166] Given the difficulties experienced in the past in agreeing on multilateral investment

---

[157] CETA Art X.9.
[158] 2012 United States Model Bilateral Investment Treaty annex B.   [159] CETA Art X.27.
[160] See M Koskenniemi, *From Apology to Utopia* (CUP 2005) 591.
[161] The principle of good governance in the ILA Delhi Declaration on Sustainable Development suggests that States and international organizations should respect due process and observe the rule of law.
[162] See *Territorial Dispute (Libyan Arab Jamahiriya v Chad)* (1994) ICJ Rep 6, 29 para 60; *Pope & Talbot Inc v The Government of Canada*, UNCITRAL, Award in Respect of Damages (31 May 2002) para 47.
[163] cf *Petrobart Limited v The Kyrgyz Republic*, SCC Case no 126/2003, Award (29 March 2005) (adoption of new law establishing that foreign investment law was to be interpreted in restrictive way).
[164] *Agoudimos and Cefallonian Sky Shipping Co v Greece* App no 38703/97 (ECHR, 28 June 2001) [29]. See also *Stran Greek Refineries and Stratis Andreadis v Greece* App no 13427/87 (ECHR, 9 December 1994) [49]–[50].
[165] See G Kaufmann-Kohler, 'Interpretative Powers of the Free Trade Commission and the Rule of Law' in E Gaillard and F Bachand (eds), *Fifteen Years of NAFTA Chapter 11 Arbitration* (Juris 2011) 194.
[166] See, for example, C Schreuer and M Weiniger (n 123) 1197f (identifying a number of these issues).

treaties,¹⁶⁷ it might be expected that it would be difficult to reach consensus on the scope of substantive protection standards. States may still be able to agree on such issues on a bilateral basis. More promising would appear to be the potential to reach consensus on various jurisdictional issues on which tribunals have reached divergent conclusions.¹⁶⁸ While investors might desire a broader scope of protection, they are ill-served when it comes to investment planning by a lack of clarity as to whether or not their investment is protected at all. For example, CETA clarifies that the MFN clause will not apply to dispute settlement.¹⁶⁹ This may also address concerns that tribunals have interpreted their jurisdictional mandates too expansively, in favour of investors.¹⁷⁰

A limited amount of inconsistency may not be a negative feature of a system, as it allows for contestation.¹⁷¹ However, a goal of the investment treaty regime should be to aspire to greater consistency. Assuming that the various political hurdles could be overcome, an appellate mechanism is likely to lead to increased consistency in decision making. However, the implementation of an appellate mechanism is no guarantee that an appellate body would not adopt unintended interpretations of investment treaty provisions. It is a truism that treaties are disagreements reduced to writing.¹⁷² If there is a political disagreement between States as to whether the fair and equitable treatment standard protects legitimate expectations, should it be for an appellate body to resolve this disagreement? A preferable approach (at least from the perspective of some States) may be to take some of the power away from both arbitrators and any appellate body. The problem of inconsistency can be ameliorated by the State parties, when negotiating treaties, providing clearer guidance on issues which have divided investment treaty tribunals.

VII. A Reintroduction of the Local Remedies Rule?

The IPFSD suggests various policy options for the drafting of investment treaties, which could be particularly supportive of sustainable development.¹⁷³ One suggested option is that States should, in light of quality of the host State's administrative and judicial system, exclude ISDS from investment treaties or make ISDS a last resort after investors have exhausted local remedies. A subsequent publication by UNCTAD suggests that introducing a local remedies requirement is one of the options for:

> limiting investor access to ISDS can help to slow down the proliferation of ISDS proceedings, reduce States' financial liabilities arising from ISDS awards and save resources.

---

¹⁶⁷ See A Newcombe and L Paradell, *Law and Practice of Investment Treaties* (Kluwer 2009) Chapter 1 (outlining various attempts to negotiate multilateral investment treaties).
¹⁶⁸ See n 156 and Van Harten (n 44) 227f. ¹⁶⁹ CETA Investment Chapter Art X.7.4
¹⁷⁰ Van Harten (n 44) 251.
¹⁷¹ See S Franck, 'The Legitimacy Crisis in Investment Treaty Arbitration' (2005) 73 Fordham Law Review 1521, 1613.
¹⁷² P Allott, 'The Concept of International Law' (1999) 10 EJIL 31, 43.
¹⁷³ IPFSD 44.

Additional benefits may be derived from these options if they are combined with assistance to strengthen the rule of law and domestic legal/judicial systems.[174]

The rule of law has been identified as an important factor contributing to development.[175] It has been suggested that domestic institutions would be strengthened by the introduction of a requirement to exhaust local remedies.[176] Would the imposition of a local remedies clause support sustainable development?

The principal justification advanced for the local remedies rule under general international law is that a potential respondent State should be given an opportunity to redress an alleged violation of international law within the framework of its own legal system before being confronted with an international claim.[177] However, investment treaty tribunals have found the general international law requirement to exhaust local remedies is inapplicable to the system of investor–State arbitration.[178] ISDS is perceived as an effective remedy for investors as it allows them to bypass domestic legal systems. As explained by the Tribunal in *Amco v Indonesia*:

One of the reasons for instituting an international arbitration procedure is precisely that parties—rightly or wrongly—feel more confident with a legal institution which is not entirely related to one of the parties.[179]

However, not infrequently investment treaties contain an analogous requirement to pursue local remedies,[180] typically for a period of twelve or eighteen months. One Tribunal has called a provision of this kind 'nonsensical from a practical point of view'.[181] Clauses imposing such a requirement have been criticized on the basis that a local remedy is unlikely to be forthcoming within such a period,[182] and that such a clause is likely only to lead to further delay and expense.[183] For example, in *Urbaser v Argentina* the applicable BIT required an investor to pursue judicial proceedings before the competent courts of the respondent State for eighteen months

---

[174] UNCTAD, 'Reform of Investor-State Dispute Settlement: In Search of a Roadmap' (2013) 2 IIA Issues Note 8.

[175] See, for example, World Bank, *Governance and Development* (1992) 28.

[176] J Wouters and N Hachez, 'The Institutionalization of Investment Arbitration and Sustainable Development' in M-C Cordonier Segger, M Gehrig, and A Newcombe (eds), *Sustainable Development in World Investment Law* (Kluwer 2011) 635.

[177] See, for example, *Interhandel (Switzerland v United States of America)* (1959) ICJ Rep 6.

[178] See, for example, *RosInvestCo UK Ltd v The Russian Federation*, SCC Case no V079/2005, Award on Jurisdiction (1 October 2007) para 153.

[179] *Amco Asia Corporation and Others v Republic of Indonesia*, ICSID Case No ARB/81/1, Award (20 November 1984) para 177.

[180] *Ambiente Ufficio SPA and Others v Argentine Republic*, ICSID Case No ARB/08/9, Decision on Jurisdiction and Admissibility (8 February) 2013 para 608.

[181] *Plama Consortium Limited v Republic of Bulgaria*, ICSID Case No ARB/03/24, Decision on Jurisdiction (8 February 2005) para 224.

[182] Australian plain packaging legislation has been the subject of both investment treaty proceedings and a constitutional challenge. The High Court of Australia handed down its judgment approximately ten months after proceedings were commenced.

[183] C Schreuer, 'Consent to Arbitration' in P Muchnlinksi, F Ortino, and C Schreuer (eds), *The Oxford Handbook of International Investment Law* (OUP 2008) 846–48.

A Reintroduction of the Local Remedies Rule? 123

before commencing arbitration.[184] However, a study published by the Argentine Government indicated that from 1985–2000 the average time for resolution of similar disputes was six years and one month and no case had been decided on the merits within eighteen months. Even without any requirement to pursue local remedies, investment treaty proceedings typically take many years.

However, leaving aside the delay and expense associated with pursuing local remedies, there are a number of advantages to the local remedies rule. International judges have recognized that it can be of great benefit to have a prior decision of a domestic tribunal.[185] Domestic tribunals possess a comparative advantage not only in relation to questions of domestic law but also often in relation to factual issues.[186] A decision of a domestic tribunal may narrow the scope of a dispute before an international tribunal. For example, such a decision may assist an international tribunal in the determination of questions of attribution, international responsibility, and quantum.[187]

The exhaustion of local remedies rule has a different aspect in the context of international human rights law.[188] Human rights treaties impose on States an obligation to provide an effective remedy,[189] which forms an essential part of the system of human rights protection.[190] Therefore, States are not only provided with an opportunity to redress an alleged violation of international law, but they are obliged to provide an effective remedy. Consequently, the European Court of Human Rights has observed that the exhaustion of local remedies rules reflects the subsidiary nature of the international mechanisms of protection.[191] Furthermore, the European Court of Human Rights has expressed a willingness to defer to decisions of domestic courts, not only on questions of fact and domestic law. In *Roche v UK* the Grand Chamber of the European Court of Human Rights was prepared to afford a considerable margin of appreciation to a decision of the House of Lords on a 'mixed question' of domestic and international law:

Where, moreover, the superior national courts have analysed in a comprehensive and convincing manner the precise nature of the impugned restriction, on the basis of the relevant

---

[184] *Urbaser SA and Consorcio de Aguas Bilbao Bizkaia, Bilbao Biskaia Ur Partzuergoa v The Argentine Republic*, ICSID Case No ARB/07/26, Decision on Jurisdiction (19 December 2012) para 196.

[185] See, for example, *Camouco (Panama v France)* (ITLOS, 7 February 2000) Dissenting Opinion of Judge Anderson; *Prince von Pless Administration (Germany v Poland)* (Preliminary Objection) (1933) PCIJ Rep Series A/B no 54 16.

[186] *Kemmache v France (No 3)* App no 17621/91 [37]; *Camouco (Panama v France)* (ITLOS, 7 February 2000) Dissenting Opinion of Judge Anderson.

[187] See R Jennings and A Watts (eds), *Oppenheim's International Law: Volume 1 Peace* (OUP 1992) 524.

[188] See C Amerasinghe, *Local Remedies in International Law* (2nd edn, CUP 2004) 430–35.

[189] See Convention for the Protection of Human Rights and Fundamental Freedoms (adopted 4 November 1950, entered into force 3 September 1953) 213 UNTS 222 Art 13; International Covenant on Civil and Political Rights (adopted 16 December 1966, entered into force 23 March 1976) 999 UNTS 171 Art 2(3); American Convention on Human Rights (adopted 22 November 1969, entered into force 18 July 1978) 1144 UNTS 123 Art 25.

[190] D Shelton, *Remedies in International Human Rights Law* (2nd edn, OUP 2005) 173.

[191] *Akdivar v Turkey* App no 21893/93 (ECHR, 16 September 1996) [65]. See also A Trindade, *The Application of the Rule of Exhaustion of Local Remedies* (CUP 1983) 56.

Convention case-law and principles drawn therefrom, this Court would need strong reasons to differ from the conclusion reached by those courts by substituting its own views for those of the national courts on a question of interpretation of domestic law and by finding, contrary to their view, that there was arguably a right recognised by domestic law.[192]

Therefore, not only is there an opportunity for States to settle the relevant dispute, but there is also an incentive to provide a well-reasoned and convincing judgment, as the European Court of Human Rights may defer to the domestic court. Giving States a role to play in the dispute settlement process, and incentivizing high quality judgments, would appear to sit well with one of the goals of sustainable development by promoting good governance.[193] Furthermore, the balancing of competing interests implicit in decisions affecting sustainable development is best taken by those most closely affected.[194] Could such a system work in the context of international investment law? There are a number of reasons why this might be problematic in the context of investment treaty arbitration.

First, State parties to the European Convention are required to provide an effective remedy. States may allow individuals to directly invoke Convention Rights before domestic courts, although this is not strictly required.[195] However, in the context of investment treaty arbitration, generally there is no such requirement. Indeed, States seem more concerned about investors having 'two bites at the cherry'; investment treaties often contain fork-in-the-road clauses. In the context of NAFTA, an investor who raises a claim based on the NAFTA investment chapter before the Mexican courts cannot subsequently make a claim under NAFTA.[196] Furthermore, Canadian and US legislation precludes domestic courts from considering a claim based on NAFTA.[197] If domestic courts are adjudicating on claims based on different causes of action, this may limit the utility of their determinations in subsequent investment treaty proceedings.[198] Furthermore, investment treaty disputes are often very complex disputes involving commercial transactions, public law issues, different legal orders, and the need for expert witnesses. If

---

[192] *Roche v The United Kingdom* App no 32555/96 (ECHR, 19 October 2005) [120]. This dicta needs to be tempered by recognition that the Chamber found 9-8 that there was no violation of Art 6(1).

[193] ILA Delhi Declaration on Sustainable Development, Principle 6.

[194] cf *Burden v The United Kingdom* App no 13378/05 (ECHR, 29 April 2008) [42]: 'it is appropriate that the national courts should initially have the opportunity to determine questions of the compatibility of domestic law with the Convention and that, if an application is nonetheless subsequently brought to Strasbourg, the European Court should have the benefit of the views of the national courts, as being in direct and continuous contact with the forces of their countries.'

[195] *Iovchev v Bulgaria* App no 41211/98 (ECHR, 2 February 2006) [142]: '[The Convention] guarantees the availability at the national level of a remedy to enforce the substance of the Convention rights and freedoms in whatever form they might happen to be secured in the domestic legal order.'

[196] North American Free Trade Agreement (adopted 17 December 1992, entered into force 1 January 1994) (NAFTA) annex 1120.1(a).

[197] See W Dodge, 'Local Remedies under NAFTA Chapter 11' in E Gaillard and F Bachand (eds), *Fifteen Years of NAFTA Chapter 11 Arbitration* (Juris 2011) 39.

[198] It would of course be open to States to allow investors to invoke investment protection standards in domestic courts directly. However, this might raise complaints of discrimination unless the ability to bring a claim based on such standards were open to all investors.

investment treaty tribunals typically take a number of years to decide on such disputes, domestic courts should not be criticized for taking a similar period of time.

In addition, the international mechanisms of protection established by the European Convention on Human Rights are intended to be subsidiary to protection at the national level.[199] Domestic authorities are intended to have the primary role in ensuring the application of the Convention. This seems perhaps inevitable in light of the extent to which human rights concerns permeate State activity and the number of cases which arise under the Convention. However, investment treaty tribunals (at least in the system as currently conceived) have the primary function in applying investment law, and ensuring that States comply with their obligations under investment treaties.

In designing ISDS mechanisms States need to bear in mind the reason that ISDS is offered to investors in the first place. This is not to say that States should automatically accede to all the wishes of foreign investors in the drafting of investment treaties. However, if investment treaties are to fulfil the function of encouraging foreign investment then they must offer an *ex ante* incentive to foreign investors. In the absence of an effective mechanism for investors to enforce their rights, investment treaties are unlikely to provide such an incentive.[200] Some prominent commentators have expressed profound scepticism about the ability of many domestic legal systems to administer justice fairly in investment disputes.[201] In circumstances in which a domestic legal system is independent and efficient, a requirement to exhaust local remedies may not undermine an investor's view that their investment has sufficient protection. For example, the possibility of international arbitration (after the exhaustion of local remedies) may be seen as a useful back-stop when a domestic court is constitutionally required to apply domestic law in breach of international law. However, in circumstances where the quality of a legal system is low and there is the greatest need for improvement in domestic legal systems, a requirement to exhaust local remedies is likely to undermine the attractiveness of ISDS to a foreign investor.[202] This suggests that the local remedies rule cannot be used as a mechanism for encouraging better governance without compromising the very purpose of ISDS.

States need to consider carefully the purpose of introducing an exhaustion of local remedies requirement in an international investment agreement (IIA). What is the purpose of such a requirement? It might offer a very rudimentary filter, and

---

[199] *Akdivar v Turkey* App no 21893/93 (ECHR, 16 September 1996) [65]. See also A Trindade, *The Application of the Rule of Exhaustion of Local Remedies* (CUP 1983) 56.

[200] See n 35.

[201] See, for example, J Paulsson, 'Enclaves of Justice' (2007) 4(5) Transnational Dispute Management: 'it would be preposterous to imagine that even half of the world's population lives in countries that provide decent justice'. See similarly, C Schreuer, 'Do We Need Investment Arbitration' (2014) 11(1) Transnational Dispute Management.

[202] Typically, a claimant is not required to pursue local remedies which are 'futile'. However, this is generally a high bar. An investor might first be forced to submit a dispute to the local courts, an investment treaty tribunal and then an award might be subject to appeal, if an appellate mechanism is introduced.

reduce the number of claims against a State. However, it may also undermine the very purpose of offering ISDS in the first place. States have independent incentives for improving their legal systems. Independent and effective legal systems will promote good governance and facilitate sustainable development. However, the incorporation of a local remedies requirement in an investment treaty is unlikely to provide an effective mechanism for achieving this.

VIII. Conclusion

The concept of sustainable development only provides broad guidance as to how ISDS should be designed. Most importantly, it suggests that the system should not be biased in favour of the protection of foreign investments; sustainable development requires that a balance be struck between economic considerations and environmental and social concerns. Sustainable development also suggests that the public should have access to information about arbitrations, and there should be mechanisms for participation. This ensures that competing interests are taken into account, and this is likely to lead to higher quality decisions.

States have now had a significant amount of experience with ISDS. There are admittedly a number of States which are seeking to withdraw from the system. However, the fact that States that have been respondents continue to enter into investment treaties which provide for investor–State arbitration indicates that, at least in their view, the system is not fundamentally flawed. While there may be benefits in having a well-designed investment court, if such a court is not appropriately designed, it may do more harm than good. At least until a well-designed investment court becomes a realistic possibility, attention should be focused on a number of areas, including ensuring that the rules for arbitrator ethics are appropriately designed to cater for the unique features of the investment treaty system.

The new UNCITRAL Transparency Rules (if adopted) are likely to provide the public with significant information about pending cases. This is important to facilitate public participation through the provision of amicus briefs. Although the UNCITRAL Transparency Rules perhaps could have gone further in allowing parties to more fully participate in arbitral proceedings, the circumstances in which such participation is needed are likely to be limited. Furthermore, there is nothing to prevent the State parties to investment treaties providing for such a possibility. The UNCITRAL Transparency Rules should be seen as a floor and not a ceiling, limiting further improvements.

It is not uncommon for investment treaties to refer to the possibility of the State parties to create some type of appellate mechanism.[203] The introduction of an appellate body of some sort has the potential to lead to increased consistency of decision and lead to the correction of errors. However, careful consideration needs to be given to the design of such a system. States may not wish to cede

---

[203] See, for example, CETA Investment Chapter Art X.42.

significant power to an appellate body, which may adopt unintended interpretations. Furthermore, if such proceedings operate in addition to annulment proceedings, an appeals phase has the potential to increase the length of what are often very lengthy proceedings. However, the problem of inconsistent decisions can be ameliorated through States entering into more detailed investment treaties.

Foreign investment can play an important role in the development of States. In formulating their investment policies and frameworks, States have a number of instruments open to them, only one of which is entering into investment treaties. It is for States to decide whether entering into investment treaties which provide for ISDS is in their best interests. States are now better informed about the nature and implications of ISDS. Many older investment treaties contained very broad provisions, effectively leaving it up to arbitral tribunals to resolve many issues. States have sought to negotiate treaties, such as CETA, which are comparatively more detailed and which address many of the criticisms which have been addressed at the investment treaty system. Indeed, States have a variety of policy options open to them in designing ISDS, including (but not limited to) those set out in the IPFSD. Equipped with such a 'toolbox', States have the means to address the deficiencies that practice has revealed. However, if investment treaties are to play a role in encouraging foreign investment, then it is important not to lose sight of the fact that investment treaties need to provide an effective means for investors to enforce their rights. This will inevitably constrain State actions, to a degree, however it need not undermine sustainable development.

On 16 September 2015, after the text of this chapter had been finalized, the European Commission published a detailed draft investment chapter for inclusion in the Transatlantic Trade and Investment Partnership. This draft chapter proposes the creation of an investment court, and an appellate body. In suggesting the creation of such institutions it addresses a number of the criticisms which have been directed at the present system of ISDS, which I have sought to address in this chapter, notably the potential (real or apprehended) for bias, and the risk of inconsistent decisions. While prima facie the creation of such a system is to be welcomed, institution building is not simply an exercise on paper. The court and appellate body will need to be staffed by appropriate people committed to the rule of law, who enjoy the confidence of not only States but also investors, if it is to serve the purpose of encouraging foreign investment.

VI

The European Commission and UNCTAD Reform Agendas

Do They Ensure Independence, Openness, and Fairness in Investor–State Arbitration?

Gus Van Harten

I. Introduction

There have been proposals to reform investment treaty arbitration since the early stages of the present wave of investor lawsuits against States. In 2001, the US, Canada, and Mexico took steps to clarify procedural and substantive aspects of the NAFTA investment chapter.[1] In 2004, the ICSID Secretariat floated a proposal to establish an appellate body at ICSID.[2] In 2008, the UN Commission on International Trade Law (UNCITRAL) initiated a process to increase transparency in treaty-based investor-State arbitrations under the UNCITRAL Rules, culminating in the transparency rules of 2014.[3] More recently, the UN Conference on Trade and Development (UNCTAD) released an investment policy framework for sustainable development in 2012 that flagged options for reform of investor–State arbitration,[4] among other things, and, in 2013, the European Commission released a consultation paper that supplemented and promoted its negotiated text on investor–State arbitration in the Canada–EU CETA.[5]

---

[1] Free Trade Commission (NAFTA FTC), *Notes of Interpretation of Certain Chapter 11 Provisions* (31 July 2001), online: Government of Canada available at: <www.international.gc.ca/trade-agreements-accords-commerciaux/topics-domaines/disp-diff/NAFTA-Interpr.aspx> accessed 4 October 2014.

[2] International Centre for Settlement of Investment Disputes (ICSID) Secretariat, Possible Improvements of the Framework for ICSID Arbitration Discussion Paper (22 October 2004).

[3] UN Commission on International Trade Law (UNCITRAL), *Rules on Transparency in Treaty-based Investor-State Arbitration* (New York 2014).

[4] UN Conference on Trade and Development (UNCTAD), *Investment Policy Framework for Sustainable Development* (United Nations 2012).

[5] European Commission, 'Public consultation on modalities for investment protection and ISDS in TTIP' (undated) ('the consultation text'), available at: <http://trade.ec.europa.eu/doclib/docs/2014/march/tradoc_152280.pdf> accessed 8 October 2014; all page number references are to the pdf version of the consultation text. Canada–European Union: Comprehensive Economic and Trade Agreement (CETA): Consolidated CETA Text, available at: Department of Foreign Affairs and International Trade (Canada) <www.international.gc.ca/trade-agreements-accords-commerciaux/agr-acc/ceta-aecg/text-texte/toc-tdm.aspx?lang=eng>accessed 8 October 2014. This paper was completed prior to a new set of ISDS reforms proposed by the European Commission in September 2015.

With limited exceptions, these official reform initiatives have been a modest and incomplete response to the central problems with the process and institutional structure of investment treaty arbitration. They focus on procedural reforms or textual clarifications that maintain the special status of foreign investors to seek public compensation in international arbitrations under the treaties and the unparalleled power of arbitrators to decide those claims and to allocate public funds accordingly. Proposed official reforms, where they address matters of process or institutional structure, tend to focus on issues of transparency, public participation, and coherence in arbitrator decision-making. These are important concerns; yet the reform parameters that they delineate do not include, let alone take meaningful steps to address, deeper problems arising from the use of arbitration, with little or no judicial oversight, to review and discipline other sovereign actors and to award compensation from public budgets.

In this chapter, I review recent approaches taken by the European Commission and UNCTAD from the perspective of often-neglected issues of process and institutional structure in investment treaty arbitration. The review is focused on the Commission's negotiated text on investor–State arbitration in the Canada–EU CETA and the Commission's supplementary consultation document and on UNCTAD's investment policy framework for sustainable development. Both of these approaches to reform are evaluated with respect to the following concerns arising from the use of arbitration to make final decisions about the legality of sovereign conduct and the proper allocation of public money.[6]

Lack of institutionalized independence: Investment treaty arbitration does not incorporate institutional safeguards of judicial independence—such as secure tenure, guaranteed and pre-set remuneration, an objective method of case assignment, and prohibitions on concurrent work as adjudicator and counsel—that are otherwise present in this type of adjudicative decision-making. The absence of these safeguards opens arbitrators' decision-making to reasonable perceptions of bias and taints decision-making outcomes.

Lack of openness:[7] The arbitration process typically allows for information which in judicial decision-making would be presumptively public—to support accountability, independence, and fairness—to be kept confidential. In some cases, confidentiality is blanket in that it extends to all documentation and even to the mere fact of the arbitration.

Lack of procedural fairness: Other than the claimant investor and respondent (usually national) government, the arbitration process does not permit parties whose rights or interests are affected by the decision-making to have standing in the process. As a result, the adjudicator may not hear all sides to the dispute.

These core concerns about the process and institutional structure of investment treaty arbitration provide a framework for evaluating official reform agendas. They

---

[6] For an elaboration of these concepts, see G Van Harten, 'Investment Treaty Arbitration, Procedural Fairness, and the Rule of Law' in SW Schill (ed), *International Investment Law and Comparative Public Law* (OUP 2010); G Van Harten, *Investment Treaty Arbitration and Public Law* (OUP 2007) 159–75.

[7] I use 'openness' synonymously with 'transparency'.

point to the question of whether the European Commission or UNCTAD acknowledges the concerns and, if so, whether they take steps to address them. In response to these questions, it is concluded here that these official actors would make investment treaty arbitration more open, albeit with important limitations (especially for the UNCTAD approach). However, the Commission and UNCTAD do not acknowledge and address the lack of institutionalized independence and fairness in the system. As a result, their approaches would expand and consolidate a system of international adjudication to resolve investor–State disputes that is reasonably open but not judicially independent and procedurally fair.

II. The Approaches to Reform

The European Commission released excerpts of the Canada–EU CETA and a supplementary consultation document in 2014.[8] In September 2014, the full negotiated text of the CETA was released following unofficial leaks.[9] In its consultation document, the Commission acknowledged various problems and laid out an agenda for reform, signalling that this agenda would be pursued in the proposed EU–US Transatlantic Trade and Investment Partnership (TTIP) as well as the Canada–EU CETA. This documentation outlined a detailed but narrowly focused approach to reform of investment treaty arbitration. For example, although the topic is beyond the scope of this chapter, the Commission limited its proposals to questions that are internal to the treaties and arbitration process and it excluded the first-order question of whether investor–State arbitration is necessary and appropriate in CETA, TTIP, or other treaties. Also, as elaborated below, the Commission did not discuss, or responded in a very limited way, to concerns about process and institutional structure in investment treaty arbitration.

UNCTAD's investment policy framework for sustainable development was released in 2012.[10] This document marked a reorientation of the focus of the UNCTAD's Division on Investment and Enterprise after the Division's earlier notorious role in promoting investment treaties and investor–State arbitration without sufficient disclosure of associated risks for States.[11] The framework includes a discussion of various issues arising from investment treaties including their potential relationship to a wider development strategy, their substantive provisions, their procedural and institutional design, and their imbalanced focus on investor rights but not responsibilities. This discussion is at times vague and overly bureaucratic.[12]

---

[8] European Commission (n 5).
[9] Department of Foreign Affairs and International Trade (Canada) (n 5).
[10] UNCTAD (n 4).
[11] Z Elkins, AT Guzman, and BA Simmons, 'Competing for Capital: The Diffusion of Bilateral Investment Treaties 1960-2000' (2006) 60 Intl Org 811, 818–19.
[12] See, for example, UNCTAD (n 4) 17 ('As economies develop, skills needs and job opportunities evolve, making a constant adaptation and upgrading of education and human development policies a necessity').

Also, the framework lays out templates of options for States to handle the various issues. The resulting formal templates for reform are sometimes narrower in their approach to reform than the discussion in the text of the framework. In any event, neither aspect of the document responds meaningfully, and often does not mention, the basic concerns about process and institutional structure that are highlighted in this chapter.

III. Independence and Impartiality

Institutional safeguards of judicial independence and procedural fairness are standard features of international tribunals and domestic courts that resolve disputes about the legality of sovereign conduct. As mentioned earlier, their absence in investment treaty arbitration is an anomaly in light of the system's adjudicative function, providing a basis to suspect inappropriate bias in the system.[13] Do the Commission or UNCTAD approaches discuss this concern and propose adequate steps to address it?

In explaining its approach to investor–State arbitration, the Commission acknowledged issues of independence in investment treaty arbitration during a discussion of arbitrator ethics, conduct, and qualifications. The Commission stated that '[t]here is concern that arbitrators on ISDS [investor–State dispute settlement] tribunals do not always act in an independent and impartial manner.'[14] Less directly, UNCTAD also noted in its investment policy framework that '[t]he institutional set-up of the ISDS system is the cause of numerous concerns including perceived lack of legitimacy'. One may read this statement as an acknowledgement of problems linked to a lack of perceived independence and impartiality, although UNCTAD does not use those terms in its discussion of concerns about investor–State arbitration.

Despite these commendable acknowledgements, the Commission and UNCTAD do not discuss any of the reasons for concern about arbitrator independence and impartiality. For example, they do not mention the role of institutional safeguards of independence in judicial decision-making or offer an explanation for why those safeguards should not be present in the CETA and other treaties that authorize investor–State arbitration. Instead, after flagging a general concern about independence, the Commission narrowed the issue considerably by focusing on arbitrator conduct at the individual level without further mention of institutional reasons for concern or the role of institutional safeguards. Similarly, UNCTAD did not elaborate any reasons for concerns about 'perceived lack of legitimacy', shifting its discussion to proposals for partial reforms that would not address the lack of institutional safeguards and do not mention the option of instituting a judicial process.

---

[13] G Van Harten (n 6).   [14] European Commission (n 5) 12.

For example, after its statement about concern, as quoted above, the Commission immediately shifted to the issue of possible bias at an individual level[15] and proposed only the use of rules to check arbitrator conduct instead of institutional reforms.[16] Alongside such rules of conduct, the Commission proposed to allow conflict of interest challenges to arbitrators. This approach emphasized concerns about arbitrators at an individual level and avoided problems of perceived bias linked to the system's non-judicial institutional structure. As such, it ignored the foundational role of safeguards of adjudicative independence in domestic courts, international courts, and some other systems of arbitration. These safeguards include:[17]

(a) secure tenure for the adjudicator instead of case-by-case appointment;

(b) set remuneration for the adjudicator instead of case-by-case (that is, for-profit) payment;

(c) an objective method of case assignment such as lottery or rotation instead of executive discretion in case assignments;

(d) prohibitions on outside lawyering by the adjudicator; and

(e) a judicial process to resolve conflict-of-interest claims instead of a process controlled by executive officials.

A set of rules of conduct cannot substitute for these institutional safeguards. Among other things, as discussed below, the Commission's proposed code would rely on executive officials—not a judicial process—to police the arbitrator conduct and self-reporting.

As a result, both the Commission and UNCTAD approaches leave in place a system whose institutional design gives rise to reasonable suspicions of bias.[18] The perceptions may operate in favour of an investor or a State depending on the circumstances. For example, because the arbitrators are appointed on a case-by-case basis and paid lucratively by the appointment, all of them—like the lawyers and experts also paid in the litigations—depend financially on whoever can trigger an actual litigation. Under investment treaties, only foreign investors have this power and only States can be ordered to pay compensation for violating the treaty. As a result, it is foreign investors who decide whether a particular litigation will take place in all cases and the investors' (or its financial backers') commitment of resources to fund the litigation must be justified ultimately based on the prospect

---

[15] ibid (emphasis added) ('Because the individuals in question may not only act as arbitrators, but also as lawyers for companies or governments, concerns have been expressed as to potential bias or conflicts of interest').

[16] ibid 13 (characterizing the problem as '[m]ost existing investment agreements do not address the issue of the conduct or behaviour of arbitrators' and stating that the Commission 'aims to establish clear rules to ensure that arbitrators are independent and act ethically'. Further: 'The EU will introduce specific requirements in the TTIP on the ethical conduct of arbitrators, including a code of conduct. This code of conduct will be binding on arbitrators in ISDS tribunals set up under TTIP').

[17] Van Harten (n 6).   [18] ibid.

of State liability. This feature of arbitrators' financial dependence operates in favour of claimants (and any financial backers), especially deep-pocketed actors who are more able to finance future litigation.

Alternatively, an arbitrator who lacks secure tenure and seeks future appointments will depend on whoever has the default power to appoint arbitrators when the disputing parties do not agree or do not appoint. On this point, the Commission approach is to grant this default authority to the Secretary-General of the World Bank's International Centre for Settlement of Investment Disputes (ICSID).[19] The ICSID Secretary-General is an executive not a judicial official and it is inconsistent with judicial independence for an executive official to choose who decides a case after learning who has sued whom and in what context. This structure of appointing power gives an opportunity for the executive official to ensure that sensitive cases are kept in safe hands depending on the power politics surrounding the claim. As such, the lack of secure tenure for arbitrators appears to operate in favour of whichever States or claimants have greater influence over the ICSID Secretary-General and, more broadly, ICSID and the World Bank. In the case of ICSID, the appointment of the Secretary-General requires the relevant individual to be nominated by the World Bank President. By convention since the Second World War, the World Bank President is effectively a nominee of the US Administration who is in turn appointed based on a decision-making process that is controlled by the major Western capital-exporting States based on the Bank's weighted voting system.[20] In this aspect of the adjudicative structure, therefore, there is reason to perceive bias in favour of the US and the other major capital-exporters and, by extension, in favour of US and Western corporate interests.

For its part, UNCTAD does not elaborate either individual or institutional reasons to doubt the independence of investor–State arbitrators.[21] Also, UNCTAD does not mention the option of a code of arbitrator conduct.[22] Its investment policy framework refers to the issue of adjudicative independence as, ironically, a rationale for replacing domestic courts with investor–State arbitrators and as an objective for regulatory institutions and government in general.[23] Yet UNCTAD expresses no concern that investor–State arbitrators themselves may have biases or conflicts of interests, especially in the absence of judicial safeguards. As a result, UNCTAD falls far short of discussing concerns about lack of independence and impartiality in investor–State arbitration. UNCTAD also does not mention the apparently logical option of using international judges, not arbitrators, where domestic judiciaries are not thought to be reliable.

---

[19] CETA (n 5) Art X.25(2) and (3).
[20] Van Harten, *Investment Treaty Arbitration and Public Law* (n 6) 170.
[21] UNCTAD (n 4) 57.   [22] ibid.
[23] ibid 34 ('In the implementation of investment policies Governments should strive to achieve: (1) integrity and impartiality across Government and independence of regulatory institutions, subject to clear reporting lines and accountability to elected officials...') and 56 ('Most [investment treaties] allow investors to bypass domestic courts or host States.... The goal is to take the dispute out of the domestic sphere, to ensure independence and impartiality of the arbitrators...').

Instead, UNCTAD lays out a more limited option of establishing 'a system with permanent or quasi-permanent arbitrators' or 'an appellate mechanism'.[24] This proposal is not accompanied by an explanation of what it would mean to have permanent arbitrators or of the anticipated structure of an appellate mechanism. For present purposes, the key question is whether these options would incorporate the safeguards of adjudicative independence that are missing at present in ISDS and that give rise to reasonable perceptions of bias. UNCTAD's avoidance of these issues is an important omission in its discussion of 'perceived lack of legitimacy' in investment treaty arbitration.

There are other reasons to suspect bias on the part of arbitrators in the absence of institutional safeguards of independence. For example, based on their financial interests, there is reason to suspect that many arbitrators depend on gatekeepers in the arbitration industry (typically senior arbitrators) to improve their prospects for future appointment.[25] Similarly, there is reason to suspect dependence on governments that have greater power to push for investment treaties that authorize investor–State arbitration. Ultimately, problems of perceived bias arise from the decision not to include the usual institutional safeguards in a context of final adjudication of disputes over the legality of sovereign action and the proper allocation of public funds. The Commission fails to address the problems by focusing exclusively on individual reasons for perceived bias, UNCTAD does the same by not elaborating on the same rationales for perceived lack of legitimacy.

The Commission acknowledges a further issue arising from the absence of institutional safeguards. This is a conflict of interest called issue conflict, which is endemic in investment treaty arbitration. The conflict arises because arbitrators work concurrently as lawyers. Indeed, repeat players in the system work regularly both as arbitrators and as lawyers.[26] Where, in their role as adjudicator, such individuals decide issues that are of potential interest to a paying client in another case, an issue conflict is created. The Commission purports to address the problem by establishing rules of arbitrator conduct to be policed by an executive official where there is a complaint by a disputing party.[27] This is an inadequate response for several reasons. For example, it assumes that the disputing parties will be able to uncover the outside counsel work of arbitrators even though investor–State arbitrations are sometimes completely confidential. Unless an arbitrator declares a situation of potential conflict, the disputing party may have no way of knowing of the arbitrator's role as counsel. Further, many investment treaty cases raise similar legal issues because they turn on commonplace treaty terms such as 'investment'

---

[24] ibid 57 (UNCTAD policy option 6.3.0: 'Improve the institutional set-up of [investor-State arbitration], for example: consider a system with permanent or quasi-permanent arbitrators and/or an appellate mechanism').

[25] Y Dezaley and B Garth, *Dealing in Virtue: International Commercial Arbitration and the Construction of a Transnational Legal Order* (University of Chicago Press 1996) 45 and 124.

[26] N Bernasconi-Osterwalder, L Johnson, and F Marshall, 'Arbitrator Independence and Impartiality: Examining the dual role of arbitrator and counsel' (International Institute for Sustainable Development 2011).

[27] CETA (n 5) Art X.25 (10).

and 'investor'. Given the frequency with which some issues arise across the system, an arbitrator who also works as counsel is reasonably presumed to have a conflict of interest.

Conflicts of interest among investor–State arbitrators could be addressed by barring individuals from working as lawyers during, and for a set period before and after, any work as an arbitrator. Put differently, the problem arises from the absence of a basic institutional safeguard of judicial independence in the system. Neither the Commission nor UNCTAD mention this straightforward option to address arbitrator conflict.

Like UNCTAD, the Commission proposes an appellate body for the EU–US TTIP (albeit without having negotiated one in the Canada–EU CETA).[28] Although presented by the Commission and UNCTAD primarily as a way to improve coherence in arbitrators' decisions, an appellate body would enhance independence in the system if it were based on a judicial model. However, there are reasons to doubt that an appellate body would be established and, importantly, that it would reflect a judicial model. First, the Commission and UNCTAD do not refer to the need for an appellate body to be based on a judicial process. Second, if the Commission were serious about establishing an appellate body, one wonders why it did not take steps toward establishing one in the CETA, which was negotiated with a far weaker party than the US. In its consultation text on CETA and TTIP, the Commission simply expresses an aspiration to propose an appellate body in future.[29] Third, the idea of an appellate body has been floated for at least ten years and appears moribund at present, especially in the US. Fourth, the Commission and UNCTAD's ambiguous proposals for an appellate body appear to maintain the role of arbitrators before any appeal. To make the system fully and reliably independent, judges would need to replace arbitrators throughout the process.

The Commission came closest to addressing some of the institutional reasons for perceived bias when it proposed a roster of investor–State arbitrators.[30] UNCTAD did the same by flagging the option of permanent or quasi-permanent arbitrators, albeit without discussion.[31] A set roster of adjudicators could be a positive step toward a judicial process. Yet the Commission says little, and UNCTAD nothing at all, about the institutional context for the roster. First, neither official actor indicates whether roster members would have tenure and set remuneration and whether they would be barred from side work as lawyers. Second, in the model negotiated by the Commission in the CETA, it is problematic that: (a) the roster will not apply to all arbitrators but only to presiding and State-appointed arbitrators; (b) an executive official will choose who is appointed from the roster case-by-case; and (c) the executive official will be able to appoint arbitrators from outside the roster if the treaty's States parties cannot agree on the roster's membership.[32]

---

[28] European Commission (n 5) 17.   [29] ibid 17.   [30] ibid 13.
[31] UNCTAD (n 4) 57.   [32] CETA (n 5) Art X.25(2)–(4).

For two decades, this loophole has apparently foiled the similar roster in NAFTA investor–State arbitration.[33] Finally, the Commission did not justify its proposal for a roster based on concerns about perceived bias but rather based on less glaring concerns about the lack of qualifications of arbitrators[34] and UNCTAD linked its suggestion for permanent or semi-permanent arbitrators primarily to the problem of inconsistency, without mentioning independence or impartiality.

These omissions to acknowledge and take meaningful steps to ensure independence and impartiality in the adjudicative process undermine the reform agenda of the Commission and UNCTAD. The implications emerge whenever that agenda depends on decision-making that should be fair and independent. For instance, the Commission has planned to address frivolous claims in investment treaty arbitration by giving arbitrators the power to decide whether a case (in which they will earn significant income) should proceed.[35] This creates a clear conflict of interest: frivolous claims should be vetted by an actor who does not have a financial stake in the outcome of the decision to vet. Also, the Commission suggests that retired judges may be well-suited to the role of arbitrator or may have relevant policy expertise.[36] Yet the Commission does not take the next step of replacing the arbitrators with judges who have expertise in the relevant area. The Commission also does not mention that a retired judge who seeks re-appointment as an arbitrator would have the same inappropriate financial incentive as other arbitrators. Lastly, both the Commission and UNCTAD promote textual clarifications of investment treaties in order to address past abuses of arbitrator power.[37] A key problem with this approach is that, in the absence of institutional safeguards, outcomes in investment treaty arbitration lack integrity regardless of the underlying text.

In essence, the approaches of the Commission and UNCTAD allow foreign investors to transfer adjudicative power from domestic and regional courts to arbitrators and executive officials, none of whom can claim the independence of a domestic or international judge who is subject to the usual safeguards. While both official actors mention the problem of perceived bias, they do not discuss the institutional reasons for this problem or highlight the straightforward solution of replacing financially dependent arbitrators with judges.

IV. Openness

The lack of openness in investment treaty arbitration has been criticized since the late 1990s. NAFTA governments responded by issuing a joint interpretation of NAFTA in 2001 to authorize disclosure of documents in investor–State arbitration and by

---

[33] North American Free Trade Agreement (signed 17 December 1992, into force 1 January 1994) (NAFTA), Art 1124(4), 32 ILM 296 and 605.
[34] European Commission (n 5) 13.
[35] ibid 14. UNCTAD (n 4) 57, makes a similar proposal.
[36] European Commission (n 5) 13.   [37] ibid 8.

incorporating provisions on transparency in new trade and investment treaties.³⁸ Similarly, in 2010, UNCITRAL issued new transparency rules for UNCITRAL investor–State arbitration although unfortunately these reforms, in contrast to other amendments of international arbitration rules, did not extend to new arbitrations under existing treaties that authorize UNCITRAL arbitration.³⁹ In the process, some European States including France and Germany took the position that investor–State arbitration should be kept confidential, without the consent of the disputing parties to make public any information about the arbitration.⁴⁰

Allowances for secrecy at the option of a party to the proceeding may be appropriate in commercial arbitration where the implications of a dispute are typically limited to the disputing parties. Yet secrecy is fundamentally misplaced in investment treaty arbitration where arbitrators regularly review decisions of legislatures, governments, and courts on matters of public interest and where they award compensation from public funds. These are among the highest powers an adjudicator can exercise.⁴¹ In a democratic adjudicative process, such powers need to be exercised publicly—subject to specific exceptions for judicially approved purposes such as national security—to ensure accountability, independence, and fairness. Even today, some investment treaty awards are not public and, to an unknown extent, the very fact of an arbitration may not be public.⁴²

In this context, one should expect clear commitments to openness from the European Commission and UNCTAD. The Commission approach delivered in this respect, with some limitations, while the UNCTAD position remained more tentative. In particular, UNCTAD took the relatively soft stance that States should 'foster accessibility of documents (for example, information about the case, party submissions, decisions and other relevant documents)'. On this point, UNCTAD noted that '[e]nhanced transparency of ISDS claims could enable broader and informed public debate as well as a more adequate representation of stakeholder

---

³⁸ NAFTA FTC (n 1). Canada recently pulled back from this position in the Canada–China BIT by permitting the host State to an arbitration claim to withhold all documents other than awards from disclosure where it decides this is in the public interest, Agreement between the Government of Canada and the Government of the People's Republic of China for the Promotion and Reciprocal Protection of Investments (signed 9 September 2012, entered in force 1 October 2014) ('Canada–China BIT') available at: <www.international.gc.ca/trade-agreements-accords-commerciaux/agr-acc/fipa-apie/china-text-chine.aspx?lang=eng> accessed 12 October 2014, Art 28(1).

³⁹ UNCITRAL, *Rules on Transparency in Treaty-based Investor-State Arbitration* (United Nations 2014).

⁴⁰ UN General Assembly, UNCITRAL Working Group II (Arbitration and Conciliation), 53rd Sess, Vienna, 4–8 October 2010, 'Settlement of commercial disputes; Transparency in treaty-based investor-State arbitration; Compilation of comments by Governments; Note by the Secretariat; Addendum' (4 August 2010), UN Doc A/CN.9/WG.II/WP.159/Add.2, 5–7.

⁴¹ Van Harten, *Investment Treaty Arbitration and Public Law* (n 6) ch 3.

⁴² In a recent empirical study, it was found that a known award on jurisdiction was not publicly available in twenty-two of 174 (13%) investment treaty cases reviewed; this would not account for unknown cases in which all awards and other documents are not publicly available. G Van Harten, 'Arbitrator Behaviour in Asymmetrical Adjudication: An Empirical Study of Investment Treaty Arbitration' (2012) 50 Osgoode Hall LJ 211, 228, 233.

interests, prevent non-transparent deals and stimulate balanced and well-reasoned arbitral decisions'.[43]

These were helpful statements by UNCTAD but they fell short of a clear commitment to openness in investment treaty arbitration. UNCTAD used the hortatory language of 'fostering' accessibility and did not mention the important links between openness on the one hand, and, on the other hand, independence and accountability. In particular, the UNCTAD position appeared to fall short of a requirement for presumptive publication of all documents arising from the adjudicative process. In these respects, UNCTAD did not endorse the principle of openness.

In clearer terms, the European Commission—in the CETA and its consultation text—accepted and responded to the problem of confidentiality in investment treaty arbitration. The Commission stated that the lack of openness jeopardizes the legitimacy and accountability of the system, prevents stakeholders from being informed about the process, and undermines consistency and predictability.[44] Also, in the CETA, the Commission negotiated for a requirement that documents and hearings be public.[45] This requirement for publication of documents, in particular, is near-comprehensive because it includes a foreign investor's request for consultation or arbitration, the submissions of the parties, and all tribunal decisions.

However, the Commission approach has limitations. Most importantly, the Commission left it to arbitrators instead of judges to decide whether documents or hearings should be redacted or closed.[46] This is an issue of independence as well as openness. A decision not to disclose documents or hearings to the public should follow from a judicial process. All arbitrators who seek reappointment may see claimants at some level as customers and claimants, as well as States, sometimes oppose openness for self-serving reasons. Further, in past cases, arbitrators have erred in favour of confidentiality instead of openness when faced with ambiguity in a treaty text.[47]

Another problem with the Commission approach is that an investment treaty claim could be brought—and a settlement reached involving payment of public money and regulatory changes—entirely off the public record. To address this, the Commission should have clarified in the CETA that the fact and terms of a settlement reached by a State, after the invocation of the treaty, would be reported to the Commission and made public. In turn, the States parties would need to assign responsibility to monitor such reporting to a domestic authority. Despite these limitations, the Commission and to a much lesser extent UNCTAD do take positive steps to address the lack of openness.

---

[43] UNCTAD (n 4) 57.   [44] European Commission (n 5) 10.
[45] ibid 11. CETA (n 5) Art X.33.   [46] CETA (n 5) Art X.33(4)–(5).
[47] See, for example, *SD Myers v Government of Canada*, UNCITRAL, Procedural Orders No 3 and 11 (10 June 1999 and 11 November 1999); *Pope & Talbot v The Government of Canada*, UNCITRAL, Merits, Phase 2 (10 April 2001), 13(4) World Trade and Arb Mat 61.

V. Procedural Fairness

Investment treaty arbitration is arguably unfair for many reasons. For example, it is grossly imbalanced in the allocation or rights and responsibilities among investors, States, and other actors. Yet the most precise reason for unfairness in the system is procedural. The treaties give full standing rights for claimant investors and respondent governments but not for anyone else whose rights or interests—including reputational interests—are affected by the decision-making process.[48] Various parties may be in this position, such as an individual accused of involvement in corruption,[49] a domestic investor in competition with foreign competitors,[50] a sub-national government alleged to have violated the treaty,[51] or an indigenous community whose land claims overlap with those of the foreign investor.[52] Such parties cannot obtain full standing in the adjudication even though their rights or interests are affected and they have a distinctive perspective relative to the claimant and respondent.

The Commission alluded to this problem but did not address it. In particular, the Commission appeared to endorse *amicus* representation, as practised in some contexts of investment treaty arbitration, by stating in its consultation text that '[i]nterested parties from civil society will be able to file submissions to make their views and arguments known to the ISDS tribunal'.[53] Similarly, UNCTAD recommended that States should 'foster public participation (for example, amicus curiae and public hearings)' in investment treaty arbitration. This emphasis on 'civil society' or 'public participation' reflected a misunderstanding or avoidance of the key issue of procedural fairness. The issue is not one of participation by the public but rather of standing for parties commensurate to their affected rights or interests.

Provisions for *amicus* representation do not require a tribunal to give full standing to a party that has a direct interest in the proceeding.[54] *Amicus* representation merely allows a party, at the discretion of the arbitrators, to participate in proceedings—the Commission said they will be able to 'file submissions'—only to the extent and in ways authorized by the arbitrators.[55] This was inadequate

---

[48] Van Harten, 'Investment Treaty Arbitration, Procedural Fairness, and the Rule of Law' (n 6) 637; CETA (n 46).

[49] *Saint Marys VCNA v Government of Canada*, Claimant submission (13 May 2011) para 1 and 33-4.

[50] *Eureko BV v Republic of Poland*, Rajski separate opinion (19 August 2005) para 11.

[51] *AbitibiBowater Inc v Government of Canada*, Claimant submission (23 April 2009) para 8-9.

[52] *Bernhard von Pezold and Others v Republic of Zimbabwe*, ICSID Case No ARB/10/15, Procedural decision (26 June 2012) para 62.

[53] European Commission (n 5) 11.

[54] P Wieland, 'Why the Amicus Curia Institution is Ill-suited to address Indigenous Peoples' Rights before Investor-State Arbitration Tribunals: *Glamis Gold* and the Right of Intervention' (2011) 3 Trade, Law & Dev 334, 344–45 and 359–60.

[55] N Blackaby and C Richard, 'Amicus Curiae: A Panacea for Legitimacy in Investment Arbitration?' in M Waibel and others (eds), *The Backlash against Investment Arbitration* (Wolters Kluwer 2010) 259–66.

because it fell short of an automatic right of full participation by all affected parties.[56] Incidentally, in actual arbitrations, *amicus* status has been used rarely and with significant restrictions.[57]

By limiting their reforms to address procedural unfairness, the Commission and UNCTAD would permit arbitrators to continue to make decisions that affect parties—other than the claimant investor and respondent government—without hearing from them. That is unfair in a very basic way. It can be addressed only by requiring public notice of investor claims and by allowing time for other parties to apply for full standing in the process on the basis that the party's rights or interests are affected in a legally significant way by the adjudication.

VI. Conclusion

The reform agendas of the Commission and UNCTAD would not make investment treaty arbitration independent and fair. In the CETA, as elaborated by the Commission in its consultation text, the Commission did not discuss institutional rationales for suspected bias and did not incorporate institutional safeguards within the adjudicative process. For its part, UNCTAD did not mention independence or impartiality at all in its discussion of concerns about investor–State arbitration and did not elaborate individual or institutional reasons for perceived bias. With respect to openness, the Commission took meaningful steps but did not ensure that all documents and hearings would be public other than in circumstances of judicially authorized confidentiality; UNCTAD did not go as far and, in particular, did not commit clearly to the publication of all documents emerging from the adjudicative process. Lastly, neither the Commission nor UNCTAD proposed a right of parties whose rights or interests are affected by an investment treaty arbitration to have full standing in the process alongside claimant investors and respondent governments.

An independent and fair model of investment treaties would have at least two elements. First, it would use a judicial process instead of financially dependent arbitrators to resolve investor–State disputes where domestic courts are shown to lack sufficient independence and impartiality. Such a process would be based on well-known institutional safeguards that make courts independent, open, and fair. Second—though the topic is beyond the scope of this chapter—the model would include robust provisions to ensure that the State's regulatory role has at least an equivalent status alongside the State's responsibilities to protect foreign investors and that foreign investors' responsibilities were enforceable in the same manner

---

[56] E Levine, '*Amicus Curiae* in International Investment Arbitration: The Implications of an Increase in Third-Party Participation' (2012) 29 Berkeley J Intl L 200, 208–14; A Salazar, 'Defragmenting International Investment Law to Protect Citizen-Consumers: The Role of *Amici Curiae* and Public Interest Groups' (2013) Osgoode Hall Law School, Comparative Research in Law & Political Economy Research Paper No 6/2013 4–8.
[57] Wieland (n 54) 341–44.

Conclusion

as their elaborate rights. Briefly, the Commission and UNCTAD approaches did not affirm clearly and unequivocally the State's right to regulate, did not stipulate binding and actionable responsibilities for foreign investors, and did not require foreign investors to go first to domestic courts where the courts offer justice and are reasonably available. As a result, these approaches would consolidate the privileged legal status of foreign investors and the exceptional power of arbitrators—operating in a non-judicial process—to review other sovereign decision-makers and allocate public money to private parties. In essence, the Commission and UNCTAD agendas appear to have been designed to re-package arbitrator power in order to preserve it.

VII

Sustainable Development Provisions in International Trade Treaties

What Lessons for International Investment Agreements?

J Anthony VanDuzer

I. Introduction

There is a burgeoning literature on the relationship between bilateral investment treaties (BITs) and sustainable development.[1] Critics of the current regime are concerned that BITs do not contribute to sustainable development in host countries, especially developing countries.[2] Part of the concern is that investment protection in BITs has not been shown to strongly encourage inward investment which is essential to development.[3] At the same time, many worry that BITs' investment protection provisions impose constraints on States that restrict their ability to ensure that investment attracted to their territory contributes to sustainable development, such as by regulating to protect the environment, labour, and human rights.[4] Critics are also concerned about the extent to which the threat of investor–State arbitration discourages States from acting to promote sustainable development.[5]

---

[1] A Van Aaken and TA Lehmann, 'Sustainable Development and International Investment Law: A Harmonious View from Economists' in R Echandi and P Sauvé (eds), *Prospects in International Investment Law and Policy* (CUP 2013) 317–39.

[2] Sacerdoti characterizes this as a 'central issue of growing concern'. See the chapter by Sacerdoti in this volume.

[3] KP Sauvant and LE Sachs, 'BITs, DTTs, and FDI Flows: An Overview' in KP Sauvant and LE Sachs (eds), *The Effect of Treaties on Foreign Direct Investment: Bilateral Investment Treaties, Double Taxation Treaties and Investment Flows* (OUP 2009); JA VanDuzer, P Simons, and G Mayeda, *Integrating Sustainable Development into International Investment Treaties: A Guide for Developing Countries* (Commonwealth Secretariat 2013) 514–23.

[4] MW Gehring and A Kent, 'Sustainable Development and IIAs: From Objective to Practice' in A de Mestral and C Levesque (eds), *Improving International Investment Agreements* (Routledge 2013) 284–302.

[5] H Mann and K von Moltke, *NAFTA's Chapter 11 and the Environment* (International Institute for Sustainable Development 2006) 5–9.

While these concerns are frequently and variously expressed, they are also contested.[6]

Regardless of one's view of the role currently played by BITs in relation to sustainable development, all observers would agree that BITs are not primarily designed as instruments to promote sustainable development.[7] Rather they are instruments intended to protect and, as a consequence, encourage investment in party States. Admittedly, there has been some revision of treaty terms in some contexts to enhance the linkage between treaty provisions and sustainable development, but these changes have been very limited so far.[8]

This same observation may be made regarding the multilateral trade regime, even though the relationship between trade and sustainable development has received much more attention over a longer period of time. For example, the original GATT contains an exception for measures necessary to protect health and exhaustible natural resources.[9] There has been a WTO committee studying trade and the environment since 1994[10] and sustainable development is identified as an objective of the trading system in the preamble to the WTO Agreement.[11] WTO members included trade and the environment on the Doha Round negotiating agenda.[12] Despite this long history, however, not much has actually been achieved in terms of the adoption of treaty provisions to ensure the compatibility of WTO rules with sustainable development.[13]

To some extent, more development has occurred in regional and bilateral preferential trade and investment treaties (PTIAs) that contain investment protection provisions. More and more PTIAs contain provisions that are directly targeted

---

[6] J Viñuales, 'Foreign Investment and the Environment in International Law: An Ambiguous Relationship' (2009) 80 British Ybk Intl L 302–09.

[7] See also the chapter by Sacerdoti in this volume.

[8] K Gordon and J Pohl, 'Environmental Concerns in International Investment Agreements: A Survey' 2011/1 OECD Working Papers on International Investment available at: <www.oecd.org/dataoecd/50/12/48083618> accessed 16 December 2014; L Cuyvers, 'The Sustainable Development Clauses in Free Trade Agreements: An EU Perspective for ASEAN?' UNU-CRIS Working Papers W-2013/10 available at: <www10.iadb.org/intal/intalcdi/PE/2013/12733.pdf> accessed 19 December 2014.

[9] General Agreement on Tariffs and Trade (1947), Art XX.

[10] Decision on Trade and the Environment (1994). In the 1996 Singapore Ministerial Declaration the WTO members decided that the competent body in relation to labour rights was the International Labour Organization and that the ILO and WTO Secretariats would continue their existing collaboration (World Trade Organization, 'Singapore WTO Ministerial 1996: Ministerial Declaration' WT/MIN/(96)/DEC, 13 December 1996 para 4).

[11] Marrakesh Agreement Establishing the World Trade Organization (15 April 1994) 1867 UNTS 154 (1994) ('WTO Agreement (1994)'), preamble. In WTO, *European Communities—Conditions for the Granting of Tariff Preferences to Developing Countries—Report of the Appellate Body* (7 April 2004) WT/DS246/AB/R, the Appellate Body determined that sustainable development is one of the objectives of the WTO itself (para 94).

[12] World Trade Organization, 'Doha WTO Ministerial 2001: Ministerial Declaration' WT/MIN(01)/DEC/1, 20 November 2001 paras 13, 31. The focus of the agenda item is on relationship between existing WTO rules and specific obligations set out in multilateral environmental agreements (MEAs).

[13] L Bartels, 'The Chapeau of Article XX GATT: A New Interpretation', University of Cambridge Faculty of Law Research Paper Series, Paper No 40/2014 available at: <http://papers.ssrn.com/sol3/papers.cfm?abstract_id=2469852> accessed 19 December 2014, 2–4.

at encouraging sustainable development by supporting the protection of human rights, labour rights, and the environment in various ways.

This paper will explore recent developments in PTIAs to see what has been done in comparison to the practice in BITs and to enquire as to whether the more thoroughgoing approach to sustainable development evident in some PTIAs might be adopted in BITs. While such an approach would mark a radical shift from the current practice of some countries, in fact, some BITs already contain provisions related to sustainable development like those found in PTIAs.[14] As well, new PTIAs and BITs are increasingly likely to contain such provisions, though there is some variation across treaties entered into by different countries.[15] In order to present a survey of sustainable development provisions, however, it is first necessary to discuss briefly what is meant by sustainable development.

II. Sustainable Development

'Sustainable development' is a highly contested term and can mean different things in different contexts.[16] It has an economic aspect: achieving sustainable development entails liberalizing trade and investment policy in order to facilitate the access of goods to markets and stimulate foreign investment flows that will generate economic development.[17] But encouraging economic growth must be reconciled with the protection of the natural environment to ensure that future generations can continue to enjoy it as present generations do.[18] Increasingly, however, sustainable development's meaning is considered to be broader than environmental sustainability. Sustainable development is understood as having a social dimension, including the protection of human and labour rights.[19]

---

[14] Fifteen of the forty-seven investment treaties signed in 2011 included provisions related to sustainable development that were suggested in UNCTAD's Investment Policy Framework for Sustainable Development: E Tuerk and R Rojid, 'Towards a New Generation of Investment Policies: UNCTAD's Investment Policy Framework for Sustainable Development' (2012) Investment Treaty News, available at: <www.iisd.org/itn/2012/10/30/towards-a-new-generation-of-investment-policies-unctads-investment-policy-framework-for-sustainable-development/> accessed 16 December 2014.

[15] V Prislan and R Zandvliet, 'Mainstreaming Sustainable Development into International Investment Agreements: What Role for Labour Provisions?' in R Hofman, C Tams, and SW Schill (eds), *International Investment Law and Development* (Edward Elgar 2014) 7–8.

[16] For a discussion of the notion of sustainable development see also the chapter by Sacerdoti in this volume.

[17] UN Secretary General, 'The Latest Developments Related to the Review Process on Financing for Development and the Implementation of the Monterrey Consensus', UN Doc A/63/179 (2008).

[18] World Commission on Environment and Development, *Our Common Future*, UN Doc GA/42/427 (1987) 43, 34.

[19] Some conceptions of sustainable development are very broad. The United Nations has articulated a *right to development*. It incorporates many aspects of the definitions of sustainable development current in the environmental, human rights, and economics literature. UN Millennium Project, *Investing in Development: A Practical Plan to Achieve the Millennium Development Goals* (Routledge 2005) 3. Sengupta defines the right to development as follows: 'The Right to Development, which is an inalienable human right, is the right to a particular process of development in which all human rights and fundamental freedoms can be fully and progressively realized', A Sengupta, 'The Human

This paper focuses on two core aspects of sustainable development: labour rights and environmental protection. These aspects were chosen because they are those most frequently and comprehensively addressed in trade and investment treaties.[20]

III. Survey of Sustainable Development Provisions in International Trade and Investment Treaties Related to Labour Standards and the Environment

a) A taxonomy of sustainable development provisions— focusing on environmental protection and labour rights

An increasing number of BITs and PTIAs now address labour and environmental standards in some way. In their 2011 survey of 1,623 international investment agreements (including both BITs and PTIAs),[21] Gordon and Pohl, found that about 50 per cent of new treaties each year include some provisions on environmental protection.[22] No comparable large survey exists with respect to labour rights provisions. Until recently only a small number of PTIAs have addressed labour standards in some way.[23] In 2007, however, UNCTAD described the protection of labour rights as an emerging issue in its survey of international investment agreements entered into between 1998 and 2006.[24] A recent ILO study found that labour provisions were included in about one-third of all trade agreements that came into force between 2005 and 2013.[25]

It is possible to identify four main categories of provisions dealing with labour and environmental rights, some with several subcategories.

Right to Development' in BA Andreassen and SP Marks (eds), *Development as a Human Right* (HUP 2009) 11.

[20] Human rights are addressed in a small but growing proportion of trade and investment treaties. See L Bartels, 'Human Rights and Sustainable Development Obligations in the EU's Free Trade Agreements' (2013) 40 Legal Issues of Economic Integration; V Barral, 'Sustainable Development in International Law: Nature and Operation of an Evolutive Legal Norm' (2012) 23 Eur J Intl L.

[21] Gordon and Pohl (n 8). [22] ibid 13–25.

[23] For a comprehensive comparison of the various labour provisions in US and EU agreements, see R Grynberg and V Qalo, 'Labour Standards in US and EU Preferential Trading Arrangements' (2006) 40 J World Trade; see also K Gordon, 'International Investment Agreements: A Survey of Environmental, Labour and Anti-Corruption Issues' in OECD, *International Investment Law: Understanding Concepts and Tracking Innovations* (OECD 2008) 135; L Bartels, 'Social Issues: Labour, Environment and Human Rights' in S Lester and B Mercurio (eds), *Bilateral and Regional Trade Agreements: Commentary, Analysis and Case Studies* (CUP 2009) 342; and for an excellent critique of these provisions, see P Alston, 'Core Labour Standards and the Transformation of the International Labour Rights Regime' (2004) 15 Eur J Intl L 497–506. Cuyvers (n 8) reports that '[o]f the 89 FTAs in the Asian Development Bank database, only 6 have provisions which relate to labour policy and 10 relating to environmental policy. Only 3 mention ILO core labour conventions: the Japan-Philippines Economic Partnership Agreement, the Singapore-Costa Rica Free Trade Agreement and the Singapore-Panama Free Trade Agreement.'

[24] UNCTAD, *International Investment Treaties 1998-2006* (United Nations 2007) 92.

[25] International Labour Organization, *Social Dimensions of Free Trade Agreements* (ILO 2013) 19–20.

1. Provisions intended to ensure that treaty parties are not prevented by their treaty obligations from acting to protect labour rights and the environment.
    a. Preambles and objectives provisions referring to the protection of labour rights and the environment—though neither preambles nor separate provisions setting out the objectives of the agreement create substantive obligations or exceptions, both are relevant for the interpretation of the provisions of agreement, encouraging interpretation in a manner consistent with sustainable development.
    b. More specific standards for State treatment of foreign investors that preserve the ability of States to take measures to protect labour rights and the environment—a few newer treaties contain investor protection provisions with new and more specific language that seeks to ensure that *bona fide* measures to achieve legitimate public policy objectives, like the protection of labour rights and the environment, will not be found contrary to the substantive investor protection obligations in the treaty.
    c. Exclusions limiting the application of treaty obligations to labour and environmental measures. These take three main forms.
        i. General exceptions relating to labour rights and environmental protection, including some modelled on GATT Article XX.
        ii. Exceptions that exclude subsidies, government procurement, tax measures, or sectors of economic activity or areas of policy-making by States from some obligations in the treaty. These kinds of provisions can be used to protect some categories of State measures to achieve sustainable development.
        iii. Country specific reservations that exclude particular State measures, sectors or areas of policy-making from some obligations in the treaty. As in ii, these kinds of provisions can be used to carve out State measures to achieve sustainable development from the obligations in the treaty.
    d. Rules that give primacy to other international treaties relating to labour or the environment over the BIT or the PTIA.
2. Commitments to ensure the effectiveness of domestic laws related to labour rights and environmental protection.
    a. Commitments regarding the enforcement of existing labour and environmental standards in domestic law—one party's failure to enforce its domestic law may be something that the other party can complain about through a dispute settlement procedure, typically separate from the other dispute settlement procedures in the treaty.
    b. No derogation from the protection of labour rights or the environment under domestic law to attract investment.
    c. Cooperation on enforcement of labour and environmental standards—some treaties contemplate cooperation between parties with respect to enforcement and even provide for the creation of institutions to

facilitate enforcement as well as commitments for investors' home States to support capacity building related to enforcement in the host States where those investors operate.
3. Commitments to comply with identified labour and environmental standards—a few treaties commit States to high levels of protection for labour rights and the environment, sometimes by reference to identified international standards. Typically, these commitments are aspirational or 'best efforts' but some recent treaties impose binding obligations on parties to ensure that their domestic law meets defined standards.
4. Cooperation on labour rights and environmental protection.

The following sections provide a survey of PTIA and BIT provisions relating to environmental protection labour rights, using this taxonomy.

b) Environmental and labour rights protection provisions in PTIAs and BITs

1. Provisions intended to ensure that treaty parties are not prevented by their treaty obligations from acting to protect labour rights and the environment.
    a. Preambles and objectives provisions referring to the protection of labour rights and the environment

Treaty preambles are the most common way in which labour rights and environmental protection are referred to in PTIAs and BITs. In most treaties, it is the only way. The impact, however, is limited. A treaty preamble sets out the overall considerations of the party States in entering the treaty and provides part of the context for interpreting treaty obligations.[26] A preamble does not create or limit obligations in the treaty directly, but the interpretation of obligations and their application in particular situations should be informed by the compatibility of the interpretation or application with the preamble. Those interpreting the treaty, including dispute resolution bodies, should prefer the interpretation that best achieves the goals set out in the preamble and is otherwise consistent with it.

The relevance of the preamble for interpreting the obligations in a treaty is set out in the Vienna Convention on the Law of Treaties ('Vienna Convention'), which provides the basic framework for interpreting international treaty obligations. Article 31(1) of the Vienna Convention requires, in part, that treaty provisions be interpreted

…in good faith in accordance with the ordinary meaning to be given to the terms of the treaty in their *context* and in light of its object and purpose. (Emphasis added.)

The Vienna Convention goes on to define the context as consisting of the preamble as well as the treaty text and any annexes to the treaty. Consistent with the

---

[26] See also the chapter by Berner in this volume.

Vienna Convention, all provisions in a treaty, including reservations and exceptions, must be interpreted in light of the expressly stated objectives of the treaty, which may appear in the preamble. Any other statements in the preamble form part of the interpretive context.[27]

Several PTIAs contain language in their preambles that recognizes the importance of protecting the environment as well as labour rights as part of sustainable development. The EC–CARIFORUM Economic Partnership Agreement (EPA) articulates the need of the parties 'to promote economic and social progress for their people in a manner consistent with sustainable development by respecting basic labour rights…and by protecting the environment'.[28] The US Model BIT adopted in 2012 contains preambular language regarding the importance of the treaty being interpreted in a manner consistent with the protection of the environment and labour rights. After reciting its objectives of providing a stable environment for investment and stimulating investment, the US Model BIT provides as follows in its preamble:

Desiring to achieve these objectives in a manner consistent with the protection of health, safety, and the environment, and the promotion of internationally recognized labor rights[29]

The preamble to the 2004 Canadian Model investment treaty, which is used by Canada to negotiate both BITS and investment chapters in PTIAs, simply recognizes that increased investment will contribute to sustainable development.[30]

---

[27] In *In the Matter of Cross-Border Trucking Services—Final Report of the Panel* (6 February 2001) USA-Mex-98-2008-01 ('*Cross-Border Trucking Services (2001)*'), the panel noted that international tribunals in other contexts frequently refer to the preamble of a treaty for the purpose of determining the principal object of the treaty, in accordance with Art 31 of the Vienna Convention on the Law of Treaties (adopted 23 May 1969, entered into force 27 January 1980) 1155 UNTS 331, citing *The Lotus Case (France v Turkey)* (1927) PCIJ Rep Series A No 10; *Free Zones of Upper Savoy and the District of Gex Case (France v Switzerland)* (Order) (1929) PCIJ Rep Series A No 22; *Asylum Case (Colombia v Perú)* (1950) ICJ Rep 266, 276, 282 (at para 219, note 233).

[28] The preamble of the United States–Morocco Free Trade Agreement expresses the desire of the parties 'to strengthen the development and enforcement of…environmental policies…promote sustainable development, and implement this Agreement in a manner consistent with environmental protection and conservation', United States-Morocco Free Trade Agreement (signed 15 June 2004, entered into force 1 January 2006) available at: <http://wits.worldbank.org/GPTAD/PDF/archive/US-Morocco.pdf> accessed 19 December 2014 ('US–Morocco FTA') preamble. See also bilateral investment treaties: for example, Agreement between the Republic of Austria and Bosnia and Herzegovina for the Promotion and Protection of Investments (signed 2 October 2000, entered into force 10 October 2002) available at: <http://investmentpolicyhub.unctad.org/Download/TreatyFile/174> accessed 19 December 2014; Agreement between the Government of the Republic of Finland and the Government of the Republic of Nicaragua for the Promotion and Protection of Investments (signed 17 September 2003, not yet in force) available at: <http://investmentpolicyhub.unctad.org/Download/TreatyFile/1204> accessed 19 December 2014.

[29] US Model Bilateral Investment Treaty 2012 available at: <www.italaw.com/sites/default/files/archive/ita1028.pdf> accessed 19 December 2014 ('US Model BIT') preamble. '[I]nternationally recognized labor rights' is not defined. In Art 13 of the US model, the parties 'reaffirm their respective obligations as members of the International Labor Organization and their commitments under the *ILO Declaration on Fundamental Principles and Rights at Work and its Follow-Up*'.

[30] Canadian model FIPA available at: <http://italaw.com/documents/Canadian2004-FIPA-model-en.pdf> accessed 19 December 2014 ('Canadian Model BIT') preamble.

Some PTIAs go beyond preambular statements to specify that sustainable development, including the protection of the environment and labour rights, is an objective of the agreement. Such an approach is rare in BITs. Like preambles, objectives provisions do not create substantive obligations but provide part of the interpretive context for the provisions in the treaty. The recent EU–Korea Free Trade Agreement provides a good example of an objectives provision expressly linking labour rights as well as environmental protection to sustainable development in its sustainability chapter.

1. ...the Parties reaffirm their commitments to promoting the development of international trade in such a way as to contribute to the objective of sustainable development and will strive to ensure that this objective is integrated and reflected at every level of their trade relationship.
2. The Parties recognise that economic development, social development and environmental protection are interdependent and mutually reinforcing components of sustainable development.[31]

Objectives provisions, as well as preambular statements that express an objective of the treaty, are likely to be given more interpretive weight than other provisions in treaty preambles.[32]

  b. More specific standards for State treatment of foreign investors that preserve the ability of States to take measures to protect labour rights and the environment

---

[31] European Union–Korea Free Trade Agreement (signed 15 October 2009, entered into force 1 July 2011) OJ L 127, 14 May 2011 ('EU–Korea FTA (2011)') Art 13(1). See also Art 13(6) linking labour standards to sustainable development. Some preambles simply refer to sustainable development. See the preamble to the Free Trade Agreement between Canada and the Republic of Colombia (signed 21 November 2008, entered into force 15 August 2011) CTS 2011/11 ('Canada–Colombia FTA (2011)') and to the United States–Colombia Trade Promotion Agreement (signed 22 November 2006, entered into force 15 May 2012) available at: <www.ustr.gov/trade-agreements/free-trade-agreements/colombia-fta/final-text> accessed 19 December 2014, as well as to the Energy Charter Protocol on Energy Efficiency and Related Environmental Aspects (signed 17 December 1994) 34 ILM 446. Other agreements refer to regulatory flexibility generally, for example, preamble to the Comprehensive Economic Cooperation Agreement Between the Republic of India and the Republic of Singapore (signed 29 June 2005, in force 1 August 2005) available at: <http://wits.worldbank.org/GPTAD/PDF/archive/India-singapore.pdf> accessed 19 December 2014 ('India–Singapore Comprehensive Economic Cooperation Agreement (2005)'). The Comprehensive Economic and Trade Agreement (negotiations concluded 26 September 2014, not yet in force) available at: <www.international.gc.ca/trade-agreements-accords-commerciaux/agr-acc/ceta-aecg/text-texte/toc-tdm.aspx?lang=eng>accessed 19 December 2014 ('Canada–Europe Comprehensive Economic and Trade Agreement') contains a specific reference to sustainable development in its preamble as well as a number of other references to the need to ensure the compatibility between the agreement and high levels of labour and environmental protection.

[32] This was the approach taken in *Cross-Border Trucking Services (2001)*. The panel in that case relied on the statements in the preamble to the North American Free Trade Agreement between the USA, Canada, and Mexico (adopted 17 December 1992, entered into force 1 January 1993) 32 ILM 289 ('NAFTA (1994)') that were consistent with the overall trade liberalizing objective of NAFTA rather than a preamble statement that the parties intended to 'preserve their flexibility to safeguard the public welfare' to adopt a restrictive approach to the interpretation of reservations to NAFTA trade liberalization obligations (at paras 216–25, 237).

Some countries, notably Canada and the United States, have adopted language in both their PTIAs and their BITs that is intended to provide more certainty regarding the ability of party States to protect labour rights or the environment without breaching their investor protection obligations. Both the Canadian and US model BITs have annexes that carve out virtually all measures of general application that seek to achieve public policy objectives from the treaty's prohibition on indirect expropriation of foreign investments without compensation to the affected investor.[33] In the US Model BIT, whether or not an indirect expropriation has occurred is to be determined using the following criteria:

- an indirect expropriation must have an effect equivalent to a direct expropriation, even though there is no formal transfer of title or an outright seizure of an investment;
- the determination of whether an indirect expropriation has occurred requires a case-by-case analysis, including a consideration of the character and economic impact of the government action and the extent to which the action 'interferes with distinct, reasonable investment-backed expectations';
- the fact that a measure or series of measures of a State party has an adverse effect on the economic value of an investment does not by itself establish that an indirect expropriation has occurred; and
- '*Except in rare circumstances, non-discriminatory regulatory measures that are designed and applied to protect legitimate public welfare objectives, such as public health, safety, and the environment, do not constitute indirect expropriations.*'[34] (Emphasis added.)

Though not enumerated, measures to protect labour rights are likely to be considered 'measures designed and applied to protect legitimate public welfare objectives.'

Increasingly PTIAs entered into by other countries have similar provisions.[35] The China–New Zealand FTA, for example, includes a similar specification of

---

[33] See Annex B of the US Model BIT; Annex B.13(1) of the Canadian Model BIT.

[34] See Annex B of the US Model BIT. The language used in the Canadian Model BIT and the Colombian model bilateral investment treaty available at: <http://italaw.com/documents/inv_model_bit_colombia.pdf> accessed 19 December 2014 is somewhat different (Annex B.13(1) of the Canadian model BIT; Art. VI.2 of the Colombian model investment agreement). Similar provisions are found in the Agreement for the Promotion and Protection of Investments Between the Republic of Colombia and the Republic of India (signed 10 November 2009, entered into force 2 July 2012) available at: <http://investmentpolicyhub.unctad.org/Download/TreatyFile/796> accessed 19 December 2014 Art VI.2(c). Certain other exclusions are also provided for (Art 8(H)).

[35] Free Trade Agreement Between the Government of The People's Republic of China and the Government of The Republic of Peru (signed 28 April 2009, entered into force 1 March 2010) available at: <http://fta.mofcom.gov.cn/bilu/annex/bilu_xdwb_en.pdf> accessed 19 December 2014 Annex 9 and the Common Market for Eastern and Southern Africa: Investment Agreement for the COMESA Common Investment Area (signed 23 May 2007, not yet in force) available at; <http://investment-policyhub.unctad.org/Download/TreatyFile/3092> accessed 19 December 2014 ('COMESA Investment Agreement (2007)') Art 20.6, and United States–Central America–Dominican Republic: Free Trade Agreement (signed 5 August 2004, entered into force (for all countries)

what constitutes indirect expropriation.³⁶ Twelve of the eighteen new PTIAs and BITs in 2013 included such a provision.³⁷

    c. Exclusions limiting the application of treaty obligations to labour and environmental measures
        i. General exceptions relating to labour rights and environmental protection, including some modelled on GATT Article XX

A few BITs and many more PTIAs include clauses that provide limited exceptions to the obligations in the treaty for measures to protect the environment and labour rights. Some of these exceptions are extremely narrow in scope. One model, common in US and Canadian treaties, is found in the US–Uruguay BIT:

[n]othing in this Treaty shall be construed to prevent a Party from adopting or maintaining, or enforcing any measure *otherwise consistent with this Treaty* that it considers appropriate to ensure that investment activity in its territory is undertaken in a manner sensitive to labor concerns.³⁸ (Emphasis added.)

An identically worded provision addresses measures to protect the environment.³⁹ This kind of provision is not truly an exception. Since it only applies to measures that are 'otherwise consistent with the treaty', it is only an interpretive direction.

---

1 January 2009) available at: <http://wits.worldbank.org/GPTAD/PDF/archive/UnitedStates-CAFTA.pdf> accessed 19 December 2014 ('US–Dominican Republic–Central America FTA'), Annex 10. See also Australia–Chile Free Trade Agreement (signed 30 July 2008, entered into force 5 March 2009) [2009] ATS 5 Annex 10-B; ASEAN Comprehensive Investment Agreement (signed 26 February 2009, entered into force 29 March 2012) available at: <http://investorstatelawguide.com/ResearchTools/ArticleCitator?toc=content&id=201&cat=investmenttreaty&subcat=regionalsectoral&docid=53#pdfanc_mainartcitOTI/0001> accessed 19 December 2014 ('ASEAN Investment Agreement (2009)'), Annex 2; Malaysia-New Zealand Free Trade Agreement (signed 26 October 2009, entered into force 31 July 2010) available at: <www.mfat.govt.nz/downloads/trade-agreement/malaysia/mnzfta-text-of-agreement.pdf> accessed 19 December 2014 Annex 7; Agreement establishing the ASEAN-Australia-New Zealand Free Trade Area (signed 27 February 2009, entered into force 1 January 2010) [2010] ATS 1 ('ASEAN–Australia–New Zealand FTA'), Annex on Expropriation and Compensation. See also other agreements listed in UNCTAD, *Expropriation: A Sequel* (United Nations 2011) 28.

³⁶ China–New Zealand Free Trade Agreement (signed 7 April 2008, entered into force 1 October 2008) available at: <www.chinafta.govt.nz/1-The-agreement/2-Text-of-the-agreement/index.php> accessed 19 December 2014 Annex 13. The ASEAN–Australia–New Zealand FTA Investment Chapter, Annex on Expropriation and Compensation goes farther, providing that *bona fide* measures of this kind *do not* constitute indirect expropriation.

³⁷ UNCTAD, *World Investment Report 2014* (United Nations 2014) 116.

³⁸ Treaty between the United States of America and the Oriental Republic of Uruguay concerning the Encouragement and Reciprocal Protection of Investment (signed 5 November 2005, entered into force 1 November 2006) available at: <http://investmentpolicyhub.unctad.org/Download/TreatyFile/2380> accessed 20 March 2015 ('US–Uruguay BIT (2004)') Art 13(3).

³⁹ US–Uruguay BIT (2004), Art 12(2). This form of provision originated in NAFTA (1994) Art 1114. Identical language is found, for example, in the United States–Singapore Free Trade Agreement (signed 6 May 2003, entered into force 1 January 2004) available at: <http://wits.worldbank.org/GPTAD/PDF/archive/US-Singapore.pdf> accessed 19 December 2014 ('US–Singapore FTA (2003)') Art 15.10. See also the Australia–United States Free Trade Agreement (signed 5 July 2004, entered into force 1 January 2005) [2005] ATS 1 ('US–Australia FTA (2005)') Art 11.11 and the Canada–Chile FTA (1997) Art G-14.1.

One might argue that such provisions should be understood to mean that a measure of a party to ensure that investment activity be 'undertaken in a manner sensitive to labor concerns' or the environment should not be found to be inconsistent with the treaty obligations of the party if the measure would be consistent with the treaty except to the extent that it was enacted to ensure that investment was sensitive to labour or environmental concerns.[40] In any case, perhaps in recognition of its limited impact, this provision is not found in recent FTAs entered into by Canada.[41] It does appear in recent US FTAs.[42]

Many PTIAs and a few BITs, mainly those negotiated by Canada,[43] contain exceptions that are based on GATT Article XX. This provision includes language that relates to environmental protection without specifically using the terms 'environment' or 'environmental protection'. GATT Article XX excludes the application of obligations in GATT to measures 'necessary to protect human, animal and plant life or health' and those 'relating to the conservation of exhaustible natural resources if such measures are made effective in conjunction with restrictions on domestic production or consumption, or the protection of natural resources'.[44] Many PTIAs either incorporate these exceptions by reference or restate them.[45] North American treaties typically specify that the first of these exceptions extends to environmental protection measures and the second includes both living and non-living exhaustible natural resources.[46] It is not obvious that this specification expands the scope of the exception.[47] WTO cases have confirmed that exhaustible natural resources generally extends to living things.[48]

---

[40] JW Salacuse, *The Law of Investment Treaties* (OUP 2010) 348 (regarding the identically worded provision in the US–Uruguay BIT (2004) on environmental measures); UNCTAD (n 24) 99.
[41] For example, Free Trade Agreement between Canada and the Republic of Panama (signed 14 May 2010, entered into force 1 April 2013) CTS 2013/9 ('Canada–Panama FTA (2013)').
[42] For example, United States–Korea Free Trade Agreement (signed 10 February 2011, entered into force 15 March 2012) available at: <www.ustr.gov/trade-agreements/free-trade-agreements/korus-fta/final-text> accessed 19 December 2014 ('US–Korea FTA') Art 11.10, US–Australia FTA (2004) Art 11.11.
[43] Canadian model BIT, Art 10. Fifteen of eighteen BITS concluded in 2013 worldwide included such a provision (UNCTAD (n 37) 116). Such provisions are also included in the Canada–Europe Comprehensive Economic and Trade Agreement (not yet in force), Chapter 32, Art X.2.
[44] GATT Art XX(b) and (g).
[45] They are restated in the India–Singapore Comprehensive Economic Cooperation Agreement (2005) Art 6.11; Free Trade Agreement Between Canada and the States of the European Free Trade Association (Iceland, Liechtenstein, Norway, and Switzerland) (signed 26 January 2008, entered into force 1 July 2009) Art 22 and the ASEAN Investment Agreement (2009) Art 17; Association Free Trade Agreement between the European Community and its Member States and Chile (signed 26 April 2002, entered into force 1 March 2005) available at: <http://wits.worldbank.org/GPTAD/PDF/archive/EC-Chile.pdf> accessed 19 December 2014 Art 91. See other PTIAs cited in Bartels (n 23).
[46] For example, NAFTA (1994) Art 2101 states that GATT Art XX(b) includes environmental measures necessary to protect human, animal, or plant life or health, and that GATT Art XX(g) applies to measures relating to the conservation of living and non-living exhaustible natural resources.
[47] Bartels (n 13) 5–6.
[48] WTO, *United States—Importation of Certain Shrimp and Shrimp Products—Report of the Appellate Body* (12 October 1998) WT/DS58/AB/R para 31.

Notably, however, most PTIAs do not extend these exceptions to the investment protection provisions.[49] Canada's treaties are an exception in this regard. Canada typically includes an exception in the following form in both its PTIAs and BITs:

3. For the purposes of Chapter Nine (Investment):
   a. a Party may adopt or enforce a measure necessary:
      i. to protect human, animal or plant life or health, which the Parties understand to include environmental measures necessary to protect human, animal or plant life or health,
      …, or
      iii. for the conservation of living or non-living exhaustible natural resources;[50]

The form and conditions for the application of these exceptions varies somewhat both from GATT Article XX and from one treaty to another. The Canadian approach illustrated above, for example, eliminates the GATT requirement that measures for the conservation of exhaustible natural resources be adopted 'in conjunction with restrictions on domestic production or consumption, or the protection of natural resources'.[51] At the same time, however, Canada's model specifies that measures must be 'necessary' for conservation just as measures must be necessary to protect human, animal or plant life or health. This is a stricter standard for States to meet than appears in the GATT itself, which requires only a measure be one 'relating to' conservation. The requirement that measures be necessary to achieve the specified objective has been the subject of a number of GATT and WTO cases. In general, a measure is necessary only if there was no alternative measure consistent with the GATT, or less inconsistent with GATT, which the country could reasonably be expected to employ to achieve its policy objectives.[52]

---

[49] For example, NAFTA (1994) incorporates GATT Art XX for the purposes of the provisions on trade in goods and technical barriers to trade only (Art 2101). These exceptions do not apply to the investment obligations in Chapter 11. A similar approach is followed in some other agreements, for example, Singapore–Taipei Free Trade Agreement (signed 19 April 2014, not yet entered into force) available at: <www.iesingapore.gov.sg/Trade-From-Singapore/ASTEP/Legal-Text> accessed 19 December 2014 Art 22.1(1) and Korea–Australia Free Trade Agreement (signed 8 April 2014, entered into force 12 December 2014) available at: <www.dfat.gov.au/fta/kafta/official-documents/index.html> accessed 19 December 2014 Art 18.1(1).

[50] Canada–Panama FTA (2013) Art 23.02(3); Canadian model BIT, Art 10. The CETA (not yet in force) simply incorporates GATT Art XX by reference (Chapter 32, Art X.2). The Canada–China BIT (2014) follows the language of GATT Art XX, Art 33.2. The Canada–Europe Comprehensive Economic and Trade Agreement (not yet in force) contains an identical exception for measures to protect human, animal, and plant health (Chapter 32, Art X.02.2(b)). The parties agreed that this extends to environmental measures. Some other PTIAs and BITS also extend these exceptions to investment, such as the India–Singapore Comprehensive Economic Cooperation Agreement (2005), Art 6.11 and the ASEAN Investment Agreement (2009), Art 17. See generally Bartels (n 13).

[51] Some other treaties follow this approach. For example, Australia–New Zealand Closer Economic Relations Trade Agreement (signed 28 March 1983, entered into force 1 January 1983) available at: <www.dfat.gov.au/trade/agreements/anzcerta/Pages/australia-new-zealand-closer-economic-relations-trade-agreement.aspx> accessed 20 March 2015 Art 18.

[52] GATT, Thailand—*Restrictions on Importation of and Internal Taxes on Cigarettes—Report of the Panel* (7 November 1990) BISD 37S/200 (1991); WTO, *European Communities—Measures*

By imposing 'necessary' as a requirement, the Canadian model agreements restrict the availability of the exception. Some other treaties have avoided using 'necessary' as a condition of the availability of the exception. The Common Market for Eastern and Southern Africa ('COMESA') Investment Agreement, for example, uses 'designed and applied'[53] which would seem to focus not on whether there were alternatives available but rather whether the State was acting in good faith in enacting the measure to achieve the indicated objective and whether there was a rational connection between how it is applied in practice and the objective. The India–Sri Lanka FTA provides even more flexibility allowing a State to take whatever measures it 'considers' necessary to achieve these objectives essentially leaving it up to the State to determine the scope of the exception, subject to an obligation to act in good faith.[54]

GATT Article XX exceptions are only available where the requirements of the so-called 'chapeau' are satisfied:

Subject to the requirement that such measures are not applied in a manner which would constitute a means of arbitrary or unjustifiable discrimination between countries where the same conditions prevail, or a disguised restriction on international trade, nothing in this Agreement shall be construed to prevent the adoption or enforcement by any contracting party of measures:...

Many PTIAs and BITS with general exception provisions contain some version of these additional 'chapeau' requirements.[55]

The GATT also contains an exception provision related to labour standards, but it has a very narrow scope. It excludes measures relating to the products of prison labour from the obligations in the agreement.[56] This provision has never been interpreted in GATT or WTO dispute settlement, but is limited to actions by States regarding goods produced by prison labour in other states permitting, for example, discrimination against such goods. Discrimination might be used to discourage such production, but the availability of the exception does not require such an intention. In any case, the exception does nothing to protect labour rights. States cannot rely on it in relation to their actions designed to promote labour standards protections. More comprehensive labour rights protections have not been adopted at the WTO.[57] FTAs that contain general

Affecting Asbestos and Products Containing Asbestos—Report of the Appellate Body (12 March 2001) WT/DS135/AB/R.

[53] Art 22.1.
[54] Free Trade Agreement Between the Republic of India and the Democratic Socialist Republic of Sri Lanka (signed 28 December 1998, entered into force 15 December 2001) available at: <http://wits.worldbank.org/GPTAD/PDF/archive/India-SriLanka.pdf> accessed 19 December 2014 Art IV.
[55] For example, Canada–Panama FTA (2010), Canadian Model BIT Art 10.
[56] GATT (1947) Art XX(e).
[57] Cuyvers (n 8) suggests this is due to concerns that broader protections would enable States to put in place protectionist measures in the form of labour standards though he notes that there have been calls for such reform to WTO rules (p 8).

exception provisions have not included this provision nor have they adopted more comprehensive exceptions regarding measures to protect labour rights.[58] Canada's general exceptions in its BITs do not extend to the products of prison labour or other labour rights.[59]

There has been no investor–State arbitration case in which a tribunal has been asked to apply these GATT-like exceptions. Some commentators have expressed scepticism regarding whether they are likely to be effective to provide greater flexibility to States to regulate to achieve sustainable development.[60] They argue, among other things, that significant flexibility is already built into the substantive investor protection provisions. As well, they note that the categories of public policy measures permitted are not limited in the investor protection provisions. GATT Article XX only protects measures in categories specifically listed in the exception.

A variation of the GATT Article XX approach appears in a few trade treaties entered into by the EU and the EFTA countries.[61] This approach follows Article 36 of the Treaty on the Functioning of the European Union (TFEU):

The Agreement shall not preclude prohibitions or restrictions on imports, exports, goods in transit or trade in used goods justified on grounds of public morality, public policy or public security; the protection of health and life of humans, animals or plants; the protection of national treasures possessing artistic, historic or archaeological value; or the protection of intellectual, industrial and commercial property or rules relating to gold and silver. Such prohibitions or restrictions shall not, however, constitute a means of arbitrary or unjustifiable discrimination where the same conditions prevail or a disguised restriction on trade between the Parties.

Notably, this provision does not refer to labour rights or the environment specifically, though 'public policy' and 'health and life of humans, animals and plants'

---

[58] For example, Free Trade Agreement between Canada and the Republic of Korea (signed 22 September 2014, entered into force 1 January 2015) available at: <www.international.gc.ca/trade-agreements-accords-commerciaux/agr-acc/korea-coree/toc-tdm.aspx?lang=eng> accessed 1 January 2015 ('Canada–Korea FTA (2015)'); EU–Korea FTA (2011).

[59] For example, Agreement between the Government of Canada and the Government of the Republic of Armenia for the Promotion and Protection of Investments (signed 8 May 1998, entered into force 1 April 1999) CTS 1999/22 Art XVII.

[60] For example, A Newcombe, 'General Exceptions in International Investment Agreements' in M-C Cordonier Segger, M Gehring, and A Newcombe (eds), *Sustainable Development in World Investment Law* (Wolters Kluwer 2012) 369.

[61] Free Trade Agreement between the States of the European Free Trade Association (Iceland, Liechtenstein, Norway, and Switzerland) and Jordan (signed 21 June 2001, entered into force 1 September 2002) available at: <http://wits.worldbank.org/GPTAD/PDF/archive/EFTA-Jordan.pdf> accessed 19 December 2014 Art 10; Free Trade Agreement between the States of the European Free Trade Association (Iceland, Liechtenstein, Norway, and Switzerland) and Tunisia (signed 17 December 2004, entered into force 1 June 2005) available at: <http://wits.worldbank.org/GPTAD/PDF/archive/EFTA-Tunisia.pdf> accessed 19 December 2014 Art 21; Agreement on Trade, Development and Cooperation Between the European Community and South Africa (signed 11 October 1999, entered into force 1 June 2000) available at: <http://wits.worldbank.org/GPTAD/PDF/archive/EC-South%20Africa.pdf> accessed 19 December 2014 Art 27.

would seem to extend to labour and environmental protection concerns. This provision does not include a necessity test but requires that measures be 'justified' on the policy grounds enumerated, likely an easier test for the State to meet. It does impose the GATT chapeau-like requirements.[62]

Bartels notes that a version of this provision is also found in some treaties entered into by countries in the Balkan peninsula. This version specifically refers to measures 'justified on grounds of…protection of the environment'.[63]

 (ii) Exceptions that exclude subsidies, government procurement, tax measures, or sectors of economic activity or areas of policy-making by States from some obligations in the treaty.

Some BITs and PTIAs contain exceptions that exclude subsidies, government procurement, tax measures, or specific sectors or areas of policy-making from some obligations in the treaty. These kinds of provisions can be relied on to protect State measures to achieve sustainable development that fall within these kinds of policies.[64]

 (iii) Country specific reservations that exclude particular State measures, sectors or areas of policy-making from some obligations in the treaty.

Some PTIAs impose broad obligations but permit each party State to list reservations that carve out specific measures, sectors of economic activity or policy areas from some of obligations in the agreement.[65] Such so-called 'negative list' agreements are commonly negotiated by Canada and the US. In NAFTA, for example, the provision of social services and programmes to support disadvantaged groups is excluded using reservations.[66] Reservations of this kind could be used to protect labour and environmental rights, but that has not been the practice to date. This approach is not found in BITs other than those entered into by Canada and the United States.[67]

 d. Rules that give primacy to other agreements relating to labour or the environment over the BIT or the PTIA.

---

[62] This standard and its interpretation by the Court of Justice of European Union are discussed extensively in M Horspool and M Humphreys, *European Union Law* (7th edn, OUP 2012) paras 10.16–10.87.

[63] For example, Art 23 Croatia–Albania Free Trade Agreement (signed 27 September 2002, entered into force 1 June 2003) available at: <http://wits.worldbank.org/GPTAD/PDF/archive/Albania-Croatia.pdf> accessed 19 December 2014. Bartels indicates that other kinds of even broader exceptions can be found in a few treaties. He notes that in the trade agreement between Egypt and Jordan parties are allowed to adopt measures for 'environmental reasons' so long as they are in conformity with domestic law (Bartels (n 13) 6).

[64] For example, NAFTA (1994) Arts 1108 (investment) and 1206 (cross-border trade in services); Canada–Europe Comprehensive Economic and Trade Agreement (not yet in force), Chapter 10, Art X.14.

[65] For example, NAFTA (1994). Some other agreements also contemplate reservations to the investment obligations. For example, India–Singapore Comprehensive Economic Cooperation Agreement (2005) Art 6.16; ASEAN Investment Agreement (2009) Art 9.

[66] For example, NAFTA (1994), Canada's Schedule to Annex II, Sector: Social Services. Some other agreements follow a similar approach, for example, Free Trade Agreement Between the EFTA States and the Republic of Chile (signed 26 June 2003, in force 1 February 2004) available at: <http://wits.worldbank.org/GPTAD/PDF/archive/EFTA-Chile.pdf> accessed 19 December 2014.

[67] For example, US–Uruguay BIT (2004) Art 14.

A final way in which PTIAs safeguard States' ability to act to promote sustainable development in a manner consistent with their obligations in the treaty is through provisions that give priority to other treaties to which they are parties that impose obligations related to the promotion of sustainable development. This is a common approach with respect to international agreements relating to environmental protection.[68] It has not been used to address labour rights. Instead, as discussed in the following section, some agreements contain provisions that encourage or require States to meet labour standards set in international agreements. Giving primacy to other treaties has not been a common feature in BITs.[69]

2. Commitments to ensure the effectiveness of domestic laws related to labour rights and environmental protection

  a. Commitments regarding the enforcement of labour and environmental standards in domestic law

One method that States have adopted to address the so-called 'race to the bottom' problem that is only found in PTIAs, is to impose requirements to enforce domestic environmental and labour laws, recognizing that weak enforcement is common and could be just as significant in practice as legislation or other positive State acts to derogate from the protection of the environment and labour rights.[70] The first approach to addressing the risk of effective derogation through weak enforcement was in the side agreements to NAFTA. Indeed, these side agreements were the first treaty provisions to link social and trade concerns and have been very influential in the subsequent development of sustainable development

---

[68] For example, NAFTA (1994) Art 104 which provides that listed environmental agreements prevail over NAFTA. A similar approach is found in many Canadian FTAs (for example, Canada–Chile FTA (1997) Art A-04). Bartels (n 13) notes that such a provision is included in the Chile–Mexico Free Trade Agreement (signed 17 April 1998, entered into force 1 August 1999) available at: <www.sice.oas.org/Trade/chmefta/indice.asp> accessed 19 December 2014 Art 1-06 and Free Trade Agreement Between the Republic of China and the Republic of Panama (signed 21 August 2003, not yet in force) available at: <http://wits.worldbank.org/GPTAD/PDF/archive/Panama-Taiwan.pdf> accessed 19 December 2014 Art 1.03 (at 9). The Canada–Europe Comprehensive Economic and Trade Agreement (not yet in force) contains a provision reaffiriming the parties commitments under such agreements but it does not give them priority (Chapter 25, Art X.3). Recent US FTAs (for example, US–Korea FTA (2012) Art 20.10) also accord priority to environmental agreements, though in a more limited way. Older US FTAs, for example, Agreement Between the United States of America and the Hashemite Kingdom of Jordan on the Establishment of a Free Trade Area (signed 24 October 2000, entered into force 17 December 2001) available at: <http://wits.worldbank.org/GPTAD/PDF/archive/UnitedStates-Jordan.pdf> accessed 19 December 2014 ('US–Jordan FTA') do not contain a provision giving priority to environmental agreements.

[69] A few BITs do address other treaties. The Belgium–Luxembourg Economic Union–Ethiopia BIT, for example, obliges each party to strive to ensure that it implements the environmental treaties to which it is party, Agreement between Belgian–Luxembourg Economic Union and the Federal Democratic Republic of Ethiopia on the Reciprocal Promotion and Protection of Investments (signed 26 October 2006, not yet in force) available at: <http://investmentpolicyhub.unctad.org/Download/TreatyFile/360> accessed 19 December 2014 Art 5.3.

[70] Enforcement is addressed in the 2012 US Model BIT, Arts 12, 13, but no actual treaties.

provisions.[71] As discussed below, these provisions are linked to commitments regarding the content of domestic laws.

The North American Agreement on Labor Cooperation (NAALC), the labour side accord to NAFTA, requires State parties to 'promote compliance with and effectively enforce' their labour laws through appropriate government measures and to ensure that judicial and non-judicial tribunal procedures are available to individuals to enforce such laws.[72] The NAALC goes on to require that each party ensure that its tribunals meet specific standards for due process and transparency. The NAALC also contemplates the establishment of several institutions, including the Commission on Labour Cooperation (CLC), consisting of a Council of the labour ministers of each party and a secretariat. The Council is the governing body of the CLC and is generally responsible for the implementation of the NAALC. The Council is supported by the Secretariat, which is also responsible for producing an Annual Report on activities of the CLC and compliance with NAALC by the parties. Each party must establish a National Administrative Office (NAO) to assist with implementation of the NAALC. Each NAO is also responsible for reviewing complaints by any citizen or organization that may relate to any labour law matter. There is no standing requirement—anyone from a NAFTA State can complain about the labour practices of a private employer or agency. Perhaps to avoid the risk of large numbers of minor complaints, however, the NAALC requires complaints about labour practices in one NAFTA jurisdiction to be made to an NAO in another NAFTA jurisdiction. The reviews are made public but there is no follow-up procedure.

With respect to the environment, the North American Agreement on Environmental Cooperation (NAAEC) creates a similar process to deal with non-enforcement. The institutions and their responsibilities, however, are somewhat different under the NAAEC. The NAAEC creates the North American Commission on Environmental Cooperation located in Montreal, with a Secretariat overseen by a Council on Environmental Cooperation (CEC), composed of the ministers of the environment from each party. Like its counterpart under the NAALC, the CEC is responsible for the implementation of the NAAEC. As well as supporting the work of the Commission and preparing annual reports on its work, the CEC Secretariat has a significant additional responsibility. It is tasked with receiving and evaluating submissions by individuals and organizations from any NAFTA party

---

[71] Bartels (n 13) 10. Approaches similar to the NAFTA side agreements have been adopted, for example, in the Peru–Korea Free Trade Agreement (signed 21 March 2011, entered into force 1 August 2011) available at: <www.sice.oas.org/TPD/PER_KOR/PER_KOR_Texts_e/PER_KOR_ToC_e.asp> accessed 19 December 2014 ('Peru–Korea FTA (2011)') Art 18.2(1); the Free Trade Agreement between the States of the European Free Trade Association (Iceland, Liechtenstein, Norway and Switzerland) and Montenegro (signed 14 November 2011, entered into force 1 September 2012 for Montenegro, Liechtenstein and Switzerland; 1 October 2012 for Iceland; 1 November 2012 for Norway) available at: <www.efta.int/media/documents/legal-texts/free-trade-relations/montenegro/montenegro-main-agreement.pdf> accessed 19 December 2014 Art 34(1).

[72] North American Agreement on Labour Cooperation (signed 14 September 1993, entered into force 1 January 1994) CTS 1994/4 ('NAALC (1994)') Arts 2 and 3.

that a party is failing to effectively enforce its environmental laws. If certain criteria are met, it can request a response from the State complained about. Based on the submission and the response, the Secretariat may decide that a 'factual record' should be prepared and recommend that to the Council. If two of the three members of the Council instruct it to do so, the Secretariat prepares a factual record and submits it to the Council. The purpose of the factual record is to provide authoritative documentation regarding the subject matter of the submission. The factual record may be made public if two of the three members of the Council agree.[73]

Many subsequent side accords on labour cooperation negotiated by Canada contain enforcement commitments that are generally based on the NAALC.[74] The US follows the same approach but recent agreements entered into by the US have incorporated provisions related to the enforcement of labour laws in the main treaty.[75]

Canada has also negotiated side agreements on environmental cooperation in relation to its subsequent FTAs that, generally, follow the structure of the NAAEC in terms of the obligations regarding domestic enforcement, but most recent agreements do not provide for a citizen submission process like that in the NAAEC.[76] By contrast, the US FTAs incorporate environmental law enforcement commitments in the treaty itself.[77] These follow the NAAEC model, including the citizen submission process,[78] and go on to provide more detailed requirements for domestic judicial and administrative procedures as well as requirements for the nature, though not the substantive content, of domestic environmental regulation.[79] For example, US treaties encourage the use of 'flexible, voluntary, incentive-based mechanisms'.

---

[73] North American Agreement on Environmental Cooperation (signed 14 September 1993, entered into force 1 January 1994) CTS 1994/3 ('NAAEC (1994)') Arts 14, 15.

[74] Agreement on Labour Cooperation between Canada and Peru (signed 29 May 2008, entered into force 1 August 2009) CTS 2009/17. The Canada–Europe Comprehensive Economic and Trade Agreement (not yet in force) provides that the parties shall not waive or otherwise derogate from its labour laws to encourage investment (Chapter 24, Art 4).

[75] For example, US–Korea FTA (2012) Chapter 19. As discussed below, one reason to include the provision in the main treaty is so that the dispute settlement provisions in the main treaty apply.

[76] For example, Agreement on Environmental Cooperation between Canada and the Republic of Honduras (signed 5 November 2013, entered into force 1 October 2014) CTS 2014/25. The Agreement on Environmental Cooperation between Canada and Chile (1997) follows the NAFTA approach (Arts 14, 15) as does the Canada–Europe Comprehensive Economic and Trade Agreement (not yet in force) (Chapter 25, Arts 13–16). The reason for this change in approach in Canada is not known. It may have been adopted because of the costs of administering the process, concerns of Canadian treaty parties or for some other reason.

[77] Some of the most recent Canadian treaties use both treaty provisions and side agreements. For example, Canada–Korea FTA (2015) available at Chapters 17, 18.

[78] For example, United States–Peru Trade Promotion Agreement (signed 12 April 2006, entered into force 1 February 2009) available at: <http://wits.worldbank.org/GPTAD/PDF/archive/US-Peru.pdf> accessed 19 December 2014 ('US–Peru FTA (2008)') Arts 18.8, 18.9.

[79] US–Peru FTA (2008) Arts 18.4, 18.5.

Commitments in side agreement are not subject to dispute settlement under the main treaty. Of course, even where labour and environmental enforcement commitments are incorporated directly in a PTIA, it is possible to carve these obligations out of the treaty's dispute settlement procedures.[80] Many PTIAs with enforcement provisions include customized dispute settlement and compliance procedures often based on those in the NAALC and the NAAEC discussed below. For example, the labour side accords to the Canada–Chile, Canada–Costa Rica, and Canada–Colombia FTAs incorporate special complaint and compliance mechanisms to ensure that States enforce their domestic labour laws that are similar to those in the NAALC.[81]

Under the NAALC, a minister (who is a member of the CLC) may initiate consultations regarding any matter covered by the NAALC. If consultations have not resolved the matter, any consulting party can request the CLC to appoint an Evaluation Committee of Experts (ECE) to examine the issue in some circumstances. Review by an ECE is only permitted if an alleged failure to enforce relates to trade in some way and to 'mutually recognized labour laws' in both countries. Following the ECE report, a party State may request consultations but only regarding whether there has been a 'persistent pattern of failure to enforce occupational health and safety, child labour or minimum wage technical labour standards' by another party State in respect of the matter addressed in the report. This can result in a complex tiered State-to-State procedure involving consultations, a meeting of the CLC, the appointment of an arbitral panel (if at least two of the Council members agree) and, following a determination by the panel that there has been persistent pattern of failure to enforce, the adoption of a mutually agreed action plan. Ultimately, if the problem persists, a monetary assessment may be imposed on the non-enforcing State and, if not paid, trade retaliation (against US and Mexico only).[82]

The NAAEC and certain US and Canadian FTAs establish a similar process to address non-enforcement in relation to environmental protection laws. Like the NAALC, the NAAEC procedures attempt to encourage the parties to find a mutually satisfactory solution.[83] However, in principle, under some side agreements

---

[80] This approach has been adopted by Canada. Even though recent Canadian FTAS have included some labour and environment commitments in the treaty itself the general dispute settlement provisions do not apply. For example, Canada–Korea FTA (2015) Art 18.24.

[81] Agreement on Labour Cooperation between Canada and Chile (1997) Art 3; Agreement on Labour Cooperation between Canada and Costa Rica (2001) Art 4; Agreement on Labour Cooperation between Canada and the Republic of Colombia (signed 21 November 2008, entered into force 15 August 2011) CTS 2011/13 Art 3; Canada–Europe Comprehensive Economic and Trade Agreement (not yet in force), Chapter 24, Arts 9–11.

[82] NAALC (1994). In practice these penalties and sanctions have never been used. The US Trade Representative recently announced the commencement of compliance proceedings against Guatemala under the US–Dominican Republic–Central America FTA. See <www.ustr.gov/about-us/press-office/press-releases/2014/September/United-States-Proceeds-with-Labor-Enforcement-Case-Against-Guatemala> accessed 19 December 2014.

[83] See NAAEC (1994) Arts 22–23; US–Australia FTA (2005) Art 18.7; United States–Chile Free Trade Agreement (signed 6 June 2003, entered into force 1 January 2004) available at: <www.ustr.gov/trade-agreements/free-trade-agreements/chile-fta/final-text> accessed 19 December 2014 ('US–Chile FTA (2003)') Art 19.5; and US–Singapore FTA (2003) Art 18.7.

and FTAs, a narrow set of disputes can go on to be the subject of arbitration[84] and could lead to the imposition of fines[85] or, in some cases, even trade sanctions to encourage compliance.[86]

More recent FTAs entered into by Canada and the US do not provide for fines or sanctions in relation to State failure to enforce its domestic laws related to labour rights and environmental protection. However, recent US FTAs do provide that parties can have recourse to the general State-to-State dispute settlement procedures in the treaty where a violation of an enforcement commitment is alleged, provided that the dispute settlement procedures in the labour or environment chapters are exhausted first without a mutually satisfactory resolution.[87] The general dispute settlement procedures can ultimately result in trade sanctions or monetary assessments.[88]

There is some variation in terms of the strength of treaty commitments regarding the enforcement of domestic laws. The current language used by the US to address weak enforcement is as follows: 'A Party shall not fail to effectively enforce its labour [or environmental] law, through a sustained or recurring course of action or inaction, in a manner affecting trade or investment between the Parties.'[89] Some of Canada's recent treaties include a stronger commitment that each party 'shall effectively enforce its labour [or environmental] laws'.[90] Some US FTAs include the following caveat, further weakening the commitment:

> The Parties recognize that each Party retains the right to exercise discretion with respect to investigatory, prosecutorial, regulatory, and compliance matters and to make decisions regarding the allocation of resources to enforcement with respect to other labour matters determined to have higher priorities. Accordingly, the Parties understand that a Party is in compliance with [its obligations to enforce its labor and environmental laws] where a course of action or inaction reflects a reasonable exercise of such discretion, or results from a bona fide decision regarding the allocation of resources.[91]

---

[84] See NAAEC (1994) Arts 24–36; Australia–US FTA (2005), Chapter 21; US–Chile FTA (2003), Chapter 22; US–Singapore FTA (2003), Chapter 20.

[85] See NAAEC (1994) Art 34(4)(b); Australia–US FTA (2005) Art 21.11(1); US–Chile FTA (2003) Art 22.15(1); US–Singapore FTA (2003) Art 20.6(1).

[86] See NAAEC (1994) Art 36; Australia–US FTA (2005) Art 21.11(2); US–Chile FTA (2003) Art 22.15(2); US–Singapore FTA (2003) Art 20.6(2).

[87] For example, under the US–Korea FTA (2012), it is possible to initiate dispute settlement proceedings after seeking to resolve the matter through the specific procedures contemplated in the labour or environmental provisions (Arts 19.7(5), 20.9(5) and 22.4). A similar approach is adopted in the US–Peru FTA (2009) Arts 17.7(7), 18.12(7) and 21.2. This differs from earlier US FTAs, which only provided a consultation process. See US–Singapore FTA (2004) Art 17.2(1)(b).

[88] US–Chile FTA (2004) Arts 22.13, 22.14.

[89] US–Korea FTA (2012) Art 20.3; US–Peru FTA (2008) Art 18.3. Identical language is used in recent EU agreements (for example, EU–Korea (2011) Art 13.7).

[90] Canada–Korea FTA (2015) Art 17.1. Some recent Canadian treaties continue to use side agreements that follow that NAFTA language, for example, Free Trade Agreement between Canada and the Republic of Honduras (signed 5 November 2013, entered into force 1 October 2014) CTS 2014/23 ('Canada–Honduras FTA (2014)'); Agreement on Labour Cooperation between Canada and the Republic of Honduras (signed 5 November 2013, entered into force 1 October 2014) CTS 2014/25 Art 3, though the environmental side agreement uses imperative language: Agreement on Environmental Cooperation between Canada and Honduras (2014) Art 4.

[91] US–Singapore FTA (2003) Art 17(2)(1)(b).

More recent US FTAs eliminate this caveat in relation to labour laws, specifying that a party State is *not* justified in failing to enforce its laws on the basis of limitations on resources or its decision to give priority to other enforcement activities.[92] A similar caveat, however, remains in relation to environmental protection.[93]

In contrast to this practice in PTIAs, most BITS, including US and Canadian BITs, do not contain any kind of enforcement obligation or mechanism to address inadequate enforcement.[94]

  b. No derogation from the protection of the labour rights or environment under domestic law to attract investment

Some PTIAs, as well as a few BITS, contain provisions acknowledging that it is inappropriate for the parties to try to encourage investment by lowering domestic environmental or labour standards and requiring parties not to waive or otherwise derogate from their domestic labour laws for this purpose. This approach to the 'race to the bottom' problem is adopted in the Economic Partnership Agreement between the EC and CARIFORUM (2008),[95] the EU–Korea FTA (2010)[96] Canada–EU CETA,[97] and several US and Canadian FTAs,[98] as well as the COMESA Investment Agreement,[99] and the model BITs of the US,[100] Austria,[101] and Belgium[102] as well as many actual BITs.[103]

---

[92] US–Peru FTA (2009) Art 17.3(1)(b).

[93] US–Korea FTA (2012) Art 20.3(1)(b). See the similar language in the Canada–Korea FTA (2015) Art 17.5(2) and Canada–Europe Comprehensive Economic and Trade Agreement (not yet in force) Chapter 25 Art X.4 and the identical caveat in relation to labour rights protection Chapter 24 Art 2.

[94] US–Uruguay BIT (2004) provides for a consultation process (Arts 13(1), 24(1) and 37(5)).

[95] Economic Partnership Agreement between the CARIFORUM states and the European Community and its Member States (signed 15 October 2008, entered into force 1 November 2008) available at: <http://wits.worldbank.org/GPTAD/PDF/archive/EC-CARIFORM.pdf> accessed 19 December 2010 ('EC-CARIFORUM EPA (2008)') Arts 73 and 193.

[96] EU–Korea FTA (2010) Arts 13.4, 13.7.

[97] Canada–Europe Comprehensive Economic and Trade Agreement (not yet in force), Chapter 24, Art 4, Chapter 25, Art X.5.

[98] See Australia–US FTA (2005); US–Dominican Republic-Central America FTA (2009) Art 16.2; US–Chile FTA (2004) Art 18.2; US–Jordan FTA (2001) Art 6; US–Morocco FTA (2006) Art 16.2 and the Canada–Colombia FTA (2011) Arts 1601–04. That agreement also references the obligations between the parties set out in the Canada–Colombia Agreement on Labour Cooperation (2011). See also Agreement on Labour Cooperation between Canada and the Republic of Peru (2008) Art 2; Agreement on Labour between the EFTA and Hong Kong, China (signed 21 June 2011, entered into force for all countries but Norway, 1 October 2012, for Norway 1 November 2012) available at: <www.efta.int/media/documents/legal-texts/free-trade-relations/hong-kong-china/Agreement%20on%20Labour.pdf> accessed 19 December 2014 Art 2; Peru–Korea FTA (2011) Art 18.2(2).

[99] COMESA Investment Agreement (not yet in force) Art 5.   [100] Art 13.

[101] Draft Agreement for the Promotion and Protection of Investment between the Republic of Austria and…available at: <http://investmentpolicyhub.unctad.org/Download/TreatyFile/2849> accessed 19 December 2014 Art 5.

[102] Belgium Model BIT Art 5.2.

[103] See Art 5 of the Agreement between the Republic of Austria and Tajikistan for the Promotion and Protection of Investments (signed 15 December 2010, entered into force 21 December 2012) available at: <www.ris.bka.gv.at/Dokumente/BgblAuth/BGBLA_2012_III_18/COO_2026_100_2_727001.

The strength of these provisions varies. Where they appear in BITs, they tend to be in the nature of a best efforts undertaking. In PTIAs, however, binding commitments are common.[104]

The US–Uruguay BIT provides an example of the approach that is common in BITs. The parties recognize that it is 'inappropriate' to encourage investment 'by weakening or reducing domestic environmental laws'.[105] The provision goes on to provide that 'each Party shall strive to ensure that it does not waive or otherwise derogate from, or offer to waive or otherwise derogate from, such laws as an encouragement for the establishment, acquisition, expansion or retention of an investment in its territory'. Where a party considers that the other party is attempting to encourage investment by lowering standards consultations may be requested. The Austrian model BIT and existing US BITS include a similarly worded provision.[106] These 'best efforts' commitments are not subject to investor–State dispute settlement but could be addressed in State-to-State dispute settlement.[107]

Some BITs entered into by the Belgium–Luxembourg Economic Union provide for expert consultations on matters related to their non-derogation provisions[108] and allow for the non-derogation provisions to be the subject of investor–State and State-to-State dispute settlement.[109] Because the non-derogation obligations only commit States to strive to ensure that they do not waive or derogate from their labour and environmental laws, dispute settlement procedures would provide only a limited review of any alleged derogation. To be in compliance, likely a State would only have to show a good faith effort not to derogate.

The US 2012 Model BIT goes somewhat further by specifically prohibiting each party from waiving or derogating from its environmental or labour laws so as to lower the protections provided by such laws to encourage investment.[110] To December 2014, no actual BIT has been concluded that follows this model.

As discussed in more detail below, recent Canadian and US FTAs go beyond non-derogation commitments to oblige the parties to ensure that their domestic labour laws 'adopt and maintain' certain identified international labour rights. The non-derogation obligation in these treaties requires parties not to derogate from their domestic laws implementing this obligation to the extent that the derogation

---

pdf> accessed 19 December 2014; as well as Art 6 of the Belgian–Luxembourg–Ethiopia BIT (not yet in force).

[104] See US–Peru FTA (2009) Arts 16.2(2), 17.2(2). Same language can also be found in the US–Panama (2011) Arts 16.2(2), 17.3(2) and US–Korea FTA (2012) Arts 19.2(2), 20.3(2).
[105] US–Uruguay BIT (2004) Arts 12, 13. The Canadian model BIT, Art 11, has a slightly different formulation.
[106] Austria model BIT. See also NAFTA (1994) Art 1114(2); US–Rwanda BIT (2008) Arts 12, 13.
[107] US–Uruguay BIT (2004) Arts 24, 37.
[108] Belgium–Luxembourg Economic Union–Mauritius BIT (2010) Art 6(4); see also US–Peru FTA (2009) Art 21.2, US–Korea FTA (2012) Art 22.4.
[109] Belgium–Luxembourg Economic Union–Mauritius BIT (2010) Arts 6(4), 12, 13.
[110] 2012 US Model BIT Arts 12, 13. See also EC–CARICOM EPA (2008) Arts 73, 188.1(a), (b); EU–Korea FTA (2011) Art 13.7; US–Chile FTA (2003) Art 19.2; US–Singapore FTA (2003) Art 18.2; Australia–US FTA (2005) Art 19.2.

would be inconsistent with the identified rights.[111] There is some variation in terms of what are considered internationally recognized labour rights.[112] For example, the Canada–Korea FTA and the US–Korea FTA both define the non-derogation obligation as applying to the maintenance of 'internationally recognized labour rights' to freedom of association, the right to collective bargaining, the elimination of child labour, the abolition of the worst forms of child labour and the elimination of discrimination in respect of employment and occupation.[113] Only the Canada–Korea FTA goes on to name acceptable minimum employment standards, the prevention of occupational injuries and illnesses, compensation in cases of occupational injuries or illnesses and non-discrimination in respect of working conditions for migrant workers as internationally recognized labour rights.[114]

The approach is somewhat different with respect to environmental laws. Non-derogation commitments apply to environmental law which is defined in a functional way. The Canada–Korea FTA, for example, defines 'environmental law' as follows:

> environmental law means any law, statutory or regulatory provision, or other legally binding measure, of a Party, the primary purpose of which is the protection of the environment, or the prevention of a danger to human life or health, through:
> (a) the prevention, abatement, or control of the release, discharge, or emission of pollutants or environmental contaminants;
> (b) the management of chemicals and waste and the dissemination of information related thereto; or
> (c) the conservation and protection of wild flora or wild fauna, including endangered species, their habitat, and protected natural areas,
> but does not include any measure directly related to worker health and safety, nor a measure the primary purpose of which is managing the commercial harvest or exploitation, or subsistence or aboriginal harvesting, of natural resources.[115]

Undoubtedly, the adoption of this functional approach reflects that absence of widely accepted basic norms for environmental protection comparable to those enshrined in the ILO Conventions.

Typically, non-derogation commitments in PTIAs can be the subject of the kind of dispute settlement procedures described in the preceding section.

---

[111] For example, US–Korea FTA (2012); Canada–Korea FTA (2015). See similarly Agreement Between Japan and the Republic of Peru for the Promotion, Protection and Liberalisation of Investment (signed 22 November 2008, entered into force 10 December 2009) available at: <http://investmentpolicyhub.unctad.org/Download/TreatyFile/1733> accessed 19 December 2014 Art 26. This approach is followed in Canada–Europe Comprehensive Economic and Trade Agreement (not yet in force) where each party commits to 'ensure that its labour laws embody and provide protection for fundamental rights at work...' as well as to seek to ensure high levels of protection (for example, Chapter 24 Arts 3, 4).

[112] Not only is there some variation across agreements entered into by different countries, there is also variation across agreements negotiated by the same country. Prislan and Zandvliet (n 15) 7–8.

[113] US–Korea FTA (2012) Art 19.2(1); Canada–Korea FTA (2015) Art 18.2.

[114] The US Model BIT includes some of these rights. The Belgium–Luxembourg–Ethiopia BIT (not yet in force) defines labour rights for the purposes of the treaty as the domestic laws regarding certain internationally recognized rights using a list which is different (Art 1).

[115] Canada–Korea FTA (2015) Art 17.17. The US Model BIT has a similar definition.

A party concerned about another party's derogation can request consultations with a view to finding a mutually satisfactory solution. If consultations are unsuccessful, an arbitration panel may be asked to rule on whether there has been a derogation. Where a panel finds a derogation, a ministerial consultation takes place with the goal of adopting an action plan to address the derogation. No penalties or trade sanctions can be imposed.[116] In US FTAs, State-to-State procedures may be used after these special procedures have failed.[117] Non-derogation obligations are usually not subject to investor–State dispute settlement.[118]

c. Co-operation on the enforcement of labour and environmental standards

A few PTIAs require cooperation among the parties on the enforcement of labour standards against investors. The EC–CARIFORUM EPA imposes an obligation on the parties both to cooperate and to take measures domestically to ensure that investors:

- Comply with the core labour standards set out in the 1998 *ILO Declaration on Fundamental Principles and Rights at Work*; and
- Do not manage or operate their investments in a manner that circumvents labour obligations arising from the international obligations of the parties.[119]

Similarly, the EC–CARIFORUM EPA imposes an obligation on the parties both to cooperate and take measures domestically to ensure that investors do not manage or operate their investments in a manner that circumvents the international labour obligations of the parties.[120] By specifically requiring both parties to take action to ensure investor compliance with international labour and environmental standards, these provisions oblige the *home State* to exercise its regulatory power in ensuring compliance by its investors with international norms in cooperation with the host State where those investors are operating.

This approach has not been followed by the EU in its recent FTA with Korea, though that treaty does provide for cooperation on a range of other issues as discussed below.[121] The US–Peru FTA does not address cooperation on enforcement generally in its cooperation provisions, but does contain an extensive annex on Forest Sector Governance, which imposes specific commitments on the US to support Peru's efforts to deal with illegal logging and trade in timber products.[122]

---

[116] Canada–Honduras FTA (2014) Art 16.
[117] US–Korea FTA (2012) Arts 19.7(5), 20.9(5), 22.4.
[118] Canada–Korea FTA (2015) Art 18.24, US–Uruguay BIT (2004) Art 24, Peru–Korea FTA (2011) Art 18.7; EFTA–Hong Kong Agreement on Labor (2011) Art 6(2).
[119] EU–CARIFORUM EPA (2008) Art 72(b), (c).
[120] EC–CARIFORUM EPA (2008) Art 72(b), (c).
[121] EU–Korea FTA (2011) Arts 13.11–13.13, Annex 13.
[122] US–Peru FTA (2008), Annex 18.3.4.

Other US FTAs provide for cooperation but no specific undertakings regarding home State enforcement.[123] Recent Canadian treaties also follow this approach.[124]

3. Commitments to comply with identified labour and environmental standards

Some PTIAs contain provisions that go beyond a prohibition on lowering standards to attract investment and requirements regarding the enforcement of domestic law to express the parties' commitment to the maintenance of high levels of labour rights and environmental protection sometimes by reference to international standards. Only a few recent treaties oblige parties to meet specific standards in their domestic law. The commitment in most treaties is aspirational or 'best efforts' only.

Under the NAALC, for example, the NAFTA States do not commit to upholding core international labour standards. Rather they agree to promote a list of principles, subject to their respective law and with the proviso that such principles do not set common minimum standards.[125] The NAALC provides that the parties must ensure that they maintain high domestic labour standards and strive to improve them, but does not further specify what this commitment means. Accordingly, it is difficult to assess its effect. A somewhat more specific approach is taken in some treaties that express aspirational or best efforts commitments regarding the implementation of certain listed international labour standards and require parties to strive to improve their labour laws.[126] Where specific standards are identified they usually include the following:

- the right of association;
- the right to organize and bargain collectively;
- prohibition of forced labour; and
- minimum age for the employment of children.[127]

---

[123] US–Korea FTA (2012) Annex 19-A, Labor Cooperation Mechanism Art 20.8 (environmental cooperation).

[124] Canada–Korea FTA (2015) Art 17.10, providing only for cooperation on matters of mutual interest related to the environment. The Canada–Europe Comprehensive Economic and Trade Agreement (not yet in force) is similar (Chapter 25, Art X.13), though the chapter on sustainability (Chapter 23) identifies enhanced enforcement of domestic labour and environmental laws as one of the goals of the labour rights and environmental protection chapters (Art 1.3.c). The Canada–Honduras FTA (2014) contemplates that the parties may develop a programme of cooperative activities related to the environment, and 'strengthening institutional capacity for enforcement' is on the indicative list of possible topics (Art 17 and Annex II). A similar approach is followed with respect to labour rights (for example, Canada–Honduras FTA (2014), Arts 19.4, Agreement on Labour Cooperation between Canada and Honduras (2014), Art 9). The same approach is followed in the Agreement on Environmental Cooperation between Canada and Panama (Art 16, Annex II).

[125] NAALC (1994) Art 2 and Annex 1 (Labour Principles).

[126] US–Jordan FTA (2001) Art 6.1

[127] Belgium–Luxembourg Economic Union-Ethiopia BIT (not yet in force) Arts 6, 1(6); US Model BIT, Art 13; Australia–US FTA (2005) Arts 18.1, 18.7; US–CAFTA–DR FTA (2009) Arts 16.1, 16.8; US–Chile FTA (2003) Arts 18.1, 18.8; US–Jordan FTA (2001) Art 6; and US–Morocco FTA (2004) Arts 16.1, 16.7. In these treaties, the parties also reaffirm their respective obligations as members of the International Labor Organization (ILO) and their commitments under the ILO Declaration on Fundamental Principles and Rights at Work and its Follow-Up, but do not otherwise tie their commitments to the specific obligations in these treaties. The EU–Korea FTA (2011)

Some treaties, however, diminish the effect of these commitments by recognizing the right of the parties to establish their own labour standards.[128]

Similar formulations are used in relation to environmental protection in FTAs.[129] The NAAEC recognizes the right of parties to establish their own domestic environmental standards, policies, and priorities, and to adopt or modify such laws and regulations, but it also requires parties to ensure that their domestic laws and regulations 'provide high levels of environmental protection' and to 'strive' to improve domestic standards.[130] Many FTAs contain aspirational obligations to strive to ensure high levels of environmental protection and to improve protection.[131] Unlike the obligations related to labour rights, the commitments on environmental protection are not tied to specific international standards.

The EC–CARIFORUM EPA provides a variation of this type of provision. Like the provisions discussed above, it requires parties to ensure that their domestic laws 'provide for and encourage high levels of social and labour standards' in line with listed international labour standards. However, it also recognizes the right of the parties 'to regulate in order to establish their own social regulations and labour standards in line with their own social development priorities and to adopt or modify accordingly their relevant laws and policies'.[132]

With respect to the environment, the EPA highlights the need for developing countries to take into account their development priorities and their level of development:

1. Recognising the right of the Parties and the Signatory CARIFORUM States to regulate in order to achieve their own level of domestic environmental and public health protection and their own sustainable development priorities, and to adopt or modify accordingly their environmental laws and policies, each Party and Signatory CARIFORUM State shall seek to ensure that its own environmental and public health laws and policies provide for and encourage high levels of environmental and public health protection and shall strive to continue to improve those laws and policies.

2. The Parties agree that the special needs and requirements of CARIFORUM States shall be taken into account in the design and implementation of measures

---

Art 13.4, goes slightly further than other US FTAs by recognizing the parties' commitments to the 2006 Ministerial Declaration of the UN Economic and Social Council on Full Employment and Decent Work and the importance of 'full and productive employment and decent work for all' for sustainable development. Other rights commonly listed include the prohibition of the worst forms of child labour; and the right to acceptable conditions of work with respect to minimum wages, hours of work, occupational safety and health.

[128] Canada–Korea FTA (2015) Art 18.2. See Art 17.2 regarding environmental protection. Belgium–Luxembourg Economic Union–Mauritius BIT (2010), is one of the few BITs to contain such a provision: Art 6(4).
[129] NAAEC Art 2.   [130] NAAEC Art 2.
[131] Canada–Korea FTA (2015) Art 17.2, US–Jordan FTA (2001) Art 5.2. The US–Korea FTA (2012) Art 20.1, is similar though states are obliged to 'adopt, maintain and implement laws…to fulfil its obligations under the multilateral environmental agreements listed in Annex 20.2.'
[132] Arts 192 and 191.

aimed at protecting environment and public health that affect trade between the Parties.[133]

The goal of these various types of provisions is not so much to improve the level of environmental protection, but to prevent competition for investment between States that will lead to a 'race to the bottom' of environmental standards. These provisions do not oblige State parties to ensure that their domestic laws and regulations reflect minimum environmental and labour standards consistent with their international obligations.

More recently, US and Canadian PTIAs have begun to require that specific labour standards be met. The US–Korea FTA, for example, provides that each party 'shall adopt and maintain in its statutes and regulations and practices' a list of labour rights like that set out above.[134] Recent US FTAs use identical language to oblige parties to fulfil their obligations under listed environmental treaties.[135] Under Canada's FTAs, however, parties are only obliged to strive to ensure that their laws provide high levels of protection consistent with listed environmental treaties.[136]

Finally, some PTIAs include general aspirational provisions on corporate social responsibility (CSR) relating to human rights, the environment, and corruption, and they may reference CSR instruments such as the OECD Guidelines for Multinational Enterprises and the Global Compact.[137] Certain US FTAs include CSR provisions that specifically target the environment. For example, the US–Australia FTA incorporates an obligation on the parties to promote 'as appropriate' the development of voluntary, market-based mechanisms that 'encourage the protection of natural resources and the environment'.[138] The US–Singapore and the US–Chile FTAs include a non-binding recommendation that parties 'encourage enterprises operating within [their] territory or subject to [their] jurisdiction to voluntarily incorporate sound principles of corporate stewardship in their internal policies, such as those principles or agreements that have been endorsed by the

---

[133] EC–CARIFORUM EPA (2008) Art 184.1. Similar language is in the EU–Korea FTA (2011) Art 13.3.

[134] US–Korea FTA (2012) Art 19.2. The list also includes elimination of discrimination in respect of employment and occupation. See similarly, US–Panama FTA (2011) Art 16.2. Canada's most recent FTAs follow this approach: Agreement on Labour Cooperation between Canada and the Republic of Colombia (2011) Art 1. Agreement on Labour Cooperation between Canada and the Republic of Honduras (2014) Art 1. In the Canada–Korea FTA (2015), this mandatory language is used but the right of each party to establish its own labour standards is expressly preserved (Art 18.2). A similar approach is followed in the Canada–Europe Comprehensive Economic and Trade Agreement (not yet in force) (Chapter 24, Art 3, 4).

[135] US–Panama FTA (2011) Art 17.2; US Korea FTA (2012) Art 20.2; Australia–US FTA (2005) Art 19.1, US–Chile FTA (2003) Art 19.1; US–Singapore FTA (2003) Art 18.1 (all use 'shall ensure').

[136] Canada–Korea FTA (2015) Art 17.2. In the Agreement on Environmental Cooperation between Canada and Honduras (2014), parties are obliged to 'ensure' that their environmental laws provide high levels of protection, but their right to set their own standards is preserved (Art 3). The Canada–Europe Comprehensive Economic and Trade Agreement (not yet in force) obliges the parties only to 'seek to ensure' that their laws provide high levels of protection (Chapter 24 Art X.4).

[137] Canada–Colombia FTA (2011) Art 816; Canada–Peru FTA (2008) Art 810.

[138] See Australia–US FTA (2005) Art 19.4.

Parties'.[139] While these provisions raise awareness of the need for environmentally responsible conduct by investors, they have no binding effect. They do not impose obligations on States to implement laws or policies on CSR. Nor do they require investors to operate in accordance with internationally accepted CSR norms.

Very few BITs contain provisions committing the parties to meet minimum standards for labour rights and environmental protection. The Belgium–Luxembourg Model BIT, however, reaffirms the parties' international commitments under environmental treaties and imposes an obligation on the parties to strive to ensure that these international environmental law obligations are implemented in domestic law.[140]

4. Co-operation between parties on labour and environmental issues

Many PTIAs establish mechanisms to enhance cooperation between the party States on labour and environmental issues. Typically, BITs do not address cooperation.

US FTAs, for example, establish a Labour Affairs Council, or a similar body of ministerial representatives or senior government officials, responsible for a Labour Cooperation and Capacity Building Mechanism. Each party is to designate a contact point within its ministry of labour. These people are responsible for developing a plan setting out cooperation priorities and specific cooperation and capacity building activities to fulfil those priorities.[141] An indicative list of activities is provided. Cooperation may take place through the exchange of information, educational activities, technical cooperation and other means. A similar approach is taken in Canadian FTAs.[142]

In parallel, the same treaties seek to enhance cooperation between the parties on environmental issues. US FTAs recognize the importance of capacity building for the purpose of environmental protection and incorporate provisions on the sharing of information relating to the environmental effects of trade agreements and policies.[143] Unlike the provisions regarding labour cooperation, however, most US FTAs do not provide any mechanism for the development of a plan to implement the parties' commitment to cooperate. The environmental cooperation provisions in the US–Chile FTA are more expansive and resemble the labour provisions found in some US FTAs, providing an indicative list of cooperative activities and a mechanism that contemplates an institutional framework for the identification

---

[139] US–Singapore FTA (2003) Art 18.9; US–Chile FTA (2003) Art 19.10. Some recent Canadian FTAs have similar provisions: for example, Agreement on Environmental Cooperation between Canada and the Republic of Honduras (2014) Art 10.

[140] Art 5(3). See also the Belgium–Luxembourg–Ethiopia BIT (not yet in force) Art 5(3).

[141] Australia–US FTA (2005) Art 18.5; US–CAFTA–DR FTA (2004) Art 16.5 and Annex 16.5; US–Chile FTA (2003) Art 18.5 and Annex 18.5; US–Morocco FTA (2004) Art 16.5 and Annex 16-A; and US–Singapore FTA (2003) Art 17.5 and Annex 17A; US–Panama FTA (2011) Art 16.6 and Annex 16.6. See also, NAALC (1994) Art 8–19.

[142] Agreement on Labour Cooperation between Canada and Honduras (2014); Canada–Korea FTA (2015) Art 18.11, Annex 18-A; Agreement on Labour Cooperation between Canada and Peru (2008) Art 9, Annex 1.

[143] The Australia–US FTA (2005) Art 19.6; US–Singapore FTA (2003) Art 18.6.

of priorities and specific activities, the development of a work plan as well as the implementation of such activities.[144] The US–Chile FTA goes further to require the parties to pursue certain identified 'cooperative projects'. These include, for example, developing a public database of chemicals that have been released into the environment, reducing the pollution from mining projects, protecting wildlife, and reducing ozone-depleting substances.[145]

Canadian FTAs tend to include more modest commitments to cooperate 'on matters of mutual interest' with areas to be determined by an Environmental Affairs Council or similar institution created under the treaty and consisting of high level officials or ministers from the party States that is responsible for the implementation of the agreement.[146] In some cases, Canada has agreed with its treaty partner to develop a work plan for cooperative activities within a specified time frame.[147] Canadian FTA commitments regarding cooperation on labour rights follow a similar pattern.[148]

The EU has taken different approaches to cooperation, seemingly dependent of the level of development of its negotiating partner. The EU–Korea FTA provides for the possibility of cooperation on a range of issues identified in an indicative list, including exchanging views on the impact of the treaty on sustainable development, cooperation in international fora responsible for social and environmental aspects of trade, the implementation of corporate social responsibility standards, trade-related aspects of sustainable fishing and logging, and labour standards.[149] There is no specific mechanism in the treaty to implement such cooperation.

By contrast, in the EU–CARIFORUM EPA, there is a wide range of specific cooperation and technical assistance commitments, some of which relate to sustainable development, and institutional arrangements are put in place to give effect to these commitments. For example, the parties agreed to work together to support the participation of CARIFORUM services suppliers in international, regional, sub-regional, bilateral, and private financing programmes to support the sustainable development of tourism.[150] With respect to labour rights, the parties agree to cooperate to strengthen domestic legislation and enhance enforcement, including 'training and capacity building initiatives of labour inspectors, and promoting corporate social responsibility through public information and reporting'.[151] Cooperation priorities and activities are to be determined by the CARIFORUM–EU Trade and Development Committee, created under the agreement and composed of representatives of the parties.[152]

---

[144] See the US–Chile FTA (2003) Art 19.5, Annex 19.3, Art 2.
[145] US–Chile FTA (2003), Annex 19.3, Art 1.
[146] For example, Canada–Korea FTA (2015) Arts 17.10, 17.11; Agreement on Environmental Cooperation between Canada and Honduras (2014) Arts 13, 17.
[147] Agreement on Environmental Cooperation between Canada and Honduras (2014) Art 7.
[148] Agreement on Labour Cooperation between Canada and Honduras (2014) Art 9, Annex 1.
[149] EU–Korea FTA (2011) Arts 13.11–13.13, Annex 13.
[150] EU–CARIFORUM EPA (2008) Art 115. See also Art 116.
[151] EU–CARIFORUM EPA (2008) Art 196.
[152] EU–CARIFORUM EPA (2008) Art 230. These commitments are supported by the European Development Fund (Art 7).

IV. Summary of Survey of Labour Rights and Environmental Protection Provisions in PTIAs and BITs

The foregoing survey discloses significant diversity in the practices followed by different countries in the BITs and PTIAs they negotiate as well those followed by a single country over time in terms of provisions relating to labour rights and environmental protection. Nevertheless, some generalizations may be made. BITs negotiated by Canada and the United States, as well as by the Belgium–Luxembourg Economic Union and a few other countries, already address aspects of sustainable development in one or more of the following ways: they (i) recognize sustainable development in their preambles, (ii) make clear that States can act to protect labour rights and the environment without being found to have been engaged in indirect expropriation for which compensation must be paid, (iii) include exceptions for certain policy tools, like subsidies, and permit country specific reservations, both of which could be used to shelter some measures relating to labour rights and environmental protection from investor protection obligations, and (iv) discourage parties from reducing the protection of labour rights and the environment in their domestic regimes to attract investment. Canadian BITs, and a small but increasing number of BITs signed by other countries, provide general exceptions for environmental measures based on GATT Article XX. Other BITs, especially older ones negotiated by European countries, include few, if any, of these kinds of provisions.

PTIAs, on the other hand, are increasingly likely to include all of these provisions, often in a stronger form, as well as a variety of others. PTIAs may include binding commitments by parties not to reduce their domestic labour and environmental standards to attract investment as opposed to the 'best efforts' undertakings in most BITs. As well, they may include commitments that domestic laws relating to labour rights and environmental protection are administered in accordance with due process and provide effective remedies. Some PTIAs even require parties to ensure that their domestic labour laws meet international norms for their substantive content and that their environmental laws reflect their commitments under international environmental agreements. PTIAs may contain State commitments to enforce their domestic laws in relation to labour rights and the environment and impose obligations on investors' home States to cooperate with the host States where their investors are operating in enforcing labour and environmental laws. PTIAs may contain obligations on both parties to cooperate more generally with the goal of improving labour rights and environmental protection. Finally, PTIAs that contain these kinds of obligations typically provide for a range of institutions and dispute settlement procedures to support the effective implementation and the enhancement of labour rights and environmental protection more generally.

It has not been possible in this short paper to canvass all the thousands of agreements in place. However, the foregoing summary identifies the main variants of provisions in PTIAs and BITS and suggests the conclusion that labour rights and environmental protection are more likely to be addressed in a thorough-going way in PTIAs than they are in BITs. In the remainder of this paper, some of the reasons for this tendency are explored with a view to assessing the likelihood that the kinds of provisions appearing in PTIAs will find their way into BITs.

V. Factors Affecting the Likelihood that PTIA Provisions Regarding Labour Rights and Environmental Protection will be Adopted in BITs

a) Introduction

A number of factors are driving change in the investment treaty regime and some of these are likely to push States towards adopting in their BITs more of the kinds of labour and environmental protection provisions currently found in PTIAs. On the other hand, the different dynamic that characterizes negotiating BITs compared to PTIAs will likely constrain the wholesale adoption of a PTIA-like approach. Typically BIT negotiations address a narrow range of investor protection issues based on a template agreement developed by one party. Parties in PTIA negotiations, by contrast, are seeking to create a comprehensive framework dealing with a broad range of issues in an agreement tailored to their particular circumstances. In the latter context, the parties are more likely to address sustainable development considerations in a thoroughgoing way.

b) Factors encouraging the adoption of labour rights and environmental protection provisions in BITs

Traditionally, BITs have been negotiated between developed capital exporting States and developing States hoping to attract investment. In this context, developed countries have tended to have a single-minded focus on the strong protection of their investors leading to the dominance of investor-protection provisions in BITs. Though BIT obligations formally applied equally to both parties, in practice, there were no developing country investors to claim the benefits of the treaty protections from developed country parties. While treaties are still entered into in this context, many treaties are now being negotiated in contexts that are dramatically different in ways that may set the stage for the inclusion in BITS of more extensive provisions addressing sustainable development provisions. FDI from developing countries and transition economies accounted for a record 39 per cent of global FDI outflows in 2013.[153] Countries like China, India, Malaysia, and others have become significant capital exporters. Countries like Canada, that have negotiated most treaties from a capital exporter's point of view, are now signing treaties with countries that are substantial sources of inward investment, forcing them to be more concerned about ensuring their ability to regulate to achieve sustainable

---

[153] UNCTAD, *IIA Issues Note: Recent Developments in Investor-state Dispute Settlement (ISDS)* (United Nations 2014) ix.

development, including the protection of labour rights and the environment, is accommodated in their treaties.[154] More generally, negotiations between countries that are both capital importers and capital exporters is occurring in an increasing number of South–South[155] and North–North contexts,[156] where all parties have an interest in ensuring the right balance between investor protection and their freedom to take action to achieve sustainable development.[157]

Another driver of change that may encourage more provisions related to labour rights and environmental protection in BITs is dissatisfaction with the BIT regime and, in particular, the balance that traditional investment agreements strike between investor protection and States' freedom to act in the public interest. Investor–State arbitration tribunals have made some awards that limited host State regulatory flexibility in surprising ways.[158] There are other sources of dissatisfaction as well. Tribunal awards have been criticized for a lack of consistency, undermining certainty regarding the content of the investor protection standards, though the degree and seriousness of this problem is subject to debate. States have also expressed concern about the high cost of defending investor claims.[159] Some very large awards have been made, including most dramatically the recent US$50 billion award against Russia,[160] and the process is costly for States even if they are successful in defending against an investor's claim.[161] Various other concerns have been expressed about investor–State arbitration, including regarding the quality and independence of the arbitrators.[162] These concerns have encouraged many countries to reconsider the costs and benefits of investment treaty protection. Some countries have reformed or are currently reforming their model treaties.[163] A few countries have even sought to opt out of the system, in whole or in part, by terminating investment treaties.[164] All countries have become more focused on

---

[154] Canada–China BIT (2014).

[155] COMESA Investment Agreement (not yet in force), ASEAN Investment Agreement (2009).

[156] NAFTA (1994), Canada–EU Comprehensive Economic and Trade Agreement (not yet in force), and the EU–US Trans-Atlantic Trade and Investment Partnership.

[157] Polanco recently found, however, that there are no consistent differences in the PTIAs and BITs negotiated by Chile with developed and developing countries (R Polanco, 'Chile's experience with South-South Trade and Investment Agreements' proceedings SIEL Working Paper 2014/26 available at: <http://papers.ssrn.com/sol3/papers.cfm?abstract_id=2474119> accessed 19 December 2014).

[158] VanDuzer and others (n 3) 102.

[159] S Franck, 'Rationalizing Costs in Investment Treaty Arbitration' (2011) 88 Washington U L Rev 769.

[160] *Yukos Universal Limited (Isle of Man) v The Russian Federation*, UNCITRAL, PCA Case No AA 227, Award (18 July 2014). This award is uncommonly large. Claims for 2013 were between US$27 million and US$1 billion (UNCTAD n 153).

[161] D Rosert, *The Stakes are High: A review of the financial costs of investment treaty arbitration* (International Institute for Sustainable Development 2014).

[162] J Wouters and N Hachez, 'Institutionalization of investment arbitration and sustainable development,' in M-C Cordonier Segger, M Gehring, and A Newcombe (eds), *Sustainable Development in World Investment Law* (Wolters Kluwer 2012).

[163] UNCTAD (n 37) 114.

[164] Many countries have rejected aspects of the system: Ecuador, Bolivia, Panama, El Salvador, Australia, India, Indonesia, and South Africa. See generally, UNCTAD (n 37) 115.

ensuring that their investment obligations accommodate their right to regulate to achieve sustainable development.

Another factor driving change is the recent initiation of investor–State claims against traditional capital exporters. As investment agreements are increasingly entered into by developed capital exporting States with countries that are significant sources of inward investment into those States, inevitably claims have begun to be made against the former. It is perhaps not surprising that the developed countries that have faced the most investor–State cases, Canada and the US, have been the leaders in seeking provisions that more clearly guarantee the policy space for regulating to achieve sustainable development. A number of Western European capital exporting States, including Belgium, France, Germany, and Greece, are facing new investor–State claims.[165] As more claims are brought against traditional capital exporting countries, their interest in provisions protecting their right to regulate to protect labour rights and the environment will likely increase.[166]

Decisions in investor–State cases and the recent initiation of cases against developed countries have generated a significant and largely critical public discourse regarding investor–State arbitration and investment treaty protection that might further encourage changes to investment treaty practice.[167] As well an explosion of wide-ranging and dynamic academic research into various aspects of the international investment regime has produced a wealth of new ideas on how to improve substantive investor protection and investor–State dispute settlement. In particular, UNCTAD's Investment Policy Framework for Sustainable Development released in 2012 has played a leading role in showing how States can incorporate sustainable development enhancing provisions in their domestic investment policy as well as in their international investment treaties and encouraging them to do so.[168]

---

[165] *Ping An Life Insurance Company of China, Limited and Ping An Insurance (Group) Company of China, Limited v Kingdom of Belgium*, ICSID Case No ARB/12/29, *Erbil Serter v French Republic*, ICSID Case No ARB/13/22, *Vattenfall AB and others v Federal Republic of Germany*, ICSID Case No ARB/12/12 (this is the third claim against Germany) and *Poštová banka, a.s. and ISTROKAPITAL SE v Hellenic Republic*, ICSID Case No ARB/13/8. Fourteen cases have been initiated against Spain.

[166] The same States may be interested in treaty commitments accommodating high standards of labour rights and environmental protection on the basis that their businesses already meet those standards while developing country businesses may not. In such a case, higher labour and environmental standards may protect developed country businesses against developing country competitors. See D Collins, 'Sustainable International Investment Law After the Pax Americana: The BOOT on the Other Foot' (2012) 13 J of World Investment and Trade 325.

[167] Providing a recent example of critical public comment, the *Economist* magazine expressed its opposition to investor–State arbitration provisions: 'A better way to arbitration: Protections for foreign investors are not horror critics claim, but they could be improved', *The Economist* available at: <www.economist.com/news/leaders/21623674-protections-foreign-investors-are-not-horror-critics-claim-they-could-be-improved> accessed 16 December 2014. The impact on policymakers is evident, for example, in recent statements of EU President Junckers, EU President-elect Junckers, Speech, 22 October 2014, available at: <http://europa.eu/rapid/press-release_SPEECH-14-705_de.htm> accessed 16 December 2014.

[168] UNCTAD, *Investment Policy Framework for Sustainable Development* (United Nations 2012). Fifteen of the forty-seven investment treaties signed in 2011 included provisions related to sustainable development that were suggested in UNCTAD's Investment Policy Framework for Sustainable Development: Tuerk and Rojid (n 14).

c) Factors discouraging the adoption of labour rights and environmental protection provisions in BITs

Despite the many factors pushing States towards the adoption of labour rights and environmental protection provisions in their BITs, several factors are likely to discourage doing so, at least in some contexts. Some developing countries may be unwilling to negotiate for more protection for sustainable development policies because they rightly understand themselves to be in a fierce competition for investment with other countries, especially similarly situated developing countries. Such countries might perceive commitments related to sustainable development in BITs as likely to cause prospective investors to devalue the protections provided and so may be reluctant to agree with them.

As well, the nature of BIT negotiations is likely to constrain the adoption of at least some of the labour rights and environmental protection provisions identified in the survey. BITs are typically negotiated on the basis of model texts proposed by one or, increasingly, both parties. While there may be some negotiation on specific provisions, negotiations are restricted to a narrow range of issues related to investment. The goal in BITs negotiations, typically, is not to create a detailed agreement uniquely customized to the needs of and conditions in the negotiating parties. By contrast, PTIA negotiations are much more complex, dealing with a wide range of issues spanning the entire trade and investment relationship between the parties. PTIA negotiations seek to establish a comprehensive framework for that relationship that is tailored to the priorities and needs of both parties. The broad scope of PTIA negotiations and the corresponding effort invested in them by the parties provides a context in which it is much more likely that issues related to sustainable development can be discussed and addressed. In the interests of establishing a framework for economic relations and sometimes to support economic development, PTIA parties are more likely to commit to cooperate regarding the enhancement of labour rights and environmental protection, to the effective enforcement of domestic rules in these areas and to create institutions involving both parties with a mandate to support such cooperation. Since BITs do not represent the same kind of engagement in relationship building, similar cooperation commitments are less likely to be negotiated.

VI. Conclusion

The question of whether the kinds of provisions found in PTIAs relating to labour rights and environmental protection will be adopted in BITs is likely to become less relevant over time. UNCTAD reports that PTIAs are growing at a faster rate than BITs.[169] As well major negotiations to create so-called 'mega-regional' PTIAs

---

[169] UNCTAD (n 37).

and the negotiation by the EU of investment commitments in its trade agreements will mean that, increasingly, PTIAs will replace many BITS worldwide.[170]

Nevertheless, to the extent that BIT negotiations continue to take place, as a consequence of the factors noted above, many of the kinds of labour rights and environmental protection commitments already found in some BITs seem likely to be adopted more broadly. These include provisions to (i) recognize sustainable development in preambles, (ii) make clear that States can act to protect labour rights and the environment without being found to have been engaged in indirect expropriation for which compensation must be paid, (iii) create exceptions for certain policy tools, like subsidies, and permit country specific reservations, both of which could be used to shelter some measures relating to labour rights and environmental protection from investor protection obligations, and general exceptions for environmental measures based on GATT Article XX, and (iv) discourage parties from reducing the protection of labour rights and the environment in their domestic regimes to attract investment. The fact that an increasing number of BITs include such provisions suggests that any factors discouraging the adoption of such provisions are not likely to be determinative.[171]

As well, some of the stronger provisions found in PTIAs that do not involve the commitment of substantial resources from the parties and are not integral to developing a long-term framework for a comprehensive economic relationship may find their way into BITs. These would include binding commitments by parties not to reduce their domestic labour and environmental standards to attract investment, to administer domestic laws relating to labour rights and environmental protection in accordance with due process and to provide effective remedies as well as commitments to ensure that their domestic labour laws meet international norms for their substantive content and that their environmental laws reflect their commitments under international environmental agreements and to enforce their domestic laws in relation to labour rights and the environment.

At the same time, however, the other sorts of provisions found in PTIAs that are related to the development of a broad economic relationship are less likely to be adopted in BITs. These include commitments to establish special dispute settlement procedures to address issues related to labour rights and environmental protection, to engage in cooperative activities related to enforcement, information exchange and technical assistance and to create institutions involving treaty parties to support such cooperation and dispute settlement.

---

[170] The Trans-Pacific Partnership negotiations involves parties that have fourteen BITs between them and the Canada–Europe Comprehensive Economic and Trade Agreement will create new investment obligations between Canada and seven EU member States that are parties to BITS with Canada (UNCTAD (n 37) 117).

[171] This is the conclusion of Fontanelli and Bianco 2014, suggesting that the 'NAFTA' model will prevail, F Fontanelli and G Bianco, 'Converging Toward NAFTA: An Analysis of FTA Chapters in the European Union and the United States' (2014) 50 Stanford J Intl L 211.

VIII

Reconciling Investment Protection and Sustainable Development

A Plea for an Interpretative U-Turn

Katharina Berner

I. Introduction

Investor–State arbitration remains an attractive option for settling international investment disputes as the high numbers of newly filed claims illustrate.[1] But despite its unbroken attractiveness, the international investment law regime has recently come under pressure. By invoking a background of alarming changes in the political and economic context as regards food security, financial crises, environmental threats, and social imbalances,[2] numerous stakeholders call for a paradigm shift away from traditional perceptions of international investment law. Once awareness had grown that international investment law should not be viewed in clinical isolation from general international law,[3] it became undeniable that international investment law also has an impact on other fields of law.[4] Against this background, it is now postulated that international investment law should abandon its preoccupation with safeguarding investors' rights and more strongly focus on sustainable development instead.[5]

Most prominently, this call for a paradigm shift has been taken up by UNCTAD's *Investment Policy Framework for Sustainable Development*, which was promulgated

---

[1] UNCTAD, 'World Investment Report 2013' (Geneva 2013) UN Doc UNCTAD/WIR/2013 110f. See also ICSID, 'Caseload—Statistics 2015-2' available at: <https://icsid.worldbank.org/ICSID>. All internet sources have been accessed on 20 August 2015.

[2] UNCTAD, *Investment Policy Framework for Sustainable Development* (July 2012) available at: <http://investmentpolicyhub.unctad.org> 3.

[3] See in particular R Hofmann and C Tams, 'International Investment Law: Situating an Exotic Special Regime within the Framework of International Law' in R Hofmann and C Tams (eds), *International Investment Law and General International Law: From Clinical Isolation to Systemic Integration?* (Nomos 2011).

[4] A Reinisch and C Knahr (eds), *International Investment Law in Context* (Eleven International Pub 2008).

[5] UNCTAD (n 2) iii.

in 2012.⁶ As its basic premise, the Framework suggests that international investment law suffers from a built-in bias favouring foreign investors and foreign investments over legitimate non-investment policy choices.⁷ Vividly depicting the current regime of international investment agreements (IIAs) as a 'straitjacket',⁸ the Framework argues, for instance, that international investment law could become 'a vehicle for the protection of interests of investors and home countries without giving due consideration to the development concerns of developing countries'.⁹ To address these alleged shortcomings, UNCTAD presents several core principles for investment policy-making that are meant to be implemented at the international level by revising existing and negotiating new IIAs.¹⁰

In this chapter, I do not purport to engage in the debates about whether a stronger focus on sustainable development concerns is really desirable. Irrespective of whether the alleged bias in favour of investment protection exists, the question to which extent international investment law should consider or even promote sustainable development concerns remains a political one. Instead, I ask whether it is truly necessary to change the substance of international investment law in order to achieve the desired paradigm shift. To start with, I argue that the rules of treaty interpretation under general public international law offer a viable alternative for reconciling investment protection and sustainable development concerns (II). Based on this observation, I then analyse whether these rules' potential has actually been used in investor–State arbitration (III). In conclusion, I contend that those who call for a stronger focus on sustainable development concerns are ill-advised to leave the current regime of international investment law as it stands (IV).

II. The Vienna Rules as a Gateway for Sustainable Development

This chapter presents an alternative to changing the substance of international investment law in order to more strongly focus on sustainable development concerns. Even under the current regime of investment protection, IIAs are not insulated against external concerns such as sustainable development.¹¹ The gateway that assists in integrating sustainable development concerns into existing agreements are the rules of treaty interpretation under general public international law.

---

⁶ UNCTAD (n 2). See also A Vanduzer, P Simons, and G Mayeda, *Integrating Sustainable Development into International Investment Agreements: A Guide for Developing Country Negotiators* (Commonwealth Secretariat 2013).
⁷ cf also SW Schill, 'Enhancing International Investment Law's Legitimacy: Conceptual and Methodological Foundations of a New Public Law Approach' (2011) 52 Va J Intl L 67.
⁸ UNCTAD (n 2) 37.   ⁹ ibid.   ¹⁰ ibid 8.
¹¹ ILC, 'Report of the Study Group on Fragmentation of International Law: Difficulties Arising from the Diversification and Expansion of International Law', finalized by Martii Koskenniemi (13 April 2006) UN Doc A/CN.4/L.682, 99f. See also Hofmann and Tams (n 3) 16.

These rules are laid down in Articles 31 to 33 of the 1969 Vienna Convention on the Law of Treaties (hereinafter referred to as the 'Vienna rules').[12]

a) Applicability of the Vienna rules

Naturally, the Vienna rules can only assist in integrating sustainable development concerns into IIAs if they apply to the interpretation of these agreements. Explaining why the Vienna rules do apply to the interpretation of many or even most IIAs is, however, not as simple and straightforward as some commentators claim.[13] In order to avoid popular fallacies, it is essential to distinguish two perspectives. On the one hand, one needs to determine whether an IIA falls within the scope of the Vienna rules. On the other hand, one needs to determine whether an arbitral tribunal is authorized (and perhaps even obliged) to apply the Vienna rules to interpret a particular agreement.

The former perspective is fairly unproblematic. Here one needs to distinguish between applying the Vienna rules in their capacity as treaty law and as a reflection

---

[12] Vienna Convention on the Law of Treaties (adopted 23 May 1969, entered into force 27 January 1980) 1155 UNTS 331 (VCLT). Arts 31 and 32 VCLT, which are more relevant to the topic under consideration than Art 33 VCLT, are reproduced below.

Article 31—General rule of interpretation
1. A treaty shall be interpreted in good faith in accordance with the ordinary meaning to be given to the terms of the treaty in their context and in the light of its object and purpose.
2. The context for the purpose of the interpretation of a treaty shall comprise, in addition to the text, including its preamble and annexes:
   (a) any agreement relating to the treaty which was made between all the parties in connection with the conclusion of the treaty;
   (b) any instrument which was made by one or more parties in connection with the conclusion of the treaty and accepted by the other parties as an instrument related to the treaty.
3. There shall be taken into account, together with the context:
   (a) any subsequent agreement between the parties regarding the interpretation of the treaty or the application of its provisions;
   (b) any subsequent practice in the application of the treaty which establishes the agreement of the parties regarding its interpretation;
   (c) any relevant rules of international law applicable in the relations between the parties.
4. A special meaning shall be given to a term if it is established that the parties so intended.

Article 32—Supplementary means of interpretation
Recourse may be had to supplementary means of interpretation, including the preparatory work of the treaty and the circumstances of its conclusion, in order to confirm the meaning resulting from the application of article 31, or to determine the meaning when the interpretation according to article 31:
(a) leaves the meaning ambiguous or obscure; or
(b) leads to a result which is manifestly absurd or unreasonable.

[13] For example, R Weeramantry, *Treaty Interpretation in Investment Arbitration* (OUP 2012) 34f; J Salacuse, *The Law of Investment Treaties* (OUP 2010) 140; C McLachlan, L Shore, and M Weiniger, *International Investment Arbitration: Substantive Principles* (OUP 2007) 66, 221; C Dugan and others, *Investor-State Arbitration* (OUP 2008) 204f.

of customary international law. In their capacity as treaty law, these rules' scope of application is limited in three respects. First, they only apply to agreements all of whose parties have also ratified the Vienna Convention.[14] Second, the Vienna rules only apply to agreements concluded between States.[15] And third, they only apply to agreements that have been concluded by States after the date on which the Vienna Convention entered into force for these States.[16] However, these limitations are hardly relevant in practice anymore. Today, it is widely recognized that Articles 31–33 VCLT reflect customary international law rules of treaty interpretation.[17] Unless the parties to an IIA choose to deviate from the Vienna rules, these rules govern the agreement's interpretation either as treaty law or as a reflection of customary international law.[18]

Establishing whether an arbitral tribunal is actually authorized (and perhaps even obliged) to apply the Vienna rules is, in contrast, more complicated. Empty phrases such as 'arbitral tribunals must apply the Vienna rules since these rules govern the interpretation of treaties',[19] albeit popular, do not help to resolve this issue. Instead, one eventually needs to determine the applicable law for each individual dispute. Since this chapter has a different focus, it must suffice at this point to briefly mention some of the factors that should be considered when determining the applicable law in investor–State arbitration.[20] First of all, one needs to recall that the creation of arbitral tribunals is governed by the principle of party autonomy.[21] Therefore, the applicable law ultimately depends on the agreement

---

[14] As of today, only 114 States have become a party to the Convention. States such as France, India, Turkey, and the USA have not ratified the Convention so far. For the current status of ratification of this and other treaties referred to in this contribution, see <http://treaties.un.org/>.

[15] Art 1 VCLT. Art 2(1)(a) VCLT further specifies that, for the purpose of the Convention, the term 'treaty' means an international agreement concluded between States in written form and governed by international law, whether embodied in a single instrument or in two or more related instruments and whatever its particular designation.

[16] Art 4 VCLT.

[17] R Gardiner, *Treaty Interpretation* (OUP 2008) 12f; see also *Legal Consequences of the Construction of a Wall in the Occupied Palestinian Territory* (Advisory Opinion) [2004] ICJ Rep 38 [94]; *Sovereignty over Pulau Litigan and Pulau Sipadan (Indonesia v Malaysia)* [2002] ICJ Rep 625 [37] with further references; *Japan—Alcoholic Beverages II*, Report of the Appellate Body (4 October 1996) WT/DS8/AB/R, WT/DS10/AB/R, WT/DS11/AB/R at Section D; *Responsibilities and Obligations of States Sponsoring Persons and Entities with Respect to Activities in the Area* (Request for Advisory Opinion submitted to the Seabed Disputes Chamber) ITLOS Case No 16 (1 February 2011) [57]; *Golder v UK* App no 4451/70 (ECtHR, 27 September 1973) [29].

[18] One such deviation, which partly supersedes the Vienna rules, is contained in Art 1131(2) NAFTA. This provision stipulates that interpretative notes issued by the Free Trade Commission (FTC) are binding on Chapter 11 arbitral tribunals. Such interpretative notes constitute a special form of subsequent agreements. Under Art 31(3)(a) VCLT, in contrast, subsequent agreements are not binding but have the same rank as the other elements of the general rule of interpretation under Art 31 VCLT; cf *Clayton v Canada*, Award on Jurisdiction and Liability, PCA Case No 2009-04 (17 March 2015) IIC 688 (2015) 430, Art 13(2) of the EU Commission's September 2015 TTIP draft (investment chapter).

[19] cf McLachlan, Shore, and Weiniger (n 13) 66, 221.

[20] See generally Y Banifatemi, 'The Law Applicable in Investment Treaty Arbitration' in K Yannaca-Small (ed), *Arbitration under International Investment Agreements: A Guide to the Key Issues* (OUP 2010); H Kjos, *Applicable Law in Investor-State Arbitration: The Interplay between National and International Law* (OUP 2013).

[21] Banifatemi (n 20) 192; Dugan and others (n 13) 201.

Vienna Rules as a Gateway for Sustainable Development 181

to arbitrate and the law that governs this agreement.[22] Further legal sources to be considered include, non-exhaustively, the respective IIA and the law governing this agreement, procedural rules chosen by the parties to the dispute, and the conflict of law rules and mandatory law of the arbitral tribunal's forum State.[23] In sum, the applicable law will thus depend on a complex interaction of various sources in the light of the principle of party autonomy.

In most instances, this complex interaction will eventually result in authorizing arbitral tribunals to apply the Vienna rules.[24] It is therefore not surprising that arbitral tribunals often quite naturally profess to apply the Vienna rules in order to interpret IIAs.[25] Nevertheless, one must not forget that applying the Vienna rules—if these rules form part of the applicable law—is not subject to a tribunal's discretion but mandatory. Hence any failure to apply or to correctly apply the Vienna rules can entail serious consequences and may even justify an annulment decision. This can be seen, for example, in the case of *Malaysian Historical Salvors Sdn Bhd v Malaysia*. In this decision, the Panel justified its decision to annul the sole arbitrator's award by pointing out that he had failed to take account of the travaux préparatoires of the ICSID Convention and therefore arrived at an interpretation that was incompatible with the travaux. Taking the Vienna rules seriously, one must object that the Panel erred in considering the sole arbitrator obliged to take the travaux into account.[26] As Article 32 VCLT clearly states, recourse *may* be had to supplementary means of interpretation such as the travaux; its consideration is therefore merely permissible under certain conditions but never mandatory.[27]

b) Meaning and legal status of sustainable development

To understand how a paradigm shift towards a stronger focus on sustainable development concerns can be implemented legally, we must in a first step define what

---

[22] cf ibid 219: 'The consent of the parties is the basis of the jurisdiction of all international arbitral tribunals.'

[23] More generally on the applicable law see ibid 201f.

[24] For example, Art 42(1) of the Convention on the Settlement of Investment Disputes between States and Nationals of Other States (adopted 18 March 1965, entered into force 14 October 1966) ('ICSID Convention') 575 UNTS 159. See also Art 1131(1) of the North American Free Trade Agreement between the USA, Canada, and Mexico (adopted 17 December 1992, entered into force 1 January 1993) 32 ILM 289 (NAFTA); Art 13(2) TTIP draft; Art X.27(1) CETA.

[25] For example, *Asian Agricultural Products Ltd ('AAPL') v Republic of Sri Lanka* (Award) IIC 18 (1990) 263 [38]. For further examples see R Dolzer and C Schreuer, *Principles of International Investment Law* (OUP 2008) 31.

[26] *Malaysian Historical Salvors Sdn Bhd v Malaysia*, ICSID Case No ARB/05/10, Decision on the Application for Annulment (16 April 2009) IIC 372 (2009) [80]. cf also *Daimler Financial Services AG v Republic of Argentina*, ICSID Case No ARB/05/1, Decision for Annulment (7 January 2015) IIC 669 (2015) 157, 161 – 62, 192 – 96.

[27] cf also C Schreuer, 'Failure to Apply the Governing Law in International Investment Arbitration' (2002) 7 ARIEL 147, 163f.

the notion 'sustainable development' actually means. In a second step, we shall try to identify its legal status to see whether the Vienna rules may help to reconcile investment protection and sustainable development.

While there are several attempts at circumscribing the notion of 'sustainable development', these attempts differ more in their level of detail than in substance.[28] An early and well-known definition has been offered by the 'Brundtland Report', which described sustainable development as 'development that meets the needs of the present without compromising the ability of future generations to meet their own needs'.[29] More refined definitions distinguish at least three key pillars upon which sustainable development rests, namely economic development, social well-being and social development, and environmental protection.[30] In its 2002 New Delhi Declaration, the International Law Association (ILA) described the notion of 'sustainable development' in even broader terms. According to this Declaration, sustainable development

> involves a comprehensive and integrated approach to economic, social and political processes, which aims at the sustainable use of natural resources of the Earth and the protection of the environment on which nature and human life as well as social and economic development depend and which seeks to realize the right of all human beings to an adequate living standard on the basis of their active, free and meaningful participation in development and in the fair distribution of benefits resulting therefrom, with due regard to the needs and interests of future generations.[31]

The various attempts at circumscribing 'sustainable development' can certainly be criticized on some points. However, this chapter does not aim at elaborating a precise definition of 'sustainable development'. Therefore, it shall be sufficient to base the following analysis on a broad understanding of sustainable development. To that end, I will regard the definitions presented above as non-exhaustive examples that may jointly be drawn on so as not to exclude potentially relevant issues from the outset.

As vaguely as the notion of 'sustainable development' comes along, so uncertain and elusive is its legal status. While few commentators have maintained that sustainable development has acquired the status of customary international law,[32] sufficient evidence of State practice and *opinio iuris* to support this view is still lacking.[33] This is illustrated by the judgment of the International Court of Justice

---

[28] See G Sacerdoti's chapter in this volume.
[29] G Brundtland, 'Report of the World Commission on Environment and Development: Our Common Future' (4 August 1987) UN Doc A/42/427/Annex available at: <http://www.un-documents.net/our-common-future.pdf> [1].
[30] MC Cordonier Segger and A Khalfan, *Sustainable Development Law* (OUP 2004) 1; UN Conference on the Human Environment, 'Declaration on the Human Environment' (Stockholm, 16 June 1972) UN Doc A/CONF.48/14/Rev.1.
[31] ILA, 'Declaration of Principles of International Law Relating to Sustainable Development' (New Delhi 2002) in (2002) 2 Intl Envtl Agreements: Pol, L & Econ 211, 212.
[32] P Sands, *Principles of International Environmental Law* (2nd edn, CUP 2003) 254.
[33] B Braune, *Rechtsfragen der nachhaltigen Entwicklung im Völkerrecht: Eine Untersuchung unter besonderer Berücksichtigung des Handels- und Investitionsrechts* (Peter Lang 2005) 70f.

(ICJ) on the *Gabčíkovo-Nagymaros Project*.[34] Whereas the Court shortly touched upon the notion's legal status, it nonetheless refrained from resolving this issue and did not acknowledge its customary international law status in the end.[35] Hence there is much to suggest that 'sustainable development' depicts, first of all, a political ideal or *leitmotif* only.[36] This is not to say, however, that individual elements of this notion may not have reached the status of customary international law or may not have been integrated into treaty law.[37]

In consequence, one cannot sweepingly invoke 'sustainable development' as such when trying to integrate sustainable development concerns into IIAs. Instead, it is necessary to carefully determine the legal status of each of those elements of sustainable development that affect the case at hand. Are we merely talking about sustainable development as a political ideal? Or does an element of this notion apply in the form of customary international law or treaty law? Sometimes, it is even possible that a particular sustainable development concern has not been legally recognized at all. In this case, it will be difficult to invoke the respective sustainable concern in accordance with the Vienna rules unless the pertinent agreement itself acknowledges this concern. This outcome may be sobering and dissatisfactory at first sight. Yet, it seems worth wondering why international investment law should be expected to accommodate concerns that have not been legally recognized by the international community so far.

c) The Vienna rules' potential to reconcile investment protection and sustainable development concerns

IIAs are usually drafted in rather vague and general terms. Hence it is not only possible but even necessary to determine and specify their meaning by way of interpretation. As a matter of fact, the more indeterminate the provisions of a treaty are the greater is the Vienna rules' potential to integrate external interests through the process of interpretation.

aa) Interpretation and conflicts of norms

Before examining more closely how this integration works, it is useful to recall what interpretation can accomplish and what it cannot. The limits of what interpretation can achieve are set out in Articles 31(1), (4), and 32 VCLT, namely by describing interpretation as an investigation into the meaning of the terms of the treaty.

---

[34] *Gabčíkovo-Nagymaros Project (Hungary v Slovakia)* [1997] ICJ Rep 7.
[35] ibid [140].
[36] U Beyerlin, 'Sustainable Development', *The Max Planck Encyclopedia of Public International Law* (2nd edn, OUP 2013) [6], [18]. Albeit an ideal that some authors have used as a battle cry heavily charged with as much force as possible and that has, correspondingly, become a provocative term for others.
[37] ibid [19]f.

The meaning of the terms of the treaty not only constitutes the logical starting point for the interpretative process.[38] At the same time, their meaning (or, more precisely, meanings) serves to distinguish permissible interpretation from impermissible formal or informal amendments.[39] When treaties are laid down in writing—as envisaged by Article 2(1)(a) VCLT—they inevitably suffer from the imperfections of written language. Words hardly ever carry only one meaning.[40] Against this background, it is the Vienna rules' objective to determine *the* ordinary or special meaning of the terms of the treaty that comes closest to giving effect to the parties' intention.[41] Conversely, the Vienna rules cannot be relied on to adopt a meaning that does not fall into the range of various possible meanings of the terms of the treaty. If this range is exceeded, the treaty is not being interpreted but in fact formally or informally amended.

As has been shown, the Vienna rules may help to *prevent* potential conflicts of norms in advance when the interpreter can choose between two or more interpretations. Yet, these rules are incapable of *solving* genuine conflicts of norms. In the worst case, we must accept that sovereign States may change their priorities or even pursue objectively incompatible aims. At this point, it is useful to recall the very rationale of treaties. This rationale is to create binding obligations and to offer some degree of legal certainty for the parties and (so they exist) third-party beneficiaries.[42] While treaty interpretation offers some flexibility to adapt treaties to different circumstances and changed priorities, the Vienna rules do not exempt States from the principle of *pacta sunt servanda*,[43] no matter how laudable the new priorities may be.

---

[38] UN Conference on the Law of Treaties (Vienna, 26 March–24 May 1968 and 9 April–22 May 1969), Official Records: Documents of the Conference, UN Doc A/CONF.39/11/Add2 at 40 [11]; see also I Sinclair in 'Summary Records of the Plenary Meetings and of the Meetings of the Committee of the Whole' UN Conference on the Law of Treaties (First session, Vienna, 26 March–24 May 1968) (1969) UN Doc A/CONF.39/11 at 177 [6]. Special Rapporteur H Waldock, 'Third Report on the Law of Treaties' [1964-II] YBILC 56 [13].

[39] G Schwarzenberger, 'Myths and Realities of Treaty Interpretation, Articles 27–29 of the Vienna Draft Convention on the Law of Treaties' (1968) 9 Va J Intl L 13; cf also, specifically concerning subsequent agreements, U Linderfalk, *On the Interpretation of Treaties* (Springer 2007) 169 and R Bernhardt, 'Interpretation and Implied (Tacit) Modification of Treaties, Comments on Arts 27, 28, 29 and 38 of the ILC's 1966 Draft Articles on the Law of Treaties' (1967) 27 ZaöRV 499.

[40] Gardiner (n 17) 164.

[41] Linderfalk (n 39) 33. See already H Grotius, *De jure belli ac pacis libri tres* (Editio nova Hein 1995) 409: 'The measure of correct interpretation is the interference of intent from the most probable indications.' Similarly E de Vattel, *The Law of Nations or the Principles of Natural Law: Applied to the Conduct and to the Affairs of Nations and of Sovereigns* (Hein & Co 1995) 201: 'The sole object of a lawful interpretation is to discover the intention of the maker or makers of the treaty.' The ultimate aim of treaty interpretation—determining the meaning of the treaty and thus giving effect to the parties' intention—must not be confused with the dispute about the proper approach to treaty interpretation. For this dispute, see P McRae, 'The Search for Meaning: Continuing Problems with the Interpretation of Treaties' (2002) 33 Victoria U Wellington L Rev 209.

[42] cf Art 37 VCLT (Revocation or modification of obligations or rights of third States).

[43] Art 26 VCLT ('Pacta sunt servanda').

bb) The Vienna rules and international investment agreements

Despite being limited to interpretation *stricto sensu*, the Vienna rules do have a great potential to reconcile investment protection and sustainable development concerns. This is because IIAs typically contain substantive clauses that do not have a single ordinary (or special) meaning. The following, non-exhaustive list of examples illustrates this.

Consulting a dictionary—a standard approach under literal interpretation—will at least convey an idea of what 'expropriation' means. In contrast, it is inevitable to use further means of interpretation to determine whether an act is 'tantamount to' or constitutes an 'indirect' expropriation.[44] The terms 'fair' and 'equitable', which make up the fair and equitable treatment (FET) standard, remain equally vague when being interpreted literally.[45] Under which conditions is an investor treated 'less favourably' than someone else who is in 'like circumstances' so that a national treatment standard is violated?[46] And what are 'goods and services' within the meaning of prohibitions of performance requirements?[47]

Yet, Article 31 VCLT not only requires interpreters to take account of the other means of interpretation when literal interpretation fails to reveal one (or more) clear meaning or meanings. Instead, Article 31 VCLT conceives interpretation as a 'single combined operation' during which all elements of the general rule are to be applied.[48] Nonetheless, a broader or vaguer meaning will automatically increase the relevance of the context and the treaty's object and purpose. Therefore, it is the object and purpose of IIAs, as well as the context of the provisions being interpreted, which are most relevant for reconciling investment protection and sustainable development concerns.

The assertion that teleological interpretation can indeed help to reconcile investment protection and sustainable development will presumably raise some doubts. Because IIAs primarily aim at investment protection—so the argument could go—their object and purpose rather prohibits than encourages consideration of sustainable development concerns. This argument, however, suffers from two flaws. First, the object and purpose of IIAs is not always one-dimensional. And second, even a one-dimensional object and purpose must not necessarily prohibit consideration of sustainable development concerns.

The impression that most IIAs solely aim at investment protection frequently results from emphasizing (or over-emphasizing) these agreements' preambular paragraphs. Indeed, it is correct that the preamble plays an important role in

---

[44] Dolzer and Schreuer (n 25) 89f.   [45] ibid 119f.   [46] ibid 178f.
[47] Salacuse (n 13) 229f.
[48] Special Rapporteur H Waldock, 'Sixth Report on the Law of Treaties' [1966-II] YbILC 219 [8]: 'The Commission, by heading the article "General rule of interpretation" in the singular and by underlining the connexion between paragraphs 1 and 2 and again between paragraph 3 and the two previous paragraphs, intended to indicate that the application of the means of interpretation in the article would be a single combined operation. All the various elements, as they were present in any given case, would be thrown into the crucible, and their interaction would give the legally relevant interpretation.'

identifying a treaty's object and purpose. Obscure as the idea of a treaty's object and purpose appears at first sight, it is important to stress that such object and purpose does not 'fall from the sky'; instead, the interpreter is required to deduce a treaty's object and purpose by looking at the treaty as a whole, including (but not limited to) its preamble and its substantive provisions.[49] Put differently, it is misguided and too narrow-minded to merely state that a preamble mentions investment protection. In the alternative, an interpreter could rely on the notion of 'economic development', which is also frequently used in preambles. Interpreted broadly, this notion may be understood as long-term or sustainable development instead of just short-term economic development.[50] But also substantive provisions of or annexes to IIAs may evidence that the agreement actually envisages more than just investment protection.[51] Even if one concluded that an agreement only aimed at investment protection, this still does not mean that its provisions cannot be interpreted in a more sustainable-development-friendly way. Let us imagine, for example, that it is unclear whether a certain protection standard prohibits a particular host State conduct motivated by sustainable development concerns. Here, a narrow object and purpose can suggest that the conduct is not prohibited because the protection standard *only* intends to protect against measures that are specifically related to this narrow object and purpose.[52]

Although these considerations show that the object and purpose of IIAs may well help to reconcile investment protection and sustainable development, systematic interpretation is, of course, much better suited for that purpose. Apart from the context in the narrow sense under Article 31(2) VCLT, it is particularly the context in the broader sense under Article 31(3)(c) VCLT which assists in integrating sustainable development concerns into IIAs. This provision invites the interpreter to take into account 'any relevant rules of international law applicable in the relations between the parties'.

With one exception, it is hardly controversial anymore under which conditions 'other rules' can be taken into account under Article 31(3)(c) VCLT. First of all, the term 'international law' only envisages the sources of public international law but not of private international law.[53] Moreover, it is widely accepted that 'other rules' are not only relevant when they concern the same subject matter as the treaty being interpreted. Expressing a principle of 'systemic integration', Article 31(3)(c) VCLT is understood more broadly so as to cover all rules that are useful for determining the meaning of the terms of the treaty. In that sense, other rules can be relevant by, for example, filling gaps, taking account of developments within the

---

[49] Gardiner (n 17) 196.
[50] D Desierto, 'Development as an International Right: Investment in the New Trade-Based IIAs' (2011) 3 Trade L & Dev 296, esp 320.
[51] For an extensive overview on environmental concerns in IIAs, see K Gordon and J Pohl, *Environmental Concerns in International Investment Agreements: A Survey* (2011) available at: <www.oecd.org/daf/investment/workingpapers>.
[52] For such unorthodox interpretation see *Lemire v Ukraine*, ICSID Case No ARB/06/18, Decision on Jurisdiction and Liability (14 January 2010) IIC 424 (2010).
[53] Gardiner (n 17) 261.

international legal system, or preventing conflicts between different rules of international law.⁵⁴ Lastly, the term 'parties' does not mean the parties to the dispute but the State parties to the treaty that is being interpreted.⁵⁵

Less obvious, in contrast, is whether the 'other rules' must apply in the relations between *all* parties to the treaty being interpreted.⁵⁶ Alternatively, one may contend that it was sufficient if they applied in the relations between those parties whose interests are concerned by the dispute giving rise to the interpretative question. Having discussed this issue abundantly, even the International Law Commission (ILC) only offered some cautious guidance. According to the ILC,

[s]uch other rules are of particular relevance where parties to the treaty under interpretation are also parties to the other treaty, where the treaty rule has passed into or expresses customary international law or where they provide evidence of the common understanding of the parties as to the object and purpose of the treaty under interpretation or as to the meaning of a particular term.⁵⁷

In view of the foregoing, arbitral tribunals must very closely consider the character of the respective IIA and of the 'other rules' to be taken into account. If the agreement is a bilateral investment agreement (BIT), the tribunal may in any event take account of rules of customary international law or of another treaty that are binding on both parties to the BIT. If the agreement is a trilateral (such as the North American Free Trade Agreement (NAFTA)) or plurilateral one (such as the Energy Charter Treaty⁵⁸), it is more difficult to satisfy the requirements under Article 31(3)(c) VCLT. In the latter case, it would, for example, be generally impermissible to rely on rules of customary international law or of another treaty that are only binding on the host State and the home State of the investor. Instead, these other rules must be binding on *all* parties to the respective agreement.

If the requirements of Article 31(3)(c) VCLT are met, the 'other rules' that can be taken into account under this provision can take various forms and relate to various manifestations of the concept of sustainable development. For instance, arbitral tribunals may take account of environmental agreements such as the 1979 Geneva Convention on Long-range Transboundary Air Pollution,⁵⁹ the 1985 Vienna Convention for the Protection of the Ozone Layer,⁶⁰ or the 1992 Rio de Janeiro Convention on Biological Diversity.⁶¹ Tribunals may also take account

---

⁵⁴ C McLachlan, 'The Principle of Systemic Integration and Article 31(3)(c) of the Vienna Convention' (2005) 54 ICLQ 279, 280; Gardiner (n 17) 260.
⁵⁵ Art 2(1)(g) VCLT.   ⁵⁶ McLachlan (n 54) 314.
⁵⁷ ILC, 'Report of the International Law Commission on the Work of its 58th Session' (2006) UN Doc A/61/10 at 414–15 [21].
⁵⁸ Energy Charter Treaty (signed 17 December 1994, entered into force 16 April 1998) 2080 UNTS 100.
⁵⁹ Convention on Long-range Transboundary Air Pollution (adopted 13 November 1979, entered into force 16 March 1983) 1302 UNTS 217.
⁶⁰ Vienna Convention for the Protection of the Ozone Layer (adopted 22 March 1985, entered into force 22 September 1988) 1513 UNTS 293.
⁶¹ Convention on Biological Diversity (adopted 5 June 1992, entered into force 29 December 1993) 1760 UNTS 79.

of agreements on cultural matters such as the 1972 Paris Convention concerning the Protection of the World Cultural and Natural Heritage,[62] the 2001 Paris Convention on the Protection of the Underwater Cultural Heritage,[63] or the 2003 Paris Convention for the Safeguarding of Intangible Cultural Heritage.[64] Or tribunals may, to mention further examples, take account of human rights treaties, treaties on educational matters, treaties setting labour standards, and so on.

III. Putting Theory into Practice: A Critical Review of Arbitral Jurisprudence

Based on the observation that the Vienna rules carry the potential to reconcile investment protection and sustainable development concerns, this part will examine whether arbitral tribunals have actually used this potential. That arbitral tribunals readily profess their adherence to the Vienna rules when setting out their approach to treaty interpretation is commonly known today.[65] Some commentators have demonstrated that arbitral tribunals' invocation of the Vienna rules is, however, often nothing more than paying lip service.[66] Thus, the way in which investment tribunals have approached treaty interpretation stands in stark contrast to the interpretative practice of other adjudicatory bodies like the European Court of Human Rights, the Iran–US Claims Tribunal, or the WTO Dispute Settlement Body, whose jurisprudence suggests that applying the Vienna rules is very well compatible with the realities of dispute settlement.[67] In the following, I solely focus on awards raising sustainable development concerns. In doing so, I do not discuss the *results* of individual cases in terms of 'right' or 'wrong', 'prudent' or 'imprudent', 'politically desirable' or 'politically undesirable'. Instead, I highlight three particularly striking features in terms of *legal reasoning*. First, the interpretative approach of arbitral tribunals tends to fall short of the single combined operation which the Vienna rules prescribe. Second, arbitral tribunals tend to only inadequately consider contextual arguments. And third, arbitral tribunals rather rely on de facto precedents instead of applying the Vienna rules.

---

[62] Convention concerning the Protection of the World Cultural and Natural Heritage (adopted 16 November 1972, entered into force 17 December 1975) 1037 UNTS 15.
[63] Convention on the Protection of the Underwater Cultural Heritage (adopted 2 November 2001, entered into force 2 January 2009) 2562 UNTS 3.
[64] Convention for the Safeguarding of Intangible Cultural Heritage (adopted 17 October 2003, entered into force 20 April 2006) 2368 UNTS 1.
[65] *AAPL* (n 25) [38]. For further examples see Dolzer and Schreuer (n 25) 31.
[66] For the case of ICSID tribunals, see O Fauchald, 'The Legal Reasoning of ICSID Tribunals—An Empirical Analysis' (2008) 19 EJIL 301, 314. See also M Waibel, 'International Investment Law and Treaty Interpretation' in R Hofmann and C Tams (n 3) 29f.
[67] ibid 29; see also G Nolte, 'Second Report for the ILC Study Group on Treaties over Time—Jurisprudence under Special Regimes relating to Subsequent Agreements and Subsequent Practice' (23 May 2011) UN Doc ILC(LXIII)/SG/TOT/INFORMAL/1 at 8, 23, 49f.

a) No single combined operation for sustainable development

The interpretative process laid down by the Vienna rules is commonly described as a 'single combined operation'.[68] This terminology illustrates that Article 31 VCLT neither stipulates a hierarchy of various distinct means of interpretation nor offers a tentative catalogue of various means of interpretation among which the interpreter may choose.[69] Article 31 VCLT, on the contrary, obliges interpreters to consider *all* potentially relevant means of interpretation that form part of the general rule and to weight all possible interpretations before eventually adopting one of them.[70]

A critical review of cases raising sustainable development concerns reveals, however, that arbitral tribunals tend not to approach interpretation as a single combined operation. What is more, arbitral tribunals often refrain from disclosing if, how, and to which extent they have taken sustainable development concerns into account. Yet, this non-transparent approach not always favours investment protection over sustainable development concerns. This can be seen in the case of *Biwater Gauff (Tanzania) Ltd v Tanzania*,[71] where the tribunal applied a rather rigorous standard for determining causation. In consequence, Biwater received no compensation although Tanzania had violated the 1994 UK–Tanzania BIT.[72] Interestingly, the award itself does not elucidate why the tribunal employed this rigorous standard; reading just the award, one may perhaps not even suspect the standard to be a particularly rigorous one or wonder about the tribunal's motivation. What casts a different light on the award is an Amicus Curiae Brief submitted by various interests groups.[73] This Amicus Curiae Brief proposed three different options for accommodating the sustainable development concerns that were at stake:

The tribunal may find the underlying investment contract invalid and thus dismiss the claims on the basis of a lack of jurisdiction or justiciability;

---

[68] See above (n 48).   [69] Gardiner (n 17) 36.
[70] ibid 142, 166. See also ILC, 'Draft Articles on the Law of Treaties with Commentaries' [1966-II] YBILC 218–23. Art 32 VCLT addresses two alternative situations in which the interpreter may have recourse to supplementary means of interpretation. In the first alternative, the interpreter may have recourse to supplementary means of interpretation only in order to confirm the meaning resulting from the application of Art 31 VCLT. Put differently, this alternative does not authorize relying on supplementary means of interpretation to support an interpretation that contradicts the meaning resulting from the application of Art 31 VCLT. In the second alternative, the interpreter may have recourse to supplementary means of interpretation to determine the meaning of the terms of the treaty when interpretation according to Art 31 VCLT leaves the meaning ambiguous or obscure or leads to a result which is manifestly absurd or unreasonable. The second alternative thus attaches greater importance to supplementary means of interpretation in that a meaning supported by supplementary means of interpretation may prevail over a meaning supported by means of interpretation that are part of the general rule.
[71] *Biwater Gauff (Tanzania) Ltd v Tanzania*, ICSID Case No ARB/05/22, Award (24 July 2008) ILC 330 (2008).
[72] Agreement between the United Kingdom of Great Britain and Northern Ireland and the United Republic of Tanzania for the Promotion and Protection of Investments (signed 7 January 1994, entered into force 2 August 1996) ('UK–Tanzania BIT') 1957 UNTS 43. See in particular *Biwater* (n 71) [788]f.
[73] Amicus Curiae Submission of the Lawyers' Environmental Action Team (LEAT), the Legal and Human Rights Centre (LHRC), the Tanzania Gender Networking Programme (TGNP), the Center for International Environmental Law (CIEL) and the International Institute for Sustainable Development (IISD) (26 March 2007) in the case of *Biwater Gauff (Tanzania) Ltd v Tanzania*, ICSID Case No ARB/05/22 available at: <http://www.ciel.org/Publications/Biwater_Amicus_26March.pdf>.

In examining the individual breaches, the tribunal may find that reproachable investor conduct affects the finding of a breach and ultimately deny the claim on the merits; or

The tribunal may reduce the damages award in consideration of the investor's conduct.[74]

Supporting these proposals, the Brief relied on contextual arguments by emphasizing Tanzania's obligations under various human rights law instruments to ensure water supply to its citizens.[75] Had the tribunal applied the Vienna rules, it would have had to take these contextual arguments into account when discussing whether Tanzania had violated the BIT and whether it had to compensate Biwater accordingly. This, in turn, may have entailed a more in-depth discussion of potentially relevant sustainable development concerns. And had the tribunal applied Article 31(3)(c) VCLT to the human rights law instruments mentioned in the Amicus Curiae Brief, it would have noticed that not all of these instruments had been ratified by the parties to the BIT, namely Tanzania and the UK. Without applying the Vienna rules, the tribunal thus not only evaded addressing the Amici's arguments. What is more, it missed the chance to openly discuss and perhaps also question the relevance of sustainable development concerns.

Another illustrative case is *Chemtura Corp v Canada*.[76] Chemtura, the claimant, was a US corporation producing lindane products for canola use in Canada. Since lindane was considered to cause serious health risks and even death, Canada adopted a policy to reduce and ban lindane. This policy included the conclusion of voluntary Withdrawal Agreements with lindane producers and a Special Review of pest control products containing lindane. Because Chemtura was subjected to a Special Review that resulted in its lindane registrations being cancelled, it contended that Canada had violated Article 1110 NAFTA; in Chemtura's view, the whole policy had not been motivated by health and environmental considerations but was the result of a trade irritant.[77] Dismissing this claim, the tribunal, however, concluded that Chemtura had not been substantially deprived of its investment because its sales from lindane products had constituted a relatively small part of its overall sales at all relevant times.[78] In an *obiter dictum*, the tribunal added that

the PMRA [the authority conducting the Special Review] took measures within its mandate, in a non-discriminatory manner, motivated by the increasing awareness of the dangers presented by lindane for human health and the environment. A measure adopted under such conditions is a valid exercise of the State's police powers and, as a result, does not constitute an expropriation.[79]

---

[74] ibid [99].
[75] ibid [96]. The instruments referred to included: African Charter on the Rights and Welfare of the Child (adopted 11 July 1990, entered into force 29 November 1999) OAU Doc CAB/LEG/24.9/49 (1990); Convention on the Elimination of All Forms of Discrimination against Women (adopted 18 December 1979, entered into force 3 September 1981) 1249 UNTS 13; Convention on the Rights of the Child (adopted 20 November 1989, entered into force 2 September 1990) 1577 UNTS 3. Tanzania had ratified all of these instruments, the UK only the latter two.
[76] *Chemtura Corp v Canada*, UNCITRAL, Award (2 August 2010) IIC 451 (2010).
[77] ibid [133].   [78] ibid [263]–[65].   [79] ibid [266] [explanation added; fn omitted].

This *obiter dictum* suggests that even if Chemtura had been substantially deprived of its investment, the tribunal would have nevertheless concluded that there had been no indirect expropriation because the cancellation, motivated by human health and environmental concerns, fell within Canada's policy powers.

The *Methanex* tribunal made a similarly apodictic statement when discussing whether the State of California, by banning the sale and use of the gasoline additive MTBE,[80] had violated Article 1110 NAFTA. The claimant, Methanex Corp, produced and sold methanol, which in turn was used to produce MTBE. Because MTBE could interchangeably be used with ethanol, a US ethanol producer had successfully lobbied for MTBE to be banned in California. Against this background, Methanex argued that the Californian ban constituted a disguised trade and investment restriction aimed at protecting and advantaging California's domestic ethanol industry through sham environmental regulations disadvantaging MTBE and methanol.[81] Like the *Chemtura* tribunal, the *Methanex* tribunal did not bother to interpret Article 1110 NAFTA by applying the Vienna rules. Rejecting Methanex' claim, it matter-of-factly remarked that

> as a matter of general international law, a non-discriminatory regulation for a public purpose, which is enacted in accordance with due process and, which affects, inter alios, a foreign investor or investment is not deemed expropriatory and compensable unless specific commitments had been given by the regulating government to the then putative investor contemplating investment that the government would refrain from such regulation.[82]

Irrespective of whether one agrees with the outcome of these cases, the tribunals' interpretation of Article 1110 NAFTA is not the most plausible one.[83] Article 1110(1) NAFTA provides:

> No Party may directly or indirectly nationalize or expropriate an investment of an investor of another Party in its territory or take a measure tantamount to nationalization or expropriation of such an investment ('expropriation'), except:
> (a) for a public purpose;
> (b) on a non-discriminatory basis;
> (c) in accordance with due process of law and Article 1105(1);
> (d) and on payment of compensation in accordance with paragraphs 2 through 6.

---

[80] MTBE is the abbreviation for methyl tertiary-butyl ether.

[81] *Methanex Corp v USA*, UNCITRAL, Partial Award (7 August 2002) IIC 166 (2002) [46].

[82] *Methanex Corp v USA*, UNCITRAL, Final Award on Jurisdiction and Merits (3 August 2005) IIC 167 (2005) (n 109) pt IV ch D Art 1110 NAFTA at [7].

[83] A Hoffmann, 'Indirect Expropriation' in A Reinisch (ed), *Standards of Protection in International Investment Law* (OUP 2008) 165, arguing that 'in modern investment arbitration there exists no general exception to the rule that investors have to be compensated for regulatory measures which have an expropriatory effect'. Similarly, see T Weiler, 'A First Look at the Interim Merits Award in *SD Myers, Inc v Canada*: It Is Possible to Balance Legitimate Environmental Concerns with Investment Protection' (2001) 24 Hastings Intl & Comp L Rev 173, 186f. For an overview on this debate, see also J Marlles, 'Public Purpose, Private Losses: Regulatory Expropriation and Environmental Regulation in International Investment Law' (2007) 16 J Transnatl L & Poly 275.

The ordinary meaning of the term 'expropriation' as well as its context thus strongly suggest that Article 1110 NAFTA clearly distinguishes between the questions of whether there has been some form of expropriation and whether such expropriation has been undertaken for a public purpose.[84] Under Article 1110 NAFTA, *any* expropriation is compensable. The public purpose, in contrast, is one of those conditions that must be met to render an expropriation lawful. Thus, the (non-) existence of a public purpose is one of the factors that determine whether the host State must pay damages. However, it does not free the host State from its obligation to compensate. Had the *Chemtura* and *Methanex* tribunals relied on the general rule to determine what an indirect expropriation or measures tantamount to expropriation mean, they could not have evaded addressing these arguments. Presumably the tribunals would have nevertheless concluded that the meaning of these terms was broad enough to envisage balancing the impact on an investor's investment with the purpose pursued by the host State. Yet, they preferred not to discuss, by applying the Vienna rules, the various arguments supporting one or the other interpretation. Thus it remains difficult to understand the tribunals' legal reasoning. On the one hand, such non-transparent approach certainly protects arbitrators from criticism concerning the weight of individual arguments and from being personally identified with a particular legal position.[85] On the other hand, such non-transparency diminishes persuasiveness and legitimacy of the tribunals' interpretation. This is because, first, they adopted their interpretations of Article 1110 NAFTA without openly applying the applicable law—that is, the Vienna rules—for arriving at these interpretations. And second, this is because they failed to discuss all legally relevant factors which they would have been obliged to take into account under the applicable law.

How implausible the tribunals' interpretations are becomes obvious if one imagined cases with express carve-outs or exceptions from indirect expropriation. Such exception is, for example, now included in Annex B of the 2012 US Model BIT.[86] Section 4(b) of the Annex provides that, '*except in rare circumstances*, non-discriminatory regulatory actions by a Party that are designed and applied to protect legitimate public welfare objectives, such as public health, safety, and the environment, do not constitute indirect expropriations'.[87] Notably, this 'exception' does not constitute a full exception but merely postulates a presumption in favour of a legitimate regulation.[88] Although the 2012 US Model BIT expressly establishes the presumption that host State action for a public purpose does not constitute an expropriation, tribunals therefore still

---

[84] In consequence, this means that the purpose for which a measure is undertaken is an ill-suited criterion to determine whether such measure qualifies as an indirect expropriation or as a measure tantamount to expropriation under IIAs that are drafted in similar terms as Art 1110(1) NAFTA.

[85] Being or not being identified with a particular legal position may be one factor influencing investors, States, or law firms when scouting arbitrators.

[86] The 2012 US Model BIT is available at: <www.italaw.com>.

[87] Emphasis added; cf also Art 2(1) and Annex I No 3 TTIP draft; Annex X.11 CETA.

[88] To the same effect, see Annex B at 13(1)(c) of the 2004 Canadian Model BIT, which is also available at: <www.italaw.com>.

need to check whether 'rare circumstances' are capable of refuting this presumption. If *no* such presumption applies, one would, in contrast, expect an even more detailed statement of legal reasons as to why the existence of a public purpose should render regulatory actions non-compensable. Yet, the *Methanex* and *Chemtura* tribunals did not provide a more detailed statement of legal reasons but gave no legal reasons at all.

In the awards just mentioned, sustainable development concerns actually prevailed over investment protection. However, cases like *Unglaube and Unglaube v Costa Rica*[89] demonstrate that tribunals may just as well subordinate sustainable development concerns to investment protection. Although *Unglaube* was an expropriation case that was decided in favour of the claimants, the tribunal's interpretative approach resembles that of the *Chemtura* and *Methanex* tribunals. Like the respondents in *Chemtura* and *Methanex*, Costa Rica had attempted to defend its case by emphasizing the environmental purpose which it had pursued when taking part of the claimants' land to include it in the neighbouring national park.[90] Quoting the *Santa Elena* Panel, the tribunal in this case, however, rejected the respondent's reasoning:

Expropriatory environmental measures—no matter how laudable and beneficial to society as a whole—are, in this respect, similar to any other expropriatory measures that a state may take in order to implement its policies...[91]

Observing that Costa Rica had not, adequately and in a timely manner, compensated the claimants, the tribunal therefore held that Costa Rica had indeed violated the Germany–Costa Rica BIT.[92]

In contrast to *Methanex* and *Chemtura*, the *Unglaube* award concerned a direct and not only an indirect expropriation or measures tantamount to expropriation. But although the term 'expropriation' possesses much clearer contours, the tribunal could still have tried to further specify its meaning by way of interpretation. Yet, the tribunal did not even mention the Vienna rules or any of its elements but merely cited other arbitral awards supporting its apodictic conclusion. As will be argued below,[93] the Vienna rules would probably not have led to a different interpretation in the end because they would have prevented the tribunal from considering the legal context invoked by Costa Rica. Nevertheless, the tribunal would have had the chance to legally explain why it was prevented from taking these sustainable development concerns into account.

---

[89] *Unglaube and Unglaube v Costa Rica*, ICSID Case Nos ARB/08/1 and ARB/09/20, Award (16 May 2012) IIC 554 (2012).
[90] ibid [103].
[91] ibid [217] quoting *Compañía del Desarrollo de Santa Elena SA v Costa Rica*, ICSID Case No ARB/96/1, Award (17 February 2000) IIC 73 (2000) [72].
[92] Agreement between the Federal Republic of Germany and the Republic of Costa Rica on the Promotion and Reciprocal Protection of Investments (signed 13 September 1995, entered into force 24 March 1998) ('Germany–Costa Rica BIT') BGBl II 1997, 1830. See *Unglaube* (n 88) [223].
[93] See below at 199f.

Fortunately, a few awards do evidence that arbitral tribunals are well capable of applying the Vienna rules to appreciate the various issues raised by a case.[94] One of these exceptions is the award in the case of *Lemire v Ukraine*.[95] The claimant challenged Article 9(1) of the 2006 Ukrainian Law on Television and Broadcasting (LRT), which imposed a 50 per cent Ukrainian music requirement on broadcasting organizations. According to the claimant, this requirement violated the prohibition of performance requirements under Article II.6 of the US–Ukraine BIT.[96] To decide whether the 50 per cent quota violated this provision, the tribunal had to determine whether the terms 'goods and services' used in Article II.6 of the BIT also applied to broadcasting music. To start with, the tribunal emphasized that 'Ukraine has the inherent right to regulate its affairs and adopt laws in order to protect the common good of its people'[97] and that '[t]he promotion of domestic music may validly reflect a State policy to preserve and strengthen cultural inheritance and national identity'.[98] Expressly citing Article 31(1) VCLT, the tribunal then proceeded by trying to determine the ordinary meaning of the contentious terms.[99] Although the ordinary meaning suggested that the music requirement did not fall under Article II.6 of the BIT, the tribunal further considered the BIT's object and purpose:

The object and purpose of Article II.6 sheds more light on its correct interpretation. The object of the BIT is to '*promote greater economic cooperation*' between the Parties (Preamble II). And the purpose of Article II.6 is trade-related: to avoid that States impose local content requirements as a protection of local industries against competing imports. When in 2006 Ukraine amended the LTR, the underlying reasons were not to protect local industries and restrict imports, but rather to promote Ukraine's cultural inheritance,[100] a purpose which is compatible with Article II.6 of the BIT.[101]

This line of reasoning is truly remarkable. Although the tribunal may have been tempted to simply adopt a literal interpretation, it nevertheless sought to reconfirm its interpretation by additionally relying on the BIT's object and purpose. Normally, one would have expected a tribunal to emphasize purposes like

---

[94] See also *SD Myers Inc v Canada*, UNCITRAL, First Partial Award and Separate Opinion (13 November 2000) IIC 249 (2000).
[95] *Lemire* (n 52).
[96] Treaty between the USA and Ukraine concerning the Encouragement and Reciprocal Protection of Investment (signed 4 March 1994, entered into force 16 November 1996) ('US-Urkaine BIT') S Treaty Doc No 103-37 (1994).
[97] *Lemire* (n 52) [505].   [98] ibid [505].   [99] ibid [509]f.
[100] On protection of cultural heritage as part of a broad concept of sustainable development, see J Hawkes, *The Fourth Pillar of Sustainability—Culture's Essential Role in Public Planning* (Cultural Development Network 2001); M Leach, 'Culture and Sustainability' in UNESCO (ed), *World Culture Report 1998—Culture, Creativity and Markets* (UNESCO Pub 1998) 93–104; K Nurse, 'Culture as the Fourth Pillar of Sustainable Development' (2006); United Cities and Local Governments, 'Agenda 21 for Culture' (8 May 2004) available at: <www.agenda21culture.net/index.php/documents/agenda-21-for-culture>; United Cities and Local Governments, 'Culture: Fourth Pillar of Sustainable Development' (2010) available at: <www.agenda21culture.net/images/a21c/4th-pilar/zz_Culture4pillarSD_eng.pdf>.
[101] *Lemire* (n 52) [510].

'promotion of economic cooperation' to prohibit the impairment of investors' interests for other reasons. But in this case, the tribunal reversed the argument by holding that the BIT was *only* meant to protect against trade- and economic-related measures. In sum, this award illustrates that applying the Vienna rules and going beyond standard and rigid interpretative patterns may well lead to atypical interpretations and thus help to accommodate concerns unrelated to investment protection.

b) Inadequate consideration of contextual arguments

Taking sustainable development concerns into account as part of an agreement's context is a particularly straightforward way of reconciling these concerns with investment protection. Compared to teleological interpretation, contextual arguments offer two advantages. First, they are more 'tangible' than an agreement's object and purpose. And second, the Vienna rules provide relatively clear guidelines for deciding which contextual arguments are admissible and which are not. Yet, it appears that arbitral tribunals do not fully appreciate these advantages.

This can, for instance, be seen in the case of *Metalclad Corp v Mexico*,[102] where the tribunal ignored the contextual arguments invoked by the host State. The facts giving rise to the dispute were as follows. In 1993, the Federal Government of Mexico granted Confinamiento Tecnico de Residuos Industriales, SA de CV (COTERIN) a permit to construct and operate a transfer station for hazardous waste and to construct and operate a landfill for this waste. When Metalclad subsequently purchased COTERIN and its permits, the Federal Government assured Metalclad that it was entitled to build and operate the landfill. The local community, however, opposed the project and demonstrators even blocked the site so that Metalclad could not operate the landfill. While Metalclad and the Federal Government entered into an agreement that provided for and allowed operation of the landfill, the Municipal Government denied permission to operate it. When all avenues to prevent the landfill's operation had been exhausted unsuccessfully, the Local Governor finally declared the region in which the site was situated a Natural Area for the protection of a rare species of cactus.

In its award, the tribunal held that the inconsistent behaviour of the Local and Federal Governments had violated the FET standard under Article 1105 NAFTA.[103] Furthermore, it held that the Ecological Decree issued by the Local Governor constituted an indirect expropriation in violation of Article 1110 NAFTA.[104] The facts of the case actually raised the impression that the Local Government's environmental motives had not been genuine but only a pretext to get rid of the landfill. Therefore, the tribunal's holding need not necessarily be criticized. What is astonishing, however, is the tribunal's legal reasoning. To defend

---

[102] *Metalclad Corp v Mexico*, ICSID Case No ARB(AF)/97/1, Award (30 August 2000) IIC 161 (2000).
[103] ibid [99].   [104] ibid [108]f.

the Decree, Mexico had emphasized its international obligations to protect the environment. Arguing, for example, that the phrase 'fair and equitable treatment' was not defined in the NAFTA, Mexico had insisted that Article 1105 NAFTA had to be interpreted according to the Vienna rules[105] and especially highlighted this provision's context:

> Other contextual elements relevant to interpreting this phrase include NAFTA Article 1114(1), the preamble, and the North American Agreement on Environmental Cooperation (the 'NAAEC'), an agreement negotiated after the conclusion of the NAFTA and which entered into force immediately after NAFTA's entry into force. All three NAFTA Parties are signatories to that agreement.[106]

But although Mexico had set out its rights and obligations under the NAAEC in detail and although this treaty satisfied all conditions for being taken into account under Article 31(3)(c) VCLT, the tribunal did not mention it at all.

Another illustrative example of how arbitral tribunals deal with contextual arguments is the case of *Grand River Enterprises Six Nations Ltd v USA*.[107] In this case, a Canadian corporation and members of the 'First Nation' challenged the terms of a settlement agreement concerning tobacco litigation that had been concluded between a number of US states and major US cigarette manufacturers. Among others, this agreement provided that tobacco corporations put funds into an escrow account. The claimants argued that this agreement breached the FET standard under Article 1105 NAFTA because the USA had failed to take account of the special rights of indigenous people. To support their claim, they

> urged further that in construing Chapter 11, the Tribunal must take into account other treaties between the United States and Canada affecting the Haudenosaunee [the tribe which the claimants belonged to], customary law rules affecting indigenous peoples and 'fundamental human rights norms, including but not limited to *jus cogens* principles.' They particularly stressed Article III of the 1794 Jay Treaty, as affirmed in the 1814 Treaty of Ghent. In the Claimant's view, Article III assured their right to carry on their cigarette business free from interference by the United States, and in particular, by the states of the United States.[108]

As regards the interpretation of Article 1105 NAFTA, they further pointed out that

> the content of the United States' obligations under Article 1105 is further shaped by US obligations under the Jay Treaty, by principles of customary international law involving indigenous peoples, and by international human rights treaties and customary principles of human rights law.... counsel urged in this regard that the minimum standard of treatment was not a standard applicable to aliens generally, but that it varied to take account the varying status and legal rights of particular claimants.[109]

---

[105] *Metalclad Corp v Mexico*, ICSID Case No ARB(AF)/97/1, Counter Memorial (17 February 1998) available at: <http://naftaclaims.com/disputes-with-mexico.html> [834]f.
[106] ibid [838] [footnotes omitted].
[107] *Grand River Enterprises Six Nations Ltd v USA*, ICSID Case No ARB/10/5, Award (12 January 2011) IIC 481 (2011).
[108] ibid [66] [explanation added].   [109] ibid [180].

The tribunal, however, took the view that the international legal context to which the claimants had referred could not influence its interpretation of Article 1105 NAFTA because 'the conception of an international minimum standard, which the tribunal must apply pursuant to the Free Trade Commission's direction'[110] could not be reconciled with according special rights to only some investors.[111] Accepting that the NAFTA was to be interpreted in accordance with the Vienna rules,[112] the tribunal emphasized that it did not understand the obligation to take into account other rules of international law

> to provide a license to import into NAFTA legal elements from other treaties, or to allow alteration of an interpretation established through the normal interpretive process of the Vienna Convention... The Tribunal is particularly mindful in this regard of the Free Trade Commission's directive that a violation of an obligation under another treaty does not give rise to a breach of Article 1105.[113]

The meaning which the tribunal apparently attached to Article 31(3)(c) VCLT is certainly surprising; in particular, it seemed to assume that Article 31(3)(c) VCLT envisaged 'importing' other rules of international law in order to 'override' an interpretation arrived at by applying the Vienna rules. Thus, the tribunal incorrectly separated Article 31(3)(c) VCLT from the remainder of the general rule and introduced the very interpretative hierarchy which the drafters of the Convention did not want to establish.[114] In contrast to what the tribunal contended, *considering* other rules of international law pursuant to Article 31(3)(c) VCLT does not mean to equate violations of these rules with violations of Article 1105 NAFTA; instead, considering other rules merely helps to elucidate the vague concept of a minimum standard of treatment to which Article 1105 NAFTA, according to the FTC note, refers.

If one gave Article 1105 NAFTA the restrictive reading which the tribunal advocated, it would become almost impossible to take non-economic concerns into account at the merits stage in cases under the FET standard.[115] But this restrictive

---

[110] ibid [181].   [111] ibid [213].   [112] ibid [69].
[113] ibid [71]. See NAFTA Free Trade Commission, 'Notes of Interpretation of Certain Chapter 11 Provisions' (July 31, 2001) available at: <www.naftalaw.org/commission.html>. As regards the interpretation of Art 1105(1) NAFTA, the note provides:

1. Article 1105(1) prescribes the customary international law minimum standard of treatment of aliens as the minimum standard of treatment to be afforded to investments of investors of another Party.
2. The concepts of 'fair and equitable treatment' and 'full protection and security' do not require treatment in addition to or beyond that which is required by the customary international law minimum standard of treatment of aliens.
3. A determination that there has been a breach of another provision of the NAFTA, or of a separate international agreement, does not establish that there has been a breach of Article 1105(1).

[114] See above at 185 and 189.
[115] Interestingly, the tribunal in the end turned out to be not completely hostile to the claimants' rights as indigenous people because it departed from the 'in principle' rule of the 1976 UNCITRAL Arbitration Rules and decided that each party shall bear its own costs and half the costs and expenses of the proceedings, although the claimants had not been successful, see *Grand River Enterprises* (n 106) [247].

and inflexible reading is not compelling at all. The FTC note's wording does not expressly refer to a universal and absolute minimum standard. Customary international law, like treaty law, evolves over time and may differ regionally.[116] Therefore, one could seek to identify a North American minimum standard under customary international law by considering the special situation of indigenous people as they have been acknowledged in numerous regional instruments, for example. Whichever view one takes on this issue, this discussion is, at first sight, of limited relevance beyond the NAFTA context and does not affect IIAs that use a different language and do not refer to the minimum standard under customary international law.[117] However, Article 5(2) of the 2012 US Model BIT and Article 5 of its Canadian counterpart, for instance, have already taken NAFTA as an example and expressly refer to customary international law, too. This suggests that the discussion will no longer be limited to the NAFTA but will become increasingly important in the future.

In other cases, arbitral tribunals not only rejected contextual arguments invoked by the host State but even completely refrained from discussing them at all. A first example of this strong reservation towards contextual arguments is the case of *Compañía del Desarrollo de Santa Elena SA v Costa Rica*.[118] Since the claim was based on customary international law, this case did not raise questions of treaty interpretation *stricto sensu*. Nonetheless, this case is noteworthy because the tribunal's ignorance towards contextual arguments is particularly striking and because it was subsequently relied on by other tribunals. The claimants in this case, Compañía del Desarrollo de Santa Elena SA (CDSE), had planned to develop large portions of their Costa Rican property as a tourist resort and a residential community. However, the property comprised a long Pacific coastline and rain forest rich in biological diversity. Therefore, Costa Rica decided to expropriate CDSE to expand the neighbouring national park. Costa Rica had offered CDSE US$1.9 million in compensation, but CDSE rejected this amount for being far too low, instead demanding US$6.4 million in compensation.[119] In the end, the tribunal held that CDSE had been expropriated and was entitled to compensation.[120] What is remarkable about the tribunal's legal reasoning is how flatly Costa Rica's international obligations to protect the environment were dismissed as irrelevant.[121] In fact, the tribunal did not even mention the evidence which Costa Rica had submitted in order to demonstrate its international obligations to protect biological diversity in the Santa Elena area.

Other sources, however, suggest that Costa Rica had invoked numerous environmental treaties,[122] including the 1940 Western Hemisphere Convention,[123] the

---

[116] *Case concerning Right of Passage over Indian Territory (Portugal v India)* (Merits) [1960] ICJ Rep 6, 39 and T Treves, 'Customary International Law', *The Max Planck Encyclopedia of Public International Law* (2nd edn, OUP 2013) [40].

[117] Dolzer and Schreuer (n 25) 125f.   [118] *CDSE* (n 90).   [119] ibid [17], [19].

[120] ibid [72].   [121] ibid [71].

[122] C Brower and J Wong, 'General Valuation Principles: The Case of Santa Elena' in T Weiler (ed), *International Investment Law and Arbitration: Leading Cases from the ICSID, NAFTA, Bilateral Treaties and Customary International Law* (Cameron May 2005) 763f.

[123] Convention on Nature Protection and Wildlife Preservation in the Western Hemisphere (adopted 12 October 1940, entered into force 3 March 1953) 161 UNTS 193.

1972 World Heritage Convention,[124] the 1971 Ramsar Convention,[125] the 1992 Biodiversity Convention,[126] and the 1993 Central American Regional Convention for the Management and Conservation of the Natural Forest Ecosystems and the Development of Forest Plantations.[127] Although this was a customary international law case, it vividly illustrates the benefits of applying the Vienna rules on interpretation. Had the case arisen under an IIA, the Vienna rules would have obliged the tribunal to assess Costa Rica's contextual arguments and to consider these treaties under Article 31(3)(c) VCLT because all but two had been ratified by Costa Rica and the USA–CDSE's State of nationality. By not discussing these contextual arguments legally and in fact not even mentioning them, one may only speculate how the tribunal arrived at the conclusion that Costa Rica's environmental obligations were irrelevant.

The same marked reservation towards contextual arguments transpires from the *Unglaube* award[128] mentioned earlier. The claimants of this case owned a property located on and close to Playa Grande beach, one of the most important nesting sites for the highly endangered leatherback turtle. Costa Rica had allegedly expropriated the claimants in order to include their land in the neighbouring national park. In defence, Costa Rica among others invoked its obligations to protect the natural environment under the 1996 Inter-American Convention for the Protection and Conservation of Sea Turtles.[129] The tribunal, however, matter-of-factly concluded that Costa Rica had indeed expropriated the claimants without compensating them and therefore violated the Germany–Costa Rica BIT.[130] Notably, the tribunal did not even address the international obligations invoked by the respondent. Hence it would not be surprising if this award had created an impression of bias towards investment protection. Had the tribunal referred to the Vienna rules, it would have been able to counteract this impression in advance. As regards the 1996 Sea Turtles Convention invoked by Costa Rica, the tribunal may then have pointed out that Germany had not ratified the Convention. Hence this instrument would not have been admissible under Article 31(3)(c) VCLT anyway and could not have influenced the interpretation of the Germany–Costa Rica BIT.

---

[124] Convention Concerning the Protection of the World Cultural and Natural Heritage (adopted 16 November 1972, entered into force 17 December 1975) 1037 UNTS 15.
[125] Convention on Wetlands of International Importance, especially as Waterfowl Habitat (adopted 2 February 1971, entered into force 21 December 1975) 996 UNTS 245.
[126] Convention on Biological Diversity (adopted 5 June 1992, entered into force 29 December 1993) 1760 UNTS 79.
[127] Central American Regional Convention for the Management and Conservation of the Natural Forest Ecosystems and the Development of Forest Plantations (adopted 29 October 1993, entered into force 15 October 1999) available at: <www.ecolex.org>.
[128] *Unglaube* (n 88).
[129] Inter-American Convention for the Protection and Conservation of Sea Turtles (signed 1 December 1996, entered into force 2 May 2001) 2164 UNTS 29. See *Unglaube* (n 88) [103].
[130] ibid [223].

c) The prominent role of de facto precedents

Before closing this review of arbitral jurisprudence, it is instructive to highlight another striking feature, namely the fact the tribunals strongly rely on de facto precedents to interpret IIAs.[131] This peculiar style of reasoning not only contradicts the Vienna rules but also risks diminishing their potential to reconcile investment protection and sustainable development concerns.

Unlike common law legal systems, international investment law is not governed by a genuine system of precedent because previous awards are not binding on other tribunals. But although the principle of *stare decisis* does not apply to investor–State disputes, arbitral tribunals nevertheless tend to acknowledge, analyse, and rely on previous awards. This peculiarity, which can be referred to as a system of de facto precedents, also dominates arbitral tribunals' legal reasoning in cases raising sustainable development concerns.[132] To specify under which conditions regulatory measures could be deemed tantamount to expropriation, the *Methanex* tribunal, for example, simply referred to the awards in the cases of *Revere Copper & Brass, Inc v OPIC*[133] and *Waste Management v Mexico*[134] instead of openly applying the Vienna rules.[135] The *Metalclad* tribunal, in contrast, strongly relied on the decision in *Biloune v Ghana Investment Centre*[136] to explain why an indirect expropriation had taken place when 'the totality of the circumstances had the effect of causing the irreparable cessation of work on the project'.[137] This tribunal even acknowledged that it was not bound by the decision in *Biloune*. Nevertheless, it regarded the *Biloune* decision as 'persuasive authority' and declared that it agreed with its analysis as well as its conclusion.[138] A particularly illustrative example is the *Nykomb* award. Here the tribunal did not even mention the previous awards that had influenced its interpretation. Instead, it simply pointed out that it had 'considered the expert legal opinions and arbitral awards rendered under similar treaties presented in this case by the parties' to explain how it had reached its understanding of 'regulatory takings' within the meaning of the ECT.[139]

Until recently, such reliance on previous awards received hardly any criticism at all. Instead, it had been argued that arbitral tribunals enhanced predictability and credibility of investor–State arbitration if they relied on or at least considered previous awards.[140] Not least under the impression of the various arbitral awards

---

[131] Schill (n 7) 82.
[132] *Biwater* (n 71) [691]f; *Chemtura* (n 76) [241]f; *Glamis Gold Ltd v USA*, UNCITRAL, Award (14 May 2009) IIC 380 (2009) [357]f.
[133] *Revere Copper & Brass, Inc v OPIC*, Award (24 August 1978) (1978) 17 ILM 1321, 1331.
[134] *Waste Management Inc v Mexico*, ICSID Case No ARB(AF)/00/3, Award (30 April 2004) IIC 270 (2004) [98]f.
[135] *Methanex*, Final Award, (n 82) at pt IV ch D Art 1110 NAFTA.
[136] *Biloune v Ghana Investment Centre*, UNCITRAL, Award on Jurisdiction and Liability (27 October 1989) (1990) 95 ILR 183, 207–10.
[137] *Metalclad* (n 101) [108].   [138] ibid [108].
[139] *Nykomb Synergetics Technology Holding AB v Latvia*, SCC Institute, Award (16 December 2003) IIC 182 (2003) 33.
[140] A Reinisch, 'The Role of Precedent in ICSID Arbitration' [2008] AAYB 495.

dealing with the Argentinian crisis, there are, however, good reasons to suspect that de facto precedents actually do not guarantee reasonably consistent arbitral decision-making. Despite the system of de facto precedents, there is now growing concern about the 'increasing number of conflicting and inconsistent interpretations by arbitral tribunals of standard principles of investment protection, not only under different treaties, but also with regard to virtually identical cases'.[141] From a doctrinal perspective, it is important to recall that judicial decisions such as arbitral awards are only recognized as a subsidiary source of international law under Article 38(1)(d) of the ICJ Statute.[142] Moreover, judicial decisions are not envisaged by the general rule of interpretation under Article 31 VCLT.

This is not to suggest, of course, that consideration of previous awards should be 'demonized' and that arbitral tribunals should completely ignore previous awards of other tribunals. Looked at in isolation, it is hardly objectionable if arbitral tribunals are aware of previous awards, consider themselves as part of an informal system of investor–State arbitration, and thus attempt to contribute to consistency of arbitral decision-making. However, referring to previous awards—sometimes even in a pick-and-choose manner—is categorically different from construing a treaty in accordance with the general rule of interpretation. As one commentator vividly remarked, '[n]either two nor two million wrongs can make a right, however much they equalize situations. Nor is the two millionth wrong somehow less wrong than the first.'[143] In consequence, tribunals must not rely on previous arbitral awards to interpret IIAs *before* they have applied the general rule of interpretation. If anything, arbitral tribunals may then cite previous awards as supplementary means of interpretation under Article 32 VCLT.[144]

---

[141] Schill (n 7) 66f. See also UNCTAD, 'Reform of Investor-State Dispute Settlement: In Search of a Roadmap' *IIA Issues Note No 2* (May 2013) available at: <http://unctad.org/en/PublicationsLibrary/webdiaepcb2013d4_en.pdf> 3; I Ten Cate, 'The Costs of Consistency: Precedent in Investment Treaty Arbitration' (2013) 51 Col J Transnatl L 418, 427; P Muchlinski, 'Corporations and the Uses of Law: International Investment Arbitration as a "Multilateral Legal Order"' (2011) Oñati Socio-Legal Series 1 (4), 7 <http://papers.ssrn.com/sol3/papers.cfm?abstract_id=1832562##> accessed 21 August 2015. A seminal work on the issue of inconsistencies is S Franck, 'The Legitimacy Crisis in Investment Treaty Arbitration: Privatizing Public International Law through Inconsistent Decisions' (2005) 73 Fordham L Rev 1521. See, however, also Reinisch (n 139) 509, who argues that 'inconsistent arbitral decisions have been rare exceptions to the general rule that tribunals seek to follow previous decisions'.

[142] The ICJ Statute is annexed to the Charter of the United Nations (adopted 26 June 1945, entered into force 24 October 1946) 1 UNTS XVI. See also M Feigerlova and A Maltais, *Obligations Undertaken by States under International Conventions for the Protection of Cultural Rights and the Environment, to What Extent they Constitute a Limitation to Investor's Rights under Bilateral or Multilateral Investment Treaties and Investment Contracts?* (Geneva 2012) available at: <http://graduateinstitute.ch/home/research/centresandprogrammes/ctei/projects-1/trade-law-clinic.html>.

[143] L Alexander, 'Constrained by Precedent' (1989) 63 S Cal L Rev 1, 10.

[144] cf *Mamidoil Jetoil Greek Petroleum Products Society SA v Republic of Albania*, ICSID Case No ARB/11/24, Award (30 March 2015) [630]. See, however, A Orakhelashvili, 'Principles of Treaty Interpretation in the NAFTA Arbitral Award on Canadian Cattlemen' (2009) 26 J Intl Arb 159, 167 f, who argued that it is not permissible to refer to previous arbitral awards under Art 32 VCLT so that relying on past decisions is not envisaged by the Vienna rules at all. A similarly critical view has been taken by Ten Cate (n 140), who argued that predictability is not a value of its own and that arbitral tribunals' reliance on past decision diminishes accuracy, sincerity, and transparency in decision-making.

But what, apart from these doctrinal objections, are the disadvantages of giving too much weight to de facto precedents? As has been argued above, applying the Vienna rules can help to reconcile investment protection with external concerns such as sustainable development. More abstractly, the Vienna rules are, in an impartial way, inherently open-minded to encompassing new developments and to adapting treaties to changed conditions. Relying on de facto precedents, in contrast, is an inherently backward looking activity and helps to perpetuate a legal status quo. In any case, a system of de facto precedents does not guarantee—unlike the Vienna rules—that relevant external concerns will at least be taken into account. Thus, tribunals diminish the chances to accommodate external concerns when they only invoke previous awards instead of faithfully applying the Vienna rules.

IV. Conclusion

Those who call for a paradigm shift towards a stronger focus on sustainable development concerns are ill-advised to leave the current regime of international investment law as it stands. However, it is not primarily the substance of international investment law which impedes such a paradigm shift.

If faithfully applied to interpret the current regime of international investment law, Articles 31–33 VCLT would offer viable alternatives for reconciling investment protection and sustainable development concerns. In fact, these rules not only facilitate the accommodation of sustainable development concerns. What is more, they even oblige arbitral tribunals to take these concerns into account once they are legally relevant. The Vienna rules cannot guarantee that sustainable development concerns will always prevail over investment protection. Yet, they require a transparent balancing process and thus help to avoid the impression of bias towards either one or the other interest. However, arbitral tribunals have been rather reluctant to use the Vienna rules' potential to reconcile investment protection and sustainable development concerns. First of all, many tribunals have not adequately addressed contextual arguments in cases raising sustainable development concerns. And second, many tribunals have not approached interpretation as a single combined operation during which all legally relevant aspects are to be considered. Instead, they have strongly relied on previous awards to explain why a particular interpretation applies. These factors taken together, it is not only difficult to understand if, how, and on which legal basis sustainable development concerns have been taken into account. What is more, there is no guarantee that arbitral tribunals would take legally relevant sustainable development concerns into account at all. Notably, this approach to interpretation has not always led tribunals to subordinate sustainable development concerns to investment protection. However, due consideration of sustainable development concerns in some cases does not eliminate the impression of bias against sustainable development concerns in other cases.

These observations may be grist to the mill of those who insist on changing the substance of international investment law to achieve a stronger focus on sustainable development concerns. To effectively ensure that sustainable development concerns are taken into account whenever they are meant to, it may indeed be necessary to re-draft IIAs in less ambiguous terms. This solution, however, entails the disadvantage of reducing flexibility and policy space for the future when it may once again be very much welcomed. And since arbitral tribunals are not even willing to comply with the Vienna rules on treaty interpretation, one may wonder why they should be induced to unreservedly implement such changes in substance in the first place. Against this background, it seems more expedient to preserve the current level of flexibility and policy space of international investment law. At the same time, it would be desirable to insist—and, if necessary, to ensure through procedural changes—that arbitral tribunals faithfully and openly apply the Vienna rules as they ought to apply any other element of the applicable law.

IX

Investment Protection and Sustainable Development

What Role for the Law of State Responsibility?

Helmut Philipp Aust[*]

I. Remedies and Regulatory Space: The UNCTAD Suggestions for Sustainable Development

The Investment Policy Framework for Sustainable Development (IPFSD)[1] of the United Nations Conference on Trade and Development (UNCTAD) seeks to develop several policy suggestions for the development of international investment law. Some of these suggestions also address questions of State responsibility. This part of general international law is concerned with the consequences of internationally wrongful acts. In other words: its rules come to apply when a primary, that is substantive, obligation has been violated. The 'secondary' rules of State responsibility then govern to whom a breach is to be attributed, whether excusing or justifying factors have been involved and what the legal consequences of this breach are. The latter question refers in particular to the content of the 'new legal relationship' which is brought about by the violation of the respective international obligation. One might argue that it is here where international law becomes a serious affair: after all, what matters is compliance and it is arguably the prospect of incurring some form of sanction that will make international law more effective.[2] The law of State responsibility is geared towards the restoration of the legal relationship as it existed before the breach. Besides cessation of the breach, reparation is owed and can take various forms. Broadly speaking, general international law knows three forms of reparation: restitution, compensation, and satisfaction. The customary international law rules on the matter are laid down in the 2001 'Articles

---

[*] I wish to thank Lisa Brahms, Georg Nolte, August Reinisch, Alejandro Rodiles, and Michael Waibel for comments and criticism. Any errors and misconceptions are mine.

[1] UNCTAD, *Investment Policy Framework for Sustainable Development* (United Nations 2012) available at <http://unctad.org/en/PublicationsLibrary/webdiaepcb2012d6_en.pdf> accessed 28 September 2013.

[2] See generally H Kelsen, 'Unrecht und Unrechtsfolge im Völkerrecht' (1932) 12 ZöR 481.

on the Responsibility of States for Internationally Wrongful Acts' (ASR)[3] of the International Law Commission (ILC).

In the investment law context, the legal consequences which may flow from treaty breaches are responsible for much of the perceived legitimacy concerns of this field of the law. The oft-lamented 'regulatory chill' of international investment law ultimately follows from significant amounts of compensation which investment arbitration tribunals award as a consequence of the violation of international investment agreements (IIAs). As Borzu Sabahi and the late Thomas Wälde have noted, 'there is nothing as likely to fuel a backlash [against investment law] as damages awards that are seen as excessive and are not founded on satisfactory reasoning'.[4] This underlines the connection between the legal consequences and the broader legitimacy of the investment protection system.[5] If the goal is to turn IIAs into vehicles of sustainable development, addressing these legitimacy concerns—which revolve around a perception of unfairness vis-à-vis host States and a lack of openness for competing policy concerns in the field of human rights and environmental protection—will be essential.

Accordingly, it is apt to consider what impact the choice of the remedies international law has to offer for what the IPFSD identifies as sustainable development. It is a matter of dispute how well-defined the notion of sustainable development is in international law.[6] For some, sustainable development is a 'well-entrenched norm of international law',[7] whereas others say that 'no one has a clue' as to its meaning and that 'everyone can thus read their own preferred meaning into the phrase'.[8] If there is anything approaching a common denominator between various understandings of the concept, it may be said that contemporary conceptions of sustainable development follow a multi-dimensional approach which aspires to bring together ecological, economic, and social development.[9]

---

[3] 'Articles on the Responsibility of States for Internationally Wrongful Acts', as taken note of by the UN General Assembly, UN Doc. A/RES/56/83 of 28 January 2002.

[4] TW Wälde and B Sabahi, 'Compensation, Damages, and Valuation' in P Muchlinski, F Ortino, and C Schreuer (eds), *The Oxford Handbook of International Investment Law* (OUP 2008) 1049, 1054–55.

[5] On the general legitimacy problems of the investment protection regime see B Kingsbury and SW Schill, 'Public Law Concepts to Balance Investors' Rights with State Regulatory Action in the Public Interest—The Concept of Proportionality' in SW Schill (ed), *International Investment Law and Comparative Public Law* (OUP 2010) 75, 75–77; M Sornarajah, *The International Law on Foreign Investment* (3rd edn, CUP 2010) 27–28; B Simma, 'Foreign Investment Arbitration: A Place for Human Rights?' (2011) 60 ICLQ 573, 575; SP Subedi, *International Investment Law—Reconciling Policy and Principle* (2nd edn, Hart 2012) 149ff.

[6] For an overview see U Beyerlin, 'Sustainable Development', *Max Planck Encyclopedia of Public International Law* vol IX (OUP 2012) 716; see also the contribution of Giorgio Sacerdoti to this volume.

[7] P Sands and J Peel, *Principles of International Environmental Law* (3rd edn, CUP 2012) 208; D Desierto, 'Deciding international investment agreement applicability: the development argument in investment' in F Baetens (ed), *Investment Law within International Law—Integrationist Perspectives* (CUP 2013) 240.

[8] J Klabbers, *International Law* (CUP 2013), 53.

[9] Beyerlin (n 6) at 9; see also M Gehring (ed), *Sustainable Development in World Investment Law* (Kluwer Law International 2010).

The IPFSD seeks to overcome definitional hurdles by mapping out certain core principles for investment policymaking. These core principles cover a large ground and range from the insight that 'the overarching objective of investment policymaking is to promote investment for inclusive growth and sustainable development' over affirmations of balanced rights and obligations of States and investors to the acceptance of a level of 'adequate protection' for established investors.[10] In this contribution, we need not go into the details of how successful these core principles can be to make the concept of sustainable development more concrete. Rather, we are concerned here with the fairly specific question of the potential role of the law of State responsibility in accommodating concerns of sustainable development in international investment law. Investment protection is just one part of IPFSD. Although the question of remedies does not take centre stage in the Framework, it does arise in a number of contexts and the IPFSD makes a number of policy suggestions, in particular in section 6.4, giving guidance on remedies and compensation. The IPFSD lists three policy options:

6.4.0 No clause.
6.4.1 Limit available remedies to monetary compensation and restitution of property (or to compensation only).
6.4.2 Provide that the amount of compensation shall be equitable in light of the circumstances of the case and set out specific rules on compensation for a treaty breach, for example:
– exclude recoverability of punitive and/or moral damages
– limit recoverability of lost profits (up to date of the award)
– ensure that the amount is commensurate with the country's level of development.

The IPFSD goes on to explain the sustainable development implications of these options. With respect to the 'no clause' option, the report notes that as 'most IIAs are silent on the issue of remedies and compensation', this would allow arbitrators to

apply any remedy they deem appropriate, including, for example, an order to the country to modify or annul its law or regulation. Remedies of the latter type could unduly intrude into the sovereign sphere of a State and impede its policy-making powers; thus, Parties to an IIA may consider limiting available remedies to monetary compensation and restitution of property (or compensation only).

This passage is illustrative of the outlook the IPFSD takes on the question of remedies. A preference for compensation—as opposed to restitution—shines through. Restitution is considered to entail possibly wide-ranging infringements on the sovereignty of host States—an argument which is familiar from other contexts. In the negotiations between the EU and Canada over a 'Comprehensive Economic

---

[10] IPFSD (n 1) at 11.

and Trade Agreement' (CETA), it was a goal of the EU negotiators to establish with 'absolute clarity' that 'a State cannot be forced to repeal a measure' due to the intervention of investor–State dispute settlement (ISDS) mechanisms. The consolidated CETA text, as it has been published by the European Commission on 26 September 2014, reflects this consideration and effectively limits the scope of restitution to the return of property (Article X.36).[11] With respect to the form and degree of compensation, the IPFSD further invites States to consider limiting compensation. In particular, the policy option 6.4.2 with the reference to 'equitable compensation' is noteworthy.

The suggestions of the IPFSD provide the background for a re-assessment of the role that the law of State responsibility has to play in the investment protection context. This contribution will first give a brief overview of the legal consequences for wrongful conduct as they are set forth in the ASR (section II). This synthesis will provide the ground for an analysis of the practice of international investment tribunals (section III). From this analysis, it will become apparent that the practice of investment tribunals is quite varied. One important consideration which will emerge from this survey is, however, that a central suggestion of the IPFSD can be challenged. The aversion against restitution as the remedy which is the most detrimental for concerns of sustainable development may not always be warranted. Accordingly, in section IV, it will be claimed that the suggestions of the IPFSD may be partly misguided. In particular, the chapter argues against the resurrection of State sovereignty in the name of sustainable development. In more general terms, the contribution holds that the necessary debate about investment protection and sustainable development should take place on the level of the primary rules of international law and not on the level of the secondary rules, to which the law of State responsibility belongs.

II. Legal Consequences in General International Law

The determination of the legal consequences of wrongful conduct is first and foremost a doctrinal question which can be discussed without any reference to the problem of sustainable development.[12] However, this question may also be assessed in the light of this overarching concern. Regardless of whether one puts great faith in the concept of sustainable development, the choice of remedy—as the different forms of reparation may also be called—can have significant policy

---

[11] See the EU Commission Fact Sheet on 'Investment Provisions in the EU-Canada Free Trade Agreement (CETA)', available at <http://trade.ec.europa.eu/doclib/docs/2013/november/tradoc_151918.pdf> accessed 21 October 2014; and consolidated CETA Text, published on 26 September 2014, available at <http://trade.ec.europa.eu/doclib/html/152806.htm> accessed 16 August 2015.

[12] See, for instance, S Hindelang, 'Restitution and Compensation—Reconstructing the Relationship in Investment Treaty Law' in R Hofmann and CJ Tams (eds), *International Investment Law and General International Law—From Clinical Isolation to Systemic Integration?* (Nomos 2011) 161.

implications.[13] In particular, the choice of a specific remedy may preserve States with more or less 'regulatory space'. It is conceivable, for instance, that a strict application of the principle of restitution—which aspires to 'turn the clock back' to the point in time before a wrongful act took place—might limit States in their regulatory efforts more than the mere order to pay compensation. It is also possible, however, that an order granting a huge sum of compensation may have crippling effects for the State and, more importantly, its population. Also the order to pay compensation may therefore deprive a State of vital means to engage in policies which are relevant for the goal of sustainable development. Before we can turn to these questions, it is however appropriate, to flesh out the basic parameters of the general regime of legal consequences as set forth in the ASR.

The building block of the international law on reparation is the dictum of the Permanent Court of International Justice (PCIJ) in its *Chorzów Factory* case. There, the Court held that 'it is a principle of international law that the breach of an engagement involves an obligation to make reparation in adequate form'.[14] At the merits stage, the PCIJ elaborated in greater detail:

The essential principle contained in the actual notion of an illegal act—a principle which seems to be established by international practice and in particular by the decisions of arbitral tribunals—is that reparation must, as far as possible, wipe out all the consequences of the illegal act and re-establish the situation which would, in all probability, have existed if that act had not been committed.[15]

These two passages are almost always cited when the customary international law on reparation is analysed.[16] The ASR also follow these principles. Article 31(1) ASR stipulates that 'the responsible State is under an obligation to make full reparation for the injury caused by the internationally wrongful act'. Article 34 ASR further states that reparation may take the forms of restitution, compensation, and satisfaction—all of which are further specified in Articles 35–37 ASR. The general idea behind the regime instituted by the ASR—which is meant to represent customary international law on the matter—is that there is a primacy of restitution. So much becomes clear from Article 36(1) ASR on compensation which provides that 'the State responsible for an internationally wrongful act is under an obligation to compensate for the damage caused thereby, insofar as such damage is not made good by restitution'. Satisfaction, in turn, is also only an option where neither restitution nor compensation has been effected.

It is fair to say, however, that the primacy of restitution only exists in theory. In practice, restitution is often not the option of choice.[17] With respect to the

---

[13] cf A van Aaken, 'Primary and Secondary Remedies in International Investment Law and National State Liability: A Functional and Comparative View' in SW Schill (ed), *International Investment Law and Comparative Public Law* (OUP 2010) 721, 746ff.
[14] *Case Concerning the Factory at Chorzów (Germany v Poland)* (Jurisdiction) PCIJ Rep Series A No 9, 21.
[15] *Factory at Chorzów (Germany v Poland)* (Merits) PCIJ Rep Series A No 17, 47.
[16] See also J Crawford, *State Responsibility—The General Part* (CUP 2013) 480–81.
[17] C Gray, 'The Different Forms of Reparation: Restitution' in J Crawford, A Pellet, and S Olleson (eds), *The Law of International Responsibility* (OUP 2010) 589.

International Court of Justice (ICJ), it even appears as if recently satisfaction has become the most frequently awarded remedy, insofar as the ICJ often only states that a certain conduct constituted a violation of international law and considers this finding to be an adequate legal consequence for the commission of a wrongful act.[18] In line with this practice, the ASR have opted for a more flexible approach,[19] which becomes apparent by the provision of Article 43(2)(b) on the notice of claim, which mentions that the injured State may specify 'what form reparation should take in accordance with the provisions of Part two'.

Before we continue with an assessment of the practice of tribunals in the field of investment law, we should make one further clarification. It is important for our topic to distinguish compensation in the context of expropriation from compensation as a remedy under the law of State responsibility.[20] The former concept of compensation is one of the criteria for the lawfulness of expropriations under both customary international law and in virtually all IIAs (besides the public purpose of the expropriation, its non-discriminatory nature and respect for due process). Although there is some uncertainty about the nature of compensation in customary international law, there still appears to be a consensus that at least in general some form of compensation has to follow an expropriation in order to make it lawful. In IIAs, it is mostly required that the compensation must be in conformity with the so-called Hull formula, that is, be 'prompt, adequate, and effective'. This notion is generally understood to require the fair market value of the property which was taken.[21]

The consequences of the law of State responsibility only come to apply when an internationally wrongful act was committed. If we presume for the moment that the ASR can find application in the investment law context—on this issue see immediately below—they will only be relevant for unlawful expropriations and other violations of the standards of protection under IIAs, that is, the standard of fair and equitable treatment, full protection and security, denial of justice as well as obligations brought under the protection of the IIA by virtue of umbrella clauses.[22]

It is important to distinguish clearly between these scenarios as also the calculation of compensation is different, depending on whether the exercise is about

---

[18] Emblematic is the finding in *Application of the Convention on the Prevention and Punishment of the Crime of Genocide (Bosnia and Herzegovina v Serbia and Montenegro)* (Merits) [2007] ICJ Rep 43, para 463.
[19] Gray (n 17) 589.
[20] A Reinisch, 'Legality of Expropriation' in A Reinisch (ed), *Standards of Investment Protection* (OUP 2008) 171, 199–204; I Marboe, 'State Responsibility and Comparative State Liability for Administrative and Legislative Harm to Economic Interests' in SW Schill (ed), *International Investment Law and Comparative Public Law* (OUP 2010) 377, 381; E de Brabandere, *Investment Treaty Arbitration as Public International Law – Procedural Aspects and Implications* (CUP 2014) 175; I Marboe, 'The System of Reparation and Questions of Terminology' in M Bungenberg, J Griebel, S Hobe, A Reinisch (eds), *International Investment Law* (Nomos 2015) 1031, para 6.
[21] R Dolzer and C Schreuer, *Principles of International Investment Law* (2nd edn, OUP 2012) 100.
[22] On the legal consequences of denial of justice see J Paulsson, *Denial of Justice in International Law* (CUP 2005), 207ff.

compensation as a criterion for the legality of an expropriation or whether it is about reparation in the sense of Articles 34, 36 ASR. In the former case, 'fair market value' is the objective standard for the calculation of compensation—a notion which may be highly hypothetical if there is no genuine market for an expropriated asset. In the latter case, the calculation takes into account the subjective situation in which the respective investor found herself at the moment at which the unlawful act was committed. This distinction can lead to markedly different results, notably with respect to the issue of lost profits.[23]

In arbitral practice, most ICSID tribunals appear to uphold this distinction.[24] That compensation may thus be considerably higher in the case of an unlawful expropriation was made abundantly clear in the *ADC v Hungary* decision, where the tribunal stressed that it was not in a position to apply the BIT provisions on 'market value' of the expropriated asset due to the unlawfulness of the expropriation. Rather, the Tribunal stated, it would have to apply the 'default standard contained in customary international law',[25] leading the Tribunal to order 'payment of a sum corresponding to the value which a restitution in kind would bear'.[26]

III. Legal Consequences of Treaty Breaches in International Investment Law

With these general observations in mind, let us now turn to the field of international investment law. Two questions stand out: first, we need to deal with the preliminary question of whether the general rules as laid down in the ASR find application in the investment law context (section a). Second, we will then look at how tribunals apply the general rules (section b).

a) Applicability of the ASR remedies

It is anything but certain that the ASR apply in investor–State arbitrations. This is owed to the fact that part two of the ASR, which deals with the content of international responsibility, is, prima facie, only directly applicable in the inter-State context.[27] Article 33(2) ASR stipulates that the provisions in part two of the ASR are 'without prejudice to any right, arising from the international responsibility of a State,

---

[23] Dolzer and Schreuer (n 21), at 100–01.
[24] For an overview see Reinisch (n 20) 202.
[25] *ADC Affiliate Limited and ADC & ADMC Management Limited v. Republic of Hungary*, ICSID Case No ARB/03/16, Award (2 October 2006) para 483.
[26] ibid para 495.
[27] J Crawford, 'Investment Arbitration and the ILC Articles on State Responsibility' (2010) 25 ICSID Rev 127, 130; Z Douglas, 'Other Specific Regimes of Responsibility: Investment Treaty Arbitration and ICSID' in J Crawford, A Pellet, and S Olleson (eds), *The Law of International Responsibility* (OUP 2010), 815, 820; U Kriebaum, 'Restitution in International Investment Law' in R Hofmann and CJ Tams (eds), *International Investment Law and General International Law—From Clinical Isolation to Systemic Integration?* (Nomos 2011) 201, 203; M Paparinskis, 'Analogies and Other

which may accrue directly to any person or entity other than a State'. The commentary notes that in

> cases where the primary obligation is owed to a non-State entity, it may be that some procedure is available where that entity can invoke the responsibility on its own account and without the intermediation of any State. This is true, for example, under human rights treaties which provide a right of petition to a court or some other body for individuals affected. It is also true in the case of rights under bilateral or regional investment protection agreements.... The articles do not deal with the possibility of the invocation of responsibility by persons or entities other than States, and paragraph 2 makes this clear. It will be a matter for the particular primary rule to determine whether and to what extent persons or entities other than States are entitled to invoke responsibility on their account.[28]

The outlook of the ASR on the matter is thus clear.[29] Whereas part one of the articles is deemed to apply in all cases where the international responsibility of States is concerned and thus regardless of the question to whom responsibility is owed, part two is specifically designed for the inter-State context. This makes sense insofar as the ASR are largely understood to represent customary international law, which has developed mostly in the inter-State context. Specific treaty regimes in the fields of human rights and investment protection may have deviated from the general rules and may have brought about special rules about the consequences of wrongful behaviour which may differ from the legal consequences of wrongful acts in the inter-State context. So much might also be inferred from Article 55 ASR which explicitly notes the possibility of lex specialis. Technically, however, this provision cannot be decisive for if part two does not apply to claims of investors against States, there is no need for lex specialis to deviate from the general rules.[30] Nonetheless, Article 55 ASR signals the openness of the general rules to make way for specific arrangements—a feature which is essential for the understanding of the ASR.[31]

That differences may have developed in this regard may become apparent in light of the different functions of 'remedies'. In the inter-State context, which is characterized mostly by a bundle of horizontal and often bilateral relationships between sovereign States,[32] the questions of wrongfulness and reparation are intimately connected with the general function of the law of State responsibility to

---

Regimes of International Law' in Z Douglas, J Pauwelyn, and JE Viñuales (eds), *The Foundations of International Investment Law* (OUP 2014) 73, 102; J Crawford and S Olleson, 'The Application of the Rules of State Responsibility' in M Bungenberg, J Griebel, S Hobe, A Reinisch (eds), *International Investment Law* (Nomos 2015) 411, para 22.

[28] 'ILC Commentary', reprinted in J Crawford, *The International Law Commission's Articles on State Responsibility* (CUP 2002) Art 33, para 4.

[29] Although it can be noted that there is a certain discrepancy between the provision which speaks of rights accruing to other entities and the commentary which refers to invocation of responsibility.

[30] Hindelang (n 12) 196, with note 122.

[31] See, in this respect, B Simma and D Pulkowski, 'Of Planets and the Universe: Self-Contained Regimes in International Law' (2006) 17 EJIL 483; HP Aust, 'Through the Prism of Diversity—The ILC Articles on State Responsibility in the Light of the ILC Fragmentation Report' (2006) 49 GYIL 165.

[32] On the bilateral origins of the law of State responsibility see G Nolte, 'From Dionisio Anzilotti to Roberto Ago: The Classical International Law of State Responsibility and Traditional Primacy of a Bilateral Conception of Inter-State Relations' (2002) 13 EJIL 1083.

preserve a climate of international legality. In the absence of a centralized and all-encompassing system of dispute settlement, the remedies set forth by the ASR are the default mode by which the international legal system aspires to bring some coherence into the mutual exchange of claims between States which find themselves at an equal footing.[33]

The situation is fundamentally different in the human rights context and also in the field of investment protection. Here, legal disputes are not characterized by the fact that they take place on a level playing field. Traditionally, especially in situations of investments abroad, foreigners were considered to require an extra amount of protection against the State which might infringe upon their rights.[34] Therefore, the central innovation of the investment protection system is the direct access of investors to arbitration which secures their legal position beyond the incalculable uncertainty of whether their home States will exercise diplomatic protection on their behalf.[35] Foreign investors may most of the times not be interested in a 'return to legality'. Especially in a country where the regulatory situation has deteriorated in a significant manner, they will probably be more interested in the termination of an investment for which they might hope to recover any financial investments they will have made until then. From this perspective, one would imagine that treaty-makers, that is States, have designed special rules for the legal consequences of treaty breaches in order to accommodate the various competing interests of investors, home as well as host States.

It is only seldom the case, however, that an IIA provides for special rules on the remedies.[36] One exception is the North American Free Trade Agreement (NAFTA), which provides in Article 1135 that only monetary damages, interest (if applicable), and restitution of property may be ordered by arbitral tribunals. It therefore creates a lex specialis regime for NAFTA which rules out the application of the general rules of State responsibility.[37] Also Article 26(8) of the Energy Charter Treaty (ECT) and a number of other agreements limit the available form of remedies.[38]

As already mentioned, most other IIAs do not include a similar provision. Hence, the question arises what remedies arbitral tribunals may order. A number of investment law tribunals have applied the rules set forth by part two of the ILC

---

[33] See further HP Aust, 'The Normative Environment for Peace—On the Contribution of the ILC's Articles on State Responsibility' in G Nolte (ed), *Peace Through International Law—The Role of the International Law Commission* (Springer 2009) 13.

[34] SW Schill, 'Investitionsschutzrecht als Entwicklungsvölkerrecht' (2012) 72 ZaöRV 261, 280.

[35] A Reinisch and L Malintoppi, 'Methods of Dispute Resolution' in P Muchlinski, F Ortino, and C Schreuer (eds), *The Oxford Handbook of International Investment Law* (OUP 2008) 691, 713; K Parlett, 'Diplomatic Protection and Investment Arbitration' in R Hofmann and CJ Tams (eds), *International Investment Law and General International Law—From Clinical Isolation to Systemic Integration?* (Nomos 2011) 211; Schill (n 34) 283.

[36] B Sabahi, *Compensation and Restitution in Investor-State Arbitration* (OUP 2011) 64.

[37] *Archer Daniels Midland Company and Tate & Lyle Ingredients Americas, Inc v United Mexican States*, ICSID Case No ARB(AF)/04/05, Award (21 November 2007) para 118.

[38] For an overview see Kriebaum (n 27) 204–05. See also the consolidated text of CETA, Art X:36 (n 11).

Articles. In these decisions, it has generally not been stated expressly on what basis this application takes place. In other words, it is not clear whether these tribunals are of the view that the ASR apply directly, or whether they apply as a matter of analogy.[39] The practice of those tribunals which rely on the ASR is pragmatic.[40] At the same time, it should be noted that other tribunals do not mention the ASR at all. This state of affairs reminds us not to generalize too much. It is a general debate whether the current investment law regime is characterized by 'fragmentation'[41] or rather by a growing convergence or 'multilateralization'.[42] The practice of arbitral tribunals with respect to the legal consequences of treaty breaches is but one facet of this debate. The decisions of tribunals who refer to the ASR might be seen as contributing to a greater coherence of the investment law regime, with general rules being introduced into the system and thus introducing a greater level of legal certainty. However, tribunals which do not refer to these rules do not necessarily place themselves at the service of fragmentation: they may have come to the conclusion that the general rules simply do not apply. In this situation, they are then more or less left alone by the current bilateral and regional treaties which in most cases, as already noted, do not specify what the alternative regime of remedies should be.

b) The choice between restitution and compensation in the practice of investment arbitration

How do arbitral tribunals then approach the question of remedies?[43] In terms of the practical outcome of the disputes, it can be noted that arbitral tribunals in most cases award compensation and thus a pecuniary remedy.[44] This does not necessarily mean, however, that they may not also order other remedies, in particular restitution. In this regard, it is possible to identify a number of different approaches: in some awards the applicability of the ASR is explicitly

---

[39] On the use of analogies see M Paparinskis, 'Investment Treaty Arbitration and the (New) Law of State Responsibility' (2013) 24 EJIL 617, 638; A Roberts, 'Clash of Paradigms: Actors and Analogies Shaping the Investment Treaty System' (2013) 107 AJIL 45, especially at 49–57.

[40] See, for instance, *MTD Equity Sdn Bhd And MTD Chile SA v Republic of Chile*, ICSID Case No ARB/01/17, Decision on Annulment (21 March 2007) para 99.

[41] ILC Study Group, 'Fragmentation of International Law: Difficulties Arising from the Diversification and Expansion of International Law' (2006) UN Doc A/CN.4/L.682.

[42] On this debate see A van Aaken, 'Fragmentation of International Law: the Case of International Investment Law' (2006) 17 FYIL 91; SW Schill, *The Multilateralization of International Investment Law* (CUP 2009); A Reinisch, 'The Proliferation of International Dispute Settlement Mechanisms: The Threat of Fragmentation vs. the Promise of a More Effective System? Some Reflections from the Perspective of Investment Arbitration' in I Buffard et al (eds), *International Law Between Universalism and Fragmentation: Festschrift in Honour of Gerhard Hafner* (Brill 2008) 107; as well as the contributions in F Baetens (ed), *Investment Law within International Law* (CUP 2013).

[43] An extremely useful analysis of arbitral practice is contained in the annex to Crawford (n 27).

[44] C Schreuer, 'Non-Pecuniary Remedies in ICSID Arbitration' (2004) 20 Arb Intl 325, 329; S Wittich, 'Investment Arbitration: Remedies' in M Bungenberg, J Griebel, S Hobe, A Reinisch (eds), *International Investment Law* (Nomos 2015) 1391, para 59.

discussed,⁴⁵ whereas other awards rely on the ASR without giving reasons.⁴⁶ Yet other tribunals do not apply them, but rather follow or make up other rules which determine the respective tribunal's findings on remedies. Non-application of the ASR is only rarely explained. An exception is the *Wintershall v Argentina* award, in which the Tribunal remarked on the quality of the ASR that they are

a detailed and official study on the subject but it [the ASR] contains no rules and regulations of State Responsibility vis-à-vis non-State actors. Tribunals are left to determine 'the ways in which State Responsibility may be invoked by non-State entities' from the provisions of the text of the particular Treaty under consideration.⁴⁷

Those tribunals which cite the ASR quite naturally refer to the customary character of the rules set forth in part two of the ASR.⁴⁸ This reference to the customary nature does not in and of itself answer the question of the applicability of the ASR, as it does not address the impact of Article 33(2) ASR. However, it indicates that these tribunals apparently consider themselves bound to apply the ASR by virtue of their belonging to the category of general international law.⁴⁹ Many bilateral investment treaties state as applicable law not just the treaty itself, but also rules of international law in general. Even if this is not the case, tribunals are directed towards the application of international law by provisions such as Article 42(1) of the ICSID Convention⁵⁰ and Article 35(1) of the UNCITRAL Arbitration Rules.⁵¹

Among those awards which rely on the ASR, some affirm the primacy of restitution. An example in this regard is *Nycomb v Latvia*:

The Arbitral Tribunal holds, and it seems to be agreed between the parties, that the question of remedies to compensate for losses or damages caused by the Respondent's violation of Article 10 of the Treaty must primarily find its solution in accordance with established principles of customary international law. Such principles have authoritatively been restated in the International Law Commission's Draft Articles on State Responsibility adopted in

---

⁴⁵ *Nycomb Synergetics Technology Holding AB v The Republic of Latvia*, SCC, Award (16 December 2003) para 5.1; *Wintershall Aktiengesellschaft v Argentine Republic*, ICSID Case No. ARB/04/14, Award (8 November 2008) para 112.
⁴⁶ See, for example, *Petrobart Limited v Kyrgyz Republic*, SCC Case No 126/2003, Award (29 March 2005) 77–78; *CME Czech Republic BV v Czech Republic*, UNCITRAL, Partial Award (13 September 2001) para 616; *Archer Daniels Midland Company and Tate & Lyle Ingredients Americas, Inc v United Mexican States*, ICSID Case No ARB(AF)/04/05, Award (21 November 2007) para 118.
⁴⁷ *Wintershall Aktiengesellschaft* (n 45) para 113.
⁴⁸ *Siemens AG v Argentine Republic*, ICSID Case No ARB/02/8, Award (6 February 2007) para 350; *Archer Daniels* (n 46) para 275; *BG Group plc v Republic of Argentina*, UNCITRAL, Final Award (24 December 2007) para 427; see also G Bücheler, *Proportionality in Investor-State Arbitration* (OUP 2015) 95.
⁴⁹ For a similar reasoning in the literature see Schill (n 42) 250.
⁵⁰ Convention on the Settlement of Investment Disputes between States and Nationals of other States (opened for Signature 18 March 1965, entered into Force 14 October 1966) ('ICSID Convention') 575 UNTS 159.
⁵¹ United Nations Commission on International Trade Law (UNCITRAL), 'Arbitration Rules' (1976) UN Doc A/RES/31/98.

November 2001...According to Articles 34 and 35 ILC restitution is considered to be the primary remedy for reparation.⁵²

Also the Tribunal in *ADC v Hungary* adopted a similar reasoning⁵³ as did the Tribunal in *CMS Gas Transmission Company v Argentina*.⁵⁴ Without expressing a clear preference for restitution, other arbitral tribunals have made reference to the general relationship between restitution and compensation under the ASR.⁵⁵ Some tribunals hold that restitution is not generally ruled out in the investment law context.⁵⁶ In an award from April 2013, the Tribunal in *Franck Charles Arif v Moldova* was faced with the situation that the respondent asked the Tribunal not to order compensation—as asked for by the claimants—but rather restitution.⁵⁷ This prompted, as the Tribunal dryly noted, 'some discussion by the Parties at the Hearing'.⁵⁸ The Tribunal noted that 'restitution is more consistent with the objectives of bilateral investment treaties, as it preserves both the investment and the relationship between the investor and the Host State'.⁵⁹ As the Tribunal did not find itself in a position to verify the possibility of restitution in the concrete case at hand, it ordered a two-step approach with a combination of restitution and compensation, the latter being suspended for a period of ninety days, thereby allowing the respondent to provide for genuine restitution.⁶⁰

Not all tribunals follow this line of reasoning, however. In the *Enron v Argentina* award, the Tribunal came to the conclusion that 'absent an agreed form of restitution by means of renegotiation of contracts or otherwise, the appropriate standard of reparation under international law is compensation'.⁶¹ Also the *CME Czech Republic v Czech Republic* award stated very clearly that 'international law requires that compensation eliminates the consequences of the wrongful act' and referred to the ASR in order to substantiate this finding.⁶² An intermediate approach which lies between the affirmation of restitution as the primary remedy and the position which takes a preference for compensation, is the recognition of the right of election of the injured party. This view is also held by some tribunals.⁶³

---

⁵² *Nycomb* (n 45).
⁵³ *ADC Affiliate Limited* (n 25) para 494; *Archer Daniels* (n 46) para 280.
⁵⁴ *CMS Gas Transmission Company v Argentine Republic*, ICSID Case No ARB/01/8, Award (12 May 2005) para 400.
⁵⁵ *LG&E Energy Corp, LG&E Capital Corp, LG&E International Inc v Argentine Republic*, ICSID Case No ARB/02/1, Award on Damages (25 July 2007) para 31; *Sempra Energy International v Argentine Republic*, ICSID Case No. ARB/02/16, Award (28 September 2007) para 401.
⁵⁶ *Occidental Petroleum Corporation and Occidental Petroleum and Exploration Company v Republic of Ecuador*, ICSID Case No ARB/06/11, Decision on Provisional Measures (17 August 2007) para 82; *Burlington Resources Oriente Limited v Ecuador and Empresa Estatal Petroleos del Ecuador*, ICSID Case No ARB/08/5, Procedural Order No 1 (29 June 2009) para 70.
⁵⁷ *Franck Charles Arif v Republic of Moldova*, ICSID Case No ARB/11/23, Award (8 April 2013) paras 561 and 564.
⁵⁸ ibid para 566.   ⁵⁹ ibid para 570.
⁶⁰ ibid para 571; on this award see also de Brabandere (n 20) 189–90; Wittich (n 44) paras 63–64.
⁶¹ *Enron Corporation and Ponderosa Assets, LP v Argentine Republic*, ICSID Case No ARB/01/03, Award (22 May 2007) para 359.
⁶² *CME Czech Republic BV v Czech Republic*, UNCITRAL, Final Award (14 March 2003) para 501.
⁶³ *LG&E Energy* (n 55) para 32.

c) Analysis

Hence, the picture is quite varied and it is not possible to identify a common approach among investment tribunals—which is quite typical for the diversity in the approaches of investment tribunals across a wide range of issues pertaining to the application of general international law. This state of affairs is mirrored in the academic literature. Some authors follow the general rules of State responsibility and argue for a prevalence of restitution.[64] Others hold the view that arbitral tribunals are not even competent to order restitution and may therefore only order compensation.[65] The third form of reparation set forth by the ASR, satisfaction, does not appear to play a significant role in the debate.[66]

The policy perspective of the two camps is markedly different: whereas the first group of authors emphasizes the integration of investment law into the international legal order, the second group flags out the investment law regime as a sub-system of international law, if not a self-contained regime. Proponents of the first approach—let us call them the integrationists here—point to the fact that most investment agreements do not specify what the legal consequences of breaches are. Accordingly, it is argued, arbitrators would be free to consider other means of reparation than just compensation. The authors falling into this camp have to acknowledge, however, that most claimants directly aim at obtaining compensation and that thus tribunals might be bound to award just this form of reparation under the ne ultra petita rule.[67]

The above-mentioned *Franck Charles Arif v Moldova* case casts a shadow of doubt on this reading, however.[68] Also the ILC was at pains to adopt a somewhat flexible solution with a general possibility for the claimant to elect the favoured remedy, without however granting absolute freedom in this regard.[69] In this connection, the question of the 'ownership' of the rights set forth in the respective IIA has a role to play. If States conclude treaties primarily for the sake of the creation of a 'healthy investment climate', it might be counterproductive if investors can always opt for compensation and walk away from investments.[70] While some situations will dictate compensation as the only appropriate remedy, restitution should not be ruled out in general.

Those who argue for the second approach—the sub-system advocates—point to the fact that the ASR are not applicable in the first place. The reliance on the PCIJ's dictum in *Chorzów Factory* would be misguided, as it would overlook the specificities of the case. Furthermore, Article 54(1) of the ICSID Convention would show that awards that would not result in compensation would be useless in many

---

[64] Hindelang (n 12) 197; V Prislan, 'Non-investment obligations in investment treaty arbitration: a greater role for States' in F Batens (ed), *Investment Law within International Law—Integrationist Perspectives* (CUP 2013) 450, 462; van Aaken (n 13) 734, 745.
[65] Douglas (n 27) 829; A Kulick, *Global Public Interest in International Investment Law* (CUP 2012) 209.
[66] See also *LG&E Energy* (n 55) para 32, note 6.   [67] Van Aaken (n 13) 734.
[68] See n 57.   [69] ILC Commentary (n 28), Art 43, paras 6–7.
[70] Hindelang (n 12) 198.

situations, as States have only agreed to enforce pecuniary obligations awarded by tribunals. This argument is inconclusive, however, as the questions of available remedy and enforcement need to be kept apart.[71]

Yet others stress the limits that flow from the sovereignty of the host State.[72] The ordering of restitution might unduly restrict the sovereignty of the respective State, as it might be forced to annul or withdraw domestic legislation. It can be wondered whether the historical origins of the law of investment protection in the protection against expropriation have a role to play in this regard. It was and is still widely recognized that States have a right to expropriate. Therefore, an emphasis on restitution could be seen as an unwarranted infringement on a central prerogative of sovereign powers. However, as was already argued above, different forms of compensation have to be kept apart. Compensation as a criterion for the lawfulness of an expropriation is a different matter than compensation as a remedy for wrongful conduct. As the reach of investment law has expanded beyond protection against expropriation, it is also conceivable that treaty breaches entail a more varied set of legal consequences. Why should, as a matter of policy, a violation of the standard of fair and equitable treatment only result in compensation? Is it not conceivable that such a violation may very well be undone and that thus a 'return to legality' could be a viable option—and thus restitution?

An intriguing comparison to the situation in investment law protection is, moreover, the state of affairs in WTO law, where the infringing State is under an obligation to bring its domestic legal framework into conformity with its international legal obligations. Only in the case of non-compliance, can compensation be awarded on the basis of Article 22 of the Dispute Settlement Understanding.[73] This mechanism could be seen as a regime-specific translation of the general relationship between restitution and compensation. Restitution and thus the 'return to legality' comes first. If this is not feasible, compensation is still viable and then marks the price a reluctant State has to pay for the breach of its international obligations.[74]

However, despite—or probably because of—the extension of the scope of investment protection, concerns about State sovereignty are also reflected in arbitral practice. In *LG&E v Argentina*, the Tribunal, for instance, held that

the judicial situation in this case would imply modification of the current legal situation by annulling or enacting legislation and administrative measures that make over the effect of

---

[71] See further, also with more details on the drafting history of the ICSID Convention, Schreuer (n 44) 325: 'it would be wrong to conclude from this provision that an ICSID tribunal may not order non-pecuniary relief'.

[72] See, for instance, Kulick (n 65) 209; see generally on the role of sovereignty in investment protection JE Viñuales, 'Sovereignty in Foreign Investment Law' in Z Douglas, J Pauwelyn, and JE Viñuales (eds), *The Foundations of International Investment Law* (OUP 2014) 317.

[73] Understanding on Rules and Procedures Governing the Settlement of Disputes, Marrakesh Agreement Establishing the World Trade Organization, Annex 2, 1869 UNTS 401, 33 ILM 1226 (1994).

[74] I am indebted to Michael Waibel for drawing my attention to this comparative aspect.

the legislation in breach. The tribunal cannot compel Argentina to do so without a sentiment of undue interference with its sovereignty.[75]

This position finds some support in the literature, where it is argued that 'a tribunal bestowed with the competency to order any remedy other than compensation or damages would be too intrusive on the host State's sovereignty and hence would be in blatant disregard of the current state of public international law'.[76] This reasoning is very questionable—also in light of the comparison with the state of affairs under WTO law.[77] There is considerable ICJ practice showing that States can very well be ordered to effect restitution or engage in specific performance of obligations they entered into.[78] Sovereignty in and of itself is never an argument to evade international obligations or the consequences flowing from breaches of the law. Rather, a State's sovereignty is defined by reference to the rights and obligations it has under international law.[79]

Between the two camps, it may not necessarily be possible to identify one correct approach. The development of the investment protection regime is still in flux and deeply rooted conceptual disagreements about the legal nature of this system impact also on our question.

This brings us back to the primordial issue to whom IIAs actually grant rights.[80] Do they provide for genuine individual rights which investors may invoke in their own name? Or do they only provide investors with the procedural capacity to invoke rights which ultimately remain vested with their respective home State? Depending on which view one takes on this issue, also the question of the applicability of part two of the ASR will be answered differently.[81] If one holds the view that IIAs guarantee individual rights of the respective investors,[82] it is sensible to argue that part two of the ASR will not apply and that we are rather within the scope of applicability of the 'no prejudice' clause of Article 33(2) ASR. If one holds the view that the protective rights set forth in IIAs are obligations which are owed at the inter-State level, then part two of the ASR of course applies.[83] In light of the many different existing IIAs it is probably not possible to answer the question in a general manner. Rather, as it has been convincingly argued, it will depend on

---

[75] *LG&E Energy* (n 55) para. 87.   [76] Kulick (n 65) 209.
[77] See also van Aaken (n 13) 747–48.
[78] *Case Concerning the Temple of Preah Vihear (Cambodia v Thailand)* [1962] ICJ Rep 5, 37; *Case Concerning United States Diplomatic and Consular Staff in Tehran (United States of America v Iran)* [1980] ICJ Rep 1, 44–45, para 95; *Case Concerning the Arrest Warrant of 11 April 2000 (Democratic Republic of the Congo v Belgium)* [2002] ICJ Rep 3, para 76; *Case Concerning Avena and other Mexican Nationals (Mexico v United States of America)* [2004] ICJ Rep 12, para 121.
[79] cf G Nolte, 'Sovereignty as Responsibility?' (2005) 99 ASIL Proc 399; Viñuales (n 72) 319.
[80] See further on this question R Volterra, 'International Law Commission Articles on State Responsibility and Investor-State Arbitration: Do Investors Have Rights?' (2010) 25 ICSID Rev 218; K Parlett, *The Individual in the International Legal System—Continuity and Change in International Law* (CUP 2011) 103–19.
[81] See Paparinskis (n 39).
[82] Z Douglas, 'The Hybrid Foundations of Investment Treaty Arbitration' (2004) 74 BYIL 151, 162ff.
[83] In this direction see Hindelang (n 12), 194–95 who ultimately leaves the question open.

the interpretation of the respective treaty provision in accordance with the general rules of interpretation set forth by Articles 31–33 of the Vienna Convention on the Law of Treaties (VCLT).[84] Guidance might be obtained from an analysis of whether the respective IIA speaks of 'rights' of the investors or whether it is formulated in a more general manner which may also allow for a construction of the rights as being placed solely on the inter-State level.[85]

Accordingly, the general rules of State responsibility might apply in some situations directly—when the rights are situated at the inter-State level—but not in others, when IIAs provide for direct rights of individuals. I would submit, however, that also in this latter category, good reasons exist for arbitral tribunals to make use of the ASR. In the absence of lex specialis, the ASR are the most important source of inspiration with respect to remedies. In the absence of special rules in the respective IIAs, arbitrators may use the general rules of the law of State responsibility by way of analogy.[86] This allows them to make creative use of the template they find in the guise of the ASR. Also in general international law, the alleged primacy of restitution has given way to a rather flexible approach.[87] Therefore, it would be too dogmatic to criticize investment tribunals for not following a strict primacy of restitution.

It is an ongoing dispute whether investment protection follows a commercial arbitration mindset[88] or should rather be carried out more in the spirit of being a part of international law,[89] or even as part of a global administrative law,[90] some might even say constitutional law.[91] Let it suffice to note here that from the perspective of general international law, investment tribunals should make a serious attempt to engage with rules and principles from outside of the investment law context.[92]

---

[84] Vienna Convention on the Law of Treaties (adopted 23 May 1969, entered into force 27 January 1980) (VCLT) 1155 UNTS 331.

[85] Parlett (n 80) 112–13. This question can also be approached in terms of the different paradigms identified by Roberts (n 39).

[86] On the criteria for the use of analogies in international law see S Vöneky, 'Analogy', *The Max Planck Encyclopedia of Public International Law* (OUP 2012) vol I, 374, paras 4–5 and 18–21.

[87] Crawford (n 16) 515–16.

[88] Simma (n 5) 576; some even speak of a 'commercial arbitration mafia': J Crawford, 'International Protection of Foreign Direct Investments: Between Clinical Isolation and Systemic Integration' in R Hofmann and CJ Tams (eds), *International Investment Law and General International Law—From Clinical Isolation to Systemic Integration?* (Nomos 2011) 17, 28; see also M Hirsch, 'Investment tribunals and human rights treaties: a sociological perspective' in F Baetens (ed), *Investment Law within International Law—Integrationist Perspectives* (CUP 2013) 85.

[89] As evidenced, for example, by authoritative interpretations of the NAFTA by the Free Trade Commission, Note of Interpretation (31 July 2001), see further M Waibel, 'International Investment Law and Treaty Interpretation' in R Hofmann and CJ Tams (eds), *International Investment Law and General International Law—From Clinical Isolation to Systemic Integration?* (Nomos 2011) 29, 47–48.

[90] G van Harten and M Loughlin, 'Investment Treaty Arbitration as a Species of Global Administrative Law' (2006) 17 EJIL 121.

[91] P Behrens, 'Towards the Constitutionalization of International Investment Protection' (2007) 45 AVR 153; for an overview of the different approaches see Kulick (n 65) 77–99; see also for the suggestion for a third way between the isolated consideration of the specific case and too ambitious attempts of integrating common concerns WM Reisman, '"Case-Specific Mandates" versus "Systemic Implications"—How Should Investment Tribunals Decide?' (2013) 29 Arb Int 131.

[92] Prislan (n 64) 462.

This follows already from the interpretive principle of systemic integration as set forth by Article 31(3)(c) VCLT.[93] This principle may have no *direct* bearing on the choice of remedies, as the direct application of this principle requires that the relevant rules be applicable in the concrete case. Nevertheless, it signals a sensibility for the existence of a broader international regulatory framework—something which might also be helpful for the attempts to bring investment protection into line with sustainable development.

IV. Rethinking the Role of State Responsibility in the Context of Investment Protection and Sustainable Development

If investment tribunals thus were to engage in such an open-minded exercise of looking towards general international law how could they proceed? And, more particularly, how could they go about in order to further the achievement of sustainable development through investment protection? Three issues stand out here and merit our attention: first, we will discuss whether the bias on the part of the IPFSD against restitution as an undue infringement of State sovereignty is warranted (section a). Second, we will question whether the law of State responsibility is the right place for the struggle for the better entrenchment of sustainable development in the investment law regime (section b). Third, we will warn against unwanted side-effects of a resurrection of State sovereignty in this context for other fields of international law (section c).

a) Restitution—an undue infringement of State sovereignty?

When we look at the suggestions of the IPFSD which were set out in the first section of this chapter, the suggestion to limit what compensation may cover will prove to be controversial. It may contribute, as the IPFSD itself acknowledges, to an 'undermining' of the 'protective quality of the IIA'. Above all, the references to the sovereignty of States and to the necessary consideration of equity in the consideration of damages are hard to reconcile with the prevailing concept of State responsibility. While States are of course free to contract out of existing international law and define the scope of compensation in narrower terms inter se, the wider implications of the suggestions of the IPFSD should nonetheless be considered. The suggestion in fact appears as an attempt to re-open the discussion about the 'New International Economic Order' (NIEO),[94] but this time

---

[93] On this principle in the investment law context see C MacLachlan, 'The Principle of Systemic Integration and Article 31(3)(c) of the Vienna Convention' (2005) 54 ICLQ 279; Simma (n 5) 584–86; JE Viñuales, *Foreign Investment and the Environment in International Law* (CUP 2012) 151–56; see also the contribution of Katharina Berner to this volume.

[94] On the attempts to redefine the protection of property in this context see Subedi (n 5) 23–26; S Pahuya, *Decolonising International Law—Development, Economic Growth and the Politics of Universality* (CUP 2011) ch 4.

not with respect to compensation for lawful expropriations, but in the context of remedies for wrongful conduct. This would be quite a wide-ranging change of the law, insofar as it is something akin to an untouched cornerstone of the law of State responsibility that wrongfulness shall entail reparation. A different matter is compensation for lawful expropriations where—at least under customary international law—it is not entirely settled whether the 'prompt, adequate and effective' compensation standard as formulated by the Hull doctrine still prevails among States.[95] As General Assembly Resolution 1803 on 'Permanent Sovereignty over Natural Resources' stated, 'appropriate compensation' is demanded as a consequence of expropriation[96]—a term which lends itself to different readings and might well accommodate also concerns of sustainable development.[97]

It is quite paradoxical that the IPFSD urges States to limit reparation to compensation and that this suggestion is seen as a step towards the better entrenchment of sustainable development concerns in the law of investment protection. As we have seen, there are only very few cases in the practice of arbitral tribunals where restitution has been ordered. In fact, most claimants also opt for compensation and do not even try to obtain restitution.[98] The IPFSD therefore strives for something which is already characterizing the current practice of investment protection. The suggestion also overlooks that in some situations full compensation may be the costlier alternative for the host State. Restitution, as it is understood in Article 35 ASR, does not necessarily presuppose a *full* restitution. Rather, it restores the status quo ante. Full compensation, in contrast, possibly extends to the hypothetical situation in which the aggrieved investor would have found herself had the wrongful act not taken place.[99] While compensation may also be granted in addition to restitution, this consideration may show that in certain situations restitution may demand less of the host State than compensation. This would especially be the case in situations where a particularly important economic sector has been affected by regulatory efforts and the State had, for example, expropriated a major international company in the oil sector. Here, full compensation could soon exceed the financial capacity of not just developing countries. The award in the *CME* case might underline this—when an US investor was awarded more than US$350 million (US$269 million damages plus interest)—a sum which was reported to be the equivalent of the entire national health budget of the Czech Republic at the time as well as three times the budget of the national ministry for the environment.[100]

---

[95] Reinisch (n 20) 194.   [96] UN Doc A/RES/1803 (14 December 1962) para 4.
[97] *Kuwait v American Independent Oil Company (Aminoil)*, Award (24 March 1982) ILM 21 (1982), 976, at 1032; Iran–US Claims Tribunal, *Shahin Shaine Ebrahimi v Government of the Islamic Republic of Iran*, Award (12 October 1994) Award No 569-44/46/47-3, 30 Iran–US CTR 1994, 170, para 88.
[98] C MacLachlan, L Shore, and M Weiniger (eds), *International Investment Arbitration—Substantive Principles* (OUP 2007) para 9.112; Dolzer and Schreuer (n 21) 294.
[99] Sabahi (n 36) at 61–62.
[100] *CME Czech Republic BV v The Czech Republic* (n 62), for the comparison with the Czech national health budget see <www.nytimes.com/2003/05/16/business/czech-republic-pays-355-million-to-media-concern.html> accessed 28 February 2014.

Even when not overwhelming a national budget in such a sense, the prospects of huge compensation claims may exert considerable pressure on States as witnessed by a settlement between Germany and Vattenfall (*Vattenfall I* case), where Germany apparently balked at the prospect of a €1.4 billion claim.[101]

The suggestion by the IPFSD not to allow for restitution as a remedy may thus be at odds with the wishes of States in concrete situations of investment arbitration. The recent *Franck Charles Arif v Moldova* award in which the respondent argued—partially successful—for the primacy of restitution as the adequate form of reparation shows that at times States may prefer this remedy over compensation.[102] In this connection, another argument against an exclusive focus on compensation is that, at least under the wide definition of sustainable development proposed by the IPFSD, there may be some situations in which restitution would actually favour sustainable development insofar as it would help to 'turn the clock back' to the situation before the regulatory action in question took place. After all, the expropriation or other form of regulatory activity need not necessarily be in the interest of sustainable development. It is at least conceivable that the continuation of a given economic activity may be as much in the interests of sustainable development as is the expropriation or the regulation of certain business activities. This brings us back to a concern expressed at the beginning of this chapter: what sustainable development means and how it is to be fostered is a question which is largely in the eye of the beholder.

b) State responsibility as a set of secondary rules

While this uncertainty should not stop us as individual lawyers, businesspeople, politicians, or activists to work towards a better entrenchment of sustainable development in international investment law, it is an argument against trying to resolve this issue in the framework of the law of State responsibility. The rules and principles of State responsibility belong to the category of the so-called secondary rules of the international legal system.[103] Following the categorization of H.L.A. Hart, they are what defines an advanced legal system as opposed to primitive legal orders which only contain primary rules of conduct, that is, the rules setting forth substantive standards.[104] As a set of secondary rules, the law of State responsibility fulfils important systemic functions for the international legal system. They are

---

[101] See MW Gehring and A Kent, 'International investment agreements and the emerging green economy: rising to the challenge' in F Baetens (ed), *Investment Law within International Law—Integrationist Perspectives* (CUP 2013) 187 214.

[102] *Franck Charles Arif v Republic of Moldova*, (n 57), paras 561–71.

[103] R Ago, 'Working Paper', [1963] YBILC, vol II, 251, 253; generally sceptical about the existence and importance of secondary rules in international law is U Linderfalk, 'State Responsibility and the Primary-Secondary Rules Terminology: The Role of Language for an Understanding of the International Legal System' (2009) 78 Nordic JIL 53; see also A Orakhelashvili, *Peremptory Norms in International Law* (OUP 2006) 80.

[104] HLA Hart, *The Concept of Law* (2nd edn, Clarendon Press 1994) 79ff.

applicable across a wide range of different international obligations, ranging from the use of force over environmental law to economic law. As Thomas Franck put it, '[i]n both mature domestic communities and in the emergent international community, these secondary rules determine and *legitimate* the processes and primary rules by which a community regulates itself'.[105] The role that secondary rules of international law have to play is captured by the four indicators of legitimacy which Franck has identified: determinacy, symbolic validation, coherence, and adherence.[106] The rules of the law of State responsibility may contribute to all four of these indicators, but especially the factors of coherence and adherence may be noted here. As long as a special regime makes use of the general rules, it should not apply them with a particularist mindset. Rather, when using general rules it should apply them with due respect for a necessary degree of systemic unity. This unity is not an all-encompassing unity in substantive terms. Such a form of unity is unlikely to emerge at the global level[107] and might also be stifling challenges to prevailing political concepts and structures. If international law should have a role to play in managing these challenges, however, it is vital that some form of common language exists which participants in this challenge can resort to. It is in this domain that the secondary rules of the international legal system have a useful role to play. They allow for cross-fertilization of judicial practice insofar as they may help to make decision-making processes more transparent. They are an invitation to other concerned parties to engage in a dialogue about the soundness and correctness of particular decisions which is easier if the decisions to be compared rest on some common basis. To paraphrase Benedict Kingsbury, 'unity of understanding and of justification' is needed even in a pluralist environment.[108]

If the rules on remedies are not to lose their capability of contributing to a minimum degree of systemic coherence of the international legal system, their application should not be overburdened with substantive debates. Policy questions and issues of substance should be discussed with respect to the primary norms.[109] In this realm, States and other involved actors can disagree over content and policy. If the secondary rules—to which also the rules on treaty interpretation belong—are re-interpreted with a specific policy goal in mind, this is likely to have unwanted spillover effects into other fields of international law. It is then preferable for specific regimes to develop special rules on the matter. An essential argument in this regard is transparency: only by disagreement about the substantive rules will the

---

[105] TM Franck, *Fairness in International Law and Institutions* (OUP 1995) 30 (emphasis in the original).
[106] ibid.
[107] See also A Nollkaemper, 'The Power of Secondary Rules to Connect the International and National Legal Orders' in T Broude and Y Shany (eds), *Multi-Sourced Equivalent Norms in International Law* (Hart 2011) 45, 46; M Prost, *The Concept of Unity in Public International Law* (Hart 2012) 66–69, who is however also sceptical of the attainability of 'formal unity', see ibid 125–28.
[108] B Kingsbury, 'International Law as Inter-Public Law' in HS Richardson and MS Williams (eds), *Moral Universalism and Pluralism* (New York University Press 2009) 167, 171; see also D Halberstam, 'Local, global and plural constitutionalism: Europe meets the world' in G de Búrca and JHH Weiler (eds), *The Worlds of European Constitutionalism* (CUP 2012) 113, 167.
[109] See also Prislan (n 64) 476.

underlying power struggles become apparent. Hiding these policy struggles behind a recourse to the seemingly neutral and technical rules of the law of State responsibility contributes to a 'managerialism'[110] whose recourse to sustainable development only serves to shield important political questions from public consideration. In doctrinal terms, the place for this debate is the one on the distinction between an indirect expropriation on the one hand and the legitimate exercise of domestic police powers on the other hand.[111] Several tribunals have recognized that States are not liable to pay compensation 'when, in the normal exercise of their regulatory powers, they adopt in a non-discriminatory manner *bona fide* regulations that are aimed at the general welfare'.[112]

A central question in this regard is the identification of legitimate purposes for which the regulatory measures were taken.[113] This question concerns the lawfulness of the expropriation, however. It thus brings us back to the distinction between lawful and unlawful expropriations and is to be determined at the level of the primary rules. The alternative view which calls for a general balancing effort in the calculus of compensation and damages overlooks this distinction.[114] Whereas the amount of compensation owed for a lawful and indirect expropriation indeed has to be appropriate, irrespective of what the respective IIA stipulates, there is no room for such a balancing effort with respect to compensation as a remedy in the sense of Articles 34, 36 ASR.[115] Here, the compensation is the consequence of a wrongful act, where reparation is owed in order to undo the effects of illegality.

c) State sovereignty and the development of international law

Finally, we should also consider any policy suggestions for the field of investment protection in the light of the greater picture of international law. In the investment protection context, one is immediately sympathetic to the preservation of 'regulatory space'. Calls to protect sovereignty against undue interferences from arbitrators—but in reality from the power exercised by transnational corporations—sound plausible. Even the once venerable but today largely irrelevant principle of in dubio mitius finds new prominence in the literature on investment protection, stipulating that international obligations should be interpreted so as not to curtail the freedom of States more than necessary.[116] Recent debates about the Transatlantic Trade and Investment Partnership (TTIP) have shown that concerns about an overreach of the system of international investment protection

---

[110] M Koskenniemi, 'The Politics of International Law—20 Years Later' (2009) 20 EJIL 7, 14–18.
[111] See further A Reinisch, 'Expropriation' in P Muchlinski, F Ortino and C Schreuer (eds), *The Oxford Handbook of International Investment Law* (OUP 2008) 407, 434.
[112] *Saluka Investments BV v Czech Republic*,UNCITRAL, Partial Award (17 March 2006) para 255.
[113] Reinisch (n 111) 434.   [114] Kulick (n 65) 209.
[115] An exception may be the calculation of the value of the investment, particularly if this investment was made in an unstable country, see further Schill (n 34) 290–91.
[116] Hindelang (n 12) 190; against both restrictive or expansive automatisms *Mondev International Ltd. v United States of America*, ICSID Case No ARB(AF)/99/2, Award (11 October 2002) para 43; see also Waibel (n 89) 39–47.

have gained currency in wide circles of the European population.[117] While an open and even heated debate about the underlying goals and values of investment protection is to be welcomed, the debate has also spurred some curious forms of resentment against ISDS as such. If we only look at the German political and juridical establishment, it is a note of concern to hear the Federal Minister for the Economy refer to ISDS as being not necessary in the relationship between States with fully developed legal systems[118] and, even more worrying, the President of the Federal Supreme Court of Justice, Bettina Limperg, mention that arbitration clauses would only be required in the dealings with 'rogue states'.[119]

When arguing along these lines, we should be cautious with respect to the world of international law into which they might take us. If we only look at the field of investment law, calls for sustainable development look 'progressive' and left-leaning. I would submit, however, that this character changes if we transpose these considerations to other fields of international law. The same proponents arguing for regulatory space and the preservation of sovereign prerogatives would be hard-pressed to accept such a vocabulary in the human rights context (even though we see mounting criticism of, for instance, the European Court of Human Rights in some EU member states as well). It is of course conceivable that the use of these argumentative techniques might remain confined to the investment law context. But this is not guaranteed. The jury is still out on the question of whether investment law really is a self-contained regime. If it is not, it is also likely to have feedback effects on general international law and on other regimes of international law.[120] More fundamentally, a plea for equitable compensation in the domain of remedies has the potential of distorting central categories of the law of State responsibility. It is an essential element of the international rule of law that wrongfulness entails an obligation to make reparation.

V. Conclusion

Despite legitimacy concerns, investment arbitration is a cornerstone of the efforts to entrench the rule of law globally. In many parts of the world, it puts a check on governments and demands of them to justify the exercise of public powers. This is in and of itself a positive contribution which, of course, should not shield international investment law from necessary discussion about the policy issues. The debate on these policy issues should however address the substantive issues head on and should not take refuge behind rather technical concepts and figures such

---

[117] F Hoffmeister, 'Wider die German Angst—Ein Plädoyer für die transatlantische Handels- und Investitionspartnerschaft (TTIP)' (2015) 53 AVR 35.
[118] See his remarks to the German Parliament on 25 September 2014, a summary is available at <www.bmwi.de/DE/Themen/aussenwirtschaft,did=656586.html> accessed 16 August 2015.
[119] See H Bubrowski, 'Muss ein Gericht ein Gebäude sein?' Frankfurter Allgemeine Zeitung (Frankfurt am Main, 13 June 2015) 10.
[120] cf Paparinskis (n 39) 646.

as the law of State responsibility. In addition, we have seen that with respect to the choice of remedies, it is not convincing to argue that compensation would generally be more conducive for sustainable development than reparation. Rather, the general rules of State responsibility do not stand in the way of the accommodation of sustainable development concerns which have been translated into the primary rules of international investment law.

X
Termination and Renegotiation of International Investment Agreements

Karsten Nowrot

I. Introduction

From the perspective of general public international law it hardly needs to be emphasized that termination and renegotiation have always been issues of considerable practical importance in the law of treaties.[1] Not least against this background, these topics have at all times also attracted significant scholarly attention. Nevertheless, as is frequently highlighted, there is no rule without at least occasional and temporary exceptions. And indeed, the validity of this statement in the present context is clearly supported when considering the realm of international investment agreements. While for example the legal issues arising from the termination as well as in particular the renegotiation of investment contracts are already for quite some time intensively and controversially debated by practitioners and scholars alike,[2] this does not apply to the respective normative challenges in connection with bilateral and multilateral investment agreements. Questions relating

---

[1] On this perception see, for example, A Aust, *Modern Treaty Law and Practice* (3rd edn, CUP 2013) 245 ('The length of this chapter [Duration and Termination] demonstrates that this is an important topic, [...].'); A Aust, 'Treaties, Termination' in R Wolfrum (ed), *Max Planck Encyclopedia of Public International Law* (June 2006) para 2 <www.mpepil.com/> accessed 11 November 2014 ('an immensely practical topic'); K Odendahl, 'Article 42' in O Dörr and K Schmalenbach (eds), *Vienna Convention on the Law of Treaties* (Springer 2012) para 20 ('the termination of treaties is of immense practical importance').

[2] From the numerous literature on these subjects see for example W Peter, *Arbitration and Renegotiation of International Investment Agreements* (2nd edn, Kluwer 1995) 51 et seq; A Kolo and TW Wälde, 'Renegotiation and Contract Adaption in International Investment Projects: Applicable Legal Principles and Industry Practices' (2000) 1 J World Inv 5; KP Berger, 'Renegotiation and Adaption of International Investment Contracts: The Role of Contract Drafters and Arbitrators' (2003) 36 Vanderbilt J Transnatl L 1347; S Kröll, 'The Renegotiation and Adaption of Investment Contracts', in N Horn (ed), *Arbitrating Foreign Investment Disputes* (Kluwer 2004) 425; ZA Al Qurashi, 'Renegotiation of International Petroleum Agreements' (2005) 22 J Intl Arb 261, each with further references.

to the termination and renegotiation of international investment treaties have so far only rarely been subject to a closer evaluation in the legal literature.[3]

The present situation of relative inattention as far as these two topics are concerned is, however, unlikely to continue for long. Due to a variety of reasons as addressed below,[4] termination and renegotiation of agreements are at least in the process of emerging as two of the key issues in the currently visible—and not only from an academic perspective rather interesting—transitional phase of international investment law; an era of reformation or 'reconceptualization'[5] that is first and foremost also characterized by intensified efforts in all parts of the world to progressively develop the international legal basis of investment protection with a view to fostering its contribution to the realization of sustainable development objectives.[6]

Already in light of these findings, it appears justified and potentially promising to take a closer look at the public international law framework applicable to these two core procedural issues paving the way to what has already been labeled a 'new generation'[7] of investment treaties. Thereby, it most certainly needs to be emphasized that 'termination and renegotiation of international investment agreements' is far too broad a topic to be discussed in the course of this comparatively short

---

[3] On this perception see also, for example, A Carska-Sheppard, 'Issues Relevant to the Termination of Bilateral Investment Treaties' (2009) 26 J Intl Arb 755 ('It appears that when it comes to the termination of a BIT, there is very little experience compared to the wealth of knowledge associated with the cancellation of investment contracts.'); J Harrison, 'The Life and Death of BITs: Legal Issues Concerning Survival Clauses and the Termination of Investment Treaties' (2012) 13 J World Inv & Trade 928, 930 ('they have received little attention in the literature to date'); FM Lavopa, LE Barreiros and M Victoria Bruno, 'How to Kill a BIT and not Die Trying: Legal and Political Challenges of Denouncing or Renegotiating Bilateral Investment Treaties' (2013) 16 J Intl Econ L 869, 872 ('less attention has been paid to the other two courses of action just mentioned, that is, denunciation and renegotiation of BITs').

[4] See under II.

[5] K Miles, 'Reconceptualising International Investment Law: Bringing the Public Interest into Private Business' in M Kolsky Lewis and S Frankel (eds), *International Economic Law and National Autonomy* (CUP 2010) 295; H Mann, 'Reconceptualizing International Investment Law: Its Role in Sustainable Development' (2013) 17 Lewis & Clark L Rev 521. See also UNCTAD World Investment Report 2014, Investing in the SDGs: An Action Plan, 2014, 126 ('The IIA regime is undergoing a period of reflection, review and reform.').

[6] Generally on these developments see for example UNCTAD World Investment Report 2012, Towards a New Generation of Investment Policies, 2012, 89 et seq; UNCTAD World Investment Report 2013, Global Value Chains: Investment and Trade for Development, 2013, 102 et seq; Integrating Sustainable Development into International Investment Agreements: A Guide for Developing Countries, Prepared for the Commonwealth Secretariat by JA VanDuzer, P Simons, and G Mayeda, August 2012, available under: <www.iisd.org/pdf/2012/6th_annual_forum_commonwealth_guide.pdf> accessed 11 November 2014; the contributions in M-C Cordonier Segger, MW Gehring, and A Newcombe (eds), *Sustainable Development in World Investment Law* (Kluwer 2011); as well as I Dubava, 'The Future of International Investment Protection Law: The Promotion of Sustainable (Economic) Development as a Public Good' in M Cremona and others (eds), *Reflections on the Constitutionalisation of International Economic Law—Liber Amicorum for Ernst-Ulrich Petersmann* (Nijhoff 2014) 389; K Nowrot, 'How to Include Environmental Protection, Human Rights and Sustainability in International Investment Law' (2014) 15 J World Inv & Trade 612.

[7] See, for example, UNCTAD, Investment Policy Framework for Sustainable Development, 2012, iii ('new generation of investment policies'); SA Spears, 'The Quest for Policy Space in a New Generation of International Investment Agreements' (2010) 13 J Intl Econ L 1037.

contribution in something even close to a comprehensive way. Rather, this article largely confines itself to presenting and discussing a number of aspects on the context of and particular legal issues arising from the current practice of an increasing number of States to terminate—as well as frequently renegotiate—their investment agreements. Against this background, the following analysis is divided into four main parts. The first part addresses the underlying reasons for the increasing practical importance of the subjects 'termination' and 'renegotiation' of treaties in the realm of international investment law (II.). Based on the findings made in this section, the subsequent three parts are devoted to an evaluation of some legal issues arising from this practice. In this connection, the second part provides some thoughts on the respective public international law framework applicable to unilateral terminations of investment treaties (III.). Subsequently, in the third part an assessment will be given of the legal rules determining the lawfulness of termination by mutual consent of the parties as well as the normative consequences of such terminations (IV.). The fourth and final section presents some alternative perspectives on possible regulatory approaches in treaty practice aimed at circumventing the respective termination clauses of the investment agreements in question (V.).

II. Reasons for the Current Importance of Termination and Renegotiation of Investment Agreements

Before turning to the underlying reasons for the currently visible rise of termination and renegotiation as increasingly prominent topics in international investment law, it seems appropriate to recall that these two issues are in principle far from being an entirely new phenomenon in investment treaty practice. In particular since the middle of the 1990s, countries like Germany, Japan and Finland have initiated a worldwide process of renegotiating many of their existing bilateral investment treaties (BITs). This trend resulted in the replacement of a considerable number of what might be called 'first generation' agreements concluded since the end of the 1950s. While for example in 1995, only five older BITs were terminated as a result of a respective renegotiation, this number rose to a total of 20 BITs in 2003.[8] According to statistical information provided by UNCTAD, between 2000 and 2008 an average of nine to fifteen BITs were replaced by new agreements, with almost one quarter of all BITs concluded in 2009 qualifying as renegotiated ones.[9] In 2013 alone, a total of 105 respective investment agreements were terminated and replaced by a new treaty.[10] To mention but one further example, Germany alone has—in the period between 1998 and 2008—as a result of renegotiations

---

[8] See UNCTAD, Recent Developments in International Investment Agreements, UNCTAD/WEB/ITE/IIT/2005/1 of 30 August 2005, 6.
[9] UNCTAD World Investment Report 2010, Investing in a Low-Carbon Economy, 2010, 86.
[10] UNCTAD World Investment Report 2014, Investing in the SDGs: An Action Plan, 2014, 133 n. 52.

terminated and replaced its older BITs with *inter alia* China, Egypt, Ethiopia, Gabon, Guinea, Indonesia, Iran, Yemen, Jordan, Madagascar, Morocco, Oman and Thailand.[11]

a) Current shift from 'second generation' to 'third generation' investment agreements

Against this background, it might seem at least at first sight slightly astonishing that legal issues arising from renegotiations and resulting terminations of investment agreements have not attracted substantial scholarly attention already in the previous two decades. In order to explain this continued lack of interest, at least two main aspects are worth highlighting. The first relevant factor relates to the material and in particular procedural modifications incorporated in the renegotiated BITs at that time. In the overwhelming majority of cases, the respective renegotiations were aimed at agreeing to—and indeed frequently achieved—an enhanced legal protection of foreign investors and their activities.[12] The previous transition period from 'first generation' to 'second generation' investment agreements was overall characterized by the introduction of improved levels of substantive guarantees for investors as well as—and particularly noteworthy—also the stipulation of investor-State dispute settlement provisions; mixed arbitration clauses that were far from common in older BITs.[13] Second, this treaty practice was based on a broad political consensus recognizing the protection of foreign investors as the sole—or at least primary—purpose pursued by international investment agreements; a perception also shared by most academics interested in the development of investment law at that time. Consequently, there was hardly anyone to regret and mourn the termination of the respective 'first generation' BITs, most certainly not the foreign investors generally benefiting from these replacements.

---

[11] See in this regard for example article 11 (4) of the Agreement between the Federal Republic of Germany and the Arab Republic of Egypt concerning the Encouragement and Reciprocal Protection of Investments of 16 June 2005

> Upon entry into force of this Agreement the Agreement between the Federal Republic of Germany and the Arab Republic of Egypt concerning the Encouragement and Reciprocal Protection of Investments of 5th July 1974, the associated Protocol and the exchange of letters of the same date shall cease to be in force.

[12] See, for example, UNCTAD, Recent Developments in International Investment Agreements, UNCTAD/WEB/ITE/IIT/2005/1 of 30 August 2005, 6 ('countries embark on their [older BITs] re-negotiation, usually agreeing to stronger commitments').

[13] On this issue see for example P Muchlinski, *Multinational Enterprises and the Law* (2nd edn, OUP 2007) 695 ('Early BITs did not cover the issue of disputes between the host state and the investor.'); C Tietje and E Sipiorski, 'The Evolution of Investment Protection based on Public International Law Treaties: Lessons to be Learned' in AK Bjorklund and A Reinisch (eds), *International Investment Law and Soft Law* (Elgar 2012) 192, 193, 205 and 217 et seq; JW Salacuse, *The Law of Investment Treaties* (OUP 2010) 373 and 380 et seq; C Tietje, K Nowrot, and C Wackernagel, *Once and Forever? The Legal Effects of a Denunciation of ICSID* (MLU Institut für Wirtschaftsrecht 2008) 18 et seq. See also pt IV.b.cc.

Quite to the contrary, the currently visible transitional phase from the 'second generation' of investment agreements mostly concluded in the previous two decades to the rise of a new 'third generation' of investment policies that increasingly also finds its manifestation in treaty practice is largely dominated by various efforts of States to regain some of their 'policy space' vis-à-vis foreign investors.[14] On the one side the foreign investors have—particularly on the basis of access to effective international legal remedies—experienced in recent years a notable strengthening of their legal status.[15] On the other side it is by now well-known that the issue arose as to the respective consequences resulting from these developments for the regulatory autonomy enjoyed by the host States. Although a number of congruent interests of investors and host States do in fact exist, international investment law has with regard to its overarching scheme always primarily been shaped and influenced by a certain tension between the economic interests pursued by investors and the necessary policy space of host States.[16] In this connection, it has more recently frequently and rightly been emphasized in the legal literature that the enhanced normative effectiveness of investment law has led to a growing influence of this branch of international economic law on the content and shape of domestic legal standards and administrative actions as well as thus, more generally, to increased constraints on the regulatory autonomy of the respective host countries.[17]

---

[14] See, for example, C Tietje, 'The Future of International Investment Protection: Stress in the System?' (2009) 24 ICSID Rev – FILJ 457, 461

> The need for a 'policy space' for governments, *i.e.* autonomy in national policy-making without constraints by international law and particularly international investment protection law, is one of the most significant consequences of the proliferation of investment law and the fragmentation of international law in general. We are currently witnessing discussions about the necessary policy space in the area of foreign investment, on both the national and international levels.

[15] See, for example, *Plama Consortium Ltd v Bulgaria*, ICSID Case No ARB/03/24, Decision on Jurisdiction (8 February 2005) para 141

> For all these reasons, Article 26 ECT provides to a covered investor an almost unprecedented remedy for its claim against a host state. [...] By any standards, Article 26 is a very important feature of the ECT which is itself a very significant treaty for investors, marking another step in their transition from objects to subjects of international law.

J Paulsson, 'Arbitration Without Privity' (1995) 10 ICSID Rev – FILJ 232; E Lauterpacht, 'International Law and Private Foreign Investment' (1997) 4 Ind J Global Legal Studies 259, 274; C Tietje, *The Applicability of the Energy Charter Treaty in ICSID Arbitration of EU Nationals vs. EU Member States* (MLU Institut für Wirtschaftsrecht 2008) 13. See thereto also see also under IV.a.

[16] On this perception see, for example, OE García-Bolívar, 'Sovereignty vs. Investment Protection: Back to Calvo?' (2009) 24 ICSID Rev – FILJ 464, 465 et seq; C Tietje, *Internationales Investitionsschutzrecht im Spannungsverhältnis von staatlicher Regelungsfreiheit und Schutz wirtschaftlicher Individualinteressen* (MLU Institut für Wirtschaftsrecht 2010) 5 et seq; M Perkams, *Internationale Investitionsschutzabkommen im Spannungsfeld zwischen effektivem Investitionsschutz und staatlichem Gemeinwohl* (Nomos 2011) 21 et seq.

[17] See thereto for example R Dolzer, 'The Impact of International Investment Treaties on Domestic Administrative Law', (2005) 37 NYU J Intl L & Pol 953; M Krajewski and J Ceyssens, 'Internationaler Investitionsschutz und innerstaatliche Regulierung' (2007) 45 AVR 180; A Kaushal, 'Revisiting History: How the Past Matters for the Present Backlash Against the Foreign Investment Regime' (2009) 50 Harv ILJ 491, 525 et seq; C Tietje, 'Grundstrukturen, Rechtsstand und aktuelle Herausforderungen des internationalen Investitionsschutzrechts' in T Giegerich (ed), *Internationales Wirtschafts- und Finanzrecht in der Krise* (Duncker & Humblot 2011) 11, 19 et seq.

In light of certain negatively perceived effects of these developments,[18] it is by now increasingly recognized among governments of industrialized and developing countries, practitioners and scholars alike, that at the level of designing investment agreements as well as in the realm of investor-State arbitration proceedings, the central challenge lawmakers and arbitrators are as of today ever more faced with is to provide for an appropriate and thus acceptable balance between the legally protected economic interests of foreign investors and the domestic steering capacity or policy space of host States to allow the later to pursue the promotion and protection of other public interest concerns like sustainable development objectives.[19] In order to illustrate the importance of this recent

---

[18] See, for example, UN Human Rights Council, Business and Human Rights: Towards Operationalizing the 'Protect, Respect and Remedy' Framework, Report of the Special Representative of the Secretary-General on the Issue of Human Rights and Transnational Corporations and Other Business Enterprises, UN Doc. A/HRC/11/13 of 22 April 2009, para 30

> Nevertheless, recent experience suggests that some treaty guarantees and contract provisions may unduly constrain the host Government's ability to achieve its legitimate policy objectives, including its international human rights obligations.

UN Human Rights Council, Protect, Respect and Remedy: A Framework for Business and Human Rights, Report of the Special Representative of the Secretary-General on the Issue of Human Rights and Transnational Corporations and Other Business Enterprises, UN Doc. A/HRC/8/5 of 7 April 2008, para 12

> Take the case of transnational corporations. Their legal rights have been expanded significantly over the past generation. This has encouraged investment and trade flows, but it has also created instances of imbalances between firms and States that may be detrimental to human rights. The more than 2,500 bilateral investment treaties currently in effect are a case in point. While providing legitimate protection to foreign investors, these treaties also permit those investors to take host States to binding international arbitration, including for alleged damages resulting from implementation of legislation to improve domestic social and environmental standards—even when the legislation applies uniformly to all businesses, foreign and domestic.

G Van Harten, *Investment Treaty Arbitration and Public Law* (OUP 2007) 45 et seq; O Chung, 'The Lopsided International Investment Law Regime and its Effect on the Future of Investor-State Arbitration' (2007) 47 Va JIL 953; J. Yackee, 'Towards a Minimalist System of International Investment Law?' (2009) 32 Suffolk Transnatl L Rev 303.

[19] For a respective example in this regard compare European Commission, Towards a Comprehensive European International Investment Policy, Communication from the Commission to the Council, the European Parliament, the European Economic and Social Committee and the Committee of the Regions, COM(2010) 343 final of 7 July 2010, 9

> A clear formulation of the balance between the different interests at stake, such as the protection of investors against unlawful expropriation or the right of each Party to regulate in the public interest, needs to be ensured. [...] Investment agreements should be consistent with the other policies of the Union and its Member States, including policies on the protection of the environment, decent work, health and safety at work, consumer protection, cultural diversity, development policy and competition policy. Investment policy will continue to allow the Union, and the Member States to adopt and enforce measures necessary to pursue public policy objectives.

Generally thereto see also for example UNCTAD World Investment Report 2010, Investing in a Low-Carbon Economy, 2010, 86 et seq; UNCTAD World Investment Report 2012, Towards a New Generation of Investment Policies, 2012, 89 et seq; UNCTAD World Investment Report 2013, Global Value Chains: Investment and Trade for Development, 2013, 102 et seq; August Reinisch, 'The Future Shape of EU Investment Agreements' (2013) 28 ICSID Rev—FILJ 179, 195; B Stern, 'The Future of International Investment Law: A Balance Between the Protection of Investors and the States' Capacity to Regulate' in JE Alvarez and KP Sauvant (eds), *The Evolving international*

reorientation in investment treaty practice, let it suffice to draw attention to the fact that all of the seventeen international investment agreements signed in 2012 for which texts are available included certain sustainable-development-oriented provisions and/or novel 'treaty elements that aim more broadly to preserve regulatory space for public policies in general or to minimize exposure to investment litigation in particular'.[20]

Nevertheless, the specific policy responses so far suggested or already implemented in this regard vary considerably from country to country. States have adopted different approaches to implement their newly revised investment policies. This finding is hardly surprising, taking into account the quite diverse political and economic backgrounds as well as preconceptions involved. A number of countries like Bolivia, Ecuador and Venezuela have not only taken the unprecedented step of withdrawing from the ICSID Convention.[21] Rather, some of them have also decided to unilaterally terminate a number of bilateral investment treaties without concluding new respective agreements; a move that was also almost unheard of in previous decades.[22] In 2008, for example, Ecuador decided to suspend negotiations of new BITs and informed nine countries—Cuba, the Dominican Republic, El Salvador, Guatemala, Honduras, Nicaragua, Paraguay, Romania and Uruguay—of its denunciation of the BITs concluded with them.[23] Two years later, a respective notice of termination was received by Finland and the denunciation by Ecuador of a number of its other BITs is likely

Investment Regime: Expectations, Realities, Options (OUP 2011) 174, 189 et seq; JE Alvarez, 'The Public International Law Regime Governing International Investment' (2009) 344 RdC 193, 308 et seq, 434 et seq; L Markert, 'The Crucial Question of Future Investment Treaties: Balancing Investor's Rights and Regulatory Interests of Host States' in M Bungenberg, J Griebel, and S Hindelang (eds), *International Investment Law and EU Law* (Nomos 2011) 145; A Kulick, *Global Public Interest in International Investment Law* (CUP 2012) 57 et seq.

[20] UNCTAD World Investment Report 2013, Global Value Chains: Investment and Trade for Development, 2013, 102–03. See also more recently UNCTAD World Investment Report 2014, Investing in the SDGs: An Action Plan, 2014, 116 ('A review of the 18 IIAs concluded in 2013 for which texts are available [...] shows that most of the treaties include sustainable-development-oriented features, [...].').

[21] Thereto as well as on the controversially debated legal implications of a denunciation of the ICSID Convention see, for example, UNCTAD, Denunciation of the ICSID Convention and BITs: Impact on Investor-State Claims, IIA Issues Note No 2, December 2010, 4 et seq; C Schreuer, 'Denunciation of the ICSID Convention and Consent to Arbitration' in M Waibel and others (eds), *The Backlash Against Investment Arbitration—Perceptions and Reality* (Kluwer 2010) 353; Tietje, Nowrot, and Wackernagel (n 13) 5 et seq; OM Garibaldi, 'On the Denunciation of the ICSID Convention, Consent to Investment Jurisdiction and the Limits of Contract Analogy' in C Binder and others (eds), *International Investment Law for the 21st Century—Essays in Honour of Christoph Schreuer* (OUP 2009) 251, each with further references.

[22] On this perception see for example the respective statement made by Salacuse (n 13) 352 ('There is no reported case of a country actually terminating an investment treaty to which it had agreed.'). For a number of BITs that have been—unilaterally or by mutual agreement of the parties—terminated prior to 2008 see UNCTAD, Recent Developments in International Investment Agreements (2008-June 2009), IIA Monitor No 3 (2009), 5.

[23] See UNCTAD World Investment Report 2008, Transnational Corporations and the Infrastructure Challenge, 2008, 65; see also, for example, K Nowrot, *International Investment Law and the Republic of Ecuador: From Arbitral Bilateralism to Judicial Regionalism* (MLU Institut für Wirtschaftsrecht 2010) 6 et seq.

to follow soon.[24] Venezuela has unilaterally terminated its BIT with the Netherlands as of 1 November 2008.[25] On 10 June 2012, the denunciation by Bolivia of its BIT with the United States became effective.[26] Already in 2009, Bolivia also terminated the respective agreement concluded with the Netherlands.[27] Furthermore, the country collectively denounced all of its remaining BITs on 6 May 2013, among them the treaties previously concluded with China, Denmark, France, Germany, Romania and the United Kingdom.[28]

However, this phenomenon of unilateral termination of international investment agreements is by now no longer confined to the realm of Latin America. The Indonesian government, for example, has informed the Netherlands in March 2014 of its decision to terminate the BIT between the two countries, effective from 1 July 2015, and is said to currently evaluate the possibility of also denouncing—or at least fundamentally renegotiating—most of its other more than sixty bilateral investment agreements in the near future.[29] In addition, South Africa, as a result of a comprehensive investment policy review started in 2009 and aimed at more appropriately securing its conformity with social and economic objectives, has denounced its BIT with Belgium and Luxemburg in September 2012[30] as well as its investment agreement with Spain in June 2013.[31] This was followed by additional notices of termination in October 2013 aimed at denouncing the respective BITs concluded by South Africa with the Netherlands, Germany and Switzerland.[32]

---

[24] See 'Ecuador Evaluates Investment Treaty Framework' (15 May 2013), available under: <www.latinarbitrationlaw.com/ecuador-evaluates-investment-treaty-framework/> accessed 11 November 2014; MJ Luque Macias, 'Current Approaches to the International Investment Regime in South America' (2014) 5 European Ybk Intl Econ L 285, 303 et seq.

[25] 'Venezuela Surprises the Netherlands with Termination Notice for BIT' *Investment Arbitration Reporter* (16 May 2008) <www.iareporter.com/articles/20091001_93> accessed 11 November 2014; T Hai Yen, *The Interpretation of Investment Treaties* (Brill 2014) 188.

[26] 'Termination of Bolivia-United States Bilateral Investment Treaty' (31 October 2012) available under: <www.latinarbitrationlaw.com/termination-of-bolivia-united-states-bilateral-investment-treaty/> accessed 11 November 2014.

[27] See N Schrijver and V Prislan, 'The Netherlands' in C Brown (ed), *Commentaries on Selected Model Investment Treaties* (OUP 2013) 535, 589.

[28] See A Orellana López, 'Bolivia Denounces its Bilateral Investment Treaties and Attempts to put an End to the Power of Corporations to Sue the Country in International Tribunals' (June 2014) available under: <http://justinvestment.org/wp-content/uploads/2014/07/Bolivia-denounces-its-Bilateral-Investment-Treaties-and-attempts-to-put-an-end-to-the-Power-of-Corporations-to-sue-the-country-in-International-Tribunals1.pdf> accessed 11 November 2014.

[29] See, for example, 'Indonesia to terminate more than 60 bilateral investment treaties' *Financial Times* (26 March 2014) <www.ft.com/cms/s/0/3755c1b2-b4e2-11e3-af92-00144feabdc0.html#axzz3Iy1ZVX5l>; 'Revamping Bilateral Treaties' (7 July 2014) available under: <www.bilaterals.org/?revamping-bilateral-treaties&lang=en> both accessed 13 November 2014.

[30] 'South Africa Pushes Phase-Out of Early Bilateral Investment Treaties after at least two Separate Brushes with Investor-State Arbitration' *Investment Arbitration Reporter* (23 September 2012) <www.iareporter.com/articles/20120924_1> accessed 11 November 2014.

[31] 'South Africa Terminates its Bilateral Investment Treaty with Spain' (27 August 2013) available under: <www.bilaterals.org/spip.php?article23728&lang=en> accessed 11 November 2014.

[32] UNCTAD, Investment Policy Monitor No 11 (November 2013), 8; UNCTAD World Investment Report 2014, Investing in the SDGs: An Action Plan, 2014, 114.

Furthermore, the government has revealed plans to terminate the investment treaties currently in force with nine other EU member states.[33]

Aside from a growing number of unilateral denunciations, another prominent—and from a legal perspective at least equally challenging[34]—policy response in the current international economic system are mutually agreed terminations of investment agreements. In the same way as in the previous transition period from first to second generation BITs, this approach finds its manifestation most certainly in the renegotiation and subsequent replacement of existing investment treaties with new BITs that include sustainable-development-oriented features. A respective example is the 'second generation' type BIT between Bangladesh and Turkey of 12 November 1987 that will be terminated as a result of replacement once the new investment treaty, signed by these two countries on 12 April 2012 and displaying a considerable number of innovative policy-space-related provisions,[35] enters into force.

b) The rise of regionalism in international investment treaty-making

In addition, however, mutually agreed terminations are in treaty practice also increasingly visible—and that constitutes a comparatively new phenomenon—as a consequence and in the context of regional economic integration agreements. This approach finds its manifestation among others in Annex 10-E of the free trade agreement concluded between Australia and Chile, entering into force on 6 March 2009 and terminating the BIT concluded between the parties on 9 July 1996.[36] Other respective stipulations worth drawing attention to in the present context include article 9.17 of the Republic of Korea-Peru free trade agreement of 21 March 2011,[37] article 10.20 of the free trade agreement between Peru and Singapore that entered into force on 1 August 2009[38] as well as already article 21.4 of the free trade agreement concluded by Chile and the Republic of Korea on 15 February 2003.[39]

---

[33] 'Move to Ease German, EU Doubts over Investor Risk in SA' (30 August 2013) available under: <www.bilaterals.org/spip.php?article23758&lang=en> accessed 11 November 2014.

[34] See pt IV.b.

[35] For details see the text of the Agreement between the Government of the People's Republic of Bangladesh and the Government of the Republic of Turkey Concerning the Reciprocal Promotion and Protection of Investments of 12 April 2012, available under: <www.moind.gov.bd/index.php?option=com_content&task=view&id=510&Itemid=567> accessed 11 November 2014.

[36] Australia-Chile Free Trade Agreement of 30 July 2008, available under: <www.dfat.gov.au/fta/aclfta/> accessed 13 November 2014.

[37] Free Trade Agreement between the Republic of Korea and the Republic of Peru, available under: <www.customs.go.kr/kcshome/main/content/ContentView.do?contentId=CONTENT_ID_000002364&layoutMenuNo=23272> accessed 13 November 2014.

[38] Peru-Singapore Free Trade Agreement of 29 May 2008, available under: </www.fta.gov.sg/fta_pesfta.asp?hl=39> accessed 13 November 2014.

[39] Chile-Korea Free Trade Agreement, available under: <www.sice.oas.org/trade/Chi-SKorea_e/ChiKoreaind_e.asp> accessed 13 November 2014.

Furthermore, also the internal and external dimension of the European Union's investment policy provides a telling example in this regard. From an internal perspective, the legal status of intra-EU BITs concluded between member States prior to their accession to the EU became more and more controversially perceived in practice as well as among academics after the number of these agreements rose from two to about 190 as a result of the two enlargement rounds in 2004 and 2007 and following increasing recourse to these treaties as a basis for investment arbitration proceedings.[40] In the wake of these developments and encouraged by the European Commission,[41] a number of member States agreed to terminate their bilateral investment treaties. To mention but a few examples, the year 2008 bore witness to the termination of the BIT between Italy and Hungary.[42] In the same year, the Czech Republic took the decision to terminate all of its BITs with other EU member States by consent of the parties. As a result, the bilateral investment agreements with *inter alia* Italy, Denmark, Slovenia, Malta and Estonia were terminated in subsequent years.[43] With regard to the external investment policy of the EU vis-à-vis third countries, it is worth recalling also in the present context the consequences of the new exclusive competences enjoyed by this supranational organization in the field of foreign direct investments under article 207 TFEU since the entry into force of the Treaty of Lisbon in December 2009. Although the member States that, taken together, currently still account for more than 1.300 bilateral agreements and thus almost half of the world's BITs[44] are not per se required to terminate their extra-EU BITs with third countries,[45] these numerous treaties will be eventually and progressively replaced by investment agreements of the EU.

---

[40] Generally thereto as well as on the legal issues arising in connection with intra-EU BITs see, for example, *EUREKO BV v. Slovak Republic*, PCA Case No 2008-13, Award on Jurisdiction, Arbitrability and Suspension (26 October 2010) paras 57 et seq, 217 et seq; *Eastern Sugar BV v Czech Republic*, UNCITRAL ad hoc Arbitration, SCC No 088/2004, Partial Award (27 March 2007) paras 115 et seq; C Söderlund, 'Intra-EU BIT Investment Protection and the EC Treaty' (2007) 24 J Intl Arb 455; H Wehland, 'Intra-EU Investment Agreements and Arbitration: Is European Community Law an Obstacle?' (2009) 58 ICLQ 297; M Burgstaller, 'The Future of Bilateral Investment Treaties of EU Member States' in M Bungenberg, J Griebel, and S Hindelang (eds), *International Investment Law and EU Law* (Nomos 2011) 55, 71 et seq; S Hindelang, 'Circumventing Primacy of EU Law and the CJEU's Judicial Monopoly by Resorting to Dispute Resolution Mechanisms Provided for in Inter-se Treaties? The Case of Intra-EU Investment Arbitration' (2012) 39 LIEI 179; R Yotova, 'The New EU Competence in Foreign Direct Investment and Intra-EU Investment Treaties: Does the Emperor have New Clothes?' in F Baetens (ed), *Investment Law within International Law—Integrationist Perspectives* (CUP 2013) 387; P Mariani, 'The Future of BITs between EU Member States: Are Intra-EU BITs Compatible with the Internal Market?' in G Sacerdoti and others (ed), *General Interests of Host States in International Investment Law* (CUP 2014) 265.
[41] See, for example, *Eastern Sugar BV v Czech Republic*, UNCITRAL ad hoc Arbitration, SCC No 088/2004, Partial Award (27 March 2007) para 126.
[42] UNCTAD, Recent Developments in International Investment Agreements (2008-June 2009), IIA Monitor No 3 (2009), 5.
[43] See for example T Fecák, 'Czech Experience with Bilateral Investment Treaties: Somewhat Bitter Taste of Investment Protection' (2011) 2 Czech Ybk Public and Private Intl L 233, 254 et seq.
[44] UNCTAD World Investment Report 2012, Towards a New Generation of Investment Policies, 2012, 85; UNCTAD World Investment Report 2011, Non-Equity Modes of International Production and Development, 2011, 100 et seq.
[45] On the respective legal framework under secondary Union law, see Regulation (EU) No 1219/2012 Establishing Transitional Arrangements for Bilateral Investment Agreements between

In this connection, a quite prominent role is again expected to be played by the phenomenon of regional integration agreements. The conclusion of the negotiations of a Comprehensive Economic and Trade Agreement (CETA) between Canada and the EU in September 2014—possibly the first EU agreement to include a substantive investment protection chapter—alone is intended to replace and thus terminate seven existing BITs previously concluded by member states with Canada in accordance with article X.07 of the CETA chapter on final provisions and the respective Annex (Y) to the agreement.[46] Furthermore, also the ongoing EU negotiations on related agreements with the United States on a Transatlantic Trade and Investment Partnership (TTIP) as well as *inter alia* with India, Thailand, Japan, Singapore, Malaysia, Vietnam and Morocco are, if successful, highly likely to result in the termination of numerous extra-EU BITs and their replacement by investment chapters in integration agreements[47]—or potentially also stand-alone investment treaties—that will provide for certain sustainable-development-oriented and policy-space-conscious features. While many economic integration agreements more recently concluded in other regions of the world do not stipulate the termination of existing BITs between the parties and thus a kind of 'parallelism' still appears to be the dominant approach in treaty practice,[48] it is nevertheless already—based on a quantitative assessment of the EU's investment policy alone—quite obvious that the 'rise of regionalism' as increasingly visible also in the realm of international investment law-making has not only the potential to contribute to a reformation and consolidation of the public international law framework on investment protection.[49] Rather, it also constitutes a notable factor to be taken into account when assessing the underlying reasons for the equally rapid rise of termination and renegotiation as central topics in the current phase of investment treaty practice.

Member States and Third Countries, OJ L 351/40 of 20 December 2012. Generally on the treaty-making powers of the EU in the field of foreign direct investments and the debate over legal status of extra-EU BITs see for example A Dimopoulos, *EU Foreign Investment Law* (OUP 2011); P Eeckhout, *EU External Relations Law* (2nd edn, OUP 2011) 62 et seq; M Bungenberg, 'The Politics of the European Union's Investment Treaty Making' in T Broude, ML Busch and A Porges (eds), *The Politics of International Economic Law* (CUP 2011) 133 et seq; as well as the contributions in M Bungenberg, J Griebel, and S Hindelang (eds), *International Investment Law and EU Law* (Nomos 2011); and M Bungenberg, A Reinisch and C Tietje (eds), *EU and International Investment Agreements—Open Questions and Remaining Challenges* (Nomos 2013).

[46] Consolidated CETA Text published on 26 September 2014, available under: <http://trade.ec.europa.eu/doclib/docs/2014/september/tradoc_152806.pdf> accessed 18 November 2014.

[47] See, for example, UNCTAD, The Rise of Regionalism in International Investment Policymaking: Consolidation or Complexity?, IIA Issues Note No 3, June 2013, 2 et seq.

[48] See thereto UNCTAD World Investment Report 2013, Global Value Chains: Investment and Trade for Development, 2013, 105 et seq; W Alschner, 'Regionalism and Overlap in Investment Treaty Law: Towards Consolidation or Contradiction?' (2014) 17 J Intl Econ L 271, 279 and 298.

[49] On the underlying 'shift in treaty-making activity from BITs towards FTAs and other economic integration treaties that combine trade and investment liberalization' see already UNCTAD World Investment Report 2008, Transnational Corporations and the Infrastructure Challenge, 2008, 17; as well as more recently for example UNCTAD, The Rise of Regionalism in International Investment Policymaking: Consolidation or Complexity?, IIA Issues Note No 3, June 2013; UNCTAD World Investment Report 2014, Investing in the SDGs: An Action Plan, 2014, 118 et seq.

Whatever approach is chosen by States and supranational organizations in implementing their investment policies—may it be bilateral or regional, static or more sustainable-development-oriented, unilateral or consensual—it should finally not go unnoticed in the present context that there is already from a quantitative perspective currently a rather wide-open 'window of opportunity' for adapting the international investment regime to changing perceptions and circumstances. According to a recent UNCTAD analysis, the overall number of BITs that can be terminated and/or renegotiated at any time has been estimated to exceed a number of 1.300 agreements at the end of 2013. In addition, between 2014 and 2018, at least another 350 BITs will reach the end of their initial minimum period of application.[50] These opportunities as well as the policy responses already adopted by States have most certainly contributed to the increasing prominence of termination and renegotiation of agreements as topics in the global discourses on investment protection.

The decisive underlying factor, however, remains the widespread recognition of the desirability and need to actively address the challenges resulting from second generation investment agreements. Whereas the previous transition period in investment treaty-making was overall characterized by and aimed at improving the legal status and protection of foreign investors, the current rise of a third generation of investment policies is expected to result in—and indeed largely also intended to—establish a new balance between host States and investors by stipulating additional limits to the legal benefits enjoyed by the latter. The respective attempts in treaty practice to 'downgrade' the legal position previously held by foreign investors under second generation investment agreements are not likely to go unchallenged. Not the least in light of this quite concrete possibility of future investment arbitration tribunals being called upon to address the legal issues arising from the termination and renegotiation of investment treaties, these questions are currently starting to attract unprecedented attention among practitioners and scholars alike. Against this background, the following parts of this article are intended to contribute to this emerging discourse by providing some thoughts on a number of related normative challenges likely to be even more intensively—and most certainly controversially—discussed in the near future.

III. 'Termination without Renegotiation': Legal Issues Arising from the Denunciation of Investment Agreements

When starting the analysis with an evaluation of the public international law framework addressing the in recent treaty practice increasingly important questions concerning the legality of a denunciation—understood as the unilateral act of a party aimed at withdrawing from a treaty[51]—of an investment

---

[50] UNCTAD, International Investment Policymaking in Transition: Challenges and Opportunities of Treaty Renewal, IIA Issues Note No 4, June 2013; see also UNCTAD World Investment Report 2013, Global Value Chains: Investment and Trade for Development, 2013, 108 et seq. On the initial fixed terms of application as stipulated in most BITs see also section III.a.

[51] See thereto LR Helfer, 'Terminating Treaties' in DB Hollis (ed), *The Oxford Guide to Treaties* (OUP 2012) 634, 635; Aust, *Modern Treaty Law and Practice* (n 1) 245; T Giegerich 'Article 54' in O Dörr and K Schmalenbach (eds), *Vienna Convention on the Law of Treaties* (Springer 2012) para 19.

agreement, two legal regimes are particularly worth drawing attention to. The first one comprises the customary international law on treaties as well as the 1969 Vienna Convention on the Law of Treaties (VCLT).[52] The possibly existing differences between these two sources of law are not to be further explored for the purposes of this contribution. Not only are they frequently disregarded in the practice of treaty negotiations. Rather, the provisions of the VCLT are also overwhelmingly considered to largely reflecting the current content of respective customary international law rules.[53] Already in light of these relevant norms of general public international law,[54] the second legal regime to be taken into account is the specific investment agreement at issue. And indeed, although most certainly caution is warranted when making generalizing statements against the background of currently already more than 3.200 investment agreements,[55] at least most of the 2900 existing BITs contain clauses that stipulate requirements of a lawful termination and address the consequences of such an act.[56] Two categories of norms are of particular significance in this regard.

a) Investment treaty provisions stipulating requirements of a lawful termination

The overwhelming majority of BITs as well as some multilateral agreements like the Energy Charter Treaty include a provision stipulating that the treaty will remain in force for an initial minimum period of time. The time frame for this initial fixed term of application normally varies from five years like in the case of article 47 (1) Energy Charter Treaty to fifteen years as for example stipulated in article 9 (2) of the BIT between China and Norway.[57] Occasionally, this initial

---

[52] Vienna Convention on the Law of Treaties of 22 May 1969, UNTS 1155, 331.
[53] On these two aspects see, for example, Aust, *Modern Treaty Law and Practice* (n 1) 10 et seq, with further references. Specifically on the customary international law status of the means of treaty interpretation as stipulated in the articles 31 to 33 VCLT see also for example *Saluka Investments BV v Czech Republic*, UNCITRAL Arbitration, Partial Award (17 March 2006) para 296; J Romesh Weeramantry, *Treaty Interpretation in Investment Arbitration* (OUP 2012) 24.
[54] See in particular the articles 42 (2) and 54 (a) VCLT, both of which are considered to codify customary international law. See thereto for example MG Kohen and S Heathcote, 'Article 42 Convention of 1969' in O Corten and P Klein (eds), *The Vienna Convention on the Law of Treaties*, vol II (OUP 2011) paras 7 et seq; V Chapaux, 'Article 54 Convention of 1969' in O Corten and P Klein (eds), *The Vienna Convention on the Law of Treaties*, vol II (OUP 2011) para 4.
[55] UNCTAD World Investment Report 2014, Investing in the SDGs: An Action Plan, 2014, 114. For more recent figures, including the BITs and other investment agreements concluded until the end of 2014, see UNCTAD, Investment Policy Monitor No 13, January 2015, 1 and 5 et seq.
[56] J Pohl, *Temporal Validity of International Investment Agreements* (OECD Working Papers on International Investment 2013/04) 7. Generally on the possible advantages as well as negative effects of stipulating termination clauses in international agreements see in particular LR Helfer, 'Exiting Treaties' (2005) 91 Va L Rev 1579, 1599 et seq; as well as for example T Meyer, 'Power, Exit Costs, and Renegotiation in International Law' (2010) 51 Harv ILJ 379, 389.
[57] See also, for example, JD Salacuse, *The Three Laws of International Investment* (OUP 2013) 400 ('Investment treaties generally provide that they shall be in force for 10 or 15 years.'); UNCTAD,

validity period even covers a timespan of up to thirty years. Such stipulations can be found, *inter alia*, in article 15 (1) of the BIT between Malaysia and the United Arab Emirates of 11 October 1991 and in article 15 (1) of the respective agreement concluded between Finland and Kuwait of 10 March 1996.

Once this initial term has expired, about sixty to eighty percent of all BITs provide for the possibility of unilateral termination at any time by notification of either party, frequently subjected to a one-year-period between the receipt of the notification by the other party and the date when the termination becomes effective.[58] Another approach occasionally to be found in investment treaty practice is the so-called 'end-of-term termination'. In that case, the investment agreement not terminated at the end of its initial minimum period will remain in force for a usually indefinite number of subsequent fixed terms and can be unilaterally terminated only towards the end of each of these subsequent periods.[59] A respective example is provided by the second sentence of article XIII (1) of the BIT between Algeria and Indonesia of 21 March 2000: 'It [the BIT] shall remain in force for a period of ten (10) years and shall continue in force thereafter for another period of ten (10) years and so forth unless denounced in writing by either Contracting Party one (01) year before its expiration.'

Considered in light of the present context, these clauses establishing initial minimum periods—as well as those providing only for the possibility of 'end-of-term terminations'—can be qualified as stipulating a temporary prohibition on the unilateral termination of the investment agreement in question.[60] Precisely because of this finding, it appears worth at least briefly drawing attention to the possibility of a denunciation under general public international law on treaties even during these fixed terms. Neither the wording of article 42 (2) VCLT, stipulating that the termination of a treaty 'may take place only as a result of the application of the provisions of the treaty or of the present Convention', nor the systematic approach adopted in the articles 54 et seq. VCLT seems to exclude the application of the additional general grounds for the termination of treaties enumerated in this convention to international (investment) agreements that provide for their own specific termination clauses.[61] In addition, it should be recalled that for example

International Investment Policymaking in Transition: Challenges and Opportunities of Treaty Renewal, IIA Issues Note No 4, June 2013, 3.

[58] See UNCTAD, International Investment Policymaking in Transition: Challenges and Opportunities of Treaty Renewal, IIA Issues Note No 4, June 2013, 3; Pohl (n 56) 7 et seq. For a respective example see article XVI (2) of the BIT between Jordan and the United States of 2 July 1997: 'A Contracting Party may terminate this Treaty at the end of the initial ten year period or at any time thereafter by giving one year's written notice to the other Contracting Party.' Similar requirements apply for example to a withdrawal by one contracting party from the Energy Charter Treaty in accordance with its article 47 (1) and (2).

[59] UNCTAD, International Investment Policymaking in Transition: Challenges and Opportunities of Treaty Renewal, IIA Issues Note No 4, June 2013, 3; Pohl (n 56) 7 et seq.

[60] Harrison (n 3) 934.

[61] See in this connection also for example Aust, *Modern Treaty Law and Practice* (n 1) 262 ('the International Law Commission did not limit it [article 62 VCLT], as had been suggested by some writers, to treaties of unlimited duration and no termination clause'); G Dahm, J Delbrück, and R Wolfrum, *Völkerrecht*, vol I/3 (de Gruyter 2002) 720; ME Villiger, *Commentary on the 1969 Vienna*

in the context of intra-EU BITs a number of investment arbitration tribunals have quite extensively discussed the prerequisites for a treaty termination under article 59 VCLT without even raising the issue of an overall applicability of this provision to the BIT at issue.[62]

Whereas an argument could be made that a denunciation based on a material breach of the BIT by the other state party under article 60 VCLT is, in light of one of the primary purposes pursued by investment agreements, excluded under article 60 (5) VCLT,[63] invoking a fundamental change of circumstances recognized as a ground for termination of treaties in article 62 VCLT serves as a vivid example to indicate the potential practical relevance of these rules of general public international law in the normative framework on investment protection.[64] Although these general grounds for denunciation of international agreements like the one enshrined in article 62 VCLT are in light of the fundamental rule of *pacta sunt servanda* (article 26 VCLT) frequently and rightly interpreted and applied rather narrowly and restrictive,[65] and despite the fact that most of them have so far played only a quite marginal role in the practice of investment dispute settlement proceedings, these admittedly only cursory reflections serve at least as an illustration that it might be necessary to look beyond the provisions of individual investment agreements when assessing the legality of their unilateral termination.

b) 'Survival clauses': treaty provisions addressing the consequences arising from denunciations

Once an investment agreement has been effectively denounced by one of its parties, a second well-known category of norms regularly incorporated in investment

---

Convention on the Law of Treaties (Nijhoff 2009) article 42, paras 10 et seq; UNCTAD, International Investment Policymaking in Transition: Challenges and Opportunities of Treaty Renewal, IIA Issues Note No 4, June 2013, 2. Either slightly misleading or expressing a different perception K Odendahl, 'Article 42' in O Dörr and K Schmalenbach (eds), *Vienna Convention on the Law of Treaties* (Springer 2012) para 24 ('If a treaty does not contain any termination, denunciation or withdrawal clauses, the rules of the VCLT apply.').

[62] See, for example, *Eastern Sugar BV v Czech Republic*, UNCITRAL ad hoc Arbitration, SCC No 088/2004, Partial Award (27 March 2007) paras 156 et seq; *Oostergetel and Laurentius v Slovak Republic*, UNCITRAL ad hoc Arbitration, Decision on Jurisdiction (30 April 20109 paras 72 et seq; *EUREKO BV v Slovak Republic*, PCA Case No 2008-13, Award on Jurisdiction, Arbitrability and Suspension (26 October 2010) paras 231 et seq. Generally on the issue of intra-EU BITs see already under section II.a.

[63] Generally on the scope of application of article 60 (5) VCLT see for example B Simma and CJ Tams, 'Article 60 Convention of 1969' in O Corten and P Klein (eds), *The Vienna Convention on the Law of Treaties*, vol II (OUP 2011) paras 41 et seq.

[64] See also briefly UNCTAD, Denunciation of the ICSID Convention and BITs: Impact on Investor-State Claims, IIA Issues Note No 2, December 2010, 3.

[65] See, for example, *Case Concerning the Gabčíkovo-Nagymaros Project (Hungary v Slovakia)* (1997) ICJ Rep 7 (65, para 104) ('The negative and conditional wording of Article 62 of the Vienna Convention on the Law of Treaties is a clear indication moreover that the stability of treaty relations requires that the plea of fundamental change of circumstances be applied only in exceptional cases.'); as well as generally thereto A Vamvoukos, *Termination of Treaties in International Law* (OUP 1985) 60 et seq; T Giegerich, 'Article 62' in O Dörr and K Schmalenbach (eds), *Vienna Convention on the Law of Treaties*

agreements and of considerable relevance in the present context comes into play. Contrary to the above mentioned provisions providing for fixed terms of application, these so-called 'survival clauses'[66]—also known as 'continuing effects clauses',[67] 'tail' period provisions[68] or 'sunset provisions'[69]—do not stipulate requirements for a lawful denunciation. Rather, they address the consequences arising from such a termination of the treaty. Generally speaking, this rather unique type of provisions grants foreign investors the possibility to continuously benefit from the respective substantive protection standards—and the frequently given availability of access to international legal remedies—in respect of investments made prior to the date of expiry of the agreement for a certain period of time after the termination becomes effective. Aimed at preventing denunciations with immediate effect, these clauses are common to most—albeit not all[70]—investment agreements. To mention but one example, article 29(3) of the 2008 BIT between Japan and Peru proscribes that '[i]n respect of investments acquired prior to the date of termination of this Agreement, the provisions of this Agreement shall continue to be effective for a period of ten years from the date of termination of this Agreement'.

It hardly needs to be emphasized that the primary reason for the frequent incorporation of these provisions lies in the specific character of the kind of economic transactions addressed by international investment agreements. As for example vividly explained by Rudolf Dolzer and Christoph Schreuer,

[m]aking a foreign investment is different in nature from engaging in a trade transaction. Whereas a trade deal typically consists of a one-time exchange of goods and money, the decision to invest in a foreign country initiates a long-term relationship between the investor and the host country. Often, the business plan of the investor is to sink substantial resources into the project at the outset of the investment, with the expectation of recouping this amount plus an acceptable rate of return during the subsequent period of investment, sometimes running up to 30 years or more.[71]

(Springer 2012) paras 1 et seq; MN Shaw, *International Law* (7th edn, CUP 2014) 688 et seq, each with numerous further references.

[66] See, for example, G Bolivar, 'The Effect of Survival and Withdrawal Clauses in Investment Treaties: Protection of Investments in Latin America' in LE Trakman and NW Ranieri (eds), *Regionalism in International Investment Law* (OUP 2013) 162, 168; T Voon, A Mitchell, and J Munro, 'Parting Ways: The Impact of Mutual Termination of Investment Treaties on Investor Rights' (2014) 29 ICSID Rev – FILJ 451, 465.

[67] See for example Salacuse (n 13) 352.

[68] LM Caplan and JK Sharpe, 'United States' in C Brown (ed), *Commentaries on Selected Model Investment Treaties* (OUP 2013) 755, 820.

[69] See, for example, FG Sourgens, 'Keep the Faith: Investment Protection Following the Denunciation of International Investment Agreements' (2013) 11 Santa Clara JIL 335, 369. See also for example T Voon and A Mitchell, 'Time to Quit? Assessing International Investment Claims Against Plain Tobacco Packaging in Australia' (2011) 14 J Intl Econ L 515, 528 ('sunset clause'); S Hamamoto and L Nottage, 'Japan' in C Brown (ed), *Commentaries on Selected Model Investment Treaties* (OUP 2013) 347, 389.

[70] A rare example of a BIT stipulating an initial minimum period of application but no survival clause is provided by the respective agreement between Egypt and Latvia of 24 April 1997.

[71] R Dolzer and C Schreuer, *Principles of International Investment Law* (2nd edn, OUP 2012) 21.

Survival clauses, but also provisions stipulating a minimum period of application, are thus first and foremost aimed at promoting long-term legal security and stability for covered investors.

Thereby, the respective extension period stipulated in survival clauses most certainly varies in treaty practice; usually they cover a timespan ranging from five years as for example enshrined in article 14(2) of the BIT between Italy and Korea of 10 January 1989 and article 15(2) of the respective agreement concluded between Italy and Malaysia of 4 January 1988 to twenty years like in the cases of article 12(3) of the 2004 BIT between Jordan and Korea as well as of article 47(3) Energy Charter Treaty. Occasionally, the provision in question even extends protection to all or at least certain types of existing investments indefinitely throughout the whole period of investment. Article 13 of the 1970 BIT between Belgium and Indonesia provides a respective example by stipulating that

[i]n case of termination of the present Agreement the provisions thereof shall continue to be effective for a period of validity of contracts concluded between the Contracting Party and the investor of the other Contracting Party prior to the notification of termination of the present Agreement.[72]

In addition it seems noteworthy that for example the Energy Charter Treaty even stipulated in the former version of its article 45(3)(b) a separate survival clause in case a signatory terminates the provisional application of this multilateral agreement[73] and that *inter alia* article 40(2) of the 2013 BIT between Canada and Tanzania covers not only existing investments but also 'commitments to invest' made prior to the date when the treaty termination becomes effective.

Whatever language is employed and independently of the individual material and temporal scope of application envisioned, these survival clauses undoubtedly—and probably undisputedly—apply to unilateral terminations made in accordance with the respective termination clause of the investment agreement at issue. Bearing in mind the additional observations made in connection with the provisions stipulating a minimum period of application, the question arises, however, whether the survival clauses also prevent denunciation with immediate effect if the unilateral termination is based on respective rules of general public international law on treaties. While the applicability has been explicitly—albeit without further reasoning—affirmed by

---

[72] An even more far reaching example is provided by article 9(4) of the BIT between France and Korea of 28 December 19177, stipulating that the provisions of the agreement shall continue to be applicable to all investments covered by its provisions and made during the period when it was in force. See also Harrison (n 3) 938.

[73] On the practical significance of this clause see, for example, *Yukos Universal Ltd (Isle of Man) v Russia*, PCA Case No AA 227, Interim Award on Jurisdiction and Admissibility (30 November 2009) para 395.

> Accordingly, the Tribunal has concluded that the ECT in its entirety applied provisionally in the Russian Federation until 19 October 2009, and that Parts III and V of the Treaty (including Article 26 thereof) remain in force until 19 October 2029 for any investments made prior to 19 October 2009. Respondent is thus bound by the investor-State arbitration provision invoked by Claimant.

See also *Yukos Universal Ltd (Isle of Man) v Russia*, PCA Case No AA 227, Final Award (18 July 2014) para 21.

at least one investment arbitration tribunal in connection with article 59 VCLT,[74] it appears acceptable to argue that at least in the very rare and 'exceptional cases'[75] in which for example the prerequisites for a denunciation based on a fundamental change of circumstances in accordance with article 62 VCLT are given, a State cannot be legitimately expected to be continuously bound by the provisions of the treaty for another decade or even longer. From a legal perspective, this arguments finds additional support for example in the more or less undisputedly held view that even the limitations imposed on treaty parties with regard to the revocation or modification of rights arising for third states in accordance with article 37(2) VCLT[76] do not hinder the parties—individually or collectively—to terminate a respective agreement without the consent of the third State on the basis of a fundamental change of circumstances under article 62 VCLT.[77] If one is willing to follow this reasoning, the often rather broadly phrased survival clauses[78] are to be—to a certain extent—narrowly interpreted in the sense of at least not covering all cases in which the unilateral termination is based on applicable general rules of the international law of treaties.

Leaving aside these quite specific and so far rather theoretical legal issues as well as disregarding the admittedly from a practical point of view very important question whether unilateral terminations of investment agreements are generally wise as a matter of policy and likely to promote a suitable balance between sustainable development and investment protection, the present analysis has revealed that, first, the legality and consequences of a denunciation are addressed in a quite detailed and unambiguous way by the provisions of most investment agreements themselves and that, second, in light of these provisions a party intending to unilaterally exit a respective treaty is—at least under normal circumstances—highly likely to be confronted with and constraint by the legal obligations it once agreed to for quite some time after the termination takes effect. Whether the same can be said with an at least comparable degree of certainty in cases of mutually agreed terminations and/or certain amendments and suspensions of international investment agreements is the subject of the following two sections.

---

[74] See *Eastern Sugar BV v Czech Republic*, UNCITRAL ad hoc Arbitration, SCC No 088/2004, Partial Award (27 March 2007) para 175 ('The Arbitral Tribunal can only reject the Czech Republic's argument that the implied termination of the BIT through accession also terminated the continuing effect expressly guaranteed by Art. 13(3) of the BIT.'). Arguably, the termination of an agreement under article 59 VCLT constitutes a case of mutually agreed termination by the parties as discussed in pt IV. Nevertheless, taking recourse to an *argumentum a maiore ad minus*, the finding of the tribunal would have been probably no different in the case of a unilateral termination based on respective rules of the general public international law on treaties.

[75] *Case Concerning the Gabčíkovo-Nagymaros Project (Hungary v Slovakia)* (1997) ICJ Rep 7 (65, para 104).

[76] See also pt IV.b.bb.

[77] See thereto for example C Chinkin, *Third Parties in International Law* (Clarendon 1993) 42; Harrison (n 3) 947; A Proelss, 'Article 37' in O Dörr and K Schmalenbach (eds), *Vienna Convention on the Law of Treaties* (Springer 2012) para 10. For a more cautious view see M Fitzmaurice, 'Third Parties and the Law of Treaties' (2002) 6 Max Planck Ybk of UN L 37, 57 ('not entirely clear').

[78] See thereto also pt IV.b.cc.

IV. 'Termination as a Result of Renegotiation': Normative Implications of Investment Treaty Termination by Mutual Consent

When evaluating the prerequisites for and normative consequences arising from the termination of investment agreements by mutual consent of the parties, it seems appropriate and useful to start with the observation that from a legal perspective there seems to be no need to differentiate between circumstances in which the ending of the treaty is merely the result of a replacement by a new respective agreement on the one side and those—comparatively rare—situations where the parties have decided, at least for the time being, to end their treaty relationships in the realm of investment protection altogether on the other side. Quite to the contrary, however, another distinction appears worth drawing attention to in the present context, namely the one between mutually agreed withdrawals in accordance with the relevant provisions of the treaty and those terminations by consent of the parties that do not conform to the applicable requirements as stipulated in the investment agreement at issue.

a) Mutually agreed terminations in accordance with the relevant treaty provisions

As for example also—and almost superfluously[79]—acknowledged by article 54 (a) VCLT, mutually agreed terminations of investment agreements—in the same way as unilateral denunciations—in accordance with the relevant treaty provisions are undoubtedly possible and from a legal perspective do in general hardly pose any noteworthy challenges. Even if one—rightly and for valid reasons—adheres to the still controversially debated perception that investment treaties are capable of and in fact frequently do create direct legal entitlements for foreign investors,[80]

---

[79] On the respective perceptions see, for example, I Sinclair, *The Vienna Convention on the Law of Treaties* (2nd edn, Manchester University Press 1984) 182 ('self-evident rule'); Chapaux (n 54) para 4 ('In addition, many members of the Commission stressed the obvious—or useless—character of this provision, which was even momentarily removed from the project, only to be finally reinserted for the sake of clarity.').

[80] See, for example, *BG Group Plc v Argentina*, UNCITRAL Arbitration, Award (24 December 2007) para 145

> The proliferation of bilateral investment treaties has effected a profound transformation of international investment law. Most significantly, under these instruments investors are entitled to seek enforcement of *their treaty rights* by directly bringing action against the State in whose territory they have invested. (emphasis by the author)

Corn Products International Inc v Mexico, ICSID Case No ARB(AF)/04/01, Decision on Responsibility (15 January 2008) paras 167 et seq.

> In the Tribunal's view, the NAFTA confers upon investors substantive rights separate and distinct from those of the State of which they are nationals. It is now clear that States are not the only entities which can hold rights under international law; individuals and corporations may also possess rights under international law. [...] In the case of Chapter XI of

this notable 'elevation' of their international normative status on the basis of these instruments does most certainly not include a protection against subsequent revocation of these treaty-based rights as a result of a termination of the investment agreement in question; at least insofar as this termination takes place in conformity with the requirements stipulated therein, among them in particular also regulations establishing initial minimum periods of application as well as survival clauses. As not infrequently—and, taking into account the at least currently still prevailing overall design of the international legal order, rightly—emphasized in particular also in connection with the options for treaty parties to terminate agreements aimed at the protection of human rights,[81] even those treaties that do not provide for a respective termination or withdrawal clause might nevertheless in principle be legally ended, and consequently the individual rights stipulated therein be abolished, with the consent of all parties.[82] In particular in the investment context, it appears furthermore rather difficult to convincingly argue in favour of a legitimate

---

the NAFTA, the Tribunal considers that the intention of the Parties was to confer substantive rights directly upon investors. That follows from the language used and is confirmed by the fact that Chapter XI confers procedural rights upon them.

Z Douglas, 'The Hybrid Foundations of Investment Treaty Arbitration' (2003) 74 British Ybk IL 151, 182; O Spiermann, 'Individual Rights, State Interests and the Power to Waive ICSID Jurisdiction under Bilateral Investment Treaties' (2004) 20 Arb Intl 179, 185 ('It would take an excessively narrow, albeit not unprecedented standard of interpretation to find that bilateral investment treaties do not vest rights in the investor as a subject of international law.'). Generally on the ongoing scholarly debates on this issue see for example Ca McLachlan, L Shore, and M Weiniger, *International Investment Arbitration* (OUP 2007) 61 et seq; Z Douglas, *The International Law of Investment Claims* (CUP 2009) 10 et seq; K Parlett, *The Individual in the International Legal System: Continuity and Change in International Law* (CUP 2011) 103 et seq; M Paparinskis, 'Investment Treaty Arbitration and the (New) Law of State Responsibility' (2013) 24 EJIL 617, 621 et seq; E De Brabandere, *Investment Treaty Arbitration as Public International Law* (CUP 2014) 55 et seq.

[81] For a quite comprehensive evaluation on this subject see, for example, Y Tyagi, 'The Denunciation of Human Rights Treaties' (2009) 79 British Ybk IL 86, with numerous further references.

[82] See, for example, Chinkin (n 77) 121–22 ('Under general treaty law and the law on State responsibility, States can amend or terminate treaties which provide rights for individuals. Individuals enjoy any benefit bestowed by treaty with the continued agreement of the States parties; [...].'); Aide Memoire of the Office of the UN Secretary General, Denunciation of the ICCPR by the Democratic People's Republic of Korea, 23 September 1997, para 13, available under: <https://treaties.un.org/doc/Publication/CN/1997/CN.467.1997-Frn.pdf> accessed 12 December 2014; E Klein, 'Denunciation of Human Rights Treaties and the Principle of Reciprocity' in U Fastenrath and others (eds), *From Bilateralism to Community Interest—Essays in Honour of Judge Bruno Simma* (OUP 2011) 477, 485 ('The fact that human rights treaties serve a community interest cannot impede the States parties from terminating the treaty by consent. Community interests as defined by treaties remain dependent on their creators as the masters of the treaty [...].'); see, however, also for a different perception with regard to human rights treaties B Hofmann, *Beendigung menschenrechtlicher Verträge* (Berliner Wissenschafts-Verlag 2009) 215 et seq; specifically for the realm of investment agreements see for example M Paparinskis, 'Investment Arbitration and the Law of Countermeasures' (2009) 79 British Ybk IL 264, 342; A Roberts, 'Power and Persuasion in Investment Treaty Interpretation: The Dual Role of States' (2010) 104 AJIL 179, 214 ('Investor rights are granted within the treaty's general regulatory framework, which includes the right of treaty parties to interpret, amend, and revoke those rights.'); R Volterra, 'International Law Commission Articles on State Responsibility and Investor-State Arbitration: Do Investors have Rights?' (2010) 25 ICSID Rev—FILJ 218, 220; TW Wälde, 'Procedural Challenges in Investment Arbitration under the Shadow of the Dual Role of the State' (2010) 26 Arb Intl 3, 16.

expectation[83] arising on the side of foreign investors that investment agreements will not be terminated by the states parties, since—as vividly stated by Mahnoush H Arsanjani and W Michael Reisman—'it is reasonable to expect (indeed, to demand) of investors that they will diligently examine the treaties that govern their investment so as to apprise themselves in advance of the scope of their rights and obligations',[84] including the expectation to take sufficiently into account—and draw the necessary conclusions from—the existence of respective termination clauses contained in the overwhelming majority of these agreements.

b) Terminations by mutual consent in disregard of applicable treaty provisions

The legal evaluation, however, appears to be considerably less straightforward and undoubted when turning to the question whether governmental or supranational treaty parties have also retained the power to terminate an investment agreement by mutual consent at any time as well as with immediate effect and thus in disregard of applicable minimum periods of application, periods of notice of termination and/or survival clauses as explicitly provided for in the treaty. It is in particular this issue that has been only recently identified as being one of the 'open questions' in this legal field in the sense of belonging to the until now unresolved topics of international investment law.[85]

aa) Doctrinal and practical relevance

And indeed, what might appear to some observers at least at first sight as a rather narrow technical question of doubtful practical relevance, can—upon closer inspection—be very well regarded as one of the central issues in the present phase of international investment treaty-making.[86] On the one side attention should

---

[83] Generally on the protection of legitimate expectations under the fair and equitable treatment standard as frequently stipulated in investment agreements see, for example, J Bonnitcha, *Substantive Protection under Investment Treaties* (CUP 2014) 167 et seq.

[84] MH Arsanjani and W Michael Reisman, 'Interpreting Treaties for the Benefit of Third Parties: The "*Salvors'* Doctrine" and the Use of Legislative History in Investment Claims' (2010) 104 AJIL 597, 603. See also, for example, Roberts (n 82) 210 ('Investor rights can be altered through various means, including interpretation, amendment, withdrawal, and termination. As parties invest in the knowledge that their treaty protections may change, they cannot legitimately expect that their treaty rights will be absolute and irrevocable.').

[85] UNCTAD, International Investment Policymaking in Transition: Challenges and Opportunities of Treaty Renewal, IIA Issues Note No 4, June 2013, 4 Fn 10 ('open question'); UNCTAD World Investment Report 2013, Global Value Chains: Investment and Trade for Development, 2013, 118 Fn 61; S Ripinsky, 'Russia' in C Brown (ed), *Commentaries on Selected Model Investment Treaties* (OUP 2013) 593, 620 ('a debatable issue not yet tested in arbitral practice'); A Roberts, 'State-to-State Investment Treaty Arbitration: A Hybrid Theory of Interdependent Rights and Shared Interpretive Authority' (2014) 55 Harv ILJ 1, 23 ('ongoing controversies'); S-I Lekkas and A Tzanakopoulos, '*Pacta sunt servanda* versus Flexibility in the Suspension and Termination of Treaties' in CJ Tams, A Tzanakopoulos, and A Zimmermann (eds), *Research Handbook on the Law of Treaties* (Edward Elgar 2014) 312, 317 Fn 27 ('interesting problems').

[86] On the current transitional phase of international investment law see already section II.a.

be drawn to the fact that the search for appropriate legal solutions to the problem whether States and supranational organizations like the European Union can mutually agree to terminate investment agreements with immediate effect is not merely a kind of recent 'sideshow' in international investment law but raises, from an overarching perspective, quite fundamental questions about what powers these governmental actors do or should in fact retain when concluding treaties that are first and foremost also aimed at protecting and benefiting private foreign investors.[87]

On the other side one has to bear in mind that these concerns are not only on a theoretical basis interesting and challenging to address. Rather, also their increasing practical importance in current investment treaty-making—and thus probably also in future investor-State dispute settlement proceedings—is close to incontrovertible. The approach of a mutually agreed termination of an investment agreement with immediate effect in disregard of a survival clause finds its manifestation in treaty practice among others in article 13(2) of the BIT between Bangladesh and Turkey of 12 April 2012, stipulating that

[t]his agreement replaces the Agreement between the Republic of Turkey and the People's Republic of Bangladesh Concerning the Reciprocal Encouragement and Protection of Investments, signed on 12th November 1987 in Ankara which shall be terminated on the date of entry into force of this Agreement. The disputes submitted to arbitration after the date of entry into force of this Agreement shall be settled in accordance with the provisions of this Agreement.

Further notable examples include the already above mentioned article 10.20 of the free trade agreement between Peru and Singapore that entered into force on 1 August 2009, article 9.17 of the Republic of Korea-Peru free trade agreement of 21 March 2011 as well as, albeit based on a more indirect stipulation, article 21.4 of the free trade agreement concluded by Chile and the Republic of Korea on 15 February 2003. In addition, a similar approach is expected to be provided for on the basis of article X.07 of the chapter on final provisions of CETA between Canada and the EU. Finally, to mention but one further example, respective arguments have already occasionally been brought forward also by countries like the Czech Republic and Egypt in the course of investment arbitration proceedings.[88]

---

[87] See thereto also, for example, JE Alvarez, *The Public International Law Regime Governing International Investment* (Hague Academy of International Law 2011) 418 ('How much power do or should Governments retain once they establish treaties to protect investors' settled or legitimate expectations against their own actions and have accepted the competence of third-party arbitrators to decide such matters?'); Roberts (n 85) 70 („it implicates fundamental, but unresolved, questions about what rights have been retained by home and host states acting individually and the treaty parties acting collectively').

[88] See *Eastern Sugar BV v Czech Republic*, UNCITRAL ad hoc Arbitration, SCC No 088/2004, Partial Award (27 March 2007) para 175; *Jan de Nul NV/Dredging International NV v Egypt*, ICSID Case No ARB/04/13, Decision on Jurisdiction (16 June 2006) para 59; *Jan de Nul NV/Dredging International NV v Egypt*, ICSID Case No ARB/04/13, Award (6 November 2008) para 126.

bb) A closer look at Article 54 (b) VCLT and its normative limitations

As already indicated above, a valid argument can be made in this connection that even the overwhelming majority of investment agreements that explicitly stipulate minimum periods of application and survival clauses nevertheless permits a denunciation by one of the parties at any time with immediate effect on the basis of a fundamental chance of circumstances.[89] Consequently, in case one accepts the respective line of reasoning, it surely does not only apply to cases of unilateral terminations but also to mutually agreed endings of the treaty relationships as long as the requirements as enshrined in article 62 VCLT are fulfilled with regard to at least one of the treaty parties concerned. If one thus adheres to the view that the general grounds for termination as laid down in the VCLT and reflecting customary international law also apply to investment agreements with own specific termination clauses,[90] the almost 'natural' starting point for an assessment of the legal implications arising from terminations by consent of the parties that do not conform to the applicable requirements as stipulated in the investment agreement at issue, in those—from a practical perspective obvious majority of—other cases not involving the exceptional circumstances of article 62 VCLT, is article 54(b) VCLT. According to this provision, whose applicability in particular also to treaties stipulating their own respective clauses is in principle beyond doubt,[91] the termination of a treaty may take place at any time by consent of all the parties. Article 54 (b) VCLT clearly mirrors the almost classical perception that the contracting parties are also the so-called 'masters of the treaty'.[92] They are collectively entitled to amend or terminate an agreement simply on the basis of mutual consent only and thus in general also in disregard of respective termination clauses as stipulated in the treaty itself.[93]

In light of these findings one might initially be quite tempted to draw the rather straightforward conclusion that the States parties to an investment agreement

---

[89] See section III.   [90] See thereto also already section III.

[91] On this perception see for example Chapaux (n 54) para 20 ('There is no doubt that Article 54 (a) cannot prevent Article 54(b) from producing effects.'); Giegerich (n 51) para 37 ('Art 54 lit b applies where the treaty either does not include provisions on termination or withdrawal at all or lays down conditions for the exercise of those rights which are not met in a given case.').

[92] See, for example, UNCTAD, Interpretation of IIAs: What States Can Do, IIA Issues Note No 3, December 2011, 3 ('In international law States are the drafters and masters of their treaties.'); Wälde (n 82) 16; Klein (n 82) 485; Giegerich (n 51) para 37; as well as J Crawford, 'A Consensualist Interpretation of Article 31 (3) of the Vienna Convention on the Law of Treaties' in G Nolte (ed), *Treaties and Subsequent Practice* (OUP 2013) 29, 31

> [I]t is too often forgotten that the parties to a treaty, that is, the states which are bound by it at the relevant time, own the treaty. It is their treaty. It is not anyone else's treaty. In the context of investment treaty arbitration there is a certain tendency to believe that investors own bilateral investment treaties, not the state parties to them. [...] That is not what international law says.

[93] See for example Aust, *Modern Treaty Law and Practice* (n 1) 254 ('A treaty may, of course, be terminated, or a party may withdraw from it, at any time by consent of all the parties (Article 54 (b)). This can be done even if the treaty provides for a minimum period of notice.'); Dahm, Delbrück, and Wolfrum (n 61) 722; Giegerich (n 51) para 37.

retain on the basis of article 54(b) VCLT also the joint powers to end their treaty relationship at any time with immediate effect despite the stipulation of respective minimum periods of application and survival clauses. However, it should be recalled at this point that these powers of the contracting parties as recognized by this provision can be subject to certain normative limitations. In particular, as for example already emphasized by Lord McNair prior to the adoption of the VCLT, the unqualified application of this rule 'presupposes that they [the treaty parties] alone are interested in the continued existence [of the agreement] and that no third party has acquired an interest in its preservation, either directly under some provision of the treaty vesting rights in favour of such a third party or indirectly [...]'.[94]

A respective restriction on the otherwise accepted freedom of the contracting parties to dispose of their agreement at will derives for example from article 37(2) VCLT, stipulating that once a right has arisen for a third state under article 36 VCLT, a revocation or modification of this third party treaty right may under certain circumstances require also the consent of the third State in question. Although it is generally recognized that article 37(2) VCLT constitutes a limitation to the exercise of the powers of the treaty parties under article 54(b) VCLT,[95] already the wording of this provision strongly suggests a comparatively narrow scope of application being confined to treaty rights arising for a 'third State' and thus does not include the present context of investment agreements as characterized by the creation of rights for private corporations, individuals and other non-State actors undertaking foreign investments. Despite respective pleas to the contrary in the recently intensified scholarly discussion on this issue,[96] there seems to be already in light of the legislative history of article 37 VCLT at least until now no sound normative basis in public international law to either enlarge the scope of application of this provision by way of analogy to treaty rights granted to foreign investors under investment agreements or to consider this stipulation as merely a kind of *pars pro toto*, signaling the existence of a general principle that would apply to all third party right holders including individuals and other foreign investors.[97]

---

[94] AD McNair, *The Law of Treaties* (OUP 1961) 506; see also subsequently for example Dahm, Delbrück and Wolfrum (n 61) 724.

[95] See, for example, Sinclair (n 79) 184; Aust, *Modern Treaty Law and Practice* (n 1) 254; Giegerich (n 51) para 39.

[96] See in particular Harrison (n 3) 943 et seq; Lavopa, Barreiros, and Bruno (n 3) 888 et seq.

[97] Generally on this perception for example Chinkin (n 77) 121

> Individuals as third parties to treaties are not in the same position as third party States or organizations. [...] Individuals are not referred to in Articles 34-7 of the Vienna Convention on the Law of Treaties, nor the Vienna Convention on International Organizations. They are not protected against revocation and modification of third party rights under Articles 36 and 37, nor any customary international law equivalent.

Dahm, Delbrück and Wolfrum (n 61) 619; P d'Argent, 'Article 36 Convention of 1969' in O Corten and P Klein (eds), *The Vienna Convention on the Law of Treaties*, vol I (OUP 2011) para 3; see also the respective evaluation of the issue by A Proelss, 'The Personal Dimension: Challenges to the *pacta tertiis* rule' in CJ Tams, A Tzanakopoulos, and A Zimmermann (eds), *Research Handbook on the Law of Treaties* (Edward Elgar 2014) 222, 235 et seq. Specifically in the context of investment agreements see, for example, Paparinskis (n 82) 342 ('It does not mean that investors have safeguards to the alteration

'Termination as a Result of Renegotiation' 251

Much the same verdict ultimately applies to another potentially illuminating stipulation enshrined in the VCLT. Article 70(1)(b) VCLT establishes a rebuttable presumption that the termination of an agreement does not 'affect any right, obligation or legal situation of the parties created through the execution of the treaty prior to its termination'. It would probably appear at first sight not too fancy to assume that this provision forms a suitable normative basis for preserving the rights of foreign investors—created by the parties through survival clauses and those providing for minimum periods of application—with regard to the prolongation of their protection under the investment agreement terminated by mutual consent, at least for the periods specified in these clauses. And indeed, at least on a rather abstract level, a certain connection between article 70(1)(b) VCLT on the one side and in particular survival clauses on the other side can hardly be denied,[98] bearing in mind that both provisions address the possible normative consequences of an ending of the treaty relationship between the parties. However, a closer look at the regulatory content relatively quickly reveals that article 70(1)(b) VCLT itself is hardly of any assistance when trying to clarify the legal issues arising in the present context of mutually agreed terminations of investment agreements. There are at least two main reasons to support this proposition. First, the reference to party autonomy in the introductory part of article 70(1) VCLT, stating in its relevant part the qualification '[u]nless [...] the parties otherwise agree', illustrates beyond reasonable doubt that the VCLT not only recognizes the right of the parties to agree on the requirements of a legally valid termination (article 54 VCLT) but also leaves it first and foremost to the contracting parties to determine the respective consequences of termination by mutual consent.[99] Consequently, this provision does not prevent the parties of an investment agreement to jointly agree on a termination with immediate effect and thus in disregard of a respective survival clause.[100] Second, and at least equally noteworthy, it is again the legislative history of this provision that clearly indicates the limited scope of application of article 70(1)(b) VCLT in the sense of only addressing the rights, obligations or legal situations in the relationship between the contracting parties and in particular being 'not in any way concerned with the question of the "vested rights" of individuals' or other private foreign investors covered and protected by investment treaties.[101]

---

of their legal rights under the investment protection law analogous to those of third parties in the more accepted sense.'); M Paparinskis, 'Analogies and Other Regimes of International Law' in Z Douglas, J Pauwelyn and JE Viñuales (eds), *The Foundations of International Investment Law* (OUP 2014) 73, 82; Voon, Mitchell and Munro (n 66) 469–70.

[98] On this connection between article 70(1)(b) VCLT and survival clauses in investment agreements see also, for example, S Wittich, 'Article 70' in O Dörr and K Schmalenbach (eds), *Vienna Convention on the Law of Treaties* (Springer 2012) paras 13 and 31.

[99] See H Ascensio, 'Article 70 Convention of 1969' in O Corten and P Klein (eds), *The Vienna Convention on the Law of Treaties*, vol II (OUP 2011) para 6 ('Provisions of the Vienna Convention do not limit the autonomy of the will of parties in this domain.'); Wittich (n 98) para 10; R Jennings and A Watts, *Oppenheim's International Law*, vol I, Parts 2 to 4 (9th edn, Longman 1992) 1311.

[100] See thereto also already Voon, Mitchell, and Munro (n 66) 467.

[101] Ybk of the ILC 1966, vol II, UN Doc. A/CN.4/SER.A/1966/Add.1, Commentary to Draft Article 66, 265 para 3

However, the fact that neither article 37(2) VCLT nor article 70(1)(b) VCLT apply to mutually agreed terminations of investment agreements does not necessarily lead to the conclusion that the powers of the contracting parties as in principle recognized by article 54(b) VCLT are in the present context not subject to other limitations under general public international law,[102] with the consequence that these treaties might ultimately be interpreted as also granting covered foreign investors the enforceable right that the agreements at issue are in principle—and thus aside from the potential relevance for example of article 62 VCLT—only jointly terminated in accordance with applicable provisions stipulating minimum periods of application and with due regard to respective survival clauses.[103] In light of the fact that the types of provisions in question are undoubtedly based on the intention of the treaty parties to promote long-term legal security and stability for foreign investors, an argument could for example be made that the contracting States have—by including them in their agreement—implicitly also agreed to an exclusion of the applicability of article 54(b) VCLT *inter se*, at least as far as the observance of minimum periods of applications and survival clauses are concerned.[104] In addition, albeit closely connected to the foregoing argument, attention could—and indeed should—be drawn to the potential relevance of general principles of law such as the doctrine of acquired rights, the concept of estoppel, considerations of legal certainty and non-retroactivity based on human rights enjoyed by foreign investors[105] and/or the possibility that the ending of an investment treaty with immediate effect by mutual consent in disregard of respective

> On the other hand, by the words 'any right, obligation or legal situation of the parties created through the execution of the treaty', the Commission wished to make it clear that paragraph 1(b) relates only to the right, obligation or legal situation of the States parties to the treaties created through the execution, and is not in any way concerned with the question of the 'vested interests' of individuals

see also Ascensio (n 99) para 20; Wittich (n 98) para 29.

[102] See also Ascensio (n 99) para 20 ('Nevertheless, pushing aside the problem [in the VCLT] does not necessarily mean denying the existence of such rights.').

[103] The distinction, made for example by UNCTAD without further reasoning, concerning the given legality of the contracting parties to investment agreements to disregard minimum periods of application on the basis of article 54 (b) VCLT on the one side and the characterization of a respective ignorance of survival clauses as an 'open question' from the perspective of public international law on the other side appears not entirely convincing already in light of the fact that in both situations the period of treaty protection enjoyed by covered investors is shortened to an equal extent. On this distinction see, for example, UNCTAD, International Investment Policymaking in Transition: Challenges and Opportunities of Treaty Renewal, IIA Issues Note No 4, June 2013, 3 Fn 8 and 4 Fn 10; World Investment Report 2013, Global Value Chains: Investment and Trade for Development, 2013, 118 Fn 59 and 61.

[104] Generally on this option under the law of treaties see for example Giegerich (n 51) para 47.

[105] On the relevance of human rights treaties and the jurisprudence of regional human rights courts in the interpretation of investment agreements in favour of foreign investors see, for example, *Mondev International Ltd v USA*, ICSID Case No ARB(AF)/99/2, Award (11 October 2002) paras 141 et seq; *Tecnicas Medioambientales Tecmed SA v Mexico*, ICSID Case No ARB(AF)/00/2, Award (29 May 2003) paras 116 et seq; *Azurix Corp v Argentina*, ICSID Case No ARB/01/12, Award (14 July 2006) paras 311 et seq; *Saipem SpA v Bangladesh*, ICSID Case No ARB/05/07, Decision on Jurisdiction and Recommendation on Provisional Measures (21 March 2007) paras 130, 132.

termination clauses might be validly perceived as an abuse of the contracting parties of their right under article 54(b) VCLT,[106] to name but one more notable good faith related principle in the present context.[107]

Admittedly, many of these lines of reasoning and legal concepts are clearly not immune to certain methodological challenges when applied in the context of jointly agreed terminations of investment agreements. With regard to a possible exclusion of the application of article 54(b) VCLT by the parties, for example, it has rightly been emphasized that 'such an intention should not be assumed lightly'.[108] Although frequently and for quite some time considered as in principle belonging to the class of general principles of law,[109] the concept of acquired rights is nevertheless also perceived to remain rather vague and illusive when trying to define its scope of application as well as the normative consequences deriving from it in a specific situation.[110] Furthermore, despite the fact that the doctrine of estoppel is commonly recognized as a general principle of law in the relationships between State actors[111] and has already occasionally been taken recourse to by investment arbitration tribunals in other contexts,[112] one cannot but agree for example with Anthea Roberts and her observation that 'it is less clear how it might apply to general relations between states and investors'.[113] Despite these reservations, however, it is currently far from certain that these and other difficulties

---

[106] Generally on the doctrine of abuse of rights in public international law see for example R Jennings and A Watts, *Oppenheim's International Law*, vol I, Introduction and Part 1 (9th edn, Longman 1992) 407 et seq; A Kiss, 'Abuse of Rights' in R Wolfrum (ed), *Max Planck Encyclopedia of Public International Law* (December 2006) <www.mpepil.com/> accessed 11 November 2014.

[107] On the qualification of these legal doctrines as good faith related concepts see, for example, M Kotzur, 'Good Faith (Bona fide)' in R Wolfrum (ed), *Max Planck Encyclopedia of Public International Law* (January 2009) paras 22 and 24 <www.mpepil.com/> accessed 11 November 2014.

[108] Giegerich (n 51) para 47.

[109] AD McNair, 'The General Principles of Law as Recognized by Civilized Nations' (1957) 33 British YBK IL 1, 16; Wittich (n 98) para 29; see however also for example M Sornarajah, *The International Law on Foreign Investment* (3rd edn, CUP 2010) 419 ('There is doubt as to whether the doctrine of acquired rights forms a part of international law at all.').

[110] See thereto already K Swan Sik, 'The Concept of Acquired Rights in International Law: A Survey' (1977) 24 Netherlands Intl L Rev 120, 140–41 ('The foregoing survey has shown that the term is used in so many different situations that it appears useless to try to achieve a generally applicable definition.'); as well as more recently for example Wittich (n 98) para 30 ('It is, however, far from clear under what conditions and requirements the doctrine of acquired rights indeed applies. Practice is too scarce and disparate as to allow to draw concrete and definite conclusions.').

[111] See, for example, *Case Concerning the Temple of Preah Vihear (Cambodia v Thailand)* (1962) ICJ Rep 6, 23 et seq; *Case Concerning the Land and Maritime Boundary between Cameroon and Nigeria (Cameroon v Nigeria)* (1998) ICJ Rep 275, 303 para 57; J Crawford, *Brownlie's Principles of Public International Law* (8th edn, OUP 2012) 420 et seq.

[112] See for example *Petrobart Limited v Kyrgyz Republic*, SCC Case No 126/2003, Award (29 March 2005) 66 et seq; *Eastern Sugar BV v Czech Republic*, UNCITRAL ad hoc Arbitration, SCC No 088/2004, Partial Award (27 March 2007) paras 140 et seq; *Government of the Province of East Kalimantan v PT Kaltim Prima Coal* et al, ICSID Case No ARB/07/3, Award (28 December 2009) paras 211 et seq; *Rachel S Grynberg* et al *v Grenada*, Award (10 December 2010) paras 7.1.1 et seq.

[113] Roberts (n 82) 214. See also for example T Cottier and JP Müller, 'Estoppel' in R Wolfrum (ed), *Max Planck Encyclopedia of Public International Law* (April 2007) para 1 <www.mpepil.com/> accessed 11 November 2014 ('In public international law, the doctrine of estoppel protects legitimate expectations of States induced by the conduct of another State.').

will not be overcome on the basis of convincing legal reasoning,[114] not the least in light of the fact that arbitration tribunals have already occasionally—albeit in the form of *obiter dicta* and without further argumentation—expressed the view that survival clauses indeed also apply to mutually agreed terminations intended by the contracting parties to have immediate effect.[115] In addition, other above mentioned legal bases such as the doctrine of abuse of rights or the relevance of human rights of foreign investors, whose application does not appear to be subject to comparable objections, might also validly not be given a light legal treatment in the present context.

cc) 'Starting all over again': on the past and present scope of application of termination clauses

Overall, there are apparently—as it is not infrequently the case—no easy answers to the rather complex legal questions arising from the termination of investment agreements by mutual consent of the parties with immediate effect. The respective discussions in the literature are in particular most recently clearly gaining momentum with as yet nothing even close to a consented perception in sight.[116] Nevertheless, it is submitted that appropriate attention also needs to be drawn to the fact that these undoubtedly interesting and challenging issues are in practice only of relevance if—and the preceding question is thus in fact whether—it can be established beyond reasonable doubt that provisions stipulating a minimum period of application and in particular also survival clauses do at all apply

---

[114] See in this connection for example the approach of an investment arbitration tribunal towards a kind of survival clause stipulated in the domestic foreign investment law of Kazakhstan in *Rumeli Telekom AS and Telsim Mobil Telekomikasyon Hizmetleri AS v Kazakhstan*, ICSID Case No ARB/05/16, Award (29 July 2008) para 335 ('Besides Article 6(1) [Foreign Investment Law], it is also well established in international law that a State may not take away accrued rights of a foreign investor by domestic legislation abrogating the law granting these rights. This is an application of the principles of good faith, estoppel *and venire factum proprium*.').

[115] See, for example, *Eastern Sugar BV v Czech Republic*, UNCITRAL ad hoc Arbitration, SCC No 088/2004, Partial Award (27 March 2007) para 175 ('The Arbitral Tribunal can only reject the Czech Republic's argument that the implied termination of the BIT through accession also terminated the continuing effect expressly guaranteed by Art. 13(3) of the BIT.'); *Walter Bau AG (In Liquidation) v Kingdom of Thailand*, UNCITRAL Arbitration, Award (1 July 2009) paras 9.5 and 9.69.

[116] The issue itself has already been raised, albeit without receiving further treatment, for example by Wälde (n 82) 16 ('it is not clear what the situation of an investor who invested on the basis of an existing BIT would be if both governments agreed to end the treaty, and even less clear what the impact of an agreed termination of the treaty would be on an ongoing case'); and Volterra (n 82) 220

> What happens if two State parties to an investment treaty decide to terminate the treaty with no continuing effect, and they make that agreement as between themselves, as of the moment they reach the agreement? Are there any continuing rights that accrue to the investor? It is hard to see how there would be.

For a subsequent more in-depth evaluation of the applicable legal framework see, for example, Voon and Mitchell (n 69) 523 et seq; Harrison (n 3) 941 et seq; TR Braun, *Ausprägungen der Globalisierung: Der Investor als partielles Subjekt im Internationalen Investitionsrecht* (Nomos 2012) 168 et seq; Lavopa, Barreiros, and Bruno (n 3) 881 et seq; Sourgens (n 69) 379 et seq; Voon, Mitchell, and Munro (n 66) 451 et seq; A Peters, *Jenseits der Menschenrechte* (Mohr Siebeck 2014) 288 et seq.

to situations of mutually agreed terminations of investment agreements in the first place.

Initially, a respective finding whether mutually agreed terminations of investment agreements with immediate effect are at all undertaken in disregard of applicable termination clauses depends most certainly on the specific wording of the treaty provisions at issue. And indeed, in particular some of the survival clauses to be found in current treaty practice are formulated in a way that suggests their applicability being confined to cases of unilateral denunciations. To mention but some examples, it has been rightly highlighted in the literature that article 14 (3) and (4) of the 1993 BIT between Australia and Hong Kong[117] as well as article 13 of the BIT between Hong Kong and New Zealand that entered into force on 5 August 1995,[118] but also among others the similarly phrased article 12(2) and (3) of the 2005 Hong Kong-Thailand BIT, article 16(1) and (2) of the 1993 BIT between Chile and Denmark, article 14(2) and (3) of the 1997 Hong Kong-Korea BIT as well as article 18(1) and (2) of the 1995 BIT between Denmark and India, are only concerned with terminations unilaterally undertaken by one of the contracting parties.[119] There appear to be—to the contrary—in current practice no investment agreements with termination clauses explicitly or at least otherwise incontrovertibly and thus beyond any doubt applying to terminations by mutual consent. Nevertheless, a considerable number of survival clauses such as for example article 12(3) of the 2004 BIT between Ethiopia and Germany[120] and in particular also provisions stipulating a minimum period of application are phrased in rather broad, encompassing terms that would, *prima facie* and based on a literal interpretation, indeed permit an understanding of their scope of application as including unilateral as well as mutually agreed terminations.[121]

---

[117] Article 14 of the Australia-Hong Kong BIT reads in its relevant parts

(3) Either Contracting Party may terminate this Agreement at any time after it has been in force for fifteen years by giving one year's written notice to the other Contracting Party. (4) Notwithstanding termination of this Agreement pursuant to paragraph (3) of this Article, the Agreement shall continue to be effective for a second and final period of fifteen years from the date of its termination in respect of investments made before the date of termination of this Agreement.

[118] Article 13 Hong Kong-New Zealand BIT

(1) This Agreement shall remain in force for a period of fifteen years and shall continue in force thereafter unless after the expiry of the initial period of fourteen years, either Contracting Party notifies in writing the other Contracting Party of its intention to terminate this Agreement. The notice of termination shall become effective one year after it has been received by the other Contracting Party. (2) In respect of investments made prior to the date when the notice of termination becomes effective, the provisions of Articles 1 to 12 shall remain in force for a further period of fifteen years from that date.

[119] See Voon and Mitchell (n 69) 526 and 528; Voon, Mitchell, and Munro (n 66) 466.

[120] Article 12 (3) Ethiopia–Germany BIT: '(3) In respect of investments made prior to the date of termination of this Treaty, the provisions of Articles 1 to 11 shall continue to be effective for a further period of fifteen years from the date of termination of this Treaty.'

[121] Generally on this perception see also Harrison (n 3) 946; Ripinsky (n 85) 620; Voon, Mitchell, and Munro (n 66) 466.

Despite their broad wording, however, an argument can be made—and is indeed suggested here—that also these last-mentioned class of termination clauses deserve in particular in light of the context of their emergence in treaty practice a more narrow interpretation in the sense of applying exclusively to unilateral denunciations of investment agreements. It has to be recalled in this connection that these provisions on termination and its consequences originally appeared in investment treaties that with regard their enforcement only provided for State-State dispute settlement.[122] Indeed, already the very first BIT concluded between Germany and Pakistan on 25 November 1959 stipulated in Article 14(2) an initial minimum period of application of ten years as well as in paragraph three of the same provision a broadly phrased survival clause.[123] These and many other 'older' termination clauses were included in the structural framework of investment agreements on the basis of the underlying assumption that—in the absence of treaty-based investor-State arbitration—the States parties themselves would decide whether to enforce or rely on them in arbitration proceedings. In light of this context, it becomes apparent that covered investors were not effectively protected against mutually agreed terminations with immediate effect, since it appears to be highly unlikely that a home State would have initiated arbitration proceedings in favour of its investors after the termination became effective. Even if a State party would have attempted to take recourse to such a remedy—which in fact never happened in practice—the respondent would have almost certainly succeeded with an objection raised on grounds of estoppel. Against this background, it can—in particular in the absence of respective statements to the contrary—very well be presumed that the contracting parties did originally never intend to understand the regulatory content of termination clauses, that they consented to include in investment treaties, as also providing for protection to covered investors against mutually agreed terminations with immediate effect.

Furthermore, it is submitted that no evidence exists suggesting that this original intention of respective parties to investment agreements was modified as a result of the subsequent incorporation of investor-State arbitration clauses in these treaties; a structural development that first materialized in the end of the 1960s[124] and became prevalent in treaty practice only since the late 1980s and early 1990s.[125] It

---

[122] See also already section II.a.
[123] Article 14 (3) of the 1959 Germany-Pakistan BIT: 'In respect of investments made prior to the date of expiry of the present Treaty, the provisions of Articles 1 to 13 shall continue to be effective for a further period of ten years from the date of expiry of the present Treaty.'
[124] The first BIT which included an unqualified state consent to investor-state arbitration was probably the investment agreement concluded between Chad and Italy on 11 June 1969. See thereto for example A Newcombe and L Paradell, *Law and Practice of Investment Treaties: Standards of Treatment* (Kluwer 2009) 45; S Hindelang, 'Study on Investor-State Dispute Settlement ("ISDS") and Alternatives of Dispute Resolution in International Investment Law' in EU Directorate-General for External Policies, *Investor-State Dispute Settlement (ISDS) Provisions in the EU's International Investment Agreements*, vol II (September 2014) 39, 48 Fn 29.
[125] See, for example, JW Yackee, 'Conceptual Difficulties in the Empirical Study of Bilateral Investment Treaties' (2008) 33 Brooklyn JIL 405, 433 ('strong BITs did not become a numerically significant phenomenon until the late 1980s and early 1990s'); Roberts (n 85) 3 Fn 4.

is noteworthy that until today there appears to be no known instances in the development of international investment law of a contracting State explicitly declaring that it considers for example survival clauses to be also applicable to mutually agreed terminations with immediate effect. Admittedly, the more recent treaty practice of some States, among them in particular the Czech Republic, aimed at what might be characterized as a kind of 'circumvention' of termination clauses could be at first sight considered as an implicit acknowledgement of a broader scope of application of survival clauses. However, a contextual understanding of the respective State practice as briefly discussed below[126] suggests that these approaches should rather be regarded as an attempt by some contracting parties to 'play safe' by engaging in a 'belts and suspenders' effort in light of the already mentioned *obiter dictum* of the Arbitral Tribunal in the case of *Eastern Sugar BV v Czech Republic*.[127] If one is willing to accept this reasoning, there is hardly any room for a convincing—and from the perspective of treaty interpretation in principle necessary[128]—assertion that the States and supranational parties to investment agreements with broadly phrased termination clauses intended to apply these provisions also to cases of termination by mutual consent. Rather, it seems considerably more reasonable to assume that the subsequent incorporation of investor-State arbitration into investment agreements, although most certainly aimed at providing covered foreign investors with a new international legal remedy in cases of a violation of what might validly regarded as their rights under the treaty at issue, was not at the same time expressing a new common will of the respective treaty parties to enlarge the original limited scope of application of termination clauses.[129]

This last-mentioned emphasis on the absence of evidence for a common will of the contracting parties to apply survival clauses also to cases of mutually agreed terminations furthermore already indicates that the approach argued for in this contribution is very far away from a simple and more or less blunt recourse to the

---

[126] See section V.b.

[127] See *Eastern Sugar BV v Czech Republic*, UNCITRAL ad hoc Arbitration, SCC No 088/2004, Partial Award (27 March 2007) para 175. On this possibility see also already LE Peterson, 'Czech Republic Terminates Investment Treaties in such a Way as to Cast Doubt on Residual Legal Protection for Existing Investments' *Investment Arbitration Reporter* (1 February 2011): 'Or were the governments simply engaging in a "belts and suspenders" effort so as to foreclose any possibility that a future arbitral tribunal might infer some residual legal protections even in cases of mutual terminations?'

[128] See thereto for example *Daimler Financial Services AG v Argentine Republic*, ICSID Case No ARB/05/1, Award (22 August 2012) paras 161 et seq, with further references. See also for an admittedly quite far reaching proposition in this regard *Plama Consortium Ltd v Bulgaria*, ICSID Case No ARB/03/24, Decision on Jurisdiction (8 February 2005) para 223 an MFN provision in a basic treaty does not incorporate by reference dispute settlement provisions in whole or in part set forth in another treaty, unless the MFN provision in the basic treaty *leaves no doubt that the Contracting Parties intended to incorporate them*') (emphasis added).

[129] For a related argumentation with regard to the scope of application of so-called 'umbrella clauses' as stipulated in investment agreements see already TW Wälde, 'The "Umbrella" Clause in Investment Arbitration—A Comment on Original Intentions and Recent Cases' (2005) 6 J World Inv & Trade 183, 188 et seq. See, however, also for a critical evaluation of the respective argumentation HJ Schramke, 'Umbrella Clauses in bilateralen Investitionsschutzabkommen' (2006) 4 German Arb J 249, 257; K Meschede, *Die Schutzwirkung von umbrella clauses für Investor-Staat-Verträge* (Nomos 2014) 100 et seq.

principle *in dubio mitius*. Although still as of today occasionally labeled as 'widely recognized in international law',[130] it has already quite frequently—and in principle rightly—been pointed out that the value of this means of interpretation and its underlying idea that treaty provisions are to be interpreted in favour of State sovereignty are becoming increasingly questionable, especially as far as treaties aimed at the protection of non-State actors are concerned.[131] However, it is equally obvious—and fortunately ever more recognized in current arbitral practice—that investment treaties are also not to be interpreted exclusively in favour of optimal investor protection based on more or less abstract policy considerations,[132] an approach that if adopted in the present context would undoubtedly favour an encompassing understanding of broadly phrased survival clauses. Rather, in the absence of a 'principle of extensive and restrictive interpretation'[133] a sober and adequate clarification has to consider one of the primary purposes pursued by investment agreements, the protection and promotion of foreign investors, within the treaty framework agreed upon by—and thus acceptable to—the contracting States; and in this regard first and foremost seek to identify the intention of the parties based on the text of the agreement at issue.[134]

In addition to the general interpretative approach as suggested and applied here and in fact closely connected to it, there appear to be at least two further arguments

---

[130] WTO, *EC—Measures Concerning Meat and Meat Products (Hormones), Report of the Appellate Body* (16 January 1998) WT/DS26 and DS48/AB/R, para 165 fn 154. See, however, already considerably more cautious WTO, *China—Measures Affecting Trading Rights and Distribution Services for Certain Publications and Audiovisual Entertainment Products*, WT/DS363/AB/R, para 11; as well as for example the qualifications made by Jennings and Watts (n 99) 1278.

[131] See, for example, R Gardiner, *Treaty Interpretation* (OUP 2008) 349 et seq; Crawford (n 111) 379 ('question-begging'); O Dörr, 'Article 31' in O Dörr and K Schmalenbach (eds), *Vienna Convention on the Law of Treaties* (Springer 2012) para 34. See also specifically in the investment context *The Loewen Group* et al *v USA*, ICSID Case No ARB(AF)/98/3, Decision on Hearing of Respondent's Objection to Competence and Jurisdiction (5 January 2001) para 51; *Aguas del Tunari SA v Bolivia*, ICSID Case No ARB/02/3, Decision on Respondent's Objections to Jurisdiction (21 October 2005) para 91; *ICS Inspection and Control Services Limited v United Kingdom*, PCA Case No 2010-9 (UNCITRAL Rules), Award on Jurisdiction (10 February 2012) para 282 ('Any general rule of restrictive treaty interpretation is plainly in conflict with the VCLT and customary international law.'); A Reinisch, 'The Impact of International Law on IIA Interpretation' in A de Mestral and C Lévesque (eds), *Improving International Investment Agreements* (Routledge 2013) 323, 330 et seq.

[132] See for example *Renta 4 SVSA* et al *v Russia*, Arbitration Institute of the Stockholm Chamber of Commerce, Award on Preliminary Objections to Jurisdiction (20 March 2009) para 93; *ICS Inspection and Control Services Limited v. United Kingdom*, PCA Case No 2010-9 (UNCITRAL Rules), Award on Jurisdiction (10 February 2012) para 277; *Daimler Financial Services AG v Argentine Republic*, ICSID Case No ARB/05/1, Award (22 August 2012) para 164.

[133] *Mondev International Ltd v USA*, ICSID Case No ARB(AF)/99/2, Award (11 October 2002) para 43.

[134] On this approach see, for example, *Telenor Mobile Communications AS v Hungary*, ICSID Case No ARB/04/15, Award (13 September 2006) para 95; *ICS Inspection and Control Services Limited v United Kingdom*, PCA Case No 2010-9 (UNCITRAL Rules), Award on Jurisdiction (10 February 2012) para 277; *Daimler Financial Services AG v Argentine Republic*, ICSID Case No ARB/05/1, Award (22 August 2012) paras 161 et seq. Generally on the presence of subject and object elements in the practice of investment treaty arbitration see for example A Mills, 'The Balancing (and Unbalancing?) of Interests in International Investment Law and Arbitration' in Z Douglas, J Pauwelyn, and JE Viñuales (eds), *The Foundations of International Investment Law* (OUP 2014) 437, 457 et seq, with further references.

that support an understanding of broadly phrased termination clauses as being only concerned with unilateral denunciations of investment agreements. Both are based on the already above mentioned—and initially only factual—observation that States are in their investment treaty practice increasingly applying mutually agreed terminations with immediate effect. When considering the conformity of this practice with their respective treaty obligations (and thereby concretizing the content of these legal commitments themselves), recourse should rightly also be taken to the concept of presumption of legality. The—rebuttable—presumption that States generally intend to perform all of their international legal obligations and that consequently their conduct is presumed to comply with applicable legal requirements finds in principle recognition in public international law[135] and seems to be even less objectionable in the case of joint actions by the parties. Applying this presumption of legality in the present context might serve as an additional indication that the respective contracting parties had never intended to extend the scope of application of these clauses to terminations by mutual consent.

Furthermore, and this concerns the second possible line of argumentation in this regard, the currently increasing practice of States to terminate their investment treaty with immediate effect can also be considered as subsequent practice to be taken into account when interpreting the regulatory content of the respective (termination) provisions under article 31(3)(b) VCLT.[136] In this regard, it is particularly noteworthy that the respective States and supranational organizations that have terminated their treaties with immediate effect as the result of a replacement by a new investment agreement have abstained from specifying the wording of provisions stipulating minimum periods of application und survival clauses in these new treaties. To mention but a few examples, article X.08(2) of the chapter on final provisions of CETA between Canada and the EU, article 13(1) and (5) of the BIT between Bangladesh and Turkey of 12 April 2012 as well as article 10.19 of the free trade agreement between Peru and Singapore that entered into force on 1 August 2009 again provide for rather broadly phrased termination clauses.

Indeed, it has been already occasionally argued for in the recent literature that—in order to avoid respective legal uncertainties for the future—the contracting parties would be well advised to specify the wording in particular of the survival clauses enshrined in their newly concluded investment agreements.[137]

---

[135] See WTO, *EC—Measures Concerning Meat and Meat Products (Hormones), Original Complaint by the United States, Decision by the Arbitrators* (12 July 1999) WT/DS26/ARB, para 9 ('WTO Members, as sovereign entities, can be *presumed* to act in conformity with their WTO obligations') (emphasis in the original); as well as for example J-M Grossen, *Les Présomptions en Droit International Public* (Delachaux et Niestlé 1954) 60 et seq; J Pauwelyn, *Conflict of Norms in Public International Law* (CUP 2003) 240 et seq; K Nowrot, 'Standard of Review as a Procedural Issue in WTO Dispute Settlement: Of Balancing Acts and Presumptions of Legality' in J Delbrück and others (eds), *Aus Kiel in die Welt: Kiel's Contribution to International Law—Essays in Honour of the 100th Anniversary of the Walther Schücking Institute for International Law* (Duncker & Humblot 2014) 607, 628 et seq.
[136] Generally on this means of interpretation see, for example, Gardiner (n 131) 225 et seq; Dörr (n 131) paras 76 et seq, each with numerous further references.
[137] See for example Ripinsky (n 85) 620 ('To avoid uncertainties, the Parties would be well advised to address this issue through explicit wording.').

Nevertheless, the 'nonchalant reluctance' displayed by the contracting parties in this regard—and in particular bearing in mind that the same countries are frequently engaging in a quite comprehensive specification process concerning substantive protection standards and dispute settlement clauses on the occasion of their newly negotiated investment agreements—can be qualified as a quite clear sign that the parties continue to consider these terminations clauses to be inapplicable to cases of mutually agreed terminations.

If one thus accepts these lines of reasoning, it becomes apparent that also the broadly phrased provisions stipulating minimum periods of application and provide for survival clauses are with regard to their scope of application not only unconcerned with certain unilateral termination based on general rules of the law of treaties[138] but also generally do not cover terminations based on the mutual consent of the contracting parties.

V. 'Renegotiation without (simultaneous) Termination': Treaty Amendments and Suspensions in Light of Termination Clauses

Again largely inspired by developments in recent investment treaty practice, a further analytical dimension worth briefly considering also in the present context concerns the respective legal issues arising from other types of conduct of contracting parties; categories of joint actions having in common that they are not intended to terminate the agreement but rather aimed at modifying and specifying the regulatory content of individual provisions or—in the case of suspensions—at temporarily deactivating the operation of the whole treaty regime[139] as a result of a renegotiation of their legal investment relationship.

a) 'Ordinary' treaty amendments and authoritative interpretations

Although BITs traditionally only seldom contained amendment clauses and respective revisions are—contrary to the already mentioned adoption of new renegotiated agreements between the parties—still a comparatively rare phenomenon in investment treaty practice,[140] it is, without doubt, in principle well-recognized under general public international law and finds its manifestation for example in

---

[138] See thereto already section III.

[139] Generally on the consequences of a suspension of a treaty as well as its distinction from terminations see article 72 VCLT; and for example I Cameron, 'Treaties, Suspension' in R Wolfrum (ed), *Max Planck Encyclopedia of Public International Law* (February 2007) para 1 <www.mpepil.com/> accessed 11 November 2014; T Giegerich 'Article 57' in O Dörr and K Schmalenbach (eds), *Vienna Convention on the Law of Treaties* (Springer 2012) para 8; J Klabbers, *International Law* (CUP 2013) 62.

[140] For a respective example see the Protocol between the Governments of the United States and of Panama Amending the 1982 Treaty concerning the Treatment and Protection of Investments of 1 June 2000, available under: <www.state.gov/documents/organization/210527.pdf> accessed on 14 November 2014.

the first sentence of article 39 VCLT that the contracting parties retain the right to jointly agree to amend treaties even in the absence of explicit stipulations in the agreement at issue. Furthermore, there are some indications that investment agreements are more recently increasingly providing for express amendment clauses, as for example evidenced by article 14(3) of the BIT between Gabon and Turkey of 18 July 2012, article 42 of the BIT signed by Canada and Nigeria on 6 May 2014 and article 52(3) of the respective treaty that entered into force between Benin and Canada on 12 May 2014.

Basically, the same findings also apply to interpretative statements as constituting another category of relevant joint actions by the contracting parties of investment agreements. Despite the fact that treaty parties enjoy the competence to jointly issue authoritative interpretations on the proper reading of respective provisions even in cases where the text of the agreement in question remains silent on this issue,[141] States have so far overall displayed a rather reluctant attitude towards actively exercising their interpretative powers in the realm of investment agreements.[142] That said, there are also certain signs that this procedural approach is in particular more recently gaining ground in investment treaty practice. Among the oldest and best-known examples is the mechanism provided for by the articles 2001(2)(c) NAFTA in connection with 1131(2) NAFTA by which the NAFTA Free Trade Commission is entitled to adopt interpretative statements that are binding on respective investment arbitration tribunals; a competence occasionally taken recourse to in the previous decade and—by and large—accepted as authoritative in arbitral practice.[143] Another more recent example is article 40(3) of the 2009 ASEAN Comprehensive Investment Agreement, stipulating that a 'joint decision of the Member States, declaring their interpretation of a provision of this Agreement shall be binding on a tribunal, and any decision or award issued by a tribunal must be consistent with that joint decision'. Additional manifestations of this regulatory approach in current investment treaty practice, to mention but a few, include article 30(3) of the 2008 BIT between Rwanda and the United States, article 15.21(2) of the free trade agreement signed by Singapore and the United States on 6 May 2003, as well as article 32(1) of the Canada–Kuwait BIT that entered into force on 19 February 2014.

---

[141] See article 31(3)(a) and (b) VCLT; as well as, for example, *Case Concerning Kasikili/Sedudu Island (Botswana v Namibia)* (1999) ICJ Rep 1045, 1075 et seq; Jennings and Watts (n 99) 1268 ('Such authentic interpretations given by the parties override general rules of interpretation'); Dörr (n 131) para 20; Nowrot (n 6) 640 et seq.

[142] On this perception see for example UNCTAD, Interpretation of IIAs: What States Can Do, IIA Issues Note No 3, December 2011, 3.

[143] See, for example, *ADF Group Inc v United States*, ICSID Case No ARB(AF)/00/1, Award (9 January 2003) para 177 ('No more authentic and authoritative source of instruction on what the Parties intended to convey in a particular provision of NAFTA, is possible.'); *Waste Management v Mexico*, ICSID Case No ARB(AF)/00/3, Award (30 April 2004) paras 90 et seq; *Merrill & Ring Forestry v Canada*, UNCITRAL Arbitration, Award (31 March 2010) paras 189 et seq; see, however, also for example the concerns voiced by the arbitration tribunal in *Pope & Talbot Inc v Canada*, UNCITRAL Arbitration, Award in Respect of Damages (31 May 2002) paras 43 et seq.

While there exists from a theoretical legal perspective a reasonably clear distinction between amendments to an agreement and the processes of treaty interpretation, it is an equally well-known fact that it can be in practice rather difficult to differentiate between the normative effectives of an authoritative interpretation by the parties on the one side and 'real' treaty amendments in the narrow sense of the meaning on the other side.[144] Consequently, it seems warranted to also list authoritative treaty interpretation among the joint regulatory approaches taken recourse to by the contracting parties in the course—or as a consequence—of what is classified here as 'renegotiation without (simultaneous) termination' of investment agreements. This appears to be even more so justified in the present context because some of the above mentioned legal issues currently discussed with regard to terminations of investment agreements by mutual consent with immediate effect, among them the doctrine of abuse of rights, the concept of estoppel as well as considerations of legal certainty and legitimate expectations, are indeed quite similar to the ones raised already for a number of years in connection with joint interpretative statements. Whereas the competence to issue subsequent authoritative interpretations most certainly constitutes a suitable and effective approach to enhance the interpretative weight to be accorded to the promotion of sustainability interests in investor-State arbitration proceedings, it is in particular the dual role of States and supranational organizations as treaty parties and actual or at least potential respondents in investment arbitration proceedings that not infrequently gives rise to concerns with regard to issues of procedural fairness, especially if treaty parties attempt to influence the litigation of ongoing cases to their benefit on the basis of interpretative statements to which retrospective effect is attributed.[145]

A more in-depth evaluation of the potential relevance of the respective legal principles in connection with authoritative interpretation is, however, beyond the scope of this contribution. Already the wording of the termination clauses as stipulated in most investment agreements indicates that these provisions are in principle not concerned with interpretative statements and treaty amendments.[146] Despite this in general more narrow scope of application of termination clauses, at least a word of caution seems appropriate also in the present context with regard to potential legal limits to the competence of contracting parties to adopt authoritative interpretations: It might be too easy to simply deduce from the above-made finding that the parties are in general entitled to jointly terminate their investment

---

[144] With regard to this perception see also, for example, A Chayes and AH Chayes, *The New Sovereignty* (Harvard University Press 1995) 209; Dahm, Delbrück, and Wolfrum (n 61) 674; Roberts (n 82) 200 et seq.

[145] On the respective concerns see for example C Schreuer, 'Diversity and Harmonization of Treaty Interpretation in Investment Arbitration' in M Fitzmaurice, O Elias, and P Merkouris (eds), *Treaty Interpretation and the Vienna Convention on the Law of Treaties: 30 Years On* (Nijhoff 2010) 129, 148 ('It is obvious that a mechanism whereby a party to a dispute is able to influence the outcome of judicial proceedings, by issuing official interpretation to the detriment of the other party, is incompatible with principles of fair procedure and is hence undesirable.'); as well as Roberts (n 82) 179 et seq, with numerous further references.

[146] See thereto also already Voon and Mitchell (n 69) 526; Lavopa, Barreiros, and Bruno (n 3) 882 et seq.

agreement at any time with immediate effect,[147] that they also enjoy—based on a kind of *argumentum a maiore ad minus*[148]—a legally unconstrained power to issue interpretative statements.

b) Treaty practice aimed at 'circumventing' termination clauses

In addition, from the broader realm of parties' conduct belonging to the category of 'renegotiation without (simultaneous) termination', two specific types of related regulatory approaches that have gained some prominence in recent investment treaty practice and potentially bear a closer relationship to termination clauses are worth mentioning here. The first method of what could be labeled as 'treaty practice aimed at "circumventing" termination clauses' has received particular attention in connection with the strategy adopted by the Czech Republic since 2008 with the aim to terminate its what are now intra-EU BITs concluded with other member States already prior to its accession to the EU.[149] According to this 'two-step' approach, implemented by the Czech Republic *inter alia* in the mutually agreed BIT termination processes with Denmark, Italy, Malta and Slovenia, the parties first agree to amend the treaty so that the respective survival clause no longer applies, and, in a second step, terminate the amended agreement with immediate effect.[150] This practice, however, is not confined to the Czech Republic and its treaty partners in the form of other EU member States. A quite similar strategy has been employed for example in the Australia-Chile Free Trade Agreement that entered into force on 6 March 2009. Annex 10-E of the agreement stipulates in its paragraph 4 a respective amendment to the survival clause enshrined in Article 12 of the BIT concluded between the two countries in July 1996 and in its paragraph 1 the termination of the said investment treaty 'on the date of entry into force of the present Agreement'.

A second notable approach in investment treaty practice consists in the mutually agreed temporary suspension, albeit for an unlimited period of time, of BITs in particular as a consequence and in the context of regional trade agreements concluded between the parties. This strategy finds its manifestation in article 27 of the investment agreement signed between the Republic of Korea, Iceland, Liechtenstein and Switzerland on 15 December 2005, stipulating that

[a]s long as it is in force or remains effective, this Agreement replaces and suspends the "Agreement between the Government of the Swiss Confederation and the Government of the Republic of Korea concerning the Encouragement and Reciprocal Protection of Investments" of 7 April 1971.

---

[147] See section IV.b.cc.
[148] Generally on the applicability of this interpretative approach in public international law see, for example, Dahm, Delbrück, and Wolfrum (n 61) 648.
[149] Generally on the issue of intra-EU BITs see already section II.c.
[150] See thereto for example Peterson (n 127); Fecák (n 43) 255 et seq; L Johnson and L Sachs, 'International Investment Agreements, 2011–2012: A Review of Trends and New Approaches' in AK Bjorklund (ed), *Yearbook on International Investment Law & Policy 2012-2013* (OUP 2014) 219, 242 Fn 142.

Other examples include article 845 of the 2008 Canada-Peru Free Trade Agreement as well as Article 9.38 of the respective agreement between Canada and Panama that entered into force on 1 April 2013. Although it is in principle generally recognized, as for example also expressed by article 57(b) VCLT, that the contracting parties retain the power to suspend the operation of a treaty by consent at any time, such an approach could nevertheless in the present context—and in particular from the perspective of affected investors—also give rise to questions as to the consequences for the application of respective survival clauses.

And indeed, both of these different regulatory strategies have in common, that they at least result in—or, in the case of the 'two step' approach taken recourse to by the Czech Republic and other countries, are even primarily aimed at—a 'neutralization' of the prolonging normative effects of termination provisions included in investment agreements. To be sure, and in order to avoid any possible misunderstandings as to the position argued for in this contribution, if one is willing to follow the arguments as advanced above in favour of a narrower understanding of termination clauses in the sense of their scope of application being confined to cases of unilateral denunciations of investment agreements and thus considers the State practice at issue merely as an attempt by some contracting parties to 'play safe',[151] neither deleting survival clauses on the basis of treaty amendments nor the mutually agreed suspension of investment treaties do in fact pose any noteworthy challenges from a legal perspective. However, in case one is not—and the present author is surely realistic enough to take into account that some readers might not be—entirely convinced by the reasoning leading to the interpretative position adhered to here, it should at least be mentioned (albeit not further analysed) also in the present contribution that a respective broader understanding of termination clauses as covering mutually agreed terminations might legitimately trigger a discussion whether in particular survival clauses should—to a certain extent beyond their ordinary meaning but in light of the object and purpose of these provisions—be interpreted as applying not only to terminations in the narrow sense of the meaning but also to some fundamental renegotiations resulting in certain amendments or suspensions of investment agreements.

VI. Conclusion

The last-mentioned suggestion might again be regarded as another *pars pro toto* for the central perception underlying the present contribution, namely the observation that the currently visible paradigmatic shift in international investment law is not only characterized by intensified efforts to strengthen and optimize the impact of this legal regime on the realization of sustainable development objectives.[152] Rather, the respective implementation processes, largely executed on the basis of renegotiations and terminations of 'first generation' and 'second generation'

---

[151] See pt. IV.b.cc.   [152] See thereto already sections I and II.

investment agreements,[153] first and foremost also results in the emerging dogmatic prominence as well as practical relevance of until recently clearly under-analysed normative issues concerning the underlying public international law framework governing these regulatory and policy approaches. Thereby, as already indicated above,[154] these normative issues arising from currently noticeable phenomena in investment treaty practice on the termination, suspension and amendment of investment agreements are not merely technical matters but give rise to quite fundamental and challenging questions about what competences the contracting (governmental) parties in fact retain after entering into treaties aimed at the protection of non-governmental actors such as private foreign investors; questions still in need to be appropriate resolved.

Viewed from an overarching research perspective, it seems somehow reassuring for scholars that the field of international investment law, although currently and in fact already for a number of years receiving considerable academic attention, still provides for numerous novel or at least so far largely neglected normative aspects and is thus also at present quite far from comprehensively analytically measured. Prominently among these only recently identified—and until now far from exhaustively evaluated—challenges are the legal questions arising in connection with the termination and renegotiation of investment agreements in light of current treaty practice. The present article is meant to be a small contribution to the discussion on this evolving issue.

---

[153] On these different generations of investment agreements see section II.a.
[154] See section IV.b.aa.

XI

The Emergence of a New Approach to Investment Protection in South Africa

Sean Woolfrey

I. Introduction

In recent years, debate around the impact of bilateral investment treaties (BITs) and the international investment arbitration regime on domestic policy space and sustainable development has intensified.[1] Growing numbers of international investment disputes[2] and the increasing prevalence of disputes against industrialized countries, such as *Vattenfall v Germany*,[3] as well as disputes over sensitive policy issues such as public health legislation,[4] have prompted a number of countries to review their use of BITs. The United States and Canada have recently made changes to their model BITs,[5] India is currently reviewing its BITs,[6] and both Bolivia and Venezuela have already terminated at least one BIT.[7]

---

[1] Many aspects of this debate are addressed in United Nations Conference on Trade and Development (UNCTAD), *World Investment Report 2012: Towards a New Generation of Investment Policies* (United Nations 2012).

[2] A record fifty-eight new investor–State disputes were filed in 2012. See UNCTAD, 'Recent Issues in Investor-State Dispute Settlement (ISDS)' *IIA Issues Note No 1* (May 2013) <http://unctad.org/en/PublicationsLibrary/webdiaepcb2013d3_en.pdf> accessed 20 June 2014.

[3] *Vattenfall AB and others v Federal Republic of Germany*, ICSID Case No ARB/12/12.

[4] Such as Phillip Morris Asia's claim against Australia (under the Australia–Hong Kong BIT) over the Australian Government's introduction of a plain-packaging law for cigarettes. See W Genova, 'Philip Morris Files Arbitration Case Vs. Australia Over Plain-Packaging Law' *International Business Times* (22 November 2011) <http://au.ibtimes.com/articles/253710/20111122/philip-morris-asia-challenges-australia-s-plan.htm#.U0qnAvmSySo> accessed 3 July 2014.

[5] United States Department of State, 'United States Concludes Review of Model Bilateral Investment Treaty' (20 April 2012) <www.state.gov/r/pa/prs/ps/2012/04/188198.htm> accessed 1 July 2014; C Titi, 'The Evolving BIT: A Commentary on Canada's Model Agreement' *Investment Treaty News* (26 June 2013) <www.iisd.org/itn/2013/06/26/the-evolving-bit-a-commentary-on-canadas-model-agreement/> accessed 1 July 2014.

[6] 'India reviewing its 83 bilateral investment pacts: Anand Sharma', *The Economic Times* (22 February 2014) <http://articles.economictimes.indiatimes.com/2014-02-22/news/47581787_1_investment-protection-bilateral-treaties-investment-promotion> accessed 2 July 2014.

[7] MJ Luque Macias, 'Current Approaches to the International Investment Regime in South America' in C Herrmann, M Krajewski, and JP Terhechte (eds), *European Yearbook of International Economic Law 2014* (Springer 2013).

Of all the countries currently exploring new approaches to investment protection, South Africa provides one of the most interesting case studies. Having undertaken a comprehensive review of its BITs and their impact on policymaking in the country, the South African Government has recently begun terminating its 'first generation' BITs—those treaties signed in the immediate post-apartheid period—and has indicated that it will refrain from entering into any new BITs in the future, except where there are 'compelling economic reasons to do so'.[8] Instead, the Government is developing legislation which aims to offer foreign (and local) investors BIT-type protection, but which also aims to ensure that the Government's capacity to regulate in the public interest is adequately safeguarded.

This chapter describes the evolution of South Africa's investment protection regime and critically assesses the new approach being adopted in the country. It provides context to the South African Government's actions by briefly discussing South Africa's experience with BITs and international investment arbitration, as well as the main findings of the Government's review of the country's BITs. It then describes the contours of the new approach to investment protection emerging in South Africa by examining the content of the Government's draft Promotion and Protection of Investment Bill as well as that of the Model BIT Template recently adopted by the Member States of the Southern African Development Community, as this gives an indication of the likely content of the model BIT being developed by the South African Government, which itself could become an important element of South Africa's dual approach to investment protection in the future.

The chapter argues that while the standards of protection contained in the draft Promotion and Protection of Investment Bill—and likely to be encapsulated in South Africa's model BIT—are consistent with the goal of ensuring greater regulatory space for the South African Government to pursue policies deemed in the public interest, including policies to redress the race-based economic inequality bequeathed by apartheid, they fall somewhat short of the standards of protection found in customary international law and contained in South Africa's existing BITs. It suggests also that the South African Government may be seeking to adopt a dual approach to investment protection, one which involves the conclusion of new generation BITs with countries in which South African companies are significant investors, but relies on domestic legislation to regulate investment flows from countries that are major exporters of capital to South Africa.

II. South Africa and BITs

Following the demise of apartheid and the African National Congress' victory in the general election of 1994, South Africa, which had no prior history of using

---

[8] 'Remarks by Dr Rob Davies at the Centre for Conflict Studies Public Dialogue on "South Africa, Africa and International Investment Agreements"', Cape Town, 17 February 2014 (Remarks by Dr Rob Davies at the CCS) <www.tralac.org/wp-content/blogs.dir/12/files/2014/02/Speech-by-Min-Davies-on-IIAS-CCR-17-Feb-2014.pdf> accessed 30 June 2014.

Table 1: South Africa's First Generation BITs with European Partners

Partner country	Date of signature	Entry into force
United Kingdom	20 September 1994	27 May 1998
Netherlands	9 May 1995	1 May 1999
Switzerland	27 June 1995	30 November 1997
Germany	11 September 1995	10 April 1998
France	11 October 1995	22 June 1997
Denmark	22 February 1996	23 April 1997
Austria	28 November 1996	30 November 1997
Italy	9 June 1997	16 March 1999
Sweden	25 May 1998	–
Belgo–Luxembourg Economic Union	14 August 1998	14 March 2003
Finland	14 September 1998	–
Spain	30 September 1998	23 December 1999
Greece	19 November 1998	6 September 2001
Czech Republic	14 December 1998	–

Source: South African Treaty Section, Office of the Chief State Law Adviser, Department of International Relations and Cooperation (DIRCO) of the Republic of South Africa

BITs, embarked on a series of BIT negotiations with major trading partners. There was significant uncertainty around the trajectory of South Africa's economic policy at this time, and signing BITs provided a way for the country to assure foreign investors that their investments would be secure under the new regime.[9] The signing of these treaties was also viewed as 'an important diplomatic signal confirming South Africa's re-entry to the international community' after years of isolation under apartheid.[10] Consequently, between September 1994 and December 1998, South Africa signed fourteen BITs with European countries (See Table 1). South Africa also negotiated a number of BITs with African, Asian, and Latin American countries during this period (and in later years), but the vast majority of these never entered into force.[11]

South Africa's first generation BITs

South Africa's first generation BITs follow the format of the Organisation for Economic Cooperation and Development (OECD) model and are very similar

---

[9] Many of South Africa's BIT negotiations were initiated before the enactment of the Constitution of the Republic of South Africa, 1996, which provides safeguards for the protection of private property and investment.

[10] 'BITs 'not decisive in attracting investment', says South Africa' *TWN Info Service on WTO and Trade Issues* (8 October 2012) <www.twnside.org.sg/title2/wto.info/2012/twninfo121001.htm> accessed 21 June 2014.

[11] South Africa has signed thirty-five BITs with non-European countries to date, but only seven have entered into force. These are South Africa's BITs with Argentina, China, Cuba, Korea, Mauritius, Nigeria, and Zimbabwe.

to one another in scope and content.¹² They focus almost exclusively on protecting the economic interests of investors against political risk, and, in line with standard principles of customary international law, guarantee covered investors *inter alia* national and most favoured nation (MFN) treatment, fair and equitable treatment, and free repatriation of funds. They also prohibit the expropriation or nationalization of investments, as well as measures having equivalent effect, except where this is carried out for a public purpose, on a non-discriminatory basis, under due process of law and against the payment of fair market value compensation. In addition, these treaties guarantee covered investors the right to take disputes against the contracting parties to arbitration under the arbitration rules of the International Centre for the Settlement of Investment Disputes (ICSID) or the United Nations Commission on International Trade Law (UNCITRAL).

The South African Government has since lamented that the officials responsible for negotiating the country's first generation BITs did not fully appreciate the 'risks posed by such treaties' for future policymaking in South Africa,¹³ and that, as a result, these treaties do not include 'the necessary safeguards to preserve flexibility in a number of critical policy areas'.¹⁴ Some of South Africa's more recent BITs make provision for limited exceptions to national treatment where domestic laws and measures grant preferences aimed at uplifting historically disadvantaged persons and communities. For example, the South Africa–Tanzania BIT,¹⁵ signed in 2005, states that the provisions on national treatment contained in the BIT:

[S]hall not be construed so as to oblige one Party to extend to the investors of the other Party the benefit of any treatment, preference or privilege resulting from...any law or other measure the purpose of which is to promote the achievement of equality in its territory, or designed to protect or advance persons, or categories of persons, disadvantaged by unfair discrimination in its territory.¹⁶

By contrast, South Africa's first generation BITs make no provision for exceptions to national treatment. Significantly, they do not provide for exceptions relating to the South African Government's Black Economic Empowerment (BEE) programme, which aims to redress the inequities of apartheid by promoting greater participation by black South Africans in the management, ownership, and control of commercial enterprises in South Africa.¹⁷ Under the BEE programme, the

---

¹² Republic of South Africa, 'Bilateral Investment Treaty Policy Framework Review: Government Position Paper' (2009) 19 <www.pmg.org.za/files/docs/090626trade-bi-lateralpolicy.pdf> accessed 28 June 2014.
¹³ ibid 5.   ¹⁴ ibid.
¹⁵ Agreement Between the Republic of South Africa and the Government of the United Republic of Tanzania for the Promotion and Reciprocal Protection of Investments (signed 22 September 2005).
¹⁶ ibid, Art 3(4)(c).
¹⁷ According to the Broad-Based Black Economic Empowerment Act 53 of 2003, which established a legislative framework for the promotion of BEE, the specific objectives of the BEE programme

Government has included a range of BEE provisions in South African legislation, including provisions requiring the transfer of certain percentages of enterprise ownership to black South Africans. The fact that South Africa's first generation BITs fail to address BEE-related policy measures has contributed to at least one investment claim against South Africa.[18]

III. South Africa Faces International Investment Arbitration under its BITs

South Africa has faced at least two claims under its BITs.[19] In 2001, a Swiss investor pursued arbitration against South Africa under the terms of the country's BIT with Switzerland.[20] The investor claimed that the South African police had ignored a spate of 'incursions, thefts and vandalism' perpetrated against a property bought by the investor for development into a game lodge and conference centre, and that the investment was subjected to expropriation due to the 'cumulative destruction' inflicted on the property or, alternatively, due to a domestic land-claims process under which a number of local residents were 'seeking all or parts of the property in question'.[21] While the expropriation claim was dismissed by the arbitration Tribunal, South Africa was found to have breached its obligation to provide 'full protection and security' to foreign investments.[22] Due to the confidential nature of the case, the arbitration proceedings and resulting award received little attention in the South African media.[23]

The *Foresti* case

One case which did receive attention in the South African media, however, was *Foresti v South Africa*.[24] The *Foresti* case began in November 2006, when several Italian nationals and a Luxembourg-based corporation ('the claimants') registered

---

are to promote the meaningful participation of black people in the South African economy, achieve greater levels of black management, ownership, and control of enterprises and productive assets, develop human resources and skills and achieve equitable representation in all occupational categories and levels in the workforce. For the purposes of BEE, 'black' refers to all racial categories discriminated against under apartheid.

[18] LE Peterson, *Bilateral Investment Treaties—Implication for Sustainable Development and Options for Regulation: FES Conference Report* (Friedrich Ebert Stiftung June 2007) 5 <www.fes-globalization.org/publications/ConferenceReports/FES%20CR%20Berlin_Peterson.pdf> accessed 27 June 2014.

[19] Given the confidential nature of some international investment arbitration proceedings, it is possible that additional claims have been brought against South Africa without having been made public.

[20] The arbitration proceedings were conducted under UNCITRAL arbitration rules, and the arbitration ruling remains confidential. For more on the dispute, see LE Peterson, 'Swiss investor prevailed in 2003 in confidential BIT arbitration over South Africa land dispute' (2008) *Investment Arbitration Reporter* 1(13) <www.iareporter.com/downloads/20100107_15> accessed 29 June 2014.

[21] ibid.   [22] ibid.   [23] ibid.

[24] *Piero Foresti, Laura de Carli and others v Republic of South Africa*, ICSID Case No ARB(AF)/07/1, Award (4 August 2010).

a request for arbitration against South Africa with ICSID.²⁵ The claimants, who at the time were involved in the South African granite mining and processing industry, registered a claim in January 2007 alleging that certain provisions in South Africa's Minerals and Petroleum Resources Development Act 28 of 2002 (MPRDA) effectively expropriated their mineral rights and violated the terms of South Africa's BITs with Italy and the Belgo-Luxembourg Economic Union.²⁶

The MPRDA, which, among other things aims to 'substantially and meaningfully expand opportunities for historically disadvantaged persons...to enter the mineral and petroleum industries and to benefit from the exploitation of the nation's mineral and petroleum resources',²⁷ established a new mineral rights regime in South Africa. Previously under South African law, private enterprises that owned land also owned the mineral resources found under that land.²⁸ Under the new regime established by the MPRDA, ownership of all mineral resources in South Africa was transferred to the State.²⁹ Private ownership of mineral rights was replaced with a licensing system administered by the Government, and mining enterprises that held old order mineral rights were required to convert these into new order rights.³⁰ Furthermore, the MPRDA introduced a number of requirements that enterprises have to fulfil in order to qualify for exploration or mining licences, including the requirement that a 26 per cent (or greater) ownership stake in the enterprise be held by black South Africans.³¹

In their Memorial, the claimants argued that through the promulgation of the MPRDA, the South African Government had expropriated their mineral rights, as the MPRDA extinguished their mineral rights while granting them, 'a procedural right to apply for conversion of their "old order mineral rights" into much-diminished "new-order mineral rights"'.³² The claimants also argued that their shares in the affected operating companies had been directly and/or indirectly expropriated by operation of the 'compulsory equity divestiture requirements' of the MPRDA in combination with the Mining Charter.³³ For these reasons, the claimants argued that the promulgation of the MPRDA contravened the provisions of South Africa's BITs with Italy and the Belgo-Luxembourg Economic Union, which provide protection against direct and indirect expropriation as well as against measures having an equivalent effect and measures limiting investors' rights of ownership, possession, control or enjoyment of their investments.³⁴

---

²⁵ ibid 3. ²⁶ ibid 16.
²⁷ Mineral and Petroleum Resources Development Act No 28 of 2002, s 2(d).
²⁸ D Vis-Dunbar, 'South African court judgment bolsters expropriation charge over Black Economic Empowerment legislation in the mining sector', *Investment Treaty News* (23 March 2010) <www.iisd.org/itn/2009/03/23/south-african-court-judgment-bolsters-expropriation-charge-over-black-economic-empowerment-legislation/> accessed 2 July 2014.
²⁹ ibid. ³⁰ ibid.
³¹ A Friedman, 'Flexible Arbitration for the Developing World: Piero Foresti and the Future of Bilateral Investment Treaties in the Global South' (2010) 7 International Law & Management Review 37, 41.
³² *Foresti* (n 24). ³³ ibid 14. ³⁴ ibid 14–15.

In its Counter-Memorial, the South African Government argued that there had been no direct or indirect expropriation of the claimants' old order mineral rights or their shares in the operating companies, as the claimants had not been substantially deprived of their rights in their investments; their shares in the operating companies had not been directly expropriated; the operating companies had retained the same fundamental entitlement to prospect for and mine granite; and the equity divestiture requirements of the MPRDA and Mining Charter did not deprive the claimants of control of their investments.[35] In addition, the Government argued that, assuming *arguendo* the claimants did have a valid claim for expropriation of their old order mineral rights and their shares in the affected operating companies, the promulgation of the MPRDA did not contravene the provisions on expropriation found in the relevant BITs, as it met the conditions under which these treaties permit expropriation, namely that the expropriation is non-discriminatory, that it is undertaken for an important public purpose, that it complies with due process requirements and that an effective mechanism for the determination of compensation is made available to the affected parties.[36]

Ultimately, the dispute at the heart of the *Foresti* case was settled outside the Tribunal, when in December 2008 the parties reached an agreement whereby the Government granted the claimants' operating companies new order mineral rights without these companies having to fully satisfy the equity divestiture requirements of the MPRDA and Mining Charter.[37] The *Foresti* case nevertheless demonstrated how foreign investors could use provisions in South Africa's BITs to pursue damages against South Africa in response to the introduction of BEE policies and other public policies which might be interpreted as contravening the terms of one or more of the country's BITs.

IV. South Africa Reviews its BIT Policy Framework

Even prior to the initiation of the *Foresti* case, the South African Government had become concerned about the risks the country's BITs posed to 'legitimate public policy making'.[38] The Government therefore decided in 2005 to initiate a comprehensive review of its BITs in order to 'fully assess the risks and benefits of these treaties',[39] and to suspend further negotiation and conclusion of BITs until the completion of this review.[40] The *Foresti* case underscored the importance of such a process, and in October 2008, the Government formally launched its multi-stakeholder Bilateral Investment Treaty Policy Framework Review ('the Review').[41]

a) The main findings of the Review

The Review came up with a number of findings. The first was that the relationship between BITs and investment flows into South Africa is 'ambiguous', as South Africa does not receive significant investment from some of the partner States with which

---

[35] ibid 19–20.   [36] ibid 17–18.   [37] ibid.
[38] 'Remarks by Dr Rob Davies at the CCS' (n 8) 4.   [39] ibid.
[40] Republic of South Africa (n 12) 12.   [41] ibid.

it has concluded a BIT, but does receive significant investment from other countries with which it has not concluded a BIT.[42] While, strictly speaking, this may be true, it is interesting to note that according to the South African Reserve Bank, the ten largest holders of South African assets (by country) at the end of 2012 were (in order): the United Kingdom, the United States, the Netherlands, Belgium, Germany, Luxembourg, Switzerland, France, China, and Japan.[43] Of these countries, only the United States and Japan have not concluded BITs with South Africa. Moreover, it is unclear whether the Review investigated whether investments in South Africa originating in countries with which South Africa has not concluded a BIT may in fact be covered by one or more of the country's BITs as indirectly controlled investments.[44]

The second significant finding of the Review was the existence of a range of 'ambiguities' in the core legal provisions of South Africa's BITs,[45] including those pertaining to the definition of investors and investments, national treatment, direct and indirect expropriation, fair and equitable treatment and compensation for expropriation.[46] Reflecting on this finding, the South African Government noted that such ambiguities create uncertainty for both investors and governments.[47] For example, the 'classical asset-based definition of investment' used by most of South Africa's first generation BITs has created some confusion in South Africa as to whether shareholders have legal standing to bring claims under a BIT if the interests of the company in which they hold shares have been adversely affected by host State regulations.[48] In the view of the South African Government these ambiguities are compounded by the shortcomings of an international investment arbitration (IIA) regime characterized by a lack of common standards, inconsistent awards, and 'divergent legal interpretations of identical or similar provisions'.[49]

A third important finding of the Review was that South Africa's BITs typically promote the commercial interests of investors over issues of public interest.[50] While some of South Africa's later BITs include exceptions to national treatment provisions where

---

[42] 'Remarks by Dr Rob Davies at the CCS' (n 8) 4.

[43] South African Reserve Bank, 'Statistical Tables: International Economic Relations' *Quarterly Bulletin* 272 <www.resbank.co.za/Lists/News%20and%20Publications/Attachments/6273/11Statistical%20tables%20%E2%80%93%20International%20economic%20relations.pdf> accessed 1 July 2014.

[44] A number of South Africa's BITs cover indirectly controlled investments. For example, Art 1(b) of the Agreement on Encouragement and Reciprocal Protection of Investments between the Republic of South Africa and the Kingdom of the Netherlands (signed 9 May 1995, entered into force 1 May 1999) states that: 'the term "investors" shall comprise with regard to either Contracting Party: i. natural persons who, according to the law of a Contracting Party, are considered to be its nationals; ii. legal persons constituted under the law of that Contracting Party; iii. *legal persons not constituted under the law of that Contracting Party but controlled, directly or indirectly, by natural persons as defined in (i) or by legal persons as defined in (ii) above* [emphasis added].'

[45] 'Remarks by Dr Rob Davies at the CCS' (n 8) 4.

[46] X Carim, 'Update on the Review of Bilateral Investment Treaties in South Africa' (Presentation to the Parliamentary Portfolio Committee on Trade and Industry, 15 February 2013) <www.thedti.gov.za/parliament/bit's_in_sa.pdf> accessed 30 June 2014.

[47] 'Remarks by Dr Rob Davies at the CCS' (n 8) 4.

[48] Republic of South Africa (n 12) 30.

[49] 'Remarks by Dr Rob Davies at the CCS' (n 8) 4–5.

[50] Republic of South Africa (n 12) 5.

domestic laws and measures aiming to promote equality or to protect or advance historically disadvantaged persons and communities are involved,[51] the country's first generation BITs do not. Furthermore, the investor–State dispute settlement provisions in South Africa's BITs allow foreign investors to circumvent South Africa's legal system and the various provisions it contains to safeguard important public policy objectives.[52] In this regard, the South African Government has expressed concern that the country's BITs 'clear the way' for foreign investors to challenge policy measures 'deemed to undermine their "expectation" of profit', and 'pose serious risks to legitimate policy making in the public interest'.[53]

The final notable finding of the Review was that certain provisions in South Africa's BITs are inconsistent with South African law.[54] Notably, the treatment of expropriation in South Africa's BITs differs from that found in the South African Constitution.[55] South Africa's BITs prohibit the expropriation or nationalization of investments as well as measures having equivalent effect to expropriation or nationalization (indirect expropriation), except where this is carried out for a public purpose, on a non-discriminatory basis, under due process of law and against the payment of fair market value compensation. For instance, the South Africa–Spain BIT states that:

> Investments and returns of investors of either Contracting Party in the territory of the other Contracting Party shall not be nationalized, expropriated or subjected to measures having an equivalent effect to nationalization or expropriation... except for public purposes, under due process of law, in a non discriminatory manner and against the payment to the investor or his legal beneficiary of prompt, adequate and effective compensation.[56]

By contrast, the South African Constitution makes no reference to nationalization or to measures having equivalent effect to expropriation or nationalization. Instead, section 25 of the Constitution, which deals with private property rights, provides that:

> (1) No one may be deprived of property except in terms of law of general application, and no law may permit arbitrary deprivation of property.
> (2) Property may be expropriated only in terms of law of general application—
>   (a) for a public purpose or in the public interest; and
>   (b) subject to compensation, the amount of which and the time and manner of payment of which have either been agreed to by those affected or decided or approved by a court ...[57]

---

[51] South Africa's BITs with Ethiopia, Nigeria, Tanzania, and Zimbabwe all explicitly state that the provisions on MFN and national treatment contained in these treaties do not oblige either contracting party to 'extend to the investors of the other party the benefit of any treatment, preference or privilege resulting from' any 'law or other measure the purpose of which is to promote the achievement of equality in its territory, or designed to protect or advance persons, or categories of persons, disadvantaged by unfair discrimination in its territory'.
[52] Republic of South Africa (n 12) 44–45.
[53] X Carim, 'South Africa and Bilateral Investment Treaties' (Presentation to the 26th Annual Labour Law Conference, 31 July 2013) <www.lexisnexis.co.za/pdf/Bilateral-investment-treaties-and-sustainable-development.ppt> accessed 1 July 2014.
[54] Carim, 'Update on the Review of Bilateral Investment Treaties in South Africa' (n 46).
[55] Constitution of the Republic of South Africa, 1996.
[56] Agreement on the Promotion and Reciprocal Protection of Investments Between the Republic of South Africa and the Kingdom of Spain (signed 30 September 1998, entered into force 23 December 1999) Art 5(1).
[57] Constitution of the Republic of South Africa, 1996, s 25.

A distinction between deprivation and expropriation within the context of the Constitution was drawn in *Agri SA v Minister of Minerals and Energy*.[58] In *Agri SA*, the Constitutional Court found that

> Deprivation within the context of section 25 includes extinguishing a right previously enjoyed, and expropriation is a subset thereof. Whereas deprivation always takes place when property or rights therein are either taken away or significantly interfered with, the same is not necessarily true of expropriation. Deprivation relates to sacrifices that holders of private property rights may have to make without compensation, whereas expropriation entails state acquisition of that property in the public interest and must always be accompanied by compensation.[59]

In addition, the Court found that 'to prove expropriation, a claimant must establish that the state has acquired the substance or core content of what it was deprived of',[60] and that '[t]here can be no expropriation in circumstances where deprivation does not result in property being acquired by the state'.[61] The implication of this finding is that the Constitution does not require the payment of compensation for indirect expropriation or regulatory taking, provided that this is carried out in accordance with section 25(1) of the Constitution (that is, through a law of general application and in a non-arbitrary way) and does not result in a direct benefit to the Government.

Furthermore, where compensation is required under South African law, the Constitution 'mandates a lesser standard' than that provided for in South Africa's BITs.[62] With regard to compensation for expropriated property, section 25(3) of the Constitution provides as follows:

> The amount of the compensation and the time and manner of payment must be just and equitable, reflecting an equitable balance between the public interest and the interests of those affected, having regard to all relevant circumstances, including –
> (a) the current use of the property;
> (b) the history of the acquisition and use of the property;
> (c) the market value of the property;
> (d) the extent of direct state investment and subsidy in the acquisition and beneficial capital improvement of the property; and
> (e) the purpose of the expropriation.[63]

As market value is just one of a number of factors to be considered in determining the value of compensation under section 25 of the Constitution, it follows that compensation awarded to claimants may be less than the market value of their expropriated property. South Africa's BITs, however, uniformly state that compensation for expropriation should amount to the full market value of the expropriated investment.

Notwithstanding these findings, the South African Government noted that due to demand from foreign governments and investors, 'some level of

---

[58] *Agri South Africa v Minister for Minerals and Energy* (CCT 51/12) [2013] ZACC 9.
[59] ibid para 48.   [60] ibid para 58.   [61] ibid para 59.
[62] Republic of South Africa (n 12) 10.
[63] Constitution of the Republic of South Africa, 1996, s 25(3).

international investor protection may be unavoidable'.[64] However, given the issues highlighted by the Review, the Government Position Paper[65] on the Review recommended that the Government reassess its approach towards BITs, clearly considering the potential downside of such instruments and subjecting them to greater scrutiny.[66] In particular, it recommended that the Government develop a model BIT which is consistent with the country's 'development needs',[67] and which balances the need for investor certainty against the Government's legitimate interest in implementing national development policies and regulating in the public interest.[68] The Government Position Paper also suggested that 'further domestic legislative intervention may be needed to ensure that such a balance is achieved',[69] and recommended that the Government develop a 'strategic investment document' that clarifies the responsibilities of all stakeholders, establishes clear policy guidelines on inward and outward investment and promotes greater coordination between investment policy, trade policy, and industrial policy.[70]

b) The 2010 Cabinet Decision

In light of the findings of the Review and the recommendations contained in the Government Position Paper, the South African Cabinet decided in mid-2010 to overhaul the legal framework for investment protection in South Africa. Specifically, the Cabinet decided that: (i) South Africa would terminate its existing BITs and would only renegotiate these treaties or enter into new BITs if there were 'compelling economic reasons to do so'; (ii) any new or renegotiated BITs entered into by South Africa would be based on a new model BIT that would address the 'risks inherent in earlier generation BITs'; (iii) a new investment law would be developed which would codify BIT-type protections into South African law and would ensure that these were consistent with the South African Constitution; and (iv) an Inter-Ministerial Committee convened by the Minister of Trade and Industry would be established to oversee this work.[71]

V. The Emergence of a New Approach to Investment Protection in South Africa

Following the 2010 Cabinet decision, the South African Government began taking steps to overhaul its policy and legislative framework for the protection of foreign investment. In 2011, it began notifying affected partners of its plans to terminate its first generation BITs in line with the termination processes set out

---

[64] Republic of South Africa (n 12) 56.   [65] Republic of South Africa (n 12) 19.
[66] ibid 55–56.   [67] ibid 55.   [68] ibid 56.   [69] ibid.   [70] ibid 24.
[71] 'Remarks by Dr Rob Davies at the CCS' (n 8) 5.

in these treaties.⁷² On 7 September 2012, the Government officially notified the Belgian Embassy in South Africa of its intention not to renew its treaty with the Belgo-Luxembourg Economic Union, and in March 2013 this became the first South African BIT to be terminated.⁷³ Over the following months, South Africa also terminated its BIT with Spain,⁷⁴ notified its intention to cancel its BITs with Germany, Switzerland, and the Netherlands,⁷⁵ and indicated that it will terminate the rest of its BITs with its European partners.⁷⁶

To fill the void created by these terminations the South African Government, through the Department of Trade and Industry, began working on the development of a national investment law that would 'strengthen South Africa's investment regime', ensuring that the country 'provides adequate protection to all investors, including foreign investors', but also that South Africa's 'constitutional obligations are upheld' and that the South African Government 'retains the policy space to regulate in the public interest'.⁷⁷ In this regard, the Government published the draft Promotion and Protection of Investment Bill (PPI Bill)⁷⁸ for public comment on 1 November 2013, and, following a lengthy consultation process, a revised version of the PPI Bill was tabled in the South African Parliament in July 2015.⁷⁹ The Government also began developing a model BIT to serve as the basis for the renegotiation of existing BITs or the negotiation of new BITs.⁸⁰

These actions reveal the emergence of a new approach to investment protection in South Africa. For almost two decades, BITs have held a prominent place in the country's investment protection framework, but now the country is in the process of replacing its current network of BITs with a national investment law containing provisions on investment protection. According to the South African Government, this change in approach has been taken in order to 'update and modernise South Africa's legal framework to protect investment in South

---

⁷² Carim, 'South Africa and Bilateral Investment Treaties' (n 53).
⁷³ P Leon, J Veeran, and E Warmington, 'South Africa Declines to Renew Bilateral Investment Treaties with European Union Member States' *Mondaq* (5 October 2012) <www.mondaq.com/x/199586/international+trade+investment/South+Africa+Declines+To+Renew+Bilateral+Investment+Treaties+With+European+Union+Member+States> accessed 2 July 2014.
⁷⁴ N Peacock and H Ambrose, 'South Africa terminates its bilateral investment treaty with Spain: second BIT terminated, as part of South Africa's planned review of its investment treaties', 21 August 2013 <www.lexology.com/library/detail.aspx?g=daf93855-71f9-425e-92d3-5368d104f8ff> accessed 3 July 2014.
⁷⁵ M Webb and R Rajen, 'South Africa: No More BITs and Pieces' *Mondaq* (2 January 2014) <www.mondaq.com/x/283892/Inward+Foreign+Investment/No+More+BITs+And+Pieces> accessed 1 July 2014.
⁷⁶ 'Remarks by Dr Rob Davies at the CCS' (n 8) 5.
⁷⁷ 'Minister Davies to address media on the draft Promotion and Protection of Investment Bill' *South African Government Online* (1 November 2013) <http://www.gov.za/minister-davies-address-media-draft-promotion-and-protection-investment-bill > accessed 3 July 2014.
⁷⁸ 'Promotion and Protection of Investment Bill, 2013' ('PPI Bill') (*Government Gazette*, Vol 581, No 36995, 1 November 2013).
⁷⁹ 'Minister Rob Davies on Promotion and Protection of Investment Bill' *South African Government Online* (28 July 2015) <www.gov.za/speeches/promotion-and-protection-investment-bill-protects-investors-minister-davies-2015-07-28-28> accessed 18 August 2015.
⁸⁰ ibid.

Africa', to clarify the 'strong protection' already provided to foreign investors by South Africa's national legislation and to better balance 'the rights of investors to protection with the right of Government to regulate and safeguard the public interest'.[81]

VI. The Draft Promotion and Protection of Investment Bill

The stated purpose of the PPI Bill is to 'promote and protect investment in a manner that is consistent with public interest and a balance between the rights and obligations of investors' and to 'ensure the equal treatment between foreign investors and citizens of the Republic, subject to applicable legislation'.[82] It sets out the rights and obligations of local and foreign investors and of the Government, and contains provisions dealing with many of the issues typically addressed in BITs, including protection of investment, national treatment, security of investment, expropriation, transfer of funds and dispute settlement. The PPI Bill has been widely criticized, however, for failing to provide the same standard of protection for foreign investors as provided for under the various BITs currently being terminated by the South African Government.[83] Much of this criticism has focused on the PPI Bill's deviation from customary international law standards on security of investment, expropriation, and dispute settlement, as well as its focus on ensuring the Government's right to regulate in the public interest. These issues are discussed below.

a) Interpretation

The PPI Bill's interpretation clause states that, when enacted, '[t]his Act must be interpreted with due regard to—(a) the Constitution; (b) international law consistent with the Constitution; (c) customary international law consistent with the Constitution; and (d) any other relevant convention or agreement to which the Republic is or becomes a party'.[84] The implication of this clause is that where principles of international law are considered to be inconsistent with the Constitution, they cannot be applied.[85] This would mean, for instance, that the principle of

---

[81] ibid.   [82] PPI Bill, s 3.
[83] P Steyn, 'The new Promotion and Protection of Investment Bill—an assessment of its implications for local and foreign investors in South Africa' *Werksmans Attorneys Legal Brief* (10 December 2013) <www.werksmans.com/legal-briefs-view/new-promotion-protection-investment-bill-assessment-implications-local-foreign-investors-south-africa/> accessed 4 July 2014. See also, J Lang, 'Bilateral Investment Treaties—A Shield or a Sword?' *Bowman Gilfillan Corporate Newsflash* 3–4 <www.bowman.co.za/FileBrowser/ArticleDocuments/South-African-Government-Canceling-Bilateral-Investment-Treaties.pdf> accessed 3 July 2014.
[84] PPI Bill, s 2.
[85] South African Institute of International Affairs (SAIIA), 'South Africa's Draft Promotion and Protection of Investment Bill 2013: A Submission by the South African Institute of International

indirect expropriation, which was found not to be part of South African law in *Agri SA*,[86] would not be applicable under the PPI Bill.

The interpretation clause also attempts to limit the interpretation of the PPI Bill to considerations of customary international law that are consistent with the South African Constitution, implying that there is customary international law that is not consistent with the Constitution.[87] This is problematic, as the Constitution itself provides that when it is interpreted, South African courts 'must consider international law',[88] meaning that when interpreting the Constitution and any legislation touching on issues of international law—as the PPI Bill does—South African courts must consider principles of customary international law such as fair and equitable treatment.[89] The formulation of the interpretation clause in the PPI Bill also suggests that South Africa may end up with legislation that does not apply international law principles, and which may be challengeable in international courts for denial of justice.[90]

b) Security of investment

International law requires States to provide security to investors' property.[91] Most BITs, including South Africa's, include an obligation on the contracting parties to provide full protection and security to investors from the other party. The PPI Bill, however, deviates from this international investment law standard and states that South Africa must accord foreign investors an 'equal level of security as may be generally provided to other investors and *subject to available resources and capacity*'.[92] This implies that the South African Government will not be liable for damages to an investor's property if resources are not sufficient.[93]

The reference to available resources and capacity probably reflects South Africa's experience as a respondent in the arbitration claim brought by a Swiss investor in 2001. As noted above, the claimant in this dispute argued that the failure of the South African police to prevent significant damage to the claimant's property constituted a breach of South Africa's obligation under the South Africa–Switzerland BIT to provide full protection and security to investments covered by the BIT.[94]

Affairs', 6 <www.thetradebeat.com/book/saiia-submission-on-south-africa-s-draft-promotion-and-protection-of-investment-bill> accessed 4 July 2014.

[86] In *Agri South Africa v Minister for Minerals and Energy* (CCT 51/12) [2013] ZACC 9, the Court ruled that under South African law, expropriation only occurs where the State acquires ownership of the property in question. See (n 61) above.

[87] SAIIA (n 85) 6.   [88] Constitution of the Republic of South Africa, 1996, s 39(1)(b).

[89] SAIIA (n 85) 6. The PPI Bill itself does not include a provision on fair and equitable treatment, but all investors in South Africa nevertheless have 'access to procedural and substantive due process provided for by the South African Constitution' (M da Gama, 'Draft Bill no Threat to Foreign Investors in South Africa' *BDLive* (1 April 2014) <www.bdlive.co.za/opinion/2014/04/01/draft-bill-no-threat-to-foreign-investors-in-south-africa> accessed 3 July 2014.

[90] SAIIA (n 85) 6.   [91] ibid 8.   [92] PPI Bill, s 7(1) (emphasis added).

[93] SAIIA (n 85) 8.

[94] Agreement between the Swiss Federal Council and the Government of the Republic of South Africa on the Promotion and Reciprocal Protection of Investment (signed 27 June 1995, entered into force 30 November 1997).

In its defence, South Africa argued that as a developing country with limited resources, some latitude should be accorded in the application of the treaty's full protection and security obligation in the South African context.[95] Although arbitral tribunals have previously considered a host State's level of development when interpreting the standard of protection it is required to provide investors under a particular BIT,[96] the Tribunal in this case rejected South Africa's argument, stating that such an interpretation would allow a State to '"escape" its responsibilities by virtue of having done "the best it could in the circumstances"' and would 'undermine the minimum requirements of public international law with respect to foreign investment protection'.[97]

The inclusion of a qualified security and protection clause in the PPI Bill appears to be an attempt by the South African Government to avoid the 'onerous burden' that a full security and protection clause would potentially place on South Africa as a developing country, and to set explicit limits to what foreign (and local) investors can legitimately expect in terms of the State's duty to protect their investments.[98]

c) **Expropriation**

Rules on expropriation are critical to any investment instrument and are particularly important in the South African context where 'proprietary rights occupy a politically contested terrain'.[99] The PPI Bill follows customary international law by providing that investments can only be expropriated 'in terms of a law of general application for public purpose or in the public interest, under due process of law, against just and equitable compensation effected in a timely manner'.[100] However, in line with the South African Constitution, and unlike South Africa's BITs, the PPI Bill makes no reference to nationalization or measures having equivalent effect to expropriation or nationalization. In so doing, it reflects the finding in *Agri SA* that the customary international law principle of indirect expropriation is not part of South African law.[101] In addition, the PPI Bill does not require that a measure be non-discriminatory in order to be considered lawful expropriation. This is another omission that is consistent with the South African Constitution, but contrary to South Africa's BITs.

The PPI Bill also deviates from common practice in customary international law by providing for the possibility of less than full market value

---

[95] Peterson, 'Swiss investor prevailed in 2003 in confidential BIT arbitration over South Africa land dispute' (n 20).
[96] In *Generation Ukraine Inc v Ukraine*, ICSID Case No ARB/00/9, Award (16 September 2003), for example, the Tribunal noted that 'it is relevant to consider the vicissitudes of the economy of the state that is host to the investment in determining the investor's legitimate expectations, the protection of which is a major concern of the minimum standards of treatment contained in bilateral investment treaties'.
[97] Peterson, 'Swiss investor prevailed in 2003 in confidential BIT arbitration over South Africa land dispute' (n 20).
[98] Lang (n 81) 3–4.   [99] SAIIA (n 85) 8.
[100] PPI Bill, s 8(1).   [101] See (n 61) above.

compensation for expropriation. In particular, section 8(3) follows the South African Constitution in stating that compensation for expropriation must be 'just and equitable',[102] and 'must reflect an equitable balance between the public interest and the interest of those affected', having regard to: '(a) the current use of the investment; (b) the history of the acquisition and use of the investment; (c) the market value of the investment; and (d) the purpose of the expropriation'.[103] By confirming that market value is just one of a number of factors to be considered in the determination of compensation, the PPI Bill permits the payment of less than market value compensation and introduces a subjective element to the process. Again, while this is consistent with the South African Constitution, it is in stark contrast to South Africa's BITs which uniformly indicate that compensation must reflect the genuine or actual market value of the property in question.

Section 8(2) of the PPI Bill also lists a number of acts which 'do not amount to acts of expropriation', including:

(a) A measure or series of measures taken by the government of the Republic that have an incidental or indirect adverse impact on the economic value of an investment;
(b) a measure aimed at protecting or enhancing legitimate public welfare objectives, such as public health or safety, environmental protection or state security;
(c) the issuance of compulsory licences granted in relation to intellectual property rights, or to the revocation, limitation or creation of intellectual property rights, to the extent that such issuance, revocation, limitation or creation is consistent with applicable international agreements on intellectual property; and
(d) any measure which results in the deprivation of property but where the State does not acquire ownership of such property provided that—(i) there is no permanent destruction of the economic value of the investment; or (ii) the investor's ability to manage, use or control his or her investment in a meaningful way is not unduly impeded.

This section is problematic for a number of reasons. For instance, the idea in subsection (a) that concerted action which has an adverse effect on the value of an investment does not constitute a form of expropriation is hard to reconcile with customary international law, wherein such action is usually deemed as 'constructive' or 'indirect' expropriation.[104] Similarly, whereas subsection (b) states that measures aimed at protecting public welfare objectives are not expropriation, in customary international law the objective of a measure is only relevant in distinguishing lawful from unlawful expropriation, and compensation is due either way.[105] Furthermore, the provision in subsection (d) specifying that a measure which does not result in State ownership of a particular property is not expropriation codifies a principle established in *Agri SA* that is not consistent with customary international law.[106] Finally, the PPI Bill indicates that the list of measures included in section 8(2) is not exhaustive, thereby adding to investor uncertainty as to what would constitute expropriation.

[102] PPI Bill, s 8(1).   [103] PPI Bill, s 8(3).   [104] SAIIA (n 85) 9.   [105] ibid.
[106] *Agri South Africa v Minister for Minerals and Energy* (CCT 51/12) [2013] ZACC 9. See (n 60) and (n 61).

In omitting any reference to indirect expropriation or to the requirement that lawful expropriation be carried out in a non-discriminatory manner, and in listing a number of measures that will not be considered expropriation, the PPI Bill provides a conceptualization of expropriation that is consistent with the South African Constitution, but which is much narrower than the conceptualization of expropriation found in the country's BITs or in customary international law. In doing so, the PPI Bill gives the South African Government significant leeway to implement, without compensation, measures which may adversely affect the value of particular investments in South Africa. Such actions could, however, fall foul of the international minimum standard of treatment in customary international law.

d) Dispute settlement

While South Africa's BITs permit covered investors to refer investment disputes to international arbitration under ICSID or UNCITRAL rules, the PPI Bill does not provide for foreign (or local) investors to refer investment disputes to international arbitration. Although the PPI Bill does not specifically prohibit the referral of disputes to international arbitration, it does not give general consent to international arbitration, and therefore such referrals would require the agreement of the South African Government. Given the Government's attitude towards international investment arbitration and the current IIA regime, it is unlikely that this consent will be granted in practice.[107] Instead, investors will probably have to rely on the provisions in the PPI Bill that provide for an investor to initiate a mediation process,[108] approach 'any court, competent, independent tribunal or statutory for the resolution of a dispute',[109] or refer a dispute to arbitration under South Africa's Arbitration Act of 1965,[110] an 'outdated' piece of legislation that has largely been used for commercial arbitration.[111] As a result of this failure to include an investor–State dispute settlement provision in the PPI Bill, where BIT provisions no longer apply, investment disputes against South Africa will be determined under South African law and not customary international law.[112]

e) Sovereign right to regulate in the public interest

The PPI Bill also puts significant emphasis on protecting the sovereign right of the South African Government to regulate in the public interest, a right that is reaffirmed in the preamble. In particular, it reserves the right of the South African Government to adopt measures to 'redress historical, social and economic inequalities', 'promote and preserve cultural heritage and practices and indigenous

---

[107] South African Minister of Trade and Industry, Dr Rob Davies, has expressed concerns over the lack of common standards in the IIA regime, inconsistency in awards granted by arbitration Panels and the possibility that arbitration awards 'could undermine democratic decision making' ('Remarks by Dr Rob Davies at the CCS' (n 8) 5).
[108] PPI Bill, s 11(1).   [109] PPI Bill, s 11(4).   [110] PPI Bill, s 11(5).
[111] SAIIA (n 85) 10.   [112] Steyn (n 83).

knowledge', 'foster economic development, industrialization and beneficiation', and 'achieve the progressive realisation of socio-economic rights'.[113] The PPI Bill does not, however, define what constitutes 'public interest'. This is problematic given the centrality of this principle to the content of the PPI Bill, and the fact that there is significant disagreement within the South African legal community as to what actually constitutes public interest.[114]

Overall, the PPI Bill reflects the South African Government's need for 'expansive regulatory space for its transformation agenda, industrial policy and the progressive realisation of socio-economic rights'.[115] Its provisions go some way towards realizing its goal in this regard, as well as the goal of ensuring that foreign investors have the same rights and obligations as local investors. However, in doing so, the provisions in the PPI Bill provide foreign (and local) investors with lower standards of protection than those found in customary international law and provided for in South Africa's BITs. The particular provisions discussed above are also likely to create significant uncertainty for investors unless they are brought in line with international investment standards before the PPI Bill is enacted into law.

VII. A South African Model BIT

The development and enactment of the PPI Bill is undoubtedly the main feature of the South African Government's overhaul of the country's investment protection regime, but it is not the only noteworthy element of this ongoing process. Although the PPI Bill, once enacted, is intended to effectively replace South Africa's BITs as the main instrument of investment protection in the country, the Government has not completely ruled out the use of BITs in the future. Indeed, as noted above, it has indicated that it is developing a model BIT to be used as the basis for negotiating future BITs where the Government feels there are 'compelling economic reasons' for the use of such instruments.[116] This is in line with the recommendation in the Government Position Paper on the Bilateral Investment Treaty Policy Framework Review that the Government develop a model BIT which is consistent with the country's 'development needs',[117] and which balances the need for investor certainty against the Government's legitimate interest in implementing national development policies and regulating in the public interest.[118]

As of mid-2015 the model BIT has yet to be published, but the South African Government did indicate in early 2014 that the model BIT would be consistent with the Southern African Development Community (SADC) Model BIT Template[119] adopted by the SADC Member States in 2012.[120] This is not

---

[113] PPI Bill, s 10(1). [114] SAIIA (n 85) 5.
[115] SAIIA (n 85) 5. [116] 'Remarks by Dr Rob Davies at the CCS' (n 8) 5.
[117] Republic of South Africa (n 12) 55. [118] ibid 56.
[119] Southern African Development Community (SADC), *SADC Model Bilateral Investment Treaty Template with Commentary* (SADC 2012).
[120] 'Remarks by Dr Rob Davies at the CCS' (n 8) 5.

surprising, as South African representatives were part of the drafting committee that developed the SADC Model BIT Template.[121]

The SADC Model BIT Template

The SADC Model BIT Template (SADC Template) is intended for use by SADC Member States in the development of their own BITs and provides a menu of different model clauses for fleshing out the provisions usually found in BITs, as well as commentary on the rationale for—and suitability of—the different options presented. It advocates an approach that aims to provide an appropriate balance between the interests of foreign investors and the SADC Member States' own development objectives. Indeed, it recommends that the preamble of SADC Member States' BITs should be used to explicitly state this aim, so as to prevent 'unintended expansive interpretation of substantive provisions in favour of investors'.[122]

The SADC Template proposes a number of deviations from the standards usually found in BITs. For example, it recommends against the inclusion of an MFN provision, arguing that BITs should not be used to establish 'unintended multilateralization'.[123] It also recommends that SADC Member States limit the scope of national treatment provisions by scheduling a list of non-conforming measures and excluded sectors to which national treatment will not apply.[124] In addition, the SADC Template cautions against the inclusion of a fair and equitable treatment provision, recommending instead the inclusion of a provision on 'fair administrative treatment'.[125] This principle, which was developed and proposed by the South African Government, is narrower in scope than the fair and equitable treatment principle in customary international law, uses the language of governance standards rather than investor rights and sets a relatively high threshold for a 'breach of natural justice'.[126]

The SADC Template follows the standard BIT approach to expropriation, with three exceptions. First, it recommends omitting the condition that an expropriation be non-discriminatory. Second, it advocates the use of a 'fair and adequate' standard of compensation and suggests that such a standard need not necessarily be determined on the basis of full market value, but could instead be determined on the basis of an 'equitable balance between the public interest and interest of those affected'.[127] Third, it recommends the inclusion of a clause stating that a non-discriminatory measure 'designed and applied to protect or enhance legitimate public welfare objectives, such as public health, safety and the environment', does not constitute indirect expropriation.[128]

In order to emphasize the goal of securing an appropriate balance between the rights and obligations of investors and host States, the SADC Template proposes the inclusion of a provision confirming that the treaty 'does not alter the Host State's basic right to regulate',[129] as well as a provision recognizing a host State's

---

[121] SADC (n 119) 3. [122] ibid 6. [123] ibid 22. [124] ibid 20–22.
[125] ibid 22–24. [126] ibid 24. [127] ibid 24–26. [128] ibid 25. [129] ibid 40.

right to take measures necessary to address 'historically based economic disparities suffered by identifiable ethnic or cultural groups' due to past 'discriminatory or oppressive measures against such groups'.[130] A provision such as the latter would be particularly relevant in the South African context given the South African Government's BEE programme and economic transformation agenda.

The SADC Template also draws on Article XX of the General Agreement on Tariffs and Trade (GATT)[131] and other regional and bilateral agreements by recommending the inclusion of a list of exceptions concerning inter alia measures relating to public morals and safety; protection of human, animal or plant life or health; conservation of natural resources; environmental protection; prudential matters; taxation measures; non-discriminatory measures of general application taken in pursuit of monetary, credit, or exchange rate policies; and protection of national security.[132]

Finally, on the critical issue of dispute settlement the SADC Template recommends against a provision granting investors the right to bring disputes directly against host States.[133] Instead, it recommends the inclusion of a State–State dispute settlement provision that allows State parties to claim damages on behalf of an investor for an alleged breach of the treaty, but only after an investor has exhausted local remedies or if the State party can demonstrate that no appropriate domestic remedies are available.[134]

The SADC Template's proposals and recommendations, and, in particular, its emphasis on host States' development objectives and right to regulate, its proposal regarding the scheduling of exceptions and its recommendations against guaranteeing market value compensation in respect of expropriation or allowing for international investor–State dispute settlement, indicate an approach at odds with both the standards of customary international law and the provisions found in South Africa's existing BITs, but consistent with the approach reflected in the PPI Bill. Consequently, it is likely that if South Africa's model BIT is consistent with the SADC Template, future South African BITs will end up providing covered investors with standards of protection in line with those found in the PPI Bill, but lower than that provided for in South Africa's existing BITs and contained in customary international law.

VIII. A Dual Investment Protection Regime?

The fact that the South African Government is introducing domestic legislation to effectively replace its existing BITs, but at the same time developing a model BIT to guide future BIT negotiations may be explained by South Africa's emergence

---

[130] ibid 40–41.
[131] General Agreement on Tariffs and Trade 1994, 15 April 1994, Marrakesh Agreement Establishing the World Trade Organization, Annex 1A, 1867 UNTS 187; 33 ILM 1153 (1994).
[132] SADC (n 119) 46–47.   [133] ibid 55.   [134] ibid 52–54.

as a significant exporter of capital to the rest of the African continent in recent years.[135] The Government has indicated that future BITs will only be negotiated where there are compelling reasons to do so. Such reasons may apply where South African firms are significant investors in African (or non-African) countries that do not have a particularly developed domestic regulatory framework for the protection of foreign investment or a well-functioning and independent domestic legal system and where, as a result, South African investors face a significant risk of expropriation. It is interesting to note in this regard, that since the beginning of 2005, South Africa has signed nine BITs with African countries and only one BIT with a non-African country (Kuwait). Furthermore, the Government has not indicated that it is seeking to terminate any of the BITs it has concluded with other African countries.[136]

If this analysis is correct, it suggests that the South African Government recognizes that BITs may be needed to protect South African investments in the rest of Africa and further afield. It also hints at a desire on the part of the Government to adopt a form of dual investment protection regime, one which involves the use of BITs with countries to which South Africa exports capital, but which relies only on domestic legislation to govern investment flows between South Africa and countries from which South Africa is mostly a capital importer. However, if this is the case, the question should be asked whether the lower standard of protection likely to be contained in any future South African BITs would be of any value to the country's outward investors.

IX. Conclusion

As a developing country with a persistent current account deficit, South Africa requires foreign investment to support the country's inclusive growth and development objectives. The South African Government understands that in order to attract foreign investment it needs to provide 'strong protection to investors, both foreign and domestic, that is in line with international standards'.[137] The fact that the Government has decided to embark on a radical overhaul of its investment protection regime by effectively replacing its network of BITs with an investment law is therefore significant. According to the Government, this change in approach has been taken in order to 'update and modernise South Africa's legal framework to protect investment in South Africa'.[138]

---

[135] According to a website annexure to the 2013 South African Budget Review (available online at <www.treasury.gov.za/documents/national%20budget/2013/review/Annexure%20W3.pdf>) South African companies undertook nearly 1 000 new investments into thirty-six African countries between 2007 and 2011.
[136] While South Africa has signed a number of BITs with other African countries, only three (those with Mauritius, Nigeria and Zimbabwe) have entered into force.
[137] 'Remarks by Dr Rob Davies at the CCS' (n 8) 2.   [138] ibid 5.

a) Balancing investment protection and sustainable development in South Africa

Globally, debates around international investment law and sustainable development focus on the impact of BITs and the IIA regime on the ability of national governments to introduce domestic regulation in areas such as public health and environmental protection. In the South African context the need to address the socio-economic legacy of apartheid is a particularly important element of the sustainable development agenda. The South African Constitution gives a mandate to the South African Government to redress the legacy of racially based social and economic inequality bequeathed by apartheid, and in line with this mandate, the Government has introduced BEE policies which seek to promote greater participation by black South Africans in the management, ownership, and control of commercial enterprises in South Africa.

South Africa's experience with investor–State arbitration under its BITs has, however, generated and reinforced concerns within the South African Government that provisions in the country's BITs can be used to impede the introduction of BEE policies and other policies crucial to its social and economic transformation agenda, and to the sustainable development of the country. Having reviewed its policy on BITs, the South African Government came to the conclusion that the risks these instruments pose to its ability to implement BEE policies and to regulate in the public interest outweigh the purported benefits of these treaties. As a result it decided to terminate these treaties and replace them with a piece of legislation, the PPI Bill, which seeks to provide a better balance between the concerns of investors and those of sustainable development.[139]

b) What does replacing BITs with the PPI Bill mean?

Through the PPI Bill, the South African Government aims to achieve two main objectives. The first is to achieve a balance between the rights of investors to protection and the rights of the Government to regulate in the public interest and pursue legitimate public policy objectives in line with constitutional requirements.[140] The second is to ensure equal treatment between foreign and local investors.[141] While the enactment of the PPI Bill in its current form—coupled with the termination of South Africa's existing BITs—would achieve the latter objective by making all investors in South Africa subject to the same rights and obligations, it is questionable to what degree this approach would achieve the former objective, or, indeed, what exactly the Government means in terms of a 'balance'.

The PPI Bill does not provide foreign (or local) investors with rights not otherwise available under South African law. Instead, it clarifies and makes

---

[139] X Carim, 'Lessons from South Africa's BIT Review' *Columbia FDI Perspectives No 109* (25 November 2013) 2 <http://ccsi.columbia.edu/files/2013/10/No_109_-_Carim_-_FINAL.pdf> accessed 7 July 2014.
[140] ibid.   [141] PPI Bill, s 3(b).

explicit the protections already provided to foreign (and local) investors by South Africa's Constitution and national legislation. The effect of this, however, is to provide a standard of investment protection that is lower than the standard found in customary international law and in South Africa's existing BITs. This is because certain principles of international law have been found not to be part of South African law. For example, the principle of expropriation is highly circumscribed in South African law and does not account for much of what would be considered indirect expropriation in customary international law. Furthermore, the South African Constitution provides for the payment of less than market value compensation in certain cases of expropriation. These deviations from the customary international law principles arise from the need in South Africa to ensure that the rights of individuals to security of property are balanced against the need to redress historical social and economic inequities.

Given that the rights contained in the PPI Bill are largely a restatement of those already provided under South African law, the impact of the South African Government's cancellation of its BITs and their replacement by the PPI Bill should be minimal from the point of view of local investors and those foreign investors not currently covered by a South African BIT. From the point of view of actual and prospective foreign investors who are (or would be) covered by one of South Africa's BITs, this approach would undoubtedly result in a diminution of the rights and protections available to them. This is not only because the standards of protection contained in the PPI Bill are lower than those provided for in South Africa's BITs, but also because these investors will not have the right under the PPI Bill to refer investment disputes against South Africa to international arbitration. Furthermore, domestic legislation can be unilaterally amended or revoked by the South African Government, and as such, cannot provide the same level of predictability and certainty as a BIT.

From the point of view of the South African Government, the replacement of its BITs with the PPI Bill certainly appears to provide greater policy space to regulate in the public interest, but at what cost? Given the importance of foreign investment to South Africa, the Government clearly believes that the reduction in the standard of protection offered to foreign investors will not have a significant and detrimental impact on investment flows into the country. However, investor concerns around land reform, the possibility of nationalization and the Government's perceived 'drift towards inward-looking trade and industrial policies' do exist.[142] The Government's efforts to achieve a balance between demands for investment protection and the need for policy space may strengthen these concerns, and could result in the country becoming a less attractive destination for foreign investment originating from countries with which South Africa currently has a BIT, many of whom are among the largest sources of foreign investment in South Africa.

---

[142] SAIIA (n 85) 4.

c) A dual approach to investment protection

While the introduction of the PPI Bill is the central pillar of the South African Government's overhaul of the country's investment protection regime, the Government has not completely ruled out the use of BITs in the future, and is currently developing a model BIT to be used as the basis for negotiating BITs where the Government feels there are 'compelling economic reasons' to do so.[143] This suggests that the Government may in fact be weighing up the adoption of a dual approach to investment protection, one which involves the conclusion of BITs with countries in which South African companies are significant investors (and which do not invest significantly in South Africa), but relies only on domestic legislation to regulate investment flows from countries that are major exporters of capital to South Africa. Such an approach would allow South Africa to benefit from BIT protections for its companies that invest in risky jurisdictions, while simultaneously reducing the potential scope for challenges to be brought against it. In a sense, it would allow South Africa to have its cake and eat it.

d) South Africa and the shifting paradigm in international investment law

The new approach to investment protection emerging in South Africa, while partly motivated by public policy imperatives and South Africa's own experience of international investment arbitration, has certainly been informed by the shift in paradigm underway in the international investment law regime, and in particular, by increasingly critical views of the impact of BITs and investor–State dispute settlement on policies directed at sustainable development. In defending the PPI Bill from criticism, the Government has stressed that the development of the Bill has occurred against an international backdrop involving 'fundamental changes to investment regimes' and 'urgent international calls from both civil society and government circles for the reform of international investment treaties, their underlying policy frameworks, and the legal frameworks for adjudication and enforcement of investment agreements'.[144] The Government has also argued that the provisions contained in the PPI Bill are in line with recent international developments, including changes made by the United States to its model BIT to circumscribe indirect expropriation.[145]

Moreover, based on the content and recommendations of the SADC Model BIT Template, the provisions likely to find their way into South Africa's model BIT reflect (although in some cases go further than) proposals by international organizations such as the United Nations Conference on Trade and Development

---

[143] 'Remarks by Dr Rob Davies at the CCS' (n 8) 5.
[144] M da Gama, 'Draft Bill no Threat to Foreign Investors in South Africa' *BDLive* (1 April 2014) <www.bdlive.co.za/opinion/2014/04/01/draft-bill-no-threat-to-foreign-investors-in-south-africa> accessed 3 July 2014.
[145] ibid.

(UNCTAD), the International Institute for Sustainable Development, and the Commonwealth Secretariat for the conclusion of new generation BITs that have a a stronger focus on balancing investor rights and sustainable development imperatives.

While both these elements of South Africa's overhaul of its investment protection regime reflect developments at the international level, the somewhat radical steps already undertaken by the South African Government also provide an example which other countries dissatisfied with the current international investment law regime may wish to emulate, and could in turn influence the trajectory of the ongoing paradigm shift in international investment law. South Africa is not only introducing alternative methods for investment protection through national law, but also looks set to develop new generation BITs which incorporate new thinking about the appropriate role of BITs and their impact on domestic policy space and sustainable development. As such, South Africa will, in the coming years, represent an important testing ground for new approaches to investment protection.

XII
Reliance on Alternative Methods for Investment Protection through National Laws, Investment Contracts, and Regional Institutions in Latin America

María José Luque Macías[*]

I. Introduction

Latin American countries have traditionally been the first to challenge the status quo of international means of investment protection. The influential Calvo doctrine applied throughout the region comprised the rejection of an international minimum standard of treatment to foreign nationals and called for recourse to national courts for protecting investors' property interests. Recently several South American countries were among the first to display dissatisfaction with international investment agreements (IIAs) and investor–State dispute settlement (ISDS) through the denunciation of bilateral investment treaties (BITs)[1] and the ICSID Convention.[2]

---

[*] The author owes gratitude to Steffen Hindelang and Markus Krajewski for the invitation to participate in the writing of this article.

[1] 'Venezuela surprises the Netherlands with termination notice for BIT; treaty has been used by many investors to "route" investments into Venezuela' *Investment Arbitration Reporter* (16 May 2008) <www.iareporter.com/articles/20091001_93> accessed 15 August 2015; P Polasek and R Mellske 'Termination of Bolivia-United States Bilateral Investment Treaty' *Latin Arbitration Law* (31 May 2012) <http://www.latinarbitrationlaw.com/termination-of-bolivia-united-states-bilateral-investment-treaty/> accessed 15 August 2015.

[2] Bolivia, Ecuador, and Venezuela denunciated the Convention on the Settlement of Investment Disputes between States and Nationals of Other States ('ICSID Convention', opened for signature 18 March 1965, entered into force 14 October 1966) on 2 May 2007, 6 July 2009, and 24 January 2012, respectively. 'Bolivia Submits a Notice under Article 71 of the ICSID Convention' *International Centre for Settlement of Investment Disputes* (16 May 2007) <https://icsid.worldbank.org/ICSID/FrontServlet?requestType=CasesRH&actionVal=OpenPage&PageType=AnnouncementsFrame&FromPage=NewsReleases&pageName=Announcement3> accessed 15 August 2015; 'Ecuador Submits a Notice under Article 71 of the ICSID Convention' *International Centre for Settlement of Investment Disputes* (9 July 2009) <https://icsid.worldbank.org/ICSID/FrontServlet?requestType=CasesRH&actionVal=OpenPage&PageType=AnnouncementsFrame&FromPage=NewsReleases&pageName=Announcement20> accessed 15 August 2015; 'Venezuela Submits a Notice under Article 71 of the ICSID

This chapter analyses recent trends in Latin American investment policies, in particular a shift to national laws, investment contracts and regional institutions. It begins with placing in context the recent discontent with BITs in Latin America and changes in the investment treaty and contractual practice of some countries (section II). Subsequently, the chapter focuses on recent approaches in the context of domestic laws and investor–State contracts of Latin American States, in particular on the ongoing investment policy review carried out by Ecuador and its implications for the protection of foreign investment (section III). The following section makes basic assumptions about the operation of the Union of South American Nations (UNASUR) Centre and the Observatory on Investment and Transnational Corporations under creation within UNASUR, and the Bolivarian Alliance for the Peoples of Our America—Peoples' Trade Treaty (ALBA-TCP), respectively, as examples of regional measures (section IV). In particular, this part of the chapter addresses theoretical problems that may arise from different types of inter-State investment claims which may probably come under the jurisdiction of the UNASUR Centre.

II. Recent Developments in Investment Treaty and Contractual Practice in Latin America

The recent manifestation of discontent with the international investment law regime in Latin America can be attributed to the high number of international legal disputes in which these countries have been involved in the last decade. Investment treaty claims faced by Argentina raised greater public awareness in Latin America of the potential negative effects of investment treaty-based arbitration on the regulatory power of host States and on an open and independent resolution of investment disputes. Some investment treaty based arbitration proceedings brought against Argentina revealed the discretionary power of arbitral tribunals to give a broad reading of IIA provisions.[3] In addition, the disqualification proceedings filed against some members of arbitral tribunals on account of their participation as counsellors or lawyers in former investment claims highlighted

---

Convention' *International Centre for Settlement of Investment Disputes* (26 January 2012) <https://icsid.worldbank.org/ICSID/FrontServlet?requestType=CasesRH&actionVal=OpenPage&PageType=AnnouncementsFrame&FromPage=Announcements&pageName=Announcement100> accessed 15 August 2015.

[3] For instance, some arbitral tribunals expansively interpreted the definition of 'investor' for exercising their jurisdiction over investment claims filed by shareholders, see *CMS Gas Transmission Company v The Republic of Argentina*, ICSID Case No ARB/01/8, Decision of the Tribunal on Objections to Jurisdiction (17 July 2003) para 788. Moreover, through a broad understanding of treaty terms such as umbrella and most-favoured-nation clause, arbitral tribunals declare themselves competent to settle breaches of investment contracts under BITs, see *El Paso Energy International Company v. Argentine Republic*, ICSID Case No ARB/03/15, Decision on Jurisdiction (27 April 2006), and they entitle foreign investors with more favourable rights granted in other BITs, see *National Grid Plc v The Argentine Republic*, UNCITRAL, Decision on Jurisdiction (20 June 2006) 82 <www.italaw.com/cases/732> accessed 15 August 2015.

the risk that a small community of legal professionals involved in their resolution might entail for the independency and impartiality of arbitrators.[4]

Notwithstanding these singular manifestations of antipathy with the international investment law regime, the majority of Latin American States firmly endorsed, either bilaterally or regionally, the instrumental suitability of IIAs for overcoming the above-mentioned concerns. Recent BITs and other type of IIAs in Latin America have been modelled after the investment chapter of the North American Free Trade Agreement (NAFTA). Furthermore, current IIAs of NAFTA member States have also indirectly influenced the drafting of IIAs in this region.[5]

In addition to introducing certain references to social and environmental public objectives in different parts of IIAs,[6] some Latin American States accord foreign investors a minimum standard of treatment pursuant to the customary international law minimum standard of treatment of aliens,[7] and introduce criteria for differentiating, in exceptional circumstances, regulatory takings from an indirect expropriation.[8]. Even the recently founded Pacific Alliance addresses these concerns in the investment chapter of the additional protocol to its constitutive treaty.[9]

At the same time, the massive ratification of BITs during the 1990s did not only enable foreign investors to bring investment treaty claims against Latin American countries, and arbitral tribunals to expansively interpret their provisions, it also had the consequence that investment laws were no longer the exclusive regulatory means of foreign investment. Only Brazil maintained its reluctance to negotiate IIAs and did not ratify any BIT, but also did not enact any specific domestic law on

---

[4] *ADF Group Inc v United States of America*, ICSID Case No ARB/00/1, Decision on Respondent's Proposal to Disqualify Arbitrator (19 January 2001) (Davis R Robinson, Seymour J Rubin) (unpublished) discussed in *Compana de Aguas del Aconquija & Vivendi Universal v The Argentine Republic*, ICSID Case No ARB/97/3, Decision on the Challenge to the President of the Committee (3 October 2001) para 23; *Azurix Corp v Argentine Republic*, ICSID Case No ARB/01/12; *Siemens AG v Argentine Republic*, ICSID Case No ARB/02/8.

[5] MJ Luque Macías, 'Current Approaches to the International Investment Regime in South America', in C Herrmann and others (eds), *European Ybk Int Econ L* (Springer 2014).

[6] See Agreement between the Republic of Guatemala and the Republic of Trinidad and Tobago on the Reciprocal Promotion and Protection of Investments, preamble, para 4, Arts 16 and 17; Free Trade Agreement between the EFTA States and the Central American States ch 5 Art 5.6.

[7] See Tratado de Libre Comercio Colombia-Panamá ch 14 Art 14.5; Acuerdo entre el Gobierno de la Republica de Singapur y el Gobierno de la Republica de Colombia sobre Promocion y Proteccion de Inversiones Art 4.

[8] Tratado de Libre Comercio entre la República de Panamá y la República del Perú ch 12 Art 12.10 and Annex 12.10.

[9] With the adoption of the constitutive treaty on 6 June 2012, the Pacific Alliance was formally founded among Chile, Colombia, Mexico, and Peru for reinforcing the presence of its member states in the Asian Pacific region. Acuerdo Marco de la Alianza del Pacífico Arts 1 and 3 para 1, lits a and b; Protocolo Comercial Arts 1.1 and 1.4. The additional protocol to the aforementioned agreement was recently signed on 10 February 2014 and entered into force on 20 July 2015. Investment issues are ruled in its ch 10. Alianza del Pacífico, Documentos, Protocolo Comercial <http://alianzapacifico.net/documentos/> accessed 15 August 2015. The investment chapter of the additional protocol to the constitutive treaty of Pacific Alliance rules in similar vein the minimum standard of treatment in Art 10.6. It also encourages its member States to promote the adoption of standards on corporate social responsibility among enterprises operating within their territories in Art 10.30. Finally, this protocol strengths the member States' regulatory power for the implementation of social and environmental regulatory objectives in Art 10.31 and Annex 10.12, respectively.

investment.¹⁰ Instead, Brazil relied on its general domestic legal framework to regulate foreign investors. In this way, Brazil became the largest recipient of foreign investment in Latin America,¹¹ setting a unique precedent regarding the protection of foreign investment within and outside Latin America.

Within Latin America, Ecuador is gradually displaying some preference for its investor–State contracts and domestic laws in the wake of the denunciation and revision of BITs.¹² Beyond Latin American borders, South Africa has also started to replace its BITs with domestic laws.¹³ It is possible that States which have recently announced their intention to terminate or have already terminated BITs, might consider moving back to investor–State contracts and domestic laws as an alternative to IIAs in the near future.¹⁴

As far as investor–State contracts and investment laws are concerned, the use of stabilization clauses have not been exempted from criticism. In addition to nongovernmental organizations,¹⁵ States have also expressed concern about the implications that ensuring legal stability over certain domestic laws may place upon their regulatory power to issue administrative measures, or to undertake legislative reforms. These considerations reflect the international debate taking place on the extent to which host State's contractual legal commitments impair the implementation of their international human rights obligations.¹⁶

---

¹⁰ Brazil signed fourteen BITs which have not been ratified. UNCTAD, Investment Policy Hub, International Investment Agreements <http://investmentpolicyhub.unctad.org/IIA/CountryBits/27#iiaInnerMenu> accessed 15 August 2015. In the same way, Brazil has not ratified any Protocol designed for the protection of foreign investment within MERCOSUR. MERCOSUR, Tratados, Protocolos y Acuerdos <www.mercosur.int/t_ligaenmarco.jsp?contentid=4823&site=1&channel=secretaria>.

¹¹ Comisión Económica para América Latina y el Caribe (CEPAL), La Inversión Extranjera Directa en América Latina y el Caribe, 2013 (LC/G.2613-P), Santiago de Chile, 2014 23.

¹² The Ecuadorian National Assembly authorized in 2010 the denunciation of BITs signed with Germany, the United Kingdom, Finland, Sweden, and France. Currently, ten BITs are under revision for their respective denunciation (BITs signed with China, Chile, Venezuela, Switzerland, Canada, Argentina, United States, Spain, Peru, and Bolivia). Asamblea Nacional de la República del Ecuador, 'Trámite General de los Tratados e Instrumentos Internacionales' <www.asambleanacional.gob.ec/tramite-general-tratados-instrumentos-internacionales-agosto2009?created=&title=> accessed 15 August 2015.

¹³ See S Woolfrey, Chapter 11.

¹⁴ See LE Trakman and K Sharma, Chapter 13. Note also LE Trakman and K Sharma, 'Indonesia's Termination of the Netherlands–Indonesia BIT: Broader Implications in the Asia-Pacific?' *Kluwer International Law* (21 August 2014) < http://kluwerarbitrationblog.com/blog/2014/08/21/indonesias-termination-of-the-netherlands-indonesia-bit-broader-implications-in-the-asia-pacific/> accessed 15 August 2015.

¹⁵ In two reports issued on 2003 and 2005, Amnesty International drew public attention over the potential negative implications of investor-state contracts related to the execution of Baku-Tbilisi-Ceyhan (BTC) and Chad-Cameroon pipelines projects over the host state´s power of implementing legal reforms pro human rights. Amnesty International, *Human Rights on the Line: The Baku-Tbilisi-Ceyhan (BTC) Pipeline Project* (2003) <http://bankwatch.org/documents/report_btc_hrights_amnesty_05_03.pdf >; *Contracting Out of Human Rights, The Chad–Cameroon pipeline project* (2005) <www.amnesty.org/ar/library/asset/POL34/012/2005/en/76f5b921-d4bf-11dd-8a23-d58a49c0d652/pol340122005en.pdf> accessed 15 August 2015.

¹⁶ The United Nations Social Representative of the Secretary-General on Business and Human rights, Professor John Ruggie, and the International Finance Corporations (IFC) sponsored a study for particularly assessing whether these contractual clauses impair host States' implementation of their

In recent years Colombia discontinued providing legal stability over domestic regulations. The Colombian domestic law on legal stability was derogated in 2012 as a reaction to a considerable decrease in tax revenues due to legal stability commitments on tax law and incentives.[17] Previously, this domestic law was also subject to certain challenges. The constitutionality of this law was reviewed on the basis of the perceived constraints that this law might pose on the legislative power to modify domestic laws stabilized under investment contracts, and over the improvement of the legal conditions of workers by new laws.[18]

This brief overview on the domestic treaty and contractual practice in Latin America suggests that Latin American countries resort to existing instruments of public international law, domestic laws, and investor–State contracts for attaining a balance between the protection and regulation of foreign investment.

III. Investment Contracts and National Laws as Legal Means for the Protection and Regulation of Foreign Investment in Latin America

a) Investment laws and dispute settlement through arbitration

The ratification of BITs in the 1990s was generally accompanied by the enactment of investment laws in Latin America. In addition to the legal rights commonly provided to foreign nationals within the host States' territory such as non-discriminatory and national treatment, as well as compensation in case of expropriation,[19] some investment laws of this period also began to accord a most-favoured nation treatment in similar fashion to BITs and a jurisdictional clause for settling potential claims before arbitral tribunals. In this way, they complemented BITs and facilitated the admission and protection of foreign investment.

Contrary to this, the substantive and procedural rights accorded to foreign investors in Brazil were exclusively determined by its Constitution and the pertinent domestic laws applicable to the respective investor–State contract. At first, foreign

---

international human rights obligations. Subsequently, this study will be referred to in this contribution as the UN–IFC study. A Shemberg, *Stabilization Clauses and Human Rights. A research project conducted for IFC and the United Nations Special Representative of the Secretary-General on Business and Human Rights* (2009).

[17] The Law 1607 derogated in its Art 166 the Law 963 of 2005 on legal stability for investors. Ley 1607 'Por la cual se expiden normas en materia tributaria y se dictan otras disposiciones', Diario Oficial No. 48.655 (26 de diciembre de 2012).

[18] Demanda de Inconstitucionalidad contra los artículos 1, 2, 3, 4 y 6 (parciales) de la Ley 963 de 2005 por la cual se instaura una ley de estabilidad jurídica para los inversionistas en Colombia, Corte Constitucional, Sentencia C-320 de 2006 (Gaceta de la Corte Constitucional, 24 de abril de 2006).

[19] See, Ley de Inversiones (Bolivia) No 1182 (17 September 1990); Ley de Inversiones (Paraguay) Ley N° 117/91 (6 December 1991); Ley de Promoción de las Inversiones Extranjeras (Peru), Decreto Legislativo N° 662 (29 August 1991) and Ley Marco para el Crecimiento de la Inversion Privada Decreto Legislativo (Peru) N°757 (8 November 1991). These investment laws and others are available at the following link: <www.sice.oas.org/Investment/natlegis_e.asp#BOL> accessed 15 August 2015.

investors were entitled to national and non-discriminatory treatment regarding ownership of property with certain restrictions in the ownership of rural land[20] and concerning foreign capital flows,[21] as well as to a fair and previous payment of pecuniary compensation in case of expropriation of property for reasons of public necessity or use, or for social interest.[22] Afterwards, the enactment of the 1996 Arbitration Act enhanced the recourse to arbitration in Brazil.[23] Subsequently, the traditional hostility encountered for this procedural alternative to domestic courts was finally overcome after higher superior courts upheld its pertinence for the settlement of investment claims against public entities.[24]

In this broad context, Ecuador also followed the investment liberalization trend of the 1990s. Nevertheless, it recently showed a strong inclination for re-designing the content of investor–State's contracts and investment laws in the wake of the denunciation of BITs. First, this country undertook significant reforms over its investment laws. Next, it published an investment contract model issued thereafter.[25] Under these new domestic regulations on investment, foreign investors are currently granted non-discriminatory treatment in the post-establishment phase,[26] and national treatment concerning legal protection, and their participation in 'non-strategic sectors'.[27] Moreover, they are entitled to have legal stability over tax incentives during fifteen years term of the investment contract[28] as well as fair and adequate compensation in cases of expropriation of immovable property for the implementation of plans in favour of social development, sustainable management of the environment, or the collective well-being.[29] With respect to foreign investor's procedural rights, even though arbitration clauses within BITs have been considered unconstitutional,[30] recourse to arbitration is guaranteed for settling disputes arising from breaches of investor–State contracts.[31]

---

[20] Constituição da República Federativa do Brasil de 1988 art 5; Lei do Capital Estrangeiro No. 4.131 art 2.
[21] Lei do Capital Estrangeiro No. 4.131, art 2; Decreto Nº 55.762 art 2.
[22] Constituição da República Federativa do Brasil de 1988 art 5 subpara XXIV.
[23] J Kleinheisterkamp, *International Commercial Arbitration in Latin America* (OUP 2005); See also, PB Casella and EL Marques, 'Brazil: Arbitration Act' (1997) 36 ILM. 1562.
[24] A review of the principal sentences and jurisprudence on this issue can be found at: A Wald and J Kalicki, 'The Settlement of Disputes between the Public Administration and Private Companies by Arbitration under Brazilian Law' (2009) 26 J Int Arb 557 Resp No 612.439 (Special Appeal), 2d Chamber of the Superior Court of Justice, reporting Justice João Otávio de Noronha, Decision of October 25, 2005, 11 Revista de Arbitragem e Mediação 176 (2007), with Arnold Wald's commentary.
[25] Código Orgánico de la Producción, Comercio e Inversiones (enacted 29 December 2010); Ministerio Coordinador de la Producción, Empleo y Competitividad 'Contrato de Inversión de Sectores Productivos (Extranjera)' (2013) <www.produccion.gob.ec/kit-del-inversionista/> accessed 15 August 2015.
[26] Código Orgánico de la Producción, Comercio e Inversiones art 17 para 1.
[27] Código Orgánico de la Producción, Comercio e Inversiones art 17 paras 1 and 3.
[28] Código Orgánico de la Producción, Comercio e Inversiones art 25 para 2 and art 26 para 1.
[29] Código Orgánico de la Producción, Comercio e Inversiones art 18.
[30] The Ecuadorian Constitution introduced the prohibition on concluding international treaties that allow the submission of contractual and commercial disputes with foreign nationals. Constitución de la República del Ecuador art 422.
[31] Código Orgánico de la Producción, Comercio e Inversiones art 27. Contrato de Inversión de Sectores Productivos (extranjera) cl 28.

This brief description provided above initially conveys the strong willingness of the Ecuadorian State to preserve its regulatory discretion while according legal protection to foreign investors and their investment. This attitude can further be observed in those legal provisions governing the conduct of investor–State contract based dispute settlement.

For instance, despite the autonomy of the contracting parties to deviate from the host State's domestic laws,[32] it could not be implied from the investment laws of Ecuador that it might be inclined to insert a choice of law clause in investor–State contracts that allow contracting parties to opt for a different legal regime as the governing law of these contracts.[33] This measure might oblige arbitral tribunals to base their judgement on the investor–State contract's terms and Ecuadorian laws, and thus prevent them from exercising certain discretion in deciding to apply other sets of rules or legal principles governing the economic relations of the disputing parties that might be pertinent for the interpretation of the issue at stake.[34]

Moreover, bringing investment contract-based disputes against Ecuador is subject to a number of procedural conditions. The recourse to arbitration pursuant to Ecuadorian laws is possible after a compulsory exhaustion of the respective administrative remedies and a subsequent mediation instance of three months.[35] Moreover, arbitration proceedings shall be conducted pursuant to the UNCITRAL rules and administered by the Permanent Court of Arbitration.[36] Assuming that arbitral tribunals enjoy more confidence as a neutral, impartial and independent forum for the settlement of contractual claims than the Ecuadorian domestic courts, foreign investors might certainly have no other available procedural alternatives than those

---

[32] *Case Concerning the Payment of Various Serbian Loans Issued in France/Case Concerning the Payment in Gold of the Brazilian Federal Loans Issued in France* (Judgment No 14) PCIJ Rep Series A No 20, 41: '[a]ny contract which is not a contract between States in their capacity as subjects of international law is based on municipal law of some country'. In the case of Brazil, the contracting parties may freely determine the applicable laws in arbitration proceedings with the sole limitation to not violate good morals and public policy. Brazilian Arbitration Act, Law No. 9.307 art 2.

[33] Código Orgánico de la Producción, Comercio e Inversiones art 25 para 1; Contrato de Inversión Extranjera Productiva (extranjera) cl 5.

[34] Under investor–State contracts with choice of law clauses that refer to a different legal regime than solely that of the State party, arbitral tribunals had recourse to international legal principles for supplementing or correcting host State's domestic law, or even prevailed these legal principles for solving conflicts of laws arising from the interaction of these legal regimes. See, *Amco v Republic of Indonesia*, (Resubmitted Case) Award (5 June 1990) 1 ICSID Report 569 40. Additionally, arbitral tribunals had applied in different manner principles of international law to the question of remedies after a breach of contract. See, *BP Exploration Company (Libya) Ltd v Government of the Libyan Arab Republic*, Award (1 August 1974) (1979) 53 ILR 297; *Libyan American Oil Company (LIAMCO) v Government of the Libyan Arab Republic*, Award (12 April 1977) (1981) 20 ILM 1; *Texaco Overseas Petroleum Company and California Asiatic Oil Company v Government of the Libyan Arab Republic*, Award (19 January 1977) (1978) 17 ILM 1.

[35] Código Orgánico de la Producción, Comercio e Inversiones art 27 paras 1 and 2. Contrato de Inversión de Sectores Productivos (extranjera) cl 28 paras 1 and 2.

[36] Código Orgánico de la Producción, Comercio e Inversiones, art 27 para 3. Contrato de Inversión de Sectores Productivos (extranjera) cl 28 subpara 28.3. The Brazilian Arbitration Act allows the contracting parties to freely determine the governing law or agree to a procedure regarding its conduct Lei de Arbitragem—Lei 9307 (1996) art 5.

laid down in these investment laws. Yet, deviating from these initial terms will considerably depend on the bargaining power of the contracting parties.

It is questionable whether current investment laws promote this country's attractiveness for oversea investors. Transnational corporations may well prove able to attain similar satisfactory legal conditions as those available under IIAs in the negotiation of investment contracts with this State. However, those investors stemming from State parties with whom Ecuador still maintain BITs in force are not affected by these domestic regulations. BITs enable them to enjoy a broader scope of legal protection regardless of their economic power.[37] On the contrary, due to their limited bargaining power, economically less powerful foreign companies may suffer a competitive disadvantage in achieving an equal legal protection under investment contracts.[38]

They might be in fact prevented to engage in economic activities in its territory, particularly when only a basic set of rights and incentives may be the only tool for claiminig legal protection against unilateral changes of domestic laws or modification of investment contracts.

Finally, foreign investors may be dissuaded to invest in this country when it maintains an inflexible constitutional stance concerning the international enforcement of investment treaty commitments before arbitral tribunals, and its intention to negotiate other type of IIAs has not yet been announced.

b) Stabilization clauses

Stabilization clauses in investor–State contracts are commonly used in the execution of long-term projects for dealing with the problem of unilateral changes of host State's domestic laws. In Latin America, stabilization clauses have mainly been adopted to ensure legal stability over fiscal and other specific economic areas.[39] To a lesser extent, some countries have also granted legal stability over their domestic labour laws applicable at the moment of recruitment of workers,[40] and even conferred a status of special law to stability contracts or contracts with stabilization clauses so that they apply as a *lex specialis* over current and subsequent legislative enactments.[41]

---

[37] Ecuador mantains sixteen BITs in force. UNCTAD, Investment Polity Hub, International Investment Agreements Navigator, Bilateral Investment Treaties (BITs), <http://investmentpolicyhub.unctad.org/IIA/CountryBits/61#iiaInnerMenu> accessed 15 August 2015.

[38] SW Schill, 'Private Enforcement of International Investment Law: Why We Need Investor Standing in BIT Dispute Settlement', in M Waibel and others (eds), *The Backlash against Investment Arbitration, Perceptions and Reality* (Kluwer Law International 2010).

[39] Estatuto de la Inversion Extranjera (Chile) Decreto Ley N 600 arts 7 and 11; Estabilidad jurídica de las inversiones (Panama) Ley N° 54 art 10 paras 2 and 3; Ley de Promoción de las Inversiones Extranjeras (Peru) Decreto Legislativo N°662 art 10 lit. (a).

[40] Estabilidad Jurídica de las Inversiones (Panamá) Ley No. 54 art 10 para 5; Ley de Promocion de las Inversiones Extranjeras (Perú) Decreto Legislativo No. 662 arts 12 lit. (a and 15.

[41] Ley Marco para el Crecimiento de la Inverión Privada (Perú) Decreto Legislativo No. 757 art 39; Constitución Política del Perú art 38 para 2.

From the marginal data of the UN–IFC study, it can be inferred that investor–State contracts with economic equilibrium clauses have prevailed in Latin America over investor–State contracts with freezing or hybrid stabilization clauses.[42] This can be explained with the effect of freezing stabilization clauses; they commonly exempt foreign investors from compliance with new laws, or require compliance only if new laws are not incompatible with the investment contract.[43] Contrary to this, economic equilibrium stabilization clauses offer host States multiple alternatives to compensate foreign investors for the financial loss in which they may incur due to the compliance with new laws.[44] Their use particularly predominates in the so-called private–public partnerships, which are investment contracts established for carrying out long-term projects. Under these investment contracts, host States assume the risk of the financial loss incurred by passing a new law; it is a form of redressing foreign investors for the compulsory adaptation of the original contractual terms of private–public partnerships to the new law.[45]

As aforementioned in the second section, stabilization clauses may pose potential risks to host States' fulfilment of their international human rights' obligations. As a result, some institutional and governmental initiatives have been developed in order to minimize their negative effects. The special Representative of the Secretary-General on the issue of human rights and transnational corporations and other business, John Ruggie, formulated a set of guiding principles for incorporating human rights considerations into the negotiation of investor–State contracts.[46] It encourages contracting parties to design stabilization clauses in a way that this legal protection accorded to foreign investors do not interfere with State's *bona fide* regulatory efforts for the realization of its human rights obligations, in a non-discriminatory manner.[47] Furthermore, Panama, for instance, restricts the legal stability of its labour regulation. It grants foreign investors legal stability on the applicable labour regulation at the time of recruitment in accordance with its domestic laws and international treaties on this subject.[48]

As far as the implementation of human rights obligations is concerned, both examples show the existence of drafting alternatives to preserve regulatory or legislative discretion without rejecting legal stability of the domestic legal framework. While this might be true, Latin American countries mostly channel their domestic

---

[42] Shemberg (n 16) 17–19 and 22–26.
[43] AFM Maniruzzaman, 'The Pursuit of Stability in International Energy Investment Contracts: A Critical Appraisal of the Emerging Trends' (2008) 1 J W E L & B 121.
[44] ibid.
[45] A Sheppard and A Crockett, 'Are Stabilization Clauses a Threat to Sustainable Development?' in MC Cordonier Segger and others (eds), *Sustainable Development in World Investment Law* (Wolter Kluwer 2010).
[46] UN Human Rights Council, *Report of the Special Representative of the Secretary-General on the issue of human rights and transnational corporations and other business enterprises, John Ruggie* (Addendum Principles for responsible contracts: integrating the management of human rights risks into State-investor contract negotiations: guidance for negotiators, A/HRC/17/31/Add.3, 2011).
[47] ibid., Annex para 31-39.
[48] Estabilidad Jurídica de Inversiones (Panama) Ley No. 54 art 10 para 5.

efforts to preserve regulatory discretion in pursuance of non-economic objectives through other legal means.

c) Addressing non-economic concerns

Without being member States of the (OECD), some Latin American countries have encouraged the implementation of the OECD Guidelines for Multinational Corporations in their territories.[49] The political commitment of these countries towards the promotion of a responsible business conduct at the international level is evidenced by the inclusion of social and environmental language in their recent IIAs.[50] At the domestic level, measures concerning the disclosure of information are adopted, such as regular reports concerning potential investment projects,[51] or periodical releases of the content of investment and legal stability contracts.[52] Moreover, initial steps have been taken to regulate corrupt practices carried out abroad.[53]

In addition to the application of the non-binding standards referred to above, Latin American countries have used their investment laws to indirectly strenght non-economic domestic obligations of foreign investors. Rather than being a current phenomenon, some investment laws enacted in the 1990s already restated the duty of foreign investors to duly observe labour and social security laws,[54] or even more precisely, obliged them to observe the right to collective bargaining, as well as to recognize national economic and social policies.[55] Moreover, other investment acts of the same period also imposed specific environmental obligations on foreign investors such as environmental impact studies prior to the development of economic activities,[56] implementing security measures in case of severe and imminent danger for the environment,[57] or obtaining certification schemes of compliance with water quality standards or waste disposal conditions.[58]

---

[49] Excluding Chile, Argentina, Brazil, Chile, Colombia, Costa Rica, Mexico, and Peru have adhered to the OECD Guidelines for Multinational Enterprises, without being non-member States of OECD, thus assuming the enforcement of these Guidelines by the creation of National Contact Points. OECD Guidelines for Multinational Corporations, National Contact Points <http://mneguidelines.oecd.org/ncps/> accessed 15 August 2015.

[50] Luque Macías (n 5).

[51] Brazilian Investment Information Network, 'Announced Investment Projects' <http://investimentos.mdic.gov.br/conteudo/index/item/34> accessed 15 August 2015.

[52] ProInversión, Agencia de Promoción de la Inversión Privada (Peru), Convenios suscritos con el Estado (Contrato de Inversión) and Convenios de Estabilidad Jurídica <www.investinperu.pe/default.aspx> accessed 15 August 2015.

[53] Brazil recently enacted the 'Clean Companies Act' for regulating acts of foreign bribery of natural and legal persons. Brazilian Clean Companies Act, Lei no L12846 (2013).

[54] Ley de Inversiones No 1182 (Bolivia) art 13; Ley de Inversiones No 117191 (Paraguay) Art 11; Ley de Inversiones Decreto Legislativo 732 (El Salvador) Art 14. Código Orgánico de la Producción, Comercio e Inversiones (Ecuador) Art 21. Contrato de Inversión de Sectores Productivos (extranjera) cl 20, subpara 20.1 lit. f.

[55] The Investment Authority Act, 2006 (Antigua and Barbuda) Sch 4 (Investment Code) 33.

[56] Ley Marco para el crecimiento de la inversión privada (Peru) Art 51.

[57] Ley Marco para el crecimiento de la inversión privada (Peru) Art 52.

[58] Ley Marco para el crecimiento de la inversión privada (Peru) Art 53.

More recently, it can also be noticed the strong inclination of Ecuador to go beyond 'indirect attempts' of reinforcing non-economic interests in investment laws. From the latest investment contract model issued by this country, it can be implied that Ecuador may not only insist on the conservation and preservation of the environment in negotiations of investment contracts; it may also demand full reparation in instances of damage to the environment and natural resources from foreign investors.[59] Ecuador also incorporates the concept of corporate social responsibility in its investment contract model. It refers to it as the duty of the investor to be responsible for the effects that their own decisions and activities might have on society and environment.[60] In performing this duty investors shall owe deference to certain principles. First, the relationship between foreign investors and workers shall be transparent, particularly with regard to recruitment. Moreover, foreign investors shall make proper use of environmental licences, and preserve the environment in accordance with national plans.[61]

Restating social and environmental obligations in investment laws—even reiterating or elaborating them in investment contracts—provides an additional method for striking a balance between private property interests and interests of the public. As such, they may have important implications for the resolution of investment-contract based arbitration proceedings. While non-economic domestic obligations might be considered in the analysis of the host State's commitments to legal stability and their effects on new laws, it is more likely they may play a more important role in the assessment of damages to be awarded to foreign investors. Respondent States might invoke these provisions to justify a regulatory measure as a response to corporate misbehaviour, and thus use it as a counterargument against the claimant investor who challenged a certain State action before arbitral tribunals.[62]

At the same time, attempts to impose obligations on foreign investors in investment laws in addition to those already enshrined by other domestic instruments might be perceived as protectionist. It is precisely for this reason that some Latin American countries merely restate non-economic obligations that are already laid down in the respective domestic instruments, or set standards of corporate social responsibility in a non-binding instrument such as an investment contract model.

Additionally, in contrast to IIAs, foreign investors can exert a significant influence on the final content of investment contracts. When they hold a considerable bargaining power, they could attain the non-inclusion of non-economic domestic obligations in investment contracts, and thus minimize the possibilities of arbitral tribunals to take them into consideration in the interpretation of contractual terms.

---

[59] Contrato de Inversión de Sectores Productivos (extranjera) cl 20 subpara 20.1, lit e.
[60] Contrato de Inversión de Sectores Productivos (extranjera) cl 21.
[61] Contrato de Inversión de Sectores Productivos (extranjera) cl 21.
[62] See *Robert Azinian and others v United Mexican States*, ICSID Case No ARB(AF)/97/2, Award (1 November 1999) 110–15; *MTD Equity Sdn Bhd & MTD Chile SA v Chile*, Award (25 May 2004) 117.

d) The future of IIAs

Admittedly, despite a lot of criticism in Latin America to IIAs and ISDS, the conclusion of BITs and other types of IIAs will not decrease in the foreseeable future.[63] A clear illustration of the fact that the negotiation of these treaties will probably remain an ongoing practice is the willingness of some Latin American countries, including the member States of the Pacific Alliance, to participate in the negotiation process of the Transpacific Partnership Agreement.[64]

Interestingly, Brazil is gradually entering into international obligations for promoting and protecting foreign investment. It recently concluded the so-called Cooperation and Facilitation Investment Agreements (CFIAs) with Angola, Malawi, Mexico, and Mozambique.[65] However, CFIAs primarily focus on investment promotion than on investment protection, and strengthen inter-State dispute settlement methods instead of ISDS.[66]

With respect to Ecuador, its half-total departure from BITs has not only involved the revision of investment law and investment contract model; it has also triggered the creation of an Audit Commission, known by its acronym CAITISA,[67] for scrutinizing BITs and investment treaty claims brought against this country.[68] To this end, CAITISA defined a methodology based on three thematic areas and designed

---

[63] Since 2010, sixteen BITs and twenty six other types of IIAs have been concluded in Latin America. This calculation is based on the data collected by UNCTAD. UNCTAD, Investment Policy Hub, International Investment Agreements, Most Recent IIAs <http://investmentpolicyhub.unctad.org/IIA/MostRecentTreaties#iiaInnerMenu> accessed 15 August 2015.

[64] This treaty under negotiation pursues the expansion of the Trans-Pacific Strategic Economic Partnership Agreement already established among Singapore, New Zealand, Brunei, and Chile, and open to access to APEC members and other countries. The Trans-Pacific Strategic Economic Partnership Agreement is in force since November 2006. Trans-Pacific Strategic Economic Partnership Agreement, Art 20, para 6. Peru formally joined the negotiation process of the Trans-Pacific Partnership Agreement in 2010; subsequently Mexico and Costa Rica expressed their intention to participate in 2011 and 2012 respectively. Organization of American States Foreign Trade Information System (SICE) 'Trade Policy Developments: Trans Pacific Partnership Agreement (TPP)—Australia, Brunei, Canada, Chile, Malaysia, Mexico, New Zealand, Peru, Singapore, the United States, and Vietnam' (Background and Negotiations) <www.sice.oas.org/TPD/TPP/TPP_e.ASP> accessed 15 August 2015.

[65] UNCTAD, Investment Policy Hub, International Investment Agreement Navigator, Brazil, Other Investment Agreements, <http://investmentpolicyhub.unctad.org/IIA/CountryOtherIias/27#iiaInnerMenu> accessed 15 August 2015.

[66] JC Hamilton and M Grando, 'Brazil and the Future of Investment Protections' *Latin Arbitration Law* <www.latinarbitrationlaw.com/brazil-and-the-future-of-investment-protections/> accessed 15 August 2015. C Trevino, 'A Closer Look at Brazil's Two New Bilateral Investment Treaties' *IAReporter* (10 April 2015) <www.iareporter.com/articles/a-closer-look-at-brazils-two-new-bilateral-investment-treaties/> accessed 15 August 2015.

[67] Comisión para la Auditoría Integral Ciudadana de los Tratados de Protección Recíproca de Inversiones y del Sistema de Arbitraje Internacional en Materia de Inversiones (CAITISA).

[68] CAITISA was created by the Ecuadorian Executive in May 2013. Registro Oficial No 958, 21 de mayo de 2013. Centro de Getión Gubernamental (CEGE), Decretos Ejecutivos, Decreto 1506 Art 2 <http://decretos.cege.gob.ec/decretos/decretos.aspx?id=2009> accessed 15 August 2015. CAITISA is mostly composed of Latin American scholars and professionals with vast experience in governmental entities and non-governmental organizations; but Muthucumaraswamy Sornorajah also participated in the elaboration of the preliminary conclusions. CAITISA, Miembros <http://caitisa.org/miembros.html> accessed 15 August 2015.

an information system about the negotiation process and content of BITs as well as other international rules covering ISDS issues.[69]

After five working sessions, this Audit Commission delivered some preliminary findings. The most significant conclusion was that BITs were not decisive drivers of foreign investment.[70] This conclusion resulted from the fact that, first, the highest investment flows into Ecuador stem from countries with which no BIT had been negotiated, and second, the level of investment flows of the countries affected by the denunciation of BITs remained unchanged.[71] As a result, CAITISA already suggested that it might probably recommend either the renegotiation of BITs with due deference to the sovereignty of States and the protection of social, cultural, and environmental rights, or the denunciation of the BITs currently in force.[72]

Whether or not the preliminary findings of CAITISA yield a definite departure of Ecuador from IIAs, and thus its complete reliance on investor–State contracts, Ecuador will still remain subject to fulfil its obligations under the denunciated BITs. After their termination, the automatic renewal clauses of these BITs commonly extend their duration for a certain period of time. In case, nevertheless, it decides to start the conclusion or the renegotiation of BITs, the two different models of IIAs described above yet exist at its disposal.

Regardless of the future direction of the Ecuadorian investment policy, the measures designed to re-orientate its policy might well provide an experimental model for those Latin American countries that already denunciated BITs or remain cautious towards the negotiation of new IIAs.

IV. Regional Initiatives in Latin America for Challenging the Status Quo of ISDS

New institutional initiatives emerging in Latin America to ensure a balanced interpretation of host States' treaty obligations, as well as a more transparent and independent resolution of investment treaty claims are equally important.

Instead of calling upon the improvement and reaffirmation of host States' domestic courts,[73] South American countries are endorsing the initiative of the

---

[69] CAITISA <www.caitisa.org/> accessed 15 August 2015.

[70] According to this press article, the principal investors in Ecuador stem from Brazil, Panama, and Mexico. 'Caitisa arroja sus primeras observaciones a los TBI' *El Telégrafo* (7 August 2014) <www.telegrafo.com.ec/politica/item/caitisa-arroja-sus-primeras-observaciones-a-los-tbi.html> accessed 15 August 2015.

[71] ibid.

[72] 'International Commission that analyzes 26 bilateral investment treaties will recommend to end agreements' *Agencia Pública de Noticias del Ecuador y Suramérica* ('ANDES') (6 August 2014) <www.andes.info.ec/en/news/international-commission-analyzes-26-bilateral-investment-treaties-will-recommend-end> accessed 15 August 2015.

[73] NM Perrone, 'La protección de la inversión extranjera, jueces nacionales y proyecto regional: el caso argentino y de la UNASUR' in JM Alvarez, M Grando, and H Hestermeyer (eds), *Estado y Futuro del Derecho Económico Internacional en América Latina* (I Conferencia Bianual de la Red Lationamericana de Derecho Económico Internacional, Universidad Exrternado de Colombia).

UNASUR for the establishment of a Centre for the Settlement of Investment Disputes (UNASUR Centre). While the negotiation process of its constitutive treaty has not been concluded, it has already been conveyed that the UNASUR Centre may settle investment disputes among its members, employing arbitration as one of the methods for their resolution.[74]

In addition to the UNASUR Centre, ALBA-TCP strongly promotes the creation of an Observatory on Investment and Transnational Corporations.

a) The UNASUR Centre for the Settlement of Investment Disputes

aa) Background

UNASUR is a treaty-based intergovernmental organization composed of all South American countries.[75] Through participation and consensus, UNASUR's primary objective is the construction of a space for integration and union in political, sociocultural, and economic fields. The organization aims at strengthening democracy, sovereignty, and independence of its member States.[76]

The institutional structure of UNASUR is based on four organs with specific duties.[77] In addition to the Secretary General,[78] the UNASUR's decision-making organ is the Summit of Heads of States and Government.[79] Moreover, UNASUR is composed of a Summit of Ministers of Foreign Affairs and the Summit of Delegates, which executes and develops initiatives and has a coordinative role in the organization, respectively.[80]

UNASUR's regulations are generally adopted by consensus.[81] Where consensus is not required, norms may be adopted by a three-quarter majority.[82] Once a UNASUR norm is adopted, it is not immediately applicable. Rather, it is only binding for its member States after they incorporate it into their domestic legal system.[83]

---

[74] UNASUR, Acta Final, VI Reunión del Grupo de Trabajo de Expertos de Alto Nivel de Solución de Controversias en Materia de Inversiones de UNASUR, 29–31 de Mayo 2013; VII Reunión del Grupo de Trabajo de Expertos Alto Nivel de Solución de Controversias en Materia de Inversiones de UNASUR, 14–16 Agosto 2013; VIII Reunión del Grupo de Trabajo de Expertos de Alto Nivel de Solución de Controversias en Materia de Inversiones de UNASUR, 18–21 de Marzo 2014.

[75] The constitutive treaty of UNASUR was signed on 23 May 2008 and entered into force on 11 March 2011.

[76] Tratado Constitutivo de la Unión de Naciones Sudamericanas Art 2. The aimed integration of UNASUR is building upon the achievements already attained by the Andean Community and MERCOSUR and is governed, among other principles, by respect to sovereignty, territorial integrity, and inviolability of its member States; their self-determination; as well as some progressive values such as universal, indivisible, and interdependence of human rights and harmony with the nature towards sustainable development. See Tratado Constitutivo de la Unión de Naciones Sudamericanas preamble paras 7 and 6, respectively.

[77] Tratado Constitutivo de la Unión de Naciones Sudamericanas art 4.
[78] Tratado Constitutivo de la Unión de Naciones Sudamericanas art 10.
[79] Tratado Constitutivo de la Unión de Naciones Sudamericanas art 5.
[80] Tratado Constitutivo de la Unión de Naciones Sudamericanas arts 8 and 9.
[81] Tratado Constitutivo de la Unión de Naciones Sudamericanas art 12 para 1.
[82] Tratado Constitutivo de la Unión de Naciones Sudamericanas art 12 para 2.
[83] Tratado Constitutivo de la Unión de Naciones Sudamericanas art 12 para 6.

Taking into account that UNASUR already provides a set of formal means for dispute settlement concerning the interpretation and application of its constitutive treaty,[84] the creation of a permanent forum in charge of the resolution of investment disputes in fact constitutes an attempt to affirm its identity at the international level.[85] To this end, the UNASUR Summit of Heads of States and Government gave a legal mandate to Ecuador in 2010 to develop a proposal for the creation of the UNASUR Centre.[86] A major motivation for this institutional initiative was that some arbitral tribunals did not show deference to certain legal principles which are perceived as highly relevant by UNASUR member States.[87] A Working Group of High Level Experts in Investment Matters ('UNASUR Working Group') was set up to discuss and develop the constitutive treaty of the UNASUR Centre with basis on the Ecuadorian draft treaty.[88]

In the absence of an official draft of the UNASUR Centre treaty, it could be argued that the legal principles established in the constitutive treaty of UNASUR may offer some guidelines on the future normative setting of the UNASUR Centre.[89] Moreover, the sovereignty of States as well as social and environmental objectives had been alluded to as the normative values which the UNASUR Centre would owe deference in the resolution of investment claims.[90]

Currently it is still open whether disputes between investors and its member States may come under the jurisdiction of the UNASUR Centre. For the time being, it has been announced that the UNASUR Centre would be able to settle investment disputes among its member States through arbitration.[91] IIAs generally contain inter-State dispute settlement clauses for disputes concerning their interpretation and application. To this purpose, some treaties had referred

---

[84] Tratado Constitutivo de la Unión de Naciones Sudamericanas art 21.
[85] Tratado Constitutivo de la Unión de Naciones Sudamericanas art 3 lit. (a and 14 para 2.
[86] UNASUR Secretaria General, Declaracion final de la reunión extraordinaria del Consejo de Jefas y Jefes de Estado de la Unión Sudamericana de Naciones (4 May 2010) para 15.
[87] UNASUR Secretaria General, Comunicado, Los cancilleres de UNASUR dejaron listo el texto de declaración presidencial de Quito (9 August 2009).
[88] 'Tratado Constitutivo de Centro de Arbitraje de UNASUR está prácticamente listo' *El Telégrafo* (16 June 2014) <www.telegrafo.com.ec/politica/item/tratado-constitutivo-de-centro-de-arbitraje-de-unasur-esta-practicamente-listo.html> accessed 15 August 2015. The first meeting of the UNASUR Working Group was held from 30 May until 1 June 2011 and was established after the Ecuadorian State submitted its proposal for the Creation of this Centre to the competent UNASUR organs. Tratado Constitutivo de la Unión de Naciones Sudamericanas (adopted 11 March 2011) Art 13 para 2.
[89] Pursuant to the UNASUR constitutive treaty, this organization is based on, among others, the legal values of full respect of State's sovereignty and its right of self-determination, as well as human rights in their universality, indivisibility, and interdependence. Tratado Constitutivo de la Unión de Naciones Sudamericanas (entered into force 11 March 2011), preamble, para 6.
[90] 'Tratado Constitutivo de Centro de Arbitraje de UNASUR está prácticamente listo' *El Telégrafo* (16 June 2014) <www.telegrafo.com.ec/politica/item/tratado-constitutivo-de-centro-de-arbitraje-de-unasur-esta-practicamente-listo.html> accessed 15 August 2015.
[91] UNASUR, VI Reunión del Grupo de Trabajo de Expertos de Alto Nivel de Solución de Controversias en Materia de Inversiones de UNASUR (Acta Final, 29–31 de Mayo 2013); VII Reunión del Grupo de Trabajo de Expertos de Alto Nivel de Solución de Controversias en Materia de Inversiones de UNASUR (Acta Final, 14–16 Agosto 2013; VIII Reunión del Grupo de Trabajo de Expertos de Alto Nivel de Solución de Controversias en Materia de Inversiones de UNASUR (Acta Final, 18–21 de marzo 2014).

to judicial forums or to ad-hoc third party arbitration. Some BITs, for instance, encourage the parties to resolve their disputes before the International Court of Justice.[92] The Common Market for Eastern and Southern Africa (COMESA) Investment Agreement refers, on the contrary, to the COMESA Court of Justice as an optional forum for the resolution of disputes among its member States concerning the interpretation or application of its provisions.[93] In the same way, few inter-State disputes have also been settled through arbitration under the UNCITRAL arbitration rules.[94]

At the same time, some IIA parties have developed their own quasi-judicial mechanisms for the same purpose. The Association of Southeast Asian Nations (ASEAN) provides a particular self-developed procedural mechanism for facilitating the resolution of legal controversies regarding economic and trade agreements.[95] Modelled after the WTO rules on dispute settlement, the ASEAN Protocol on Enhanced Dispute Settlement Procedure serves ASEAN member States to settle disputes concerning the interpretation and application of the ASEAN Comprehensive Investment Agreement.[96]

bb) Structure and basic principles

The internal structure of the UNASUR Centre will depend on whether this Centre is conceived as a permanent body of judges or panel members to decide these claims without stipulating the procedural rules, or as a forum providing procedural rules for exclusively facilitating their resolution. Regardless of its final institutional purpose, the UNASUR Centre may have at least one division that gives support on administrative and technical areas for the good functioning of the Centre,[97] and another division in charge of adopting necessary rules for the institution of proceedings and procedures provided.[98] Besides, the UNASUR Centre

---

[92] Agreement between the Islamic Republic of Pakistan and the Federal Republic of Germany on the Encouragement and Reciprocal Protection of Investments (signed 25 November 1959, entered into force 28 April 1962) Art 9 paras 2 and 3.

[93] Investment Agreement For the COMESA Common Investment Area A|rt 27 para 1 lit. iii.

[94] Treaty between the United States of America and the Republic of Ecuador concerning the Encouragement and Reciprocal Protection of Investment (signed 27 August 1993, entered into force 11 May 1997) Art VII para 1.

[95] 2004 ASEAN Protocol on Enhanced Dispute Settlement Mechanism (adopted 29 November 2004, entered into force 29 November 2004) ('ASEAN EDSM') Art 1 para 1 and Appendix I para 31. GJ Naldi, 'The Asean Protocol on Dispute Settlement Mechanisms: An Appraisal' (2014) J I D S 5, 105–38.

[96] 2009 ASEAN Comprehensive Investment Agreement (adopted 26 February 2009, entered into force 29 March 2012) ('ASEAN Comprehensive Investment Agreement 2009') Art 27.

[97] ICSID Convention Art 11; The Hague Convention for the Pacific Settlement of International Disputes of 1899 (concluded 29 July 1899, entered into force 4 September 1900) ('Pacific Settlement of International Disputes—1899') Art 22; The Hague Convention for the Pacific Settlement of International Disputes of 1907 (concluded 18 October 1907, entered into force 26 January 1910) ('Pacific Settlement of International Disputes—1907') Art 43.

[98] ICSID Convention Art 11. Pacific Settlement of International Disputes—1899 art 28; Pacific Settlement of International Disputes—1907 Art 49; ASEAN EDSM Art 2.

may also offer a list of potential arbitrators to its member States for facilitating the appointment of arbitral tribunals.[99]

Equally important, the UNASUR Centre may also ensure certain guarantees on independency and impartiality of arbitrators, in particular after the concerns raised by some South American countries relating to potential conflict of interest of arbitrators in ISDS.[100] The initial Ecuadorian draft treaty of the UNASUR Centre included a code of conduct similar to WTO practice defining the essential requirements for the appointment of arbitrators.[101] It follows that the UNASUR Centre may also undertake attempts to ensure the independency and impartiality of arbitrators in inter-State dispute settlement as already exist in the ISDS context.[102] Likewise, it can also be assumed that the UNASUR Centre may also devote efforts towards increasing transparency and public participation in inter-State disputes.[103]

---

[99] Ministerio de Relaciones Exteriores y Movilidad Humana (Ecuador), 'Representantes de Unasur analizan proyecto de Acuerdo Constitutivo del Centro de Solución de Controversias en Materia de Inversiones de UNASUR' (22 de Agosto de 2014) <http://cancilleria.gob.ec/representantes-de-unasur-analizan-proyecto-de-acuerdo-constitutivo-del-centro-de-solucion-de-controversias-en-materia-de-inversiones-de-unasur/> accessed 15 August 2015.

[100] Some Latin American countries have regarded ISDS as illegitimate. Ministerio de Relaciones Exteriores y Movilidad Humana (Ecuador), 'Latinoamérica avanza en la creación de un Observatorio del Sur de Transnacionales' (6 May 2014) <http://cancilleria.gob.ec/es/latinoamerica-avanza-en-la-creacion-de-un-observatorio-del-sur-de-transnacionales/> accessed 15 August 2015. They have supported this contention by referring to the Eberhardt-Olivet study which attempted to ascertain the strong bias of arbitrators towards investment protection. C Olivet and P Eberhardt, *Profiting from Injustice: How Law Firms, Arbitrators and Financiers are Fuelling an Investment Arbitration Boom* (Transnational Institute 2012) <www.tni.org/briefing/profiting-injustice> accessed 15 August 2015.

[101] SK Fiezzoni, 'The Challenge of UNASUR Member Countries to Replace ICSID Arbitration' (2011) Beijing L Rev <www.scirp.org/journal/PaperInformation.aspx?PaperID=7722> accessed 15 August 2015). WTO, Understanding on Rules and Procedures Governing the Settlement of Disputes, 1869 UNTS 401 ('WTO DSU') Arts 6 and 11. See also, WTO, Rules of Conduct for the Understanding on Rules and Procedures governing the Settlement of Disputes (11 December 1996), WT/DSB/RC/1, provision IV.

[102] The ICSID Convention introduced the duty of disclosure on arbitrators in order to facilitate the disputing parties the advance awareness of potential conflicts of interest related to their independency after the acceptance of their appointment as a member of the tribunal, whereas UNCITRAL rules demand from potential arbitral tribunals' members the compliance with this requirement before their appointment, concerning any circumstance that might raise doubts on their impartiality and independence. ICSID Convention Art 14 para 1 and ICSID Rules of Procedure for Arbitration Proceedings ('ICSID Arbitration Rules') (April 2006) rule 6; UNCITRAL Arbitration Rules (as revised in 2010) Arts 9 and 11, respectively. See also, WTO DSU Art 8.

[103] Traditionally, ICSID has made significant advances in regularly updating the status of the registered cases and excerpts of the legal rules applicable on arbitral awards. ICSID Arbitration Rules rule 48 para 4; ICSID Additional Facility Rules Art 53 para 3. Currently the UN have also made efforts towards greater transparency in ISDS conducted under the UNCITRAL Arbitration Rules by including the UNCITRAL Rules on Transparency as an additional requirement for their employment in treaty-based investor-State arbitration. As a result, the UN Secretary-General, through the UNCITRAL secretariat, created the Transparency Registry for publishing information and related documents concerning treaty-based investment claims initiated under UNCITRAL Rules. General Assembly Resolution 68/109, [on the report of the Sixth Committee (A/68/462)] 68/109. UNCITRAL Rules on Transparency in Treaty-based Investor-State Arbitration and UNCITRAL Arbitration Rules (as revised in 2010, with new Art 1, para 4, as adopted in 2013) Art 8.

cc) Potential scope of jurisdiction

As already mentioned, State–State dispute settlement clauses have generally been established in IIAs for legal disputes that arise between the treaty parties concerning the interpretation and/or application of their provisions.

By filing an inter-State claim, the claimant State must initially demonstrate the existence of a 'dispute' as a precondition for the establishment of the arbitral tribunal's jurisdiction. In addressing this initial question, the UNASUR Centre may folllow the reading of the term 'dispute' given by the Permanent Court of International Justice and the International Court of Justice.[104] For instance, the *Ecuador v United States* tribunal argued that a dispute requires that the disputing parties hold opposing views concerning the interpretation of a treaty obligation.[105] Once the UNASUR Centre is confronted with this initial question and finds that it has jurisdiction over an inter-State investment claim, it may face the considerable challenge to look for adequate answers to three different types of claims.

First, the UNASUR Centre may exercise jurisdiction over inter-State claims concerning the interpretation of a treaty provision in direct connection with a party's alleged treaty violation as in the aforementioned case. Besides, it may also be confronted with purely interpretative questions concerning the general meaning of a treaty provision. In the *Lucchetti v Peru* case, the Chilean investor, Lucchetti, commenced an investor–State arbitration proceeding against Peru under the Chile–Peru BIT after two years of its entry into force.[106] Peru, on the contrary, countered the allegations of the claimant investor by asserting that the dispute did not fall into the scope of the treaty's application since it arose before the treaty was in force for the parties.[107] Shortly after the submission of the investor–State claim, Peru initiated an inter-State arbitration claim against Chile in order to obtain an authoritative interpretation on whether this investor–State claim was outside the jurisdiction of the investor–State tribunal set up for resolving this dispute.[108] This case example makes aware of the potential duty of the UNASUR Centre to rule on the interaction between inter-State and investor–State claims if it also has

---

[104] For the Permanent Court of International Justice (PCIJ), a dispute constituted a 'disagreement on a point of law or fact, a conflict of legal views or interests between two persons'. *Mavrommatis Palestine Concessions (Greece v Gr Brit)* (1924) PCIJ Series A No 2, 1. In similar vein, the International Court of Justice maintained that a dispute amounts to a situation in which two sides held clearly opposite views concerning the question of performance or non-performance of a treaty obligation. *Interpretation of Peace Treaties with Bulgaria, Hungary and Romania* (Advisory Opinion) (1950) ICJ Rep 65, 74.
[105] See J Hepburn and LE Peterson, 'U.S.-Ecuador Inter-State Investment Treaty Award, Released to Parties; Tribunal Members Part Ways on Key Issues' *Investment Arbitration Reporter* (30 October 2012) <www.iareporter.com/articles/20121030_1> accessed 15 August 2015. This inter-State dispute had its origin in the *Chevron v Ecuador* case. In this investor–State dispute, Ecuador was held liable by the Chevron Tribunal for its failure to provide Chevron effective means for asserting claims and enforcing its rights on account of the lengthy delays incurred by its domestic courts in deciding some investment-contract based claims. *Chevron Corporation (USA) and Texaco Petroleum Company (USA) v Republic of Ecuador*, PCA Case No 34877, Partial Award on Merits (30 March 2010).
[106] *Industria Nacional de Alimentos SA and Indalsa Perú SA (formerly Empresas Lucchetti SA and Lucchetti Peru SA) v The Republic of Peru*, ICSID Case No ARB/03/4, Award (7 February 2005).
[107] ibid 25–37.   [108] ibid 7.

jurisdiction over investor–State disputes. This question will be discussed in the following section.

Second, the UNASUR may not only have the task of settling inter-State disputes concerning the application of IIAs in which treaty parties assert their own direct interests. Diplomatic protection claims may also come under its jurisdiction since a home State may seek recourse to inter-State arbitration on behalf of investors to review the compliance of the host State with its treaty obligations.[109] An illustration of such an inter-State dispute is the *Italy v Cuba* case. Italy filed an inter-State claim against Cuba seeking legal protection in its own name and on behalf of a group of Italian companies.[110]

In this type of inter-State investment claim, the UNASUR Centre may have to deal with the application of customary international rules of diplomatic protection over investment treaty provisions for determining the admissibility of a diplomatic protection claim under IIAs.[111] The *Italy v Cuba* Tribunal set out some guidelines in this regard. Concerning the nationality requirement, the Tribunal dismissed the diplomatic protection claim of Italy on behalf of two companies controlled by Italian nationals but whose place of incorporation was located in two Latin American countries.[112] It maintained the customary place-of-incorporation criteria,[113] thereby disregarding the broad definition of investor provided in the Cuba–Italy BIT.[114] With respect to exhaustion of local remedies, the Tribunal pointed out that it was not an obligation for Italian investors under ISDS clauses in case they wanted to bring an investment claim against Cuba. However, this Tribunal held that satisfying this procedural requirement was indispensable for Italy in order to bring a diplomatic protection claim under this treaty on behalf of its nationals.[115] Following this

---

[109] CJ Trevino, 'State-to-State Investment Treaty Arbitration and the Interplay with Investor-State Arbitration under the same Treaty' (2014) 5 J I D S 206.
[110] *Republic of Italy v Republic of Cuba*, Ad Hoc Arbitration, Sentence préliminaire [Interim Award] (15 March 2005), 24–25 <www.italaw.com/sites/default/files/case-documents/ita0434_0.pdf> accessed 15 August 2015.
[111] Under customary international law, the nationality of a company exits where it has its place of incorporation and will ordinarily maintain a registered office. *Barcelona Traction, Light and Power Company, Limited (Belg v Spain)* (Judgment) (1970) ICJ Rep 3, 90. In this regard, Art 9 of the Draft Articles on Diplomatic Protection adds to this definition that the State of Nationality of a company, which is controlled by nationals of another State and has no substantial business activities in its place of incorporation, is that State where it has its seat of management and financial control are both located. International Law Commission, 2006 Draft Articles on Diplomatic Protection with commentaries, UN Doc A/61/10 ('2006 ILC Draft Articles') Art 9, 38. Only the State where the company was incorporated is entitled to bring a diplomatic protection claim. Ibid Art 11, 1.
[112] *Republic of Italy v Republic of Cuba*, Ad Hoc Arbitration, Sentence finale [Final Award] (1 January 2008) 200–21 <http://italaw.com/sites/default/files/case-documents/ita0435_0.pdf> accessed 15 August 2015.
[113] *Republic of Italy v Republic of Cuba*, Ad Hoc Arbitration, Sentence finale, Dissenting Opinion of Attila Tanzi) 31 <http://italaw.com/sites/default/files/case-documents/ita0436_0.pdf> accessed 15 August 2015.
[114] ibid 35.
[115] *Republic of Italy v Republic of Cuba*, Ad Hoc Arbitration, Sentence préliminaire [Interim Award] (15 March 2005), 88–89.

reasoning, the Tribunal thus dismissed Italy's argument that the ISDS clause of the Cuba–Italy BIT serves as a waiver to the customary international law requirement of exhausting domestic remedies for seeking recourse to diplomatic protection under this treaty. It maintained that the treaty parties have not included any provision that expressly exclude the exhaustion of their domestic remedies for resorting to diplomatic protection.[116]

Accordingly, the UNASUR Centre may have to decide whether it adopts the *Italy v Cuba* Tribunal's reasoning which strongly relied on the customary international rules on diplomatic protection, or whether it follows existing jurisprudence which already acknowledges that a special agreement between treaty parties concerning the scope of this term excludes the application of customary international rules.[117]

Finally, the UNASUR Centre could possibly also have to decide on inter-State claims pursuing a declaration on whether a treaty party's action or omission constitutes a breach of its treaty obligations.[118] Some Latin American countries prevent ISDS over taxation measures by imposing upon any arbitral tribunal the duty to follow the joint determination of the competent authorities, established in the respective IIA, on whether a State party has breached a treaty obligation by the undertaking of taxation measures.[119] This type of investment claim contributes to clarifying the underlying motivations of a host State's measure that could lead to an investor–State treaty claim.[120] Whether or not this determination is binding to inter-State arbitral tribunals will be part of the discussion below.

dd) Relationship between inter-State and investor–State disputes

Implying that the UNASUR Centre may also have jurisdiction over investor–State disputes, and depending on the type of inter-State investment claim and the stage of the investor–State arbitration proceedings, it follows that it would have the additional challenging duty to rule on the interaction between inter-State and investor–State claims.

Within the context of the ICSID Convention, the contracting parties are prevented from according diplomatic protection if an investment claim is brought by an investor, unless the respondent State did not comply with the arbitral award issued in this dispute.[121] Many investment treaties actually restate the wording of the ICSID Convention by providing that an investor–State treaty claim precludes the recourse of the home State to diplomatic protection for its national.[122] In this respect, the *Italy v Cuba* Tribunal confirmed this reading by asserting that the

---

[116] ibid 90.   [117] Trevino (n 108).
[118] A Roberts, 'State-to-State Investment Treaty Arbitration: A Hybrid Theory of Interdependent Rights and Shared Interpretive Authority' (2014) 55 Harv I L J.
[119] See Agreement between Canada and the Republic of Peru for the Promotion and Protection of Investments (adopted 14 November 2006, entered into force on 20 June 2007) Art 16 para 4.
[120] Roberts (n 117).   [121] ICSID Convention Art 27 para 1.
[122] See M Potestà, 'State-to-State Dispute Settlement pursuant to Bilateral Investment Treaties: Is there Potential?' in N Boschiero and T Scovarazzi (eds), *International Courts and the Development of International Law—Essays in Honour of Tullio Treves* (TMC Asser Press 2012) 763–64.

investor's home country could have recourse to diplomatic protection under a BIT inter-State dispute settlement clause if the investor did not submit a claim against the host State.[123] Accordingly, a diplomatic protection claim under IIA provisions following this treaty language may be admissible *before* the submission of an investor–State treaty claim and *only after* in such cases if the arbitral award already rendered was not honoured by the respondent State.

Treaty parties which do not include a procedural provision with similar terms may probably be allowed to bring diplomatic protection claims before investor–State arbitral tribunal's final decision on a particular case. However, in case of compliance with the award, inter-State tribunals would find it difficult to determine the existence of an 'international wrongful act' of the respondent State in a previous investor–State claim. An inter-State tribunal would thus dismiss a home State's diplomatic protection claim for damages already redressed to its national,[124] yet, an inter-State tribunal could also consider a diplomatic protection claim motivated by an unfavourable award as an abuse of process of the investor's home State.[125]

An alternative scenario could be constructed concerning the interaction of an inter-State claim pursuing a treaty interpretation or a declaration of a treaty violation with ISDS. IIA provisions generally establish that inter-State arbitral awards are binding without further enlightening as to whom they apply. While this might be true, it has been argued that an inter-State arbitral award on interpretative questions would be authoritative, at least for an investor–State tribunal. While some scholars contended that an inter-State arbitral award about the interpretation of a treaty term should be considered as a direct agreement between treaty parties due to their consent already given for that purpose in IIAs,[126] few arbitral tribunals had denied the obligatory nature of treaty parties' joint determination of the scope of a particular treaty term.[127]

Taking these considerations into account, some authors[128] have recommended that an investor–State tribunal should owe deference to an inter-State arbitration claim with interpretative purposes, or to await the outcome of such a dispute based on the consent given by the disputing treaties parties to the later tribunal for doing so. These propositions recognize the legitimate right of treaty parties in seeking an interpretation of their rights and obligations through the means they had agreed,

---

[123] *Republic of Italy v Republic of Cuba*, Ad Hoc Arbitration, Sentence préliminaire [Interim Award] (15 March 2005) 65.
[124] 2006 ILC Draft Articles Art 1. [125] Trevino (n 108). [126] ibid 221, 225.
[127] To illustrate, the *Pope & Talbot* Tribunal rejected the interpretation given by the NAFTA Free Trade Commission concerning the content of the NAFTA's 'minimum standard of treatment' by arguing that its purpose was its retroactive amendment in order to interfere with an ongoing case. *Pope & Talbot Inc v The Government of Canada*, UNCITRAL, Award in Respect of Damages (31 May 2002) 47 <www.italaw.com/cases/863> accessed 15 August 2015. Contrarily, other arbitral tribunals recognized the same treaty term's interpretation as authoritative and thus, binding. *ADF Group Inc v United States of America*, ICSID Case No ARB (AF)/00/1, Award (9 January 2003), 77. *Methanex Corp v United States of America*, UNCITRAL, Final Award of the Tribunal on Jurisdiction and Merits (3 August 2005) 20 <www.italaw.com/cases/683> accessed 15 August 2015.
[128] Trevino (n 108). Based on the rules of the Vienna Convention and existing case law, supporters of this reading sustain this reasoning by equating an inter-State arbitral award with a direct agreement between the parties about the interpretation of a treaty term achieved after its conclusion. Ibid 221, 225. See also, Roberts (n 117) 61–63.

namely before an inter-State tribunal, but at the same time, acknowledge the discretionary power of an investor–State tribunal to decide on whether an inter-State tribunal's interpretation is compatible or not with the treaty's text or treaty party's intended understanding.[129]

On the other hand, bringing an inter-State interpretative dispute may not be successful after commencing an investor–State arbitration claim or once an award has been rendered. As already mentioned, the ICSID Convention explicitly rules on the interaction between an international claim and an investment claim already brought before its jurisdiction.[130] This provision might be understood as to exclude an arbitration proceeding between States and another proceeding between an investor and a State, when both investment claims arise from the same investment treaty.[131] Under this reading, an inter-State arbitral tribunal may not exercise jurisdiction on an inter-State investment claim, when this claim has the purpose of avoiding, obstructing, or exercising certain influence on an investor–State treaty claim previously filed pursuant to these procedural rules, or affecting the implementation of an arbitral award rendered by an ICSID tribunal.[132]

Even though no official information is available concerning the *Peru v Chile* case, the *Lucchetti v Peru* Tribunal confirmed this understanding about the interaction between an inter-State and investor–State tribunal when it rejected Peru's pretension to suspend the investment claim filed by the investor.[133] Therefore, a similar outcome could be expected in the future since some IIAs also exclude the possibility of submitting an inter-State claim when an investor–State claim has already been filed.[134]

ee) Outlook

The creation of the UNASUR Centre constitutes a joint endeavour of South American countries, beyond the reforms introduced in IIAs, to ensure a counterbalance to the perceived expansive interpretation of arbitral tribunals of the legal commitments honoured within these international treaties.

The UNASUR Centre constitutes an ambitious project due to the fact that it is hitherto intended to have jurisdiction on inter-State investment disputes and is strongly oriented towards State's sovereignty and non-economic policy objectives in the resolution of these disputes. As such, it is expected to address to which extent it will differ from the traditional constitutive treaties of arbitration institutions, or the existing international arbitration rules. It is only in this way that it will

---

[129] ibid 225–26.   [130] ICSID Convention Art 27.
[131] C Schreuer, 'The ICSID Convention: A Commentary on the Convention on the Settlement of Investment Disputes between States and Nationals of other States' (2nd edn, CUP 2009) [Art 27, 420].
[132] ibid 421.
[133] *Industria Nacional de Alimentos SA and Indalsa Perú SA (formerly Empresas Lucchetti SA and Lucchetti Peru SA) v The Republic of Peru*, ICSID Case No ARB/03/4, Award (7 February 2005) 7 and 9.
[134] Already the ASEAN Comprehensive Investment Agreement includes a provision in such terms. The ASEAN Comprehensive Investment Agreement (2009) Art 34 para 3.

be possible to assess the institutional and legal implications that a regional forum of such nature will have for the international investment law regime.

Moreover, some structural reforms are required for achieving these ambitious aims. The jurisdiction of future UNASUR arbitral tribunals would require that its member States reform their IIAs, unless inter-State arbitration clauses are drafted in such a broad way that they could imply their jurisdiction from its content.

Consequently, there is a lot of work ahead for all policymakers and legal professionals involved in the consolidation of this South American project.

b) Observatory on Transnational Corporations

The ALBA-TCP has also become active in introducing concrete initiatives to achieve greater transparency in ISDS. It encourages the creation of the Observatory on Investment and Transnational Corporations for monitoring the actions of arbitral tribunals through a regular update of investment claims filed against their potential member States.[135] Moreover, the it may also be in charge of providing counselling services to its member States.[136]

The observable fact that Latin America has suffered the highest rate of investment treaty claims filed up to the present time[137] exposes the lacking abilities of these States to prevent or manage these complex international disputes. Presumably, the idea of creating this entity within ALBA-TCP was brought by Ecuador in 2009 when this country proposed in 2009 setting up a counselling centre to complement the operation of the UNASUR Centre.[138] This initiative may facilitate its potential members to gain a better understanding of the scope of their investment treaty obligations and thus take them into account when adopting or implementing regulatory policies or measures, as well as exercise more caution when negotiating new IIAs.[139]

Certainly, the ALBA-TCP did not exclude the involvement of countries from other regions. In its latest meeting, some African and Asian States also participated

---

[135] V Villaruel, 'El Observatorio sobre Inversión y Transnacionales y su Importancia para el Desarrollo Regional' (Diplomacia Ciudadana, Revista bimestral No 9, Ministerio de Relaciones Exteriores y Movilidad Humana, 2009).
[136] ibid.
[137] UNCTAD 'Recent Developments in Investor-State Dispute Settlement' (2014) 1 IIA Issues Note <http://unctad.org/en/PublicationsLibrary/webdiaepcb2014d3_en.pdf > accessed 15 August 2015.
[138] Fiezzoni (n 99). Considering the strong WTO approach adopted by Ecuador when drawing up the first draft treaty of the UNASUR Centre, it could even be envisaged that the Advisory Centre on WTO Law might serve as a model for defining the structure and financing of this Observatory. The Advisory Centre on WTO Law is composed of a general assembly, a management board, and an executive director, and is financed, among other sources, with the contributions of its member States, depending on their level of development. Advisory Centre on WTO Law <www.acwl.ch/e/index.html> accessed 15 August 2015. See also, CP Brown, *Self-Enforcing Trade Developing Countries and Dispute Settlement* (Brookings Institution Press 2006) 142–45.
[139] ibid 165–67.

in the discussion of this initiative.¹⁴⁰ This development opens up a new path in the wide range of existing alternatives. Through South–South cooperation, some Latin American countries aim at subjecting arbitrators to public scrutiny for their actions in the resolution of investment claims, and in decreasing the probabilities of being respondent States of investment treaty claims.

V. Conclusion

The expansive interpretation of investment treaty obligations and potential deficiencies in an independent and impartial resolution of investor–State treaty claims build the main foundations for concerns over IIAs and ISDS in Latin America. These adverse circumstances have not led to a decrease in the conclusion of IIAs. Rather, the majority of Latin American States currently address both issues with a cautious negotiation of treaty provisions.

Even though IIAs still enjoy great confidence in Latin America as a legal means for the protection of foreign investment, a nascent tendency can be identified in Ecuador towards the reassertion of investment contracts and domestic laws as measures for mitigating the concerns relating to the predominant model in current international investment law. To this end, it redefined its investment policy by amending its investment law and enacting an investment contract model, as well as establishing an Audit Commission for assessing to which extent the BITs signed by this country attract investment flows into its territory. While the Ecuadorian attitude towards IIAs remains under revision, its definite departure from IIAs may have the effect of preventing the engagement of economically less powerful foreign companies in economic activities within its territory. In contrast to transnational corporations, they usually lack the necessary bargaining power to surpass the modest legal protection domestically accorded to foreign investment.

Additionally, guarantees of legal stability on the domestic legal framework have also come under scrutiny and subject to reforms in Latin America due to the potential constrains that they might pose on regulatory power. Also, reinforcing the non-economic domestic legal obligations of foreign investors is a common practice in investment laws. Interestingly, incipient attempts can also be observed in investment contract models to regulate the corporate conduct of foreign investors.

Despite the heterogeneity of investment policy approaches, Latin American countries seem to share the willingness to consolidate two institutional alternatives

---

¹⁴⁰ 'Países del Sur buscan en Venezuela crear observatorio sobre Inversiones y Transnacionales' Agencia Pública Nacional de Noticias del Ecuador y Sudamérica ANDES (11 September 2014) <www.andes.info.ec/es/noticias/paises-sur-buscan-venezuela-crear-observatorio-sobre-inversiones-transnacionales.html> accessed 15 August 2015. 'Southern Observatory on Transnational Corporations to redress balance between states and companies' Agencia Venezolana de Noticias (AVN) (10 September 2014) <www.avn.info.ve/contenido/southern-observatory-transnational-corporations-redress-balance-between-states-and-compani> accessed 15 August 2015.

for jointly mitigating the perceived deficiencies of investment treaty-based arbitration. The first relates to the establishment of the UNASUR Centre for the settlement of investment disputes that aims at resolving investment treaty disputes that arise between its member States. The second refers to the creation of an Observatory on Investment and Transnational Corporations which pursues reinforcing the accountability of arbitrators and improving the understanding of investment treaty obligations of its future members.

Although the inter-State investment dispute settlement mechanism has been restricted in the past to the resolution of residual issues such as non-compliance with an arbitral award,[141] the establishment of the UNASUR Centre could revive the debate about the potential of inter-State dispute settlement as an instrument for attaining greater consistency in treaty interpretation.

Taking for granted that the UNASUR Centre will have jurisdiction over inter-State investment claims, it may resolve interpretative questions directly related to an investment treaty violation, or make a mere abstract interpretation of a treaty provision in addition to inter-State claims seeking declaratory relief. Furthermore, this forum may decide on inter-State claims concerning the application of IIAs, in which the claimant State vindicates its own direct interests, or has recourse to diplomatic protection on behalf of its national. In the latter case, the UNASUR Centre may also be called to decide the weight that it would give to the customary international law rules on diplomatic protection.

Finally, if the UNASUR Centre also exercises jurisdiction on investor–State claims, it will thus be compelled to decide on the interaction of the two dispute settlement mechanisms. This may give the impression of increasing, rather than lessening, the inconsistency concerns already voiced over arbitral tribunal interpretation of IIAs. While this might be true, States parties of IIAs also have the legitimate interest in seeking an interpretation of their treaty rights and obligations before arbitral tribunals. Faced with this dilemma, the UNASUR Centre should be able to provide at least guarantees on procedural fairness in order to prevent the aforementioned incompatibilities, and thus its ultimate failure.

---

[141] *Republic of Ecuador v United States of America*, PCA Case No 2012-5, Expert Opinion with Respect to Jurisdiction, Prof. W Michael Reisman (24 April 2012) 20–21, 10, 4.

XIII
Jumping Back and Forth between Domestic Courts and ISDS
Mixed Signals from the Asia-Pacific Region

*Leon E. Trakman and Kunal Sharma**

I. Introduction

It is uncontroversial that cross-border investments engender the possibility of disputes arising between investors and host States. What is unclear is whether such disputes should be characterized as being unique or distinctive because they involve foreign investors. What is further in controversy is whether there should be a customized mechanism to resolve such disputes. The institution of investor–State dispute settlement (ISDS), which has for some time enjoyed popularity as a way of resolving investor–State disputes, has come under renewed scrutiny over the past few years as a result of dissatisfaction articulated by a number of countries.

Many South American and Asian countries have expressed concerns over the nature of ISDS and the organizations that facilitate it.[1] This includes Nicaragua and Venezuela signalling an intention to terminate existing bilateral investment treaties (BITs),[2] and Ecuador denouncing the International Centre for Settlement of Investment Disputes (ICSID) established by the World Bank, which is the primary source of investment arbitration.[3] In 2007, the Philippines negotiated to exclude ISDS in its free trade

---

* This chapter is part of ongoing research related to a discovery grant awarded by the Australian Research Council (2014–16) (DP140102526). The authors thank Luke Nottage for his comments and suggestions.

[1] See LE Trakman, 'Choosing Domestic Courts over Investor-State Arbitration: Australia's Repudiation of the Status Quo' (2012) 35 UNSW LJ 979; LE Trakman, 'The ICSID under Siege' (2012) 45 Cornell Intl LJ 603.

[2] For commentary on these events, as well as investment arbitration in Latin America generally, see S Appleton, *Latin American Arbitration: The Story Behind the Headlines*, International Bar Association <www.ibanet.org/Article/Detail.aspx?ArticleUid=78296258-3B37-4608-A5EE-3C92D5D0B979> accessed 20 October 2014.

[3] See ICSID in Crisis: Straight-Jacket or Investment Protection?' *Bretton Woods Project* (10 July 2009) <www.brettonwoodsproject.org/art-564878>. See also S Hamamoto and L Nottage, 'Foreign Investment in and out of Japan: Economic Backdrop, Domestic Law, and International Treaty-Based Investor-State Dispute Resolution' (2011) 5 Transn Disp Mgmt <www.transnational-dispute-management.com/article.asp?key=1766> accessed 11 July 2014.

agreement with Japan.⁴ In March 2014, Indonesia indicated that it would terminate its BIT with the Netherlands and likely implement a scheme of terminating all of its remaining BITs as they become due to expire.⁵

In 2011, the Commonwealth Government of Australia stated in a Trade Policy Statement ('the Policy') that Australia would no longer agree to the inclusion of ISDS in its future bilateral and regional trade agreements (BRTAs), choosing instead to rely on alternatives to ISDS.⁶ After a change in Australia's Government in 2013, two years after the Policy was announced, the new Liberal–National Coalition Government has retreated from that Policy notably by including an ISDS regime in the Korea–Australia Free Trade Agreement (KAFTA) concluded on 5 December 2013, and the China–Australia Free Trade Agreement (ChAFTA) concluded on 17 June 2015.⁷ References to the Policy have been removed from the Department of Foreign Affairs and Trade's official website, which indicates instead that it will consider the inclusion of ISDS on a case-by-case basis.⁸ Further, the Government has categorically stated that Australia's ability to pass public interest legislation, such as in the areas of national security, public health, and environmental protection, will not be compromised. Notably, the Japan–Australia Economic Partnership Agreement (JAEPA), concluded in April 2014, does not include an ISDS regime.⁹ Australia is currently in bilateral negotiations with Indonesia and India, as well as having a stake in the imminent Trans Pacific Partnership Agreement (TPPA).¹⁰ It is not clear what negotiation stance the Australian Government is likely to take with respect to these instruments.

In formulating national investment policy, including with respect to ISDS, governments should seek to adopt measures that pursue broader economic development, encourage responsible investor behaviour, and are practical in ensuring policy effectiveness. These principles, addressing concerns about investment policy generally and ISDS in particular, are reflected in the global debate over

---

⁴ See Hamamoto and Nottage (n 3).
⁵ Netherlands Embassy in Jakarta, Indonesia, 'Termination Bilateral Investment Treaty' <http://indonesia.nlembassy.org/organization/departments/economic-affairs/termination-bilateral-investment-treaty.html> accessed 11 July 2014.
⁶ Department of Foreign Affairs and Trade (Australia), 'Gillard Government Trade Policy Statement: Trading Our Way to More Jobs and Prosperity' (April 2011).
⁷ Korea–Australia Free Trade Agreement (signed 8 April 2014, entered into force 12 December 2014) (KAFTA) [2014] ATNIF 4, ch 11; China–Australia Free Trade Agreement (signed 17 June 2015, not yet entered into force) ch 9.
⁸ Department of Foreign Affairs and Trade (Australia), 'Frequently Asked Questions on Investor-State Dispute Settlement (ISDS)' <http://dfat.gov.au/fta/isds-faq.html> accessed 11 July 2014. For comments on the Policy by the Coalition Government elected in 2013 see R Callick, 'Korea Ready to Talk Turkey After FTA Hurdle Removed' *The Australian* (1 November 2013) <www.theaustralian.com.au/business/economics/korea-ready-to-talk-turkey-after-fta-hurdle-removed/story-e6frg926-1226750841630#> accessed 11 July 2014.
⁹ Japan–Australia Economic Partnership Agreement (signed 8 July 2014, entered into force 15 January 2015) (JAEPA) [2014] ATNIA 14. See also Department of Foreign Affairs and Trade (Australia), 'Conclusion of Negotiations' <www.dfat.gov.au/fta/jaepa/> accessed 11 July 2014.
¹⁰ Department of Foreign Affairs and Trade (Australia), 'Australia's Trade Agreements' <www.dfat.gov.au/fta/> accessed 11 July 2014.

sustainable development, notably in the UNCTAD's Investment Policy Framework for Sustainable Development (IPFSD).[11]

In light of a broader framework for sustainable development of investment policy, this chapter will consider the value of ISDS in resolving disputes between host States and foreign investors, particularly in the Asia Pacific region. It will argue that the oscillation between ISDS and domestic courts serves to destabilize international commerce as well as comity between states. It will recommend, in response, potential developments to the substantive and procedural execution of ISDS provisions. The chapter will focus on the policies articulated by Australia in its Policy Statement in 2011 and then in 2013. The chapter will also construe the positions adopted by a number of Asian countries as examples of developments taking place within the region and the potential future of ISDS regionally as well as internationally.

II. The Practical Value of ISDS

Domestic policies and international accord in relation to ISDS have a direct impact on trade and investment, both within the region and globally.[12] Countries within the Asia Pacific region have the capacity to influence each other's investment regimes, as well as having an impact on investment practices outside the region.[13] As a method of resolving investor–State disputes, ISDS is arguably directed at promoting a healthy cross-border flow of FDI and providing investors with a viable and fair platform for dispute resolution.[14] A foreign investor can lodge a claim against a host State to be resolved through a specialized and expert international investment tribunal, without the need to mobilize its home State to take diplomatic action or to pursue inter-State dispute resolution, including through the WTO.

ISDS has been increasingly incorporated into trade and investment agreements worldwide, including countries in Asia, which historically resisted ISDS due to

---

[11] See UNCTAD, Investment Policy Framework for Sustainable Development (IPFSD) <http://unctad.org/en/Pages/DIAE/International%20Investment%20Agreements%20%28IIA%29/IIA-IPFSD.aspx> accessed 20 October 2014.

[12] See R Abbott, F Erixon, and M Francesca Ferracane, 'Demystifying Investor-State Dispute Settlement (ISDS)' (2014) ECIPE Occasional Paper 5/2014, <www.ecipe.org/media/publication_pdfs/OCC52014__1.pdf>; Seventh Annual Forum of Developing Countries Investment Negotiators, sponsored by the International Institute for Sustainable Development, the Ministry of Foreign Affairs for Indonesia and the South Centre, Jakarta, 4–6 November 2013 <www.iisd.org/pdf/2013/7th_annual_forum_report.pdf>.

[13] On the extent to which global economic and political norms are adopted regionally, such as in Asia, or lead to norm diffusion, see D Capie, 'When Does Track Two Matter? Structure, Agency and Asian Regionalism' (2010) 17 Rev Intl Pol Econ 291.

[14] See Trakman, 'Choosing Domestic Courts' (n 1); LE Trakman, 'Investor State Arbitration or Local Courts: Will Australia Set a New Trend?' (2012) 46 JWT 83; L Nottage, 'Throwing the Baby Out with the Bathwater: Australia's New Policy on Treaty-Based Arbitration and its Impact in Asia' (2013) 37 Asian Stud Rev 253; M Burch, L Nottage, and B Williams, 'Appropriate Treaty-Based Dispute Resolution for Asia-Pacific Commerce in the 21st Century' (2012) 35 UNSW LJ 1013.

various ideological and economic considerations.[15] It is now a commonly used method of investor–State dispute resolution in the region, and is perceived to have some distinct benefits over the alternatives.

ISDS can insulate States in general from diplomatic involvement in investment disputes by giving their investors an alternative pathway to resolve their grievances against host States. ISDS can also obviate the need for outbound investors to seek domestic legal remedies in foreign States which they may view as less impartial than international investment arbitration.[16] As a result, foreign investors may be attracted to invest in certain markets, including countries in the Asia Pacific region, because of the availability of ISDS mechanisms, on the assumption that they would not be exposed to unfair or unprincipled treatment at the hands of domestic courts.[17] In addition, ISDS can confer substantive protections on foreign investors, such as most-favoured-nation or national treatment guarantees under international investment law. As such, a rejection of ISDS by States in the Asian region does not simply exclude that *process* of dispute settlement; it excludes the substantive protections that investment treaties and international law more generally often confer on foreign investors in light of their vulnerable position, including when facing the domestic courts of host States in Asia.

A country such as Australia, which has a dualist system, does not provide for international laws to be directly applied in domestic courts. Clauses such as those providing for most-favoured-nation treatment cannot be enforced in its domestic courts unless there is domestic legislation providing for such protection. Thus, a rejection of ISDS in a treaty between Australia and an Asian treaty partner is also a rejection of many of the substantive protections that a community of nations has invested decades in developing.[18] Such a position proceeds on the subtext that foreign investors should not be given additional protections or incentives for investment beyond those given to domestic investors, even where their inbound investments could be exposed to unfair government interference or expropriation. Problematically, the impugned conduct may often not be unlawful under the domestic laws of the host country engaged in such interference, including through changes in legislation effected for that very purpose. Certainly, Australia and other countries within the Asia Pacific region are unlikely to target foreign investors in this manner, particularly where robust protections are entrenched in the State's constitutional framework. The potential for this occurrence, however, is not far-fetched.

---

[15] See L Nottage and R Weeramantry, 'Investment Arbitration in Asia: Five Perspectives on Law and Practice (2012) 28(1) Arb Int 19.

[16] J Kurtz, 'Australia's Rejection of Investor–State Arbitration: Causation, Omission and Implication' (2012) 27(1) ICSID Rev 65; Trakman 'Investor State Arbitration or Local Courts' (n 14).

[17] On treaty provisions for ISDS across Asia, including a critique of the practice, by the Chief Justice of Australia, see R S French, 'Investor State Dispute Settlement: A Cut Above the Courts?', Speech at the Supreme and Federal Courts Judges' Conference (Darwin 9 July 2014) <www.hcourt.gov.au/assets/publications/speeches/current-justices/frenchcj/frenchcj09jul14.pdf>.

[18] See LE Trakman, 'Investor-State Arbitration: Evaluating Australia's Evolving Position' (2014) 15 J World Inv & Trade152, 173.

The above is not intended to suggest that ISDS is without shortcomings or critics. Certainly, the power imbalance between States and investors is not always in favour of host States. Many developing countries do not have the resources that wealthy investors have. As a result, in recent years a number of developing States, including in Asia, have become critical of ISDS and rejected the process as well as challenging the tribunals that deliver it on procedural grounds, not least of all for conflicts of interest: these States have also adopted alternative dispute resolution models to ISDS.[19]

This chapter contends that criticisms of ISDS, however justified in particular cases, should not be universally adopted as a means of rejecting it, without close further examination. The merits of ISDS relative to resolution of disputes by domestic courts are considered in section IV below.

III. Domestic Policies—Australia and the Asia Pacific

a) Australian Labor Party's 2011 trade policy

The Australian Government, led by Prime Minister Julia Gillard, articulated its aversion to ISDS in the 2011 Policy, providing that Australia would no longer negotiate treaty protections 'that confer greater legal rights on foreign businesses than those available to domestic businesses' or rights that would 'constrain the ability of the Australian Government to make laws on social, environmental, and economic matters in circumstances where those laws do not discriminate between domestic and foreign businesses'.[20]

One of the aims of the Policy was to prevent foreign investors from invoking ISDS to challenge Australia's regulatory autonomy over public safety, health, and the environment.[21] The Policy was informed, to some degree, by an increase in FDI flows into Australia, particularly in the resources and energy sectors,[22] and by the significant potential for investors to institute claims against Australia challenging domestic environmental and health legislation. By declining to incorporate ISDS in its BRTAs, Australia would have greater latitude in designing sustainable measures to preserve its public interests, thereby avoiding pressures created by the so-called 'regulatory chill' arising from the perceived threat of having to defend against costly and intrusive ISDS claims.[23]

---

[19] See Trakman (nn 1, 14, 18). For a general overview of this trend see M Waibel (ed), *The Backlash Against Investment Arbitration: Perceptions and Reality* (Kluwer Law International 2010).
[20] ibid 1–2.
[21] See L Nottage, 'Investor-State Arbitration Policy and Practice after *Philip Morris Asia v Australia*' in LE Trakman and N Ranieri (eds), *Regionalism in International Investment Law* (OUP 2013) ch 15, 452.
[22] K Tienhaara, 'Regulatory Chill and the Threat of Arbitration: A View from Political Science' in C Brown and K Miles (eds), *Evolution in Investment Treaty Law and Arbitration* (CUP 2012) ch 26, 606.
[23] ibid.

These concerns are reflected in wider global concerns, notably in UNCTAD's IPFSD, which recognizes that 'ISDS claims can be used by foreign investors in unanticipated ways'. Noting that '[a] number of recent cases have challenged measures adopted in the public interest (for example, measures to promote social equity, foster environmental protection or protect public health)', the IPFSD observes that 'the borderline between protection from political risk and undue interference with legitimate domestic polices is becoming increasingly blurred'.[24] They are also illustrated in part by Philip Morris' ISDS claim against Australia under the Hong Kong–Australia BIT over Australia's decision to require the plain packaging of cigarettes on public health grounds[25] and recent WTO challenges against Australia initiated by Ukraine and now including, among others, Indonesia, over the same issue.[26] While the Philip Morris case provides a good illustration of the challenges envisaged by the critics of ISDS, certainly one ISDS claim is not sufficient to show that a systemic problem exists, jeopardizing Australia's ability to legislate on public health grounds in the national interest. Aside from the fact that it is the very purpose of ISDS to facilitate challenges against host States where other avenues are not available, it is unusual to reject the institution of ISDS on the basis of one claim that the Government may perceive to be unsubstantiated. Certainly, few of Australia's regional neighbours and trading partners who are parties to BITs providing for ISDS have reacted so strongly when a claim has been brought against them.[27]

Australia has further concerns that foreign drug companies could invoke ISDS to contest restrictions on foreign manufactured drugs under Australia's Pharmaceutical Benefits Scheme (PBS), which selectively restricts public access to some pharmaceuticals while subsidizing others.[28] Such concerns have been articulated with renewed emphasis in the context of the TPPA negotiations.[29] The

---

[24] UNCTAD (n 11) 40.
[25] On Philip Morris' ongoing action against Australia under the Australia–Hong Kong Free Trade Agreement, see Philip Morris International News Release, 'Philip Morris Asia Initiates Legal Action Against the Australian Government Over Plain Packaging' (27 June 2011) <www.pmi.com/eng/media_center/press_releases/pages/PM_Asia_plain_packaging.aspx> accessed 11 July 2014. On Philip Morris' unsuccessful action against the Australia Government, see *Philip Morris Limited and Prime Minister* [2011] AATA 556. See also *JT International SA v Commonwealth of Australia* [2012] HCA 43. On the earlier claim brought against the Republic of Uruguay under the Switzerland–Uruguay BIT, see *FTR Holdings SA (Switzerland) v Oriental Republic of Uruguay*, ICSID Case No ARB/10/7, Request for Arbitration (19 February 2010). FTR Holding SA is a subsidiary of Philip Morris International Inc (PMI). PMI's Operation's Centre is in Switzerland. See also AD Mitchell and SM Wurzberger, 'Boxed in? Australia's Plain Tobacco Packaging Initiative and International Investment Law' (2011) 27 Arb Int 623; T Voon and A Mitchell, 'Implications of WTO Law for Plain Packaging of Tobacco Products' in A Mitchell, T Voon, and J Liberman (eds), *Public Health and Plain Packaging of Cigarettes: Legal Issues* (Edward Elgar 2012) ch 6, 109.
[26] WTO, *Australia: Certain Measures Concerning Trademarks and Other Plain Packaging Requirements Applicable to Tobacco Products and Packaging'* (9 May 2014) WT/DS434 <www.wto.org/english/tratop_e/dispu_e/cases_e/ds434_e.htm> accessed 11 July 2014.
[27] Nottage (n 14) 257.
[28] On the PBS see Department of Health (Australia) 'Pharmaceutical Benefits Scheme: PBS News Updates' <www.pbs.gov.au> accessed 11 July 2014.
[29] G Chan, 'Leaked Trade Deal Terms Prompt Fears for Pharmaceutical Benefits Scheme' *The Guardian* (11 June 2015) <www.theguardian.com/business/2015/jun/11/pacific-trade-deal-raises-fears-over-future-of-pharmaceutical-benefits-scheme> accessed 16 August 2015.

Government also has ongoing disquiet about foreign investors securing a controlling interest in the Australian media and in core financial markets such as the stock exchange (exemplified by Australia's refusal to permit the takeover, expressed as an amalgamation, of the Australian Stock Exchange by its Singaporean counterpart).[30]

The proposition underlying the Gillard Government's policy in 2011 was that Australian courts would be more likely to protect domestic public policy in cases brought by foreign investors against the Australian Government than international ISDS tribunals. Ancillary to this view was its supposition that domestic courts in Australia are more likely to take account of national security legislation, administrative regulations, and prior domestic court decisions in Australia in so deciding, whereas international ISDS tribunals are less likely to so respond to such domestic requirements or expectations.

b) The Coalition Government's current policy

The current Liberal–National Coalition Government appears to have adopted a more tempered approach to ISDS. Whereas the Gillard Government took an in-principle approach in indicating that it would not agree to the incorporation of ISDS into its future BRTAs, the Coalition Government has indicated that it will take a contextual or 'case-by-case' approach regarding the incorporation of ISDS in future BITs.[31] In this spirit, it has adopted ISDS in its recent BIT with the Republic of Korea.[32] Illustrating the case-by-case approach, the agreement with Japan that soon followed did not include an ISDS regime.[33] This may, however, be of limited significance if an ISDS mechanism is ultimately included in the Trans-Pacific Partnership Agreement (TPPA), and if neither Japan nor Australia, as TPPA negotiating parties, are exempted from ISDS.

The fact that JAEPA does not include ISDS provisions intially gave rise to renewed criticisms of ISDS, including comments that it is no longer being sought by Asian countries.[34] However, this is far from established, particularly in light of the ISDS inclusions in KAFTA and ChAFTA. Certainly, ISDS is an important negotiating point in the TPPA, which remains one of the most significant regional agreements ever contemplated. As such, it is difficult to accept that Australia can abandon ISDS without repercussions.

---

[30] See LE Trakman, 'National Good No Issue in ASX Deal' *The Australian* (2 November 2010) <www.theaustralian.com.au/business/national-good-no-issue-in-asx-deal/story-e6frg8zx-1225946362212> accessed 11 July 2014.
[31] See 'Frequently Asked Questions on Investor-State Dispute Settlement (ISDS)' (n 8).
[32] See KAFTA (n 7) ch 11 (Investment).
[33] P Martin, 'ISDS: The Trap that Australia–Japan Free Trade Agreement Escaped' *Sydney Morning Herald* (10 April 2014) <www.smh.com.au/federal-politics/political-opinion/isds-the-trap-the-australiajapan-free-trade-agreement-escaped-20140407-zqrwk.html> accessed 11 July 2014; D Crowe, 'Tony Abbott Concludes Free Trade Agreement with Japan' *The Australian* (7 April 2014) <www.theaustralian.com.au/national-affairs/policy/tony-abbott-concludes-free-trade-agreement-with-japan/story-fn59nm2j-1226877009701#> accessed 11 July 2014.
[34] See Martin ibid. See also P Martin, 'Free Trading Cards Laid on the Table, but Beware the Ace Up the Sleeve' *Sydney Morning Herald* (9 April 2014) <www.smh.com.au/business/free-trading-cards-laid-on-the-table-but-beware-the-ace-up-the-sleeve-20140408-36b6v.html> accessed 11 July 2014.

The Coalition Government's approach presumably presupposes that, in deciding whether to adopt ISDS on a case-by-case basis, the Australian Government will consider discrete national interests, such as the nature of national security, environmental, or public health protection in relation to each treaty it negotiates. It will also pay heed to the kind of treaty partner in issue, including the political system, economic development, and treatment accorded to foreign investors by the particular negotiating partner State in the past.

While it appears superficially attractive, this case-by-case approach can be challenging for treaty partners, foreign investors, and domestic interests. The approach assumes that, while negotiating a treaty, the Australian Government will be able to determine in advance the nature of investor–State disputes that are likely to eventuate, and whether the Australian Government ought to negotiate for ISDS or domestic courts in anticipating such disputes. It is unclear how the Government will decide, in relation to inbound investment, whether investors from a particular State party will be more likely to invoke ISDS against Australia. It is also unclear, in relation to outbound investment, what protections courts of foreign States in Asia are likely to confer upon Australian outbound investors. Generally speaking, the nature of the State party, such as its developing economic status or high corruption index, and its historical actions are insufficient bases upon which to determine whether ISDS or domestic courts should be the chosen method of dispute settlement in the future. There is simply insufficient evidence to predict with any confidence how differently ISDS and domestic courts will resolve investor–State disputes in Asia.

The current contextual approach is nevertheless an improvement on the seemingly rigid stand articulated by the Gillard Government in its 2011 Policy. It at least facilitates negotiation around ISDS and domestic courts, and enables the negotiating parties to weigh up the risks and benefits of each. Admittedly, it does not eliminate predictive uncertainty, notably in how Australian or foreign domestic courts are likely to adjudicate public policy debates. It does however enable reflection on such factors as pre-existing national legislation in negotiating treaty States that demonstrate protectionism.

c) Australia's regional investment interests

The countries of the Asia Pacific region have strong trade relations. In 2013, Australia's top five two-way trading partners were China, Japan, the US, Korea, and Singapore.[35] Australia's top three export markets were China, Japan, and South Korea,[36] and top three import sources were China, the US, and Japan.[37] Indeed two-way trade with the Asian region accounted for 62.8 per cent of Australia's total trade in 2013.[38] Needless to say, China is integral to Australian trade and

---

[35] Department of Foreign Affairs and Trade (Australia), *Trade at a Glance 2014*, 5 <http://dfat.gov.au/about-us/publications/trade-investment/trade-at-a-glance/trade-at-a-glance-2014/Pages/trade-at-a-glance-2014.aspx> accessed 16 August 2015.
[36] ibid 20.   [37] ibid 24.   [38] ibid 27.

investment, given that it is Australia's largest two-way trading partner. While there are healthy two-way trading links between Australia and the Asian region as well as the US, longer-term outbound investments in Asian countries by Australian investors could be improved,[39] and so could longer-term inbound investment by Asian investors in Australia.[40]

Australia should recognize its regional interests in formulating its policy on ISDS. In addition to having a considerable bearing on Australia's international trade and investment, it is noteworthy that countries in the Asian region have increasingly provided for ISDS protection in treaties, though admittedly some, such as India and Indonesia, continue to remain cautious.[41]

Significantly, the final version of the Australia–Japan trade agreement, hailed as being supremely advantageous for both the Australian and Japanese economies,[42] does not include an ISDS regime. Notably, however, Japan had requested ISDS at least until the tenth round of negotiations[43] and dispute settlement was still a point of concern until the sixteenth round.[44] Japan has also favoured ISDS in its other investment treaties in the recent past, preferring to allow for resolution of investor–State disputes through independent channels.[45] Ultimately, however, Japan agreed to conclude JAEPA without an ISDS regime, potentially because it considered that insisting on ISDS was not worth any additional concessions it may have to provide.[46] There has been suggestion that Japan was satisfied that Australia's rule of law tradition would secure sufficient protections for Japan's investors, rendering an ISDS regime unnecessary[47] (though this seems entirely speculative, particularly in light of Japan's earlier requests for ISDS).

As a result, whatever else may be extrapolated from the JAEPA negotiation process, it cannot be said that Japan now holds ISDS in disfavour. Its willingness to exclude ISDS from JAEPA shows at best that the economic and political advantages of securing a trade and investment agreement with Australia were greater

---

[39] ibid 32.   [40] ibid 36.

[41] LE Trakman and K Sharma, 'Locating Australia on the Pacific Rim: Trade, Investment and the Asian Century' (2015) Transn Disp Mgmt 1 (online at <www.transnational-dispute-management.com/article.asp?key=2178> accessed 15 August 2015); Nottage (n 11) 257.

[42] See Crowe (n 27).

[43] Department of Foreign Affairs and Trade (Australia) 'Newsletter Update 10: Australia-Japan Free Trade Agreement, Tenth Negotiating Round' (17–25 November 2012) <www.dfat.gov.au/fta/jaepa/newsletters/update_10.html> accessed 11 July 2014.

[44] Department of Foreign Affairs and Trade (Australia) 'Sixteenth round of negotiations—13–15 June 20' <www.dfat.gov.au/fta/jaepa/#news> accessed 11 July 2014.

[45] See Agreement between the Government of Malaysia and the Government of Japan for an Economic Partnership (signed 13 December 2005, entered into force 13 July 2006) Art 85; Agreement between Japan and the Republic of Indonesia for an Economic Partnership (signed 20 August 2007, entered into force 1 July 2008) Art 69; Comprehensive Economic Partnership Agreement between Japan and the Republic of India (signed 16 February 2011, entered into force 1 August 2008) Art 96. Japan's FTAs are available at Ministry of Foreign Relations of Japan, 'Japan–Asia Relations' <www.mofa.go.jp/region/asia-paci/index.html> accessed 11 July 2014. See also, Hamamoto and Nottage (n 3).

[46] L Nottage, 'Investor–State Arbitration: Not in the Australia–Japan Free Trade Agreement, and Not Ever for Australia?' (2014) 19 J Japanese L 37.

[47] Martin, 'Free Trading Cards' (n 33).

than insistence on ISDS. The fact that Australia's legal system is generally regarded as being independent, transparent, and reliable may have given some comfort to Japanese negotiators, but this view is not likely to be universally convincing.

A converse illustration to JAEPA is the KAFTA concluded in December 2013, which does include ISDS provisions and upon which Korea reportedly insisted.[48] Given Korea's position as a key trading partner of Australia and the potential it offers for significant investment opportunities, it was certainly prudent for the Australian Government to endorse a balanced ISDS outcome.

Australia has also recently concluded a trade agreement with China,[49] which includes an ISDS regime. China is a particularly significant regional trading partner of Australia. It is a major investor in Australia and is heavily involved in its natural resources sector. While Australia's investment in China still lags behind other States in the region, in 2010 Australia's FDI in China reached AU$17 billion.[50] Although China only invested AU$19 billion in Australia at that time, this rate is three times higher than what it was in 2007.[51]

FDI flows from China into Australia are also growing exponentially and are making a major contribution to Australia's recent high economic growth, commonly referred to as the natural resources boom. Considering China's demand for natural resources, it is unlikely that this trend will be reversed in the near future as China acquires more of Australia's natural resources. Even more broadly, China's desire to increase its investments in Australia is seen in its insistence during the ChAFTA negotiations that the Foreign Investment Review Board (FIRB) threshold for investments from China should be increased to match the thresholds available to US and New Zealand investors (equivalent concessions were extracted by Japan and Korea as part of their respective agreements relating to investments by private entities in non-sensitive industries); this concession was granted in the final agreement.[52] The sticking point during negotiations was that much of the inbound investment into Australia was likely to come from State-owned enterprises (SOEs), which China insisted should be treated in the same manner as private enterprises.[53]

---

[48] See Callick (n 8).
[49] See ChAFTA (n 7) <http://dfat.gov.au/trade/agreements/chafta/official-documents/Pages/official-documents.aspx> accessed 16 August 2015.
[50] Australian Government, *Australia in the Asian Century, Foreign Direct Investment Fact Sheet*, (October 2012) <www.asiancentury.dpmc.gov.au/sites/default/files/fact-sheets/20.-Foreign-investment-in-Australia.pdf> accessed 11 July 2014.
[51] ibid.
[52] See M Janda, 'Investment Threshold Lifted above $1b under Korea–Australia FTA' *ABC News* (17 February 2014) <www.abc.net.au/news/2014-02-17/government-releases-details-of-korea-australia-fta/5264840> accessed 11 July 2014; M Kenny and P Wen, 'Japan, Korea and Now a Free Trade Deal with China is in Sight' *Sydney Morning Herald* (10 April 2014) <www.smh.com.au/federal-politics/political-news/japan-korea-and-now-a-free-trade-deal-with-china-is-in-sight-20140409-36djp.html> accessed 11 April 2014; B Fan, 'Foreign Investment Review Changes for Chinese Investors under the China-Australia Free Trade Agreement' *Herbert Smith Freehills* (28 November 2014) <www.herbertsmithfreehills.com/insights/legal-briefings/foreign-investment-review-changes-for-chinese-investors-under-the-china-australia-fta> accessed 16 August 2015.
[53] K Murphy, 'Tony Abbott Goes to China "to be a Friend", Not to Chase Deals' *The Guardian* (10 April 2014)<www.theguardian.com/world/2014/apr/10/tony-abbott-goes-to-china-to-be-friend-not-chase-deals> accessed 11 July 2014.

Leading up to the finalization of the agreement, the Coalition Government indicated it was no longer averse to investment from SOEs;[54] however in the final agreement, the relaxation of the FIRB threshold was not accorded to investments by SOEs, this provision to be reviewed by the parties in three years' time.

Over the past two decades, China has shown a trend towards trade liberalization, even if this movement has been slow, at least according to some western countries.[55] The inclusion of ISDS in ChAFTA was understandable. Chinese investors have made a number of high-profile investments in Australia and it is reasonable to surmise that China wants to ensure independent protections for them.

On the flip side, while the Asian region has immense economic opportunities, Australia's outbound investment into some Asian countries is not without risks. According to the 2013 Transparency International Corruption Perceptions Index, the majority of countries in Asia scored between ten and fifty points out of a possible 100.[56] Other studies conducted by the World Justice Project provide similarly troubling assessments.[57] The World Bank's Ease of Doing Business rankings of East Asia and the Pacific paints an even bleaker picture: only four countries in the region managed to score in the top twenty, with other key regional economic partners of Australia falling behind by a significant margin.[58] While the methodology of these rankings is not without controversy,[59] these surveys portray a similar story: Asia is still lagging behind other parts of the world in the development of its legal institutions and in the protections accorded to foreign investors.

In the absence of ISDS, Australia's outbound investors located in Asia may encounter resistance in securing relief from regulation by host States, including before their local courts. While some investors may move their businesses to intermediary States to avoid the courts of partner States, many smaller Australian investors lack such mobility and will have to resolve their disputes in the local courts of their host States.[60] Thus, one of the practical challenges that Australia faces, if it

---

[54] K Murphy, 'Tony Abbott Says China's State-Owned Enterprises Are Welcome in Australia' *The Guardian* (11 April 2014) <http://www.theguardian.com/world/2014/apr/11/abbott-says-chinas-state-owned-enterprises-welcome> accessed 11 July 2014; P Coorey, 'Side Deal May Open Door for China State-Owned Firms' *Australian Financial Review* (12 April 2014) <www.afr.com/p/national/side_deal_may_open_door_for_china_0TUDkjLssijS9698OcJqEO> accessed 11 July 2014.

[55] LE Trakman, 'China and Foreign Direct Investment: Does Distance Lend Enchantment to the View?' (2014) 2 Chin J Comp L1; LE Trakman, 'China and Investor State Arbitration' (2012) University of New South Wales Faculty of Law Research Series No 48.

[56] See Transparency International, *Corruption Perceptions Index 2013* <http://cpi.transparency.org/cpi2013/results/> accessed 11 July 2014.

[57] See World Justice Project, *WJP Rule of Law Index 2014* <http://data.worldjusticeproject.org/> accessed 11 July 2014.

[58] See International Finance Corporation and the World Bank, 'Economy Rankings' *Doing Business* (June 2013) <www.doingbusiness.org/rankings> accessed 11 July 2014.

[59] See T Thompson and A Shah, 'Transparency International's Corruption Perceptions Index: Whose Perceptions are they Anyway?' World Bank Discussion Draft 2005 <http://siteresources.worldbank.org/INTWBIGOVANTCOR/Resources/TransparencyInternationalCorruptionIndex.pdf> accessed 11 July 2014.

[60] Investors may base these decisions on various grounds, including but not limited to corruption, transparency, and rule of law indices: see (nn 58–60).

remains determined to retire ISDS, lies in protecting its outbound investors in Asia who lack the capacity to protect themselves.

d) Australia not alone—Indonesia's apparent aversion to ISDS

Recently, Indonesia, another key regional player, has shown some aversion to the current state of its investment agreements and to ISDS in particular. Early in 2014, the Netherlands embassy in Jakarta announced that the Indonesian Government had informed the Netherlands that it intended to terminate the Netherlands–Indonesia BIT,[61] from 1 July 2015, which is when the BIT expires.[62] The Netherlands embassy also stated that the Indonesian Government had mentioned it intended to terminate all of its sixty-seven BITs.

In the aftermath of that announcement, there was widespread discussion around the intentions of the Indonesian Government and what may have motivated its decision to cancel the Netherlands BIT. It was proposed that, in part at least, the *Churchill Mining PLC and Planet Mining Pty Ltd v Republic of Indonesia* cases[63] may have motivated the Indonesian Government to review its current treaty portfolio.[64] The Churchill claim, which has caused some concern in Indonesia, is for over $1 billion, not including interest.[65] Certainly, there have been emphatic calls for Indonesia to immediately withdraw from the ICSID and continue to treat BITs with caution.[66] Some of the reasons articulated are comparable to those expressed by the Australian Government as part of its 2011 Policy. These include equal treatment of foreign and domestic investors and the restraints placed on the Government as a result of having international claims lodged against it. More particularly, however, there is a view that, in light of the economic power it now has, Indonesia no longer needs to forsake its regulatory autonomy to attract foreign investment.

Termination of its BITs by Indonesia would not mean a complete withdrawal from all investment protection obligations and mechanisms. Existing investors would continue to be protected by the 'survival clauses' that have been included

---

[61] Agreement between the Government of the Republic Indonesia and the Government of the Kingdom of the Netherlands on Promotion and Protection of Investment (signed 6 April 1994, entered into force 1 July 1995) ('Netherlands–Indonesia BIT').
[62] 'Termination Bilateral Investment Treaty' (n 5).
[63] ICSID Case No ARB/12/14 and 12/40 <www.italaw.com/cases/1479> accessed 11 July 2014.
[64] C Tevendale and V Naish, 'Indonesia Indicates Intention to Terminate all of its Bilateral Investment Treaties?' *Herbert Smith Freehills Dispute Resolution* (20 March 2014) <http://hsfnotes.com/arbitration/2014/03/20/indonesia-indicates-intention-to-terminate-all-of-its-bilateral-investment-treaties/> accessed 11 July 2014; B Bland and S Donnan, 'Indonesia to Terminate More Than 60 Bilateral Investment Treaties' *Financial Times* (26 March 2014) <www.ft.com/intl/cms/s/0/3755c1b2-b4e2-11e3-af92-00144feabdc0.html?siteedition=uk#axzz36C9e5Oos> accessed 11 July 2014.
[65] Tevendale and Naish (n 65).
[66] H Juwana, 'Indonesia Should Withdraw from the ICSID Now!' *Jakarta Post* (2 April 2014) <www.thejakartapost.com/news/2014/04/02/indonesia-should-withdraw-icsid.html> accessed 11 July 2014.

in many of the BITs. For example, under the Netherlands BIT, the investments under the BIT will be protected by a sunset period of fifteen years after the BIT's termination.[67] Further, even if all of its BITs were terminated, Indonesia would still be subject to its obligations under the ASEAN Comprehensive Investment Agreement and the ASEAN–Australia–New Zealand Free Trade Agreement.[68]

In any case, the more likely view is that Indonesia does not intend to withdraw from its regime of investment agreements altogether. It is undertaking a termination programme so that it can renegotiate its BITs with greater State protections. Indonesia is now economically stable and powerful enough to assert its regulatory autonomy. It has been suggested that Indonesia intends to renegotiate its BITs to provide greater capacity to regulate in the 'public interest for health, the environment or financial reasons'.[69] Again, Indonesia's motivations in this respect are analogous to Australia's position enunciated in its 2011 Policy Statement. As stated previously, the Australian Government made it clear that it would not limit its ability to legislate in the public interest. Despite having moved away from the 2011 Policy considerably, the Coalition Government elected in 2013 has expressed analogous sentiments about not restricting its ability to legislate in the public interest. Even the ISDS regime it recently negotiated as part of the KAFTA includes carve-outs to allow State parties some freedom of regulating in the public interest, subject to investment arbitrators construing those carve-outs restrictively.[70]

e) Regional concerns—the Trans-Pacific Partnership Agreement

The potential for a multilateral accord promised by the TPPA is a considerable one, not least because the TPP countries represent 39 per cent of the world GDP, account for 25.8 per cent of world trade, and, for Australia, include five of its top ten trading partners.[71]

There had been some optimism that the TPPA would be concluded by early 2015,[72] but this has not come to pass. After the latest meeting of Chief Negotiators in May 2015, followed by a meeting of the Ministers in July 2015, the agreement has not yet been finalized.

Indonesia is unlikely to join negotiations at this late stage, though it may seek to ratify it in its agreed form. Certainly, the TPPA poses a significant geopolitical

---

[67] Tevendale and Naish (n 65).
[68] ASEAN Comprehensive Investment Agreement (signed 26 February 2009, entered into force 29 March 2012); Agreement Establishing the ASEAN–Australia–New Zealand Free Trade Area (signed 27 February 2009, entered into force 1 January 2010) [2010] ATS 1.
[69] M Ewing-Chow and JJ Losari, 'Indonesia is Letting its Bilateral Treaties Lapse so as to Renegotiate Better Ones' *Financial Times* (15 April 2014) <www.ft.com/intl/cms/s/0/20c6c518-c1 6c-11e3-97b2-00144feabdc0.html?siteedition=intl#axzz34NvIWeHB> accessed 11 July 2014.
[70] KAFTA (n 7) ch 22 (General Provisions and Exceptions).
[71] Department of Foreign Affairs and Trade (Australia) 'Trans-Pacific Partnership Agreement Negotiations' <www.dfat.gov.au/fta/tpp/> accessed 11 July 2014.
[72] R Taylor, 'Australia's Trade Minister Expects Long Slog for Trade Deal' *The Wall Street Journal* (18 June 2014) <http://online.wsj.com/articles/australias-trade-minister-expects-long-slog-for-trade-deal-1403073241> accessed 11 July 2014.

challenge for Australia, which is a negotiating party. The challenge lies in the contest between Australia potentially favouring domestic courts over ISDS and other TPPA member countries, in particular the US, favouring ISDS.[73] JAEPA, expressed by Australia and Japan as creating significant economic opportunities for both countries, has apparently been dismissed by the US as detracting from the TPPA.[74] The US has observed that the benefits created by JAEPA are 'significantly less ambitious' than those envisaged for the TPPA.[75]

Australia's new bilateral relationships with Asian countries have tended to reinforce a somewhat populist view that Australia does not need to worry about the TPPA, given it now has bilateral or regional treaties with most of the countries who are parties to the TPPA.[76] However, aside from the fact that Australia does not have trade agreements with Canada, Mexico, and Peru, all parties to the TPPA, the value of a multilateral regional accord should not be underplayed.

There is an indication that the TPPA negotiating parties are likely to favour the inclusion of an ISDS regime.[77] Officially, Australia commenced negotiating the TPPA with the understanding that it would be exempt from any ISDS provisions in the TPPA. It is difficult to speculate whether the Coalition Government will agree to ISDS in the TPPA, though it may do so, subject to securing trade and investment concessions from the treaty partners, such as gaining access to the US beef and dairy markets.

On the other hand, if pursued, an exemption for Australia from ISDS would not itself be extraordinary. Country-specific reservations and exemptions are part and parcel of multilateral negotiating processes. Furthermore, the parties negotiating the TPPA have rejected a one-size-fits-all TPPA in order to accommodate the domestic interests of negotiating States.[78] Thus, on the surface, the exemption

---

[73] See MK Lewis, 'The Trans-Pacific Partnership: New Paradigm or Wolf in Sheep's Clothing?' (2011) 34 Boston College Intl & Comp L Rev 27, 34; P Ranald, 'The Trans-Pacific Partnership Agreement: Contradictions in Australia and in the Asia Pacific Region' (2011) 22(1) Econ Lab Relat Rev 81. On the US negotiating position generally, see D Gantz, 'Trans-Pacific Partnership Negotiations: Progress, But No End in Sight' *Kluwer Arbitration Blog* (22 June 2014) <kluwerarbitrationblog.com/blog/2012/06/22/trans-pacific-partnership-negotiations-progress-but-no-end-in-sight/> accessed 11 July 2014; see also the US position on ISDS generally: Office of the United States Trade Representative, 'The Facts on Investor-State Dispute Settlement: Safeguarding the Public Interest and Protecting Investors' (27 March 2014) <www.ustr.gov/about-us/press-office/blog/2014/March/Facts-Investor-State%20Dispute-Settlement-Safeguarding-Public-Interest-Protecting-Investors> accessed 11 July 2014.

[74] S Donnan, 'Japan-Australia Trade Deal Is Dismissed by the US' *Financial Times* (London, 7 April 2014) <www.ft.com/intl/cms/s/0/5e4023b6-be43-11e3-b44a-00144feabdc0.html#axzz2yehuWuKc> accessed 11 July 2014.

[75] ibid. [76] Martin 'Free Trading Cards' (n 33).

[77] B Cubitt, 'Potential Investor-State Dispute Settlement Provisions in Trans-Pacific Partnership Agreement—A Change in Policy for Australia?' *Kluwer Arbitration Blog* (14 February 2014) <http://kluwerarbitrationblog.com/blog/2014/02/14/potential-investor-state-dispute-settlement-provisions-in-trans-pacific-partnership-agreement-a-change-in-policy-for-australia/> accessed 11 July 2014.

[78] State-by-state negotiations notwithstanding, each 'round' of TPPA negotiations includes all participating countries. The most recent round of TPP Negotiations took place in Ottawa, Canada, from 3 to 12 July 2014. See further LE Trakman, 'The Transpacific Partnership Agreement: Significance for International Investment' (2013) 4(4) J Intl Comm L 1.

that Australia originally sought from ISDS could be justified in light of exemptions from other provisions in the TPPA potentially sought by the other parties. Nevertheless, the costs of Australia securing an exemption from ISDS may outweigh its anticipated benefits.[79]

First, reservations and exemptions from treaties are often strategically determined by State parties to such treaties in general and by States seeking specific reservations and exemptions in particular. As a result, participating countries are likely to grant exemptions depending on the perceived benefit to them of doing so. However, a TPPA that is replete with country-specific exemptions can neutralize its value as an umbrella agreement, undermine its uniformity, and lead to multiple side-agreements that are inconsistent with it.

The potential drawback of a TPPA that obfuscates a one-size-fits-all agreement is that it will be downgraded to a loose framework agreement with multi-tiered exemptions and side agreements. Such an eventuality could seriously undermine its economic and legal stature as a multilateral agreement purporting to rival in part a faltering WTO. For many observers, the TPPA represents an attempt to reinvigorate the Doha Round of trade negotiations and promote greater harmonization among the various standards that were created in the spaghetti bowl of BRTAs. While the TPPA falls short of a WTO-style agreement, its proponents envisage that it will lead to greater harmony in trade and investment, offsetting disparities among pre-existing investment treaties, improving dispute resolution processes, and involving key States, including in Asia, in these decision-making processes.

IV. ISDS or Domestic Courts

A move away from ISDS does not automatically mean that foreign investors can have resort only to the domestic courts of host States, including in countries of the Asia Pacific. There are likely to be other avenues, both for dispute resolution and avoidance. These could include political risk insurance, diplomatic intervention by home States, investor–State contracts, as well as other mechanisms of mediation and negotiation that might be available in particular contexts. However, these avenues are likely to be onerous or inaccessible for many investors. In practice, therefore, domestic courts are going to be the most likely alternative to ISDS.

Before setting out the debate briefly, it is worth reiterating that the contest is perhaps more formal than substantive. ISDS and domestic courts are not simply different forums, but rather have different tools available to them. As noted above, if investment disputes are to be resolved by domestic courts, as when foreign investors are required to submit investor–State disputes to the courts of the host State,

---

[79] For arguments in support of Australia opting out of investor–State arbitration see K Tienhaara, 'Submission to the Department of Foreign Affairs and Trade: Investor-State Dispute Settlement in the Trans-Pacific Partnership Agreement' <www.dfat.gov.au/fta/tpp/subs/tpp_sub_tienhaara_100519.pdf> accessed 11 July 2014.

in a country such as Australia that subscribes to a dualist system, the courts would apply domestic law including its substantive law rules. They would not directly apply investor protections provided for by treaty except insofar as domestic laws incorporate international investment law, such as standards of protection embodied in investment treaties, into domestic law. As such, we truly are comparing apples and oranges.

Further, by choosing resort to domestic courts as the preferred manner of resolving investment disputes, a country such as Australia would presumably accept that foreign courts will apply their own laws to Australian investors in those foreign countries, whatever those laws may be. In declining to agree to ISDS in investment treaties, the Australian Government could not effectively draw a distinction between countries that apply a 'rule of law' jurisprudence that is comparable to that applied in Australia and those countries that do not subscribe to such a tradition.[80]

Certainly, ISDS is far from perfect and numerous objections can be raised with respect to it. Some of these criticisms were identified by the Australian Productivity Commission (APC) in its draft and final reports, on which the Gillard Government based its 2011 Policy. These included the large size of investor claims, the latitude of investment tribunals in determining the amount of compensation, the lack of rigorous rules governing the conduct of ISDS, the absence of an appeals process, and the threat of 'institutional biases and conflicts of interest, inconsistency and matters of jurisdiction, a lack of transparency and the costs incurred by participants'.[81] The APC concluded that 'experience in other countries demonstrates that there are considerable policy and financial risks arising from ISDS provisions'.[82]

In addition, it could be argued there are numerous reasons for preferring resort to domestic courts over ISDS. First, on principled grounds, it could be said that investors ought to be subject to the territorial sovereignty of the State in which they invest.[83] Second, a domestic court of a State party is the appropriate forum to resolve an investment dispute, in the same manner as it resolves other disputes between that State and other private or corporate claimants.[84] Third, foreign

---

[80] LE Trakman, 'Foreign Direct Investment: An Australian Perspective' (2010) 13 Intl Trade & Bus L Rev 31, 39–43. See also T Westcott, 'Foreign Investment Issues in the Australia–United States Free Trade Agreement' (Summer 2004–05) Economic Roundup 69 <http://archive.treasury.gov.au/documents/958/PDF/06_Foreign_investment_policy_AUSFTA.pdf> accessed 11 July 2014.

[81] Productivity Commission, 'Australian Government, Bilateral and Regional Trade Agreements: Final Research Report' (13 December 2010) 272 <www.pc.gov.au/projects/study/trade-agreements> accessed 11 July 2014.

[82] ibid 274.

[83] On the complexity of sovereignty in international investment law, see, for example, W Shan, P Simons, and D Singh, *Redefining Sovereignty in International Economic Law* (Hart 2008) (see especially Part Four for commentary on the complexity of sovereignty in international investment law); R Stumberg, 'Sovereignty by Subtraction: The Multilateral Agreement on Investment' (1998) 31 Cornell Intl L J 491, 503–04, 523–25. See too RH Jackson, *Quasi-States: Sovereignty, International Relations and the Third World* (CUP 1990); JH Jackson, *The Jurisprudence of GATT and the WTO: Insights on Treaty Law and Economic Relations* (CUP 2000); M Reisman, 'International Arbitration and Sovereignty' (2002) 18 Arb Intl 231; R Jennings and A Watts (eds), *Oppenheim's International Law* (Longman 1992) 927.

[84] On these arguments in relation to the Australia–United States Free Trade Agreement, see Trakman, 'Foreign Direct Investment: An Australian Perspective' (n 81), 48–53; Westcott (n 81).

investors should not receive investment benefits beyond those provided to domestic investors. Such treatment is conceivably unfair, as is evidenced historically by the privileges accorded by less developed countries to multinational corporations at the expense of local subjects who were competitively disadvantaged.

Finally, domestic courts are bound by established forum procedures and rules of evidence to protect the rights of foreign investors in accordance with domestic public policy that usually includes a right of appeal to a higher court. Arguably, ISDS is not subject to comparable procedural and substantive constraints as domestic courts. Investment arbitrators may decide in favour of foreign investors on grounds that undermine the public interest of home States. There are no appeals from ISDS awards, except for an arbitrator's failure to exercise, or abuse of, jurisdiction (leading to a review by the ICSID Annulment Committee where ISDS is conducted under the ICSID).[85] Annulment proceedings are an extraordinary process and more limited in scope than appeals to a domestic court.

Attacking a plethora of domestic legal systems and courts is more challenging than impugning ISDS as a mechanism, especially where foreign investors may be subject to a multitude of domestic legal systems with divergent procedures and substantive investment jurisprudence. However, this multiplicity of domestic legal options is itself problematic, in forsaking uniformity among inevitably divergent legal systems including across Asia. These deficiencies of domestic legal systems stand starkly in contrast to ISDS institutions that seek to limit the proliferation of international investment laws. As such, ISDS serves as a unifying framework within which multiple BITs are subject to largely uniform ISDS provisions that derive significantly from the global experience of foreign investors, as well as host and home States. Acting as a levelling force, ISDS is founded on principles, standards, and rules of investment jurisprudence that, formally at least, are not

---

[85] On the absence of an appeal from ICSID arbitration, see Convention on the Settlement of Investment Disputes between States and Nationals of Other States (opened for signature 18 March 1965, entered into force 14 October 1966) ('ICSID Convention') Art 53(1). Art 53 provides: 'The award…shall not be subject to any appeal or to any other remedy except those provided for in this Convention.' The most significant remedy under the ICSID is the annulment of an award under Art 53. The ICSID provides instead for a review of an investment award by an Annulment Committee which is set up specifically for that purpose, with the power to modify or nullify an ICSID award on limited procedural grounds under Art 75 of the ICSID Convention. Either party can request that the award be annulled. However, the grounds for such a challenge are restricted and fall short of an appeal. They include that:

(1) the ICSID tribunal was not properly constituted;
(2) the tribunal manifestly exceeded its powers;
(3) there was corruption on the part of a tribunal member;
(4) there was a serious departure from a fundamental rule of procedure; or
(5) the award failed to state the reasons on which it was based.

ICSID Annulment Committees traditionally have interpreted these grounds for a challenge liberally, permitting a series of challenges, although such challenges have dissipated in recent years. Resort to domestic courts is not an option under the ICSID. See ICSID Convention, Art 75. For ICSID documents generally, see <http://icsid.worldbank.org/ICSID/Index.jsp> accessed 21 October 2014. See also J Crawford and K Lee, ICSID Reports (2004) vol 6. On the ICSID Additional Facility, see <http://icsid.worldbank.org/ICSID/ICSID/AdditionalFacilityRules.jsp.> accessed 21 October 2014.

ordinarily sublimated by domestic legal systems and rules of procedure. ISDS is also conceived as more certain and stable than a myriad of different domestic laws and rules that might otherwise govern direct foreign investment.[86]

Notwithstanding the absence of judicial precedent in ISDS as common lawyers conceive of it, ISDS is still likely to be more coherent than a multiplicity of different State laws applied by local courts to foreign investment. However difficult it is to identify cohesive ISDS principles out of ad hoc and sometimes unpublished arbitration awards, and however arbitrators may fragment standards of treatment under different BITs, ICSID and UNCITRAL arbitration have been used over a considerable period of time to resolve investment disputes in often complex investment cases.[87] That task of investment arbitration is accomplished notwithstanding the plethora of BITs in existence and their susceptibility to different kinds of interpretation.[88] Nor should institutions like the ICSID be blamed for inconsistent reasoning that is sometimes adopted by ISDS tribunals that, while guided by ICSID and UNCITRAL rules, exercise independent discretion in deciding investment disputes.

The principled argument that the domestic courts of sovereign States ought to decide investment disputes based on domestic laws and judicial procedures is offset by the observation that international arbitrators are also subject to domestic laws that are encompassed within a BIT or investor–State agreement. Far from being insulated from domestic laws and procedures, ISDS principles and standards of treatment accorded to foreign investors inhere not only in international jurisprudence, but both evolve from and are incorporated into domestic law as well.[89] As a result, ISDS arbitrators cannot summarily disregard domestic laws that are expressly or impliedly integrated into applicable BITs or investor–State agreements.[90]

The rationale that domestic courts are expert in law including investment law is counterbalanced by the contention that investment arbitrators are expert in international investment law in a manner that domestic judges, even courts of

---

[86] Vandevelde writes that from 1959 to 1969 only seventy-five BITs were concluded. During the 1970s, nine BITs were negotiated each year; that rate more than doubled in the 1980s and has been increasing geometrically ever since then: see K Vandevelde, 'A Brief History of International Investment Agreements' (2005) 12 UC Davis J of Intl L & Poly157, 172. See also UNCTAD 'World Investment Report 2010' (24 June 2014) UNCTAD/WIR/2014, xxv <http://unctad.org/en/pages/PublicationWebflyer.aspx?publicationid=937> accessed 11 July 2014.

[87] On such authorities, see, for example, M Sornarajah, 'The Case against a Regime on International Investment Law' in Trakman and Ranieri (n 21) ch 4, 59; C Schreuer and R Dolzer, *Principles of International Investment Law* (OUP 2008), ch 1; SW Schill, *The Multilateralization of International Investment Law* (CUP 2009) chs 1–2.

[88] See, A Antonietti, 'The 2006 Amendments of the ICSID Rules and Regulations and the Additional Facility Rules' (2006) 21 ICSID Rev 427; E Baldwin, M Kantor, and M Nolan, 'Limits to Enforcement of ICSID Awards' (2006) 23 J Intl Arb 1 (discussing 'tactics' that may be employed in attempts to 'delay' or 'avoid' compliance with ICSID Awards).

[89] See W Shan, P Simons, and D Singh (eds), *Redefining Sovereignty in International Economic Law* (Hart 2008) ch 11 (Shan), ch 17 (Schneiderman).

[90] See, C Schreuer, *The ICSID Convention: A Commentary* (CUP 2001) 357.

commercial jurisdiction, are not.[91] Even the rationale that domestic courts are subject to tried and tested rules of evidence and procedure is offset in part by the observation that investment arbitration is guided by ICSID or UNCITRAL rules that take into account the complexities of investment law. Insofar as the decisions of domestic courts are subject to appeal, the awards of investment arbitrators are subject to extraordinary challenge or annulment proceedings for non-compliance albeit constrained by limited powers of review.[92]

V. The Future of ISDS for Australia

What can be said in defence of ISDS is that, while it does not lead to judicial precedent as common lawyers conceive of it, ISDS is likely to be more stable in nature than a plethora of different local laws and procedures that domestic courts apply to foreign investment. However fragmentary may be the application of international standards of treatment to foreign investors and however difficult it may be to identify cohesive principles out of ad hoc and sometimes unpublished arbitration awards, an international investment jurisprudence has evolved, inconsistencies notwithstanding.[93] Given the multitude of BITs currently in existence and their disparate clauses, ICSID and UNCITRAL arbitrations have promoted the successful resolution of investment disputes in a series of complex cases. As such, ISDS has helped to develop a more cohesive construction of BITs internationally than has the jurisprudence of divergent domestic legal systems and their courts.

However, it cannot be contended that investment arbitration is beyond reproach. What can be said is that it has considerable practical value in resolving investment disputes, and has the capacity to be transformed and developed further. As such, it would be profitable to endeavour to improve ISDS rather than abandon it.[94]

A preferable approach for a State like Australia would be to pursue a programme of multi-tiered, qualified access to ISDS including in its treaties with partner States in the Pacific Rim. This would be embodied in an overarching Australian BIT policy that would serve as a flexible template for negotiating FTAs and BITs, including with dominant States that have their own model BITs. Australia could also develop

---

[91] On the case for investor–State arbitration, see generally C Dugan, D Wallace, and N Rubins, *Investor-State Arbitration* (OUP 2008); P Muchlinski, F Ortino, and C Schreuer (eds), *Oxford Handbook of International Investment Law* (OUP 2008); C McLachlan, L Shore, and M Weiniger, *International Investment Arbitration: Substantive Principles* (OUP 2008); P Kahn and TW Walde (eds), *New Aspects of International Investment Law* (Martinus Nijhoff 2007); G Van Harten, *Investment Treaty Arbitration and Public Law* (OUP 2007); RD Bishop, J Crawford, and WM Reisman, *Foreign Investment Disputes: Cases, Materials and Commentary* (Kluwer 2005); T Weiler (ed), *International Investment Law and Arbitration: Leading Cases from the ICSID, NAFTA, Bilateral Treaties and Customary International Law* (Cameron May 2005); N Horn (ed), *Arbitrating Foreign Investment Disputes* (Kluwer 2004).
[92] On the ICSID, see (n 87).   [93] See (n 89).
[94] See UNCTAD (n 11), 43: The IPFSD recognized that 'the ISDS system has more recently displayed serious shortcomings' and proposed a number of ways to reform it. But see 44, where the IPFSD points out that 'no ISDS' or ISDS as a last resort may be appropriate in certain situations.

model clauses to incorporate into its BITs that encourage dispute prevention and avoidance measures, such as requiring investor–State parties to undertake negotiations and/or conciliation prior to resorting to either domestic litigation or ISDS.

Australia should also develop model rules of procedure to apply during formal ISDS proceedings that include: setting limits on the standing of foreign investors to bring ISDS claims; requiring public notice of ISDS complaints; providing for public participation in ISDS proceedings; and requiring publication of ISDS awards. It may also design model BIT clauses that provide for interim measures; create budgetary limits on the costs of ISDS in order to avoid cost overruns; and address dilatory ISDS processes including lengthy adjournments. In addition to modification of the procedural rules regulating ISDS, Australia may provide for the stay of ISDS proceedings to allow for investor–State settlement. In addition, to ensure that ISDS proceedings do not produce absurd or unjust decisions, it could provide for bilateral challenge committees to hear challenges to ISDS decisions, such as on grounds of a denial of due process, including rules to govern the functioning of such challenge committees.[95]

This multi-tiered approach to resolving investor–State disputes has the advantage of allowing the Australian Government to redress many of the limitations associated with ISDS, while avoiding the problems arising from a complete rejection of it. For example, one of the broader benefits of resorting to illustrative BIT rules and clauses governing ISDS is a greater commitment to transparency, not only for foreign States and their foreign investors, but also for Australians expressing their rights in a democracy, beyond protecting the economic interests of Australian investors abroad. A comprehensive BIT policy could also serve as a signal to both States and investors that Australia has adopted a balanced approach to dispute resolution in its BITs, including support for stable trade and investment relations, which it shares with other States and impacted investors.

Importantly, Australia's adoption of a BIT policy and illustrative BIT clauses could provide inducements for foreign investment in the domestic Australian economy such as by adopting a market-based definition of 'investment' and by espousing an investor-sensitive conception of a 'direct or indirect expropriation'. Conversely, it could provide for Australia's public interest defences to foreign investor claims in order to protect its predominately resource-based economy from foreign investor incursions.

Such a proposed BIT policy has strategic benefits for Australia, encouraging further economic integration between Australia and its key economic allies in the region. Such a policy would also make it easier for Australia to engage in TPPA negotiations in which the majority of members have opted for ISDS.

The purpose of the proposed BIT policy would be to identify Australia's preferred position in negotiating BITs—including BIT variations to meet specific

---

[95] On such a challenge process, see UNCTAD, 'Reform of Investor-State Dispute Settlement: In Search of a Roadmap' *IIA Issues Note* 4 <unctad.org/en/PublicationsLibrary/webdiaepcb2013d4_en.pdf> accessed 11 July 2014.

domestic and/or foreign party requirements—not unlike, but with more flexibility than, the US Model BIT. It would also assist Australian negotiators to frame BIT provisions, and would provide domestic courts and ISDS tribunals with a point of reference when applying treaties to specific investor–State disputes. In addition, it would enable Australia to negotiate for its preferred dispute avoidance provisions in concluding BITs with other States.

The authors have previously made specific recommendations on the framework of a potential BIT policy.[96] While the adoption of a detailed BIT policy is encouraged, the policy should be neither uncompromising nor mechanically applied to all of Australia's ensuing treaties. Some States, like the US, strongly adhere to a Model BIT template in negotiating BITs with partner States. Other States, like China, sometimes diverge extensively from their Model BITs when they negotiate individual BITs. This was the case in China's BIT with Canada, concluded in 2012,[97] and will most likely be repeated in China's investment treaty negotiations with the EU, launched in November 2013.[98]

Australia should adopt a middle position by utilizing a BIT policy that includes illustrative and non-binding BIT clauses, given the likelihood that it will conclude negotiations with different kinds of BIT partners in the foreseeable future. Thus, Australia's BIT policy should not be drafted as a declaration upon which Australia's national identity is inextricably dependent.

Furthermore, the policy should be subject to ongoing examination and refinement. In particular, to ensure that the proposed BIT policy is properly adopted and implemented, it would need to be monitored on a continuing basis in light of its application to particular BITs and the subsequent interpretation of those BITs by domestic courts and ISDS tribunals. The policy would also need to be regularly re-evaluated in light of its impact on national policy and the flow of FDI into and out of Australia.

VI. Conclusion

This chapter has discussed a trend of oscillation between ISDS and domestic courts to resolve investment disputes, with a perceptible shift towards a preference for the

---

[96] See LE Trakman and K Sharma, (n 40); Trakman, 'Choosing Domestic Courts' (n 1).

[97] The China–Canada Bilateral Investment Treaty was concluded in September 2012, although Canada has not yet adopted it. See Agreement Between the Government of Canada and the Government of the People's Republic of China for the Promotion and Reciprocal Protection of Investments, agreed 9 September 2012, <www.international.gc.ca/trade-agreements-accords-commerciaux/agr-acc/fipa-apie/china-text-chine.aspx?lang=eng> accessed 11 July 2014. See also 'Chinese premier urges Canada to approve investment treaty' *Xinhuanet* (28 October 2013) <http://news.xinhuanet.com/english/china/2013-10/18/c_132811261.htm> accessed 11 July 2014.

[98] See P Bentley and F Schoneveld, 'A Giant Leap: EU-China Bilateral Investment Treaty Negotiations to Be Launched Formally' *National Law Review* (23 November 2013) <www.natlawreview.com/article/giant-leap-eu-china-bilateral-investment-treaty-negotiations-to-be-launched-formally> accessed 11 July 2014.

latter, both within and outside the Asia Pacific region. This shift is most noticeable in the Policy Statement adopted by the Australian Government in 2011, which the subsequent Coalition Government has tempered to apply on a case-by-case basis. This has led to the exclusion of ISDS from the 2014 JAEPA and its potential exclusion from the impending TPPA. Further marking this shift away from ISDS is Indonesia's decision in 2014 to terminate its BIT with the Netherlands and to undertake a termination and renegotiation programme in general, in light of its recent experiences with ISDS.

The central argument in this chapter is not that ISDS is inherently superior to litigation before domestic courts of host States, or the converse. Indeed, both options have limitations, whether in protecting foreign investors from regulation by host States or in insulating host States from regulating in the public interest. All other factors being constant, domestic courts on balance are more likely than ISDS tribunals to recognize national security, public health, and environmental protection invoked by host States. Conversely, ISDS tribunals, on balance, are more likely to recognize and apply investor protections in BITs that favour foreign investors. However, these likelihoods are nowhere close to being guarantees. Much will depend on the nature of the BIT or FTA in issue, the State parties to it, and the manner in which domestic courts or ISDS tribunals apply the protections available.

One central argument in this chapter is that, notwithstanding its imperfections, ISDS has key systemic advantages over domestic courts in deciding investor–State disputes, all other factors being constant. These include an extensive ISDS jurisprudence that has evolved to regulate international investment practice; specialist institutions such as the ICSID whose rules regulate such practice; and expert ISDS tribunals that decide investor–State disputes between a range of foreign investors and host States. Nevertheless, these benefits of ISDS are not self-determining. Nor are they invariably superior to determinations by domestic courts. The second central argument, therefore, is in favour of a BIT policy that includes different and graduated dispute resolution options, not limited to either domestic courts or ISDS.

The chapter concludes with recommendations for a graduated method of resolving investor–State disputes. Whether States will adopt variants of these recommendations will depend on how they perceive economic, social, and political benefits arising from such a graduated approach in negotiating BITs and FTAs. The goal should be to ensure that investment policy is devised in a manner that pursues sustainable development as outlined in the IPFSD.

The evidence to date is that some States in the Pacific Rim, such as Australia, may resist ISDS selectively in favour of domestic courts, asserting that domestic courts are more likely to comply with the rule of law, to recognize domestic public policy, and to avoid the allegedly high costs of ISDS proceedings. Other States, such as Indonesia, are likely to resist ISDS due to the more explicit concern that inbound investors will secure ISDS remedies that undermine domestic public policy, and lead to crippling awards against host States. This concern, of losing ISDS cases to foreign investors, is not entirely novel, tracing back to positions adopted by Ecuador, Venezuela, and Bolivia between 2008 and 2010, whereby they all rejected ISDS. What is different from those cases is the economic, social, and political context in which the Pacific Rim states find themselves today, including investment disputes that have taken place since 2010, as well as prospective future developments that may include one of the largest trade pacts attempted in the Pacific region, the Trans-Pacific Partnership.

XIV
The 'Generalization' of International Investment Law in Constitutional Perspective

Peter-Tobias Stoll and Till Patrik Holterhus

I. Introduction

For a long time, international investment law has emerged as a rather distinct and specific element of international economic law and general international law. Accordingly, its merits, shortcomings, and improvements were mainly discussed and analysed with a view to this system and the situations and objectives, which it was understood/meant to address. A number of developments have resulted in a broadening of the perspective. The apparent interlinkage of investment law with other areas of international law may be mentioned here as well as cases where investment law was put to practice against States with a highly developed legal system.

However, the most significant developments in this regard can be seen in the negotiations on the Comprehensive and Economic Trade Agreement (CETA), the Trans-Pacific Partnership (TPP), and theTransatlantic Trade and Investment Partnership (TTIP), as they imply a 'generalization' of international investment law. As will be shown, this generalization is characterized by two distinct elements: first, that the international investment law is now conceived as providing a legal framework for investments vis-à-vis all States, whereas it was originally meant to mitigate an adverse investment climate particularly in countries where the legal system revealed shortcomings as to legal certainty and predictability. Second, that investment protection sides with trade rules in one common framework, namely a preferential trade agreement.

In order to properly address these significant changes, a 'constitutional' view is suggested here,[1] which brings into play elements of constitutional thought in order to critically assess both the interfaces between such a 'generalized' investment law and the domestic and the EU legal order and its relation to other parts

---

[1] See in particular Section III.

of international law, including human rights and particular questions concerning the context of a right to property.[2]

II. From Splendid Isolation to Centre Stage

a) Splendid isolation and reform

International investment law and scholarly reflection on it has largely developed in recent years. For a long time, improvements to the system itself, both in terms of substantive law and procedure, have only been induced by arbitration tribunals in their decisions, by amendments to the ICSID Convention and by new language in bilateral investment treaties (BITs). These developments have been closely followed by academia. To name but a few of them, the limitation of coverage by the definition of investments in the Salini test,[3] clarifications on the scope of indirect expropriation and the standard of fair and equitable treatment, the safeguards in favour of a national policy space, as well as the annulment of ICSID awards and rules to ensure the independence and impartiality of arbitrators must be mentioned.[4] These improvements have been discussed and reflected on largely with a view to analysing the effectivity, efficiency, justice, and appropriateness of the system of investment law alone.

b) Interlinkages to other areas of international economic law and general international law

However, over the last couple of years, there has been a growing tendency to look at international investment law in its context with other areas of international law.[5] From this perspective, the interrelation between international investment law and environmental law,[6] the international law on sustainable development,[7] labour

---

[2] See in particular section VIII.
[3] See, for instance the Salini test, which defined and thereby delineated the covered investments, *Salini Costruttori SpA and Italstrade SpA v Kingdom of Morocco*, ICSID Case No ARB/00/4, Decision of Jurisdiction (23 July 2001).
[4] See for a comprehensive overview: S Hindelang, 'Part II: Study on Investor-State Dispute Settlement ("ISDS") and Alternatives of Dispute Resolution in International Investment Law', in *European Parliament, Directorate General for External Policies of the Union, Study Investor-State Dispute Settlement (ISDS) Provisions in the EU's International Investment Agreements* (European Commission 2014) 46 <http://ssrn.com/abstract=2525063> accessed 17 February 2015.
[5] See recently F Baetens (ed), *Investment Law within International Law—Integrationist Perspectives* (CUP 2013).
[6] S Di Benedetto, *International Investment Law and the Environment* (Edward Elgar 2013); JE Viñuales, *Foreign Investment and the Environment in International Law* (CUP 2012).
[7] M-C Cordonier Segger, MW Gehring, and A Newcombe (eds), *Sustainable Development in World Investment Law* (Kluwer Law International 2011); JA VanDuzer, P Simons, and G Mayeda (eds), *Integrating Sustainable Development into International Investment Agreements: A Commonwealth Guide for Developing Country Negotiators* (Commonwealth Secretariat 2013).

standards,⁸ human rights,⁹ and culture¹⁰ have been discussed both in academia and in the general public. These discussions have resulted in a number of cases and new treaty language in BITs and free trade agreements.¹¹ Another strand of discussion has addressed the ever-closer relationship between international investment law and international trade law.¹²

c) Recent experiences of the application of international investment law

Lastly, we have seen discussions on the impact of international investment law on national law, which have recently been fuelled by investment arbitrations being initiated against Canada,¹³ Australia,¹⁴ and Germany.¹⁵ Of course, the initiation of investment arbitration procedures could have been foreseen, as BITs are drafted in a reciprocal way and impose the very same rights and obligations on either contracting party.¹⁶ For a long time, however, it has probably been believed that investment law would come to practice primarily in (that is, against) countries whose legal systems were considered to be less capable of securing the rights of investors.

In the public and academia, particularly the aforementioned cases have given rise to questioning the impact of international investment law on sovereignty, democracy, and on maintaining appropriate margins for national regulatory policies. Of course, these issues have been of relevance ever since Calvo's influential work.¹⁷ However, opposite to the situation in some Latin American States, policymakers, academia, and the general public in those States which were among the initiators of modern investment law and of bilateral investment agreements, have

---

⁸ V Prislan and R Zandvliet, 'Labor Provisions in International Investment Agreements: Prospects for Sustainable Development' (2013) 2012/2013 Yearbook of International Investment Law and Policy <http://papers.ssrn.com/sol3/papers.cfm?abstract_id=2171716> accessed 17 February 2015.

⁹ P-M Dupuy, E-U Petersmann, and F Francioni (eds), *Human Rights in International Investment Law and Arbitration* (OUP 2009); E De Brabandere, 'Human Rights Considerations in International Investment Arbitration' in M Fitzmaurice and P Merkouris (eds), *The Interpretation and Application of the European Convention of Human Rights: Legal and Practical Implications* (Martinus Nijhoff 2012) <http://ssrn.com/abstract=2230305> accessed 17 February 2015.

¹⁰ V Vadi, *Cultural Heritage in International Investment Law and Arbitration* (CUP 2014).

¹¹ See, for example, the 2012 American Model BIT, which contains environmental (Art 12) and labour (Art 13) provisions <www.state.gov/documents/organization/188371.pdf> accessed 17 February 2014. See also T Stoll, H Krüger, and Jia Xu, 'Freihandelsabkommen und ihre Umweltschutzregelungen' (2014) ZUR 387 387.

¹² R Leal-Arcas, *International Trade and Investment Law: Multilateral, Regional and Bilateral Governance* (Edward Elgar 2011).

¹³ *Lone Pine Resources Inc v The Government of Canada*, UNCITRAL case, Notice of Arbitration (6 September 2013).

¹⁴ PCA Case No 2012-12—*Phillip Morris Asia Ltda v The Commonwealth of Australia*.

¹⁵ *Vattenfall AB and others v Federal Republic of Germany*, ICSID Case No ARB/12/12, Notice of Arbitration (31 May 2012).

¹⁶ BM Cremades, 'Disputes Arising out of Foreign Direct Investment in Latin America: A New Look at the Calvo Doctrine and other Jurisdictional Issues' (2004) 59 Disp Resol J 78 79.

¹⁷ C Calvo, *Derecho Internacional Teórico y Práctico de Europa y América* (D´Amyot Librarie Diplomatique—Durand et Pèdone-Lauriel 1868).

not addressed these questions in depth so far. While, for instance, in Germany the relation between domestic law and international agreements and international courts and tribunals has been the subject of constitutional provisions, a rich jurisprudence of the Federal Constitutional Court and an equally rich academic literature, the likely impact of the application of international investment law has so far not been the subject of much debate.

d) Generalization: CETA, TTIP, and others

All those developments are highly relevant in the current situation, as a number of negotiations involving investment chapters are under way. The EU–Canadian CETA[18] as well as the EU–Singapore Free Trade Agreement,[19] the projects most close to finalization, which in the economic perspective are little more than a prelude, nevertheless are templates, pioneering exercises, which hardly can be ignored in the negotiations on the EU–US TTIP and will doubtlessly serve as a model in further negotiations with Japan and others. Also, intense negotiations on further standalone EU-BITs have just started or will take place soon, a potential partner being the Peoples Republic of China. In a number of public statements, the expectation has been voiced that TTIP will define a 'gold standard' for international investment law, which then can be brought to the table in future negotiations with other partners.[20]

These developments are quite remarkable. So far, while having concluded numerous bilateral investment agreements, OECD countries were nevertheless selective. With some notable but yet rather specific exceptions, including NAFTA and the Energy Charter Treaty, they did usually not conclude such agreements among each other. Probably, this was due to the perception that asking each other for additional international protection of investors would have meant to unnecessarily put into question the reputation of national legal systems, which were seen to have a by and large good record in effectively protecting foreign investors. Departing from this long-established policy, the CETA and TTIP negotiations

---

[18] Consolidated CETA, published on 26 September 2014, made available to the public by the European Commission at <http://trade.ec.europa.eu/doclib/html/152806.htm> accessed 17 February 2015.

[19] Chapter IX on Investment Protection, published on 17 December 2014, made available to the public by the European Commission at <http://trade.ec.europa.eu/doclib/press/index.cfm?id=961> accessed 17 February 2015.

[20] 'The investment chapter of the TTIP should eventually serve as the "gold standard" for other investment agreements.' Statement of the US Chamber of Commerce on the Transatlantic Trade & Investment Partnership to the Office of the US Trade Representative, 10 May 2013 <hwww.regulations.gov/#!documentDetail;D=USTR-2013-0019-0241> accessed 17 February 2015 and the statement of Peter Robinson, President and CEO, United States Council for International Business (USCIB) on 'USCIB's Foreign Direct Investment Policy Agenda' at the UNCTAD World Investment Forum on 16 October 2014: 'We strongly support the ongoing efforts of the U.S. Government to negotiate the Trans-Pacific Partnership (TPP) and the Transatlantic Trade and Investment Partnership (TTIP), as well as gold standard BITs with key partner countries, including advanced developing countries', 1 <http://unctad-worldinvestmentforum.org/wp-content/uploads/2014/10/Robinson.pdf> accessed 17 February 2015.

indeed mark a turning point. In the absence of any more conclusive explanations, it does not make much sense to discuss the potential reasons behind this policy shift. In particular, there is no indication that negotiators now believe that the *niveau* of protection of investors in the US or the EU has deteriorated compared to earlier times. And it would certainly go beyond the limits of this chapter to find out whether this is true and what kind of a yardstick to use to answer this question.

Rather, it is sufficient to note that this turnaround results in a generalization. This generalization firstly implies that, rather than excluding themselves from those rules as they widely did in the past, Canada, the US, and the EU now head for making applicable international investment law among themselves. This way, they—secondly—seem to aim at setting standards to be brought to the table in negotiations with third countries. Taking this one step further, this—thirdly—implies that, by consequence, Canada, the US, and the EU accept as a general rule that foreign investors will enjoy additional protection under international investment law in all respective jurisdictions and that international investment law might de facto become an element of general application in international economic law after all, sometimes even referred to as a 'global ius commune'.[21]

III. A 'Constitutional' View

In view of this tendency of generalization, the questions which came up recently with the investment arbitral proceedings initiated against Canada, Australia, and Germany became more general, too, and more pressing as might be indicated by the vivid debate within the EU, which prompted the Commission to halt the TTIP negotiations on this point in order to undertake a public consultation. There is now time to explore the relation between international investment law and national constitutional law. This debate is going on at the moment in Germany,[22] where quite diverse positions are taken as to the compatibility of Germany's existing and newly proposed commitments under various BITs

---

[21] I Pernice, 'Part III: Study on International Investment Protection Agreements and EU Law', in European Parliament, Directorate General for External Policies of the Union, *Study Investor-State Dispute Settlement (ISDS) Provisions in the EU's International Investment Agreements* (European Commission 2014) 158 <www.jura.fu-berlin.de/fachbereich/einrichtungen/oeffentliches-recht/lehrende/hindelangs/Studie-fuer-Europaeisches-Parlament/Volume-2-Studies.pdf> accessed 17 February 2015.

[22] See, for example, the differing legal opinions by M Krajewski, September 2014 <www.gruenebundestag.de/fileadmin/media/gruenebundestag_de/themen_az/EU-USA_Freihandelsabkommen/Thesenpapier_Klageprivilegien_in_CETA.PDF> accessed 5 February 2015. A Fischer-Lescano and J Horst, October 2014 <www.attac.de/uploads/media/CETA-Rechtsgutachten_Oktober_2014_Fischer-Lescano_Uni_Bremen.pdf> accessed 5 February 2015 and SW Schill, September 2014 <www.bmwi.de/BMWi/Redaktion/PDF/C-D/ceta-gutachten-investitionsschutz,property=pdf,bereich=bmwi2012,sprache=de,rwb=true.pdf> accessed 17 February 2015. Additionally see the debate on 'verfassungsblog.de' <www.verfassungsblog.de/category/schwerpunkte/investitionsschutz-im-ttip-in-der-kritik/> accessed 5 February 2015 and on the arbitration in German administrative KH Möller, *Echte Schiedsgerichtsbarkeit im Verwaltungsrecht: Eine Studie zu Rechtsrahmen und Kontrolle nichtstaatlicher Streitentscheidung im Verwaltungsrecht* (Duncker & Humblot 2014) 38.

and preferential trade agreements—CETA and TTIP in particular—in view of a number of provisions of the German Basic Law.[23] Beyond these rather recent, complex, but well-defined questions of the constitutionality of commitments under international investment law and related activities by international investment arbitration, the public debate has a tendency to more generally address the merits of existing and proposed international investment protection as to their (potential) impact on sovereignty, democracy, legitimacy, due process, and the rule of law. These terms have not least emerged in the context of national constitutional law as well as constitutional thought and cannot be taken to the international level without careful consideration. However, it has been widely acknowledged for quite some time that in addition to national bodies, international rules and institutions have their own and distinctive part to play in the exercise of public authority and consequently should be subjected to principles and rules similar to those of national constitutions and national constitutional discourse.[24] This is evident in the likely case that the constitutionality of commitments under international investment protection rules and procedures has to be assessed by taking into account the very structure and details of the international rules and procedures. However, in a more general way, the constitutionalist perspective, with all caution, is also a viable tool for analysis of international investment law more generally, as it might show parallels and departures of that law in view of principles, which can be derived from national constitutional thought but may also be mirrored by international legal principles.[25] Research in this direction can build on recent (quite differing) approaches in the area of comparative public law[26] as well as from insights regarding the international administrative law approach.[27]

The approach taken here is quite complex, as it requires seeing the international and national rules and procedures on investment protection in their interplay and analysing them in view of national as well as international rules and principles. It also entails a number of questions, which so far have not been considered in depth. Therefore, the following discussion can only provide for some preliminary insights, which will focus on a few issues that appear to be most significant.

---

[23] In particular Art 20 para 3 (rule of law), Art 20 para 1 (principle of democracy), Art 19 para 4 (access to justice), Art 92 (judicial power vested in the judges) and Art 101 para 1 (right to a lawful judge) of the Basic Law for the Federal Republic of Germany 1949.
[24] M Loughlin, 'What is Constitutionalisation?' in P Dobner and M Loughlin (eds), *The Twilight of Constitutionalism?* (OUP 2010) 63.
[25] See on a further constitutional approach in international investment law D Schneiderman, 'A New Global Constitutional Order?' in T Ginsburg and R Dixon (eds), *Comparative Constitutional Law: Research Handbook in Comparative Constitutional* Law (Edward Elgar 2011) 189–207 and D Schneiderman, 'Investment Rules and the New Constitutionalism' (2000) 25 Law & Soc Inquiry 757, 757.
[26] See the differing approaches of SW Schill (ed), *International Investment Law and Comparative Public Law* (OUP 2010) and G Van Harten, *Investment Treaty Arbitration and Public Law* (OUP 2007).
[27] G Van Harten and M Loughlin, 'Investment Treaty Arbitration as a Species of Global Administrative Law' (2006) 17 EJIL 121; see for a discussion of the merits of the different approaches JW Yackee, 'Controlling the International Investment Law Agency' (2012) 53 Harv Intl L J 392, 396.

IV. Aspects of Sovereignty, Democracy, and Legitimation

In the current public debate, international investment law has occasionally been criticized for threatening sovereignty and democracy and for lacking legitimation. From a legal perspective, these three issues are closely interlinked, but require a more precise and distinct reflection.

Sovereignty indeed has been an issue in international investment protection ever since Calvo referred to it in his influential doctrine.[28] From an international perspective, sovereignty, rather than putting into question international commitments of the State per se, would imply that a State can independently decide on such commitments, including to subject itself to related dispute settlement procedures at an international level.[29] However, in the interest of their continued exercise and control of public authority, most States, when accepting international commitments or subjecting themselves to international dispute settlement procedures, are required by their internal constitutional law to ensure that these commitments or procedures are well-defined, predictable, and legitimate.[30] This is often mandated at the constitutional level on the basis of such diverse constitutional rules as a national guarantee of sovereignty, a requirement inherent in the exercise of foreign relations powers or as an emanation of the principle of democratic governance.

Whether concerns arise in this regard very much depends on how intensively international obligations and procedures will interfere with the exercise of power and the legal system at the national level and how these international commitments and procedures will be defined and limited in order to make them foreseeable and legitimate.

Regarding the potential degree of interference, it is often held that States face more severe impacts under regimes such as the WTO. Indeed, under the WTO, a State, when found to have acted inconsistently with WTO agreements in a WTO dispute settlement, will be ordered to bring such measure into conformity with its obligations,[31] while awards in investment arbitration will very likely be limited to awarding damages or compensation. However, this argument is a rather formalistic one. It hardly takes into account appropriately that investment arbitration tribunals would incidentally rule on the consistency of a State's measure with applicable law and that the compensation granted by an award can reach a considerably high amount. Furthermore, the award, at least in the case of ICSID, enjoys the rather unique privilege of being directly enforceable in all member States. This has a considerable impact on the financial autonomy of States and could cause a chilling effect.[32]

---

[28] Calvo (n 17). [29] Pernice (n 21) 134. [30] Hindelang (n 4) 72.
[31] Understanding on Rules and Procedures Governing the Settlement of Disputes (15 April 1994) LT/UR/A-2/DS/U/1 art 19 <https://docsonline.wto.org>.
[32] Pernice (n 21) 139.

Because of this considerable impact, the proper delimitation and definition of international investment standards and procedures is of critical importance. The number of recent reform proposals, addressing various issues in this regard, is worth noting. Indeed, efforts to define substantive standards such as indirect expropriation, fair and equitable treatment more clearly and more concisely, as well as to provide for an explicit safeguard for the national public policy space can be welcomed. This would especially address legitimate concerns in view of interference with the national democratic process. Also noteworthy are the various proposals and tendencies to improve the procedure by securing the independence and impartiality of arbitrators, by providing for transparency and by even employing some sort of an authoritative interpretation by Parties as well as by envisioning a review procedure.

V. Review of the Exercise of Public Authority— by an Arbitral Body?

One particular aspect merits a closer look. International investment law involves a review of the exercise of public authority—which is undertaken by an arbitral body. The critical relevance of this point is increased by the fact that also (highest) court rulings are to be understood as public authority in this context and, hence, can be subject to the arbitral body's review, even if the courts' ruling did explicitly not grant appeal.[33]

Several and distinct legal issues arise at this point.

a) The Autonomy of the EU Legal Order

A specific, but nonetheless significant issue of the problematic situation that court rulings are subject to an arbitral body's review unfolds, as far as the EU is concerned, in the context of the autonomy of the EU legal order,[34] especially when taking into account the European Court of Justice's opinions 1/91,[35] 1/92,[36] 1/00,[37] 1/09[38]

---

[33] This can be illustrated by *Eli Lilly and Company v Government of Canada*, where a company claimed compensation under NAFTA for the invalidation of patents by the Canadian Federal and the Federal Appeals Courts, while the Supreme Court of Canada did not grant appeal. Case No UNCT/14/2, Canada's Statement of Defence of 30 June 2014<www.international.gc.ca/trade-agreements-accords-commerciaux/topics-domaines/disp-diff/eli-statement-declaration.aspx?lang=eng> accessed 5 February 2015.

[34] See on the specific problem of the interrelation between EU legal order and international investment law: S Hindelang, 'Der primärrechtliche Rahmen einer EU Investitionsschutzpolitik: Zulässigkeit und Grenzen von Investor-Staat-Schiedsverfahren aufgrund künftiger EU Abkommen' (2010) WHI Paper 01/11, 17 <www.whi-berlin.eu/tl_files/documents/whi-paper0111.pdf> accessed 17 February 2015; J Ahner, *Investor-Staat-Schiedsverfahren nach Europäischem Unionsrecht* (Mohr Siebeck 2015) 204ff.

[35] Council Opinion (EEC) 1/91 opinion pursuant to Art 228 of the EEC treaty [1991] OJ I-6099.
[36] Council Opinion (EEC) 1/92 opinion of the court [1992] OJ I-2838.
[37] Council Opinion (ECAA) 1/00 [2002] OJ I-3493.
[38] Council Opinion (European and Community Patents Court) 1/09 [2011] OJ I-1137.

and in particular the most recent opinion 2/13, issued on 18 December 2014.[39] All these opinions made clear that the autonomous EU legal order—preserving the specific characteristics of EU law and ensuring the competences of the EU and the powers of its institutions[40]—must usually not be limited through international obligations and/or treaties. The recent opinion 2/13 concerns the compatibility of the draft agreement on the accession of the European Union to the European Convention for the Protection of Human Rights and Fundamental Freedoms (ECHR) with the TEU and TFEU. As the court held:

> the competence of the EU in the field of international relations and its capacity to conclude international agreements necessarily entail the power to submit to the decisions of a court which is created or designated by such agreements as regards the interpretation and application of their provisions.[41]

Yet, the Court went on stating:

> Nevertheless, the Court of Justice has also declared that an international agreement may affect its own powers only if the indispensable conditions for safeguarding the essential character of those powers are satisfied and, consequently, there is no adverse effect on the autonomy of the EU legal order.[42]

Furthermore, the Court stated in view of the European Court on Human Rights:

> In particular, any action by the bodies given decision-making powers by the ECHR, as provided for in the agreement envisaged, must not have the effect of binding the EU and its institutions, in the exercise of their internal powers, to a particular interpretation of the rules of EU law.[43]

Clearly, the award of an investment arbitration tribunal, when dealing exclusively with damages or compensation, would not bind the EU and its institutions to a particular interpretation of the rules of EU law. However, the de facto impact on the autonomy of the legal order may be considerable, even surmounting the one of WTO dispute settlement and perhaps, as is voiced sometimes, going even beyond the possible implications of an accession of the EU to the ECHR in view of the direct enforceability of awards.[44]

b) The Arbitration Procedure

While this issue can be seen as a specific limit with regard to the possible scope of adjudication of an international dispute settlement procedure, the more serious concern with regard to investment arbitration is the procedure.

---

[39] Council Opinion 2/13 (ECtHR) [2014] ECLI:EU:C:2014:2454.   [40] ibid para 161.
[41] ibid para 182.
[42] ibid para 183. The Court in this regard referred to its Opinions 1/00, EU:C:2002:231, paras 21, 23 and 26, and Opinion 1/09, EU:C:2011:123, para 76 and furthermore to the judgment in *Kadi and Al Barakaat International Foundation* v *Council and Commission*, EU:C:2008:461, para 282.
[43] ibid para 184.   [44] Pernice (n 21) 146.

Indeed, as a rule, the review of the exercise of public authority will be reserved to courts and judges in most jurisdictions. Often, constitutional rules provide that there is access to justice and that jurisprudence should be generally in the hands of courts and judges, which in most countries will have a special and privileged status and are often selected in a way to secure their democratic accountability. These rules generally reflect that dispute settlement and law enforcement are core public functions of a State. Concerning private and commercial disputes, most jurisdictions allow for mediation and arbitration as alternative modes of dispute resolution in view of the fact that private interests are at stake. However, with regard to administrative or other public matters, such alternative modes of dispute resolution are pretty uncommon.[45] This may be said to reflect the conviction that the conduct of public authority should be reviewed by institutions with a high profile of independence, impartiality, and democratic legitimacy.

This does not automatically mean that arbitration with regard to issues of the exercise of public authority should be impermissible once and forever. But it certainly implies that good reasons should be required to employ the method of dispute settlement. The speedy procedure is often put forward in this regard, which indeed is a considerable advantage of arbitration over a normal court procedure. However, when balancing this legitimate interest of a claimant with the public interests reflected by the normal court procedure, the latter will likely have an advantage, in particular, where claims to damages and compensation (and probably consequential chilling effects) are at stake.[46] This is at least the case where national courts exist that are competent to hear the cases.

In this context the proposal to establish an international investment court, which has been made more than once, has to be mentioned, as it would importantly improve the legitimacy of international investment adjudication.[47] If this turns out to be impossible to establish, an investment appellate body could be imagined, along the lines of the WTO Appellate Body, which is a standing adjudicating body, which decides about appeals against WTO panel decisions, which in some way may be considered to come close to arbitral tribunals in investment law.

---

[45] See on the rareness of arbitration in German administrative law Möller (n 22) 31 and SW Schill, 'Öffentlich-rechtliche Schiedsverfahren zwischen Risikobewältigung und Rechtsrisiko' (2010) DÖV 1013, 1013.

[46] G Van Harten (n 26) 175ff; with a sceptical approach on German law see Möller (n 22) 48,132.

[47] See European Commission, 'Commission draft text TTIP— investment' (September 2015) <http://trade.ec.europa.eu/doclib/docs/2015/september/tradoc_153807.pdf> accessed 1 October 2015. G Van Harten, 'A Case for an International Investment Court' (2008) Society of International Economic Law (SIEL) Inaugural Conference Working Paper 22/08 <http://papers.ssrn.com/sol3/papers.cfm?abstract_id=1153424> accessed 17 February 2015; M Krajewski, *Modell-Investitionsschutzvertrag mit Investor-Staat-Schiedsverfahren für Industriestaaten unter Berücksichtigung der USA* (German Federal Ministry for Economic Affairs and Energy 2015) <www.bmwi.de/BMWi/Redaktion/PDF/M-O/modell-investitionsschutzvertrag-mit-investor-staat-schiedsverfahren-gutachten,property=pdf,bereich=bmwi2012,sprache=de,rwb=true.pdf> accessed 19 August 2015.

VI. A Fast Track to Compensation?

Another aspect concerns the fact that international investment law is very much focused on compensation.[48] Indeed, most investment cases concern the issue of compensation while only few of them address issues concerning the legality of the measure or even require a host State to do something about its measure in case it is found to be in breach with applicable rules. This limitation is hardly warranted by the ICSID convention itself, which is far more open in defining the tasks and powers and mandates of the tribunals. Sometimes, the focus on compensation is due to provisions in underlying BITs, which may define the mandate of tribunals to be confined to issues of compensation. Furthermore, however, the focus on compensation is in many cases the result of the claims put forward by investors. Where it is possible to claim compensation without ado, this opportunity will often be preferred, presumably because at the point of initiation of the proceedings, investors might already doubt whether continuing the investment is a good idea. This is very much in line with the traditional understanding of international investment law as it means to 'ensure' investments by guaranteeing at least a monetary compensation in cases where the investment has to be terminated. It is also in line with the institutional developments, since the establishment of ICSID was accompanied by the Mulitlateral Investment Guarantee Agency (MIGA) as a pure investment guarantee insurance scheme.

This traditional ratio and current practice in international investment law is in stark contrast to the approach of most national laws and the law of the European Union. Rather than allowing a fast track avenue to compensation, national laws usually require an enterprise to challenge the legality of the measure before proceeding to compensation claims.[49] Such an approach is seen to have some merits. First of all, it may allow for a timely correction of the measure and thus prevent undue losses on the part of the investor as well as on the part of the taxpayer. Also, it allows for a clarification of the legality of the measure in the interest of the enterprise concerned but also in the more general interest of the public in striking a clear and predictable balance between individual rights and the public interest. Furthermore, it is understood sometimes to prevent some sort of rent-seeking attitude.

These principles are also reflected in international law. The articles on State responsibility do prefer restitution over compensation.[50] The exhaustion of local remedies is required by customary international law in the area of diplomatic protection and furthermore is applied by explicit rule in the area of human

---

[48] See chapter by Aust in this volume.
[49] J Kleinheisterkamp, 'Financial Responsibility in the European International Investment Policy' (2013) LSE Law, Society and Economy Working Papers 15/2013 <www.lse.ac.uk/collections/law/wps/WPS2013-15_Kleinheisterkamp.pdf> accessed 17 February 2015 and Pernice (n 21) 147.
[50] UNGA Res 56/83 (12 December 2001) UN Doc A/RES/56/83, 'Responsibility of States for Internationally Wrongful Acts' Art 36 para 1.

rights. While it does not directly advocate a preference of primary remedies over secondary ones, it nevertheless would allow States to pursue that preference at national level.

In contrast, in investment arbitration under ICSID, the exhaustion of local remedies is not required unless specifically required by a State party in accordance with Article 26 second sentence of the ICSID Convention. Only a small number of rather old BITs did require such exhaustion of local remedies.

Two other mechanisms are used and discussed in this context of giving incentives to using primary remedies over secondary ones. Waiting periods (so-called cooling-off periods) are contained in several BITs and may be considered to encourage investors to turn to national courts or to seek amicable settlement with national authorities. Their effectivity in this regard, however, is put into question, as such waiting periods are often seen as a pure procedural device and not as a jurisdictional requirement.

The same holds true for those cases where a BIT combines such waiting periods with the duty to seek relief in national courts. This requirement has been at issue in several arbitrations in view of the interplay with Article 26 second sentence of the ICSID convention and with regard to MFN clauses. Also, in a number of cases, the requirement has been seen as a slight modification of the waiting period only and treated accordingly as a mere procedural issue.

Lastly, so-called fork-in-the-road provisions must be mentioned, which require investors to make a choice between international arbitration and national courts. However, under such provisions, investors are often expected to opt for arbitration. Also, it should be noted that the effect of these clauses depends on whether arbitral tribunals will halt or terminate the arbitration on grounds of *lis alibi pendens*. Where an arbitral tribunal does not consider the other pending case identical, no limits whatsoever would be imposed by a fork-in-the-road clause. In sum, international investment law as it stands appears to offer little to favour the use of primary remedies over secondary ones.

As regards recent developments, the current discussions within the European Union are of some relevance, as the EU is becoming a strong actor in international investment law due to its newly attained competence in this field (Article 207 para 1 TFEU) and the high number of trade agreements currently under negotiation. On the occasion of a public consultation held in 2014, the European Commission explained that its approach would include favouring domestic courts.[51] While not exactly reflecting the idea of a preference for primary remedies, this statement can nevertheless be welcomed, as it would allow States and presumably also the European Union as such to be in a position to review the case at hand, to correct its decision and to settle the issue according to its own standards and procedures

---

[51] European Commission, 'Public consultation on modalities for investment protection and ISDS in TTIP', Public Consultation B Investor-to-state dispute settlement (ISDS), Introduction (2014) 5<http://trade.ec.europa.eu/doclib/docs/2014/march/tradoc_152280.pdf> accessed 17 February 2015.

at the regional or domestic levels. The European Commission understands the CETA draft to widely conform to this approach.[52] Indeed, the agreement applies a rather restrictive approach by only allowing international arbitration for claims for loss and damage suffered due to a violation of several of the agreement's main disciplines for the treatment of foreign investors. Furthermore, in view of such claims, Article X.21 of the investment chapter of the CETA draft requires investors to waive their right to access domestic or international courts with regard to claims for damages and compensation upon the initiation of an arbitration procedure. Furthermore, there is a waiting period of 180 days. This has been seen as a considerable incentive to bring similar claims at the domestic level first in order not to lose this opportunity. Doubts arise at this point, however, in view of the considerable duration of national administrative court proceedings.

Also, as the investment arbitration rules are confined to claims for losses and damages arising from a violation of the agreement, investors are understood to be free to bring claims under national law and in view of primary remedies at the domestic level at any time. While these rules can be understood to encourage investors to try national or EU remedies first, it results in a remarkable split-up between primary and secondary remedies. Altogether, it is questionable whether these rules and international investment law in general can achieve, what the priority for primary remedies at national and EU level is all about.

VII. 'Reverse discrimination' as an Aspect of Non-discrimination

While the point has hardly played a role in academic analysis so far, the discrimination of domestic investors[53] surfaces as a major concern when looking on international investment law from a constitutional perspective. Evidently, exclusively foreign investors benefit from international investment law. While foreign investors who face adverse State measures on a national level are regularly entitled to take legal action under international investment law *as well as* the particular national law, domestic investors are limited to pursue their interests via the

---

[52] European Commission, 'Investment Provisions in the EU-Canada Free Trade Agreement (CETA)' (2014) 4 <http://trade.ec.europa.eu/doclib/docs/2013/november/tradoc_151918.pdf> accessed 17 February 2015.

[53] See, however, SP Subedi, *International Investment Law: Reconciling Policy and Principle* (Hart Publishing 2008) 182; V Been and JC Beauvais, 'The Global Fifth Amendment? NAFTA's Investment Protections and the Misguided Quest for an International "Regulatory Takings" Doctrine'(2003) 78 NYU L Rev 30, 129; Workshop on Global Administrative Law Issues in Latin America, 'What international investment law and Latin America can and should demand from each other: Updating the Bell/Calvo doctrine in the BIT generation' (2007) <www.iilj.org/gal/documents/SantiagoMontt.GAL.pdf> accessed 17 February 2015; A Epiney, *Umgekehrte Diskriminierungen: Zulässigkeit und Grenzen der discrimination à rebours nach europäischem Gemeinschaftsrecht und nationalem Verfassungsrecht* (Heymann 1995) 4; WTO Doc WT/WGTI/W/122 submitted by the Permanent Delegation of the European Commission, 2 and Pernice (n 21) 144.

particular national law alone.⁵⁴ Regardless of the particular extent of *substantive* protection granted by the applicable investment treaties and/or national laws, foreign investors hence usually have an additional *procedural* option that domestic companies don't. Whatever option to define the relation between domestic courts and international investment arbitration as discussed above will be chosen, domestic investors will, hence, face a considerable disadvantage.

Indeed, one could argue that almost every BIT 'mirrors' (and therefore counterbalances) such an inferior treatment of domestic investors in their home State by the potential superior treatment when finding themselves in the role of foreign investors in the other contracting State's territory. But, first, circumstances where a potential mirrored superior treatment results in an 'equal' treatment overall, are almost impossible to find, considering the wide differences in structure and extent of the particular State's legal remedies.

And, second, this argument would mean approaching the concept of non-discrimination from a systemic rather than an individual perspective, which conflicts with the concept of non-discrimination as an individual right. The proposed application of a possible generalized 'global standard' of investment law around the globe will make this disadvantage even more significant, and in particular, not make the problem disappear: the expectation to enjoy such privileged treatment in *multiple* other States can hardly be considered to outweigh or justify discriminatory effects at home. Hence, aside from discriminatory effects, the issue also raises concerns in view of competition.⁵⁵

The problem at hand relates to the issue of reverse discrimination,⁵⁶ that is, the phenomenon that a host State's own nationals are treated less favourably than foreign investors. The issue is complex and still awaits a comprehensive in-depth analysis. While an impressive number of standards on non-discrimination exists, both in international human rights law, including particularly the Additional Protocol 12 to the ECHR, as well as in primary (Article 18 TFEU) and secondary EU law, taking into consideration also the EU Charter of Fundamental Rights (Article 21

---

⁵⁴ R Dolzer and C Schreuer, *Principles of International Investment Law* (2nd edn, OUP 2012) 44.

⁵⁵ The argument of a competitive disadvantage has already been made by the European Commission in view of intra-EU BIT's between its Member States <http://ec.europa.eu/internal_market/capital/analysis/monitoring_activities_and_analysis/index_en.htm> accessed 17 February 2015. See in this context also C Binder, *Die Grenzen der Vertragstreue im Völkerrecht* (Springer 2013) 561 with further references; C Tietje, 'Bilaterale Investitionsschutzverträge zwischen EU Mitgliedstaaten (Intra-EU-BITs) als Herausforderung im Mehrebenensystem des Rechts', in C Tietje, G Kraft, and M Lehmann, *Beiträge zum Transnationalen Wirtschaftsrecht*, vol 104, (Bibliografische Information der Deutschen Bibliothek 2011); H Wehland, 'Schiedsverfahren auf der Grundlage bilateraler Investitionsschutzabkommen zwischen EU-Mitgliedstaaten und die Einwendung des entgegenstehenden Gemeinschaftsrechts' (2008) SchiedsVZ 222, 229.

⁵⁶ O De Shutter, *International Human Rights Law* (1st edn, OUP 2010) 681; Epiney (n 53) 4; C Hammerl, *Inländerdiskriminierung* (Duncker & Humblot 1997) 27 with further references, 95; T Cottier and M Oesch, 'Direct and Indirect Discrimination in WTO Law and EU Law' (2011) NCCR Trade Regulation Working Paper No. 2011/16 <www.wti.org/fileadmin/user_upload/nccr-trade.ch/

paragraph 2), the issue of reverse discrimination has scarcely ever been addressed in case law or in scholarly writing.

Especially when recognizing the shifted competences in the field of a Common Commercial Policy (Articles 206, 207 TFEU), including foreign direct investments, it is not the Member States anymore but now the EU that is getting into the centre of attention when it comes to questions of reverse discrimination in the context of investment law. It could be considered, that if the EU concludes an investment treaty with a particular State, this treaty solely entitles foreign investors to take legal action under international investment law and therefore treats all domestic European investors inferior to the foreign investors of the contracting State, this might be a violation of primary and/or secondary EU non-discrimination laws by the EU itself. A thorough analysis is urgently warranted to understand the implications of investment law in this regard.

VIII. International Constitutional Dimensions

Our discussion has so far concerned the interplay between international investment law and national legal systems as being addressed by national and partly also by international norms and principles. One may call this a multi-level exercise and undoubtedly, a constitutional view has proven to be useful to see the interaction of national as well as international principles in perspective. This discussion may be complemented by a somewhat horizontal view, where international investment law may be regarded in the context of the international legal system. Understanding international law with its many different and often fragmented parts and elements as a system may be useful to understand, how it does perform certain functions and how it is or should be determined by common principles and values. Without claiming here that international law should be or already is a constitutional system, constitutional thought nevertheless is a welcome analytical aide. Investment law, in this perspective, is often and correctly understood to mainly serve the interest of the protection of property. In this regard, in a constitutional view, we may ask, how it is related to the protection of property in international law more generally. At the same time, we might see international investment law as part of international economic law and more specifically as a particular individual economic right.

a) Investors' rights as a substitute for a human right to property— or the other way round?

Even though modern international investment law covers issues like fair and equitable treatment and non-discrimination as well, its core objective is still the protection of the property of a foreign investor. From a constitutional perspective, the proximity between the protection of foreign investors and a right to property comes to mind immediately. This suggests to question how property is protected in international law more generally and what role international investment law does play or should play in this regard.[57]

Property is protected as a human right or a fundamental right by most constitutions around the world. However, one would be ill advised to expect such right to also exist at the international level. Indeed, for a number of historical reasons, the global bill of rights—the number of multilateral human rights treaties—do not contain a right to property.[58] While Article 17 of the 1948 Universal Declaration of Human Rights did state in paragraph 1 that 'everyone has a right to own property alone as well as in association with others' and paragraph 2 added that 'no one should be arbitrarily deprived of his property', this right has not been taken up in the further development of the global human rights instruments and particularly not in the drafting of the International Covenant of Economic, Social and Cultural Rights of 1966. The reluctance to guarantee a right to property has even been felt in the Council of Europe, where such right was not included in the ECHR as such but was only added later by the First Protocol to the Convention of 1952, which entered into force in 1954. The right has ever since played a prominent role in the jurisprudence of the European Court of Human Rights, which can issue binding judgments and may award just satisfaction under Article 41 ECHR.[59] In addition, it should be mentioned that the American, African, and Arab regional human rights instruments contain similar guarantees of the right to property.[60] These laudable developments at a regional level are far from filling the gap at the global level, let alone that their effectivity may be questioned in some regards.

International investment law, being based on the customary international law rules on the protection of aliens and their belongings, could with all its undoubted effectivity be seen as a substitute in this regard. Rather than bothering about the disillusioning state of the development of a human right to property, one could see investment law to fill the gap.

However, a closer look reveals that the protection of foreign investors and a human right to property are of quite a different nature in conceptual terms.[61] First of all, the protection under international investment law by its very nature covers only foreign investors and investments. It thus offers no protection to domestic investors. As explained above, the latter also suffer from reverse discrimination, as they are not entitled to protection on an equal footing. In contrast, human rights imply the idea of non-discrimination and are thus applicable to nationals and foreigners alike. Also, rather than bypassing the national legal order by offering a shortcut in

---

hi/CottierOeschNCCRWP16.pdf> accessed 17 February 2015; A Tryfonidou, *Reverse Discrimination in EC Law* (Kluwer Law International 2009).

[57] See generally T Cottier, K Gehne, and M Schultheiss, 'The Protection of Property in International Law: The Missing Pieces' in HP Hestermeyer, D König, N Matz-Lück, V Röben, A Seibert-Fohr, PT Stoll, and S Vöneky (eds), *Coexistence, Cooperation and Solidarity, Liber Amicorum Rüdiger Wolfrum* (Martinus Nijhoff 2012) 367–96.

[58] ibid 377.

[59] See A Riza Çoban, *Protection of Property Rights within the European Convention on Human Rights* (Ashgate 2004).

[60] Cottier, Gehne, and Schultheiss (n 57) 379.

[61] See generally U Kriebaum, *Eigentumsschutz im Völkerrecht: Eine vergleichende Untersuchung zum internationalen Investitionsrecht sowie zum Menschenrechtsschutz* (Duncker & Humblot 2008).

the form of international investment arbitration, human rights enforcement, while certainly including safeguards against a denial of justice, would nevertheless rely on the exhaustion of local remedies. It might therefore be concluded that investment law can hardly be seen as a legitimate substitute for a human right to property. Investment law and all its welcome developments thus do not put into question the urgent need to further develop and strengthen a human right to property. This is not least the case, because recent economic research indicates that reliable and efficient rights to property are key in economic development.[62] Even more, a human rights-type protection of property appears to be also preferable in cases where the protection of property is already secured at the domestic level in order to prevent discriminatory effects that result from the application of investment law.

In sum, this comparison of the concepts of investment law and a human right to property would suggest preferring the latter. Of course, such a proposal appears to be overly academic and it could be doubted, whether it could count on support and consensus under real-world conditions. However, an approach of pulling the protection of (international) investments entirely on the level of an international human right to property could start with a few parties, which act somewhat as pioneers and convince other States to join just in the same way as the investment chapters in the CETA draft and TTIP negotiations are aimed at setting a 'gold standard' for international investment protection.

b) A proper role for the individual in an international economic law for the global marketplace

In the overly fragmented landscape of international economic law, international investment law is one of the rare exceptions where the individual is given a role as a subject of law. In all other areas, particularly in trade, individuals depend on governments and their willingness to enforce commitments regarding market access and non-discrimination. When seen from a bird's eye perspective, one could even conclude that international economic law applies as a 'default rule' mechanism which comes quite close to diplomatic protection, a state of affairs which international investment law has surmounted long ago. Even more, investors may receive compensation, whereas those who are hit by a sudden and unexpected denial of market access usually go away empty-handed.[63] In a global marketplace, where investors may also be traders or inventors and vice versa, and where they act in global supply chains, policymaking would be ill advised to focus exclusively on investors and their well-understood interests. However, likewise, it would be highly questionable whether extending the scope of investment law to issues such as market access or the protection of intellectual property rights would be the solution. More coherent approaches have to be explored to give a voice to those who

---

[62] See T Besley and M Ghatak, 'Property Rights and Economic Development' in D Rodrik and M Rosenzweig (eds), *Handbook of Development Economics, Vol 5* (North-Holland 2010) 4525–95 and A Sen, 'Property and Hunger' (1988) 4 Econ Philos 57.

[63] PT Stoll, 'Le droit international économique face aux défis de la mondialisation' (2009) 113 RGDIP 273, 279.

depend on open markets, non-discrimination, and the protection of their property as well as their legitimate expectations. Such a scenario, however, would hardly be convincing without offering a role to those too, who are part of the global marketplace and its governance as workers, consumers, and citizens.

IX. Outlook

International investment law has met with quite some criticism recently, which has been focusing on certain cases and more particular on the initiation of investment arbitration procedures against Australia, Canada, and Germany. At the same time, the negotiation and conclusion of CETA and TTIP can be said to foster a generalization of international investment law, as both agreements also will include investment protection rules that OECD countries so far were usually reluctant to conclude among themselves and which are aimed at setting a standard to be used in negotiations with third countries in the future. In contrast to the earlier selective approach, international investment protection is now envisioned to become a regular element of international economic relations and by implication is accepted as a standard, which generally foreign investors will enjoy also within their developed host jurisdictions. This tendency has further fuelled criticism in public. It arguably also marks a turning point, a change in quality, which requires looking at the matter in a different way. It is argued that a constitutional approach is required at this point to see international investment protection and national legal orders in their interplay and to analyse them in view of national as well as of international rules and principles instead of looking at it as an isolated subject. Issues of sovereignty, democracy, and legitimation are addressed in this perspective as well as the review of public authority by arbitration tribunals, the fast track to compensation, and the intricate issue of reverse discrimination. The discussion is complemented by a look at the international legal order. It addresses the issue of a human right to property as well as the more general aspect of the proper role that individuals should be given in international economic law. As the developments discussed here are recent and have not been the subject of much scholarly reflection and debate yet, no definite answer could be expected. The merit of the approach advocated here and the discussion of some of the issues may be seen in raising questions rather than in answering them.

Tentatively, one may conclude, that the shortcomings of international investment law, namely the circumvention of local remedies, the possible shortcut to compensation, the arbitration procedure, and the discrimination of domestic investors become even more visible and critical, where such law in the sense of a generalization is applied among market economies with highly developed rule of law systems such as Canada, the US, and the EU. At the same time, an increase of investment flows, as has been traditionally seen to justify the system, can hardly be expected. Very likely, the unique opportunity for these three main players in the world economy to work towards a new, ambitious, and coherent definition of the role of the individual to play in international economic relations will pass by unused.

XV

The Contribution of EU Trade Agreements to the Development of International Investment Law

Frank Hoffmeister

I. Introduction

Once a special field of a few academics, government lawyers, and private associates, international investment law has nowadays become a hot topic in Europe. One figure may illustrate this: when the European Commission launched a public consultation on investment protection matters in the EU–US Free Trade Agreement in spring 2014, it received almost 150,000 replies within three months![1] In comparison: when the Organisation for Economic Co-operation and Development (OECD) asked for public comments on investor–State dispute settlement in summer 2012, a mere twenty comments were received and published by the Paris-based organization.[2]

There may be a number of reasons for this spectacular rise in public attention in Europe. For the first time, cases are brought against Western European States whose companies have been regularly on the other side of litigation—the list includes for example *Vattenfall v Germany*[3] and *Ping An v Belgium*.[4] As those cases raise important questions of public policy, the debate about the proper balance between investor protection and policy space for European democracies has come to the forefront. Many citizens ask whether democratic principles would be threatened if international investment tribunals were to overturn democratically enacted laws or

---

[1] European Commission, 'Report on the Online Public Consultation on Investment Protection and Investor-State Dispute Settlement in the Transatlantic Trade and Investment Partnership (TTIP)' (July 2014) <http://trade.ec.europa.eu/doclib/docs/2014/july/tradoc_152693.pdf> accessed 28 October 2014.

[2] OECD, Investor-State Dispute Settlement Public Consultation, Comments received as of 30 August 2012 <www.oecd.org/daf/inv/investment-policy/ISDSconsultationcomments_web.pdf> accessed 28 October 2014.

[3] *Vattenfall AB and others v Federal Republic of Germany*, ICSID Case No ARB/12/12.

[4] *Ping An Life Insurance Company of China, Limited and Ping An Insurance (Group) Company of China, Limited v Kingdom of Belgium*, ICSID Case No ARB/12/29.

crucial government action. Second, the absolute figure of investment cases worldwide is on the rise.[5] As cases are actually brought by companies, there is a growing feeling that multinationals may get an undue advantage by relying on additional rights to fight public measures. This, in turn, feeds into a broader uneasiness of some globalization critics who traditionally fight the perceived unlimited powers of internationally active (bad) companies over locally rooted (good) States. Not surprisingly, such anti-globalization groups have now detected investment protection as another target for campaigning.[6] Third, the European Union is about to implement its new competence for foreign direct investment that it derives—since 2009—from the Treaty of Lisbon.[7] Leaving aside the intra-EU debate on the precise scope of this competence,[8] developing investment policy at the European level naturally opens the possibility to review the existing system and to come up with proposals to develop it further from a European perspective. Most visibly, that can be done through a new generation of investment protection treaties with third States. At the time of writing, EU negotiations within the broader framework of trade agreements are far advanced with Canada and Singapore, and they have begun with Japan, a number of ASEAN countries, and the United States (paused). The Council has also adopted negotiation directives on investment with four Euromed countries (Morocco, Jordan, Tunisia, and Egypt).[9] Moreover, negotiations on a self-standing investment protection agreement have been launched with China and Myanmar.

In the present contribution, we will look at Europe's transformative power. Following the main theme of the book, section II will investigate how the EU deals with the interrelationship between investment protection and sustainable development. A short reflection about the importance of international law for EU investment agreements will follow in section III. The important question of dispute settlement alternatives will then be looked at in section IV before concluding. In doing so, it should be recalled that no single EU investment protection chapter has yet entered into force. However, on 26 September 2014, the Commission published texts from the draft agreement with Canada (Comprehensive Economic and

---

[5] United Nations Conference on Trade and Development (UNCTAD), *World Investment Report 2013* (United Nations 2013) 111 with an interesting table on known ISDS cases from 1987–2012.

[6] Compare, for example, the open letter of a number of European and American NGOs to US Trade Representative Froman and EU Trade Commissioner De Gucht of 16 December 2013, available at: <http://www.s2bnetwork.org/wp-content/uploads/2014/11/CivilSociety_TTIP_Investment_Letter_Dec16-2013_Final.pdf> accessed 25 August 2015, claiming that investment protection in the EU–US Agreement would undermine democratic decision-making.

[7] Art 207 (1) TFEU.

[8] See F Hoffmeister and G Unuvar, 'From BITS and Pieces towards European Investment Agreements' in M Bungenberg, A Reinisch, and C Tietje (eds), *EU and Investment Agreements* (Nomos 2013) 65–70, claiming EU only competence for all investment protection matters on the one hand, and N Lavranos, 'The Remaining Decisive Role of Member States in Negotiating and Concluding EU Investment Agreement' in ibid 165 claiming that 'national procedural law, expropriation and compensation' are still within the competence of the Member States or are at most 'areas of shared competence', on the other hand.

[9] See details on the investment homepage of the European Commission at <http://ec.europa.eu/trade/policy/accessing-markets/investment/> accessed 24 November 2014.

Trade Agreement (CETA)).[10] As the CETA text is sufficiently stable and publicly accessible, all quotes from EU practice may be made from it, although details will, of course, differ when it comes to future EU agreements with other third States.

II. The Concept of Sustainable Development in EU Agreements

a) Definition of sustainable development

Abstract definitions of the concept of sustainable development may vary considerably. Originally, the notion found its place in political theories on development and slowly emerged into a notion of international environmental law.[11] In the investment law context, it may well have another nuance. Hence, it is important to clarify briefly what the notion may and may not encapsulate from a European perspective.

aa) UNCTAD Report 2012

In its policy report of 2012 on investment and sustainable development,[12] UNCTAD put forward a rather broad understanding. It argues that sustainable development issues include 'environmental, social and poverty alleviation concerns as well as investor responsibility'.[13] It then identifies 'design criteria' for investment policies at the national and international levels. For the latter, it proposes a number of policy options 'to operationalize sustainable development objectives in international investment agreements'.[14] This list focuses on:

(i) adjusting existing provisions to make them 'more sustainable development friendly through clauses that safeguard policy space and limit State liability';
(ii) adding new provisions on new 'stronger paragraphs within provisions for sustainable development purposes to balance investor rights and responsibilities, promote responsible investment and strengthen home-country support';
(iii) introducing special and differential treatment for the less developed party 'to calibrate the level of obligations to the country's level of development'.

While not delving into the details of the examples given by UNCTAD, it is obvious that all the proposals are State-friendly. The UN body, whose membership is

---

[10] Consolidated CETA Text of 26 September 2014 <http://trade.ec.europa.eu/doclib/docs/2014/september/tradoc_152806.pdf> accessed 11 March 2015.
[11] See U Beyerlin, 'The Concept of Sustainable Development' in R Wolfrum (ed), *Enforcing Environmental Standards: Economic Mechanisms as Viable Means?* (Springer 1996) 95–121.
[12] UNCTAD, *Investment Policy Framework for Sustainable Development* (United Nations 2012).
[13] ibid 5.   [14] ibid 43–64 with an overview table at 45.

dominated by developing countries, gives advice to States on how to preserve more policy space, to demand more responsibility from investors, and to reduce one's own commitment. All this is presented as being conducive to sustainable development which appears as a catch-all phrase to justify a single-sided reorientation of international investment policy.

bb) The Brussels Consensus

In the EU, the starting point is different. Between 2010 and 2011 the Commission, Council, and Parliament set out their respective views on Europe's international investment policy.[15] From those statements, a Brussels consensus emerged that EU investment agreements should:

(1) provide a high level of protection for EU investors through standard clauses;
(2) respect the right to regulate in order to meet legitimate public policy objectives;
(3) increase legal certainty for both investors and host States;
(4) be consistent with broader principles and objectives of the Union's external action; and
(5) include a state-of-the-art dispute settlement chapter with investor-to-State procedures.[16]

The fourth topic is *sedes materiae* for our discussion. Under Article 207 (1) second sentence TFEU, the EU's Common Commercial Policy (CCP) should be conducted in line with its external action objectives more broadly—another Lisbon novelty.[17] Among those objectives we find the eradication of poverty by fostering the sustainable economic, social and environmental development of developing countries (Article 21(2)(d) TEU) and the sustainable management of global natural resources in order to ensure sustainable development (Article 21(2)(f) TFEU). It has thus become a primary law task to support sustainable development also within the realm of the EU's investment policy. In other words, Article 21 TEU enhances the importance of environmental and development goals as non-trade objectives of the CCP.[18] This is a remarkable difference to a number of Member

---

[15] European Commission, 'Towards a comprehensive European International Investment Policy', (Communication) COM (2010) 343 final; Council of the European Union, Conclusions on a Comprehensive European International Investment Policy, 3041st Foreign Affairs Council Meeting (25 October 2010); European Parliament resolution P7_TA(2011)0141 of 6 April 2011 on the Future European International Investment Policy.

[16] For details on the positions of the three EU institutions see F Hoffmeister and G Alexandru, 'A First Glimpse of Light on the Emerging Invisible EU Model BIT' (2014) 15 J World Inv & Trade 379, 381–82.

[17] For details on this clause see C Vedder, 'Die außenpolitische Zielbindung der gemeinsamen Handelspolitik' in M Bungenberg and C Herrmann (eds), *Die Gemeinsame Handelspolitik der Europäischen Union nach Lissabon* (Nomos 2011) 121–56.

[18] A Dimopoulos, 'The Effects of the Lisbon Treaty on the Principles and Objectives of the Common Commercial Policy' (2010) 15 E F A Rev 153, 164.

State BITs which operate investment protection standards on a stand-alone basis disconnected from broader foreign policy considerations.

In practice, the Commission operationalizes this orientation by negotiating a sustainable development chapter to which we now turn to.

b) The EU sustainable development chapter

aa) Free Trade Agreements (FTAs)

In EU practice, a sustainable development chapter has already become part of a number of trade agreements pre-dating the Lisbon Treaty. Importantly, Article 3 (1) of the Economic Partnership Agreement with the CARIFORUM States mentions sustainable development as one objective of the treaty.[19] Being probably the most innovative feature,[20] Article 72 requires investors to 'act in accordance with ILO core standards', and parties are required not to relax core labour standards either (Article 73). Moreover, Articles 191–196 of the CARIFORUM EPA deal with social aspects of trade.

The EU–Korea Free Trade Agreement[21] contains a whole chapter on the topic with similarly innovative clauses. For example, Article 13.7 stipulates that neither side shall lower its social or environmental standards in order to attract more trade or investment. The FTA also encompasses a civil society dialogue mechanism (Article 13.13). Comparable provisions can also be found in the EU FTA with Peru and Colombia.[22] It recalls the right to regulate (Article 268), contains the 'no-lowering-down of standards' clause (Article 277), and also works with the civil society to ensure proper implementation (Articles 281–282). On the other hand, it has to be stressed that a breach of the sustainable development chapter will not enable the other side to adopt hard sanctions as such an enforcement machinery is usually not acceptable for the EU's treaty partners.[23] Rather, the central idea is to induce compliance through an institutionalized dialogue.

In the post-Lisbon negotiations, such chapters are also pursued next to the relevant investment chapter. As both the investment chapter and the sustainable development chapter form part of one treaty, it is possible to read them together. In particular, the sustainable development chapter may contain additional principles

---

[19] Economic Partnership Agreement between the CARIFORUM States, of the one part, and the European Community and its Member States, of the other part [2008] OJ L289/81 ('CARIFORUM EPA').

[20] J Kenner, 'Economic Partnership Agreements: Enhancing the Labour Dimension of Global Governance?' in B Van Vooren, S Blockmans, and J Wouters (eds), *The EU's Role in Global Governance. The Legal Dimension* (OUP 2013) 306, 320.

[21] Free Trade Agreement between the European Union and its Member States, of the one part, and the Republic of Korea, of the other part [2011] OJ L127/6 ('EU–Korea Free Trade Agreement').

[22] Trade Agreement between the European Union and its Member States, of the one part, and Colombia and Peru, of the other part [2012] OJ L354/3. The agreement with Peru is applied provisionally since 1 March 2013, with Colombia since 1 August 2013.

[23] F Hoffmeister, 'Der Beitrag der EU zur Entwicklung des besonderen Völkerrechts' in W Obwexer (ed), *Die Europäische Union im Völkerrecht, Europarecht Beiheft 2/2012* 247, 257.

that are relevant in context under Article 31(1) VCLT[24] when conducting a balancing exercise in the application and interpretation of an investment standard. Moreover, the preamble of the agreement may be construed in a way that sustainable development references are directly relevant to ensure the right to regulate in the investment context.

For example, under the CETA preamble, the parties resolve to build their relationship on the WTO agreements and to build an expanded and secure market for goods and services through the reduction or elimination of barriers to trade by agreeing clear, transparent, and mutually advantageous rules (first to third indent). The fourth to sixth indents then read:

Reaffirming their commitment to promote sustainable development and the development of international trade in such a way as to contribute to sustainable development in its economic, social and environmental dimensions;

Determined to implement this Agreement in a manner consistent with the enhancement of the levels of labour and environmental protection and the enforcement of their labour and environmental laws and policies, building on their international commitments on labour and environmental matters;

Encourage enterprises operating within their territory or subject to their jurisdiction to respect internationally recognized standards and principles of corporate social responsibility, notably the OECD Guidelines for multinational enterprises and to pursue best practices of responsible business conduct.

Indent 7 recognizes that investment protection stimulates mutually beneficial business activity and following two indents addressing human rights and security issues, indent 10 and 11 say this:

Recognising that the provisions of this Agreement preserve the right to regulate within their territories and resolving to preserve their flexibility to achieve legitimate public policy objectives, such as public health, safety, environment, public morals and the promotion and protection of cultural diversity;

Affirming their commitment as Parties to the UNESCO Convention on the Protection and Promotion of the Diversity of Cultural Expressions and recognizing that states have the right to preserve, develop and implement their cultural policies, and to support their cultural industries for the purpose of strengthening the diversity of cultural expressions, and preserving their cultural identity, including through the use of regulatory measures and financial support.

Such formulations have a number of important legal consequences. First, the EU does not present the concept of sustainable development as simply serving host State interests. Rather, as the fourth indent shows, international trade and investment is portrayed as contributing to sustainable development. This means that private activity from investors is generally regarded as positive and not detrimental for the host State. Moreover, the reduction or elimination of barriers to trade and investment (through the agreement) mentioned in the second indent has the clear

---

[24] Vienna Convention on the Law of Treaties (adopted 23 May 1969, entered into force 27 January 1980) 1155 UNTS 331 (VCLT).

objective to further foster private cross-border investment. At the same time, the tenth and eleventh indent recall in clear terms the right to regulate of the host State, first in general terms and then specifically with respect to cultural diversity. Moreover, the fifth indent makes an express reference that the Agreement should be implemented consistent with national and international labour and environmental standards.

As the preamble can be used to discern the object and purpose of an investment protection treaty[25] such reference therein can encourage a regulatory-friendly interpretation of various provisions of an investment protection agreement.[26] In the European context, investment protections shall neither freeze the legislative environment of the investor nor produce a 'chilling effect' that the enactment of stricter regulation may run the risk of triggering State liability. Rather, policy space is emphasized as parties can always choose a level of protection which 'preserves their flexibility to achieve legitimate policy objectives' which are mentioned in a non-exhaustive list, as the formulation 'such as' in the tenth indent makes clear.

bb) Investment Protection Agreements

The situation is slightly different when it comes to a stand-alone BIT, such as the one currently in negotiation with China. Should the EU have a sustainable development clause next to the investment standards? A probable answer is that a number of elements can indeed be integrated. In particular, provisions to ensure that the parties shall not encourage foreign direct investment by weakening or reducing domestic environmental or labour legislation make sense. In this context, relaxing core labour standards or failing to effectively enforce them could be a case in point. Moreover, support to internationally agreed standards in the social and environmental domain of specific relevance for investment and their effective implementation can be announced in a stand-alone EU investment agreement. Finally, in line with the relevant EU strategy,[27] recalling internationally recognized standards of corporate social responsibility can usefully fit into the sustainable development context. That means putting a reference to the OECD guidelines for multinational enterprises[28] in an appropriate place in an EU investment agreement.

A tricky issue is human rights. Drawing on similar formulations in the former EC and EU Treaty, Article 21(2)(b) TEU (Lisbon version) mainstreams them into the EU's entire external action. For a long time, human rights considerations have entered into EU external relations, both in its development policy[29] and its trade

---

[25] *Saluka Investments BV v The Czech Republic*, UNCITRAL, Partial Award (17 March 2006) para 299.
[26] C Titi, *The Right To Regulate in International Investment Law* (Nomos 2014) 122.
[27] European Commission, 'A Renewed EU Strategy 2011-14 for Corporate Social Responsibility' (Communication) COM (2011) 681 final (25 October 2011) 14.
[28] OECD, *Guidelines for Multinational Enterprises* (OECD 2011), available at <www.oecd.org/daf/inv/mne/48004323.pdf> accessed 24 November 2014.
[29] B Simma and C Schulte, 'Human Rights Considerations in the Development Cooperation Activities of the EC' in P Alston (ed), *The EU And Human Rights* (OUP 2004) 571–626.

policy through the general human rights clause. Such clause declares universal human rights standards as incorporated in the 1948 UN Declaration to constitute an essential element of an agreement, sometimes coupled with a specific suspension clause which allows either party to suspend the agreement if it considers that there is a serious breach by the other side.[30] Against that background, the question of human rights and labour standards has, for example, played a prominent role in the recent ratification phase of the EU–Colombia/Peru Free Trade Agreement. In particular, in the European Parliament the human rights record of Colombia was intensively discussed with civil society. In the end, after Colombia had adopted a specific roadmap on the protection and improvement of human rights, labour standards, and the environment, as demanded by the European Parliament in June 2012,[31] the European Parliament ratified the agreement in December 2012, pointing also to the significant decrease in the number of murders of trade unionists from forty-nine (2010), to twenty-nine (2011), and nineteen (2012).[32] This is a clear example of human rights and trade agreements interplaying in EU practice.

What is now the situation with respect to the new investment policy? The joint Human Rights Communication of the High Representative and the Commission of December 2011 makes the point that also 'the EU's common investment policy should be guided by the principles and objectives of the Union's external action, including human rights'.[33] In its EU Strategic Framework and Action Plan on Human Rights and Democracy, the Council agreed with this point in June 2012. It promised to 'integrate human rights in all areas of its external action without exception', mentioning specifically the promotion of human rights 'into trade, investment,...'.[34]

While there is political consensus that investment protection policy is thus not 'isolated' from general human rights policy, it is less clear how exactly human rights considerations can be integrated into a self-standing investment protection agreement. At first sight, the easiest would be to incorporate the standard human rights clause also into an investment agreement, as apparently advocated by the European Parliament.[35]

---

[30] For details compare L Bartels, *Human Rights Conditionality in the EU's International Agreements* (OUP 2005).

[31] European Parliament resolution P7_TA(2012)0249 of 13 June 2012 on the EU Trade Agreement with Colombia and Peru.

[32] P Pagotto, 'EU Trade Policy and Labour Standards: The Case of the Free Trade Agreement with Colombia and Peru' (2013) European Ybk of Human Rights 255, 264.

[33] Joint Communication of the European Commission and the High Representative of the European Union for Foreign Affairs and Security Policy, COM (2011) 886 final (12 December 2011) 12.

[34] Council of the European Union Press Release 11855/12, 'EU Strategic Framework and Action Plan on Human Rights and Democracy' (25 June 2012) 2.

[35] European Parliament resolution P7_TA(2010)0434 of 25 November 2010 on Human Rights, Social and Environmental Standards in International Trade Agreements para 12: 'reaffirms that these clauses must also be included in all trade and sectoral agreements' and para 13: 'underlines the fact that the same approach of systematic inclusion should also be applied to the chapters on sustainable development in bilateral agreements'; European Parliament resolution P7_TA-PROV(2013)0411 of 9 October 2013 on EU–China Negotiations for a Bilateral Investment Agreement para 23.

Human rights would then constitute an essential element of the relationship, and persistent and grave breaches of the agreed human rights standard would entitle either party to suspend the agreement in line with Article 60 of the VCLT or on the basis of a specifically designed suspension clause. However, at second sight, this reasoning is self-defeating. Why should the EU take away investment protection from its own investors if the host-State engages in human rights violations? And the threat of suspending the investment protection standards for investors of the other State in Europe will probably not induce the host State government to stop its human rights violations. In other words, the operational mechanism of a human rights standard is not suitable to deliver any likely result.

Hence, it seems more useful to enrich the traditional references to social, labour, and environmental standards with the notion of human rights. Either the preamble or a treaty article could recall that parties should not attract foreign direct investment by lowering social, labour, environmental, *or human rights* standards. Similarly, the protection of human rights can be mentioned as a legitimate public policy objective when recalling the right to regulate. Moreover, references to corporate social responsibility are linked to UN human rights standards bearing on the investor. Hence, a clarification that universal human rights standards are also bearing on the two parties could be pursued by the EU, even though partners with a starkly different human rights approach are likely to resist such references.

c) Further EU reforms

Going beyond the strict confines of a sustainable development chapter or clause, it should be added that the EU is also engaging in a broader policy reform. When announcing its public consultation on TTIP in March 2014, the European Commission announced developing a new and innovative approach to 'clarify and improve investment protection rules so as to guarantee that the right to regulate is not undermined' and to 'build a modern, transparent and efficient ISDS system'.[36]

However, this is not done under the UNCTAD 'chapeau' of being more receptive to sustainable development in third States. Rather, the EU reform agenda is an expression of an internal policy discussion about public preferences with respect to granting rights to investors against European measures. In this context, there is an attempt to provide more legal certainty on certain substantive standards. Accordingly, certain standard clauses are formulated in a more precise manner, which coincides with some of the UNCTAD suggestions in substance.

---

[36] European Commission Press Release IP/14/292, 'European Commission launches public online consultation on investor protection in TTIP' (27 March 2014).

aa) Fair and equitable treatment

For example, in order to mitigate potentials for abuse in litigation arising from the present vague formulation in many Member State BITs,[37] the CETA text on fair and equitable treatment reads:

> Article X.9 of the CETA text on fair and equitable treatment says this:
> 1. Each Party shall accord in its territory to covered investments of the other Party and to investors with respect to their covered investments fair and equitable treatment and full protection and security in accordance with paragraphs 2 to 7.
> 2. A Party breaches the obligation of fair and equitable treatment referred to in paragraph 1 where a measure or series of measures constitutes:
>   (a) Denial of justice in criminal, civil or administrative proceedings;
>   (b) Fundamental breach of due process, including a fundamental breach of transparency, in judicial and administrative proceedings;
>   (c) Manifest arbitrariness;
>   (d) Targeted discrimination on manifestly wrongful grounds, such as gender, race or religious belief;
>   (e) Abusive treatment of investors, such as coercion, duress and harassment; or
>   (f) A breach of any further elements of the fair and equitable treatment obligation adopted by the Parties in accordance with paragraph 3 of this Article.
> 3. The Parties shall regularly, or upon request of a Party, review the content of the obligation to provide fair and equitable treatment.
> 4. When applying the above fair and equitable treatment obligation, a tribunal may take into account whether a Party made a specific representation to an investor to induce a covered investment, that created legitimate expectation, and upon which the investor relied in deciding to make or maintain the covered investment, but that the Party subsequently frustrated.
> 5. For greater certainty, 'full protection and security' refers to the Party's obligations relating to physical security of investors and covered investments.
> 6. For greater certainty, a breach of another provision of this Agreement, or of a separate international Agreement, does not establish that there has been a breach of this Article.

A number of points are noteworthy in this EU text. While falling short of simply omitting FET (one radical option offered by UNCTAD), it follows in substance other more moderate UNCTAD recommendations[38] to a certain degree.

First, it establishes the FET clause as an exhaustive list of additional indicators. That list includes access to justice, due process, absence of manifest arbitrariness, non-discrimination on prohibited grounds, and a prohibition of abuse. Within that list, there are certain filters, such as the word 'fundamental' breach of due process, 'manifest' arbitrariness, and 'targeted' discrimination. These filters stress

---

[37] R Dolzer noted in 2005: 'In current litigation practice, hardly any lawsuit based on an international investment treaty is filed these days without invocation of the relevant treaty clause requiring fair and equitable treatment' in 'Fair and Equitable Treatment: A Key Standard in Investment Treaties' (2005) 39 Intl L 87. See also the comprehensive study from R Kläger, *Fair and Equitable Treatment in International Investment Law* (CUP 2011).

[38] UNCTAD, *Investment Policy Framework* (n 12) 44.

that FET is designed as a safety-belt for investors to defend themselves against egregious State behaviour. This means that mere inconveniences or disadvantages for an investor cannot turn into a treaty breach. Rather, a certain threshold of gravity must be met. On the other hand, with the exception of legitimate expectations which are dealt with in paragraph 4, the five indicators in paragraph 2 cover the broad spectrum of issues that has been hitherto identified in investment jurisprudence.[39]

Hence, the EU is going beyond narrower concepts to link FET with 'minimum standards' or international law on aliens. In other words, the carefully formulated and selected indicators mitigate the double risk that the FET standard would be lowered down to 'minimum standards' as feared by the investors or be blown up into a catch-all standard unwarranted by the host States.[40]

Second, the text takes a restrictive position on the controversial issue of protecting legitimate expectations. According to paragraph 4, such expectations cannot relate to regulatory stability. The investor can hence not expect that a State will not enact new or higher legislative or regulatory standards that affect the operation of his business. Such action is an exercise of the host State's right to regulate. Rather, legitimate expectations can only arise when 'specific representations' upon which the investor relied before making his investment are being subsequently frustrated. This 'cas de figure' covers the much narrower scenario when a government breaks the promises it made to a specific investor.

Third, paragraph 5 gives short shrift to the idea that 'security' could also include 'legal security', thereby widening the door again that was just closed in paragraph 4. Rather, this standard is specifically restricted to protecting the physical security of investors and their covered agreement. In practice, this standard is only rarely invoked, as for example in the *AAPL v Sri Lanka* case,[41] where rebels physically destroyed an investor's farm and the question of the host State responsibility came up.

bb) Expropriation

In line with the overall reform intention to guarantee that the right to regulate is not undermined, the EU also designs some novelties in the formulation on the expropriation standard. The CETA text contains the following Article X.11:

1. Neither Party may nationalize or expropriate a covered investment either directly, or indirectly through measures having an effect equivalent to nationalization or expropriation, except:
    (a) for a public purpose;
    (b) under due process of law;

---

[39] See the description of specific applications of the FET standard in R Dolzer and C Schreuer, *Principles of International Investment Law* (OUP 2008) 133–49.
[40] Hoffmeister and Alexandru (n 16) 392.
[41] *Asian Agricultural Products Ltd v Republic of Sri Lanka*, ICSID Case No ARB/87/3, Award (27 June 1990) paras 45ff.

(c) in a non-discriminatory manner; and
(d) against payment of prompt, adequate and effective compensation.
For greater certainty, this paragraph shall be interpreted in accordance with Annex X.11 on the clarification of expropriation...

The said Annex then stipulates:

The Parties confirm their shared understanding that:
  a) direct expropriation occurs when an investment is nationalised or otherwise directly expropriated through formal transfer of title or outright seizure; and
  b) indirect expropriation occurs where a measure or series of measures by Party has an effect equivalent to direct expropriation, in that it substantially deprives the investor of the fundamental attributes of property in its investment, including the right to use, enjoy and dispose of its investment, without formal transfer of title or outright seizure.
2. The determination of whether a measure or a series of measures by a Party, in a specific fact situation, constitutes an indirect expropriation requires a case-by-case, fact based inquiry that considers, among other factors:
  a) the economic impact of the measure or series of measures, although the sole fact that a measure or series of measures of a Party has an adverse effect on the economic value of an investment does not establish that an indirect expropriation has occurred;
  b) the duration of the measure or series of measures by a Party;
  c) the extent to which the measure or series of measures interferes with distinct, reasonable investment backed expectations; and
  d) the character of the measure or series of measures, notably their object, context and intent.
3. For greater certainty, except in the rare circumstance where the impact of the measure or series of measures is so severe in light of its purpose that it appears manifestly excessive, non-discriminatory measures by a Party that are designed and applied to protect legitimate public welfare objectives, such as health, safety and the environment, do not constitute indirect expropriations.

While the need to compensate investors for direct expropriations forms a large consensus in Europe, the concept of indirect expropriation is more controversial. For example, the leading candidate of the Green Party for the European elections, Mrs Keller, argued in the campaign against TTIP with the allegation that the agreement would entitle investors to get indemnification for lost gains whenever a State measure would jeopardize their investment.[42] The same wrong understanding has also been put forward by green NGOs before German regional parliaments in expert hearings.[43] While such a right has never existed in international investment

---

[42] P Pinzler, 'Extrarechte für Multis—Das Handelsabkommen mit Amerika soll US-Investoren besonders schützen—sogar vor deutschen Gesetzen' *Die Zeit* (16 December 2013) quoting Mrs Keller: 'Amerikanische Unternehmen könnten beispielsweise klagen, wenn EU-Umweltgesetze ihre Gewinnaussichten schmälern'.

[43] J Maier, Forum Umwelt & Entwicklung, Answers to the questions of the Parliament of Brandenburg, 11 June 2014, 7: 'Unter "indirekter Enteignung" kann alles subsummiert werden, was darauf hinausläuft, dass die "legitimen Gewinnerwartungen" eines Unternehmens reduziert werden

law, claims to the contrary nevertheless triggered the need for the EU institutions to clarify that such right is not contemplated in EU investment chapters.

Hence, while not being perceived as a sustainable development issue, the EU text incorporates in substance one more UNCTAD recommendation,[44] namely to specify (in paragraph 3 of the interpretative understanding) that non-discriminatory good faith regulations pursuing public policy objectives do not constitute indirect expropriation. In addition, the definition of indirect expropriation takes a clear stance in favour of the 'substantial deprivation' standard[45] (paragraph 1b). Other important restraining factors are paragraphs 2a and 2d of the understanding. By dismissing the 'sole effects' doctrine and by looking at the object, context, 'and intent' of the measure, mere side effects of State action regularly do not constitute indirect expropriation. Investment jurisprudence, which has declared a government's intention as being immaterial when interpreting the general notion of indirect expropriation,[46] would thus have no basis in the EU definition. Rather, the idea behind the standard is to catch wilful State behaviour, where an investor is knowingly harmed through other ways and means than by taking away his property.

III. Importance of International Law

As any under international agreement of the European Union, an investment agreement or an investment chapter within a trade agreement shall be interpreted in line with the directions given by Article 31 of the VCLT. Although the Convention is not binding on the EU as an international organization, its substance is relevant for EU agreements since it incorporates customary international law.[47] Hence, the wording, context, and object and purpose of a specific provision are important. Together with the context also 'any relevant rules of international law applicable in the relation between the Parties' shall be taken into account (Article 31(3)(c)).

This rule of 'systemic integration'[48] allows in particular bringing into the dispute rules derived from multilateral conventions or—more rarely bilateral agreements—to

---

oder werden könnten'. Such 'expertise' is evidently not helping a Parliament to make an objective assessment on the matter.

[44] UNCTAD, *Investment Policy Framework* (n 12) 45, Table 5: 'clarifications'.

[45] *Metalclad Corporation v The United Mexican States*, ICSID Case No ARB(AF)/97/1, Award (30 August 2000) para 103; *Telenor Mobile Communications AS v The Republic of Hungary*, ICSID Case No ARB/04/15, Award (13 September 2006) para 65.

[46] *Tecnicas Medioambientales Tecmed SA v The United Mexican States*, ICSID Case NoARB (AF)/00/2, Award (29 May 2003) para 116; *Siemens AG v The Argentine Republic*, ICSID Case No ARB/02/8, Award (6 February 2007) para 270.

[47] F Hoffmeister, 'The Contribution of EU Practice to International Law' in M Cremona (ed), *Developments in EU External Relations Law* (OUP 2008) 37, 57 with further references and examples from EU practice.

[48] International Law Commission, *Conclusion of the Work of the Study Group on Fragmentation of International Law: Difficulties Arising from the Diversification and Expansion of International Law* (United Nations 2006) point 17.

which the EU and the other side are parties. In the WTO context, the EU has already convinced the Appellate Body to this effect on the occasion of the *Airbus* case.[49] A similar argument can be made for investment agreements, which is further sustained by treaty language in the preamble. As cited above,[50] the parties desire to promote trade and investment 'mindful of high levels of environmental and labour protection and relevant internationally recognised standards and agreements to which they are parties'. That formulation is a useful reminder to solve investment disputes when issues of internationally recognized standards are invoked by a party. One could imagine, for example, that a factory output is suffering from a general protest of its workers, claiming higher salaries. In such a situation, an arbitration tribunal dealing with an investment protection claim[51] would have to take into account whether the host government had ratified ILO Convention No 87 on the Freedom of Association.[52] If so, allowing associated workers to protest in line with international commitments could not at the same time constitute a breach of the investment protection standard.

Aside from incorporating certain conventional rules applicable between the parties, Article 31(3)(c) VCLT also allows the application of concepts of customary international law,[53] which are by definition binding on all international law subjects. In that respect, the EU does not differ from States—customary rules of international law are binding on it both as a matter of international law and as a matter of EU law.[54] Hence, just as customary international law concerning State responsibility as largely laid down in the ILC Articles on State Responsibility[55] may be looked at,[56] tribunals may have a look at the relevant ILC Articles on the Responsibility of International Organisations,[57] insofar as they codify customary law. In the case of the European Union, though, certain supranational features distinguish it from an ordinary international organization. Accordingly, due regard must be paid to any existing *lex specialis*, as also noted in Article 63 of the ILC's Articles.[58]

---

[49] WTO—*Appellate Body, EC and certain Member States, Measures affecting trade in certain large civil aircraft*, WT/DS316/AB/R, para 846.
[50] Section II.b of this chapter.
[51] See, for example, the claim made in *Plama Consortium Limited v Republic of Bulgaria*, ICSID Case No ARB/03/24, Award (27 August 2008) para 236. The claimant alleged that the insufficient action of the Bulgarian police against 'worker riots' had constituted a breach of the constant protection and security standard. The Tribunal did not have to decide on that claim given conflicting evidence on the facts (para 249).
[52] International Labour Organization Freedom of Association and Protection of the Right to Organise Convention C87 (adopted 9 July 1948, entered into force 4 July 1950).
[53] See on this point generally C McLachlan, 'Investment Treaties and General International Law' (2008) 57 Intl & Comp L Q 361f.
[54] Case C-162/96 *Racke* [1998] ECR I-3688, 3704, paras 45-46; Case C-366/10 *ATAA* [2011] ECR I-13755, para 101.
[55] International Law Commission 'Draft Articles on the Responsibility of States for Internationally Wrongful Acts' (2001) UN Doc A/56/10.
[56] *Chevron Corporation (USA) and Texaco Petroleum Company (USA) v The Republic of Ecuador*, UNCITRAL, PCA Case No 34877, Interim Award (1 December 2008) para 118.
[57] International Law Commission 'Draft Articles on the Responsibility of International Organizations' (2011) UN Doc A/66/10.
[58] F Hoffmeister, 'Litigating Against the European Union and its Member States—Who Responds under the ILC's Draft Articles on International Responsibility of International Organisations?' (2010) 21 EJIL 723, 739f.

Moreover, general international law concepts can only be properly applied in an EU investment dispute if there are no specific deviations in an investment agreement itself. With respect to CETA one may note, for example, that the parties have explicitly laid down that an award cannot go as far as forcing a party to repeal a measure.[59] That means that customary law concepts of *restitutio in integrum* cannot be applicable in a potential CETA dispute. Rather, a tribunal can award damages to compensate for an illegal act of a party.

IV. Enforcement

As recalled above, an effective enforcement chapter with investor–State dispute settlement (ISDS) provisions forms also part of the Brussels investment consensus. In particular, all EU Member States (except Poland) are parties to the ICSID Convention[60] and the Energy Charter Treaty.[61] Moreover, virtually all bilateral BITs of Member States include ISDS mechanisms. There is also no legal impediment to include such clauses at the EU level. As the European Court of Justice has held several times, the EU's competence to conclude international agreements necessarily entails the power to submit itself to the decisions of a court which is created or designated by such agreements as regards the interpretation and application of their provisions.[62] Whether such courts or tribunals are activated by a government decision or by a decision of a private party does not make any difference as long as the autonomy of the European Court of Justice to interpret EU law proper is safeguarded.[63] Against that background, the Commission shared with its first negotiating partners (Canada, Singapore, India) the first EU proposal in July 2012 after intense consultation with the Council and the Parliament.[64] Moreover, the EU prepared internally for the hypothesis that such ISDS chapters were to be concluded in EU agreements. Based on a proposal from the Commission,[65] the Council and the Parliament adopted the relevant

---

[59] European Commission memorandum on investment provisions in CETA (3 December 2013) Point 10, available at: <http://trade.ec.europa.eu/doclib/docs/2013/november/tradoc_151918.pdf> accessed 24 November 2014.

[60] Convention on the Settlement of Investment Disputes Between States and Nationals of Other States (opened for signature 18 March 1965, entered into force 14 October 1966) 575 UNTS 159.

[61] Energy Charter Treaty (adopted 17 December 1994, entered into force 16 April 1998) 2080 UNTS 95.

[62] Opinion 1/91, ECR 1991 I-6079 para 40; Opinion 1/09, ECR 2009 I-1137 paras 74–78.

[63] For an in-depth discussion of the EU primary law framework see S Hindelang, 'The Autonomy of the European Legal Order—EU Constitutional Limits to Investor-State Arbitration on the Basis of Future EU-Investment-related Agreements' in M Bungenberg and C Herrmann (eds), *Common Commercial Policy 'After Lisbon', Special Issue of the European Yearbook of International Economic Law* (Springer 2013) 187f.

[64] C Brown and I Naglis, 'Dispute Settlement in Future EU Investment Agreements' in M Bungenberg, A Reinisch and C Tietje (n 8) 24.

[65] Commission Proposal of 21 July 2012, COM (2012) 335. For details on that proposal compare Brown and Naglis ibid 29–34.

regulation on financial responsibility in future ISDS disputes against the Union in July 2014.[66]

However, in the same time span, more and more critical voices have been questioning the need for ISDS. For example, when the European Parliament adopted its (non-binding) resolution on the EU–China investment negotiation directives, a significant number of MEPs from the European Left, the Greens, and the Socialist group tried to delete a reference to ISDS as an appropriate feature in the EU agreement. At the level of the Trade Committee the relevant amendment was rejected in September 2013 with 18:12 votes, and also at the plenary session in October the conservative–liberal majority of the House turned this motion down. According to the adopted resolution the Parliament thus:[67]

Considers that the agreement should include, as a key priority, effective state-to-state and investor-to-state dispute settlement mechanisms in order, on the one hand, to prevent frivolous claims from leading to unjustified arbitration, and, on the other, to ensure that all investors have access to a fair trial, followed by enforcement of all arbitration awards without delay.

Although the parliamentary majority won the vote in this case, the episode shows that ISDS has come under closer public scrutiny. Against that background, the Commission devoted half of its questions in the public consultation on TTIP to this complex. In line with the topic of this book, we will now concentrate on the question how the EU deals with possible alternative approaches to ISDS.

a) Mediation

Article X.19 of the CETA text contains a specific provision on mediation reading:

1. The disputing parties may at any time agree to have recourse to mediation.
2. Recourse to mediation is without prejudice to the legal position or rights of either disputing party under this chapter and shall be governed by the rules agreed to by the disputing parties, including, if available, the rules established by the Services and Investment Committee pursuant to Article X.42(3)(c).
3. The mediator is appointed by agreement of the disputing parties. Such appointment may including appointing a mediator from the roster established pursuant to Article X.25 (Constitution of the Tribunal) or requesting the Secretary-General of ICSID to appoint a mediator from the list of chairpersons established pursuant to Article X.25 (Constitution of the Tribunal).
4. Disputing parties shall endeavour to reach a resolution to the dispute within 60 days from the appointment of the mediator.

---

[66] Regulation No 912/2014 of the European Parliament and of the Council of 23 July 2014 establishing a framework for managing financial responsibility linked to investor-state dispute settlement tribunals established by international agreements to which the European Union is party [2014] OJ 257/121.
[67] European Parliament Resolution P7_TA-PROV(2013)0411 of 9 October 2013 on EU-China Negotiations for a Bilateral Investment Agreement para 42.

5. If the disputing parties agree to have recourse to mediation, Articles X.18(5) and X.18(7) (Consultations) shall not apply from the date on which the disputing parties agreed to have recourse to mediation to the date on which either party decides to terminate the mediation, by way of a letter to the mediator and the other disputing party.

The above text contains a rather generous possibility to go to mediation at any time by using the roster of arbitrators. Moreover, according to paragraph 5, the time of mediation effectively counts as consultations required if a party nevertheless decides to go to arbitration afterwards. Two conclusions can be drawn therefrom. First, the EU tries to make mediation easily accessible, thereby providing an incentive to seek an amicable solution to a dispute. Second, mediation does not shut off the door to arbitration. Hence, it is an additional option, but not a strict alternative, which would force the investor to choose between mediation or arbitration.

b) Domestic Remedies

Another salient feature is the relationship to domestic remedies which has recently attracted wide academic attention as well.[68] On that point Article X.21 of the CETA text contains the following language:

1. An investor may submit a claim to arbitration under Article X.22 (Submission of a Claim to Arbitration) only if the investor:
   a) delivers to the respondent with the submission of a claim to arbitration, its consent to arbitration with the procedures set out in this Chapter;
   b) allows at least 180 days to elapse from the submission of the request for consultations and, where applicable, at least 90 days to elapse from the submission of the notice requesting a determination;
   c) fulfils the requirements of the notice requesting a determination of the respondent;
   d) fulfils the requirement related to the request for consultations;
   e) does not identify measures in its claim to arbitration that were not identified in its request for consultations;
   f) provides a declaration, where it has initiated a claim or proceeding, seeking compensation or damages before a tribunal or court under domestic or international law with respect to any measure alleged to constitute a breach referred to in its claim to arbitration that:
      i. a final award, judgment or decision has been made; or
      ii. it has withdrawn any such claim or proceeding;
         The declaration shall contain, as applicable, proof that a final award, judgment or decision has been made or proof of withdrawal of any such claim or proceeding; and
   g) waives its right to initiate any claim or proceeding seeking compensation or damages before a tribunal or court under domestic or international law with respect to any measure alleged to constitute a breach referred to in its claim to arbitration...

---

[68] H Bubrowski, *Internationale Schiedsverfahren und nationale Gerichte* (Mohr Siebeck 2003).

The provision again sets a number of incentives to settle the dispute through domestic remedies. Before activating at least 180 days of consultations must have tried under littera b—if the investor does not want to 'lose' six months, he might opt to seize a domestic court right away. Moreover, ISDS cannot be triggered while a domestic case is pending. On the other hand, littera f also makes clear that an ISDS case is possible if a final domestic award has been made. However, an exhaustion of domestic remedies is not *required*.

What can be the reasons for this approach? In the introduction to this topic in question 7 of the consultation questionnaire, the Commission mentions the risk that an investment agreement cannot be invoked before domestic courts. For example, in the dualist US system, direct effect will not be granted to provisions of an international trade agreement. Rather, there needs to be transposition into national legislation, which can be lacking on certain aspects. But even in the European Union, the question of direct effect of investment protection standards is anything but settled. Under the Court's case law, a provision from an EU international agreement can be invoked if it is sufficiently precise, having regard to its context and the object and purpose of the treaty.[69] A priori, that should be possible for investment protection standards which can be compared with other provisions which contain unconditional commitments. On the other hand, in the trade field, there is a countertendency not to grant direct effect to individual provisions, as this could upset the delicate balance between contracting parties. Famously, the Court has thus denied direct effect of the WTO agreement in the EU legal order,[70] citing as a confirmation of its finding also a recital in the Council's conclusion decision which stated that 'by its nature, the WTO Agreement, including the Annexes thereto, is not susceptible to being directly invoked in Community or Member State courts'.[71]

The latter reasoning can probably be transposed to an EU investment chapter in an agreement where the treaty partner denies direct effect in its domestic law. For example, if the EU were to allow direct effect inside the EU legal system, whereas the United States excludes it, such disparity could allow the US investors to enforce their rights also before domestic courts in Europe, whereas European investors would not benefit from such a remedy in the United States. That is not in line with reciprocity and deemed politically unfair. Hence, from a European perspective, it would make sense to exclude direct effect of investment protection guarantees in an EU–US agreement either in the treaty itself, or at least by a recital in the Council decision concluding such an agreement. In return, if both parties exclude direct effect before their domestic courts, it would make no sense to require investors to actually exhaust local remedies when the international standards may not be invoked before national tribunals anyway.

---

[69] Case 104/81 *Hauptzollamt Mainz v. Kupferberg* [1982] ECR 1982 3641, paras 19–23. For a presentation and discussion of this case and subsequent case law, see PJ Kuijper and others (eds), *The Law of External Relations, Cases, Materials and Commentary on the EU as an International Actor* (OUP 2013) 930f.
[70] Case C-149/96 *Portugal v Council* [1999] ECR I-8395, paras 36–48.
[71] Council Decision 94/800/EC of 22 December 1994, OJ 1994 L 336, 1.

On the other hand, in well-functioning States governed by the rule of law, there may be equivalent investment protection standards available under domestic law. In that hypothesis, there may be a political reflection whether using the local court system would not satisfy the need of judicial protection of the investors. However, Member State BITs do not contain any exhaustion of local remedies rule. If the EU was to adopt one, an EU agreement would unlikely to be considered of equivalence and meet resistance in the Council at the ratification stage. Moreover, the existence of ISDS may also help to resolve disputes at the pre-litigation state. Finally, EU investors would face disadvantages vis-à-vis investors from other States such as NAFTA or Pacific States, if those partners entertain an ISDS system with America but Europe does not.

c) Improved Enforcement Mechanism

It follows from the above, that the Commission is not considering doing away with ISDS. Rather than presenting mediation or the reliance on domestic remedies as a functional substitute, those issues are tackled in order to provide clarity about their relationship with ISDS. Nevertheless, the EU acknowledges at the same time that a number of ISDS features need to be improved. Those elements relate to establishing certain filters on prudential matters and providing for elements of inadmissibility of frivolous or manifestly unfounded claims. Furthermore, a number of proposals are made to improve the administration of justice in Commission practice (selection and ethics of arbitrators, transparency of proceedings, appellate system)[72] and in policy proposals to the European Parliament.[73] Finally, in the framework of TTIP, the Commission also put forward the idea to establish a standing appellate body which could lead to a World Investment Court in the long term..[74]

V. Conclusion

The European Union is gradually establishing itself as an important player in the international investment protection scene. Pulling together the experience of twenty-eight Member States under their bilateral investment agreements, the European Commission has begun to seriously reform the traditional approach to investment protection under bilateral agreements of individual EU nations with third countries. Moreover, the Commission also combines investment protection chapters with larger FTAs, which allows for putting the sustainable development chapter on par with an investment protection chapter in one agreement. These two strands of development (new European template derived from Member State experience; integration of investment chapters into broader trade agreements) have produced quite a new approach in Europe. As witnessed by the published draft

---

[72] For details see Hoffmeister and Alexandru (n 16) 396–400.
[73] S Hindelang, 'Study on Investor-State Dispute Settlement ("ISDS") and Alternatives of Dispute Resolution in International Investment Law' in EU Directorate-General for External Policies, Investor-State Dispute Settlement (ISDS) Provisions in the EU's International Investment Agreements, vol II (September 2014).
[74] This paper was completed prior to this development.

CETA text, EU agreements tend to be enriched by a full sustainable development chapter and will focus with much tighter language on the protection of a right to regulate. The traditional EU approach to be open to conventional and general international law can also be felt in the investment field, albeit with lesser emphasis. Finally, the relationship to alternative methods of enforcement are looked at in detail—here, the general line is to set incentives for negotiating friendly settlements, going for mediation or making use of local remedies, while at the same time offering an improved enforcement system.

Does all this contribute to shifting paradigms in international investment law itself? Insofar as the EU approach will be put into the agreement with Canada, the United States, and China, these texts are likely to exercise some influence worldwide. However, before getting there, Europe must first ratify these agreements at home. This, in turn, may prove highly controversial given that a number of TTIP opponents have identified investment protection as the target for their anti-globalization and anti-capitalism campaigns. Gaining a majority in the European Parliament—and in national parliaments insofar as a given agreement were to be of mixed competence—thus stands and falls with convincing the European public that the above-mentioned reforms are benefitting the European economy, its companies, and ultimately the European citizen. It is thus hoped that the European Commission will find convincing answers to the 150,000 submissions it received on the topic with respect to TTIP. If it succeeds, it would probably not only give European investment policy a further push, but would also have bigger ramifications on the international scene.

As sketched here, the EU contribution would probably help in finding a new balance between the protection of the investor and the interests of the host State to maintain regulatory space. Stopping short of a simple 'rollback', more up-to-date formulations on certain key investment protection standards would go hand in hand with an enrichment of the text with references to the right to regulate, corporate social responsibility of investors and the integration of international environmental and labour standards which are binding on the parties. Moreover, the EU would also become a proponent of a reformed ISDS system with more transparency, a better administration of justice and tighter interpretative control of arbitration panels. Thus, Europe would not turn into a detractor of the international investment system that its Member States helped to build over the decades. Rather it would put its weight behind the efforts to further improve the international rule of law by limiting the potential for abuse and putting more disciplines on investors and arbitration panels. Such deep reforms could help gain the confidence of the European public which is used to a high level of quality and impartiality of judges whose task is to provide justice in the name of the people.

Conclusion and Outlook

Whither International Investment Law?

Steffen Hindelang and Markus Krajewski

I. Where Do We Stand?

It is really just twenty-five years ago that we could witness the beginning of a remarkable process of proliferation of international investment agreements (IIAs), mostly bilateral, around the globe. In parallel, the number of investor–State dispute settlement (ISDS) cases has also been growing tremendously. Indeed, the field of international investment law as we know it today is young on years but might have gotten already a bit long in the tooth. For a sub-field of public international economic law, a quarter of a century is a relatively short period of time, a blink of the eye really. Many scholars and practitioners of general public international law would still describe it as the 'new kid on the block'. Yet, international investment law is facing serious challenges concerning the legitimacy of its underlying objectives and the mechanisms through which investment disputes are adjudicated: parts of civil society, some parliamentarians and the public more generally increasingly question the current—'traditional'—approach of foreign investment protection. Arbitration lawyers, many businesses, and governments defend, however, the general features of the system as they stand today; albeit with some modifications. In contrast, countries in South America, Africa, and Asia openly question the current international investment law regime and reach out for alternative models at national and regional levels.[1] International organizations such as UNCTAD or the Commonwealth Secretariat develop new models aiming at accommodating different policy objectives while wanting to preserve international treaties as the means of choice to regulate foreign investment.[2] At the same time, the signing of investment agreements continues, though at a slower pace than just a few years ago. However, many recently signed investment agreements differ significantly from the models used in the 1990s and early 2000s. Many of the new agreements

---

[1] See the chapters by S Woolfrey, MJ Luque Macías, and LE Trakman and K Sharma in this volume.
[2] See the chapter by P Muchlinski in this volume.

contain more detailed language defining the standards of investment protection, include references to sustainable development, and stipulate transparency requirements for dispute settlement mechanisms.

It is at this truly exciting yet confusing moment that this volume set itself the task to aptly analyse and discuss the legal principles and concepts which lie at the heart of the current debate on the past, present, and future of international investment law. The individual contributions took on the debate from a variety of perspectives: they centred on the scope of substantive provisions in investment agreements, the ISDS mechanism, and the use of general public international law concepts in investment law, as well as on a recourse to national law instruments for the protection and regulation of foreign investment. On this basis, which conclusions can be drawn in light of the current status of international investment law? Do recent developments indeed indicate shifting paradigms, as our working hypothesis suggested? Are these changes evidence of a trend towards a more balanced, less isolated, and increasingly diversified investment regime?

At a first glance, the picture seems blurry: There is evidence of a significant crisis of the traditional international investment law regime. However, will the crisis lead to a gradual decline of the practical relevance of the regime or to a fundamental reform with a view to rebalancing the system by taking new or different objectives into account? The answers to these questions lie—as often—in the eye of the beholder. They depend on the observer's perspective and on the trends and developments he or she focuses on. Apart from the signs of a general legitimacy crisis and evidence of a major reform movement, there are also signs signalling 'business as usual'.

Adapting a term coined by *Habermas*, one could call this the period of 'new obscurity' (*neue Unübersichtlichkeit*)[3] of investment law. In fact, the contributions to this book are to a certain extent evidence of this: some authors seem to argue that there is little need to reform the system as it is, by and large, functioning well. *Stifter* and *Reinisch* argue, for example, that modern expropriation clauses 'are unlikely to pose a major obstacle to host States adopting measures aimed at sustainable development'. In the same vein, after discussing a number of reform options for ISDS, *Ketcheson* concludes 'that IIAs need to provide an effective means for investors to enforce their rights. This will inevitably constrain State actions, to a degree, however it need not undermine sustainable development'. In addition, *Trakman* and *Sharma* argue that 'notwithstanding its imperfections, ISDS has key systemic advantages over domestic courts in deciding investor–State disputes, all other factors being constant'. It seems fair to conclude that these authors generally concur with the current approach of investment law without denying that some elements of investment agreements can always be improved.

---

[3] J Habermas, *Die Neue Unübersichtlichkeit* (Suhrkamp 1985) and J Habermas, 'The New Obscurity: The Crisis of the Welfare State and the Exhaustion of Utopian Energies: translated by Phillip Jacobs' (1986) 11 Phil & Soc Criticism 1–18.

Other contributions, however, articulate a clearer need for change. The current system would disfavour sustainable development and the State's right to regulate. However, they do not see a fundamental contradiction between investment protection and sustainable development. *Muchlinski* states that 'the investment-sustainable development "trade-off" may be an inaccurate and exaggerated contestation. Rather, the balance between the two needs to be further clarified'. He argues that the approaches taken by UNCTAD and the Commonwealth Secretariat do exactly that. In this context the new approach of the EU is also worth mentioning. *Hoffmeister* sees the EU in a position to 'help in finding a new balance between the protection of the investor and the interests of the host State to maintain regulatory space'. He disfavours a 'simple "roll back"' and calls for 'more up-to-date formulations on certain key investment protection standards' as well as 'a reformed ISDS system with more transparency, a better administration of justice and tighter interpretative control of arbitration panels'.

This does not go far enough for critical scholars who fundamentally oppose the current approach and call for a new system. One of them is *Van Harten* who rejects the reform agendas of UNCTAD and the European Commission because they 'consolidate the privileged legal status of foreign investors and the exceptional power of arbitrators—operating in a non-judicial process—to review other sovereign decision-makers and allocate uncapped amounts of public money to private parties'. These approaches 'appear designed to re-package arbitrator power in order to preserve it'. Similarly, *Stoll* and *Holterhus* see 'shortcomings of international investment law, namely the circumvention of local remedies, the possible shortcut to compensation, the arbitration procedure, and the discrimination of domestic investors'. They suggest that investment protection needs to fulfil constitutional standards of the rule of law.

a) More balanced

Given these rather distinct appreciations of the current regime, it can easily be grasped that the regime is in a state of re-evaluation. However, despite the 'new obscurity' tied to such process, it appears that some developments chartered in the course of this volume came to stay. The first major change to the regime in recent years is a broadening of the objectives investment law is tailored towards. The objective of investment agreements until the 1990s was only, or at least predominantly, to protect foreign investors and their investments against illegitimate actions of the host State, most notably expropriations without compensation. In that respect, the model of investment law was in its structure linear and one-dimensional: individual economic interests needed to be protected against the State. This paradigm of investment law was part of a general development in international law which increasingly recognized individual interests and rights.[4] However, the focus on

---

[4] A Peters, *Jenseits der Menschenrechte—Die Rechtsstellung des Individuums im Völkerrecht* (Mohr Siebeck 2014) 257 et seq.

the protection of private property interests and the limitation of State regulatory powers interfering with private business was also a central element of an economic thought heavily focusing on market freedom. Despite the continued attractiveness of this approach for some policymakers and academics it seems that international investment law is no longer characterized by such a 'pensée unique'.[5] New treaties (more) explicitly recognize sustainable development objectives and public policy goals more generally; reform agendas of a number of key international players and a vivid scholarly debate demonstrate an increasingly diversified picture or other further evidence of this shift.

If the focus on the objective of protecting individual economic interests is not the predominant paradigm of investment law any more, what has come to replace it? Here, the picture becomes blurry again. One new trend is certainly the focus on sustainable development. Even though the exact contours of the legal concept remains fuzzy,[6] sustainable development is a central policy objective of global governance. Hence, international investment agreements are increasingly focusing on balancing economic, ecologic, and social development perspectives. As shown by *Van Duzer*, new agreements increasingly recognize sustainable development in their preambles, clarify that States can act in a diligent manner in order to protect labour rights and the environment without being found to having been engaged in indirect expropriation, agreements include exceptions for certain policy tools and discourage parties from reducing the protection of labour rights and the environment in their domestic regimes to attract investment. One particularly noteworthy example of the development towards such new treaty language is the approach of European Union applied to the Canada–EU Comprehensive Economic and Trade Agreement (CETA).[7] As a 'late-comer' to the field of international investment law-making the EU tries to avoid the broad and general language of many first generation investment agreements. The EU may hence become an important contributor to the reform movement of international investment treaties.

One of the most visible signs evidencing this recalibration of the objectives of international investment law away from the 'pensée unique' is UNCTAD's Investment Policy Framework for Sustainable Development (IPFSD).[8] Its perspective is on reform of the current system, not on its complete abandonment or reinvention. Hence, the framework focuses on existing substantive and procedural elements of investment agreements and puts forward a spectrum of possible variations of the respective standard provisions. In this context, it is worth recalling that UNCTAD itself underwent a remarkable policy change. While the organization

---

[5] I Ramonet, 'La Pensée Unique' *Le Monde Diplomatique* (January 1995) <www.monde-diplomatique.fr/1995/01/RAMONET/1144> accessed 25 March 2015.

[6] *Case Concerning the Gabčíkovo-Nagymaros Project (Hungary v Slovakia)* (1997) ICJ Rep 7, 77 para 140. See also the chapter by G Sacerdoti in this Volume.

[7] See the chapter by F Hoffmeister, in this volume.

[8] UNCTAD, *Investment Policy Framework for Sustainable Development* (United Nations 2012) <http://unctad.org/en/PublicationsLibrary/diaepcb2012d5_en.pdf> accessed 27 April 2015.

was supporting the conclusion of 'unqualified' investment agreements in the 1990s, its new approach is clearly more balanced.

If and how UNCTAD's and other reform proposals will contribute to a sustainable development is still open to debate. The contributions on fair and equitable treatment, expropriation, and ISDS in this book provide most valuable reflections on UNCTAD's proposals. They point out the proposal's benefits, but also indicate shortcomings and problems. In other words, UNCTAD's reform proposals are not the end of a new development, but rather the beginning.

While we are not arguing that rewriting international investment law in terms of sustainable development objectives is *the* new emerging paradigm of investment law, it seems however reasonably clear—especially when considering the intensified activities of (State-driven) international organizations such as UNCTAD—that sustainable development is a policy goal embraced by a rather large number of governments which hold the potential to reshape and recalibrate the theory and practice of international investment law significantly. Notwithstanding the openness of the concept of sustainable development, it appears widely accepted that such regulatory approaches in investment agreements, or the interpretation thereof, which would focus only on the investor's individual economic interests would fall short of this concept. The concept of sustainable development calls for a balancing of the diverse set of economic, social, environmental, and other interests present when carrying out a foreign investment. Recognizing sustainable development as a policy objective in investment agreements is therefore a clear signal towards a more balanced approach. Approaches which conceptualized investment law solely from the perspective of the protection of individual economic and property rights are no longer dominating. Rather, we seem to be in a period of 'greater diversification' in which 'sole objective approaches' have been replaced by more nuanced ones. In this sense, the shift of paradigms might be envisaged in international investment law's drift towards a more balanced reconciliation of private and public interests.

In a similar way, but with a slightly different tone, other attempts to refocus international investment agreements centre on the State's ability to regulate. This approach often refers to the recognition of the 'right to regulate' in international agreements even though a 'right' of the State to regulate has never been disputed. In fact, a 'right to regulate' does not need to be specifically recognized in international agreements, as such a right is inherent in State sovereignty. If anything, international law may confer a duty to regulate on a State, for example, to protect human rights and essential services. Therefore, what is behind this debate about the 'right to regulate' and international investment law is the question of permissible instruments through which the State regulates. In other words, the debate behind the 'label' of a 'right to regulate' is actually about the impact of investment agreements and ISDS on the State's autonomy to use regulatory instruments. Understood in this way, a recognition of the 'right to regulate' in international investment law indicates a similar if not the same paradigm shift as with regards to sustainable development: It should not be seen (or misused) as embracing unfettered or unchecked public powers, but it can be understood as relating to a *more balanced* approach which not only focuses on the rights of the investor but also on the obligation of the State to regulate economic activities in a public interest. Again, it appears that balancing, or indeed also rebalancing private and public interests is one of the key elements of modern international investment law.

b) More diversified

In addition to what might be termed a 'more balanced'-approach, a second current trend is that the field of investment law is no longer predominantly a domain of public international law. More precisely, regional and domestic regulation of foreign investment play an increasingly important role where previously treaties in public international law were the means of choice. Yet, related public and academic discourses do not always attract instant attention beyond the geographical or linguistic boundaries of respective regions or national jurisdictions. This trend might therefore be a bit less conspicuous but by no means negligible. At the domestic level, the approach taken by South Africa can serve as an example in this respect; probably as one more widely known and studied. That model clearly embraces the notion of investment protection. It even accepts that foreign investment should be protected in a different way than its domestic counterpart. However, in doing so it (predominately) relies on domestic courts to apply investment protection standards. As argued by *Woolfrey*, the approach is dramatically deviating from the status quo if seen in a global context and might inspire other countries. Despite the renunciation of the traditional investment agreement regime, at least to a larger extent, South Africa is not rejecting investment protection as such.

Similarly, the new regional approaches taken in Latin America, discussed by *Luque*, also still aim at protecting foreign investment. Unlike the nineteenth-century approach of Latin America, based on the *Calvo* doctrine, the regional investment protection initiatives would offer foreign investors more than just national treatment. Regional approaches are not limited to Latin America. The Arab Investment Court established on the basis of the Unified Agreement for the Investment of Arab Capital in the Arab States is another example even though its practical relevance has so far been limited.[9] Europe will also have to address the question of regional investment protection in the foreseeable future: Bilateral investment protection agreements concluded among the EU Member States do not sit easily with their obligations flowing from EU law.[10] Hence, these agreements have to be terminated earlier rather than later. The crucial question would be whether there will be some sort of a replacement on a regional basis or whether investment protection will be left (entirely) to domestic courts applying national and EU law.

---

[9] W Ben Hamida, 'The First Arab Investment Court Decision' (2006) 6 J World Inv & Trade 699–721.
[10] S Hindelang, 'Circumventing Primacy of EU Law and the CJEU's Judicial Monopoly by Resorting to Dispute Resolution Mechanisms Provided for in Inter-se Treaties? The Case of Intra-EU Investment Arbitration' (2012) 39 LIEI 179 et seq.

An apparently contrarian drift can be witnessed among industrialized countries which have traditionally enjoyed high standards in terms of the domestic rule of law. Countries such as the USA, Canada, Japan, or regional integration organizations like the European Union have agreed to embark on large-scale negotiations of so-called mega-regional agreements such as the Transatlantic Trade and Investment Partnership (TTIP), CETA, and the Transpacific Partnership (TPP). At least some of the governments involved have started talks with the view to establishing investment protection and investor–State arbitration in public international law also between such countries where domestic remedies to protect foreign investment have been deemed sufficient.

As of writing, it is not clear whether all of the abovementioned agreements will ultimately contain investment protection chapters and if so how these will look like.[11] The (pre-legal scrubbing) CETA text of September 2014 suggests that there will be an investment chapter with ISDS as an alternative avenue even to domestic jurisdictions which have not widely been known for an excessive degrees of corruption, discrimination, or incompetency. A recently leaked text of the TPP indicates that the negotiators included a chapter on investment protection with ISDS built on existing investment agreements but with certain limitations. In particular, ISDS would be restricted to treaty breaches and countries would be permitted to exclude certain sectors from ISDS.[12] Mega-regional agreements with investment protection including ISDS would have a significant impact on international economic law simply because of the sheer magnitude of investment relations in the Transatlantic and Transpacific arena. It would be difficult for other countries to ignore them completely. They would certainly provide a new driver for regulating investment protection by means of public international law.

The emergence of 'mega-regionals' even raises the question of the potential and the desirability of a renewed attempt towards the multilateralization of investment protection, which would mean an even stronger trend towards public international law. Could mega-regional agreements such as TPP and TTIP, with investment chapters including ISDS, become the nucleus of a (new attempt towards a) multilateral investment protection agreement? For the time being, no such initiative has been launched and there are no governments or international organizations openly pursuing such an agenda. This does not seem surprising. In light of the legitimacy crisis and the many challenges international investment law is currently facing and the general fatigue of States with multilateralism, the situation remains too fragile and unpredictable to expect bold calls for new multilateral initiatives on investment law.

However, the development could also go into a very different direction. The impact of the TTIP, CETA, and other agreements between developed countries

---

[11] See the chapters by LE Trakman and K Sharma and by F Hoffmeister.
[12] See 'TPP Investment Leak Reveals Remaining Issues Are ISDS Scope, Capital Controls' *Inside US Trade* (27 March 2015).

would be equally significant if these agreements were not to contain investment protection chapters including ISDS. In particular, if ISDS will not be deemed necessary in agreements between countries with mature legal systems, the focus of investor protection may get a stronger spin towards the domestic legal system, in particular constitutional safeguards. Indeed, if a legal system contains a strong protection for property rights and treats national and foreign investors on equal footing and if these standards are guaranteed by constitutional law and are effectively enforceable, the need for agreements in public international law may actually be less pressing.[13] In that vein, *Stoll* and *Holterhus* in their contribution to this book are critical of the idea of protecting foreign investors in a different—that is, possibly in a more favourable—way than domestic investors. They argue that domestic constitutional law standards are sufficient—at least in developed legal systems which are firmly based on the rule of law.

Establishing a clear trend among governments towards affording protection of foreign investors exclusively or predominately at a national or regional level in lieu of bilateral investment treaties, or the latter just being a subsidiary means, would be bold; too bold indeed. Some countries that previously made use of treaties in public international law are now turning away from these. Others—in particular some governments currently involved in negotiating mega-regionals—now aim at protecting foreign investors by means of public international law although no such means have been deemed necessary in the past. For the time being, what can be deduced from these developments is that there is no longer a 'one-way route' to ever more investment protection treaties (except for the classical outriders Brazil and most OECD countries for their dealing among each other) which has existed since the early 1960s and fortified in particular after the Iron Curtain came down. Rather, governments seem to be more flexible in the choice of means—domestic, regional, and international—to protect foreign investment. Each of the 'protection layers' of this multi-layered governance system may provide for a different balance between the private and public interests. States will continue to make policy choices into one direction or another within such a multi-layered system thereby facing the challenging task of coordinating different regulatory layers with each other. Investors may in turn have to adapt to an increasingly diversified system.

c) Less isolated?

In their contributions, *Berner* and *Aust* both emphasized the capacity of general public international law for refocusing international investment law. The Vienna

---

[13] See the chapter by PT Stoll and TP Holterhus. Note also S Hindelang; *Stellungnahme, Öffentliche Anhörung des Ausschusses für Wirtschaft und Energie des Deutschen Bundestages zum Comprehensive Economic and Trade Agreement ('CETA') zwischen der EU und Kanada* <https://www.bundestag.de/blob/345496/2f9d17704429c70693d11e18755bbc3b/steffen-hindelang--fu-berlin-data.pdf> accessed 23 April 2015.

Rules on the interpretation of treaties, for example, provide a workable gateway for leading international investment law out of some sort of 'isolation' within the broader field of public international law; until recently shielded from too much 'outside influence'. The Vienna Rules allow for considering other interests next to the private ones of the investor, the earlier of which recognized and mirrored in other international treaties concluded between the State parties to an investment agreement, such as those on environmental protection, human rights, or labour standards.

The proper application of these general rules can ultimately hardly be ensured by including explicit language in investment agreements demanding a matter of course: the application of the law.[14] Rather, it is the willingness and ability of the adjudicators to apply them in substance instead of just paying lip service which would make a difference. Potential methodological weaknesses have increasingly been recognized by State parties and explicitly addressed in international investment treaties by actually demanding an adjudicator having knowledge or expertise in public international law in general and international investment law in particular. If enforced rigorously—for example by nominating only well-regarded experts in public international law for a possible roster of adjudicators—this could indeed lead to a stronger 're-integration' of international investment law in public international law. However, past experiences with the nomination of judges of international courts and tribunals teaches us that such a task is everything else than easy.

While *Aust* convincingly demonstrates that sticking to the choice of remedies offered in general public international law would be conductive for developing a more balanced approach in international investment law, most recent treaty language—for example in the CETA text—appears to suggest that States wanted to 'cement' a *Sonderregime* in that respect by only allowing for compensation as a possible remedy. Such approach ties in with some controversial awards, in which the tribunal found that compensation would be the only legitimate remedy in international investment law, despite the fact that the respective investment treaties did not make any explicit choice.[15]

In any event, our two test beds have delivered mixed responses on whether we will see an international investment law regime being less isolated from other rules of public international law in the future. Far from being exhaustive in analysis and hence with all disclaimers applying, it appears that a claim suggesting a paradigm shift towards a less isolated regime is still very much ideal rather than reality.

---

[14] cf Art X.27 (1) CETA text which states 'A Tribunal established under this chapter shall render its decision consistent with this Agreement as interpreted in accordance with the Vienna Convention on the Law of Treaties, and other rules and principles of international law applicable between the Parties.'

[15] S Hindelang, 'Restitution and Compensation—Reconstructing the Relationship in International Investment Law' in R Hofmann und C Tams (eds), *International Investment Law and General International Law: From Clinical Isolation to Systemic Integration* (Nomos 2011) 161–99.

II. Where Do We Go from Here?

The great Danish physicist *Niels Bohr* once claimed: 'Predictions are difficult, especially if they concern the future.'[16] The same holds true for predicting the future of international investment law. We see an investment law regime emerging, which can indeed be described in tendency as more balanced, more diverse, not necessarily less isolated though. But where do we go from here? As also evidenced in many contributions to this volume, the future of international investment law is most palpable in three areas. The first area concerns the reformulation and reconstruction of substantive provisions of investment agreements in order to (even) better balance investor interests and regulatory interests of the State. The second area relates to the reform of the current system of ISDS with the view to ensuring that a dispute settlement mechanism is firmly based on openness, neutrality, and the rule of law. In this context, new institutional settings including the establishment of an appellate mechanism would need to be developed and discussed. Finally—and somewhat related to the reform of ISDS—a recalibration of the relationship between ISDS and domestic courts appears to be appropriate.[17]

a) The protection of the State's ability to regulate

Concerning the first area, the contributions in this volume, in particular the analyses of the fair and equitable treatment standard and the protection against expropriation[18] showed that new treaty language might help to clarify standards and take the State's regulatory interests into account. Recent treaty practice suggests that new investment agreements will contain more detailed definitions of investment protection standards.[19]

However, it has also been demonstrated that even within the framework of *existing* provisions, ISDS tribunals could resort to general public international law and accommodate the State's right to regulate and objectives of sustainable development based on more holistic and integrated interpretations of the respective provisions.[20] Whether through reformed languages or a change of the interpretation of existing language, there seems to be a general consensus among policymakers and commentators on the need to clarify the contents of the most relevant substantive provisions of investment agreements. It can hence be assumed that this area of reform will prove to be less controversial than others.

---

[16] Circulating in a multitude of variations, the quote is most likely a Danish proverb appropriated by Bohr, see F Shapiro (ed), *The Yale Book of Quotations* (YUP 2006) 92.
[17] For a similar assessment see European Commission, 'Commission Staff Working Report, Online public consultation on investment protection and investor-to-state dispute settlement (ISDS) in the Transatlantic Trade and Investment Partnership Agreement (TTIP)' SWD (2015) 3 final, 4 <http://trade.ec.europa.eu/doclib/docs/2015/january/tradoc_153044.pdf> accessed 27 April 2015.
[18] See chapters by R Kläger and L Stifter and A Reinisch, in this volume.
[19] See chapter by F Hoffmeister, in this Volume.
[20] See the chapters by K Berner on interpretation and H Aust on the law of State responsibility.

b) Reform of the dispute settlement system

The second element of the current reform agenda is also gaining support in public and academic debates.[21] Many observers seem to agree that the intrinsic elements of commercial arbitration are not or no longer suitable for investor–State disputes because of their inherent public nature. The central features of commercial arbitration—ad hoc constitution of the tribunal, selection of the arbitrators by the parties, and the privacy of the proceedings—do not seem to meet the requirements of adjudication of disputes which concern the review of the exercise of public authority. At the same time, the practice of investment arbitration is perceived as a closed shop with only few individuals acting as counsel and arbitrators.[22] This criticism as well as doubts about a sufficient degree of independence of the arbitrators and concerns of a perception in the public of the ISDS regime being inherently systemically biased towards the investor due to an at least theoretical link between the number of cases adjudicated and the personal gain of adjudicators. In any event, a consensus seems to be emerging that stricter rules are required to secure the independence and neutrality of arbitrators and to more substantially address situations which might cause a conflict of interest.[23]

Another element of a reformed ISDS mechanism which gained significant support in a remarkably short period of time concerns the transparency of the proceedings. Traditionally, the general rule was that proceedings were held in private and documents were usually not disclosed. Even the awards were not made public by default. An almost complete reversal of this approach is now underway. The UNCITRAL Rules on Transparency in Treaty-Based Investor-State Arbitration, effective since 2014, are the most prominent indication of this new trend. These rules reverse the traditional rule-exception relationship and provide for transparency of ISDS proceedings as default. Most documents need to be disclosed and hearings are generally public. The CETA even went beyond the requirements of the UNCITRAL rules and demands not just the publication of the written submissions but also that of exhibits. The willingness of States to establish transparency as

---

[21] See, for example, G Bottini, 'Reform of the Investor-State Arbitration Regime: The Appeal Proposal in Reform of Investor-State Dispute Settlement: In Search of a Roadmap' (2014) 11(1) Transn Disp Mgmt; UNCTAD, 'Reform of Investor-State Dispute Settlement: In Search of a Roadmap' (2013) 2 IIA Issues Note <unctad.org/en/PublicationsLibrary/webdiaepcb2013d4_en.pdf> accessed 11 July 2014; UNCTAD, 'Reform of the IIA Regime: Four Paths of Action and a Way Forward' (2014) 3 IIA Issues Note <http://unctad.org/en/PublicationsLibrary/webdiaepcb2014d6_en.pdf> accessed 12 November 2014; G Kaufmann-Kohler, 'In Search of Transparency and Consistency: ICSID Reform Proposal' (2005) 2 Trans Disp Mgmt; N Bernasconi-Osterwalder and D Rosert, *Investment Treaty Arbitration: Opportunities to reform arbitral rules and processes* (International Institute for Sustainable Development 2014) <www.iisd.org/sites/default/files/pdf/2014/investment_treaty_arbitration.pdf> accessed 7 May 2015; European Parliament Research Service, 'Investor-State Dispute Settlement (ISDS)—State of Play and Prospects for Reform' (Briefing, 21 January 2014) <www.europarl.europa.eu/RegData/bibliotheque/briefing/2014/130710/LDM_BRI%282014%29130710_REV2_EN.pdf> accessed 7 May 2015.

[22] S Puig, 'Social Capital in the Arbitration Market' (2014) 25 EJIL 387–424.

[23] For a depiction of the issue of a publicly perceived bias in ISDS see the chapter by G van Harten in this volume.

a rule in ISDS can also be seen in the rapidly gaining acceptance of the Mauritius Convention on Transparency in Treaty-Based Investor-State Arbitration of 2014.[24]

Whereas stricter rules on arbitrator neutrality and conflict of interests as well as greater transparency are increasingly accepted as key elements of a reform agenda, the adequate institutional setting of dispute settlement mechanisms is still subject to debate. Recent proposals focus on establishing an investment court with pre-determined judges instead of party-selected arbitrators. For example, trade ministers from six EU countries issued a paper entitled 'Improvements to CETA and Beyond: Making a Milestone for Modern Investment Protection' which calls for a 'Trade and Investment Court'.[25] In September 2015, the European Commission published similar ideas possibly informing the position to be taken in upcoming TTIP negotiation rounds.[26] If such a court would only be based on a bilateral agreement, it would obviously be deficient in the eyes of all those cherishing the idea of a multinational investment court. However, it could be a step in that direction. So far, investment agreements have not established an institution of this kind. An institutional role model for such a bilateral arbitral setting could be the Iran–United States Claims Tribunal established in January 1981.[27] Yet, further research and political consensus-building seems necessary to develop or render more precisely the idea and concept of a bilateral investment court or tribunal with predetermined judges or arbitrators. One could argue that jurisprudence of a permanent international investment court would be less prone to State influence than that of an ad hoc system of arbitration panels, because States—like investors—could not choose the judges on an ad hoc basis anymore but would have to live with their choices for a while. However, as experience with NAFTA has colourfully demonstrated, it can be doubted that ad hoc tribunals effectively perform the claimed role of a guardian of the State parties' intentions. On the contrary, if tribunals had respected the intentions of the State parties in interpreting an investment instrument, there would not have been the need for the NAFTA Free Trade Commission—bringing together the State parties to NAFTA to authoritatively decide on questions of interpretation—to fix the substantive treatment standards of fair and equitable treatment and full protection and security to the customary international law minimum standard of treatment of aliens.[28] Rather, in order to effectively check and balance a permanent investment court, State parties would need to install an effective mechanism to issue authoritative interpretations.

Another aspect of a reformed ISDS system relates to the establishment of an appeals mechanism. While some investment agreements provide for the possibility

---

[24] On 31 March 2015, nine States had signed the convention, among them Canada, the US, and a number of EU countries, see <www.uncitral.org/uncitral/en/uncitral_texts/arbitration/2014Transparency_Convention_status.html> accessed 31 March 2015.

[25] See 'Improvements to CETA and beyond: Making a milestone for modern investment protection' <www.libre-echange.info/IMG/pdf/s_d_position_on_isds_1_.pdf> accessed 27 April 2015.

[26] European Commission, 'Commission draft text TTIP—investment' (September 2015) <http://trade.ec.europa.eu/doclib/docs/2015/september/tradoc_153807.pdf> accessed 1 October 2015.>.

[27] For further information see <www.iusct.net/>.

[28] S Hindelang, 'Study on Investor-State Dispute Settlement ("ISDS") and Alternatives of Dispute Resolution in International Investment Law' in EU Directorate-General for External Policies, *Investor-State Dispute Settlement (ISDS) Provisions in the EU's International Investment Agreements*

of negotiations on the establishment of such a mechanism, it has never been pursued further. ICSID Member States rejected the idea when it was proposed by the ICSID Secretariat in 2004.[29] However, in the debates about the CETA and TTIP investment chapters, the idea remerged. Yet, the only existing model of such a mechanism in international economic law is the Appellate Body of the WTO. However, institutional differences between the multilateral trading system and the investment law regime would have to be taken into account. The WTO's Appellate Body, for example, can rely on the infrastructure of the WTO Secretariat and is part of a larger institutional framework. Nothing of the like exists in the context of the international investment regime as of yet.

c) Relationship between investment protection and domestic legal remedies

The final element of the current reform agenda concerns the relationship between ISDS and domestic courts. In this respect, broadly two general models can be distinguished: the exhaustion of local remedies on the one side and so-called fork-in-the-road or waiver clauses on the other.

The classic model of public international law requires the exhaustion of local remedies before recourse can be sought through international measures. Traditionally, this model has been rejected in most investment agreements, because the very rationale of investor protection was to spare the investor the difficulties of seeking remedies before the domestic courts of the host State which were often perceived as or actually were biased in favour of the host State.

However, it might be worth considering whether the exhaustion of local remedies would not be a more adequate procedural requirement for investment agreements between States with developed legal systems and strong constitutional protection of foreign investors at the domestic level.[30] Yet, it should be kept in mind that investment tribunals will then adjudicate a case after the highest courts of the host State have already decided on the matter. This might lead to a situation that could easily be misunderstood as giving investment tribunals the power to rule over national supreme and constitutional courts. However, it should be stressed that international courts usually do not exercise appeals power over domestic courts. Instead, they decide about a possible violation of the international legal obligations of the State only; a model already well known and widely accepted in the human rights context.

The models usually used in international investment agreements to delineate the domestic courts and investment tribunals are provisions which either require the investor to choose between the domestic and the international legal protection

---

(European Parliament 2014) <www.jura.fu-berlin.de/fachbereich/einrichtungen/oeffentliches-recht/lehrende/hindelangs/Studie-fuer-Europaeisches-Parlament/Volume-2-Studies.pdf> accessed 24 April 2013 61 et seq.

[29] C Tams, 'An Appealing Option? The Debate about an ICSID Appellate Structure' in C Tietje; G Kraft, and R Sethe (eds), *Beiträge zum Transnationalen Wirtschaftsrecht, Heft 57* <www.economiclaw.uni-halle.de/sites/default/files/altbestand/Heft57.pdf> accessed 27 April 2015.

[30] See for the proposal of a flexible exhaustion of local remedies rule Hindelang, 'Study on Investor-State Dispute Settlement' (n 28).

at the outset ('true' fork-in-the-road clause) or to waive any right to return to domestic courts after arbitration was initiated (waiver clause). The problem of both arrangements is that it gives the investor the possibility to bypass the domestic legal system and to preclude domestic courts from assessing the measure challenged by the investor based on domestic law. In addition, such a mechanism might lead to divergent decisions if the measure is challenged by a foreign investor before an international tribunal and by domestic investors in front of domestic courts. If the foreign investor is, as usually is the case, locally incorporated it may even be able to use the domestic and the international avenue. This can be shown by the example of the Swedish State-owned energy company *Vattenfall* which seeks damages for the alteration of its licences to operate nuclear power plants in Germany after Germany decided to phase out the production of nuclear energy. *Vattenfall* has initiated ICSID proceedings and applied to the Federal Constitutional Court to review the German law on the basis of the German constitution.

In light of the difficulties and challenges to manage the interface between the domestic legal system and ISDS, there is not yet a clear consensus emerging which basic model should be used. The usual argument against an exhaustion of local remedies seems less convincing in the context of a mature and developed legal system; on the contrary.[31]

In terms of substantive standards, at least advanced legal systems provide for a multitude of safeguards for investors against an abuse of governmental powers, such as the right to property or the freedom of profession enshrined in domestic constitutions. When appreciating an investor's claim the domestic court will usually consider it against the background of the whole domestic legal system. Such a system reflects an elaborate, complex and refined balance of private and public interests to which the society in which the foreigner voluntarily chose to do its business agreed in a democratic process. When a court decides a case, its holding would echo this societal consensus and is more likely to be accepted and perceived as legitimate by the public. Investments are frequently also protected by international or supranational law such as regional or global human rights conventions or the fundamental freedoms in the Treaty on the Functioning of the European Union. States may of course choose to even further fortify protection of (specifically foreign) investors by concluding international investment instruments stipulating substantive standards for the treatment of foreign investment. If domestic courts are allowed—and here traditions vary greatly among States—also to apply and interpret international treaties including any given investment instrument one single forum would exist in which a dispute is adjudicated in respect of whether the host State measure was in compliance with domestic laws and international obligations of the host State. Domestic courts of a considerable number of States even engage in interpreting domestic law in accordance with international treaties despite the fact that those might not be directly applicable in the domestic forum.

---

[31] The following sections draw on Hindelang, 'Study on Investor-State Dispute Settlement' (n 28) 76 et seq, 88 et seq.

Domestic courts, at least in advanced systems, may operate in a legal environment more consistent and predictable than current ISDS practice. Also, in contrast to the current ISDS model, erroneous decisions can be corrected by appeals mechanisms.

Furthermore, by charging domestic courts with the task of adjudicating disputes involving foreign and domestic investors alike, criticism that investment instruments favour foreigners over locals by granting additional legal remedies could be mitigated.

However, as already pointed out earlier, domestic courts may also fail to impartially adjudicate a conflict between a host State and a foreign investor. They might be, rightly or wrongly, perceived by investors as being biased towards the host State government. Domestic courts may also be corrupt or lack expertise in resolving a dispute in reasonable quality and time.

What is necessary is to respond to the varying capacities of domestic courts. On a pragmatic level, one could consider a solution which avoids hard choices by going beyond the classic options of 'no local remedies', 'full exhaustion of local remedies' and requiring a fixed time period in which the investor has to pursue domestic remedies before proceeding to arbitration.

A pragmatic solution could involve prescribing for an 'elastic' local remedies rule. Such a rule would link the obligation to pursue local remedies to a third-party index that measures the potential of domestic courts to produce effective solutions to claims of foreign investors. In the end, an international investment court or arbitral tribunal—similar to the European Court of Human Rights—could evaluate in the individual case whether the foreign investor just wants enjoy 'a shortcut' or is indeed prevented from seeking an effective legal remedy in domestic courts.

However, regardless of how one designs a future and reformed system of ISDS, it should be remembered that ISDS will always give foreign investors a legal remedy which is not available for domestic investors. In this light, every State negotiating an investment agreement with a special dispute settlement system that is only available for foreign investors needs to assess the benefits and downsides of such a system. It would not be a claim too bold to argue that no matter how the reformed ISDS looks, a dispute settlement mechanism will be included in an investor's strategy if it is available. One should not be too surprised if it is actually used.

Bibliography

—— 'Articles on the Responsibility of States for Internationally Wrongful Acts', as taken note of by the UN General Assembly, UN Doc. A/RES/56/83 of 28 January 2002.
'BITs "not decisive in attracting investment", says South Africa' *TWN Info Service on WTO and Trade Issues* (8 October 2012) <www.twnside.org.sg/title2/wto.info/2012/twninfo121001.htm> accessed 21 June 2014.
—— 'Bolivia Submits a Notice under Article 71 of the ICSID Convention' *International Centre for Settlement of Investment Disputes* (16 May 2007) <https://icsid.worldbank.org/apps/ICSIDWEB/Pages/News.aspx?CID=113&ListID=74f1e8b5-96d0-4f0a-8f0c-2f3a92d84773&variation=en_us> accessed 28 August 2015.
—— 'Caitisa arroja sus primeras observaciones a los TBI' *El Telégrafo* (7 August 2014) <www.telegrafo.com.ec/politica/item/caitisa-arroja-sus-primeras-observaciones-a-los-tbi.html> accessed 1 September 2014.
—— 'Chinese premier urges Canada to approve investment treaty' *Xinhuanet* (28 October 2013) <http://news.xinhuanet.com/english/china/2013-10/18/c_132811261.htm> accessed 11 July 2014.
—— 'Ecuador Evaluates Investment Treaty Framework' (15 May 2013), available under: <www.latinarbitrationlaw.com/ecuador-evaluates-investment-treaty-framework/> accessed 11 November 2014.
—— 'Ecuador Submits a Notice under Article 71 of the ICSID Convention' *International Centre for Settlement of Investment Disputes* (9 July 2009) <https://icsid.worldbank.org/apps/ICSIDWEB/Pages/News.aspx?CID=97&ListID=74f1e8b5-96d0-4f0a-8f0c-2f3a92d84773&variation=en_us> accessed 21 August 2015.
—— 'ICSID in Crisis: Straight-Jacket or Investment Protection?' *Bretton Woods Project* (10 July 2009) <www.brettonwoodsproject.org/art-564878> accessed 24 March 2015.
—— 'Improvements to CETA and beyond: Making a milestone for modern investment protection' <www.libre-echange.info/IMG/pdf/s_d_position_on_isds_1_.pdf> accessed 27 April 2015.
—— 'India reviewing its 83 bilateral investment pacts: Anand Sharma' *The Economic Times* (22 February 2014) <http://articles.economictimes.indiatimes.com/2014-02-22/news/47581787_1_investment-protection-bilateral-treaties-investment-promotion> accessed 2 July 2014.
—— 'Indonesia to terminate more than 60 bilateral investment treaties' *Financial Times* (26 March 2014) <www.ft.com/cms/s/0/3755c1b2-b4e2-11e3-af92-00144feabdc0.html#axzz3Iy1ZVX5l>.
—— 'International Commission that analyzes 26 bilateral investment treaties will recommend to end agreements' *Agencia Pública de Noticias del Ecuador y Suramérica* ('ANDES') (6 August 2014) <www.andes.info.ec/en/news/international-commission-analyzes-26-bilateral-investment-treaties-will-recommend-end> accessed 1 September 2014.
—— 'Lessons from South Africa's BIT Review' *Columbia FDI Perspectives* No 109 (25 November 2013) <http://ccsi.columbia.edu/files/2013/10/No_109_-_Carim_-_FINAL.pdf> accessed 7 July 2014.

—— 'Move to Ease German, EU Doubts over Investor Risk in SA' (30 August 2013) available under: <www.bilaterals.org/spip.php?article23758&lang=en> accessed 11 November 2014.

—— 'Ninth Annual Columbia International Investment Conference: "Raising the Bar: Home Country Efforts to Regulate Foreign Investment for Sustainable Development"' <http://ccsi.columbia.edu/2014/11/12/raising-the-bar-home-country-efforts-to-regulate-foreign-investment-for-sustainable-development/> accessed 23 March 2015.

—— 'Países del Sur buscan en Venezuela crear observatorio sobre Inversiones y Transnacionales' *Agencia Pública Nacional de Noticias del Ecuador y Sudamérica ANDES* (11 September 2014) <www.andes.info.ec/es/noticias/paises-sur-buscan-venezuela-crear-observatorio-sobre-inversiones-transnacionales.html> accessed 11 September 2014.

—— 'Remarks by Dr Rob Davies at the Centre for Conflict Studies Public Dialogue on "South Africa, Africa and International Investment Agreements"', Cape Town, 17 February 2014 <www.tralac.org/wp-content/blogs.dir/12/files/2014/02/Speech-by-Min-Davies-on-IIAS-CCR-17-Feb-2014.pdf> accessed 30 June 2014.

—— 'Revamping Bilateral Treaties' (7 July 2014) available under: <www.bilaterals.org/?revamping-bilateral-treaties&lang=en> both accessed 13 November 2014.

—— 'South Africa and Bilateral Investment Treaties' (Presentation to the 26th Annual Labour Law Conference, 31 July 2013) <www.lexisnexis.co.za/pdf/Bilateral-investment-treaties-and-sustainable-development.ppt> accessed 1 July 2014.

—— 'South Africa Pushes Phase-Out of Early Bilateral Investment Treaties after at least two Separate Brushes with Investor-State Arbitration' *Investment Arbitration Reporter* (23 September 2012) <www.iareporter.com/articles/20120924_1> accessed 11 November 2014.

—— 'South Africa Terminates its Bilateral Investment Treaty with Spain' (27 August 2013) available under: <www.bilaterals.org/spip.php?article23728&lang=en> accessed 11 November 2014.

—— 'Southern Observatory on Transnational Corporations to redress balance between states and companies' *Agencia Venezolana de Noticias ('AVN')* (10 September 2014) <www.avn.info.ve/contenido/southern-observatory-transnational-corporations-redress-balance-between-states-and-compani> accessed 11 September 2014.

—— 'Special Issue: Towards Better BITs?—Making International Investment Law Responsive to Sustainable Development Objectives' (2014), 15 J World Inv & Tr 795–1126.

—— 'Swiss investor prevailed in 2003 in confidential BIT arbitration over South Africa land dispute' (2008) *Investment Arbitration Reporter* Vol 1, No 13, October 22, 2008 <www.iareporter.com/downloads/20100107_15> accessed 29 June 2014.

—— 'Termination of Bolivia-United States Bilateral Investment Treaty' (31 October 2012) available under: <www.latinarbitrationlaw.com/termination-of-bolivia-united-states-bilateral-investment-treaty/> accessed 11 November 2014.

—— 'TPP Investment Leak Reveals Remaining Issues Are ISDS Scope, Capital Controls' *Inside US Trade* (27 March 2015).

—— 'Tratado Constitutivo de Centro de Arbitraje de UNASUR está prácticamente listo' *El Telégrafo* (16 June 2014) <www.telegrafo.com.ec/politica/item/tratado-constitutivo-de-centro-de-arbitraje-de-unasur-esta-practicamente-listo.html> accessed 1 September 2014.

—— 'Venezuela Submits a Notice under Article 71 of the ICSID Convention' *International Centre for Settlement of Investment Disputes* (26 January 2012) <https://icsid.worldbank.org/ICSID/FrontServlet?requestType=CasesRH&actionVal=OpenPage&PageType=AnnouncementsFrame&FromPage=Announcements&pageName=Announcement100> accessed 1 September 2014.

—— 'Venezuela Surprises the Netherlands with Termination Notice for BIT' *Investment Arbitration Reporter* (16 May 2008) <www.iareporter.com/articles/20091001_93> accessed 11 November 2014.

—— 'Venezuela surprises the Netherlands with termination notice for BIT; treaty has been used by many investors to "route" investments into Venezuela' *Investment Arbitration Reporter* (16 May 2008) <www.iareporter.com/articles/20091001_93> accessed 1 September 2014.

Abbott R, F Erixon, and M Francesca Ferracane, 'Demystifying Investor-State Dispute Settlement (ISDS)'(2014) ECIPE Occasional Paper 5/2014.

Acconci P, 'The "Unexpected" Development-Friendly Definition of Investment in the 2013 Resolution of the Institut de droit international' (2014) 23 Italian Ybk Int L 69–90.

Ago R, 'Working Paper', [1963] YBILC, vol II.

Ahner J, *Investor-Staat-Schiedsverfahren nach Europäischem Unionsrecht* (Mohr Siebeck 2015).

Aide Memoire of the Office of the UN Secretary General, 'Denunciation of the ICCPR by the Democratic People's Republic of Korea' (23 September 1997) <https://treaties.un.org/doc/Publication/CN/1997/CN.467.1997-Frn.pdf> accessed 12 December 2014.

Al Qurashi ZA, 'Renegotiation of International Petroleum Agreements' (2005) 22 J Intl Arb 261–300.

Alexander L, 'Constrained by Precedent' (1989) 63 S Cal L Rev 3–64.

Allott P, 'The Concept of International Law' (1999) 10 EJIL 31–50.

Alschner W, 'Regionalism and Overlap in Investment Treaty Law: Towards Consolidation or Contradiction?' (2014) 17 J Intl Econ L 271–98.

Alston P, 'Core Labour Standards and the Transformation of the International Labour Rights Regime' (2004) 15 Eur J Intl L 457–521.

Alvarez J and T Brink, 'Revisiting the Necessity Defense' (2010–2011) 3 Ybk on Intl L and Inv Poly.

Alvarez JE, *International Organizations as Law-Makers* (OUP 2006).

Alvarez JE, 'The Public International Law Regime Governing International Investment' (2009) 344 RdC.

Alvarez JE, *The Public International Law Regime Governing International Investment* (Hague Academy of International Law 2011).

Amerasinghe C, *Local Remedies in International Law* (2nd edn, CUP 2004).

Americans for Tax Reform Foundation, *International Property Rights Index* <internationalpropertyrightsindex.org> accessed 23 March 2015.

Amicus Curiae Submission of the Lawyers' Environmental Action Team (LEAT), the Legal and Human Rights Centre (LHRC), the Tanzania Gender Networking Programme (TGNP), the Center for International Environmental Law (CIEL) and the International Institute for Sustainable Development (IISD) (26 March 2007) in the case of *Biwater Gauff (Tanzania) Ltd v Tanzania*, ICSID Case No ARB/05/22 <www.ciel.org/Publications/Biwater_Amicus_26March.pdf> accessed 15 July 2014.

Amnesty International, *Contracting Out of Human Rights, The Chad–Cameroon pipeline project* (2005) <www.amnesty.org/ar/library/asset/POL34/012/2005/en/76f5b921-d4bf-11dd-8a23-d58a49c0d652/pol340122005en.pdf> accessed 1 September 2014.

Amnesty International, *Human Rights on the Line: The Baku-Tbilisi-Ceyhan (BTC) Pipeline Project* (2003) <www.amnesty.org.uk/images/ul/H/Human_Rights_on_the_Line.pdf> accessed 1 September 2014.

Antonietti A, 'The 2006 Amendments of the ICSID Rules and Regulations and the Additional Facility Rules' (2006) 21 ICSID Rev 427–48.

Appleton S, *Latin American Arbitration: The Story Behind the Headlines*, International Bar Association, <www.ibanet.org/Article/Detail.aspx?ArticleUid=78296258-3B37-4608-A5EE-3C92D5D0B979> accessed 20 October 2014.

Arsanjani MH and W Michael Reisman, 'Interpreting Treaties for the Benefit of Third Parties: The "*Salvors*' Doctrine" and the Use of Legislative History in Investment Claims' (2010) 104 AJIL 597–604.

Asamblea Nacional de la República del Ecuador, 'Trámite General de los Tratados e Instrumentos Internacionales' <www.asambleanacional.gob.ec/tramite-general-tratados-instrumentos-internacionales-agosto2009?created=&title=> accessed 1 September 2014.

Ascensio H, 'Article 70 Convention of 1969' in O Corten and P Klein (eds), *The Vienna Convention on the Law of Treaties*, vol II (OUP 2011) 1585–609.

Aust A, 'Treaties, Termination' in R Wolfrum (ed), *Max Planck Encyclopedia of Public International Law* (June 2006) para 2 <www.mpepil.com/> accessed 11 November 2014.

Aust A, *Modern Treaty Law and Practice* (3rd edn, CUP 2013).

Aust HP, 'Through the Prism of Diversity—The ILC Articles on State Responsibility in the Light of the ILC Fragmentation Report' (2006) 49 GYIL 165–200.

Aust HP, 'The Normative Environment for Peace—On the Contribution of the ILC's Articles on State Responsibility' in G Nolte (ed), *Peace Through International Law—The Role of the International Law Commission* (Springer 2009) 13–46.

Australian Department of Foreign Affairs and Trade, 'AUSFTA fact sheets: investment' (31 December 2012) <www.dfat.gov.au/fta/ausfta/outcomes/09_investment.html> accessed 20 December 2014.

Australian Government, *Australia in the Asian Century, Foreign Direct Investment Fact Sheet*, (October 2012) <www.asiancentury.dpmc.gov.au/sites/default/files/fact-sheets/20.-Foreign-investment-in-Australia.pdf> accessed 11 July 2014.

Baetens F (ed.), *Investment Law within International Law—Integrationist Perspectives* (CUP 2013).

Baldwin E, M Kantor, and M Nolan, 'Limits to Enforcement of ICSID Awards' (2006) 23 J Intl Arb 1–24.

Banifatemi Y, 'The Law Applicable in Investment Treaty Arbitration' in K Yannaca-Small (ed), *Arbitration under International Investment Agreements: A Guide to the Key Issues* (OUP 2010) 191–210.

Barral V, 'Sustainable Development in International Law: Nature and Operation of an Evolutive Legal Norm' (2012) 23 Eur J Intl L 377–400.

Bartels L, *Human Rights Conditionality in the EU's International Agreements* (OUP 2005).

Bartels L, 'Social Issues: Labour, Environment and Human Rights' in S Lester and B Mercurio (eds), *Bilateral and Regional Trade Agreements: Commentary, Analysis and Case Studies* (Cambridge University Press 2009) 342–66.

Bartels L, 'Human Rights and Sustainable Development Obligations in the EU's Free Bartels L, Trade Agreements' (2013) 40 Legal Issues of Economic Integration 297–313.

Bartels L, 'The Chapeau of Article XX GATT: A New Interpretation', University of Cambridge Faculty of Law Research Paper Series, Paper No 40/2014 <http://papers.ssrn.com/sol3/papers.cfm?abstract_id=2469852> accessed 19 December 2014).

Been V and JC Beauvais, 'The Global Fifth Amendment? NAFTA's Investment Protections and the Misguided Quest for an International 'Regulatory Takings' Doctrine' (2003) 78 NYU L Rev 30–143.

Behrens P, 'Towards the Constitutionalization of International Investment Protection' (2007) 45 AVR 153–79.

Ben Hamida W, 'The First Arab Investment Court Decision' (2006) 6 J World Inv & Trade 699–721.
Bentley P, 'A Giant Leap: EU-China Bilateral Investment Treaty Negotiations to Be Launched Formally' *The National Law Review* (17 November 2013) <www.natlawreview.com/article/giant-leap-eu-china-bilateral-investment-treaty-negotiations-to-be-launched-formally> accessed 11 July 2014.
Bentley P and F Schoneveld, 'A Giant Leap: EU–China Bilateral Investment Treaty Negotiations to Be Launched Formally' *National Law Review* (23 November 2013).
Benvinisti E and GW Downs, 'The Empire's New Clothes: Political Economy and the Fragmentation of International Law' (2007) 60 Stan L Rev 595–631.
Berger KP, 'Renegotiation and Adaption of International Investment Contracts: The Role of Contract Drafters and Arbitrators' (2003) 36 Vanderbilt J Transnatl L 1347–80.
Bernasconi-Osterwalder N, L Johnson, and F Marshall, *Arbitrator Independence and Impartiality: Examining the dual role of arbitrator and counsel* (International Institute for Sustainable Development 2011).
Bernasconi-Osterwalder N and D Rosert, *Investment Treaty Arbitration: Opportunities to reform arbitral rules and processes* (International Institute for Sustainable Development 2014) <www.iisd.org/sites/default/files/pdf/2014/investment_treaty_arbitration.pdf> accessed 7 May 2015.
Bernhardt R, 'Interpretation and Implied (Tacit) Modification of Treaties, Comments on Arts 27, 28, 29 and 38 of the ILC's 1966 Draft Articles on the Law of Treaties' (1967) 27 ZaöRV 491–506.
Besley T and M Ghatak, 'Property Rights and Economic Development', in D Rodrik and M Rosenzweig (eds): *Handbook of Development Economics, Vol. 5* (North-Holland 2010) 4525–95.
Beyerlin U, 'The Concept of Sustainable Development' in: R Wolfrum (ed), *Enforcing Environmental Standards: Economic Mechanisms as Viable Means?* (Springer 1996) 39–93.
Beyerlin U, 'Sustainable Development', *Max Planck Encyclopedia of Public International Law* (OUP 2009).
Beyerlin U, 'Sustainable Development', *Max Planck Encyclopedia of Public International Law*, (OUP 2012) vol IX.
Beyerlin U, 'Sustainable Development' in Rüdiger Wolfrum (ed), *The Max Planck Encyclopedia of Public International Law* (2nd edn, OUP 2013) 716–21.
Binder C, *Die Grenzen der Vertragstreue im Völkerrecht* (Springer 2013).
Birnie P, A Boyle and C Redgwell, *International Law and the Environment* (3rd edn, OUP 2009).
Bishop RD, J Crawford, and WM Reisman, *Foreign Investment Disputes: Cases, Materials and Commentary* (Kluwer 2005).
Blackaby N and C Richard, 'Amicus Curiae: A Panacea for Legitimacy in Investment Arbitration?' in M Waibel, A Kaushal, K Chung, and C Balchin (eds), *The Backlash against Investment Arbitration* (Kluwer 2010) 253–74.
Bland B and S Donnan, 'Indonesia to Terminate More Than 60 Bilateral Investment Treaties' *Financial Times* (26 March 2014) <www.ft.com/intl/cms/s/0/3755c1b2-b4e2-11e3-af92-00144feabdc0.html?siteedition=uk#axzz36C9e5Oos> accessed 11 July 2014.
Bolivar G, 'The Effect of Survival and Withdrawal Clauses in Investment Treaties: Protection of Investments in Latin America' in LE Trakman and NW Ranieri (eds), *Regionalism in International Investment Law* (OUP 2013) 162–81.

Bonnitcha J, 'Outline of normative framework for evaluating interpretations of investment treaty protections' in C Brown and K Miles (eds), *Evolution in Investment Treaty Law and Arbitration* (CUP 2011) 117–44.

Bonnitcha J, *Substantive Protection under Investment Treaties—A Legal and Economic Analysis* (CUP 2014).

Borensztein E, J De Gregorio, and J Lee, 'How does Foreign Direct Investment Affect Economic Growth?' (1998) 45 J Int Econ 115–35.

Bottini G, 'Reform of the investor-State arbitration regime: the appeal proposal in Reform of Investor-State Dispute Settlement: In Search of A Roadmap' (2014) 11(1) Transn Disp Mgmt.

de Brabandere E, *Investment Treaty Arbitration as Public International Law—Procedural Aspects and Implications* (CUP 2014).

Braun TR, *Ausprägungen der Globalisierung: Der Investor als partielles Subjekt im Internationalen Investitionsrecht* (Nomos 2012).

Braune B, *Rechtsfragen der nachhaltigen Entwicklung im Völkerrecht: Eine Untersuchung unter besonderer Berücksichtigung des Handels- und Investitionsrechts* (Peter Lang 2005).

Brazilian Investment Information Network, 'Announced Investment Projects' <http://investimentos.mdic.gov.br/conteudo/index/item/34> accessed 1 September 2014.

Brian N (ed), *A Comprehensive Dictionary of Economics* (Abhishek Publications 2009).

Brower C and J Wong, 'General Valuation Principles: The Case of Santa Elena' in Todd Weiler (ed), *International Investment Law and Arbitration: Leading Cases from the ICSID, NAFTA, Bilateral Treaties and Customary International Law* (Cameron May 2005) 747–76.

Brower C and SW Schill, 'Is Arbitration a Threat or a Boon to the Legitimacy of International Investment Law?' (2009) 9 Chicago JIL 471–98.

Brown C and I Naglis, 'Dispute Settlement in Future EU Investment Agreements' in: M Bungenberg, A Reinisch and C Tietje, *EU and International Investment Agreements—Open Questions and Remaining Challenges* (Nomos 2013) 17–35.

Brown C, *Self-Enforcing Trade Developing Countries and Dispute Settlement* (Brookings Institution Press 2006).

Brundtland G, 'Report of the World Commission on Environment and Development: Our Common Future' (4 August 1987) UN Doc A/42/427/Annex <www.un-documents.net/our-common-future.pdf> accessed 15 July 2014.

Bubrowski H, *Internationale Schiedsverfahren und nationale Gerichte* (Mohr Siebeck 2003).

Bubrowski H, 'Muss ein Gericht ein Gebäude sein?' *Frankfurter Allgemeine Zeitung* (Frankfurt am Main, 13 June 2015).

Bücheler G, *Proportionality in Investor-State Arbitration* (OUP 2015).

Bundesverband der Deutschen Industrie e.V., *Positionspapier: Schutz europäischer Investitionen im Ausland: Anforderungen an Investitionsabkommen der EU* (BDI 2014) <www.bdi.eu/download_content/GlobalisierungMaerkteUndHandel/Schutz_europaeischer_Investitionen_im_Ausland.pdf> accessed 23 April 2014.

Bungenberg M, 'The Politics of the European Union's Investment Treaty Making' in T Broude, ML Busch, and A Porges (eds), *The Politics of International Economic Law* (CUP 2011) 133–61.

Bungenberg M, J Griebel, and S Hindelang (eds), *International Investment Law and EU Law* (Nomos 2011).

Bungenberg M and A Reinisch, 'Special Issue: The Anatomy of the (Invisible) EU Model BIT' (2014) 15 J World Inv & Trade 375–78.

Bungenberg M, A Reinisch, and C Tietje (eds), *EU and International Investment Agreements—Open Questions and Remaining Challenges* (Nomos 2013).

Burch M, L Nottage, and B Williams, 'Appropriate Treaty-Based Dispute Resolution for Asia-Pacific Commerce in the 21st Century' (2012) 35 UNSW LJ 1013–43.

Burgstaller M, 'The Future of Bilateral Investment Treaties of EU Member States' in M Business and Human Rights Initiative, *How to Do Business with Respect for Human Rights* (Global Compact Network Netherlands 2010).

Burke-White W, 'The Argentine Financial Crisis: State Liability under BITs and the Legitimacy of the ICSID System' in M Waibel, A Kaushal, K Chung, and C Balchin (eds), *The Backlash against Investment Arbitration* (Kluwer 2010) 407–32.

Callick R, 'Korea Ready to Talk Turkey After FTA Hurdle Removed' *The Australian* (1 November 2013) <www.theaustralian.com.au/business/economics/korea-ready-to-talk-turkey-after-fta-hurdle-removed/story-e6frg926-1226750841630#> accessed 11 July 2014.

Calvo C, *Derecho Internacional Teórico y Práctico de Europa y América* (D'Amyot Librarie Diplomatique—Durand et Pèdone-Lauriel, 1868).

Cameron I, 'Treaties, Suspension' in R Wolfrum (ed), *Max Planck Encyclopedia of Public International Law* (February 2007) para 1 <www.mpepil.com/> accessed 11 November 2014.

Capie D, 'When Does Track Two Matter? Structure, Agency and Asian Regionalism' (2010) 17 Rev Intl Pol Econ 291–318.

Caplan LM and JK Sharpe, 'United States' in C Brown (ed), *Commentaries on Selected Model Investment Treaties* (OUP 2013).

Carim X, 'Update on the Review of Bilateral Investment Treaties in South Africa' (Presentation to the Parliamentary Portfolio Committee on Trade and Industry, 15 February 2013) <www.thedti.gov.za/parliament/bit's_in_sa.pdf> accessed 30 June 2014.

Carska-Sheppard A, 'Issues Relevant to the Termination of Bilateral Investment Treaties' (2009) 26 J Intl Arb 755–71.

Casella PB, EL Marques, 'Brazil: Arbitration Act' (1997) 36 ILM 1562–77.

Chan G, 'Leaked Trade Deal Terms Prompt Fears for Pharmaceutical Benefits Scheme' *The Guardian* (London, 11 June 2015) <www.theguardian.com/business/2015/jun/11/pacific-trade-deal-raises-fears-over-future-of-pharmaceutical-benefits-scheme> accessed 16 August 2015.

Chapaux V, 'Article 54 Convention of 1969' in O Corten and P Klein (eds), *The Vienna Convention on the Law of Treaties*, vol II (OUP 2011) 1236–45.

Chayes A and AH Chayes, *The New Sovereignty* (HUP 1995).

Chinkin C, *Third Parties in International Law* (Clarendon 1993).

Chung O, 'The Lopsided International Investment Law Regime and its Effect on the Future of Investor-State Arbitration' (2007) 47 Va JIL 953.

Clarkson S and S Hindelang, 'How Parallel Lines Intersect: Investor-State Dispute Settlement and Regional Social Policy' in: AC Bianculli and A Ribeiro Hoffmann (eds), *Regional Organizations and Social Policy in Europe and Latin America: A Space for Social Citizenship?* (Palgrave, 2015) 25–45.

Clifton D, 'Representing a Sustainable World—A Typology Approach', (2010) 3 J Sustainable Dev 40–57.

Collins D, 'Sustainable International Investment Law After the Pax Americana: The BOOT on the Other Foot' (2012) 13 J World Inv & Trade 325–48.

Comisión Económica para América Latina y el Caribe ('CEPAL'), La Inversión Extranjera Directa en América Latina y el Caribe, 2013 (LC/G.2613-P), Santiago de Chile, 2014.

Comisión para la Auditoría Integral Ciudadana de los Tratados de Protección Recíproca de Inversiones y del Sistema de Arbitraje Internacional en Materia de Inversiones ('CAITISA') Miembros, <http://caitisa.org/miembros.html> accessed 1 September 2014.

Commonwealth Secretariat Press Release, 'Commonwealth investment guide launched at trade workshop in Vanuatu' (7 February 2013) <http://thecommonwealth.org/media/news/commonwealth-investment-guide-launched-trade-workshop-vanuatu#sthash.zGBw9CG9.dpuf> accessed 12 November 2014.

Commonwealth Secretariat, *Integrating Sustainable Development into International Investment Agreements: A Guide for Developing Countries* (2012) <https://publications.thecommonwealth.org> accessed 4 November 2014.

Commonwealth Secretariat, *Integrating Sustainable Development into International Investment Agreements: A Guide for Developing Country Negotiators* (Commonwealth Secretariat, 2013).

Coorey P, 'Side Deal May Open Door for China State-Owned Firms' *Australian Financial Review* (12 April 2014) <www.afr.com/p/national/side_deal_may_open_door_for_china_0TUDkjLssijS9698OcJqEO> accessed 11 July 2014.

Cordonier Segger M-C and Khalfan A, *Sustainable Development Law: Principles, Practices & Prospects* (OUP 2004).

Cordonier Segger M-C, MW Gehring, and A Newcombe (eds), *Sustainable Development in World Investment Law* (Wolters Kluwer 2011).

Cottier T, K Gehne, and M Schultheiss, 'The Protection of Property in International Law: The Missing Pieces', in HP Hestermeyer, D König, N Matz-Lück, V Röben, A Seibert-Fohr, PT Stoll, and S Vöneky (eds), *Coexistence, Cooperation and Solidarity, Liber Amicorum Rüdiger Wolfrum* (Martinus Nijhoff 2012).

Cottier T and JP Müller, 'Estoppel' in R Wolfrum (ed), *Max Planck Encyclopedia of Public International Law* (April 2007) <www.mpepil.com/> accessed 11 November 2014.

Cottier T and M Oesch, 'Direct and Indirect Discrimination in WTO Law and EU Law' (2011) NCCR Trade Regulation Working Paper No. 2011/16 <www.wti.org/fileadmin/user_upload/nccr-trade.ch/hi/CottierOeschNCCRWP16.pdf> accessed 17 February 2015.

Cotula L and K Tienhaara, 'Reconfiguring Investment Contracts to Promote Sustainable Development' in K Sauvant (ed), *Yearbook on International Investment Law and Policy 2011–2012* (OUP 2013) 281–310.

Council of the European Union Decision 94/800/EC of 22 December 1994, OJ 1994 L 336, 1.

Council of the European Union Conclusions on a Comprehensive European International Investment Policy, 3041st Foreign Affairs Council Meeting (25 October 2010).

Council of the European Union Press Release 11855/12, 'EU Strategic Framework and Action Plan on Human Rights and Democracy' (25 June 2012).

Council of the European Union 'Directives for the negotiation on the Transatlantic Trade and Investment Partnership between the European Union and the United States of America', ST 11103/13 RESTREINT UE/EU RESTRICTED (17 June 2013) <http://data.consilium.europa.eu/doc/document/ST-11103-2013-DCL-1/en/pdf> accessed 23 April 2015.

Crawford J, *The International Law Commission's Articles on State Responsibility* (CUP 2002).

Crawford J, 'Investment Arbitration and the ILC Articles on State Responsibility' (2010) 25 ICSID Rev 127–99.

Crawford J and S Olleson, 'The Application of the Rules of State Responsibility' in M Bungenberg, J Gabriel, S Hobe, and A Reinisch (eds), *International Investment Law* (Nomos 2015) 411–41.

Crawford J, 'International Protection of Foreign Direct Investments: Between Clinical Isolation and Systemic Integration' in R Hofmann and C Tams (eds), *International*

Investment Law and General International Law—From Clinical Isolation to Systemic Integration? (Nomos 2011) 17–28.

Crawford J, *Brownlie's Principles of Public International Law* (8th edn, OUP 2012).

Crawford J, 'A Consensualist Interpretation of Article 31 (3) of the Vienna Convention on the Law of Treaties' in G Nolte (ed), *Treaties and Subsequent Practice* (OUP 2013) 29–33.

Crawford J *State Responsibility—The General Part* (CUP 2013).

Crawford J and K Lee, ICSID Reports (2004) vol 6.

Crawford J and J McIntyre, 'The Independence and Impartiality of the International Judiciary' in S Shetreet and C Forsyth, *The Culture of Judicial Independence: Conceptual Foundations and Practical Challenges* (Nijhoff 2011) 189–214.

Cremades BM, 'Disputes arising out of Foreign Direct Investment in Latin America: a new look at the Calvo Doctrine and other Jurisdicional Issues' (2004) 59 Disp Resol J 78.

Crowe D, 'Tony Abbott Concludes Free Trade Agreement with Japan' *The Australian* (7 April 2014) <www.theaustralian.com.au/national-affairs/policy/tony-abbott-concludes-free-trade-agreement-with-japan/story-fn59nm2j-1226877009701#> accessed 11 July 2014.

Cubitt B, 'Potential Investor-State Dispute Settlement Provisions in Trans-Pacific Partnership Agreement—A Change in Policy for Australia?' *Kluwer Arbitration Blog* (14 February 2014) <http://kluwerarbitrationblog.com/blog/2014/02/14/potential-investor-state-dispute-settlement-provisions-in-trans-pacific-partnership-agreement-a-change-in-policy-for-australia/> accessed 11 July 2014.

Cuyvers L, 'The Sustainable Development Clauses in Free Trade Agreements: An EU Perspective for ASEAN?' UNU-CRIS Working Papers W-2013/10 <www10.iadb.org/intal/intalcdi/PE/2013/12733.pdf> accessed 19 December 2014.

d'Argent P, 'Article 36 Convention of 1969' in O Corten and P Klein (eds), *The Vienna Convention on the Law of Treaties*, vol I (OUP 2011) 929–40.

da Gama M, 'Draft Bill no Threat to Foreign Investors in South Africa' *BDLive* (1 April 2014) <www.bdlive.co.za/opinion/2014/04/01/draft-bill-no-threat-to-foreign-investors-in-south-africa> accessed 3 July 2014.

Dahm G, J Delbrück, and R Wolfrum, *Völkerrecht*, vol I/3 (de Gruyter 2002).

De Brabandere E, 'Human Rights Considerations in International Investment Arbitration' in M Fitzmaurice and P Merkouris (eds), *The Interpretation and Application of the European Convention of Human Rights: Legal and Practical Implications* (Martinus Nijhoff 2012) <http://ssrn.com/abstract=2230305> accessed 17 February 2015.

De Brabandere E, *Investment Treaty Arbitration as Public International Law* (CUP 2014).

De Luca A, 'Integrating non-trade objectives in the oncoming EU Investment Policy: what policy options for the EU?' (2013/14) CLEER Working Papers (Asser Institute).

De Shutter O, *International Human Rights Law* (1st ed, OUP 2010).

de Vattel E, *The Law of Nations or the Principles of Natural Law: Applied to the Conduct and to the Affairs of Nations and of Sovereigns* (Hein & Co 1995).

Department of Foreign Affairs and Trade (Australia) 'Newsletter Update 10: Australia-Japan Free Trade Agreement, Tenth Negotiating Round' (17-25 November 2012), <www.dfat.gov.au/fta/jaepa/newsletters/update_10.html> accessed 11 July 2014.

Department of Foreign Affairs and Trade (Australia) 'Sixteenth round of negotiations' <www.dfat.gov.au/fta/jaepa/#news> accessed 11 July 2014.

Department of Foreign Affairs and Trade (Australia) 'Australia's Trade Agreements' <www.dfat.gov.au/fta/> accessed 11 July 2014.

Department of Foreign Affairs and Trade (Australia) 'Conclusion of Negotiations' <www.dfat.gov.au/fta/jaepa/> accessed 11 July 2014.

Department of Foreign Affairs and Trade (Australia) 'Frequently Asked Questions on Investor-State Dispute Settlement (ISDS)' <http://dfat.gov.au/fta/isds-faq.html> accessed 11 July 2014.

Department of Foreign Affairs and Trade (Australia) 'Gillard Government Trade Policy Statement: Trading Our Way to More Jobs and Prosperity' (April 2011).

Department of Foreign Affairs and Trade (Australia) *Trade at a Glance 2014* <http://dfat.gov.au/about-us/publications/trade-investment/trade-at-a-glance/trade-at-a-glance-2014/Pages/trade-at-a-glance-2014.aspx> accessed 16 August 2015.

Department of Foreign Affairs and Trade (Australia) 'Trans-Pacific Partnership Agreement Negotiations' <www.dfat.gov.au/fta/tpp/> accessed 11 July 2014.

Department of Foreign Affairs and Trade (Australia) 'Regional Comprehensive Economic Partnership' <http://dfat.gov.au/trade/agreements/rcep/Pages/regional-comprehensive-economic-partnership.aspx#news> accessed 24 April 2015.

Department of Health (Australia) 'Pharmaceutical Benefits Scheme: PBS News Updates' <*www.pbs.gov.au*> accessed 11 July 2014.

Desierto D, 'Development as an International Right: Investment in the New Trade-Based IIAs' (2011) 3 Trade L & Dev 296–333.

Desierto D, 'Deciding international investment agreement applicability: the development argument in investment' in F Baetens (ed), *Investment Law within International Law—Integrationist Perspectives* (CUP 2013) 240–56.

Dezaley Y and B Garth, *Dealing in Virtue: International Commercial Arbitration and the Construction of a Transnational Legal Order* (niversity of Chicago Press 1996).

Dhooge L, 'Foreign Investors versus Environmentalists: Whose Green Counts in the North American Free Trade Agreement?' (2001) 10 Minn J Global Trade 209–89.

Di Benedetto S, *International Investment Law and the Environment* (Edward Elgar 2013).

Diehl A, *The Core Standard of International Investment Protection* (Kluwer 2012).

Dimopoulos A, 'The Effects of the Lisbon Treaty on the Principles and Objectives of the Common Commercial Policy' (2010) 15 E F A Rev 153–70.

Dimopoulos A, *EU Foreign Investment Law* (OUP 2011).

Dodge W, 'Investor-State Dispute Settlement Between Developed Countries: Reflections on the Australia United States Free Trade Agreement' (2006) 39 Vanderbilt J of Transnatl L 1–37.

Dodge W, 'Local Remedies under NAFTA Chapter 11' in E Gaillard and F Bachand (eds), *Fifteen Years of NAFTA Chapter 11 Arbitration* (Juris 2011).

Dolzer R, *Eigentum, Enteignung und Entschädigung im geltenden Völkerrecht/Property, Expropriation and Compensation in Current International Law* (Springer 1985).

Dolzer R, 'Indirect Expropriations: New Developments?' (2003) 11 NYU Env LJ 64.

Dolzer R, 'Fair and Equitable Treatment: A Key Standard in Investment Treaties' (2005) 39 Intl L 87–106.

Dolzer R, 'The Impact of International Investment Treaties on Domestic Administrative Law', (2005) 37 NYU J Intl L & Pol 953–72.

Dolzer R and C Schreuer, *Principles of International Investment Law* (OUP 2008).

Dolzer R and C Schreuer, *Principles of International Investment Law* (2nd edn, OUP 2012).

Dolzer R and M Stevens, *Bilateral Investment Treaties* (Nijhoff 1995).

Donnan S, 'Japan-Australia Trade Deal Is Dismissed by the US' *Financial Times* (London, 7 April 2014) <www.ft.com/intl/cms/s/0/5e4023b6-be43-11e3-b44a-00144feabdc0.html#axzz2yehuWuKc> accessed 11 July 2014.

Dörr O, 'Article 31' in O Dörr and K Schmalenbach (eds), *Vienna Convention on the Law of Treaties* (Springer 2012) 521–70.

Douglas Z, 'The Hybrid Foundations of Investment Treaty Arbitration' (2004) 74 BYIL.
Douglas Z, *The International Law of Investment Claims* (CUP 2009).
Douglas Z, 'Other Specific Regimes of Responsibility: Investment Treaty Arbitration and ICSID' in J Crawford J, A Pellet, and S Olleson (eds), *The Law of International Responsibility* (OUP 2010) 815–42.
Dubava I, 'The Future of International Investment Protection Law: The Promotion of Sustainable (Economic) Development as a Public Good' in M Cremona and others (eds), *Reflections on the Constitutionalisation of International Economic Law—Liber Amicorum for Ernst-Ulrich Petersmann* (Nijhoff 2014) 389–402.
Dugan C, D Wallace and N Rubins, *Investor-State Arbitration* (OUP 2008).
Dumberry P, *The Fair and Equitable Treatment Standard: A Guide to NAFTA Case Law on Article 1105* (Kluwer 2013).
Dupuy P-M, E-U Petersmann, and F Francioni (eds.), *Human Rights in International Investment Law and Arbitration* (OUP 2009).
Ebert F, and A Posthuma, Labour Provisions in Trade Arrangements: Current Trends and Perspectives (International Labour Organization 2011) <www.ilo.org/wcmsp5/groups/public/---dgreports/---inst/documents/publication/wcms_192807.pdf> accessed 19 December 2014.
Economist Magazine, 'A better way to arbitration: Protections for foreign investors are not horror critics claim, but they could be improved,' <www.economist.com/news/leaders/21623674-protections-foreign-investors-are-not-horror-critics-claim-they-could-be-improved> accessed 16 December 2014.
Eeckhout P, *EU External Relations Law* (2nd edn, OUP 2011).
Elkins Z, AT Guzman, and BA Simmons, 'Competing for Capital: The Diffusion of Bilateral Investment Treaties 1960-2000' (2006) 60 Intl Org 811–46.
Epiney A, *Umgekehrte Diskriminierungen: Zulässigkeit und Grenzen der discrimination à rebours nach europäischem Gemeinschaftsrecht und nationalem Verfassungsrecht* (Heymann 1995).
European Commission, 'Investment Provisions in the EU-Canada Free Trade Agreement (CETA)', <http://trade.ec.europa.eu/doclib/docs/2013/november/tradoc_151918.pdf> accessed 21 October 2014.
European Commission, 'Towards a comprehensive European International Investment Policy', (Communication) COM (2010) 343 final.
European Commission, Press Release IP/14/292, 'European Commission launches public online consultation on investor protection in TTIP' (27 March 2014).
European Commission, Proposal of 21 July 2012, COM (2012) 335.
European Commission, 'A renewed EU strategy 2011–14 for Corporate Social Responsibility' (Communication) COM (2011) 681 final (25 October 2011).
European Commission, Memo, 'EU Investment Negotiations with China and ASEAN' (18 October 2013) <http://europa.eu/rapid/press-release_MEMO-13-913_en.htm> accessed 23 April 2015.
European Commission, 'Investment Protection and Investor-to-State Dispute Settlement in EU Agreements—Fact Sheet' (November 2013) <http://trade.ec.europa.eu/doclib/cfm/doclib_results.cfm?docid=151916> accessed 30 June 2014.
European Commission, 'Investment Provisions in the EU-Canada Free Trade Agreement (CETA)' (2014) <http://trade.ec.europa.eu/doclib/docs/2013/november/tradoc_151918.pdf> accessed 17 February 2015.
European Commission, 'Online public consultation on investment protection and investor-to-state dispute settlement (ISDS) in the Transatlantic Trade and Investment

Partnership Agreement (TTIP)' (13 July 2014) <http://trade.ec.europa.eu/consultations/index.cfm?consul_id=179> accessed 30 June 2014.

European Commission, 'Public consultation on modalities for investment protection and ISDS in TTIP', Public Consultation B Investor-to-state dispute settlement (ISDS), Introduction (2014) 5<http://trade.ec.europa.eu/doclib/docs/2014/march/tradoc_152280.pdf> accessed 17 February 2015.

European Commission, 'Public consultation on modalities for investment protection and ISDS in TTIP' (undated), available online: http://trade.ec.europa.eu/doclib/docs/2014/march/tradoc_152280.pdf accessed 8 October 2014.

European Commission, 'Report on the Online Public Consultation on Investment Protection and Investor-State Dispute Settlement in the Transatlantic Trade and Investment Partnership (TTIP)' (July 2014) <http://trade.ec.europa.eu/doclib/docs/2014/july/tradoc_152693.pdf> accessed 28 October 2014.

European Commission, Memo, '9th Round Transatlantic Trade and Investment Partnership Negotiations' (7 April 2015) <http://trade.ec.europa.eu/doclib/events/index.cfm?id=1287> accessed 24 April 2015.

European Commission, Concept Paper 'Investment in TTIP and beyond–the path for reform' (May 2015) <http://trade.ec.europa.eu/doclib/docs/2015/may/tradoc_153408.PDF> accessed 24 August 2015.

European Commission, 'Commission Staff Working Report, Online public consultation on investment protection and investor-to-state dispute settlement (ISDS) in the Transatlantic Trade and Investment Partnership Agreement (TTIP)' SWD (2015) 3 final, 4 <http://trade.ec.europa.eu/doclib/docs/2015/january/tradoc_153044.pdf> accessed 27 April 2015.

European Commission, 'Monitoring Activities and Analysis: Foreign Direct Investment' <http://ec.europa.eu/internal_market/capital/analysis/monitoring_activities_and_analysis/index_en.htm> accessed 17 February 2015.

European Commission, 'Commission draft text TTIP—investment' (September 2015) <http://trade.ec.europa.eu/doclib/docs/2015/september/tradoc_153807.pdf> accessed 1 October 2015.

European Parliament Research Service, 'Investor-State Dispute Settlement (ISDS)—State of play and prospects for reform' (Briefing, 21 January 2014) <www.europarl.europa.eu/RegData/bibliotheque/briefing/2014/130710/LDM_BRI%282014%29130710_REV2_EN.pdf> accessed 7 May 2015.

European Trade Union Confederation Press Release, 'European Trade Union Calls for a Fundamental Rethink of Canadian and US Trade Deals' (17 November 2014) <www.etuc.org/press/european-trade-union-calls-fundamental-rethink-canadian-and-us-trade-deals#.VTjoyfAgcg8> accessed 23 April 2015.

European Union President-elect Junckers, Speech, 22 October 2014, <http://europa.eu/rapid/press-release_SPEECH-14-705_de.htm> accessed 16 December 2014.

Ewing-Chow M and JJ Losari, 'Indonesia is Letting its Bilateral Treaties Lapse so as to Renegotiate Better Ones' *Financial Times* (15 April 2014) <www.ft.com/intl/cms/s/0/20c6c518-c16c-11e3-97b2-00144feabdc0.html?siteedition=intl#axzz34NvIWeHB> accessed 11 July 2014.

Fan B, 'Foreign Investment Review Changes for Chinese Investors under the China-Australia Free Trade Agreement' *Herbert Smith Freehills* (28 November 2014) <www.herbertsmithfreehills.com/insights/legal-briefings/foreign-investment-review-changes-for-chinese-investors-under-the-china-australia-fta> accessed 16 August 2015.

Fauchald O, 'The Legal Reasoning of ICSID Tribunals—An Empirical Analysis' (2008) 19 EJIL 301–64.

Fecák T, 'Czech Experience with Bilateral Investment Treaties: Somewhat Bitter Taste of Investment Protection' (2011) 2 Czech Ybk Public and Private Intl L 233–67.

Feigerlova M and A Maltais, *Obligations Undertaken by States under International Conventions for the Protection of Cultural Rights and the Environment, to What Extent they Constitute a Limitation to Investor's Rights under Bilateral or Multilateral Investment Treaties and Investment Contracts?* (Geneva 2012) <http://graduateinstitute.ch/home/research/centresandprogrammes/ctei/projects-1/trade-law-clinic.html> accessed 15 July 2014.

Fiezzoni SK, 'The Challenge of UNASUR Member Countries to Replace ICSID Arbitration' (2011) Beijing L Rev <www.scirp.org/journal/PaperInformation.aspx?PaperID=7722> accessed 1 September 2014).

Fiezzoni SK, 'UNASUR Arbitration Centre: The Present Situation and the Principal Characteristics of Ecuador's Proposal' (*International Institute for Sustainable Development*, 12 January 2012) <www.iisd.org/itn/2012/01/12/unasur/> accessed 8 March 2015.

Fischer-Lescano A and J Horst, *Europa—und verfassungsrechtliche Vorgaben für das Comprehensive Economic and Trade Agreement der EU und Kanada (CETA)* <www.attac.de/uploads/media/CETA-Rechtsgutachten_Oktober_2014_Fischer-Lescano_Uni_Bremen.pdf> accessed 5 February 2015.

Fitzmaurice M, 'Third Parties and the Law of Treaties' (2002) 6 Max Planck Ybk of UN L 37–137.

Fontanelli F and G Bianco, 'Converging Toward NAFTA: An Analysis of FTA Chapters in the European Union and the United States' (2014) 50 Stanford J Intl L 211–245.

Foreign Affairs, Trade and Development Canada Press Release, 'Canada Ratifies Important International Treaty on Investment Disputes' (1 November 2013) <www.international.gc.ca/media/comm/news-communiques/2013/11/01a.aspx?lang=eng> accessed 23 April 2015.

Foreign Affairs, Trade and Development Canada Press Release, 'Trans-Pacific Partnership (TPP) Free Trade Negotiations' <www.international.gc.ca/trade-agreements-accords-commerciaux/agr-acc/tpp-ptp/rounds-series.aspx?lang=eng> accessed 24 April 2015.

Fortier LY and SL Drymer, 'Indirect Expropriation in the Law of International Investment: I Know It When I See It, or Caveat Investor' (2004) 19 ICSID Rev—FILJ 293–327.

Francioni F, 'Foreign Investments, Sovereignty and the Public Good' (2014) 23 Italian Ybk Int L 1–22.

Franck S, 'The Legitimacy Crisis in Investment Treaty Arbitration: Privatizing Public International Law through Inconsistent Decisions' (2005) 73 Fordham L Rev 1521–1625.

Franck S, 'Development and Outcomes of Investment Treaty Arbitration' (2009) 50 HILJ 435.

Franck S, 'Rationalizing Costs in Investment Treaty Arbitration' (2011) 88 Washington U L Rev 769–852.

Franck TM, *Fairness in International Law and Institutions* (OUP 1995).

French R, 'Investor-State Dispute Settlement—A Cut Above the Courts?' (Supreme and Federal Court Judges' Conference, Darwin, 9 July 2014) <www.hcourt.gov.au/assets/publications/speeches/current-justices/frenchcj/frenchcj09jul14.pdf> accessed 8 March 2015.

Friedman A, 'Flexible Arbitration for the Developing World: Piero Foresti and the Future of Bilateral Investment Treaties in the Global South' (2010) 7 Intl L & Mgmt Rev 37–51.

Füracker M, 'Relevance and Structure of Bilateral Investment Treaties—The German Approach' (2006) 4 SchiedsVZ 236–47.

Gantz D, 'Trans-Pacific Partnership Negotiations: Progress, But No End in Sight' *Kluwer Arbitration Blog* (22 June 2014) <kluwerarbitrationblog.com/blog/2012/06/22/trans-pacific-partnership-negotiations-progress-but-no-end-in-sight/> accessed 11 July 2014.

García-Bolívar OE, 'Sovereignty vs. Investment Protection: Back to Calvo?' (2009) 24 ICSID Rev–FILJ 464–88.

Gardiner R, *Treaty Interpretation* (OUP 2008).

Garibaldi OM, 'On the Denunciation of the ICSID Convention, Consent to Investment Jurisdiction and the Limits of Contract Analogy' in C Binder and others (eds), *International Investment Law for the 21st Century—Essays in Honour of Christoph Schreuer* (OUP 2009).

Gehring MW (ed), *Sustainable Development in World Investment Law* (Kluwer Law International 2010).

Gehring MW and A Kent, 'International investment agreements and the emerging green economy: rising to the challenge' in F Baetens (ed), *Investment Law within International Law—Integrationist Perspectives* (CUP 2013) 187–216.

Gehring MW and A Kent, 'Sustainable development and IIAs: from objective to practice' in A de Mestral and C Levesque (eds), *Improving International Investment Agreements* (Routledge 2013) 284–302.

Genova W, 'Philip Morris Files Arbitration Case Vs. Australia Over Plain-Packaging Law' *International Business Times*, 22 November 2011. <http://au.ibtimes.com/articles/253710/20111122/philip-morris-asia-challenges-australia-s-plan.htm#.U0qnAvmSySo> accessed 3 July 2014.

Giegerich T, 'Article 54' in O Dörr and K Schmalenbach (eds), *Vienna Convention on the Law of Treaties* (Springer 2012) 945–62.

Giegerich T, 'Article 57' in O Dörr and K Schmalenbach (eds), *Vienna Convention on the Law of Treaties* (Springer 2012) 989–95.

Giegerich T, 'Article 62' in O Dörr and K Schmalenbach (eds), *Vienna Convention on the Law of Treaties* (Springer 2012) 1067–104.

Gordon K, 'International Investment Agreements: A Survey of Environmental, Labour and Anti-Corruption Issues' in OECD, *International Investment Law: Understanding Concepts and Tracking Innovations* (OECD 2008) 135–240.

Gordon K and J Pohl, 'Environmental Concerns in International Investment Agreements: A Survey' 2011/1 OECD Working Papers on International Investment, <www.oecd.org/dataoecd/50/12/48083618> accessed 16 December 2014.

Gray C, 'The Different Forms of Reparation: Restitution' in J Crawford, A Pellet, and S Olleson (eds), *The Law of International Responsibility* (OUP 2010) 589–97.

Green P, 'Czech Republic Pays $355 Million to Media Concern' *The New York Times* (16 May 2003) <www.nytimes.com/2003/05/16/business/czech-republic-pays-355-million-to-media-concern.html> accessed 28 February 2014.

Greierson-Weiler TJ and IA Laird, 'Standards of Treatment' in P Muchlinski, F Ortino, and C Schreuer (eds), *The Oxford Handbook of International Investment Law* (OUP 2008) 259–304.

Grossen J-M, *Les Présomptions en Droit International Public* (Delachaux et Niestlé 1954).

Grotius H, *De jure belli ac pacis libri tres* (Editio nova Hein 1995).

Group of Eight, 'Responsible Leadership for A Sustainable Future' <www.g8italia2009.it/static/G8_Allegato/G8_Declaration_08_07_09_final,0.pdf> accessed 27 April 2015

Group of Twenty, 'G20 Leaders Statement: The Pittsburgh Summit, September 24-25, 2009, Pittsburgh, Annex: Core Values for Sustainable Economic Activity' <www.g20.utoronto.ca/2009/2009communique0925.html#annex> accessed 27 April 2015.

Grynberg R, and V Qalo, 'Labour Standards in US and EU Preferential Trading Arrangements' (2006) 40 J World Trade 619–53.

Guzman AT, 'Why LDCs sign treaties that hurt them: explaining the popularity of BITs' (1998) 38 Va JIL 639–688.

Habermas J, *Die Neue Unübersichtlichkeit* (Suhrkamp 1985).

Habermas J, 'The New Obscurity: The Crisis of the Welfare State and the Exhaustion of Utopian Energies: translated by Phillip Jacobs' (1986) 11 Phil & Soc Criticism 1–18.

Haeri H, 'A Tale of Two Standards: 'Fair and Equitable Treatment' and the Minimum Standard in International Law' (2011) 27 Arb Int 27–46.

Hai Yen T, *The Interpretation of Investment Treaties* (Brill 2014).

Halberstam D, 'Local, global and plural constitutionalism: Europe meets the world' in G de Búrca and JHH Weiler (eds), *The Worlds of European Constitutionalism* (CUP 2012) 150–202.

Hamamoto S and L Nottage, 'Foreign Investment in and out of Japan: Economic Backdrop, Domestic Law, and International Treaty-Based Investor-State Dispute Resolution' (2011) 5 Transn Disp Mgmt <www.transnational-dispute-management.com/article.asp?key=1766> accessed 11 July 2014.

Hamamoto S and L Nottage, 'Japan' in C Brown (ed), *Commentaries on Selected Model Investment Treaties* (OUP 2013).

Hammerl C, *Inländerdiskriminierung* (Duncker & Humblot 1997).

Hamilton JC and M Grando, 'Brazil and the Future of Investment Protections' *Latin Arbitration Law* <www.latinarbitrationlaw.com/brazil-and-the-future-of-investment-protections/> accessed 15 August 2015.

Harrison J, 'The Life and Death of BITs: Legal Issues Concerning Survival Clauses and the Termination of Investment Treaties' (2012) 13 J World Inv & Trade 928–50.

Hart HLA, *The Concept of Law* (2nd edn, OUP/Clarendon Press 1994).

Hawkes J, *The Fourth Pillar of Sustainability—Culture's Essential Role in Public Planning* (Cultural Development Network 2001).

Helfer LR, 'Exiting Treaties' (2005) 91 Va L Rev 1579–1648.

Helfer LR, 'Terminating Treaties' in DB Hollis (ed), *The Oxford Guide to Treaties* (OUP 2012) 634–49.

Henckels C, 'Balancing Investment Protection and the Public Interest: The Role of the Standard of Review and the Importance of Deference in Investor-State Arbitration' (2013) 4 JIDS 197–215.

Hepburn J and LE Peterson, 'U.S.-Ecuador Inter-State Investment Treaty Award, Released to Parties; Tribunal Members Part Ways on Key Issues' *Investment Arbitration Reporter* (30 October 2012) <www.iareporter.com/articles/20121030_1> accessed 1 September 2014.

Hindelang S, 'Der primärrechtliche Rahmen einer EU Investitionsschutzpolitik: Zulässigke it und Grenzen von Investor-Staat-Schiedsverfahren aufgrund künftiger EU Abkommen' (2010) WHI Paper 01/11, 17 <www.whi-berlin.eu/tl_files/documents/whi-paper0111.pdf> accessed 17 February 2015.

Hindelang S, 'Restitution and Compensation—Reconstructing the Relationship in Investment Treaty Law' in R Hofmann and C Tams (eds), *International Investment Law and General International Law—From Clinical Isolation to Systemic Integration?* (Nomos 2011) 161–99.

Hindelang S, 'Circumventing Primacy of EU Law and the CJEU's Judicial Monopoly by Resorting to Dispute Resolution Mechanisms Provided for in Inter-se Treaties? The Case of Intra-EU Investment Arbitration' (2012) 39 LIEI 179–206.

Hindelang S, 'The Autonomy of the European Legal Order—EU Constitutional Limits to Investor-State Arbitration on the Basis of Future EU- Investment-related Agreements' in

M Bungenberg and C Herrmann (eds), *Common Commercial Policy 'After Lisbon', Special Issue of the European Yearbook of International Economic Law* (Springer 2013) 187–98.

Hindelang S, 'Study on Investor-State Dispute Settlement ('ISDS') and Alternatives of Dispute Resolution in International Investment Law' in EU Directorate-General for External Policies, *Investor-State Dispute Settlement (ISDS) Provisions in the EU's International Investment Agreements* (European Parliament 2014) <http://ssrn.com/abstract=2525063> accessed 17 February 2015.

Hindelang S, *Stellungnahme, Öffentliche Anhörung des Ausschusses für Wirtschaft und Energie des Deutschen Bundestages zum Comprehensive Economic and Trade Agreement ('CETA') zwischen der EU und Kanada* <https://www.bundestag.de/blob/345496/2f9d17704429c70693d11e18755bbc3b/steffen-hindelang--fu-berlin-data.pdf> accessed 23 April 2015.

Hindelang S and S Wernicke (eds), 'Outlines of Modern Investment Protection—Harnack-Haus Reflections (2015)', available at <http://tinyurl.com/ofzq7k3> accessed 1 October 2015.

Hirsch M, 'Investment tribunals and human rights treaties: a sociological perspective' in F Baetens (ed), *Investment Law within International Law—Integrationist Perspectives* (CUP 2013) 85–105.

Hodgson M, 'Counting the costs of investment treaty arbitration' (2014) 9(2) Global Arb Rev.

Hoffmann A, 'Indirect Expropriation' in August Reinisch (ed), *Standards of Protection in International Investment Law* (OUP 2008) 151–70.

Hoffmeister F, 'The Contribution of EU Practice to International Law' in M Cremona (ed), *Developments in EU External Relations Law* (OUP 2008) 37–127.

Hoffmeister F, 'Litigating Against the European Union and Its Member States—Who responds under the ILC's Draft Articles on International Responsibility of International Organisations?' (2010) 21 EJIL 723–47.

Hoffmeister F, 'Der Beitrag der EU zur Entwicklung des besonderen Völkerrechts' in W Obwexer (ed), *Die Europäische Union im Völkerrecht, Europarecht Beiheft 2/2012* (Nomos 2012) 247–62.

Hoffmeister F and G Alexandru, 'A First Glimpse of Light on the Emerging Invisible EU Model BIT' (2014) 15 J World Inv & Trade 379–402.

Hoffmeister F and G Unuvar, 'From BITS and Pieces towards European Investment Agreements' in: M Bungenberg, A Reinisch, and C Tietje, *EU and Investment Agreements* (Nomos 2013) 57–85.

Hoffmeister F 'Wider die German Angst–Ein Plädoyer für die transatlantische Handels- und Investitionspartnerschaft (TTIP)' (2015) 53 AVR 35–67.

Hofmann B, *Beendigung menschenrechtlicher Verträge* (Berliner Wissenschafts-Verlag 2009).

Hofmann R and C Tams, 'International Investment Law: Situating an Exotic Special Regime within the Framework of International Law' in R Hofmann and C Tams (eds), *International Investment Law and General International Law: From Clinical Isolation to Systemic Integration?* (Nomos 2011) 9–16.

Horn N (ed), *Arbitrating Foreign Investment Disputes* (Kluwer 2004).

Horspool M, and M Humphreys, *European Union Law* (7th edn OUP 2012).

International Centre for Settlement of Investment Disputes Secretariat, 'Possible Improvements of the Framework for ICSID Arbitration' (2004) ICSID Secretariat Discussion Paper <https://icsid.worldbank.org/apps/ICSIDWEB/resources/Documents/Possible%20Improvements%20of%20the%20Framework%20of%20ICSID%20Arbitration.pdf> accessed 23 March 2015.

International Centre for Settlement of Investment Disputes Secretariat 'Suggested Changes to the ICSID Rules and Regulations' (2005) Working Paper of the ICSID Secretariat

<https://icsid.worldbank.org/apps/ICSIDWEB/resources/Documents/Suggested%20 Changes%20to%20the%20ICSID%20Rules%20and%20Regulations.pdf> accessed 23 March 2015.

International Centre for Settlement of Investment Disputes Secretariat 'Caseload—Statistics 2014-1' <https://icsid.worldbank.org/ICSID/FrontServlet#> accessed 15 July 2015.

International Monetary Fund, 'Looming Ahead. Five Nobel Prize winners discuss what they each see as the biggest problem facing the global economy of the future' (September 2014) 51 Finance & Development 14–19.

International Chamber of Commerce, *ICC Guidelines for International Investment* (2012).

International Finance Corporation and the World Bank, 'Economy Rankings' *Doing Business* (June 2013) <www.doingbusiness.org/rankings> accessed 11 July 2014.

International Finance Corporation, *Guide to Human Rights Impact Assessment and Management (HRIAM)* available at <www.ifc.org/wps/wcm/connect/8ecd35004c 0cb230884bc9ec6f601fe4/hriam-guide-092011.pdf?MOD= AJPERES> accessed 12 November 2014.

International Institute for Sustainable Development, *Model International Agreement on Investment for Sustainable Development. Negotiators Handbook* (2nd edn, IISD 2005, revised 2006), available at: www.iisd.org/pdf/2005/investment_model_int_agreement. pdf accessed 12 November 2014.

International Institute for Sustainable Development, the Ministry of Foreign Affairs for Indonesia and the South Centre, 'Seventh Annual Forum of Developing Countries Investment Negotiators, Jakarta, 4–6 November 2013' <www.iisd.org/pdf/2013/7th_ annual_forum_report.pdf> accessed 11 July 2014.

International Labour Organization, *Social Dimensions of Free Trade Agreements* (ILO 2013).

International Law Association, 'Declaration of Principles of International Law Relating to Sustainable Development, 2 April 2002' (2002) 2 International Environmental Agreements: Politics, Law and Economics 211–16.

International Law Commission, 'Draft Articles on the Law of Treaties with Commentaries' (1966) vol II YBILC.

International Law Commission, *Yearbook of the International Law Commission 1966, vol II*, UN Doc. A/CN.4/SER.A/1966/Add.1.

International Law Commission, *Conclusion of the Work of the Study Group on Fragmentation of International Law: Difficulties Arising from the Diversification and Expansion of International Law* (United Nations 2006).

International Law Commission, 'Report of the International Law Commission on the Work of its 58th Session' (2006) UN Doc A/61/10.

International Law Commission, 'Report of the Study Group on Fragmentation of International Law: Difficulties Arising from the Diversification and Expansion of International Law', finalized by Martii Koskenniemi (13 April 2006) UN Doc A/CN.4/L.682.

Jackson JH, *The Jurisprudence of GATT and the WTO: Insights on Treaty Law and Economic Relations* (CUP 2000).

Jackson RH, *Quasi-States: Sovereignty, International Relations and the Third World* (CUP 1990).

Janda M, 'Investment Threshold Lifted above $1b under Korea—Australia FTA' *ABC News* (17 February 2014) <www.abc.net.au/news/2014-02-17/government-releases-details-of-korea-australia-fta/5264840> accessed 11 July 2014.

Jenkins BW, 'The Next Generation of Chilling Uncertainty: Indirect Expropriation Under CAFTA and Its Potential Impact on Environmental Protection' (2007) 12 (2) Ocean and Coastal LJ 269–304.

Jennings R and A Watts (eds), *Oppenheim's International Law, Volume I* (9th edn, Longman 1992).
Jennings R and A Watts (eds), *Oppenheim's International Law: Volume 1 Peace* (OUP 1992).
Johnson L and L Sachs, 'International Investment Agreements, 2011-2012: A Review of Trends and New Approaches' in AK Bjorklund (ed), *Yearbook on International Investment Law & Policy 2012-2013* (OUP 2014) 219–62.
Jin B, F Garcia, and R Salomon, 'Do Host Countries Really Benefit from Inward Foreign Direct Investment?' (2013) 98 Columbia FDI Perspectives 1–3.
Joint Communication of the European Commission and the High Representative of the European Union for Foreign Affairs and Security Policy, COM (2011) 886 final (12 December 2011).
Joubin-Bret A and JE Kalicki 'Introduction TDM Special issue on 'Reform of Investor-State Dispute Settlement: In Search of a Roadmap" (January 2014)
Juwana H, 'Indonesia Should Withdraw from the ICSID Now!' *Jakarta Post* (2 April 2014) <www.thejakartapost.com/news/2014/04/02/indonesia-should-withdraw-icsid.html> accessed 11 July 2014.
Kahn P and TW Walde (eds), *New Aspects of International Investment Law* (Martinus Nijhoff 2007).
Kantor M, 'The Transparency Agenda for UNCITRAL Investment Arbitrations Looking in all the Wrong Places' (2011) <www.iilj.org/research/documents/IF2010-11.Kantor.pdf> accessed 8 March 2015.
Karamanian S, 'The Place of Human Rights in Investor-State Arbitration' (2013) 17 Lewis & Clark L Rev 423–47.
Katz Cogan J, 'Competition and Control in International Adjudication' (2009) 48 Va JIL 411–49.
Kaufmann-Kohler G, 'In Search of Transparency and Consistency: ICSID reform proposal' (2005) 2 Trans Disp Mgmt 1–8.
Kaufmann-Kohler G, 'Interpretative Powers of the Free Trade Commission and the Rule of Law' in E Gaillard and F Bachand (eds), *Fifteen Years of NAFTA Chapter 11 Arbitration* (Juris 2011).
Kaushal A, 'Revisiting History: How the Past Matters for the Present Backlash Against the Foreign Investment Regime' (2009) 50 Harv ILJ 491–534.
Kelsen H, 'Unrecht und Unrechtsfolge im Völkerrecht' (1932) 12 ZöR 481–608.
Kenner J, 'Economic Partnership Agreements: Enhancing the Labour Dimension of Global Governance?' in: B Van Vooren, S Blockmans, and J Wouters (eds) *The EU's Role in Global Governance. The Legal Dimension* (OUP 2013) 306–21.
Kenny M and P Wen, 'Japan, Korea and Now a Free Trade Deal with China Is in Sight' *Sydney Morning Herald* (10 April 2014) <www.smh.com.au/federal-politics/political-news/japan-korea-and-now-a-free-trade-deal-with-china-is-in-sight-20140409-36djp.html> (11 April 2014).
Khalil MI, 'Treatment of Foreign Investment in Bilateral Investment Treaties' (1992) 8 ICSID Rev 339–383.
Kingsbury B, 'International Law as Inter-Public Law' in HS Richardson and MS Williams (eds), *Moral Universalism and Pluralism* (New York University Press 2009) 167–204.
Kingsbury B and SW Schill, 'Investor–State Arbitration as Governance: Fair and Equitable Treatment, Proportionality and the Emerging Global Administrative Law' (2009) New York University School of Law Institute for International Law and Justice, Working Paper 2009/6.
Kingsbury B and SW Schill, 'Public Law Concepts to Balance Investors' Rights with State Regulatory Action in the Public Interest—The Concept of Proportionality' in SW Schill (ed), *International Investment Law and Comparative Public Law* (OUP 2010) 75–104.

Kiss A, 'Abuse of Rights' in R Wolfrum (ed), *Max Planck Encyclopedia of Public International Law* (December 2006) <www.mpepil.com/> accessed 11 November 2014.

Kjos H, *Applicable Law in Investor-State Arbitration: The Interplay between National and International Law* (OUP 2013).

Klabbers J, *International Law* (CUP 2013).

Kläger R, *Fair and Equitable Treatment in International Investment Law* (CUP 2011).

Kläger R, 'Fair and Equitable Treatment' and Sustainable Development', in: M-C Cordonier Segger, M Gehring, and A Newcombe (eds), *Sustainable Development in World Investment Law* (Kluwer 2011) 237–259.

Klein E, 'Denunciation of Human Rights Treaties and the Principle of Reciprocity' in U Fastenrath and others (eds), *From Bilateralism to Community Interest—Essays in Honour of Judge Bruno Simma* (OUP 2011) 477–87.

Kleinheisterkamp J, *International Commercial Arbitration in Latin America* (OUP 2005).

Kleinheisterkamp J, 'Financial Responsibility in the European International Investment Policy', (2013) LSE Law, Society and Economy Working Papers 15/2013 <www.lse.ac.uk/collections/law/wps/WPS2013-15_Kleinheisterkamp.pdf> accessed 17 February 2015.

Kohen MG and S Heathcote, 'Article 42 Convention of 1969' in O Corten and P Klein (eds), *The Vienna Convention on the Law of Treaties*, vol II (OUP 2011) 1015–28.

Kolo A and TW Wälde, 'Renegotiation and Contract Adaption in International Investment Projects: Applicable Legal Principles and Industry Practices' (2000) 1 J World Inv 5–57.

Koskenniemi M, *From Apology to Utopia* (CUP 2005).

Koskenniemi M, 'The Politics of International Law—20 Years Later' (2009) 20 EJIL 7–19.

Kotzur M, 'Good Faith (Bona fide)' in R Wolfrum (ed), *Max Planck Encyclopedia of Public International Law* (January 2009) paras 22 and 24 <www.mpepil.com/> accessed 11 November 2014.

Krajewski M, *Anmerkungen zum Gutachten von Dr. Stephan Schill zu den Auswirkungen der Bestimmungen zum Investitionsschutz und zu den Investor-Staat-Schiedsverfahren im Entwurf des CETA auf den Handlungsspielraum des Gesetzgebers vom 22.9.2014* <www.gruene-bundestag.de/fileadmin/media/gruenebundestag_de/themen_az/EU-USA_Freihandelsabkommen/Thesenpapier_Klageprivilegien_in_CETA.PDF> accessed 5 February 2015.

Krajewski M and J Ceyssens, 'Internationaler Investitionsschutz und innerstaatliche Regulierung' (2007) 45 AVR 180–216.

Krajewski M, *Modell-Investitionsschutzvertrag mit Investor-Staat-Schiedsverfahren für Industriestaaten unter Berücksichtigung der USA* (German Federal Ministry for Economic Affairs and Energy 2015) <www.bmwi.de/BMWi/Redaktion/PDF/M-O/modell-investitionsschutzvertrag-mit-investor-staat-schiedsverfahren-gutachten,property=pdf,bereich=bmwi2012,sprache=de,rwb=true.pdf> accessed 19 August 2015.

Kriebaum U, 'Regulatory Takings: Balancing the Interests of the Investor and the State' (2007) 8 J World Inv & Trade 717–44.

Kriebaum U, *Eigentumsschutz im Völkerrecht: Eine vergleichende Untersuchung zum internationalen Investitionsrecht sowie zum Menschenrechtsschutz* (Duncker & Humblot 2008).

Kriebaum U, 'Restitution in International Investment Law' in R Hofmann and C Tams (eds), *International Investment Law and General International Law—From Clinical Isolation to Systemic Integration?* (Nomos 2011) 201–10.

Kriebaum U, 'Expropriation' in M Bungenberg, J Gabriel, S Hobe, A Reinisch (eds), *International Investment Law* (Nomos 2015) 959–1030.

Kröll S, 'The Renegotiation and Adaption of Investment Contracts', in N Horn (ed), *Arbitrating Foreign Investment Disputes* (Kluwer 2004) 425–70.

Kuijper PJ and others (eds), *The Law of External Relations, Cases, Materials and Commentary on the EU as an International Actor* (OUP 2013).

Kuijper PJ and others (eds) 'Part I: Study on Investment Protection Agreements as Instruments of International Economic Law', in *European Parliament, Directorate General for External Policies of the Union, Study Investor-State Dispute Settlement (ISDS) Provisions in the EU's International Investment Agreements* (European Commission 2014) <www.jura.fu-berlin.de/fachbereich/einrichtungen/oeffentliches-recht/lehrende/hindelangs/Studie-fuer-Europaeisches-Parlament/Volume-2-Studies.pdf> accessed 24 April 2015.

Kulick A, *Global Public Interest in International Investment Law* (CUP 2012).

Kurtz J, 'Australia's Rejection of Investor–State Arbitration: Causation, Omission and Implication' (2012) 27 ICSID Rev 65–86.

Lang J, 'Bilateral Investment Treaties—A Shield or a Sword?' *Bowman Gilfillan Corporate Newsflash* <www.bowman.co.za/FileBrowser/ArticleDocuments/South-African-Government-Canceling-Bilateral-Investment-Treaties.pdf> accessed 3 July 2014.

Lauterpacht E, *Aspects of the Administration of International Justice* (CUP 1991).

Lauterpacht E, 'International Law and Private Foreign Investment' (1997) 4 Ind J Global Legal Studies 259–76.

Lavopa FM, LE Barreiros, and M Victoria Bruno, 'How to Kill a BIT and not Die Trying: Legal and Political Challenges of Denouncing or Renegotiating Bilateral Investment Treaties' (2013) 16 J Intl Econ L 869–91.

Lavranos N, 'The Remaining Decisive Role of Member States in Negotiating and Concluding EU Investment Agreement' in: M Bungenberg, A Reinisch, and C Tietje, *EU and Investment Agreements* (Nomos 2013) 165–68.

Leach M, 'Culture and Sustainability' in UNESCO (ed), *World Culture Report 1998—Culture, Creativity and Markets* (UNESCO Pub 1998) 93–104.

Leal-Arcas R, *International Trade And Investment Law: Multilateral, Regional and Bilateral Governance* (Edward Elgar 2011).

Legg A, The Margin of Appreciation in International Human Rights Law (OUP 2012).

Legum B, 'Options to Establish an Appellate Mechanism for Investment Disputes' in K Sauvant (ed), *Appeals Mechanism in International Investment Disputes* (OUP 2008) 231–40.

Legum B and I Petculescu, 'GATT Art. XX and International Investment Law' in A de Mestral and C Levesque (eds), *Improving International Investment Agreements* (Routledge 2013) 340–62.

Lekkas S-I and A Tzanakopoulos, '*Pacta sunt servanda* versus Flexibility in the Suspension and Termination of Treaties' in C Tams, A Tzanakopoulos and A Zimmermann (eds), *Research Handbook on the Law of Treaties* (Edward Elgar 2014) 312–40.

Leon P, J Veeran and E Warmington, 'South Africa Declines to Renew Bilateral Investment Treaties with European Union Member States' *Mondaq* (5 October 2012) <www.mondaq.com/x/199586/international+trade+investment/South+Africa+Declines+To+Renew+Bilateral+Investment+Treaties+With+European+Union+Member+States> accessed 2 July 2014.

Letter for the Swiss Secretariat for Economic Affairs to the ICSID Deputy Secretary-General of 1 October 2003, Mealey's International Arbitration Reports (February 2003).

Lévesque C and A Newcombe, 'Canada', in C Brown (ed), *Commentaries on Selected Model Investment Treaties* (OUP 2013) 53–130.

Levine E, '*Amicus Curiae* in International Investment Arbitration: The Implications of an Increase in Third-Party Participation' (2012) 29 Berkeley J Intl L 200–224.
Lewis MK, 'The Trans-Pacific Partnership: New Paradigm or Wolf in Sheep's Clothing?' (2011) 34 Boston College Intl & Comp L Rev 27–52.
Linderfalk U, *On the Interpretation of Treaties* (Springer 2007).
Linderfalk U, 'State Responsibility and the Primary-Secondary Rules Terminology: The Role of Language for an Understanding of the International Legal System' (2009) 78 Nordic JIL 53–72.
Lipson C, *Standing Guard: Protecting Foreign Capital in the Nineteenth and Twentieth Centuries* (University of California Press 1985).
Loughlin M, 'What is Constitutionalisation?' in P Dobner and M Loughlin (eds), *The Twilight of Constitutionalism?* (OUP 2010) 47–72.
Lowe V, 'Sustainable Development and Unsustainable Arguments' in A Boyle and D Freestone (eds), *International Law and Sustainable Development: Past Achievements and Future Challenges* (OUP 1999) 19–38.
Lowenfeld A, *International Economic Law* (2nd edn, OUP 2008).
Luque Macias MJ, 'Current Approaches to the International Investment Regime in South America' in C Herrmann, M Krajewski, and JP Terhechte (eds.) *European Yearbook of International Economic Law 2014* (Springer 2013) 285–308.
Mahoney P, 'The International Judiciary: Independence and Accountability' (2008) 7 The Law and Practice of International Courts and Tribunals 313–49.
Malik M, 'IISD Model International Agreement on Investment for Sustainable Development' in M-C Cordonier Segger, M Gehring, and A Newcombe (eds), *Sustainable Development in World Investment Law* (Kluwer Law International 2011) 561–84.
Maniruzzaman AFM, 'The pursuit of stability in international energy investment contracts: A critical appraisal of the emerging trends' (2008) 1 J W E L & B 121–157.
Mann H, 'Reconceptualizing International Investment Law: Its Role in Sustainable Development' (2013) 17 Lewis & Clark L Rev 521–544.
Mann H and K von Moltke, *NAFTA's Chapter 11 and the Environment* (International Institute for Sustainable Development 2006).
Marais J, 'South Africa pays dearly after scrapping trade treaties' *Business Day* (21 July 2013) <www.bdlive.co.za/business/trade/2013/07/21/south-africa-pays-dearly-after-scrapping-trade-treaties> accessed 6 July 2014.
Marboe I, 'State Responsibility and Comparative State Liability for Administrative and Legislative Harm to Economic Interests' in SW Schill (ed), *International Investment Law and Comparative Public Law* (OUP 2010) 377–412.
Marboe I, 'The System of Reparation and Questions of Terminology' in M Bungenberg, J Gabriel, S Hobe, A Reinisch (eds), *International Investment Law* (Nomos 2015) 1031–44.
Mariani P, 'The Future of BITs between EU Member States: Are Intra-EU BITs Compatible with the Internal Market?' in G Sacerdoti and others (ed), *General Interests of Host States in International Investment Law* (CUP 2014) 265–86.
Markert L, 'The Crucial Question of Future Investment Treaties: Balancing Investor's Rights and Regulatory Interests of Host States' in M Bungenberg, J Griebel, and S Hindelang (eds), *International Investment Law and EU Law* (Nomos 2011) 145–71.
Marlles J, 'Public Purpose, Private Losses: Regulatory Expropriation and Environmental Regulation in International Investment Law' (2007) 16 J Transnatl L & Poly 275–336.
Martin P, 'Free Trading Cards Laid on the Table, but Beware the Ace Up the Sleeve' *Sydney Morning Herald* (9 April 2014) <www.smh.com.au/business/free-trading-

cards-laid-on-the-table-but-beware-the-ace-up-the-sleeve-20140408-36b6v.html> accessed 11 July 2014.

Martin P, 'ISDS: The Trap that Australia–Japan Free Trade Agreement Escaped' *Sydney Morning Herald* (10 April 2014) <www.smh.com.au/federal-politics/political-opinion/isds-the-trap-the-australiajapan-free-trade-agreement-escaped-20140407-zqrwk.html> accessed 11 July 2014.

McDonagh T, *Unfair, Unsustainable and Under the Radar—How Corporations use Global Investment Rules to Undermine a Sustainable Future* (The Democracy Center 2013) <http://democracyctr.org/wp/wp-content/uploads/2013/05/Under_The_Radar_English_Final.pdf> accessed 23 April 2015.

McKenzie R, K Malleson, P Martin, and P Sands, *Selecting International Judges: Principles, Process, and Politics* (OUP 2010).

McLachlan C, 'The Principle of Systemic Integration and Article 31(3)(c) of the Vienna Convention' (2005) 54 ICLQ 279–320.

McLachlan C, 'Investment Treaties and General International Law' (2008) 57 ICLQ 361–401.

McLachlan C, L Shore, and M Weiniger, *International Investment Arbitration: Substantive Principles* (OUP 2007).

McNair AD, 'The General Principles of Law as Recognized by Civilized Nations' (1957) 33 British Ybk IL.

McNair AD, *The Law of Treaties* (OUP 1961).

McRae P, 'The Search for Meaning: Continuing Problems with the Interpretation of Treaties' (2002) 33 Victoria U Wellington L Rev 209–260.

MERCOSUR, Tratados, Protocolos y Acuerdos <www.mercosur.int/t_ligaenmarco.jsp?contentid=4823&site=1&channel=secretaria>.

Meschede K, *Die Schutzwirkung von umbrella clauses für Investor-Staat-Verträge* (Nomos 2014).

Meyer T, 'Power, Exit Costs, and Renegotiation in International Law' (2010) 51 Harv ILJ 379–425.

Miles K, 'Reconceptualising International Investment Law: Bringing the Public Interest into Private Business' in M Kolsky Lewis and S Frankel (eds), *International Economic Law and National Autonomy* (CUP 2010) 295–319.

Mills A, 'The Balancing (and Unbalancing?) of Interests in International Investment Law and Arbitration' in Z Douglas, J Pauwelyn and JE Viñuales (eds), *The Foundations of International Investment Law* (OUP 2014) 437–466.

Ministério do Desenvolvimento, Indústria e Comércio Exterior (Brasil), Cooperation and Facilitation Investment Agreement (CFIA), Presentation at the UNCTAD World Investment Forum 2015, <http://unctad-worldinvestmentforum.org/wp-content/uploads/2015/03/Brazil_side-event-Wednesday_model-agreements.pdf> accessed 24 April 2015.

Ministerio de Relaciones Exteriores y Movilidad Humana (Ecuador) 'UNASUR analiza la creación del Centro de Solución de Controversias en Materia de Inversiones' (18 March 2014) <http://cancilleria.gob.ec/unasur-analiza-la-creacion-del-centro-de-solucion-de-controversias-en-materia-de-inversiones/> accessed 1 September 2014.

Ministerio de Relaciones Exteriores y Movilidad Humana (Ecuador) 'Latinoamérica avanza en la creación de un Observatorio del Sur de Transnacionales' (6 May 2014) <http://cancilleria.gob.ec/es/latinoamerica-avanza-en-la-creacion-de-un-observatorio-del-sur-de-transnacionales/> accessed 1 September 2014.

Ministerio de Relaciones Exteriores y Movilidad Humana (Ecuador) 'Representantes de Unasur analizan proyecto de Acuerdo Constitutivo del Centro de Solución de Controversias en Materia de Inversiones de UNASUR' (22 August 2014) <http://cancilleria.gob.ec/representantes-de-unasur-analizan-proyecto-de-acuerdo-constitutivo-del-centro-de-solucion-de-controversias-en-materia-de-inversiones-de-unasur/> accessed 1 September 2014.

Mitchell AD and SM Wurzberger, 'Boxed in? Australia's Plain Tobacco Packaging Initiative and International Investment Law' (2011) 27 Arb Int 623–52.

Möller KH, *Echte Schiedsgerichtsbarkeit im Verwaltungsrecht: Eine Studie zu Rechtsrahmen und Kontrolle nichtstaatlicher Streitentscheidung im Verwaltungsrecht* (Duncker & Humblot 2014).

Montt S, 'What International Investment Law and Latin America Can and Should Demand from Each Other: Updating the Bell/Calvo Doctrine in the BIT Generation' (2007) <www.iilj.org/gal/documents/SantiagoMontt.GAL.pdf> accessed 17 February 2015.

Moran TH, EM Graham, and M Blomstrom (eds), *Does Foreign Direct Investment Promote Development?* (IIE 2005).

Muchlinski P, '"Caveat Investor"? The Relevance of the Conduct of the Investor Under the Fair and Equitable Treatment Standard' (2006) 55 ICLQ 527–58.

Muchlinski P, *Multinational Enterprises and the Law* (2nd edn, OUP 2007).

Muchlinski P, 'Holistic Approaches to Development and International Investment Law: the Role of International Investment Agreements' in J Faundez and C Tan (eds), *International Economic Law, Globalization and Developing Countries* (Edward Elgar 2010) 180–204.

Muchlinski P, 'Corporations and the Uses of Law: International Investment Arbitration as a "Multilateral Legal Order"' (2011) Oñati Socio-Legal Series 1 (4) <http://papers.ssrn.com/sol3/papers.cfm?abstract_id=1832562##> accessed 21 August 2015.

Muchlinski P, 'Implementing the New UN Corporate Human Rights Framework: Implications for Corporate Law, Governance and Regulation' (2012) 22(1) Bus Ethics Q 145–77.

Muchlinski P, 'The Role of Preferential Trade and Investment Agreements in International Investment Law: From Unforeseen Historical Developments to Uncertain Future' in R Hofman, SW Schill, and C Tams (eds), *Preferential Trade and Investment Agreements: From Recalibration to Reintegration* (Nomos 2013).

Muchlinski P, 'Towards a Coherent International Investment System: Key Issues in the Reform of International Investment Law' in R Echandi and P Suave (eds), *Prospects in International Investment Law and Policy: World Trade Forum* (CUP 2013) 411–42.

Muchlinski P, F Ortino, and C Schreuer (eds), *Oxford Handbook of International Investment Law* (OUP 2008).

Muchlinski P and V Rouas, 'Foreign Direct-Liability Litigation Toward the Transnationalisation of Corporate Legal Responsibility' in L Blecher, NK Stafford, and GC Bellamy (eds), *Corporate Responsibility for Human Rights Impacts: New Expectations and Paradigms* (ABA Chicago 2014) 357–92.

Murphy K, 'Tony Abbott Goes to China "to Be a Friend", Not to Chase Deals' *The Guardian* (10 April 2014) <www.theguardian.com/world/2014/apr/10/tony-abbott-goes-to-china-to-be-friend-not-chase-deals> accessed 11 July 2014.

Murphy K, 'Tony Abbott Says China's State-Owned Enterprises Are Welcome in Australia' *The Guardian* (11 April 2014) <www.theguardian.com/world/2014/apr/11/abbott-says-chinas-state-owned-enterprises-welcome> accessed 11 July 2014.

NAFTA Free Trade Commission (NAFTA FTC), 'Notes of Interpretation of Certain Chapter 11 Provisions' (31 July 2001) <www.international.gc.ca/trade-

agreements-accords-commerciaux/topics-domaines/disp-diff/NAFTA-Interpr.aspx> accessed 4 October 2014.

NAFTA Free Trade Commission, 'Joint Statement on the Decade of Achievement', 16 July 2004.

Naldi GJ, 'The Asean Protocol on Dispute Settlement Mechanisms: An Appraisal' (2014) 5 JIDS 105–38.

Netherlands Embassy in Jakarta, Indonesia, 'Termination Bilateral Investment Treaty' <http://indonesia.nlembassy.org/organization/departments/economic-affairs/termination-bilateral-investment-treaty.html> accessed 11 July 2014.

Newcombe A, 'The Boundaries of Regulatory Expropriation in International Investment Law' (2005) 20 ICSID Rev 1–57.

Newcombe A, 'Sustainable Development and Investment Treaty Law' (2008) 8 J World Inv & Tr 357–407.

Newcombe A, 'An Integrated Agenda for Sustainable Development in International Law' in M-C Cordonier Segger, M Gehrig, and A Newcombe (eds) *Sustainable Development in World Investment Law* (Kluwer 2011) 99–142.

Newcombe A, 'General Exceptions in International Investment Agreements' in M-C Cordonier Segger, M Gehring, and A Newcombe (eds), *Sustainable Development in World Investment Law* (Wolters Kluwer 2012) 351–70.

Newcombe A and L Paradell, *Law and Practice of Investment Treaties: Standards of Treatment* (Kluwer 2009).

Nollkaemper A, 'The Power of Secondary Rules to Connect the International and National Legal Orders' in T Broude and Y Shany (eds), *Multi-Sourced Equivalent Norms in International Law* (Hart 2011) 45–68.

Nolte G, 'From Dionisio Anzilotti to Roberto Ago: The Classical International Law of State Responsibility and Traditional Primacy of a Bilateral Conception of Inter-State Relations' (2002) 13 EJIL 1083–1098.

Nolte G, 'Sovereignty as Responsibility?' (2005) 99 ASIL Proc 389–92.

Nolte G, 'Second Report for the ILC Study Group on Treaties over Time—Jurisprudence under Special Regimes relating to Subsequent Agreements and Subsequent Practice' (23 May 2011) UN Doc ILC(LXIII)/SG/TOT/INFORMAL/1.

Nottage L, 'Investor-State Arbitration Policy and Practice after *Philip Morris Asia v Australia*' in LE Trakman and N Ranieri (eds), *Regionalism in International Investment Law* (OUP 2013) 452–74.

Nottage L, 'Throwing the Baby Out with the Bathwater: Australia's New Policy on Treaty-Based Arbitration and its Impact in Asia' (2013) 37 Asian Stud Rev 253–72.

Nottage L, 'Investor–State Arbitration: Not in the Australia–Japan Free Trade Agreement, and Not Ever for Australia?' (2014) 19 J Japanese L 37–52.

Nottage L and R Weeramantry, 'Investment Arbitration in Asia: Five Perspectives on Law and Practice' (2012) 28(1) Arb Int 19–62.

Nowrot K, *International Investment Law and the Republic of Ecuador: From Arbitral Bilateralism to Judicial Regionalism* (MLU Institut für Wirtschaftsrecht 2010).

Nowrot K, 'How to Include Environmental Protection, Human Rights and Sustainability in International Investment Law' (2014) 15 J World Inv & Trade 612–44.

Nowrot K, 'Standard of Review as a Procedural Issue in WTO Dispute Settlement: Of Balancing Acts and Presumptions of Legality' in J Delbrück and others (eds), *Aus Kiel in die Welt: Kiel's Contribution to International Law—Essays in Honour of the 100th Anniversary of the Walther Schücking Institute for International Law* (Duncker & Humblot 2014) 607–33.

Nurse K, 'Culture as the Fourth Pillar of Sustainable Development' (2006); United Cities and Local Governments, 'Agenda 21 for Culture' (8 May 2004) <www.agenda21culture.net/index.php/documents/agenda-21-for-culture> accessed 15 July 2014.

Odendahl K, 'Article 42' in O Dörr and K Schmalenbach (eds), *Vienna Convention on the Law of Treaties* (Springer 2012) 733–44.

Organisation for Economic Co-operation and Development, *Guidelines for Multinational Enterprises* (OECD 2011) <www.oecd.org/daf/inv/mne/48004323.pdf> accessed 24 November 2014.

Organisation for Economic Co-operation and Development, *Guidelines for Multinational Enterprises, National Contact Points* <http://mneguidelines.oecd.org/ncps/> accessed 1 September 2014.

Organisation for Economic Co-operation and Development, Investor-State Dispute Settlement Public Consultation, Comments received as of 30 August 2012, <www.oecd.org/daf/inv/investment-policy/ISDSconsultationcomments_web.pdf> accessed 28 October 2014.

Organisation for Economic Co-operation and Development, 'Official Development Assistance 2013' <www.oecd.org/statistics/datalab/oda2012.htm> accessed 5 November 2014.

Organisation for Economic Co-operation and Development, Informal Ministerial Meeting on Responsible Business Conduct, 'Investment treaty law, sustainable development and responsible business conduct: A fact finding survey' (26 June 2014) available at <www.oecd.org/investment/2014RBCMinisterial-TreatyRBC.pdf> accessed 12 November 2014.

Office of the United States Trade Representative, 'The Facts on Investor-State Dispute Settlement: Safeguarding the Public Interest and Protecting Investors' (27 March 2014) <www.ustr.gov/about-us/press-office/blog/2014/March/Facts-Investor-State%20Dispute-Settlement-Safeguarding-Public-Interest-Protecting-Investors> accessed 11 July 2014.

Official Records of the United Nations Conference on the Law of Treaties, First Session, Summary Records of the Plenary Meetings and of the Meetings of the Committee of the Whole (1969) UN Doc A/CONF.39/11.

Olivet C and P Eberhardt, *Profiting from Injustice: How Law Firms, Arbitrators and Financiers are Fuelling an Investment Arbitration Boom* (Transnational Institute 2012) <www.tni.org/briefing/profiting-injustice> accessed 1 September 2014.

Orakhelashvili A, *Peremptory Norms in International Law* (OUP 2006).

Orakhelashvili A, 'Principles of Treaty Interpretation in the NAFTA Arbitral Award on Canadian Cattlemen' (2009) 26 J Intl Arb 159–73.

Orellana López A, 'Bolivia Denounces its Bilateral Investment Treaties and Attempts to put an End to the Power of Corporations to Sue the Country in International Tribunals' (June 2014) available under: <http://justinvestment.org/wp-content/uploads/2014/07/Bolivia-denounces-its-Bilateral-Investment-Treaties-and-attempts-to-put-an-end-to-the-Power-of-Corporations-to-sue-the-country-in-International-Tribunals1.pdf> accessed 11 November 2014.

Organization of American States Foreign Trade Information System, 'Trade Policy Developments: Trans Pacific Partnership Agreement (TPP)—Australia, Brunei, Canada, Chile, Malaysia, Mexico, New Zealand, Peru, Singapore, the United States, and Vietnam' (Background and Negotiations) <www.sice.oas.org/TPD/TPP/TPP_e.ASP> accessed 1 September 2014.

Osgoode Hall Law School, 'Public Statement on the International Investment Regime' (31 August 2010) <www.transnational-dispute-management.com/article.asp?key=1657> accessed 23 March 2015.

Pagotto P, 'EU Trade Policy and Labour Standards: The Case of the Free Trade Agreement with Colombia and Peru' (2013) 5 European Ybk on Human Rights 255–70.

Pahuya S, *Decolonising International Law—Development, Economic Growth and the Politics of Universality* (CUP 2011).

Paparinskis M, 'Investment Arbitration and the Law of Countermeasures' (2009) 79 British Ybk IL 264–352.

Paparinskis M, 'Regulatory Expropriation and Sustainable Development', in MC Segger, M Gehring, A Newcombe (eds) *Sustainable Development in World Investment Law* (Wolters Kluwer 2011) 295–328.

Paparinskis M, 'Investment Treaty Arbitration and the (New) Law of State Responsibility' (2013) 24 EJIL 617–47.

Paparinskis M, *The International Minimum Standard* (OUP 2013).

Paparinskis M, 'Analogies and Other Regimes of International Law' in Z Douglas, J Pauwelyn and JE Viñuales (eds), *The Foundations of International Investment Law* (OUP 2014) 73–108.

Park W, 'Arbitrator Integrity' in M Waibel, A Kaushal, K Chung, and C Balchin (eds), *The Backlash against Investment Arbitration* (Kluwer 2010) 189–252.

Parlett K, 'Diplomatic Protection and Investment Arbitration' in R Hofmann and C Tams (eds), *International Investment Law and General International Law—From Clinical Isolation to Systemic Integration?* (Nomos 2011) 211–229.

Parlett K, *The Individual in the International Legal System—Continuity and Change in International Law* (CUP 2011).

Pasquino P, 'Prolegomena to a Theory of Judicial Power' (2003) 2 The Law and Practice of International Courts and Tribunals 11–26.

Pathak S, A Laplume, and E Xavier-Oliviera, 'Inward Foreign Direct Investment: Does it Enable or Constrain Domestic Technology Entrepreneurship?' (2012) 84 Columbia FDI Perspectives 1–4.

Paulsson J, 'Arbitration Without Privity' (1995) 10 ICSID Rev–FILJ 232–57.

Paulsson J, *Denial of Justice in International Law* (CUP 2005).

Paulsson J, 'Enclaves of Justice' (2007) 4 (5)Transn Disp Mgmt.

Paulsson J, 'Moral Hazard in International Dispute Resolution' (2010) 25 ICSID Rev 339–55.

Pauwelyn J, *Conflict of Norms in Public International Law* (CUP 2003).

Pavoni R, 'Environment Rights, Sustainable Development and Investor-State Case Law: A Critical Appraisal' in PM Dupuy, EU Petersmann, and F Francioni (eds), *Human Rights in International Investment Law and Arbitration* (OUP 2009) 525–56.

Peacock N and Ambrose H, 'South Africa terminates its bilateral investment treaty with Spain: second BIT terminated, as part of South Africa's planned review of its investment treaties' (21 August 2013) <www.lexology.com/library/detail.aspx?g=daf93855-71f9-4 25e-92d3-5368d104f8ff> accessed 3 July 2014.

Perfetti A, 'Ensuring the consistency of the EU Investment Policy within the EU External Action: The relevance of non-trade values' in Sacerdoti G and others (eds), *General Interests of Host States in International Investment Law* (CUP 2014) 308–24.

Perkams M, *Internationale Investitionsschutzabkommen im Spannungsfeld zwischen effektivem Investitionsschutz und staatlichem Gemeinwohl* (Nomos 2011).

Pernice I, 'Part III: Study on International Investment Protection Agreements and EU Law', in European Parliament, Directorate General for External Policies of the Union, *Study Investor-State Dispute Settlement (ISDS) Provisions in the EU's International Investment Agreements* (European Commission 2014) <www.

jura.fu-berlin.de/fachbereich/einrichtungen/oeffentliches-recht/lehrende/hindelangs/Studie-fuer-Europaeisches-Parlament/Volume-2-Studies.pdf> accessed 17 February 2015.

Perrone NM, 'La protección de la inversión extranjera, jueces nacionales y proyecto regional: el caso argentino y de la UNASUR', in JM Alvarez, M Grando, H Hestermeyer (eds), *Estado y Futuro del Derecho Económico Internacional en América Latina* (I Conferencia Bianual de la Red Lationamericana de Derecho Económico Internacional, Universidad Exrternado de Colombia).

Peter W, *Arbitration and Renegotiation of International Investment Agreements* (2nd edn, Kluwer 1995).

Peters A, *Jenseits der Menschenrechte—Die Rechtsstellung des Individuums im Völkerrecht* (Mohr Siebeck 2014).

Peterson LE, 'Bilateral Investment Treaties—Implication for Sustainable Development and Options for Regulation: FES Conference Report' *Friedrich Ebert Stiftung* (June 2007) <www.fes-globalization.org/publications/ConferenceReports/FES%20CR%20Berlin_Peterson.pdf> accessed 27 June 2014.

Peterson LE, 'Out of Order' in M Waibel, A Kaushal, K Chung, and C Balchin (eds), *The Backlash against Investment Arbitration* (Kluwer 2010) 483–88.

Peterson LE, 'Czech Republic Terminates Investment Treaties in such a Way as to Cast Doubt on Residual Legal Protection for Existing Investments' *Investment Arbitration Reporter* (1 February 2011).

Philip Morris International News Release, 'Philip Morris Asia Initiates Legal Action Against the Australian Government Over Plain Packaging' (27 June 2011) <www.pmi.com/eng/media_center/press_releases/pages/PM_Asia_plain_packaging.aspx> accessed 11 July 2014.

Pinzler P, 'Extrarechte für Multis—Das Handelsabkommen mit Amerika soll US-Investoren besonders schützen—sogar vor deutschen Gesetzen' 50 *Die Zeit* (Hamburg, 16 December 2013).

Pohl J, 'Temporal Validity of International Investment Agreements' 2013/4 OECD Working Papers on International Investment.

Pohl J, K Mashigo, and A Nohen, 'Dispute Settlement Provisions in International Investment Agreements: A Large Sample Survey' 2012/2 OECD Working Papers on International Investment.

Polanco R, 'Chile's experience with South-South Trade and Investment Agreements' proceedings SIEL Working Paper 2014/26 <http://papers.ssrn.com/sol3/papers.cfm?abstract_id=2474119> accessed 19 December 2014.

Polanco R, 'Is There a Life for Latin American Countries After Denouncing the ICSID Convention?' (2014) 11(1) Transn Disp Mgmt.

Polasek P and R Mellske 'Termination of Bolivia–United States Bilateral Investment Treaty' *Latin Arbitration Law* (31 May 2012) <www.latinarbitrationlaw.com/termination-of-bolivia-united-states-bilateral-investment-treaty/> accessed 1 September 2014.

Portal Brasil, 'Brasil e Angola assinam acordo bilateral' (2 April 2015) <www.brasil.gov.br/governo/2015/04/brasil-e-angola-assinam-acordo-bilateral> accessed 24 April 2015.

Posner E and M de Figueiredo, 'Is the International Court of Justice Biased?' (2005) 34 JLS 599–630.

Potestà M, 'State-to-State Dispute Settlement pursuant to Bilateral Investment Treaties: Is there Potential?' in N Boschiero and T Scovarazzi (eds), *International Courts and the Development of International Law—Essays in Honour of Tullio Treves* (TMC Asser Press 2012) 753–68.

Prislan V, 'Non-investment obligations in investment treaty arbitration: a greater role for States' in F Baetens F (ed), *Investment Law within International Law—Integrationist Perspectives* (CUP 2013) 450–81.

Prislan V and R Zandvliet, 'Labor Provisions in International Investment Agreements: Prospects for Sustainable Development' (2013) 2012/2013 Yearbook of International Investment Law and Policy <http://ssrn.com/abstract=2171716 orhttp://dx.doi.org/10.2139/ssrn.2171716> accessed 17 February 2015.

Prislan V and R Zandvlilet, 'Mainstreaming Sustainable Development into International Investment Agreements: What Role for Labour Provisions?'in R Hofmann, C Tams, and S Schill (eds), *International Investment Law and Development* (Edward Elgar 2015).

Productivity Commission, 'Australian Government, Bilateral and Regional Trade Agreements: Final Research Report' (13 December 2010) 272 <www.pc.gov.au/projects/study/trade-agreements> accessed 11 July 2014.

Proelss A, 'Article 37' in O Dörr and K Schmalenbach (eds), *Vienna Convention on the Law of Treaties* (Springer 2012) 637–84.

Proelss A, 'The Personal Dimension: Challenges to the *pacta tertiis* rule' in C Tams, A Tzanakopoulos and A Zimmermann (eds), *Research Handbook on the Law of Treaties* (Edward Elgar 2014) 222–54.

ProInversión, Agencia de Promoción de la Inversión Privada (Peru), Convenios suscritos con el Estado (Contrato de Inversión) and Convenios de Estabilidad Jurídica <www.investinperu.pe/default.aspx> accessed 1 September 2014.

Prost M, *The Concept of Unity in Public International Law* (Hart 2012).

Puig S, 'Social Capital in the Arbitration Market' (2014) 25 EJIL 387–424.

Puvimanasinghe S, *Foreign Investment, Human Rights and the Environment: A Perspective from South Asia on the Role of Public International Law for Development* (Martinus Nijhoff Publishers 2007).

Ramonet I, 'La Pensée Unique' Le Monde Diplomatique (January 1995) <www.monde-diplomatique.fr/1995/01/RAMONET/1144> accessed 25 March 2015.

Ranald P, 'The Trans-Pacific Partnership Agreement: Contradictions in Australia and in the Asia Pacific Region' (2011) 22(1) Econ Lab Relat Rev 81–98.

Reed L, J Paulsson, and N Blackaby, *Guide to ICSID Arbitration* (Kluwer 2010).

Reinisch A, 'Back to Basics: From the Notion of "Investment" to the Purpose of Annulment—ICSID Arbitration in 2007' (2008) 8 The Global Community. Ybk of Intl L & Jurisprudence 1591–1614.

Reinisch A, 'Expropriation' in P Muchlinski, F Ortino, and C Schreuer (eds), *The Oxford Handbook of International Investment Law* (OUP 2008) 407–58.

Reinisch A, 'Legality of Expropriations', in: A Reinisch (ed), *Standards of Investment Protection* (OUP 2008) 171–208.

Reinisch A, 'The Proliferation of International Dispute Settlement Mechanisms: the Threat of Fragmentation vs. the Promise of a More Effective System? Some Reflections from the Perspective of Investment Arbitration' in I Buffard et al. (eds), *International Law Between Universalism and Fragmentation: Festschrift in Honour of Gerhard Hafner* (Brill 2008) 107–125.

Reinisch A, 'The Role of Precedent in ICSID Arbitration' [2008] 2 AAYB 495–510.

Reinisch A, 'The Future Shape of EU Investment Agreements' (2013) 28 ICSID Rev–FILJ 179–96.

Reinisch A, 'The Impact of International Law on IIA Interpretation' in A de Mestral and C Lévesque (eds), *Improving International Investment Agreements* (Routledge 2013) 323–41.

Reinisch A and C Knahr (eds), *International Investment Law in Context* (Eleven International Pub 2008).
Reinisch A and L Malintoppi, 'Methods of Dispute Resolution' in P Muchlinski, F Ortino, and C Schreuer (eds), *The Oxford Handbook of International Investment Law* (OUP 2008) 691–721.
Reisman WM, 'International Arbitration and Sovereignty' (2002) 18 Arb Intl 231–39.
Reisman WM, '"Case-Specific Mandates" versus "Systemic Implications"—How Should Investment Tribunals Decide?' (2013) 29 Arb Int 131–52.
Republic of South Africa, 'Bilateral Investment Treaty Policy Framework Review: Government Position Paper' (2009) <www.pmg.org.za/files/docs/090626trade-bi-lateralpolicy.pdf> accessed 28 June 2014.
Resmini L, 'Il ruolo degli investimenti diretti esteri' in G Venturini (ed) *Le nuove forme di sostegno allo sviluppo nella prospettiva del diritto internazionale* (Giappichelli 2009) 67–81.
Ripinsky S, 'Russia' in C Brown (ed), *Commentaries on Selected Model Investment Treaties* (OUP 2013) 593–622.
Riza. Çoban A, *Protection of Property Rights within the European Convention on Human Rights* (Ashgate 2004).
Roberts A, 'Power and Persuasion in Investment Treaty Interpretation: The Dual Role of States' (2010) 104 AJIL 179–225.
Roberts A, 'Clash of Paradigms: Actors and Analogies Shaping the Investment Treaty System' (2013) 107 AJIL 45–94.
Roberts A, 'State-to-State Investment Treaty Arbitration: A Hybrid Theory of Interdependent Rights and Shared Interpretive Authority' (2014) 55 Harv ILJ 1–70.
Rogers C, 'Transparency in International Commercial Arbitration' (2005–06) 54 U Kan L Rev.
Rogers C, 'The Politics of International Investment Arbitrators' (2014) 12 Santa Clara JIL 223–262.
Romesh Weeramantry J, *Treaty Interpretation in Investment Arbitration* (OUP 2012).
Rosert D, *The Stakes are High: A review of the financial costs of investment treaty arbitration* (International Institute for Sustainable Development 2014).
Sabahi B, *Compensation and Restitution in Investor-State Arbitration* (OUP 2011).
Sacerdoti G, 'Bilateral Treaties and Multilateral Instruments on Investment Protection' (1997) 269 RdC.
Sacerdoti G, 'Precedent in the Settlement of International Economic Disputes: the WTO and the Investment Arbitration Models' in A Rovine (ed), *Contemporary Issues in International Arbitration and Mediation: The Fordham Papers 2010* (Martinus Nijhoff 2011) 225–46.
Sacerdoti G and M Recanati, 'From Annulment to Appeal in Investor-State Arbitration: Is the WTO Appeal Mechanism a Model?' in JA Huerta-Goldman, A Romanetti, and F Stirnimann (eds), *WTO Litigation, Investment and Commercial Arbitration* (Kluwer 2013) 327–56.
Sacerdoti G and others (eds), *General Interests of Host States in International Investment Law* (CUP 2014).
Salacuse JW, *The Law of Investment Treaties* (OUP 2010).
Salacuse JW, *The Three Laws of International Investment* (OUP 2013).
Salacuse JW, *The Law of Investment Treaties* (OUP 2nd ed 2015).
Salasky J and C Montineri, 'UN Commission on International Trade Law and Multilateral Rule-making' (2014) 11(1) Transn Disp Mgmt.
Salazar A, 'Defragmenting International Investment Law to Protect Citizen-Consumers: The Role of *Amici Curiae* and Public Interest Groups' (2013) Osgoode Hall Law School, Comparative Research in Law & Political Economy Research Paper No 6/2013.

Sands P, *Principles of International Environmental Law* (2nd edn, CUP 2003).
Sands P and J Peel, *Principles of International Environmental Law* (3rd edn, CUP 2012).
Sauvant KP and F Ortino, *Improving the International Investment Law and Policy Regime: Options for the Future* (Formin 2013).
Sauvant KP and LE Sachs, 'BITs, DTTs, and FDI Flows: An Overview' in KP Sauvant, and LE Sachs (eds), *The Effect of Treaties on Foreign Direct Investment: Bilateral Investment Treaties, Double Taxation Treaties and Investment Flows* (OUP 2009) xxvii–2.
Sauvant KP and LE Sachs (eds), *The Effect of Treaties on Foreign Direct Investment: Bilateral Investment Treaties, Double Taxation Treaties, and Investment Flows* (OUP 2009).
Shemberg A, *Stabilization Clauses and Human Rights. A research project conducted for IFC and the United Nations Special Representative of the Secretary-General on Business and Human Rights* (United Nations/International Finance Corporation 2009).
Schill SW, 'Do Investment Treaties Chill Unilateral State Regulation to Mitigate Climate Change?' (2007) 24 J of Intl Arb 469–77.
Schill SW, *The Multilateralization of International Investment Law* (CUP 2009).
Schill SW, 'Fair and Equitable Treatment, The Rule of Law and Comparative Public Law', in: SW Schill (ed), *International Investment Law and Comparative Public Law* (OUP 2010) 151–82.
Schill SW (ed.), *International Investment Law and Comparative Public Law* (OUP 2010).
Schill SW, 'Öffentlich-rechtliche Schiedsverfahren zwischen Risikobewältigung und Rechtsrisiko' (2010) 63 DÖV 1013–18.
Schill SW, 'Private Enforcement of International Investment Law: Why We Need Investor Standing in BIT Dispute Settlement', in M Waibel and others (eds), *The Backlash against Investment Arbitration, Perceptions and Reality* (Kluwer 2010) 29–50.
Schill SW, 'Enhancing International Investment Law's Legitimacy: Conceptual and Methodological Foundations of a New Public Law Approach' (2011) 52 Va J Int'l L 57–102.
Schill SW, 'Investitionsschutzrecht als Entwicklungsvölkerrecht' (2012) 72 ZaöRV 261–308.
Schill SW, 'The Virtues of Investor-State Arbitration' (*EJIL: Talk!*, 19 November 2013) <www.ejiltalk.org/the-virtues-of-investor-state-arbitration/> accessed 8 March 2015.
Schill SW, 'International Investment Law as International Development Law' in A Bjorklund (ed), 5 *Yearbook on International Investment Law and Policy* 2012–2013 (5–6) (2014) 327–356.
Schill SW, *Auswirkungen der Bestimmungen zum Investitionsschutz und zu den Investor-Staat-Schiedsverfahren im Entwurf des Freihandelsabkommens zwischen der EU und Kanada (CETA) auf den Handlungsspielraum des Gesetzgebers (Kurzgutachten)* <www.bmwi.de/BMWi/Redaktion/PDF/C-D/ceta-gutachten-investitionsschutz,property=pdf,bereich=bmwi2012,sprache=de,rwb=true.pdf> accessed 17 February 2015.
Schneiderman D, 'Investment Rules and the New Constitutionalism' (2000) 25 Law & Soc Inquiry 757–87.
Schneiderman D, 'A New Global Constitutional Order?' in T Ginsburg and R Dixon (eds.), *Comparative Constitutional Law: Research Handbook in Comparative Constitutional* Law (Edward Elgar 2011) 186–207.
Schramke HJ, 'Umbrella Clauses in bilateralen Investitionsschutzabkommen' (2006) 4 German Arb J 249–257.
Schreuer C, *The ICSID Convention: A Commentary* (CUP 2001).
Schreuer C, 'Failure to Apply the Governing Law in International Investment Arbitration' (2002) 7 ARIEL 147–96.

Schreuer C, 'Non-Pecuniary Remedies in ICSID Arbitration' (2004) 20 Arb Intl 325–332.
Schreuer C, 'Consent to Arbitration' in P Muchlinksi, F Ortino, and C Schreuer (eds), *The Oxford Handbook of International Investment Law* (OUP 2008) 830–67.
Schreuer C, *The ICSID Convention: A Commentary on the Convention on the Settlement of Investment Disputes between States and Nationals of other States* (2nd edn, CUP 2009).
Schreuer C, 'Denunciation of the ICSID Convention and Consent to Arbitration' in M Waibel and others (eds), *The Backlash Against Investment Arbitration—Perceptions and Reality* (Kluwer 2010) 353–68.
Schreuer C, 'Diversity and Harmonization of Treaty Interpretation in Investment Arbitration' in M Fitzmaurice, O Elias, and P Merkouris (eds), *Treaty Interpretation and the Vienna Convention on the Law of Treaties: 30 Years On* (Nijhoff 2010) 129–151.
Schreuer C, 'Do We Need Investment Arbitration' (2014) 11(1) Transn Disp Mgmt.
Schreuer C and R Dolzer, *Principles of International Investment Law* (OUP 2008).
Schreuer C, L Malintoppi, A Reinisch, and A Sinclair, *The ICSID Convention: A Commentary* (2nd edn, CUP 2009).
Schreuer C and M Weiniger, 'A doctrine of precedent?' in P Muchlinski, F Ortino, C Shreuer (eds), *The Oxford Handbook of International Investment Law* (OUP 2008) 1188–1206.
Schrijver N and V Prislan, 'The Netherlands' in C Brown (ed), *Commentaries on Selected Model Investment Treaties* (OUP 2013) 535–92.
Schrijver N, V Prislan, and F Weiss (eds), *International Law and Sustainable Development, Principles and Practice* (M Nijhoff 2004).
Schwarzenberger G, 'Myths and Realities of Treaty Interpretation, Articles 27–29 of the Vienna Draft Convention on the Law of Treaties' (1968) 9 Va J Intl L 1–19.
Schwebel S, 'Ad Hoc Chambers of the International Court of Justice' (1987) 81 AJIL 831–54.
Sen A, 'Property and Hunger' (1988) 4 Econ Philos 57–68.
Sengupta A, 'The Human Right to Development' in BA Andreassen and SP Marks (eds), *Development as a Human Right* (Harvard University Press 2009).
Shan W, P Simons and D Singh (eds.), *Redefining Sovereignty in International Economic Law* (Hart 2008).
Shany Y, 'Towards a General Margin of Appreciation Doctrine in International Law' (2006) 16 EJIL 907–40.
Shapiro F (ed), *The Yale Book of Quotations* (YUP 2006).
Shaw MN, *International Law* (7th edn, CUP 2014).
Shelton D, *Remedies in International Human Rights Law* (2nd edn, OUP 2005).
Sheppard A and A Crockett, 'Are Stabilization Clauses a Threat to Sustainable Development?' in M-C Cordonier Segger and others (eds), *Sustainable Development in World Investment Law* (Wolter Kluwer 2010) 329–50.
Simma B, 'Foreign Investment Arbitration: A Place for Human Rights?' (2011) 60 ICLQ 573–96.
Simma B and D Pulkowski, 'Of Planets and the Universe: Self-Contained Regimes in International Law' (2006) 17 EJIL 483–529.
Simma B and C Schulte, 'Human Rights considerations in the development cooperation activities of the EC' in P Alston (ed) *The EU And Human Rights* (OUP 2004) 571–626.
Simma B and C Tams, 'Article 60 Convention of 1969' in O Corten and P Klein (eds), *The Vienna Convention on the Law of Treaties, Volume II* (OUP 2011) 1351–78.
Sinclair I, *The Vienna Convention on the Law of Treaties* (2nd edn, Manchester University Press 1984).

Söderlund C, 'Intra-EU BIT Investment Protection and the EC Treaty' (2007) 24 J Intl Arb 455–68.
Sornarajah M, *The International Law on Foreign Investment* (3rd edn, CUP 2010).
Sornarajah M, 'Mutations of Neo-Liberalism in International Investment Law' (2011) 3 Trade L & Dev 203–232.
Sornarajah M, 'The Case against a Regime on International Investment Law' in LE Trakman and N Ranieri (eds), *Regionalism in International Investment Law* (OUP 2013) 475–98.
Sourgens FG, 'Keep the Faith: Investment Protection Following the Denunciation of International Investment Agreements' (2013) 11 Santa Clara JIL 335–96.
South African Government, 'Minister Davies to address media on the draft Promotion and Protection of Investment Bill' (1 November 2013) <www.gov.za/minister-davies- address-media-draft-promotion-and-protection-investment-bill www> accessed 3 July 2014.
South African Government, 'Minister Rob Davies on Promotion and Protection of Investment Bill' (28 July 2015) <www.gov.za/speeches/promotion-and-protection-investment-bill-protects-investors-minister-davies-2015-07-28-28> accessed 18 August 2015.
South African Institute of International Affairs (SAIIA), 'South Africa's Draft Promotion and Protection of Investment Bill 2013: A Submission by the South African Institute of International Affairs', <www.thetradebeat.com/book/saiia-submission-on-south-africa-s-draft-promotion-and-protection-of-investment-bill> accessed 4 July 2014.
South African Reserve Bank, 'Statistical Tables: International Economic Relations', *Quarterly Bulletin* 272, <https://www.resbank.co.za/Lists/News%20and%20Publications/Attachments/6273/11Statistical%20tables%20%E2%80%93%20International%20 economic%20relations.pdf> accessed 1 July 2014.
Southern African Development Community (SADC), 'SADC Model Bilateral Investment Treaty Template with Commentary' (SADC 2012).
Spears SA, 'The Quest for Policy Space in a New Generation of International Investment Agreements' (2010) 13 J Intl Econ L 1037–75.
Special Rapporteur H Waldock, 'Third Report on the Law of Treaties' (1964) vol II YbILC.
Special Rapporteur H Waldock, 'Sixth Report on the Law of Treaties' (1966) vol II YbILC.
Spiermann O, 'Individual Rights, State Interests and the Power to Waive ICSID Jurisdiction under Bilateral Investment Treaties' (2004) 20 Arb Intl 179–212.
Statement of Peter Robinson, President and CEO, United States Council for International Business (USCIB) on 'USCIB's Foreign Direct Investment Policy Agenda', UNCTAD World Investment Forum, 16 October 2014 <http://unctad-worldinvestmentforum.org/wp-content/uploads/2014/10/Robinson.pdf> accessed 17 February 2015.
Statement of the U.S. Chamber of Commerce on the Transatlantic Trade & Investment Partnership to the Office of the U.S. Trade Representative, 10 May 2013 <www.regulations.gov/#!documentDetail;D=USTR-2013-0019-0241> accessed 17 February 2015.
Stern B, 'The Future of International Investment Law: A Balance Between the Protection of Investors and the States' Capacity to Regulate' in JE Alvarez and KP Sauvant (eds), *The Evolving international Investment Regime: Expectations, Realities, Options* (OUP 2011) 174–92.
Steyn P, 'The new Promotion and Protection of Investment Bill—an assessment of its implications for local and foreign investors in South Africa' *Werksmans Attorneys Legal Brief* (10 December 2013) <www.werksmans.com/legal-briefs-view/new-promotion-protection-investment-bill-assessment-implications-local-foreign-investors-south-africa/> accessed 4 July 2014.

Stoll PT, 'Le droit international économique face aux défis de la mondialisation' (2009) 113 RGDIP.

Stoll PT, H Krüger, and Jia Xu, 'Freihandelsabkommen und ihre Umweltschutzregelungen' (2014) 7 ZUR 387–95.

Strik D, 'Investment Protection of Sovereign Debt and Its Implications on the Future of Investment Law in the EU' (2012) 29 (2) J Intl Arb 183–204.

Stumberg R, 'Sovereignty by Subtraction: The Multilateral Agreement on Investment' (1998) 31 Cornell Intl LJ 491–598.

Subedi SP, *International Investment Law: Reconciling Policy and Principle* (Hart Publishing 2008).

Subedi SP, *International Investment Law—Reconciling Policy and Principle* (2nd edn, Hart 2012).

Swan Sik K, 'The Concept of Acquired Rights in International Law: A Survey' (1977) 24 Netherlands Intl L Rev 120–42.

Sweet AS, 'Investor-State Arbitration: Proportionality's New Frontier' (2010) 4 L & Ethics Hum Rts 47–76.

Tams C, 'An Appealing Option? A debate about an ICSID Appellate System' (2006) Essays in Transnational Economic Law No 57, 19 <http://papers.ssrn.com/sol3/papers.cfm?abstract_id=1413694> accessed 23 March 2015.

Tams C 'An Appealing Option? The Debate about an ICSID Appellate Structure' in C Tietje; G Kraft, and R Sethe (eds), *Beiträge zum Transnationalen Wirtschaftsrecht, Heft 57* <www.economiclaw.uni-halle.de/sites/default/files/altbestand/Heft57.pdf> accessed 27 April 2015.

Taylor R, 'Australia's Trade Minister Expects Long Slog for Trade Deal' *The Wall Street Journal* (18 June 2014) <http://online.wsj.com/articles/australias-trade-minister-expects-long-slog-for-trade-deal-1403073241> accessed 11 July 2014.

Ten Cate I, 'International Arbitration and the Ends of Appellate Review' (2012) 44 Intl L and Poly 1109–1204.

Ten Cate I, 'The Costs of Consistency: Precedent in Investment Treaty Arbitration' (2013) 51 Col J Transnatl L 418–478.

Tevendale C and V Naish, 'Indonesia Indicates Intention to Terminate all of its Bilateral Investment Treaties?' *Herbert Smith Freehills Dispute Resolution* (20 March 2014) <http://hsfnotes.com/arbitration/2014/03/20/indonesia-indicates-intention-to-terminate-all-of-its-bilateral-investment-treaties/> accessed 11 July 2014.

Thompson T and A Shah, 'Transparency International's Corruption Perceptions Index: Whose Perceptions Are They Anyway?' World Bank Discussion Draft 2005, http://siteresources.worldbank.org/INTWBIGOVANTCOR/Resources/TransparencyInternationalCorruptionIndex.pdf> accessed 11 July 2014.

Tienhaara K, 'Regulatory Chill and the Threat of Arbitration: A View from Political Science' in C Brown and K Miles (eds), *Evolution in Investment Treaty Law and Arbitration* (CUP 2012) 606–28.

Tienhaara K, 'Submission to the Department of Foreign Affairs and Trade: Investor-State Dispute Settlement in the Trans-Pacific Partnership Agreement' <www.dfat.gov.au/fta/tpp/subs/tpp_sub_tienhaara_100519.pdf> accessed 11 July 2014.

Tietje C, *The Applicability of the Energy Charter Treaty in ICSID Arbitration of EU Nationals vs. EU Member States* (MLU Institut für Wirtschaftsrecht 2008).

Tietje C, 'The Future of International Investment Protection: Stress in the System?' (2009) 24 ICSID Rev–FILJ 457–63.

Tietje C, *Internationales Investitionsschutzrecht im Spannungsverhältnis von staatlicher Regelungsfreiheit und Schutz wirtschaftlicher Individualinteressen* (MLU Institut für Wirtschaftsrecht 2010).

Tietje C, 'Bilaterale Investitionsschutzverträge zwischen EU Mitgliedstaaten (Intra-EU-BITs) als Herausforderung im Mehrebenensystem des Rechts', in C Tietje, G Kraft, and M Lehmann, *Beiträge zum Transnationalen Wirtschaftsrecht*, vol. 104, (Bibliografische Information der Deutschen Bibliothek 2011) 128–35.

Tietje C, 'Grundstrukturen, Rechtsstand und aktuelle Herausforderungen des internationalen Investitionsschutzrechts' in T Giegerich (ed), *Internationales Wirtschafts- und Finanzrecht in der Krise* (Duncker & Humblot 2011) 11–33.

Tietje C, 'The Right to Development within the International Legal Order' in M Cremona and others (eds), *Reflections on the Constitutionalisation of International Economic Law: Liber Amicorum, EU Petersmann* (Brill 2014) 543–57.

Tietje C, K Nowrot, and C Wackernagel, *Once and Forever? The Legal Effects of a Denunciation of ICSID* (MLU Institut für Wirtschaftsrecht 2008).

Tietje C, and E Sipiorski, 'The Evolution of Investment Protection based on Public International Law Treaties: Lessons to be Learned' in AK Bjorklund and A Reinisch (eds), *International Investment Law and Soft Law* (Elgar 2012) 192–237.

Titi C, 'The Evolving BIT: A Commentary on Canada's Model Agreement' *Investment Treaty News* (26 June 2013) <www.iisd.org/itn/2013/06/26/the-evolving-bit-a-commentary-on-canadas-model-agreement/> accessed 1 July 2014.

Titi C, *The Right To Regulate in International Investment Law* (Nomos 2014).

Toral M and T Schultz, 'The State, a Perpetual Respondent in Investment Arbitration? Some Unorthodox Considerations' in M Waibel, A Kaushal, K.H. Chung, and C Balchin, (eds) *The Backlash against Investment Arbitration: Perceptions and Reality* (Kluwer 2010) 577–602.

Trachtman J, 'The Domain of WTO Dispute Resolution' (1999) 40 HILJ 333–76.

Trakman LE, 'Foreign Direct Investment: An Australian Perspective' (2010) 13 Intl Trade & Bus L Rev.

Trakman LE, 'National Good No Issue in ASX Deal' *The Australian* (2 November 2010) <www.theaustralian.com.au/business/national-good-no-issue-in-asx-deal/story-e6frg8zx-1225946362212> accessed 11 July 2014.

Trakman LE, 'China and Investor State Arbitration' (2012) University of New South Wales Faculty of Law Research Series No 48.

Trakman LE, 'Choosing Domestic Courts over Investor-State Arbitration: Australia's Repudiation of the Status Quo' (2012) 35 UNSW LJ 979–1012.

Trakman LE, 'Investor State Arbitration or Local Courts: Will Australia Set a New Trend?' (2012) 46 JWT 83–120.

Trakman LE, 'The ICSID under Siege' (2012) 45 Cornell Intl LJ 603–665.

Trakman LE, 'The Transpacific Partnership Agreement: Significance for International Investment' (2013) 4(4) J Intl Comm L 1–38.

Trakman LE 'China and Foreign Direct Investment: Does Distance Lend Enchantment to the View?' (2014) 2 Chin J Comp L 1–20.

Trakman LE, 'Investor-State Arbitration: Evaluating Australia's Evolving Position' (2014) 15 J World Inv & Trade 152–92.

Trakman LE and K Sharma, 'Indonesia's Termination of the Netherlands–Indonesia BIT: Broader Implications in the Asia-Pacific?' *Kluwer International Law* (21 August 2014) <http://kluwerarbitrationblog.com/blog/author/leontrakman/> accessed 1 September 2014.

Trakman LE and K Sharma, 'Locating Australia on the Pacific Rim: Trade, Investment and the Asian Century' (2015) 1 Transn Disp Mgmt.

Transparency International, *Corruption Perceptions Index 2013* <http://cpi.transparency.org/cpi2013/results/> accessed 11 July 2014.

Treves T, 'Customary International Law' in Rüdiger Wolfrum (ed), *The Max Planck Encyclopedia of Public International Law* (2nd edn, OUP 2013) 937–56.

Trevino CJ, 'State-to-State Investment Treaty Arbitration and the Interplay with Investor-State Arbitration under the same Treaty' (2014) 5 JIDS 199–233.

Trevino CJ, 'A Closer Look at Brazil's Two New Bilateral Investment Treaties' *IAReporter* (10 April 2015) <www.iareporter.com/articles/a-closer-look-at-brazils-two-new-bilateral-investment-treaties/> accessed 15 August 2015.

Trindade A, *The Application of the Rule of Exhaustion of Local Remedies* (CUP 1983).

Tryfonidou A, *Reverse Discrimination in EC Law* (Kluwer Law International 2009).

Tudor I, *The Fair and Equitable Treatment Standard in the International Law of Foreign Investment* (OUP 2008).

Tuerk E and R Rojid, Towards a New Generation of Investment Policies: UNCTAD's Investment Policy Framework for Sustainable Development, (2012) Investment Treaty News, <www.iisd.org/itn/2012/10/30/towards-a-new-generation-of-investment-policies-unctads-investment-policy-framework-for-sustainable-development/> accessed 16 December 2014.

Tyagi Y, 'The Denunciation of Human Rights Treaties' (2009) 79 British Ybk IL 86–193.

United Nations, *Monterrey Consensus of the International Conference on Financing for Development, Report of the International Conference on Financing for Development, Monterrey, Mexico, 18-22 March 2002 (UN Doc. A/CONF.198/11, chapter 1, resolution 1, annex)* (United Nations 2003) <www.un.org/esa/ffd/monterrey/MonterreyConsensus.pdf> accessed 27 April 2015.

United Nations, *Development and the Implementation of the Monterrey Consensus*, UN Doc. A/63/179 (2008).

United Nations, 'Johannesburg Declaration on Sustainable Development' (2002) UN Doc A/CONF.199/20 (2002).

United Nations Commission on International Trade Law, *Rules on Transparency in Treaty-based Investor-State Arbitration* (UNCITRAL 2014) <www.uncitral.org/pdf/english/texts/arbitration/rules-on-transparency/Rules-on-Transparency-E.pdf> accessed 12 November 2014.

United Nations Conference on Environment and Development, *Agenda 21: Programme of Ac-tion for Sustainable Development* (United Nations 1992) <https://sustainabledevelopment.un.org/content/documents/Agenda21.pdf> accessed 8 May 2015.

United Nations Conference on the Human Environment, 'Declaration on the Human Environment' (Stockholm, 16 June 1972) UN Doc A/CONF.48/14/Rev.

United Nations Conference on the Law of Treaties (Vienna, 26 March–24 May 1968 and 9 April–22 May 1969), Official Records: Documents of the Conference, UN Doc A/CONF.39/11/Add2.

United Nations Conference on Trade and Development, *Foreign Direct Investment and Development*, UNCTAD/ITE/IIT/10 (vol. I, 1999).

United Nations Conference on Trade and Development, *Bilateral Investment Treaties 1959–1999* (United Nations 2000).

United Nations Conference on Trade and Development, *Taking of Property* (United Nations 2000).

United Nations Conference on Trade and Development, *World Investment Report 2003, FDI Policies for Development: National and International Perspectives* (United Nations 2003).
United Nations Conference on Trade and Development, *International Investment Agreements: Key Issues* (United Nations 2004).
United Nations Conference on Trade and Development, *Recent Developments in International Investment Agreements* (30 August 2005), UNCTAD/WEB/ITE/IIT/2005/1.
United Nations Conference on Trade and Development, *International Investment Treaties 1998-2006* (United Nations 2007).
United Nations Conference on Trade and Development, *International Investment Rule-Making* UNCTAD/ITE/IIT2007/3 (2008).
United Nations Conference on Trade and Development, *World Investment Report 2008, Transnational Corporations and the Infrastructure Challenge* (United Nations 2008).
United Nations Conference on Trade and Development, 'IIA Monitor No 3: Recent Developments in International Investment Agreements (2008-June 2009)', (2009) <http://unctad.org/en/Docs/webdiaeia20098_en.pdf> accessed 24 March 2015.
United Nations Conference on Trade and Development, *The Role of Investment Agreements in Attracting Foreign Direct Investment* (United Nations 2009).
United Nations Conference on Trade and Development, 'Denunciation of the ICSID Convention and BITs: Impact on Investor-State Claims' (2010) 2 IIA Issues Note <http://unctad.org/en/Docs/webdiaeia20106_en.pdf> accessed 24 March 2015.
United Nations Conference on Trade and Development, *Most-Favoured-Nation Treatment: A Sequel* (United Nations 2010).
United Nations Conference on Trade and Development, *World Investment Report 2010, Investing in a Low-Carbon Economy* (United Nations 2010).
United Nations Conference on Trade and Development, *World Investment Report 2010* UNCTAD/WIR/2014 <http://unctad.org/en/pages/PublicationWebflyer.aspx?publicationid=937> accessed 11 July 2014.
United Nations Conference on Trade and Development, *Expropriation: A Sequel* (United Nations 2011).
United Nations Conference on Trade and Development, 'Interpretation of IIAs: What States Can Do' (2011) 3 IIA Issues Note <http://unctad.org/en/docs/webdiaeia2011d10_en.pdf> accessed 24 March 2015.
United Nations Conference on Trade and Development, *Scope and Definition: A Sequel* (United Nations 2011).
United Nations Conference on Trade and Development, 'Sovereign debt restructuring and international investment agreements' (2011) 2 IIA Issues Note <http://unctad.org/en/Docs/webdiaepcb2011d3_en.pdf> accessed 12 November 2014.
United Nations Conference on Trade and Development, *Fair and Equitable Treatment: A Sequel* (United Nations 2012).
United Nations Conference on Trade and Development, *Fair and Equitable Treatment. UNCTAD Series on Issues in International Investment Agreements II* (United Nations 2012).
United Nations Conference on Trade and Development, *Investment Policy Framework for Sustainable Development* (United Nations 2012).
United Nations Conference on Trade and Development, *International Policy Framework for Sustainable Development* (2012) <http://unctad.org/en/Pages/DIAE/International%20Investment%20Agreements%20%28IIA%29/IIA-IPFSD.aspx> accessed on 30 June 2014.
United Nations Conference on Trade and Development, *Investment Policy Framework for Sustainable Development* (United Nations 2012) <http://investmentpolicyhub.unctad.org> accessed 15 July 2015.

United Nations Conference on Trade and Development, *Investment Policy Framework for Sustainable Development* (United Nations 2012) available at <http://unctad.org/en/PublicationsLibrary/webdiaepcb2012d6_en.pdf> accessed 28 September 2013.

United Nations Conference on Trade and Development, *Investment Policy Framework for Sustainable Development* (United Nations 2012) UN Pub. UNCTAD/DIAE/PCB/2012/5 available at: <http://unctad.org/en/PublicationsLibrary/diaepcb2012d5_en.pdf> accessed 12 November 2014.

United Nations Conference on Trade and Development, *Investment Policy Framework for Sustainable Development* (United Nations 2012) <http://unctad.org/en/Pages/DIAE/International%20Investment%20Agreements%20%28IIA%29/IIA-IPFSD.aspx> accessed 20 October 2014.

United Nations Conference on Trade and Development, *Investment Policy Framework for Sustainable Development* (United Nations 2012) <http://unctad.org/en/PublicationsLibrary/diaepcb2012d5_en.pdf> accessed 16 December 2014.

United Nations Conference on Trade and Development, *World Investment Report 2012, Towards a New Generation of Investment Policies* (United Nations 2012).

United Nations Conference on Trade and Development, *International Investment Agreements Negotiators Handbook* (APEC Project CTI 15/2010T APEC/UNCTAD, 2013) <http://investmentpolicyhub.unctad.org/Upload/Documents/UNCTAD_APEC%20Handbook.pdf> accessed 23. March 2015.

United Nations Conference on Trade and Development, 'International Investment Policymaking in Transition: Challenges and Opportunities of Treaty Renewal' (2013) 4 IIA Issues Note <http://unctad.org/en/PublicationsLibrary/webdiaepcb2013d9_en.pdf> accessed 24 March 2015.

United Nations Conference on Trade and Development, 'Investment Policy Monitor No 11' (2013). <http://unctad.org/en/PublicationsLibrary/webdiaepcb2013d11_en.pdf> accessed 24 March 2015.

United Nations Conference on Trade and Development, 'Recent Developments in Investor-State Dispute Settlement (ISDS)' (2013) 1 Issues Note <http://unctad.org/en/publicationslibrary/webdiaepcb2013d3_en.pdf> accessed 24 March 2015.

United Nations Conference on Trade and Development, 'The Rise of Regionalism in International Investment Policymaking: Consolidation or Complexity?' (2013) 3 IIA Issues Note <http://unctad.org/en/PublicationsLibrary/webdiaepcb2013d8_en.pdf> accessed 24 March 2015.

United Nations Conference on Trade and Development, 'Reform of Investor-State Dispute Settlement: In Search of a Roadmap' (2013) 2 IIA Issues Note <unctad.org/en/PublicationsLibrary/webdiaepcb2013d4_en.pdf> accessed 11 July 2014.

United Nations Conference on Trade and Development, *World Investment Report 2013, Global Value Chains: Investment and Trade for Development* (United Nations 2013).

United Nations Conference on Trade and Development, *World Investment Report 2013* UN Doc UNCTAD/WIR/2013.

United Nations Conference on Trade and Development, *Investor-State Dispute Settlement* (United Nations 2014).

United Nations Conference on Trade and Development, *Recent Developments in Investor-State Dispute Settlement* (United Nations 2014).

United Nations Conference on Trade and Development, 'Recent Developments in Investor-State Dispute Settlement' (2014) 1 IIA Issues Note <http://unctad.org/en/PublicationsLibrary/webdiaepcb2014d3_en.pdf> accessed 24 April 2015.

United Nations Conference on Trade and Development, 'Reform of the IIA Regime: Four Paths of Action and a Way Forward' (2014) 3 IIA Issues Note <http://unctad.org/en/PublicationsLibrary/webdiaepcb2014d6_en.pdf> accessed 12 November 2014.

United Nations Conference on Trade and Development, *World Investment Report 2014, Investing in the SDGs: An Action Plan* (United Nations 2014).

United Nations Conference on Trade and Development, *World Investment Report 2015, Reforming Inernational Investment Governance* (United Nations 2015).

United Nations Conference on Trade and Development, *Investment Policy Framework for Sustainable Development* (United Nations 2015) <http://investmentpolicyhub.unctad.org/Upload/Documents/INVESTMENT%20POLICY%20FRAMEWORK%202015%20WEB_VERSION.pdf> accessed 13 August 2015.

United Nations Conference on Trade and Development, 'Investment Policy Monitor No 13' (2015) <http://unctad.org/en/PublicationsLibrary/webdiaepcb2015d13_en.pdf> accessed 24 March 2015.

United Nations Conference on Trade and Development, 'Recent Trends in IIAs and ISDS' (2015) 1 IIA Issues Note 1 <http://unctad.org/en/PublicationsLibrary/webdiaepcb2015d1_en.pdf> accessed 23 April 2014.

United Nations Conference on Trade and Development, *Investment Policy Hub, International Investment Agreements, Most Recent IIAs* <http://investmentpolicyhub.unctad.org/IIA/MostRecentTreaties#iiaInnerMenu> accessed 1 September 2014.

United Nations Conference on Trade and Development, *Investment Policy Hub, International Investment Agreements* <http://investmentpolicyhub.unctad.org/IIA> accessed 21 August 2015.

United Nations General Assembly, UNCITRAL Working Group II (Arbitration and Conciliation), 53rd Sess., Vienna, 4-8 October 2010, 'Settlement of commercial disputes; Transparency in treaty-based investor-State arbitration; Compilation of comments by Governments; Note by the Secretariat; Addendum', (4 August 2010), UN Doc A/CN.9/WG.II/WP.159/Add.2.

United Nations General Assembly Res 66/288, 'The Future We Want' (27 July 2012) UN Doc A/RES/66/288.

United Nations Human Rights Council, 'Protect, Respect and Remedy: A Framework for Business and Human Rights, Report of the Special Representative of the Secretary-General on the Issue of Human Rights and Transnational Corporations and Other Business Enterprises', UN Doc. A/HRC/8/5 (7 April 2008).

United Nations Human Rights Council, 'Business and Human Rights: Towards Operationalizing the "Protect, Respect and Remedy" Framework, Report of the Special Representative of the Secretary-General on the Issue of Human Rights and Transnational Corporations and Other Business Enterprises', UN Doc. A/HRC/11/13 (22 April 2009).

United Nations Human Rights Council, 'Report of the Special Representative of the Secretary-General on the issue of human rights and transnational corporations and other business enterprises, John Ruggie' (21 March 2011) UN Doc. A/HRC/17/31.

United Nations Human Rights Council, 'Seventeenth Session 21 March 2011: Guiding Principles on Business and Human Rights Implementing the United Nations "Protect, Respect and Remedy" Framework' <www.ohchr.org/documents/issues/business/A.HRC.17.31.pdf> accessed 12 November 2014.

United Nations Human Rights Council, 'Guiding Principle 17, adopted by Resolution 17/4 of the Human Rights Council 16 June 2011' UN Doc A/HRC/RES/17/4 <www.business-humanrights.org/media/documents/un-human-rights-council-resolution-re-human-rights-transnational-corps-eng-6-jul-2011.pdf> accessed 12 November 2014.

United Nations Millennium Project, *Investing in Development: A Practical Plan to Achieve the Millennium Development Goals* (Routledge 2005).

United Nations Secretary General, *The Latest Developments Related to the Review Process on Financing for Development and the Implementation of the Monterrey Consensus* (United Nations 2008) <www.un-ngls.org/IMG/pdf/SGreport_25JUL2008.pdf> accessed 24 March 2015.

United Nations Sub-Commission on the Promotion and Protection of Human Rights, *Norms on the Responsibilities of Transnational Corporations and Other Business Enterprises with Regard to Human Rights*, ECOSOC, UN Doc E/CN.4/Sub.2/2003/12/Rev.2 (2003).

United Nations Sub-Commission on the Promotion and Protection of Human Rights, *Commentary on the Norms on the Responsibilities of Transnational Corporations and Other Business Enterprises with Regard to Human Rights*, UN Doc. E/CN.4/Sub.2/2003/38/Rev.2, (2003).

United Nations World Summit for Sustainable Development, *Plan of Implementation of the World Summit for Sustainable Development* (United Nations 2002) <www.un.org/esa/sustdev/documents/WSSD_POI_PD/English/WSSD_PlanImpl.pdf> accessed 8 May 2015.

Unión de Naciones Suramericanas Secretaria General, 'Comunicado, Los cancilleres de UNASUR dejaron listo el texto de declaración presidencial de Quito' (9 August 2009) <www.unasursg.org/index.php?option=com_content&view=article&id=278:cancilleres-dejan-lista-declaraciasn-de-quito&catid=68:comunicados> accessed 28 February 2013.

Unión de Naciones Suramericanas Secretaria General, 'Declaracion final de la reunión extraordinaria del Consejo de Jefas y Jefes de Estado de la Unión Sudamericana de Naciones' (4 May 2010) www.unasursg.org/index.php?option=com_content&view=article&id=359:declaracion-final-de-la-reunion-extraordinaria-del-consejo-de-jefas-y-jefes-de-estado-de-unasur-los-cardales-mayo-2010&catid=96:declaraciones> accessed 28 February 2013.

United States Department of State, 'United States Concludes Review of Model Bilateral Investment Treaty, 20 April 2012 <www.state.gov/r/pa/prs/ps/2012/04/188198.htm> accessed 1 July 2014.

United Cities and Local Governments, 'Culture: Fourth Pillar of Sustainable Development' (2010) <www.agenda21culture.net/images/a21c/4th-pilar/zz_Culture4pillarSD_eng.pdf> accessed 15 July 2014.

Vadi V, *Cultural Heritage in International Investment Law and Arbitration* (CUP 2014).

Valencia-Ospina E, 'The use of Chambers of the International Court of Justice' in V Lowe and M Fitzmaurice (eds), *Fifty years of the International Court of Justice* (CUP 1996) 503–27.

Vamvoukos A, *Termination of Treaties in International Law* (OUP 1985).

van Aaken A, 'Fragmentation of International Law: the Case of International Investment Law' (2006) 17 FYIL 409–24.

van Aaken A, 'Primary and Secondary Remedies in International Investment Law and National State Liability: A Functional and Comparative View' in SW Schill (ed), *International Investment Law and Comparative Public Law* (OUP 2010) 721–54.

van Aaken A and TA Lehmann, 'Sustainable development and international investment law: a harmonious view from economists' in R Echandi and P Sauvé (eds), *Prospects in International Investment Law and Policy* (CUP 2013) 317–39.

van den Berg A, 'Dissenting Opinions by Party-Appointed Arbitrators in Investment Arbitration' in M Arsanjani, J Katz Cogan, R Sloane, and S Wiessner (eds), *Looking to the Future: Essays in Honour of W. Michael Reisman* (Brill 2010) 821–43.

Van Harten G, *Investment Treaty Arbitration and Public Law* (OUP 2007).
Van Harten G, 'A Case for an International Investment Court' (2008) Society of International Economic Law (SIEL) Inaugural Conference Working Paper 22/08 <http://papers.ssrn.com/sol3/papers.cfm?abstract_id=1153424> accessed 17 February 2015.
Van Harten G, 'Investment Treaty Arbitration, Procedural Fairness, and the Rule of Law' in SW Schill (ed) *International Investment Law and Comparative Public Law* (OUP 2010) 627–58.
Van Harten G, 'Arbitrator Behaviour in Asymmetrical Adjudication: An Empirical Study of Investment Treaty Arbitration' (2012) 50 Osgoode Hall LJ 211–68.
Van Harten G and M Loughlin, 'Investment Treaty Arbitration as a Species of Global Administrative Law' (2006) 17 EJIL 121–50.
Vandevelde K, 'A Brief History of International Investment Agreements' (2005) 12 UC Davis J of Intl L & Poly 157–94.
Vandevelde K, 'A Unified Theory of Fair and Equitable Treatment' (2010) 42 Intl L & Pol 43–106.
VanDuzer JA, P Simons, and G Mayeda (eds), *Integrating Sustainable Development into International Investment Agreements: A Commenwealth Guide for Developing Country Negotiators* (Commonwealth Secretariat 2013).
VanDuzer JA, P Simons, and G Mayeda, *Integrating Sustainable Development into International Investment Agreements: A Guide for Developing Countries*, Prepared for the Commonwealth Secretariat (August 2012) <www.iisd.org/pdf/2012/6th_annual_forum_commonwealth_guide.pdf> accessed 11 November 2014.
VanDuzer JA, P Simons, and G Mayeda, *Integrating Sustainable Development into International Investment Treaties: A Guide for Developing Countries* (Commonwealth Secretariat 2013).
Vedder C, 'Die außenpolitische Zielbindung der gemeinsamen Handelspolitik' in M Bungenberg and C Herrmann (eds), *Die Gemeinsame Handelspolitik der Europäischen Union nach Lissabon* (Nomos 2011) 121–56.
Villaruel V, 'El Observatorio sobre Inversión y Transnacionales y su Importancia para el Desarrollo Regional' (Diplomacia Ciudadana, Revista bimestral No. 9, Ministerio de Relaciones Exteriores y Movilidad Humana, 2009) 10–13.
Villiger ME, *Commentary on the 1969 Vienna Convention on the Law of Treaties* (Nijhoff 2009).
Viñuales JE, 'Foreign Investment and the Environment in International Law: An ambiguous relationship' (2009) 80 British Ybk Intl L 244–332.
Viñuales JE, *Foreign Investment and the Environment in International Law* (CUP 2012).
Viñuales JE, 'The Environmental Regulation of Foreign Investment Schemes under International Law' in: P-M Dupuy and JE Viñuales (eds.), *Harnessing Foreign Investment to Promote Environmental Protection: Incentives and Safeguards* (CUP 2013) 273–320.
Viñuales JE, 'Sovereignty in Foreign Investment Law' in Z Douglas, J Pauwelyn, and JE Viñuales (eds), *The Foundations of International Investment Law* (OUP 2014) 317–62.
Vis-Dunbar D, 'South African court judgment bolsters expropriation charge over Black Economic Empowerment legislation in the mining sector' *Investment Treaty News* (23 March 2010) <www.iisd.org/itn/2009/03/23/south-african-court-judgment-bolsters-expropriation-charge-over-black-economic-empowerment-legislation/> accessed 2 July 2014.
Voeten E, 'The Politics of International Judicial Appointments' (2007) 61 Int Org 669–701.
Volterra R, 'International Law Commission Articles on State Responsibility and Investor-State Arbitration: Do Investors Have Rights?' (2010) 25 ICSID Rev 218–23.

Völkeny S, 'Analogy', *The Max Planck Encyclopedia of Public International Law* (OUP 2012) vol I.

Voon T and A Mitchell, 'Implications of WTO Law for Plain Packaging of Tobacco Products' in A Mitchell, T Voon, and J Liberman (eds), *Public Health and Plain Packaging of Cigarettes: Legal Issues* (Edward Elgar 2012) 109–36.

Voon T and A Mitchell, 'Time to Quit? Assessing International Investment Claims Against Plain Tobacco Packaging in Australia' (2011) 14 J Intl Econ L 515–52.

Voon T, A Mitchell, and J Munro, 'Parting Ways: The Impact of Mutual Termination of Investment Treaties on Investor Rights' (2014) 29 ICSID Rev–FILJ 451–73.

Waibel M, A Kaushal, K Chung, and C Balchin (eds), *The Backlash against Investment Arbitration* (Kluwer 2010).

Waibel M, A Kaushal, K Chung, and C Balchin (eds), 'International Investment Law and Treaty Interpretation' in R Hofmann and C Tams (eds), *International Investment Law and General International Law—From Clinical Isolation to Systemic Integration?* (Nomos 2011) 29–52.

Wald A and J Kalicki, 'The Settlement of Disputes between the Public Administration and Private Companies by Arbitration under Brazilian Law' (2009) 26 J Int Arb 557–78.

Wälde TW, 'The "Umbrella" Clause in Investment Arbitration—A Comment on Original Intentions and Recent Cases' (2005) 6 J World Inv & Trade 183–236.

Wälde TW, 'Procedural Challenges in Investment Arbitration under the Shadow of the Dual Role of the State' (2010) 26 Arb Intl 3–42.

Wälde TW and B Sabahi, 'Compensation, Damages, and Valuation' in P Muchlinski, F Ortino, and C Schreuer (eds), *The Oxford Handbook of International Investment Law* (OUP 2008) 1049–1124.

Webb M and R Rajen, 'South Africa: No More BITs and Pieces' *Mondaq* (2 January 2014) <www.mondaq.com/x/283892/Inward+Foreign+Investment/No+More+BITs+And+Pieces> accessed 1 July 2014.

Weeramantry R, *Treaty Interpretation in Investment Arbitration* (OUP 2012).

Wehland H, 'Schiedsverfahren auf der Grundlage bilateraler Investitionsschutzabkommen zwischen EU-Mitgliedstaaten und die Einwendung des entgegenstehenden Gemeinschaftsrechts' (2008) 6 SchiedsVZ 222–33.

Wehland H, 'Intra-EU Investment Agreements and Arbitration: Is European Community Law an Obstacle?' (2009) 58 ICLQ 297–320.

Weiler T, 'A First Look at the Interim Merits Award in *SD Myers, Inc v Canada*: It Is Possible to Balance Legitimate Environmental Concerns with Investment Protection' (2001) 24 Hastings Intl & Comp L Rev 173.

Weiler T (ed), *International Investment Law and Arbitration: Leading Cases from the ICSID, NAFTA, Bilateral Treaties and Customary International Law* (Cameron May 2005).

Westcott T, 'Foreign Investment Issues in the Australia–United States Free Trade Agreement' (Summer 2004–05) Economic Roundup 69 <http://archive.treasury.gov.au/documents/958/PDF/06_Foreign_investment_policy_AUSFTA.pdf> accessed 11 July 2014.

Wieland P, 'Why the Amicus Curia Institution is Ill-suited to address Indigenous Peoples' Rights before Investor-State Arbitration Tribunals: *Glamis Gold* and the Right of Intervention' (2011) 3 Trade, Law & Dev 334–66.

Wittich S, 'Article 70' in O Dörr and K Schmalenbach (eds), *Vienna Convention on the Law of Treaties* (Springer 2012) 1195–1210.

Wittich S, 'Investment Arbitration: Remedies' in M Bungenberg, J Gabriel, S Hobe, A Reinisch (eds), *International Investment Law* (Nomos 2015) 1391–1430.

World Bank, *Governance and Development* (World Bank 1992).

World Justice Project, *WJP Rule of Law Index 2014* <http://data.worldjusticeproject.org/> accessed 11 July 2014.

World Trade Organization, Doha WTO Ministerial 2001: Ministerial Declaration WT/MIN(01)/DEC/1, 20 November 2001.

World Trade Organization, Singapore WTO Ministerial 1996: Ministerial Declaration WT/MIN/(96)/DEC, 13 December 1996.

World Trade Organization, Working Group on the Relationship between Trade and Investment, 'Communication from the European Community and its Member States—Concept Paper on Non-Discrimination' WT/WGTI/W/122 <http://trade.ec.europa.eu/doclib/docs/2004/july/tradoc_113951.pdf> accessed 23 March 2015.

Wouters J and N Hachez, 'The Institutionalization of Investment Arbitration and Sustainable Development' in M-C Cordonier Segger, M Gehrig, and A Newcombe (eds) *Sustainable Development in World Investment Law* (Kluwer 2011) 611–40.

Yackee JW, 'Conceptual Difficulties in the Empirical Study of Bilateral Investment Treaties' (2008) 33 Brooklyn JIL.

Yackee JW, 'Towards a Minimalist System of International Investment Law?' (2009) 32 Suffolk Transnatl L Rev 303–40.

Yackee JW, 'Controlling the International Investment Law Agency', (2012) 53 Harv Intl L J 392–448.

Yannaca-Small K, '"Indirect Expropriation" and the "Right to Regulate" in International Investment Law' in OECD (ed), *International Investment Law. A Changing Landscape* (OECD Paris 2005) 43–72.

Yannaca-Small K, 'Indirect Expropriation and the Right to Regulate: How to Draw the Line?' in K Yannaca-Small (ed), *Arbitration under International Investment Agreements: A Guide to Key Issues* (OUP 2010) 445–77.

Yotova R, 'The New EU Competence in Foreign Direct Investment and Intra-EU Investment Treaties: Does the Emperor have New Clothes?' in F Baetens (ed), *Investment Law within International Law—Integrationist Perspectives* (CUP 2013) 387–414.

Zhan J, 'Investment Policies for Sustainable Development: Addressing Policy Challenges in a New Investment Landscape' in R Echandi and P Sauvé (eds), *Prospects in International Investment Law and Policy* (CUP 2013) 13–29.

Ziegler A, 'Better BITS?—Making International Investment Law Responsive to Sustainable Development Objectives' (2014) 15 JWIT 803–08.

Index

Tables are indicated by an italic *t* following the page number.

acquired rights, concept of 253
arbitration, *see* dispute settlement
arbitrators; *see also* ICSID Convention
   alternative to present appointment system 108–09
   appointing authorities, and 107–08
   appointment 105
   chairperson appointment 107
   disqualification 105
   dissents 106
   independence and impartiality 104–05, 108, 307
   interpretative guidelines on FET 75–77
   reputation 107–08
   role 105–06
   views on questions of law 106–07
Articles on the Responsibility of States for Internationally Wrongful Acts' (ASR), *see* State responsibility
Asia-Pacific region:
   trade relations 323–27
   Trans-Pacific Partnership Agreement (TPPA) 302, 317, 321, 322, 328–30, 337, 338
Australia:
   dispute settlement
      current policy 322–23, 337
      domestic courts as alternative 330–34, 336–37
      future policy 334–36, 337–38
      previous policy 317, 320–22, 337
   regional trade relations 323–27
   sovereign right to regulate in public interest 317
   Trade Policy Statement of 2011 317, 320–22
   Trans-Pacific Partnership Agreement (TPPA) 302, 317, 321, 322, 328–30, 337, 338
   treaty negotiations 317

balance of private/State interests, *see* investor protection; sustainable development
bilateral investment treaties (BITs):
   critiques 142–43
   denunciation 291
   discrimination against domestic investors 351–53
   dispute settlement clauses 3
   emergence 3
   environmental and labour rights protection provisions
   factors against adoption 175, 176
   factors for adoption 172–74, 176
   summary of 171–72
   survey of 147–70
   taxonomy of 145–47
   EU sustainable development chapter 363–65
   evolution of scope 32–37
   foreign investment 38
   growth in use 175
   model BIT
      development of 283
      template 283–85
   replacement by national legislation, *see* South Africa
   replacement by PTIAs 176
   reviews of use 266
   rise in numbers 1, 3–4
   South Africa, *see* South Africa
   sustainable development 38, 142–44
   termination 266, 291, 316–17

Calvo doctrine 291, 345
Commonwealth Secretariat:
   definition of sustainable development 44
   proposals for reform of IIAs 41, 43
   sustainable development guide 42–43, 63
compensation:
   concept 349–51
   emphasis on 349–51
comprehensive free trade agreements, *see* free trade agreements
contracts, stabilization clauses 298–300
cooperative institutional structures, IIA reform 59
courts, *see* State regulation

definition clauses, *see* scope and definition clauses
democracy, concerns over 345–46, 357–58
differential treatment provisions, IIA reform 60
discrimination against domestic investors 351–53
dispute settlement; *see also* arbitrators; international investment court
   appellate body 115–21
   applicability of ASR remedies 210–13
   arbitration as suitable format 104–10
   arguments for continued use 109, 126
   Australia, *see* Australia
   balance of private/State interests 126
   bias 104–05

Index

dispute settlement *(cont.)*:
  choice of restitution or compensation 213–15
  clauses in BITs 3
  compensation, emphasis on 349–51
  constraint on sustainable development 97–98
  critiques of investor–State dispute settlement (ISDS) 42, 316–20, 337
  domestic courts as alternative 330–34, 336–37
  EU legal order, and 346–47
  exhaustion of local remedies rule 123–26
  growth in use 97, 357–58
  inclusion or omission from treaties? 101–03
  Indonesia, *see* Indonesia
  international investment court, proposals for 42
  interpretative approach of tribunals
    consideration of contextual arguments 195–99
    de facto precedents, role of 200–02
    features 188
    'single combined operation' 189–95
  investor consent for proceedings 83
  investor's right to initiate 97
  Latin America, *see* Latin America
  local remedies requirement 121–26
  new model 98, 109–10, 127
  procedure, concerns over 347–48
  proportionality 80
  public participation and access 110–14
  reform
    approaches 130–31, 387–89
    fairness 129, 139–40
    independence and impartiality 129, 131–36, 140, 307
    initiatives 128–30, 140–41
    openness 129, 136–38, 140
  review of exercise of public authority, as
    arbitration procedure, concerns over 347–48
    autonomy of EU legal order 346–47
    domestic court rulings as public authority 346
  rise in numbers of disputes 1
  South Africa 270–72, 282
  success of system 4
  sustainable development, and 98–101, 126–27
  UNASUR Centre for the Settlement of Investment Disputes, *see* Latin America
  UNCITRAL Arbitration Rules 107, 112, 306
  UNCITRAL Transparency Rules 112–14, 126, 128
  value of 318–20, 337
  Vienna Rules and 188
domestic law, *see* State

economic law, *see* international economic law
environmental law, definition 164
environmental protection:
  impact assessments 60
  Latin America 292–95, 300–01, 302–03
  sustainable development provisions in PTIAs and BITs
    summary of 171–72
    survey of 147–70
    taxonomy of 145–47
  treaties with provisions for 145
European Commission (EC), dispute settlement reform 128–41
European Union (EU):
  autonomy of legal order 346–47
  balance of private/State interests 376
  definition of sustainable development 360–61
  democracy, concerns over 357–58
  dispute settlement
    alternatives to 372–75
    improved mechanism 375
    provisions 371–72
  domestic remedies, use of 373–75
  expropriation 367–69
  fair and equitable treatment (FET) 366–67
  foreign direct investment, competence for 358
  importance of international investment law 357
  international law, and 369–71
  investment protection rules reform 365–69, 375–76
  investment protection treaties 358–59, 361–65
  mediation 372–73
  non-discrimination 352–53
  sustainable development chapter
    BITs 363–65
    FTAs 361–63
exceptions clauses, IIA reform 56–57
expropriation:
  concept 94
  definition 192
  EU provisions 367–69
  IIA commitments as restraint 83
  IIA reform 50–52, 90–96
  indirect expropriation
    clause 85–90
    concept 52, 335, 368
    definition 92, 94, 369
  police powers doctrine 88–90
  sole effects doctrine 86–88
  South African draft legislation 280–82
  sustainable development, and 84–85

fair and equitable treatment (FET):
  concept 65–66, 70–71, 73, 77, 197 n 113
  definition 50, 67–68, 71, 196
  equitableness, concept of 73
  EU provisions 366–67
  exhaustive list of State obligations 74–75
  fairness, concept of 73
  IIA reform 48–50

Index 437

interpretative guidelines for arbitrators 75–77
IPFSD policy options 65, 68, 79
liability threshold 79–80
omission of references to 77–79
problems 67–68
proportionality test 80
reasonableness, concept of 73
reference to international law principles or minimum standards 70–73
unqualified clauses 68–70
variations 66–67
foreign investment; *see also* investor protection
BITs, use of 38
EU competence 358
government's policy responsibility 37
international protection and regulation 28–32
investment law reform proposals 38–40
role 19–23
sustainable development, and 7–9, 19–40
UN principles 37
foreign owned assets, expropriation,
see expropriation
free trade agreements (FTAs):
EU sustainable development chapter 361–63
rise in numbers 1
'full protection and security', concept of 71, 197 n 113

'good governance':
concept of 21
social development, and 99

home State obligations, IIA reform 59
human rights:
autonomy of EU legal order, and 347
dispute settlement and 188, 190, 196, 225, 389
exhaustion of local remedies rule 123–26
fair and equitable treatment, and 70
foreign investors, of 252, 254
IIAs and 8, 39, 44, 52, 145 n 20, 168, 205, 212, 232 n 18, 363–65
international investment law, and 13, 340, 341
investor protection and 390–91
non-discrimination 352–53
property, to 353–56
property protection and 18
protection of 22 n 47, 57–58, 62, 109, 114, 120, 142, 144, 211, 246, 381, 385
respect for 24, 37
social development, and 99
State obligations 295, 299
sustainability assessment 60–61
sustainable development, and 26, 45 n 25, 59
UN Guiding Principles 57, 76 n 49

ICSID Convention:
accessions 1
alternatives to 109–10

appeals 117, 118
commencement 32
constraints on Arbitration Rules reform 112
denunciation 291
drafting 98
preamble 102
withdrawals 2, 16–17, 107, 109
indirect expropriation, *see* expropriation
Indonesia:
dispute settlement, policy on 327–28, 337
termination of BITs 317, 337
International Centre for Settlement of Investment Disputes, *see* ICSID
international economic law:
individual's role 355–56
international investment law and 339, 340–41
international investment agreements (IIAs);
see also bilateral investment treaties;
free trade agreements; preferential trade and investment treaties (PTIAs)
amendment of treaty language 79
emphasis on private property protection 4
handbook for negotiators 63–64
initiatives for reform of 41–43
interpretation 185–88
new model 41–64
prospects for reform 63–64
reference to social and environmental development 82–83
regional policies as to, *see* Latin America
renegotiation, *see* termination
rise in numbers 1
sustainable development, and
cooperative institutional structures 59
differential treatment provisions 60
dispute settlement reform 61–63
enforcement issues 83
exceptions clauses 56–57
expropriation, *see* expropriation
fair and equitable treatment (FET) provisions 48–50
home State obligations 59
IIA reform proposals 43–46
investor obligations and responsibilities 57–59
most-favoured-nation (MFN) treatment 53
national treatment clauses 54
new sustainable development oriented provisions 56
no lowering of standards clauses 59
preambles, revised wording 46–47
pre-establishment rights 47–48
progress on treaty reform 143
scope and definition clauses 54–55
special treatment provisions 60
sustainability assessment 60–61
treaty design 46
treaty interpretation controversies 48
termination, *see* termination

Index

international investment agreements
(IIAs) (*cont.*):
  treaty design
    objectives for 63–64
    sustainable development 46
  Vienna Rules 185–88
international investment court:
  mandate 108–09
  proposals for 42, 79
international investment law
  balance of private/State interests 4–5, 82
  'constitutional' view of 339–40, 343–44, 353, 356
  contributions to current study summarized 9–18
  current state 377–79
  distinctiveness 339
  future of 386
  general international law, and 177, 339, 340–41
  'generalization' of 339–40, 342–43, 356
  growth in controversies 2–3
  growth in importance 1–2
  'internal' sources of reform 340
  international economic law, and 339, 340–41
  investor protection as current paradigm 5
  legitimation, concerns as to 345–46
  less isolated 5, 384–85
  lines of development 6
  more balanced 5, 379–82
  more diversified 5, 382–84
  origins 3
  recent applications 341–42
  shifting paradigms, and 5–6, 379–385
  'state of transition' 3
  sustainable development as new paradigm 5–6, 9, 177–78
international law:
  international investment law and 177, 339, 340–41
  reference to principles or minimum standards of 70–73
  State responsibility, *see* State responsibility
  sustainable development as norm 205
  treaty interpretation rules, *see* Vienna Rules
International Law Commission (ILC), *see* State responsibility
international trade treaties, *see* preferential trade and investment treaties
interpretation:
  clause 278–79
  controversies as to IIAs 48
  rules of general international law, *see* Vienna Rules
  tribunal practice, *see* dispute settlement
investment arbitration, *see* dispute settlement
Investment Policy Framework for Sustainable Development (IPSFD):
  basic premise 177–78
  definition of sustainable development 44, 359–60
  dispute settlement critique 42
  handbook for IIA negotiators 63
  IIA reform 82
  investment law proposals 5–6
  policy options 65, 68, 79, 128, 204, 206
  States' rights and obligations 83
investments:
  concept, scope of 48
  definition 29, 54–55, 273, 335, 340
  Salini test 340
investor obligations and responsibilities, IIA reform 57–59
investor protection:
  Australia, *see* Australia
  balance with sustainable development 4–5, 82, 126, 183–88, 202–03, 376
  BITs, *see* bilateral investment treaties
  current investment law paradigm, as 5
  definition of 'investor' 292 n 3, 309, 310
  discrimination against domestic investors 351–53
  domestic legal remedies, and 389–91
  Draft Promotion and Protection of Investment Bill (PPI Bill), *see* South Africa
  'full protection and security', concept of 71, 197 n 113
  'good governance', concept of 21
  human rights and 390–91
  Indonesia, *see* Indonesia
  Latin America, *see* Latin America
  South Africa, *see* South Africa
investors' rights:
  legitimate expectations, concept of 49, 95
  right to property, and 353–55
investor–State contracts, stabilization clauses 298–300
investor–State dispute settlement (ISDS), *see* dispute settlement

labour rights:
  'internationally' recognized labour rights', definition of 148 n 29
  sustainable development provisions in PTIAs and BITs
    summary of 171–72
    survey of 147–70
    taxonomy of 145–47
  treaties with provisions for 145
language:
  amendment of treaty language 79
  imprecision of treaty language 79
Latin America:
  approaches to IIAs 314
  Calvo doctrine 291, 345
  challenges to international investment regime 291, 302, 303, 313–14, 316

contractual practice 294–95
dispute settlement
  arbitration 295–98
  Observatory on Investment
    and Transnational
    Corporations 313–14, 315
  regional initiatives 303–4
  UNASUR Centre 304–13, 315
environmental measures 300–01
future of IIAs 302–03
investment laws 295–98
Observatory on Investment and Transnational
  Corporations 313–14, 315
social measures 300–01
stabilization clauses in investor–State
  contracts 298–300
treaty practice 292–94
UNASUR Centre for the Settlement of
  Investment Disputes
  background 304–06
  establishment 304, 315
  future development 312–13
  inter-State and investor–State
    disputes 310–12
  jurisdiction 308–10, 315
  principles 307
  structure 306–07
legitimate expectations, concept of 49, 95
**liability threshold, fair and equitable
  treatment** 79–80

**more balanced, less isolated, and increasingly
  diversified regime**
**most-favoured-nation (MFN) treatment, IIA
  reform** 53

national law, *see* State
national treatment clauses, IIA reform 54
**no lowering of standards clauses, IIA
  reform** 59
non-discrimination, approach to 352–53

omission of references:
  dispute settlement, to 101–03
  fair and equitable treatment, to 77–79

paradigm shift, *see* international investment law
permanent investment court, *see* international
  investment court
preambles, IIA reform 46–47
pre-establishment rights, IIA reform 47–48
**preferential trade and investment treaties
  (PTIAs):**
  environmental and labour rights protection
    provisions
    summary of 171–72
    survey of 147–70
    taxonomy of 145–47
  growth in use 175–76

replacement of BITs 175–76
sustainable development 143–44
private property:
  right to property, investors' rights,
    and 353–56
  treaty emphasis on 4
**proportionality test, fair and equitable
  treatment** 80
public authority, review of exercise of, *see*
  dispute settlement
public international law, *see* international law

remedies:
  applicability of ASR remedies 210–13
  choice of restitution or
    compensation 213–15
  compensation
    concept 349–51
    emphasis on 349–51
  domestic legal remedies, investor protection
    and 389–91
  exhaustion of local remedies rule 123–26
  reparation, forms of 204
  restitution as infringement of State
    sovereignty, as 220–22
renegotiation, *see* termination
**reverse discrimination against domestic
  investors** 351–53
**right to development, sustainable development
  and** 144 n 19
right to property, investors' rights, and 353–56

SADC, *see* Southern African Development
  Community
Salini test 340
**scope and definition clauses, IIA
  reform** 54–55
shifting paradigms, *see* international
  investment law
social legislation in Latin America 300–01
South Africa:
  balance of private/State interests 287
  continued use of BITs 285–86
  Draft Promotion and Protection of
    Investment Bill (PPI Bill)
    critique 278
    dispute settlement 282
    expropriation 280–82
    implications for BITs 287–88
    interpretation clause 278–79
    purpose 278
    scope 278
    security for investment 279–80
    sovereign right to regulate in public
      interest 282–83
  dual approach to investment
    protection 285–86, 289
  'first generation' BITs 267, 268–70, 268*t*
  investment arbitration 270–72

South Africa: *(cont.)*:
model BIT
development of 283
Southern African Development
Community (SADC) Model BIT
Template 283–85
new investment law paradigm, and 289–90
new investment protection
regime 267, 276–78
replacement of BITs by PPI Bill 287–88
review of BITs 267, 272–76
termination of BITs 267
usage of BITs 267–70
Southern African Development Community (SADC), Model BIT Template 283–85
sovereignty, *see* State sovereignty
special treatment provisions, IIA reform 60
stabilization clauses in investor–State contracts 298–300
State obligations:
balanced with rights 83
list of 74–75
State regulation:
court rulings as public authority 346
domestic legal remedies, investor protection and 389–91
Draft Promotion and Protection of Investment Bill (PPI Bill), *see* South Africa
'good governance', concept of 21
necessity, as 83
sovereign right to regulate in public interest 282–83, 317–18, 386
State responsibility:
applicability of ASR remedies 210–13
choice of restitution or compensation 213–15
home State obligations, IIA reform 59
ILC Articles (ASR) 204–05
investment law and 205
investment tribunal practice analysed 216–20
IPFSD policy options 206–07
legal consequences of wrongful conduct
general international law 207–10
international investment law 210–20
reparation, forms of 204
restitution
compensation, or 213–15
form of reparation, as 204
infringement of State sovereignty, as 220–22
scope 204
'secondary' rules 204, 222–24
State sovereignty and international law 224–25
sustainable development, and 205, 225–26
State sovereignty:
concerns as to 345–46
definition 218

international law and 224–25
restitution as infringement 220–22
sovereign right to regulate in public interest 282–83, 317–18, 386
State–investor contracts, stabilization clauses 298–300
subsidiarity, sustainable development and 100
sustainability assessment, IIA reform 60–61
sustainable development:
balance with investor protection 4–5, 82, 126, 183–88, 202–03, 376
BITs, limitations of 38
Commonwealth Secretariat guidance 42–43
concept 5–7, 9–12, 19, 23–25, 98–99, 187, 381
controversy 7
definitions 7, 23, 25–28, 44, 67 n 12, 81, 98–99, 144–45, 181–83, 205, 359–61
foreign investment, and 7–9, 19–40
'good governance' and 99
government's policy responsibility 37
IIA reform, and 41–64
international law norm, as 205
investment law reform proposals 38–40
new investment law paradigm, as 5–6, 9, 177–78
private sector involvement 81–82
right to development, and 144 n 19
subsidiarity 100
treaty references 7
UNCTAD Policy Framework, *see* Investment Policy Framework for Sustainable Development

taking of assets, *see* expropriation
termination:
denunciation, legality of 238–39
IIA provisions for 239–41
key issue, as 228–30
law of treaties, and 227–28
mutual agreement as per treaty provisions 245–47
mutual agreement outside treaty provisions
application of termination clauses 254–60
issues as to 247
limitation under VCLT provisions 249–54
relevance for treaty-making 247–48
new model of IIAs 230–35
regional IIAs 235–38
renegotiation following termination 245–60
renegotiation without termination
amendment clauses 260–63
categories of 260
circumvention of termination clauses 263–64
interpretative statements 260–63
South African BITs 267
survival clauses 241–44
sustainable development, and 228, 264–65
without renegotiation 238–41

Trans-Pacific Partnership Agreement (TPPA), *see* Asia-Pacific region
Transparency Rules, *see* UNCITRAL Transparency Rules
treaty design, IIA reform 46

UNCITRAL Arbitration Rules 107, 112, 306
UNCITRAL Transparency Rules 112–14, 126, 128
Union of South American Nations (UNASUR), *see* Latin America
United Nations (UN), foreign investment principles 37
United Nations Conference on Trade and Development (UNCTAD):
dispute settlement reform 128–41
Policy Framework, *see* Investment Policy Framework for Sustainable Development (IPSFD)
proposals for reform of IIAs 41

United Nations Human Rights Council, Guiding Principles for Business and Human Rights 57, 76 n 49
unqualified clauses, fair and equitable treatment 68–70

Vienna Convention on the Law of Treaties (VCLT):
acquired rights, concept of 253
limitation on mutual agreements to terminate treaties 249–54
rules on treaty interpretation, *see* Vienna Rules
Vienna Rules:
applicability 179–81
balance of private/State interests 183–88, 202–03
conflicts of norms, and 183–84
dispute settlement and 188
IIAs 185–88
limits of interpretation 183–84